ISLAMIC LEGENDS CONCERNING ALEXANDER THE GREAT

Taken from Two Medieval Arabic Manuscripts in Madrid

INTRODUCTION, EDITION, TRANSLATION, AND NOTES

by

Z. DAVID ZUWIYYA

State University of New York Press

Library of Congress Cataloging-in-Publication Data

Islamic legends concerning Alexander the Great : taken from two medieval Arabic manuscripts in Madrid / introduction, edition, translation, and notes by Z. David Zuwiyya.

p. cm.

Includes bibliographical references and index.

ISBN 1-58684-132-7 (pbk. : alk. paper)

1. Dhū al-Qarnayn in the Koran. 2. Alexander, the Great, 356-323 B.C.--Legends. I. Zuwiyya, Z. David (Zachary David), 1964- II. Alexander the Great (Arabic version). English & Arabic.

BP133.7.A42 I85 2001

398.22--dc21

2001004124

For information, contact

State University of New York Press, Albany, NY

www.sunypress.edu

TABLE OF CONTENTS

PREFACE

This book to which I have given the title *Islamic Legends Concerning Alexander the Great* is essentially the story of Alexander, *Qiṣṣat Dhulqarnayn*, containing various interpolated Islamic texts. This project began as an offshoot of my doctoral dissertation on the Aljamiado-Morisco *Rrekontamiento del rrey Ališandre.* It turned out that *Qiṣṣat Dhulqarnayn* was the closest Arabic legend to the *Rrekontamiento.* As I had spent considerable time reading and outlining the manuscript containing *Qiṣṣat Dhulqarnayn*, I decided to pursue it further by ordering a microfiche of the second recension from another Madrid library.

I have tried to govern my life by what James Michener once (in so many words) wrote in an essay: Do not be afraid to take on long-term projects that may seem to stretch one's abilities, and whose completion is unimaginable at the time of conception, because with time people grow. And this is how large projects get done.

At the same time, from my professors at the University of California, Santa Barbara, I understood that one of the most important duties of the medievalist is to bring to light unedited manuscripts. Here was a text complete from beginning to end, quite legible, existing in two nearly identical versions, and which in content was substantially different from the only other modern edition of an Arabic Alexander romance. I am referring to Emilio García Gómez' *Un texto árabe occidental de la leyenda de Alejandro Magno*, which is missing the first few pages of the manuscript. Their difference rests, in part, on the inclusion or omission of certain episodes, and in part, on the fact that the transmitter of *Qiṣṣat Dhulqarnayn* cites sources for nearly every account he reports, which is of tremendous value even though the veracity of these sources will no doubt be a matter of debate. Moreover, the whole body of literature on Alexander in Arabic, in all its richness and diversity, has no translation in English, and, subsequently, is not given adequate treatment in the general works on Alexander.

And so my reading of Arabic Alexander romances took on the specific goal of an eventual edition, translation and study of the legend edited here. My intention has been to produce a first edition to awaken the interest of scholars in the field. It is hoped that with this edition an Arabist more knowledgeable than I will take up the publication of one of the other Arabic manuscripts containing Alexander's story. Until all the manuscripts are published, it is unlikely that we will be able to describe with any certainty the path of evolution of the Alexander romance in Arabic. In this sense the Arabists are far behind the scholars of the Latin, Greek and Romance texts.

I must confess that the many hours I spent reading Arabic manuscripts with dictionary in hand were made more enjoyable by the fact that I knew my knowledge of Arabic was improving with every page. To get answers to the questions that inevitably arose, I kept a notebook of those passages for which I had doubt, and eventually went to see first Fawzi Abdulrazak, former Arabic Language Specialist at Harvard University library and managing editor of *Mundus Arabicus*, as he is a good friend of my father. Subsequently, I visited F. Corriente of the Universidad de Zaragoza, who was kind enough to sit with me for two days and go through the microfiche copies of the manuscripts. Additionally, for many hours I sat with family members in Sidon, Lebanon who helped me to understand parts of the Arabic manuscript. To these people, especially my aunt Bihan and my father, who read the entire Arabic manuscript, I am very grateful. I am also indebted to my mother, Dr. Nancy Zuwiyya, who read the English translation, as well as to my neighbor, the French medievalist Michel Raby, who read and commented on the introductory study. Finally, I must offer many thanks to my friend Juan Pedro Monferrer Sala in Arabic at the Universidad de Córdoba, who in addition to reading the Arabic edition made many valuable suggestions regarding editorial criteria. Additional thanks go to Ignacio Ferrando of the Universidad de Cádiz for pointing out errors and inconsistencies in the edition. To my Arabic professors in Santa Barbara, Juan and Magda Campo, and Dwight Reynolds, who went out of their way to make my study of Arabic possible, thank you. I have mentioned the names of some very knowledgeable people and I need to make clear that any mistakes in the translation and edition are entirely of my own doing. It would be wrong for me to omit mention of Auburn University, and in particular the Department of Foreign Languages and Literatures, which has been very supportive of this project in every respect.

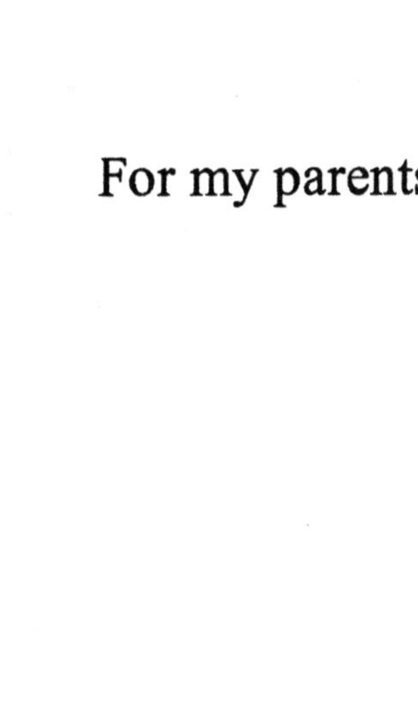

For my parents

﴿ وَقُل رَّبِّ زِدْنِي عِلْماً ﴾

("O my Lord! Advance me in knowledge.")

Qur'ān 20:114;
Qiṣṣat Dhulqarnayn, Arabic text, f. 9

TRANSLITERATION OF ARABIC WORDS AND NAMES

The system used is that of ‘Abd Allah Yusuf ‘Alī in his edition and translation of the Qur’ān (p. 23), with the exception of the consonants ‘th’ ‘kh’ and ‘dh’., which are not underlined.

ا = Alif = a
= ā (long vowel)

ب = Bā’ = b

ت = Tā’ = t

ث = Thā’ = th

ج = Jīm = j

ح = Ḥā’ = ḥ

خ = Khā’ = kh

د = Dāl = d

ذ = Dhāl = dh

ر = Rā’ = r

ز = Zāy = z

س = Sīn = s

ش = Shīn = sh

ص = Ṣād = ṣ

ض = Ḍād = ḍ

ط = Ṭā’ = ṭ

ظ = Ẓā’ = ẓ

ع = ‘Ayn = ‘ (inverted apostrophe)

غ = Ghayn = gh

ف = Fā’ = f

ق = Qāf = q

ك = Kāf = k

ل = Lām = l

م = Mīm = m

ن = Nūn = n

ه = Hā’ = h

و = Wāw = w (consonantal)
= ū (long vowel)

ي = Yā’ = y (consonantal)
= ī (long vowel)

ء = hamza = ‘ (apostrophe)

Short vowels: َ__ (fatḥah) = a

ِ__ (kasrah) = i

ُ__ (ḍammah) = u

BIBLIOGRAPHY

The principal modern editions of ancient and medieval works are listed under their author, or in the case of anonymous works under the name of the editor(s).

Manuscripts Consulted Containing Versions of the Arabic Alexander Legend

Ibn al-Jawzī. *Mir'āt al-zamān fī ta'rīkh al-a'yān.* London: British Library, Or. 4215. ff. 77-85.

Qiṣṣat Dhulqarnayn. Madrid: Real Academia de la Historia, Colección Gayangos 61. Also, in Ms. 5378 of the Biblioteca Nacional de Madrid.

Al-Ṣūrī, Ibrāhīm Mufarrij. *Kitāb ta'rīkh al-Iskandar Dhī al-Qarnayn wa wazīrihi al-Khiḍir.* Arabic manuscript num-ber Add. 7366 of the British Museum.

'Umāra b. Zayd. *Qiṣṣat al-Iskandar wa mā fīhā min al-'amr al-'ajīb.* London: British Library, Add. 5928.

Electronic Resources

HE: *Mawsū'at al-hadīth al-sharīf: Hadith Encyclopedia.* Cairo: Harf Information Technology, 1998. Version 2.1.

Bibliography for the Study of the Arabic Alexander Legend

Abbott, N. "Wahb b. Munabbih: A Review Article," *Journal of Near Eastern Studies* 36 (1977): 103-112.

Abel, A. "Dū'l Qarnayn, Prophète de l'Universalité." *Annuaire de l'Institut de Philologie et d'Histoire Orientales et Slaves* 11 (1951): 6-18.

Abu Muhammad b. Yusuf b. Mu'ayyid Nizami-'d-Din. *The Sikandar Nama, E Bara, or Book of Alexander the Great.* Ed. Captain H. Wilberforce Clarke. New Delhi: V. I. Publications 1979. First published in 1881.

Alfonso X el Sabio. *La historia novelada de Alejandro Magno.* Eds. Tomás González Rolán and Pilar Saquero Suárez-Somonte. Madrid: Editorial de la Universidad Complutense, 1982.

Anderson, Andrew Runni. *Alexander's Gate, Gog and Magog, and the Inclosed Nations.* Cambridge: The Medieval Academy of America, 1932.

--"Alexander at the Caspian Gates." *Transactions of the American Philological Association* 59 (1928): 130-163.

--"Alexander's Horns." *Transactions of the American Philological Association* 58 (1927): 100-122.

--"The Arabic History of Dulcarnain and the Ethiopian History of Alexander." *Speculum* 6 (1931): 434-445.

Arioli, Angelo, ed. and trans. *Le Isole Mirabili: Periplo arabo medievale.* Torino: Giulio Einaudi, 1989.

Al-Bakrī, Abū 'Ubayd Allah. *Kitāb al-Mugrib fī dhikr bilād Ifrīqiyā wa-l-Magrib. Description de l'Afrique septentrionale,* ed. and trans. B. de Slane. Paris, 1911.

Beeston, A.F.L. "The Arabic Book" in *The Cambridge History of Arabic Literature: Arabic Literature to the End of the Umayyad Period.* Cambridge UP, 1983. pp. 22-26.

Blau, Joshua. *A Grammar of Christian Arabic. Based Mainly on South-Palestinian Texts from the First Millennium.* 3 vols. Lovaina, 1966-67.

--"The State of Research in the Field of the Linguistic Structure of Middle Arabic." *Arabica* 28 (1981): 187-203.

--"The Status and Linguistic Study of Middle Arabic." *Jerusalem Studies in Arabic and Islam* 23 (1999): 221-227.

Bonebakker, Seeger A. "Some Medieval Views on Fantastic Stories." *Quaderni di Studi Arabi* 10 (1992): 21-43.

Boyle, J.A. "The Alexander Romance in the East and West." *Bulletin of the John Rylands University Library* 60 (1977): 13-27.

Bridges, M. and J.C. Bürgel. *The Problematics of Power: Eastern and Western Representations of Alexander the Great.* Bern, 1996.

Brockelmann, Carl. *Geschichte der Arabischen Litteratur. Zweite den Supplementänden Angepasste Auflage.* 2 vols. Leiden: E.J. Brill, 1943.

Budge, Ernest A. Wallis. *The History of Alexander the Great Being the Syriac Version, Edited from Five Manuscripts of the Pseudo-Callisthenes with an English Translation.* Cambridge, 1889. Reprinted by Philo Press in Amsterdam, 1976.

-- *The Life and Exploits of Alexander the Great Being a Series of Ethiopic Texts Edited from Manuscripts in the British Museum and the Bibliothèque Nationaled, Paris.* 2 vols. New York/ London: Benjamin Blom, 1968. First Published in 1896.

The Cambridge History of Arabic Literature: Arabic Literature to the End of the Umayyad Period. Eds. A.F.L. Beeston, T.M. Johnstone, R.B. Serjeant and G.R. Smith. Cambridge UP, 1983.

The Cambridge History of Arabic Literature: Religion, Learning and Science in the 'Abbasid Period. Eds. M.J.L. Young, J.D. Latham and R.B. Serjeant. Cambridge UP, 1990.

Cameron, A.J. *Abū Dharr al-Ghifārī: An Examination of His Image in the Hagiographyof Islam.* London: Royal Asiatic Society, 1973.

Cary, George. *The Medieval Alexander.* New York & London: Garland Publishing, 1987. [With extensive bibliography pp. 378-93.]

Casari, Mario. *Alessandro e Utopia nei romanzi persiani medievali.* Rome: Bardi Editore, 1999. Supplement 1 to the *Revista degli Studi Orientali* 72.

Castillo Castillo, Concepción. "El profeta Idrís y "su viaje" al Más Allá" in *Actas XVI Congreso UEAI (Salamanca 27 agosto-2 septiembre 1992).* Salamanca, 1995. pp. 125-136.

--"Algunos aspectos de la angelología islámica, según Shihāb al-Dīn al-Ash'arī." *Miscelánea de Estudios Árabes y Hebraicos* 26-27 (1977-79): 423-431.

Chapira, Bernard. "Légendes Bibliques attribuées a Ka'b el-Aḥbar." *Revue des Études Juives* 69 (1919): 86-107.

Corriente Córdoba, F. *Diccionario árabe-español.* 2nd ed. Madrid: Instituto Hispano-Árabe de Cultura, 1986.

--*A Dictionary of Andalusi Arabic.* Leiden: Brill, 1997.

--*A Grammatical Sketch of the Spanish Arabic Dialect Bundle.* Madrid: Instituto Hispano-Arabe de Cultura, 1977.

--, ed. *Relatos píos y profanos del manuscrito de Urrea de Jalón.* Córdoba: Institución Fernando el Católico, 1990.

Al-Dīnawarī, Abū Ḥanīfan Aḥmad b. Dā'ūd. *Kitāb al-akhbār al-ṭiwāl.* Cairo, 1960.

De Polignac, F. "L'image d'Alexandre dans la littérature arabe: l'Orient face à l'hellenisme?" *Arabica* 39 (1982): 296-306.

Dozy, R. *Supplément aux dictionnaires arabes.* 2 vols. Beirut: Libraire du Liban, 1991. Reproduction of the original edition of E.J. Brill, 1881.

Dugat, G. *Histoire des philosophes et des théologiens musulmanes de 632 à 1258.* Amsterdam, 1973. First published in Paris, 1878.

Finazzi, Rosa Bianca and Alfredo Valvo, eds. *La diffusione dell'eredità classica nell'età tardoantica e medievale. Il Romanzo di Alessandro e altri scritti: Atti del Seminario Internazionale di Studio, Roma-Napoli, 25-27 settembre 1997.* Alexandria: Edizione dell'Orso, 1998.

EI: *The Encyclopaedia of Islam: A Dictionary of the Geography, Ethnography and Biography of the Muhammadan Peoples.* 4 vols. Eds. M.Th. Houtsma, T.W. Arnold, R. Basset and R. Hartmann. Leiden: E.J. Brill, 1913.

--EI : *Encylopaedia of Islam: New Edition.* Ed. H.A.R. Gibb, et al. Leiden: E.J. Brill, 1960-.

Ferro, Isabel. "The Introduction of ḥadīth in al-Andalus: 2nd/8th- 3rd/9th centuries." *Der Islam* 66 (1989): 68-93.

Fraenkel, S. "Recensione a 'Nöldeke, Th., Beiträge zur Geschichte des Alexanderromans.'" *Zeitschrift der Deutschen Morgenländischen Gesellschaft* 45 (1891): 309-330.

Friedlaender, Israel. *Die Chadhirlegende und der Alexanderroman.* Leipzig: B.G. Teubner, 1913.

Galmés de Fuentes, Alvaro. "La literatura aljamiado-morisca, literatura tradicional" in *Les Morisques et leur temps: table ronde internationale, 4-7 juillet 1981.* Ed. Louis Cardaillac. Paris: Editions du Centre Nationale de la Recherche Scientifique, 1983. pp. 15-27.

García Gómez, Emilio, ed. and trans. *Un texto árabe occidental de la leyenda de Alejandro Magno.* Madrid: Instituto de Valencia de D. Juan, 1929.

Gaster, M. "An Old Hebrew Romance of Alexander." *Journal of the Royal Asiatic Society of Great Britain* (1897): 485-549.

Ginzberg, L. *The Legends of the Jews.* 7 vols. Philadelphia, 1925-47.

Goldfeld, Isaiah. "The Tafsīr of Abdallah b. 'Abbās." *Der Islam* 58 (1981): 125-35.

Goldziher, Ignace. *A Short History of Classical Arabic Literature.* Trans. by Joseph Desomogyi. Berlin: Georg Olms Verlagsbuchhandlung Hildesheim, 1966.

Godolphin, Francis R.B., ed. *The Greek Historians. The Complete and Unabridged Historical Works of Herodotus, Thucydides, Xenophon, Arrian.* 2 vols. New York: Random House, 1942.

Grignaschi, M. "Le Roman Epistolaire Classique conservé dans la version arabe de Sālim Abū-l-'Alā'. " *Le Muséon* 80 (1967): 211-264.

Von Grunebaum, G.E. "Literature in the Context of Islamic Civilization." *Oriens: Zeitschrift der internationalen Gesellschaft für Orientforschung* 20 (1967): 1-14.

Gunderson, Lloyd L. *Alexander's Letter to Aristotle about India.* Hain: Meisenheim am Glan, 1980.

Hartmann, R. "Alexander und der Rätselstein aus dem Paradies" in *Oriental Studies Presented to E.G. Browne.* Cambridge, 1922. pp. 179-85.

Hilka, Dr. A. "Studien Zur Alexandersage." *Romanische Forschungen* 39 (1911): 1-71.

Huart, Cl. *Le livre de la Création et de l'histoire de Motahhar Ben Tāhir el-Maqdisī.* 5 vols. Paris, 1899-1916.

Ibn al-Faqīh al-Hamadhānī, Abu Bakr Aḥmad b. Muḥammad. *Kitāb al-buldān.* Ed. M.J. de Goeje. London: E.J. Brill, 1967.

Ibn Ḥajar, Aḥmad b. 'Ali. *Tahdhīb al-Tahdhīb.* 12 vols. Beirut: Dār Ṣādir, 1968.

Ibn Ḥibbān al-Bustī, Muhammad. *Kitāb al-majrūḥīn min al-muḥaddithīn wa-l-ḍu'afā' wa-l-matrūkīn.* Ḥalab: Dār al-wa'y, 1981.

Ibn Isḥāq, Abū 'Abd Allah Muhammad. *Sīra rasūl Allah. [The Life of Muhammad.]* Trans. A. Guillaume. Karachi: Oxford UP, 1970.

Kassis, Hanna E. and Karl I. Kobbervig. *Las concordancias del Corán.* Madrid: Instituto Hispano-Arabe de Cultura, 1987.

Ibn Khallikān, Aḥmad b. Muhammad b. Ibrāhīm Shams al-Dīn Abū'l-'Abbās. *A Biographical Dictionary.* Trans. Bn. MacGuckin de Slane. 4 vols. New York: Johnson Reprint Corp., 1961. Originally published in Paris and London,1843-71.

Idrīsī. *Description de l'Afrique et de l'Espagne.* Eds. R. Dozy and M.J. de Goeje. Leiden: Brill, 1968. First edition 1866.

Juynboll, G.H.A. *Muslim Tradition: Studies in Chronology, Provenance and Authorship of Early Hadīth.* Cambridge UP, 1983.

Khoury, R.G. "Pour une nouvelle comprénsion de la transmission des texts dans les trois premiers siècles islamiques." *Arabica* 34 (1987): 181-196.

Kisa'ī, Muhammad b. 'Abd Allah. *Qiṣaṣ al-anbiya': The Tales of the Prophets of al-Kisai.* Trans. W.M. Thackston, Jr. Boston: Twayne Publishers, 1978.

Knust, Hermann, ed. "De Alixandre" in *Bocados de oro. Mittheilungen aus dem Eskurial.* Tübingen, 1879. pp. 277-316.

--ed. "Los ensennamientos de Alixandre" in *El libro de los buenos proverbios. Mittheilungen aus dem Eskurial.* Tübingen, 1879. pp. 36-59.

Lazarus-Yafeh, Hava. *Intertwined Worlds: Medieval Islam and Bible Criticism.* Princeton: Princeton UP, 1992.

Lévi, Israel. "La legende d'Alexandre dans le Talmud." *Revue des Études Juives* 2 (1881): 293-300.

--"La legende d'Alexandre dans le Talmud et le Midrasch." *Revue des Études Juives* 7 (1883): 78-93.

--"Les traductiones hebraiques de l'histoire legendaire d'Alexandre." *Revue des Études Juives* 3 (1881): 238-75.

Lidzbarski, M. "Zu den arabischen Alexandergeschichten." *Zeitschrift für Assyriologie* 8 (1893): 263-312.

Margoliouth, D.S. "The Use of the Apocrypha by Moslem Writers." *The Moslem World* 5 (1915): 404-8.

Marín, Manuela. "Ṣaḥaba et tābi'ūn dans al-Andalus: Histoire et Légende." *Studia Islamica* 54 (1981): 5-49.

Massignon, L. "Les sept dormants, apocalypse de l'Islam" in *Opera Minora.* Beirut, 1963. Vol. 3, pp. 104-118.

Mas'ūdī, Abū'l-Ḥasan 'Alī b. al-Ḥusayn. *Murūj al-dhahab wa ma'ādin al-jawāhir.* 7 vols. Ed. Barbier de Meynard and Pavet de Courteilled. Beirut: Publications de l'Universite Libanaise, 1979. Text revised and corrected by Charles Pellat.

--*Les Praires d'or.* 9 vols. Ed. and trans. C. Barbier de Meynard and Pavet de Courteille. Paris, 1861-77. Alexander story in vol. 2, pp. 242-78.

Meillet, Gabriel. "L'Ascension d'Alexandre le Grand." *Syriac* 4 (1923): 85-123.

Meissner, Bruno. "Mubashshirs Aḫbār el-Iskender." *Zeitschrift der Deutschen Morgenländischen Gesellschaft* 49 (1896): 583-627.

Müller, Karl, ed. *Reliqua Arriani, et Sciptorum de rebus Alexandri Magni fragmenta: Pseudo-Callisthenis Historiam Fabulosam, Itinerarium Alexandri.* Paris, 1846.

Nagel, T. *Alexander der Grosse in der frühislamischen Volksliteratur.* Walldorf-Hessen, 1978.

Newby, Gordon, ed. *The Making of the Last Prophet: A Reconstruction of the Earliest Biography of Muhammad.* Columbia, South Carolina: U of South Carolina Press, 1989.

--"Tafsīr 'isrā'īlīyāt." *Journal of the American Academy of Religion, Thematic Issue S* 47:4 (December 1979): 685-97.

The New Oxford Annotated Bible. Eds. Bruce M. Metzger and Roland E. Murphy. New York: Oxford University Press, 1994.

Nöldeke, Theodor. "Beiträge zur Geschichte des Alexanderromans." *Denkschriften der kaiserlichen Akademie der Wissenschaftern in Wien* 38 (Vienna, 1890).

Nykl, A.R. ed. *Rrekontamiento del rrey Alisandre* in *Revue Hispanique* 77 (1929): 409-611.

Pederson, Johannes. *The Arabic Book.* Trans. Geoffrey French. Ed. Robert Hillenbrand. Princeton, NJ: Princeton UP, 1984.

Penrice, John. *A Dictionary and Glossary of the Korān with Copious Grammatical References and Explanations of the Text.* New York: Biblo and Tannen, 1969. First published in 1873.

Perlmann, Moshe. "A Legendary Story of Ka'b al-Aḥbār's Conversion to Islam" in *The Joshua Starr Memorial Volume.* NY, 1953. pp. 85-99.

Piemontese, A. "La figura di Alessandro nelle letterature d'area islamica" in *Alessandro Magno. Storia e Mito.* Rome, 1995. pp. 177-183.

Porter, J.R. "Pre-Islamic Arabic Historical Traditions and the Early Historical Narratives of the Old Testament." *Journal of Biblical Literature* 87 (1968): 17-26.

Pritchard, R. Telefryn, trans. *The History of Alexander's Battles:* Historia de preliis—*The J Version.* Toronto: Pontifical Institute of Medieval Studies, 1992.

Pseudo-Callisthenes (rec. C), see Müller (1846).

Pseudo-Callisthenes (Syriac), see Budge (1889).

Pseudo-Callisthenes (Ethiopic), see Budge (1896)

Pseudo-Callisthenes (rec. α), ed. W. Kroll. *Historia Alexandri Magni.* Berlin, 1926.

Pseudo-Callisthenes (rec. λ), ed. H. van Thiel. *Die Rezension λ des Pseudo-Kallisthenes.* Bonn, 1959.

Pseudo-Callisthenes (rec. β), ed. L. Bergson. *Der griechische Alexanderroman, Rezension β.* Stockholm, 1965.

Pseudo-Callisthenes (Armenian), see Wolohojian.

Pseudo-Callisthenes (J version, called *Historia de preliis*), see Pritchard.

Pseudo-Callisthenes (ms. L), ed. and trans. M. Centanni. *Il romanzo di Alessandro.* Torino, 1991.

Rrekontamiento del rrey Alisandre, see Nykl.

Ribera y Tarragó, J. "La enseñanza entre los musulmanes españoles" in *Disertaciones y opúsculos: Edición colectiva que en su jubilación del profesorado le ofrecen sus discípulos y amigos.* 2 vols. Madrid: Imprenta de E. Maestre, 1928. Vol. 1, pp. 229-359.

Ross, D.J.A. *Alexander Historiatus: A Guide to Medieval Illustrated Alexander Literature.* London, 1963.

Rubanovich, Julia. "The Reconstruction of a Storytelling Event in Medieval Persian Prose Romance: The Case of the *Iskandarnāma.*" *Edebiyāt* 9 (1998): 215-47.

Ruggini, I.C. "Sulla cristianizzazione della cultura pagana. Il mito greco e latino di Alessandro dall'età antonina al medioevo." *Athenaeum* 43 (1965): 3-80.

Scarcia Amoretti, B. "Nota a Corano, XVIII, 94." *Annali della Facolta' di Lingue e Letterature Straniere di Ca' Foscari* 9 (1970): 13-21.

Schaeder, H. Heinrich. "Ḥasan al-Basrī, Studien zur Frügeschichte des Islam," *Der Islam*, 14 (1925): 1-75.

Stetkevych, Jaroslav. *Muhammad and the Golden Bough: Reconstructing Arabian Myth.* Bloomington, Indiana: Indiana UP, 1996.

Al-Suyūṭī, Jalāl al-Dīn. *Bugyat al-wu'āt fī ṭabaqāt al-lugawiyyīn wa-l-nuḥāt.* 2 vols. Ed. Muḥammad Abū l-Faḍl Ibrāhīm. Cairo: Maṭba'at 'Isa al-Bābī al-Ḥalabī wa-shurakā-hi, 1964.

Al-Ṭabarī, Abū Ja'far Muḥammad b. Jarir. *Jāmi' al-bayān fī tafsīr al-Qur'ān.* 30 vols. Cairo: Mustafa al-Halabi and Sons, 1954.

--*Annales quos scripsit.* Ed. M.J. de Goeje. 15 vols. Leiden: E.J. Brill, 1964-65. Reprint of edition from 1879-1901.

--*The History of al-Ṭabarī (Ta'rīkh al-rusul wa'l-mulūk) vol. 4: The Ancient Kingdoms.* Trans. Moshe Perlmann. Albany: SUNY Press, 1987.

Al-Tha'labī, Ibn Isḥāq Aḥmad b. Muhammad Ibrahim. *Qiṣaṣ al-anbiyā' al-musamma bi al-'Ara'is.* Cairo: Maktaba al-Jumhuriyya al-'Arabiyya bi al-'Azhār, 19--?

Wansborough, John. *Quranic Studies: Sources and Methods of Scriptural Interpretation.* Oxford: Oxford UP, 1977.

Wehr, Hans. *A Dictionary of Modern Written Arabic.* 4th edition. Ithaca, NY: Spoken Languages Services Inc., 1979.

Weymann, K.F. *Die aethiopische und arabische Uebersetzung des* Pseudo-Callisthenes. Kirchhain, 1901.

Wilson, C.E. "The Wall of Alexander Against Gog and Magog; and the Expedition Sent out to Find It by the Khalif Wāthiq in 842 A.D" in *Hirth Anniversary Volume.* London: Probsthain & Co., 1922. pp. 575-612.

Wolohojian, Albert Mugrdich, trans. *The Romance of Alexander the Great by Pseudo-Callisthenes: Translated from the Armenian.* New York and London: Columbia University Press, 1969.

Zuwiyya, Z. David. *Western and Oriental Aspects of the* Rrekontamiento del rrey Ališandre. Dissertation completed at the University of California, Santa Barbara, August 1995.

INTRODUCTION

History and Genre of the Alexander Romance in Arabic

The story of Alexander reached Mecca probably in oral form sometime before the revelation of the Qur'ān, as it is included in the Muslim holy book in Sura 18:83-98,[1] which begins: "They ask thee concerning Dhulqarnayn. Say, 'I will rehearse to you something of his story.' Verily We established his power on earth, and We gave him the ways and means to all ends." At the beginning of the seventh century, the Alexander legend deriving from a Greek work known as the *Pseudo-Callisthenes*[2] (PC) was circulating in a number of languages, including Greek, Latin,[3] Armenian,[4] and Syriac. It is well known that the Quranic story of Dhulqarnayn shows greatest similarity to the Syriac Alexander legends.[5] Once Muhammad's revelation was complete and the Qur'ān came to circulate, first orally and then in writing, the followers of the new religion began to inquire about the details of the many fragmentary episodes that make up the Qur'ān. The Prophet's style was to allude to more than narrate in full the lives of prophets and peoples. In light of the fact that the protagonists of many Quranic stories were from the Judeo-Christian tradition, some Muslims during the formative years of Islam turned to the People of the Book for exegesis of Muhammad's revelation.[6] As suggested in the Qur'ān 4:51-57, God did not distinguish among the prophets, all of whom received a "portion of the Book,"[7] taught the same monotheistic religion, and attempted to warn man of the penalty of rejecting God's signs. Thus the Judeo-Christian legendary and prophetic tradition could help to understand Islam. Among those who most eagerly sought the literature of the Jews and Christians were Companions of Muhammad such as Ibn 'Abbās (d. 687-88 A.D.), converted Jews such as the Yemenite Ka'b al-Aḥbār (d. circa 652 A.D.),[8] pre-Islamic monotheists such as Abū Dharr (d. 653 A.D.), and scholars of the generation after Muhammad, such as the Persian Jewish convert Wahb b. Munabbih (d. circa 730), learned in the lore of South Arabia, and Ibn Ishāq (d.

---

[1] Qur'ān 18:59-63 dealing with Moses and al-Khiḍr also derives from the Alexander romance. Cf. I. Friedlaender, *Chadhirlegende*, pp. 61-67.

[2] Wolohojian dates the PC to "sometime before the fourth century A.D." (p. 1); Pritchard sees the second century A.D. as a *terminus post quem* (p. 3). Budge (1889) believes the anonymous work to be of Egyptian origin (pp. 35-51).

[3] The Latin Translation of Julius Valerius belongs to between 270-330 A.D.

[4] The existence of an Armenian Alexander romance relating, among other episodes, Alexander's dialogue as a youth with the sages and Alexander's arrival to paradise was demonstrated by I. Levi (1881), p. 297. The work has since been identified and published as one the versions of the PC most faithful to a Greek original. See Wolohojian, *The Romance of Alexander the Great.*

[5] These were the Syriac "Christian Legend Concerning Alexander," the "Brief Life of Alexander," and a work in verse attributed to Jacob of Serūgh (died A.D. 521), all edited with English translation in Budge (1889). For their relationship to the Qur'ān, Cf. Nöldeke, p. 24 ff.

[6] Public sentiment turned against the use of Judeo-Christian tradition to elucidate Quranic passages by the end of the second Islamic century. Cf. Newby, *Making of the Last Prophet*, p. 4.

[7] This idea is reiterated in 4:44, and 3:23. Regarding Arabaham, the Qur'ān says: "We had already given the people of Abraham the Book and Wisdom" (4: 54).

[8] Among the transmitters listed here, Ibn 'Abbās, Wahb b. Munabbih, and Ibn Isḥāq were disciples of Ka'b. Cf. Chapira, "Légendes Bibliques attribuées a Ka'b el-Aḥbar," p. 90.

circa 767), author of the biography of the Prophet.[9] The stories of the ancient prophets and kings that entered Islam by way of scholars of Judeo-Christian origin came to be known as the genre *qiṣaṣ al-anbiyā'*, or the *isrā'īlīyāt*.[10]

That the story of Alexander in Arabic belonged to this genre is suggested in part by the fact that all of the above cited transmitters are mentioned in *Qiṣṣat Dhulqarnayn* (QDh) as sources. Additionally, there is an explicit reference in QDh to the origin of one of its stories that reads as follows: "Abū 'Abd al-Malik said: Ka'b al-Aḥbār told me that in *some of the books of the Banī Isrā'īl* it states that God sent Adam and the serpent down to earth on the same day" (f. 133). The content of the "books of the Banī Isrā'īl" was precisely the *isrā'īlīyāt* literature. The story of Alexander in Arabic along with other *isrā'īlīyāt* legends was actively transmitted among Muslims during the formative period of Islam.[11] It often circulated in abridged form in collections of *qiṣaṣ al-anbiyā'*, such as those written by Ka'b al-Aḥbār,[12] Waḥb b. Munabbih,[13] Muhammad b. Isḥāq, al-Tha'labī, and al-Kisa'ī. Alexander also appears among the ancient kings in historical works by al-Ṭabarī, al-Mas'ūdī,[14] al-Dinawārī, and Mubashshir. In the domain of philosophy, there is also a work by Hunayn b. Isḥāq containing portions of the Alexander romance, which has survived in Old Spanish translation.[15] Full-length versions of the Arabic legend are those of 'Umāra,[16] 'Abd al-Raḥmān b. Ziyād,[17] al-Ṣūrī, the version edited by García Gómez in *Un texto árabe occidental*, the Arabic original for the *Rrekontamiento del rrey Ališandre*, an Aljamiado Morisco work edited by A.R. Nykl. It is also likely that full-length lives of Alexander were written by al-Mas'ūdī, contained in his *Akhbār al-zamān* and also in his *Kitāb al-awsaṭ*,[18] and in a history by the physician Mubashshir b. Fātik,[19] although neither of these works is extant. In Arabic texts, Alexander

---

[9] Cf. Newby, *Making of the Last Prophet*, p. 10.

[10] For a discussion of the *qiṣaṣ al-anbiyā'* and *isrā'īlīyāt*, see Newby, *Making of the Last Prophet*, pp. 3, 10-11; and especially his "*Tafsīr Isrā'īlīyāt* "

[11] B. Chapira, p. 93.

[12] The existence of a seventh-century History of the Prophets attributable to Ka'b al-Aḥbār is suggested by B. Chapira. Cf. his "Légendes Bibliques attribuées a Ka'b el-Aḥbar" (p. 94).

[13] Wahb was known as author of a work on the prophets known as *Mubtada'*. Cf. Newby, "Tafsīr Isrā'īlīyāt," p. 686.

[14] Al-Mas'ūdī had at his disposal the knowledge of the People of the Book. For example, in an explanation of Alexander's two horns he says: "Nous nous bornerons pour le moment à parler de la dissidence des deux doctrines émises par les peuples du Libre (les juifs et les chrétiens)," trans. Barbier de Meynard (1861), 2, p. 249.

[15] Cf. Knust, *Mittheilungen aus dem Eskurial*.

[16] See below, "Comparison with 'Umāra's Version of the Alexander Legend."

[17] The last transmitter of the Arabic Alexander legend edited here. See note to f. 1 of the translation. See also below, "Towards an Identification of the Sources for *Qiṣṣat Dhulqarnayn*."

[18] In the chapters of *Murūj al-dhahab* dedicated to Alexander/ Dhulqarnayn, al-Mas'ūdī refers on several occasions to the extensive *Akhbār al-zamān*. Cf. *Murūj al-dhahab* (1979) 1, p. 73. Regarding the content of the Alexander story in *Kitāb al-awsaṭ*, al-Mas'ūdī says "nous avons rapporté toutes les circonstances du massacre de Dara et des rois de l'Inde, ainsi que des princes de l'Orient qui, faisaient cause commune avec eux," trans. Barbier de Meynard from 1861, 2, p. 248.

[19] Mubashshir himself refers the reader to the more extensive Alexander romance found in his *Ta'rīkh al-kabīr*. With respect to Alexander's story he writes, وهو كتاب طويل وقد ذكرته وغيره من كتبه

usually goes by the name, Dhulqarnayn, i.e., the Two-Horned. Arab scholars and storytellers took the pagan hero of the PC and gave him an Islamic identity. The Two-Horned became a saint, or some would say a prophet, who knew and professed the testimony of Islamic faith: "There is no god but God, and Muhammad is his Messenger." He led the Army of God and preached Islam to the peoples he conquered. The process by which Alexander became a Muslim was, on the one hand, the reflection of the Christianization of Alexander in the hands of Syriac Christians,[20] and on the other, the direct result of exegesis of the Qur'ān, where he receives God's praise.

The narration of the lives of the prophets during Islam's early years not only informed the Muslim community of the tradition they had inherited, but also gave transmitters the opportunity to shape traditional material in such a way as to show that the line of biblical prophets led inequivocally to Islam. The way in which this was done shows similarity to Judeo-Christian typology.[21] The lives of the prophets were rewritten with details added to point to the life of Muhammad and the precepts of Islam. In Alexander's case, he is given a lineage reaching back to Abraham. The expansion of his empire and the message God commands him to spread throughout the earth prefigure Muhammad's message and the expansion of Islam. On one occasion, Alexander is made to ascend into the heavens with an angel, and, on another, to ride the same mythical animal Muhammad rode, the *al-burāq*. The Macedonian hero is even given the name Aḥmad, coming from the same root as Muhammad. By establishing a parallel between the lives of Alexander/Dhulqarnayn and the Prophet, the early Quranic interpreters proved that the message of Islam had always been on earth, and that even the Jews of antiquity had known, or had had opportunity to know, that Islam was the straight path.

It is not known to what degree the authors of the longer Arabic Alexander romances synthesized and augmented the material they inherited from their early sources such as Ka'b al-Aḥbār, and his disciples (Ibn 'Abbās, Wahb, and Ibn Isḥāq), or Muqātil b. Sulaymān, whom they frequently cited. In part the lack of knowledge is due to the remoteness of the ninth century, but it is also a direct result of the posthumous disrepute that fell upon the scholars of the seventh and eighth centuries who had made use of *isrā'īlīyāt* literature, among whose ranks were nearly all of the above transmitters. If Ka'b, Wahb or Muqātil put into

---

في تأريخي الكبير علـــى التمـــام (Meissner, p. 601). He also refers to the longer story of Alexander on p. 602.

[20] For the Christianization of the Alexander legend, Cf. Budge (1889, pp. 57-62; 77-83), Cary, *The Medieval Alexander* (pp. 80-83), and I.C. Ruggini in "Sulla cristianizzazione della cultura pagana. Il mito greco e latino di Alessandro."

[21] The use of typology in early Islam has not been adequately studied. Hava Lazarus-Yafeh (p. 110) and John Wansborough (p. 33) both state that Islam never attempted a complete typological approach to Scripture. At the same time, Wansborough cites several examples of typological imagery in Islam (pp. 3-4), as does Jaroslav Stetkevych (p. 33). Newby avoids the term 'typology' but describes relationships between Islamic and Judeo-Christian events and personages that suggest typology (pp. 16-19). I have a done a study of Arabic *qiṣaṣ al-anbiyā'* in their Aljamiado-Morisco translation that seeks to demonstrate that early Arabic authors of stories of the prophets did indeed rewrite Judeo-Christian legends with typology in mind (forthcoming in the journal *Qurṭuba*, fall 2001).

writing any of the mass of *isrā'īlīyāt* material they transmitted, we cannot know this because their works have not survived, perhaps because of their ostracization.[22] Such mythical literature, inasmuch as it narrated the mythical past of the Pagan, Biblical and Quranic peoples, never came to be acknowledged in a canonical sense among the Arabs.[23] For the serious Muslim scholar, the ancient myth with supernatural elements[24] was, and still is for many, nonsense. Had Dhulqarnayn not been mentioned in the Qur'ān, this attitude would have wiped out the Alexander legend in Arabic. Indeed, the discovery of a number of Aljamiado texts in Spain at the end of the nineteenth century revealed a large body of Arab-Islamic literature concerning the prophets that had disappeared in the original Arabic.[25] The question that needs to be raised is, if the purpose of recasting the stories of the prophets into Arabic was to underscore the veracity of Muhammad and Islam, then why did the seemingly useful literary genre produce so few surviving texts? With the expansion of the Islamic empire, the consolidation of its power and wealth, and the growth of its urban intellectual community with resources such as libraries and the support of patrons at their disposal, Muslim exegetes ceased to rely on Judeo-Christian tradition to aid in interpreting the Qur'ān. There was no need for a technique like typology to prove that Judeo-Christianity led to Islam: the Qur'ān, the *hadīth* and sunna[26] were sufficient in and of themselves. The preservation of Islamic truths was legitimized by the *isnād*, or chain of authority, preferably reaching back to a Companion of the Prophet without any weak links. This assertion of the self-contained integrity of Islam, and the move to distance itself from Judeo-Christian

---

[22] The negative reaction among Muslim scholars towards the *isrā'īlīyāt* and the *qiṣaṣ al-anbiyā'* is common knowledge among Arabists. For a discussion of the popular reception of this genre of narrative prose, see S.A. Bonebakker, "Some Medieval Views on Fantastic Stories," pp. 22-25.

[23] Regarding the type of literature discussed here, G.E. von Grunebaum says: "Islam has not added any mythological element. The nearest kin to mythology, the hagiographic image of the Prophet, was evolved without affecting the belles lettres of the classical Islamic age to any significant extent, unless one wishes to identify the biography of Muhammad written by Ibn Isḥāq and edited by Ibn Hishām as "literature" which would hardly be in accordance with the authors' intent. Only some centuries later could one argue that lives of the saints, the life of the caliph 'Alī, and the life of the Prophet as it appears in popular consciousness exhibit "mythological" traits and are allowed to enter literature—although hardly ever in a form that would qualify them as "standard" writing" (p. 12).

[24] There is much material in *Qiṣṣat Dhulqarnayn* relating the stories of the children of Noah and the foundations of cities and peoples that classifies as mythology. See, for instance, the chapter, "Dhulqarnayn's Journey to the Land of the Banī Mansik" below.

[25] Cf. Alvaro Galmés de Fuentes, "La literatura aljamiado-morisca, literatura tradicional" (p, 22). While Galmés de Fuentes' claim that Aljamiado legendary material was transmitted orally in Arabic is polemic, his observation that the Aljamiado texts have preserved lost Arabic texts has not been questioned. J.P. Monferrer Sala also spoke of an Aljamiado text that preserved an Arabic work from early Islam in his paper "'Laora ke la olyó muyó.' Una leyenda oriental sobre la muerte de Moisés en el *Ms. misceláneo 774 de la BNF*. Notas para el estudio de las fuentes musulmanas en la literatura aljamiada" delivered at the VIII Simposio Internacional de Mudejarismo in Teruel, Sept. 15-17, 1999. The printed article should appear in the *Actas del VIII Simposio Internacional de Mudejarismo*, forthcoming.

[26] According to custom, Muhammad's sunna comprises his deeds, utterances (*hadīth*), and his unspoken approval. For a discussion of sunna and the the relationship between hadīth and sunna, see EI 4, pp. 555-57, (Wensinck).

interpretation, coincided with the rise of the Abbasid dynasty. After that point, transmitted literature that had been constructed with Judeo-Christian knowledge would be rejected by serious scholars. In some cases, portions of larger works, valuable in their content but relying on Judeo-Christian transmitters, were purged.[27] Despite these developments, the stories of the prophets, especially that of Alexander, remained popular outside of canonical Arabic literature at least until the seventeenth century.

Mode of Transmission

As a hero who was at once a sacred personage in the Qur'ān and a protagonist in a mainly fictitious legend, Dhulqarnayn was the subject of both Islamic scholars and storytellers. Quranic commentators transmitted their interpretation of passages in Sura XVIII: 83-98 in the manner evident in the following excerpt from QDh:

> Ibn Isḥāq, on the authority of 'Abd al-Malik, who reported from Muqātil b. Sulaymān, who said on the authority of al-Ḍaḥḥāk b. Muzāḥim, who related on the authority of Ibn 'Abbās, may God be satisfied with him, said: The Messenger of God, God bless him and grant him salvation, was asked about the story of Dhulqarnayn and what happened during his life. He responded: He was one of the emirs of the Rūm people. Rūm scholars found in their books and in the common knowledge of the Rūm people that God, the Almighty and Exalted, would send among them a man whose name was Dhulqarnayn, the Knowledgeable One, who would reach the ends of the earth, east and west. There were well-informed men familiar with his story that spoke of him and related his feats and deeds. (ff. 14-15)

Using the *samā'–qirā'a* method,[28] by which one would hear and recite back traditions relative to the Prophet, 'Abd al-Malik, citing the appropriate authorities, taught Ibn Isḥāq a portion of Dhulqarnayn's story. For Ibn Isḥāq to earn the right to transmit on 'Abd al-Malik's authority, as he does here, it is understood that he had to recite what he had learned back to his teacher. Upon successful recitation, he would receive an *ijāza*, or permission, to pass on to others the content of the lesson. 'Abd al-Malik would have gone through the same process with his source, Muqātil b. Sulaymān, and Muqātil from al-Ḍaḥḥak, etc. The method was the same for an entire book, with the complication that transmitters often became authors in their own right. Along with the text they had permission to recite, they would interpolate their own material. With the passage of time, it became difficult to distinguish what a scholar was transmitting and what the scholar

---

[27] The classic example is Ibn Hishām's elimination of Ibn Isḥāq's *Kitāb al-mubtada'*, the compilation of stories from the lives of the prophets that served as beginning to *Sīrat rasūl Allah*. It was cut because it was based on Judeo-Christian authorities. Cf. Newby, *Making of the Last Prophet*, pp. 1-4; 16-22.

[28] The comments given here regarding the transmission of knowledge in early Islam follow chapter 3 of J. Pedersen's *The Arabic Book*.

offered himself, as the books often carried the same title. This confusion is present in QDh, as, on occasions, the reader is unable to clarify who the narrator is.[29] For scholars, who were afraid of having their work rejected, the option to abridge and/or augment an existing acceptable work was a way to conform to tradition and, at the same time, to introduce some novelty. The exigencies of *isnāds* did not prevent interpolations. On the contrary, the citing of a proper *isnād* would have served the intentions of the interpolator well.[30]

One begins to see the tremendous opportunity the façade of *tafsīr* and *hadīth* transmission offered the storyteller, or qāṣṣ. If the *hadīth* transmitter, or Quranic interpreter, was also a storyteller--as was sometimes the case--the recasting of legendary material as Islamic tradition could produce an especially effective narrative. In the case of the Alexander legend, fictitious material from the *Pseudo-Callisthenes* and exegesis of Quranic passages were treated equally in the narration. The effect was that only the most knowledgeable readers could distinguish the two.

Strong chains of authority resisted this sort of interpolation better than weak ones. As an example, consider the *Tafsīr* of Ibn ʻAbbās. A strong *isnād* for a citation from this work might be one confirmed in al-Bukhārī, or Qays b. Muslim through ʻAṭā' b. al-Sā'ib on the authority of Saʻīd b. Jubayr, and Muhammad b. Isḥāq through Muhammad b. Abī Muhammad on the authority of either ʻIkrima or Saʻīd b. Jubayr. Weak chains of transmitters are: Muhammad b. al-Sā'ib al-Kalbī on the authority of Abū Ṣaliḥ or worse—Muhammad b. Marwān al-Ṣuddī through al-Kalbī on the authority of Abū Ṣāliḥ,[31] as well as *isnāds* including Muqātil b. Sulaymān, and al-Ḍaḥḥāk.[32] As one of the most respected depositories of the wisdom of the Companions, Ibn ʻAbbās was frequently cited with no legitimate basis for invoking his authority. It is illuminating to look at the case of Ibn ʻAbbās because one recognizes each of the names given among the weak chains of transmitters as sources cited in QDh.

Thus, while the prominence given to the *samāʻ—qirā'a* method throughout QDh indicates that its transmitters likely worked in the intellectual environment of the *tafsīr* and *hadīth*, and may have passed the text off as solid scholarship, one must be careful not to take all the *isnāds* at face value. Rather, the consistent citing of sources can be seen as a structural device the transmitters imposed on the legend to legitimize a text whose pagan Greek sources were ultimately untrustworthy, but whose message was essentially Islamic and attractive to the Muslim public.

---

[29] Cf. folios 49 & 58.

[30] The discussion on the addition of material during the process of transmission is a summary of Isaiah Goldfeld, "The *Tafsīr* of ʻAbdallah b. ʻAbbās," pp. 125-27.

[31] G. Newby points out that this was known as the "Chain of Falsehood" (*silsilat al-kadhib*). "Tafsīr Isrā'īlīyāt," p. 689.

[32] Cf. "The *Tafsīr* of ʻAbdallah b. ʻAbbās" p. 129.

Alexander or Dhulqarnayn?

Before the revelation of the Qur'ān, Arabic literature had attributed no more importance to Alexander the Great, the Two-Horned,[33] than to any of the other ancient kings or prophets. His name in Arabic, Dhulqarnayn, literally 'the one possessing two horns,' did not necessarily have any transcendental meaning for Arabs, other than being the translation of the Greek. The Arabs of the *jāhilīya* composed no known Alexander romance. It is possible, however, that fragments of the PC preserved from the Syriac recensions circulated among them in popular oral tradition. In short, there is no indication that there was any ambiguity regarding his identity as the pagan conqueror.

With the Quranic mention of Dhulqarnayn, the pagan Greek king quickly assumed the role of the Islamic conqueror at the head of the Army of God, on a mission to traverse the world, submitting its peoples and delivering God's message. Some Muslim writers attributed to Dhulqarnayn superhuman powers, such as the ability to command the darkness to envelop his enemies before he would attack in a blaze of light;[34] the ability to ascend into the heavens with an angel; and the ability to walk on water and even to pound tent pegs into the sea.[35] During the early years of Islam, the first *hadīth* transmitters and Quranic exegetes communicated with sages in Syria and Mesopotamia to fill in details of the many fragmentary Quranic episodes. They took care, in their interpretation, not to contradict the words of the Prophet. For even on those occasions when Muhammad seemed to err,[36] the word of God was incorrigible and sacred. The efforts of Quranic exegetes to identify the Quranic figure of Dhulqarnayn revealed, on the one hand, that he was the hero of a Christian Syriac legend, whose character swung between orthodox Christian and strict ascetic.[37] On the other hand, the exegetes discovered that he was also the hero of the PC, motivated by an uncontrolled ambition to conquer the world and to spread pagan Greek culture. Unknown to them was the fact that the saintly Syriac image of Alexander derived from the pagan hero of the PC.[38]

This confusion was resolved in different manners. Some scholars attributed to Dhulqarnayn superhuman longevity of up to 1600 years.[39] The

---

[33] There has been much discussion of how Alexander came to be called the Two-Horned. See the translation, ff. 58-59 including footnotes, and also García Gómez, p. 48, n. 1.

[34] Cf. al-Tha'labī, p. 363.

[35] These miraculous feats are narrated in QDh. For the ascension see f. 24 sq. For the march across the water see f. 29. For the securing of the tent pegs in the water, see f. 30.

[36] For example, in attributing to Moses in Sura 18: 60-63 the episode in which Alexander's chef brings a dead fish to life by washing it in the water of the Fountain of Life. The episode comes from the PC (ed. Müller), 2, pp. 39-41, as pointed out by A. Abel, p. 6.

[37] García Gómez, p. 39.

[38] García Gómez, p. 40.

[39] Many of the details provided here come from García Gómez' indispensable study of Dhulqarnayn in early Islam, pp. 40-48.

young and rash PC hero learned from his mistakes, and later in life became a pious servant of God. A more natural way to reconcile the two incompatible natures of Dhulqarnayn was to consider the possibility that there were two Dhulqarnayns. The older one was the protagonist of the Quranic episodes and the younger one was Alexander the Great. The creation of a new personage allowed ample space for scholars to invent his history. 'Umāra tells us that there were those who thought he was a Yemenite, others who thought he was Persian, others who claimed he was Spanish, and still others who believed he was from the Banī Isrā'īl.[40] Ibn al-Jawzī offers several possible identifications. He identifies him as 'Alī Karam (according to al-Ḍaḥḥak), 'Abbās b. Qaysar (i.e., son of caesar) where his father was the first of the caesars (according to Muhammed b. 'Alī b. al-Ḥussayn b. Zayn al-'Abidīn), and finally S'ab b. al-Qalmis (according to Ibn Abī Haythim).[41] Other scholars have also identified him with the South Arabian kings Tubba As'ad[42] and Tubba al-Akrān, as well as with Marzaban b. Mardabah al-Yunānī from the offspring of Yunān, son of Japheth, son of Noah.[43] It would seem that each tribe claimed the Quranic hero as one of its own.

By the time of al-Ṭabarī (d. 923 A.D.), the separation of the Quranic Dhulqarnayn from the protagonist of the Greek romance was complete.[44] In his history of prophets and kings, al-Ṭabarī narrates the story of the Pseudo-Callisthenian Alexander.[45] He includes the episode of the Persian campaign, and makes reference to the slaying of the Indian king and to the conquest of China. One notices that the fantastic elements of Dhulqarnayn's story have been reduced to a minimum. The ascension with the angel is not mentioned. The expedition to the Fountain of Life is treated as just another geographical exploit; and the celebrated journey into the darkness is described as a simple march through the North Pole region where the sunlight is poor. Al-Ṭabarī's Quranic commentary, the *Tafsīr*,[46] shows no overlap with the material in his *History*. The lineage given for Dhulqarnayn is different, and the itinerary he follows is also completely different. This is because al-Ṭabarī in his *Tafsīr* is narrating the story of the Quranic personage endowed by God with supernatural powers, with a divine mission to carry the message of Islam to the people of the world. As historian and Quranic commentator, al-Ṭabarī had in hand material coming from the PC tradition that had been augmented with legends attached to the figure of the Two-Horned by Syriac and Persian authors, as well as by transmitters of the *qiṣaṣ al-anbiyā'*, such as Ka'b al-Aḥbār, Wahb b. Munnabih, and Muqātil b. Sulaymān. From this body of diverse material, al-Ṭabarī attributed the more historical

---

[40] f. 3r. See below, "Comparison of QDh with 'Umāra's version."

[41] According to Ibn al-Jawzī in *Mir'āt al-zamān*, f. 77v.

[42] García Gómez gives the name as 'Asaab,' without a source. Al-Mas'ūdī, in *Murūj al-dhahab* identifies a pious Himyarite king, Tubba As'ad (1, p. 76), which is likely the reference intended in García Gómez (p. 41). The Himyarite king Tibān al-As'ad is mentioned in al-Ṭabarī, 4, p. 79.

[43] Given in both García Gómez (p. 41) and Newby, *Making of the Last Prophet*, p. 193.

[44] Abel has pointed out the distinction that al-Ṭabarī makes between the hero of the PC and the Qur'ān in "Dhū'l Qarnayn, Prophète de l'Universalité" (pp. 12-13).

[45] Al-Ṭabarī's story of Dhulqarnayn is found in *Annales* 1, pp. 694-702. In English, it may be found in *The History of al-Ṭabarī: The Ancient Kingdoms*, pp. 88-95.

[46] The story of Dhulqarnayn is found in his *Tafsīr*, 16, p. 9 and pp. 17-21.

episodes to Dhulqarnayn/Alexander and included these in his *History.* The material of a fantastic nature he attributed to the Quranic personage and included in his *Tafsīr.* The result was two distinct accounts belonging to two distinct figures.

However, one hundred or so years later in al-Tha'labī's version in *Qiṣaṣ al-anbiyā',* Alexander/ Dhulqarnayn was again one person. As his career unfolds, he is first conqueror and later prophet. Regarding his status in God's eyes, al-Tha'labī acknowledges the diversity of opinion. Some say he was just a pious king. Others believed that he was a prophet, but that he was not sent to a specific people (*ghayr mursal*). In other words, he manifested through his actions that he was a sign of the Lord, but without being a bearer of a message destined for a specific people, as was the case with Abraham, Moses, Ṣāliḥ, Jesus and Muhammad.[47] For al-Tha'labī, the preferred name was Dhulqarnayn, although he makes reference to Alexander when discussing his name and ancestry. Al-Tha'labī worked towards the reconciliation of Alexander/ Dhularnayn's ambition and piety, the two seemingly contradictory aspects of his character. This was achieved by making him a saintly king whose ambitious project to visit the farthest removed places on the earth, even some that were forbidden,[48] was by order of his Lord.[49] He had a special relationship with God embodied in his regular communication with an angel. Since he was not from Mecca or Jerusalem, and could not, therefore, be a prophet, Dhulqarnayn did not receive visits from the angel Gabriel, who only appeared to prophets. In Gabriel's place came the angel Raphael, often corrupted to Zayāqīl in Arabic legends. The relationship he shared with God was also embodied in the epithet that his soldiers and ministers used, 'friend of God,' وليّ الله ,[50] similar to Abraham's epithet, *Khalīl Allah,* meaning also 'friend of God.'

After the millennium, the growth of Arabic historiography and philosophy, facilitated by extensive translation from Greek and the accumulation of ancient world knowledge in book form, would make it difficult to deny the

---

[47] Cf. Abel, p. 13, n. 4.

[48] When Dhulqarnayn tells al-Khiḍr that he is entering the darkness, his advisor replies, "Fear God, Dhulqarnayn! Do not go places that God has forbidden" (f. 185). Another example of his ambition to tread upon forbidden lands is his meeting with the angel of the horn. The angel asks, "What do you want from this land? Is it that you would like to extend your kingdom to the angels of heaven, whom God with his blessing has veiled from the view of his chosen creatures?" (f. 197).

[49] He tells a bird perched in a castle in which neither human being nor jinn had ever set foot that "my Lord brought me here because He wanted someone to fulfill his command, and for that purpose I came, and He is the One whose dictums are carried out" (f. 194). The seemingly Islamic defense by posturing that one acts only upon God's command may have originated in the PC. When Dhulqarnayn defends his conquests to the Brachmans, he says, "This is not determined by us but by Providence above, so that we are servants of its command; for the sea does not move if the wind does not blow, and trees do not stir if the air is still. Man achieves nothing unless he executes the will of Providence" (PC, Wolohojian, p. 123). The same passage is found translated into romance in the *Rrekontamiento* (f. 78).

[50] For examples in QDh, see ff. 30, 191, 205. This idea is also conveyed in the *Rrekontamiento,* where in answer to the question about whether or not he was a prophet, the transmitter says "no, enpero era amigo de sus amigos, rrey sabidor" (f. 6). The Spanish scribe has rendered the Arabic expression ولي من أولياء الله into romance as "amigo de sus amigos."

identification of the Quranic Dhulqarnayn with the Macedon, Alexander the Two-Horned. This identification was further strengthened by the wide circulation of the Alexander romance in Latin, Persian, and Hebrew. However, a more sophisticated knowledge of his Greek origins did not give occasion to the writing of an Arabic romance that eliminated the many anachronisms present in the Arabic Alexander romances and more accurately reflected the PC. The pervasive influence of the Qur'ān would never admit to a version that directly contradicted Sura 18: 83-98.

Sequence of Episodes in *Qiṣṣat Dhulqarnayn*

[Introduction]

Commonplace of praise to God, and admonishment to the reader (ff. 1-3); frame story in which People of the Book come to Muhammad to pose questions (ff. 3-14); Dhulqarnayn's advent foretold (f. 15); Dhulqarnayn's youth and his relationship with Aristotle (ff. 15-17).

Dhulqarnayn and the Building of Alexandria

The kings and governors of his day pay him hommage (f. 17); the clergymen and monks of Rūm pose questions to the young king (ff. 18-19); Aristotle poses questions to Dhulqarnayn (ff. 19-20); Dhulqarnayn builds Alexandria (f. 20).

The Means Given to Dhulqarnayn and How He Achieved So Many Wondrous Things

Dhulqarnayn asks himself if he should begin his campaigns in the east or the west and exchanges letters with Aristotle on the question (ff. 20-24); Dhulqarnayn meets the angel Zayāqīl and flies high above the earth beneath the angel's wing (24-26); Dhulqarnayn is overwhelmed with the mission revealed to him and asks God how he could bear such a burden (f. 26); God's reassurance and the mission he is to be assigned (ff. 27-28); the army departs on its journey and Dhulqarnayn walks on water (f. 29); the whinnying of the horses keeps the men from sleeping, and the miracle by which the men are made to pound their tent pegs into the water as if it were solid earth (f. 30); Dhulqarnayn's ancestry and lineage (f. 31); castle with the revolving doors and spiraling motion containing Sitrūn's plaque foretelling Muhammad and Islam including the stories of Qātūr, Sitrūn and Sām b. Noah (ff. 33-39).

Dhulqarnayn's Trip to the City of Jābalqā

Dhulqarnayn arrives at Jābalqā and prepares to attack (ff. 39-42); the people of Jābalqā explain that they had closed their doors because they thought their enemy had come to threaten them (f. 43); Dhulqarnayn rides the Alborak (ff. 45-46); he sees the sun set in black mud and hears the clamor of the people that live nearby (ff. 46-48); he converses with a 1163 yr. old sheikh named Jūdib b. Jūdib (ff. 48-55); he orders his men to hang their weapons on the Pleiades (ff. 48-57); several reasons to explain the name Dhulqarnayn (57-59); he enters Jābalqā and has a conversation with the old man unimpressed by the Macedonian's arrival (ff. 59-61); stories of Hūd, Ṣāliḥ, and the Thamūd and the etymology of the toponyms Jābalqā and Jābarṣā (ff. 61-66).

Dhulqarnayn's Trip from Jābalqā to the East

Zayāqīl brings orders from God for Dhulqarnayn to go to the people of Bārish (f. 66); written correspondence with the Bārish (ff. 67-71); Dhulqarnayn meets the Bārish and learns their story (ff. 71-74); Dhulqarnayn observes the Bārish's pious and ascetic way of life (f. 74); dialogue with the Bārish and departure (ff. 74-77); arrival to the Mārib Plain where Dhulqarnayn builds the Mārib barrier (ff. 77-80); Dhulqarnayn writes to the Tārish who harass their enemies the Bārish (ff. 82-83); the Tārish write back to Dhulqarnayn (ff. 82-83); interpolated prophecy about the coming of the Anti-Christ and God's protection of Medina and Mekka (ff. 84-85); description of the Tārish and warning that they will break their accord when the Macedonian army leaves (ff. 85-87); the Bārish offer to collect a tax to pay for the construction of a barrier to keep the Tārish out (ff. 87-90); construction of the barrier (ff. 90-92).

Dhulqarnayn's Journey to the People of Yāwīl.

Dhulqarnayn writes letter to the people of Yāwīl and disguises himself as messenger (ff. 92-96); he learns that the Yāwīl have many cities and that their king is Nawwāsh b. 'Amlāq (f. 97); Description of the city's fortifications, including the cave retreat in the city's center (ff. 98-99); King Nawwāsh b. 'Amlāq writes to Dhulqarnayn (ff. 99-100); Dhulqarnayn accepts the surrender of King Nawwāsh, and appoints Nawwāsh's nephew as division leader in his army (ff. 100-102).

Dhulqarnayn's Journey to the People of Tāwīl

Dhulqarnayn comes to the island of the Tāwīl (ff. 103-105); he writes to their king Shūrash b. Sharīsh (f. 106); Shūrash consults with his people and they vote to oppose Dhulqarnayn. Although Shurāsh is against the idea of fighting Dhulqarnayn, as king he agrees to attack the invaders (ff. 107-108); in the midst of battle, Shurāsh surrenders and Dhulqarnayn accepts and honors him (ff. 108-110).

Dhulqarnayn's Journey to the Banī Mansik

Dhulqarnayn comes to a pair of islands inhabited by the Mansik (ff. 110-111); he sends them a letter (ff. 111-112); the messenger sits with the Mansik king who is a most beautiful young man (ff. 113-115); their king, Dahqān b. 'Ālaj b. Khawlān b. Jad'ān b. Mansik b. Artakhshad b. Sām b. Noah, travels to meet Dhulqarnayn, and tells him the history of the Mansik tribe (ff. 115-118); Dahqān informs Dhulqarnayn that a serpent attacks his people (ff. 118-119); story of the fishermen who once traveled to Mt. Qāf and were sequestered by a giant bird, the 'Anaqā (ff. 119-128); Dhulqarnayn builds a canal to protect them from the serpents (ff. 129-30); history of the serpents (ff. 130-35); distribution of the earth's land among the creatures (ff. 135-37); prediction that the end of the world is near and that barbarians will swarm the earth through a hole in the Gog and Magog barrier (ff. 137-38); Zayāqīl informs Dhulqarnayn that his next mission is to visit the lands of the Naghāsh tribe (f. 139).

Dhulqarnayn's Journey to the Lands of the al-Naghāsh

Dhulqarnayn comes upon a people who spend their lives fighting cranes and storks that eat their crops (ff. 139-40); Dhulqarnayn sends them a letter and they surrender (ff. 140-42); Dhulqarnayn comes to the city of Rome and writes to all the kings of the Rūm lands (ff. 142-44); He writes to Jerusalem (ff. 144-45); He consults with his advisors and they decide that the first place they will attack is Persia (ff. 145-46); Darius learns of Dhulqarnayn and underestimates the threat he poses (ff. 147-48); Darius marches forward with his army until he comes to a river called the Bişwariş, from where he writes to Dhulqarnayn and sends him gifts including sesame seeds (ff. 148-149); Dhulqarnayn imprisons Darius' messengers and pretends that he plans to kill them (ff. 150-51); he writes two letters to Darius and sends them with the messengers (ff. 151-55); the Macedonians meet the Persians in battle and the Persians are forced into retreat (ff. 155-57); Darius and his men escape safely to Persia (f. 157).

Dhulqarnayn's Journey to the Land of Katāba[51]

Dhulqarnayn enters the region of Mount Sinai where he subdues the people and imposes a *kharaj* tax (f. 157); he comes to the land of Fadūma, inhabited by the Naqrūn people whom he subdues and on whom he imposes a *kharaj* tax (f. 158); he departs from there and comes to a people called the al-Qaylūn in the land of al-Qablī with whom he makes a pact to pay him tribute and tax every year (f. 158); he leaves them and comes to a land called Qadūmā, governed by King Falaş, which is towards where the Rūm people have their roots. He promises them he will not enter the gates of their city until he has conquered their king, Darius (ff. 158-59); he travels to a city called Qasamṭīna in the land of Majrān where the troops begin to starve. They leave to look for food and travel to a city called Taṭūsh, where they find a temple. Dhulqarnayn threatens to destroy the temple if his future is not foretold, but then hears a voice that tells him he will achieve great things (ff. 159-61); he leaves there and travels to the land of Amānīsh where the people reject Dhulqarnayn's proposal for peace. They lose the battle and write to Darius for help (ff. 161-63); Macedonians and the Persians meet in a fierce battle at which Darius is routed and forced to flee across a dangerous river (ff. 163-65); Darius offers to surrender to Dhulqarnayn if his troops will cease to attack the Persians (ff. 165-66); Darius retreats to a temple in Persia where he sees no choice but to write a letter of surrender to Dhulqarnayn. Afterwards, he reconsiders and writes to Labūr, King of India, for help (ff. 166-69).

Dhulqarnayn's Journey to the City of Jābarṣā

Dhulqarnayn travels and draws near the city of Jābarṣā. The city has ten thousand doors with a distance between each door of three parasangs (ff. 169-70); story about Hūd, Ṣaliḥ and the founding of Jābalqā and Jābarṣā (ff. 171-74); we return to the main narrative and find Dhulqarnayn has approached Jābarṣā whose people close the city doors thinking it is the army of their enemies the Jābalqāns (f. 174); Dhulqarnayn writes them a letter (f. 175); from the letter's contents they know it is not their enemy and the king goes to see Dhulqarnayn, who asks him about his people, his religion and the city (ff. 175-B:65r); Dhulqarnayn learns that the darkness is nearby (f. 65v); Dhulqarnayn asks the angel Zayāqīl about the darkness and learns that it contains the Fountain of Life (ff. 65v-66r); Dhulqarnayn leaves Jābarṣā and travels until he comes near the darkness (ff. B:66r-A:178); Dhulqarnayn asks the angel more questions about the darkness (ff. 178-80); Dhulqarnayn asks his wisemen and Afshakhīr about the darkness. Afshakhīr demonstrates that he knows as much as the angel about the darkness and warns the king not to enter (ff. 180-84); al-

[51] This is perhaps a corruption of Kināna, referring to Egypt, land of the Kinana tribe.

Khiḍr also admonishes him not to enter (ff. 185-86); Dhulqarnayn chooses his best men and horses, and takes out a magical stone capable of lighting the darkness and gives it to al-Khiḍr (186-87); Lātiqūn will stay behind in control of the troops (ff. 187-88).

Dhulqarnayn's Journey to the Island of the Darkness

The army of Dhulqarnayn approaches the darkness and enter with al-Khiḍr at the lead (ff.188-89); al-Khiḍr goes off by himself and finds the Fountain of Life, drinks from it and does the ritual ablutions in its waters (ff. 190-91); al-Khiḍr rejoins the troops and leads them with the light of the stone on a twenty day march out of the darkness (ff. 191-92); they come to a sandy white land and find a castle (f. 192).

The Wonders Dhulqarnayn Saw in the Castle

Dhulqarnayn finds a door to the castle and enters to discover a bird hanging upside down that asks him why he has come there. They have a dialogue about the moral state of the people on earth. First, the bird expands in size to fill the entire chamber with its body, and subsequently contracts back to original size. Then the bird directs Dhulqarnayn to climb a stairwell (ff. 193-96); Dhulqarnayn climbs the stairs to a lofty terrace and meets the boy of the horn with whom he has a conversation, upon completion of which the hornblower gives Dhulqarnayn a bunch of grapes to feed his troops and their animals, as well as a stone said to be made in his image (ff. 196-99); Dhulqarnayn feeds the troops magically with a single bunch of grapes (ff. 199-200); the wisemen congregate to determine the mystery of the stone (ff. 200-201); al-Khiḍr interprets for him the secret of the stone and Dhulqarnayn breaks down and cries and is said to become an ascetic (ff. 201-205); the army crosses a riverbed of precious gems and Dhulqarnayn says that he who gathers will regret and he who does not will also regret (ff. 205-206); Dhulqarnayn comes to the people of the two mountains and the narrator recalls briefly some details of that earlier episode (ff. 206-208); Darius' request has reached India and King Labūr sends his nephews to aid the Persians. In the meantime, Dhulqarnayn has learned of his rival's duplicity and has intensified his search for the Persian king (ff. 208-209); With Dhulqarnayn in hot pursuit, Darius' ministers slay their leader and Dhulqarnayn comes upon him in his last moments before death and promises revenge and care for his family (ff. 209-211); Darius is given a fitting burial (ff. 211-213); Dhulqarnayn writes to the cities of Persia with a promise to rebuild their country and a request for arms, soldiers and horses (ff. 213-215); Dhulqarnayn tricks the assassins into turning themselves in so that he can crucify them (ff. 215-216); Dhulqarnayn and Darius' mother exchange correspondence (ff. 216-218); Dhulqarnayn sends his own mother a letter and some money with a request to prepare the trousseau for his marriage to Rashīqa, daughter of Darius (f. 218).

Dhulqarnayn's Attack against Labūr, King of India.

Dhulqarnayn and Labūr exchange letters and the Macedonians begin the invasion of India (ff. 218-222).

Dhulqarnayn's Campaign against Labūr, King of India, and What Happened Therein.

Narrator tells us that Dhulqarnayn has met his mother and consummated his marriage to Darius' daughter (f. 222); account of how the Indians harvest pepper that has washed down from the mountains (f. 223-24); Dhulqarnayn asks an Indian man about Labūr and about the Indian people and their army (ff. 224-26); Dhulqarnayn reassures his frightened soldiers that Labūr and the Indians are no better than the other armies they have defeated, and that they should not be intimidated by mere words (f. 226); Dhulqarnayn writes to Labūr (ff. 226-27); description of the Indian army with its lions and elephants (ff. 227-28); Dhulqarnayn outfits his army with firey statue-like images of wild beasts to fight the Indians (ff. 228-31); Dhulqarnayn's army marches into combat, beating their drums and professing God's oneness (f. 231); the battle rages on and both sides suffer terrible casualties, such that Dhulqarnayn's men consider for a moment betraying their leader (ff. 231-33); Dhulqarnayn yells to Labūr and asks him to solve their dispute by means of single combat between the two kings (f. 233); Dhulqarnayn slaughters Labūr when the Indian king is momentarily distracted (ff. 234-35); the Macedonians collect booty from the battle (f. 235); Dhulqarnayn writes to Aristotle with his news (ff. 235-36); Dhulqarnayn heads west and comes to the Berbers, known in that era as the Libyans, who are a savage people that scoff at lions and ride them and consider mankind to be their enemy (ff. 236-37); he fought the Berbers, subdued them and obliged them to pay him tribute and then continued on his way to Ifrīqīyā (ff. 237-38).

Dhulqarnayn's Campaign to the Lands of Ifrīqīyā.

Dhulqarnayn leaves Libya and enters the lands of Ifrīqīyā where he meets many interconnected tribes among whom were the Kutāma and the Muzāna. Some embrace his religion and others refuse and face the sword. He exacts tribute and the *kharaj* tax (f. 238); he leaves and comes to the Hajyasa people who quickly submit to his conditions (f. 239); he leaves them and comes to a mountain in the al-Dara region called Jarjara, where he finds a people called Zawāra whom he subdues and from whom he collects tribute (f. 239); from there he travels until he comes to the Kutāma tribe, who are governed by a man named Khīdān b. Kīdād Senior who pays him tribute (f. 239); leaving Khīdān, he comes to the coast to a place called Nakara, whose name has since been changed to Naldar. Here live people who are of Rūm lineage called the al-Zarāha[52] (f. 239); a short distance further along the coast, he finds a people living there who are called the Nafza (f. 239); he sails along the coast and conquers Kafāl b. Ghuwwān, who had settled there with his people in the time of Ba'tīsh. He stays there for a year and three months, until he conquers the inhabitants of the Morroccan mountains (f. 240); he conquers the city of Aylān (f. 241); he crosses the strait to disembark on the distant shore (f. 241).

Dhulqarnayn's Campaign into al-Andalus

Dhulqarnayn comes to the shores of Mount al-Fataḥa, inhabited by the people called the al-Andalus, also known as the al-Anbār (f. 241); Zayāqīl comes to him and commands him to order the soldiers led by Ghaydāf b. Māzin b. Arūm to leave behind their horse stakes in the ground. The stakes of Dhulqarnayn's horses were made from the wood of the olive tree and grew into trees and the place took the name of the military commander (ff. 241-42); the al-Anbār obey Dhulqarnayn, and upon his request, narrate their tribal history to the Macedon. Finally, they tell him of another people in the area called the Zawābra, of blue skin, who live on an island behind Mount Shāmakh. They warn him of the danger of climbing the mountain because of the extreme winds that have caused the death of all those

---

[52] Perhaps this is a corruption of Zarhūn, a well-known mountain in Morocco.

who attempt its ascent (ff. 242-45); he climbs the mountain and loses one hundred men and is only saved after falling to his knees and praying to God for help (f. 245); his general, Philon, takes a patrol group out into the sea to look for more marvelous things. The patrol comes across a city built on ships that moves across the face of the sea (ff. 245-47); Philon meets the king of the floating city, who assures the patrol that his people believe in Dhulqarnayn's religion and that they will pay tribute (ff. 247-50); afterwards they set sail into a great sea flowing into the Ocean towards the land of Taqlīs, said to be on the coast in the eastern lands of the Rūm (f. 250); the Macedonians go in search of water and come to an island populated with many tigers, beasts, and hungry wild animals, where there is a spring of excellent water (f. 250); in a cave they discover a statue of Kūsh, whose kingdom and knowledge spread from there to al-Shūs in the West and to China in the East (ff. 250-52); they settle in to make camp in the vicinity of a lake with high winds and a harsh climate, and are attacked by an elephant sized beast at night. They manage to keep the beast away till morning, but then it attacks again and kills forty men before they slaughter it and find a giant serpent in its belly (ff. 252-53); from there, they sail into the seas until they land in an area with great deserts and dry lands along the coast. They make camp there and find cannibals with fangs and faces like dogs, and whose color is black like the crow. These are the Abyssinians from Kūsh and although they agree to believe in Dhulqarnayn's religion, the Macedon calls them atrocious and leaves them because they do not bury their dead (ff. 253-55); departing from there, he comes to a river valley with great cliffs, many rocks, and treacherous mountain paths. There are no sowed fields or buildings, but fruit grows abundantly. They make camp in the valley beside the riverbed and eat dates and fruits. They are attacked by a beast larger than an elephant with hair like a pig. It carries away a woman from the army and kills her before they manage to kill it (ff. 255-56); they come to a great body of land in the mountains, with many river valleys and springs. Inhabiting those lands is a people that belong to mankind, but their bodies are covered with feet from top to bottom and they are black and have no nose. Their language is incomprehensible. They do not live in houses, but in the fields like wild animals. They throw rocks at the Macedonian army, killing a number of soldiers. So Dhulqarnayn attacks them and causes them great loss of life. They enter caves and remain in impregnable underground shelters (ff. 256-57); Dhulqarnayn comes across trees that grow and/or shrink according to the position of the sun in the sky. Dhulqarnayn orders his men to take fruit from the magical trees but rocks rain down on them from the sky and a voice admonishes them not to touch the fruit (ff. 258-59); Dhulqarnayn comes to Babel and finds a temple in which the King of the Jinn is laid out on a bed in a golden chamber. Dhulqarnayn finds a pile of red sulphur alongside the bed and takes it, and later discovers it to be a cure for leprosy (ff. 259-61); at sea, Dhulqarnayn comes upon an isthmus over which the waves crash and produce eggs; some hatch and become beautiful maidens, and others become vulture-like birds that snatch the maidens and fly away (ff. 261-63); leaving from there with great curiousity, he sails until he reaches the end of the sea, where a mountain rises high into the sky. There he encounters an angel, sitting in a chair. On each of the four legs of the chair there is a snake. Dhulqarnayn learns from the angel that by means of those snakes and that angel, God anchors the mountains of the earth and causes earthquakes. The angel also tells him that the mountain in front of him is Mt. Qāf. Dhulqarnayn asks about the maidens and the angel says that nobody knows for sure, but they are believed to be the hūries, found in paradise (ff. 264-65); Dhulqarnayn comes to a land of abundant fruit and cold weather and orders the Rūm soldiers to settle there (ff. 266-67); Dhulqarnayn comes to the land of the Jinn and is told by Zayāqīl to look after his soul (ff. 267-68); Dhulqarnayn orders his men to gather the treasures and he writes his name on each item in the treasury and records everything in a book and goes with the book towards his homeland. He sends the treasure to his mother with a letter (ff. 268-69); Dhulqarnayn and his army invade China where he receives a letter from his mother in which she gives him her approval and guidance (ff. 269-70); story of the buyer of a house who complains that the seller left a fortune in the house and is unwilling to claim it or remove it (ff. 270-72); Following Alexander's conquest of China, and upon his return, he feels ill and so complains. When he lays down to sleep a sign comes to him in his dreams. It says: "May God take pity on you, for you will die upon new ground above which is green." When he awakes in the morning he tells his scribe to write a letter of consolation to his mother (ff. 272-75); in another account, Alexander meets Abraham at the Ka'ba (f. 275); several transmitters maintain that Dhulqarnayn did not die until he reached Jerusalem (ff. 275-77); letter from Alexander to his mother (f. 277); Alexander's mother throws a party for all the women who do not grieve for someone (ff. 278-79); speculation on why Alexander was not a prophet (f. 279); conclusion (f. 279).

Collation of *Qiṣṣat Dhulqarnayn* with Other Versions of the Arabic Alexander Romance

Comparison of *Qiṣṣat Dhulqarnayn* with the Syriac Version Called *History of Alexander the Great*

Ernest A. Wallis Budge edited and translated the Syriac version of the legend of Alexander in 1889. In his introduction he provided a survey of the major non-European works concerning the Alexander romance. Some forty years later A.R. Nykl[53] and Emilio García Gómez[54] both concurred with Budge[55] in his belief that the story of Alexander entered Arabic through a Syriac version of the PC made in the sixth century by a Christian monk. The Christianized Syriac Alexander is said to be the one alluded to in the Qur'ān, which explains how a pagan conqueror and proselytizer of Greek culture managed to be praised in the Muslim holy book. Nykl has placed the Arabic rendition of the Syriac circa 800 A.D. and before Hunayn b. Isḥāq (809-873), who is believed to have included material from an Arabic Alexander romance for the part of his work relating aphorisms of the philosophers.[56]

---

[53] *Rrekontamiento*, p. 445.

[54] *Un texto árabe occidental*, p. xxxi

[55] "That it (i.e., the Ethiopic) was made from the Arabic, there is little doubt" *The Life and Exploits of Alexander the Great* (xxiv). Also, see Budge's *History of Alexander*, p. xc.

[56] This is the work from which derive the Spanish *Bocados de oro* and *Buenos proverbios*. The narrative material intercalated in this philosophical work are the episode relating Alexander's encounter with the old man stirring bones (below ff. 59-60) and the letters from Dhulqarnayn to his mother. Cf. Nykl, p. 445; García Gómez pp. 66, 67, 153-56.

The Syriac Alexander legend is in many ways more faithful to the PC than the Arabic texts deriving from it. The Syriac text offers a fairly complete and accurate account of Olympias' affair with the Egyptian king Nectanebus, as related in the PC. This material pointed to an adulterous birth for Alexander and, consequently, was unsuitable for the Islamic versions of the legend in which the hero is portrayed as either prophet or saint with untainted ancestry reaching back to Noah. Thus, it has been cut from the Arabic romances. The youth of Alexander, inasmuch as it concerns the prince's relationship to his father Philip, is present in the Syriac romance (p. 18) but has been eliminated from the Arabic legends, although there is an allusion in QDh (f. 145) and in the *Rrekontamiento* (f. 43v.) to Aristotle's identification of astrological signs foretelling Alexander's rise to power as a youth. Alexander's relationship to his tutor Aristotle is present in the Syriac text and in QDh. In the latter, Aristotle is portrayed as the most pious and righteous man among the Rūm people, and is said to be Alexander's cousin (f. 15-16). The events in Pisa together with the death of Nicolaus, and Philip's attempt to kill his son, present in the Syriac, are altogether absent from QDh, as well as from other Arabic Alexander romances. Of the narrative material that follows Philip's quarrel with his son in the Syriac text, only the founding of Alexandria is present in QDh, and even here the resemblance is slight. The Arabs' dramatic transformation of the PC material can be explained as an attempt to Islamicize the legend. For a Muslim translator, the contents of the Greek PC, as rendered into the Syriac, contained many references to pagan idols and auguries (such as the one foretelling the construction of Alexandria) and would need to be recast in an Islamic light.

At this point in the Syriac text, the campaign begins against Darius, King of Persia. As is to be expected, the Syriac is much closer to the PC than to any of the Arabic versions, none of which can be said to be more than an abridgement of the Persian campaign in the PC.[57] Some of the most important material eliminated from the Arabic romances is Alexander's destruction of Thebes and the submission of the Athenians.

In contrast, the campaign against the king of India has been expanded in QDh rather than abridged, perhaps because of the Arabs' fascination with the processes of metallurgy used to make animal figures. The letters between the Macedonian and Indian king are longer and insist on Dhulqarnayn's Islamic message. The preparation of the brazen images of the beasts to be used to combat the Indian elephants and wild beasts is more elaborate. The battle includes more gruesome detail. Alexander kills the Indian king by decapitation rather than running him through with a sword. On the whole, QDh is quite faithful in detail to the Syriac with respect to the campaign against the Indians.[58]

In the Syriac text, after Alexander buries the king of India he travels to meet the Brahmans. In addition to having been moved in the narrative sequence-- the encounter with the Brahmans is inserted in QDh before the Persian and Indian

---

[57] For a detailed comparison of *Qiṣṣat Dhulqarnayn*, the *Rrekontamiento*, the PC, the Syriac and the Ethiopian with respect to the campaign against Darius, see my dissertation pp. 160-204.

[58] 'Umāra's version of the Indian campaign is much closer in detail to the Syriac than *Qiṣṣat Dhulqarnayn*. See 'Umāra ff. 38v-41v.

campaigns, as opposed to immediately after the death of the king of India as in the Syriac--, the episode has been greatly transformed in QDh and hardly resembles the Syriac, except for the unparalleled piety of the tribe ("He observed a people who without doubt constituted the most pious of nations" f. 74).[59] The letters exchanged between Alexander and the Brahmans have disappeared. The questions Dhulqarnayn poses are almost entirely different.[60] Where in the Syriac (p. 92) it says that the Brahmans "were all naked, ... their wives and children went about the plain like sheep," in QDh (f. 74) it says that "their livestock roamed without shepherds" and the men "were equal in their earnings, strength, and dress." Even the name 'Brahman' does not appear in QDh, as the "naked sages" have been transferred from India to a land called Bārish.

Upon leaving the Brahmans, the Syriac Alexander writes to Aristotle to inform him of the wonders of India. This letter is very long and includes events that traverse India, Asia, China, Samarkand. The letter's ending is not marked, but flows into the episode of Candace, Queen of Samira, where the narration switches back from first to third person. In QDh after the Indian triumph, without mention of the Brahmans, Dhulqarnayn heads west where he meets the Berbers, as well as the people of Ifrīqīyā and al-Andalus. This material is altogether lacking in the Syriac. However, after his trip to al-Andalus, QDh narrates several episodes that recall the Syriac, although the details have been significantly reworked. There is the naval patrol of Philon (f. 245); the city floating on the sea (ff. 246-250) which has been in form and content liberally adapted; the discovery of the pillar of Sesonchosis while Alexander's army is dying of thirst in a land of terrible beasts that attack the Macedonian army in the middle of the night (f. 251); the beast that attacked and ate one of the women accompanying Alexander's troops (f. 256); the tree that either grew or diminished in size according to the time of day (f. 258); and Alexander in the temple of Dionysius, who is transformed in the Arabic text into the king of the Jinn (f. 260). The arrival of Alexander to China is only alluded to in QDh (f. 269). Missing is his encounter and dialogue with the Chinese emperor. Also missing is the construction of Samarkand, his visit to Sebazaz, Sogd, the crossing of the river Bartesitos, the slaying of Paryog, and the building of Maro -- among other things.

As mentioned above, the letter concerning the wonders of India runs into the story of Alexander and Candace, Queen of Samira. There is no mention in QDh of Samira or Candace, or of Alexander's subsequent encounter in the Syriac with the Amazon women. These two episodes originating in the PC, in which Alexander is sexually tempted, were apparently not suitable to the prophet-like stature the Islamic authors wished to create for their hero.

---

[59] 'Umāra's version of the Brahman's episode (41v. 46r) is very close in detail to the Syriac. The *Rrekontamiento* is also close to the Syriac, although the tribe is called the Turjamānīn, i.e., the intrepreters. See *Rrekontamiento* ff. 74v-85. *Qiṣṣat Dhulqarnayn* mentions the Turjamānīn, but omits the episode: "You should know that I have not reached the kingdom of Syria, nor the kingdom of China nor the Turjamānīn. But I am heading there, God Almighty willing" (f. 143). The Ethiopic text here also closely resembles the Syriac (pp. 126-142).

[60] Where the dialogues in the two texts agree, at least in content, is with regards to the proximity of the Brahman's graves and houses. Cf. the Syriac, p. 92 and QDh, f. 74.

The final sequence in the Syriac work consists of Aristotle's letter to Alexander admonishing him to thank the Gods for the favor they have shown him. This is followed by Alexander's letter to his mother relating a number of adventures. Finally, there is the poisoning of Alexander, the writing of his testament, his instructions for burial, his death and the list of cities he erected. All of this is missing from QDh.

Budge has suggested the possibility of identifying passages from the original Arabic translation made from the Syriac text. This might be done by comparing the proper names given in the Syriac with the Arabic text in question and comparing these in turn with the Ethiopic text, known to be a translation of an early Arabic text.[61] Great similarities would indicate proximity in filiation. A review of proper names in our text reveals that they are quite different from both the Syriac and the Ethiopic:

Syriac	**QDh**	**Ethiopic**
Alexander	Dhulqarnayn/Alexander	Two-Horned/Alexander
Philip	Nabbāsh	Philip
Olympias	Al-Ghaydā'	Olympias
Roshnak (Alexander's wife)	Rashīq(a)	Rasīq
Porus (King of India)	Labūr	Porus
Sesankos (Sesonchosis, (King of the World)	Kūsh	Kūs
Achaia	Katāba[62] (first stop in side excursion after success in battle against Darius)	Not mentioned
"A certain river"	Tiqrān River (Darius narrowly escapes across this river)	"A mighty river"
Anṭognaya	Lāṭīqūn	El-Anṭikon
Akranṭis (site of Apollo's temple)	Taṭūsh	Not mentioned
Philon	Aflaṭūn	"one of my councillors"

It is to be noted that comparison is sometimes obstructed by the frequent omission of proper nouns: where one text mentions a person or place-name, another gives no name at all. Thus, although each text has dozens of proper names, it is difficult to find even a handful of narrative moments in which two or three of the texts coincide. From those that have been located, there is a stark contrast between Akranṭis and Taṭūsh, Olympias and al-Ghaydā', Achaia and Katāba. The

[61] García Gómez has conjectured from a comparison of *Hadīth Dhulqarnayn* with the Syriac Alexander legend that certain episodes in the work he edits "pueden representar quizá la primitiva versión arábiga del célebre texto, procedente del siríaco, que se consideraba perdida. Ningún episodio tiene, sin embargo, el interés que el evidentemente derivado de la leyenda cristianosiríaca. Causa cierta sorpresa encontrar una versión casi completa y bastante fiel de este texto venerable, que influyó en el Alcorán, en un manuscrito aragonés del siglo XV, cuando, según Nöldeke, apenas quedan rastros suyos en la literatura islámica" (p. 156). One must proceed with caution here. One of the episodes he believes may reflect the original Arabic translation of the Syriac legend relates the construction of the wall of Gog and Magog. This episode appears in nearly all Arabic accounts of Dhulqarnayn's life, precisely because of its mention in the Qur'ān. For instance, see QDh below ff. 87-92.

[62] See note 51 above.

variation in other toponyms and proper names, such as with Alexander's wife Roxana, Sesonchosis, Antigonus, Philon, Porus and Philip,[63] can be explained as corruptions.

In conclusion, the few similarities in proper names, together with the many distinctions pointed out above with respect to the two narratives would seem to indicate that QDh is somewhat distant in filiation from any Arabic recension of the Alexander romance made of the Syriac text.

Comparison of *Qiṣṣat Dhulqarnayn* and *The Life and Exploits of Alexander the Great Being a Series of Ethiopic Texts*

The Ethiopic Alexander romance was edited and translated into English by E.A. Wallis Budge in 1896. It is a lengthy Christianized rendition of the Macedon's tale occupying more than 350 pages in Budge's English translation. Said to have been rendered from Arabic into Ethiopic, and relating many episodes common to QDh, the work merits a close scrutiny.

Like the PC and the Syriac romances, the Ethiopic story of Alexander begins by narrating Olympias' affair with Nectanebus the Egyptian, followed by Alexander's youth, with minor variation from the Syriac and PC.[64] That this material is present in the Ethiopic indicates that it must have passed into Arabic, although none of the Arabic legends that I have examined mentions Alexander's mother's adulterous relationship with the former Egyptian king. As in the PC, following Philip's death Alexander makes a series of speeches to his troops and writes his army a letter. This material is not included in QDh. Their first common narrative element is the letter from Alexander to all kings calling them to obedience. Thus, the episodes related in the first 140 pages of QDh –including his ancestry and lineage linking him to Noah, the building of Alexandria in Egypt, his journey to Jābalqā, his visit to the Bārish, his journey to the lands of the people called Yāwīl and Tāwil and to the Banī Mansik-- are not present in the Ethiopic.

The Ethiopic version of the campaigns against the Persians is not substantially different from QDh. Notable variations are that in the middle of the Persian campaign, where in QDh as in the PC,[65] Alexander makes a side incursion into the lands of the East, in the Ethiopic this excusion is to Jerusalem. The Ethiopic author inserts Alexander's encounter and dialogue with the Jews of the Holy City to convert them, not present in the PC, the Syriac or QDh. The Ethiopic text also shows considerable development in the relationship between Alexander and his wife to be, Roxana, including the exchange of several letters.

The campaign against Porus, King of India, is also very similar to the version found in QDh, although as is generally the case, the Ethiopic text shows more elaboration. In the Ethiopic, Alexander's horse Bucephalus is bewitched by

---

[63] See Proper Names below.

[64] See the Ethiopic text especially pp. 38, 39, 45 for the early development of Alexander's Christian character.

[65] PC p. 66. QDh ff. 158-162.

Porus' sorcery, a detail which is lost in QDh and other Arabic legends, perhaps because Alexander's acquisition of Bucephalus falls in the first chapters of the PC which are universally cut from the Arabic texts. It is also to be noted that Alexander kills Porus by running him through with the spear, as in the Syriac, which is in contrast to QDh where he dies decapitated.

The following episodes in the Ethiopic include Dhulqarnayn's adventures with the Brahmans, with the king of China, with the Queen of Samira (Candace), and with the Amazon women. None of this material appears in QDh. Regarding Alexander's epistle to Aristotle narrating the wonders of India, the Ethiopic shares with QDh the discovery of a city supported in mid air above the sea, the lake upon whose shore was the pillar of Kush, King of the World (including the terrifying night(s) the Macedon army spent fighting the beasts that came down to the lake to drink), the slaughter of the enormous beast whose belly contains snakes, the woman who is taken and eaten by a monstrous beast "like unto that of a wild boar," the trees which grow and diminish according to time of day, the arrival of Dhulqarnayn to the temple of Enoch atop a mountain.[66] Missing from the epistle are the cave dwellers, the Greek-speaking golden birds, the whirlwind, the black lightening cloud, the snow storm and the trees of the sun and the moon.[67] Even for those episodes that coincide, the details show such variation as to be recognizable only as having a remote common source.

Alexander's voyage into the foetid sea in the Ethiopic includes passages pointing to the hero's uncontrolled ambition to dominate the entire world. Perhaps for this reason, the episode does not figure in QDh, where the intent is to portray a pious "evangelical" Muslim.

On the other hand, the episode of Alexander's journey to the western end of the earth where he sees the sun set in the spring of muddy water is of great interest to the transmitters of all the Arabic romances, as it appears in the Qur'ān. QDh, as other Arabic romances, dedicates long passages to his arrival to the people who live in the lands of the setting sun. The Christian monk who authored the Ethiopic text allows for only brief reference to this episode (less than one paragraph), a testament to the fact that as Christian, he is not impressed by material mentioned in the Qur'ān. Instead, the Ethiopic text makes Alexander out to be an astronomer in passages such as this one:

> "And he went up still higher, and saw the heavens and the orbits thereof, and the stars and their stations, and the courses thereof, and he wrote down the calculations concerning them which Nimrod, the mighty man, had made, and the times in which they revolved in their orbits in years, and months, and days. Now he had knowledge of all these things, and he wrote it down and established it, and he taught it unto the wise men his friends." (228)

Alexander's inclination for astronomy likely derives from the training he received as a youth from his father, Nectanebus, the Egyptian king, skilled in sorcery.

In his description of the women of Gog and Magog, the Ethiopic author provides details (for instance, that they have knives hung upon their hands and neck, for purposes of quick reach in combat), which bring his text closer to the PC

[66] This is the temple of Dionysius in the Syriac and PC.

[67] These last three adventures are related in the Aljmiado-Morisco *Rrekontamiento* ff. 111-113v.

than to texts from the Arabic tradition.[68] The building of the barrier of Gog and Magog is similarly developed in both texts to the point that they concurr in details as fine as the sharpened tongues with which these barbaric tribes lick the wall trying to escape their confines. However, the Ethiopic author has Alexander make a prophecy concerning the coming of Judgment Day when the barrier of Gog and Magog would come down (it will be in the eight hundred and sixty fourth year).[69] Such prophecy is not nor could be made in QDh, as the appointed time is clearly stated to be beyond human cognition:

> "Regarding your question about the Hour of Resurrection, and when is its appointed time, that knowledge is forbidden to man. The mystery of time is above all but the Almighty and Exalted One. It is one of the five secrets unknown to man. No one has ever known or will ever know when time will come to its end. Neither kings who rule with God's favor nor prophets sent down from heaven are an exception!" (f. 13)

In the episode of Alexander's voyage into the land of darkness there are several important distinctions between the two texts. In QDh, Alexander penetrates the darkness and, after climbing a stairwell to a lofty balcony atop a castle, meets and converses with the angel entrusted with blowing the horn on Judgment Day. In the Ethiopic text, instead of at the castle Alexander meets the angel on top of a mountain. In their ensuing conversation, the angel alludes to several biblical passages identified by Wallis Budge (Ezequiel 1:10, p. 247; Isaiah 40:5 and Psalm 104:32, p. 248; Leviticus 22:30 and Matthew 6:34, p. 257). These references are understandably missing from the Islamic texts like QDh, as are the angel's history of creation and the mountain. The latter of these is certainly a reference to Mt. Qāf, the mountain surrounding the world, often referred to in the Arabic Alexander legends. The central figures in the episode of the land of darkness besides Alexander are Arfshakhīr and al-Khiḍr in QDh. The former provides Alexander with a detailed account of the nature of the darkness and the marvelous things it contains, most importantly, the location of the Fountain of Life within the darkness. In the Ethiopic, Arfshakhīr is called Maṭun the Sage, who later in the episode is clearly identified to be the same person as al-Khiḍr.[70] At the Fountain of Life, the motif of the fish brought back to life as it is washed in the waters recalls Alexander's cook, Andreas, from the PC,[71] who had disappeared along with the revived fish motif from Arabic legendary material on Alexander.[72] Perhaps the accidental way in which Andreas attains immortality was unsatisfactory to Islamic writers who saw divine intervention as an integral part of life. So al-Khiḍr in QDh receives a visit from the angel Gabriel,

---

[68] Compare Ethiopic p. 231-232 with the PC (Müller), Bk iii, chpt. 29.

[69] In the Syriac, also said to be the work of a Christian author, the crumbling of the wall will happen in 826 years (p. 154). The Ethiopic text cites the Bible, Jeremiah 1:14, as authority for this prediction (p. 241).

[70] "So Maṭun, that is to say El-Khiḍr..." pp. 267, 268, 269. The Ethiopic scribe seems to be confused here because in the preceding pages (263-66) Maṭun and al-Khiḍīr are treated as two separate characters.

[71] PC, Müller, p. 90.

[72] The role of al-Khiḍr, the Green One, in the Alexander romance has been masterfully studied by I. Friedlaender in *Die Chadhirlegende und der Alexanderroman.*

> "When he had gone twenty days God gave revelation to al-Khiḍr, bless him. This was because he was an honorable prophet. Gabriel came to him, bless him, and said: 'Oh Khiḍr! In this darkness there is only one river and you are close to it. In this river there is a well. It is the only water there, since the riverbed is dry and filled with sand and gravel.'" (f. 189-190)

In the end, "al-Khiḍr [...] fulfilled the purpose which God had intended for him throughout his life. Indeed, it had been written in God's Book that he and no other would bathe in the Fountain of Life" (QDh, f. 192).

The episode of the land of darkness ends in many legends with a parable revolving around a mysterious small stone that when placed on a balance outweighs any number and size of rocks placed on the opposing plate of the balance. The interpretation of the parable with its resulting message strikes a resonant tone among Arab writers. Thus the narrative here is long and dramatic (the hero breaks down and cries no less than three times!). In contrast, the parable receives little attention in the Ethiopic, and at the conclusion of al-Khiḍr's comparatively brief interpretation, the hero is said only to be "terrifed at the parable," but does not cry.[73]

The motif of Alexander's flight into the air is common in both European and Oriental medieval romances. In the Arabic QDh, Alexander's flight is beneath the wing of his guardian angel Zayāqīl, and serves as a revelation of the mission God has designed for him. He sees the lands he will conquer.[74] In the Ethiopic, the ascension is related as a passing adventure, not an integral part of Dhulqarnayn's revelation. The text does not even describe how he flies: "Now when he flew through the air he took with him three eagles and their young" (281). One might assume that he is hoisted into the air by the eagles, as in the *Historia de preliis.*[75]

Also common is Alexander's descent into the sea in a glass cage from which he is able to watch the great monsters of the sea parade before him. This episode is present in the Ethiopic and in HD,[76] where it is followed by Alexander's conversation with the Angel of the Sea.[77] Alexander makes far more sea voyages in QDh than in other legends, such as the Ethiopic, the Syriac and the PC. However, his descent into the sea is not mentioned in QDh.[78]

---

[73] Compare the Ethiopic p. 282 with QDh ff. 200-204.

[74] His flight in the Arabic is designed to recall, or essentially, to foretell the flight or *mi'rāj* that the Prophet Muhammed would take upon birth.

[75] "Then he had the idea of devising a kind of contrivance by which griffins could lift him up to the sky so that he could view the nature of the sky that is above us..." (f. 114). In agreement with the censure of ambition characteristic of the *Historia de Preliis,* Alexander falls to the ground from great heights along with the birds, but suffers no harm because he was protected in a cage of iron bars. In terms of their narrative sequence, the flights in the Ethiopic and the *Historia de Preliis* both follow Alexander's voyage in the Ocean.

[76] Ethiopic, p. 282; HD pp. 59-61

[77] The Ethiopic author uses a parallel structure, as the conversation with the Angel of the Sea follows the conversation with the Angel of the Mountain.

[78] The *Historia de Dulcarnain* in García Gómez' *Un texto árabe occidental,* relates both Alexander's conversation with the Angel of the Mountain (pp. 36-44) and his underwater expedition in which he converses with the Angel of the Sea (pp. 58-61). The Ethiopic and García Gómez' texts show very interesting similarities here.

The remaining episodes in the Ethiopic include an account of the eight wonders of Babylon; a very long speech Alexander delivers to his scribe, Raḥaman; Alexander's illness in Iraq; Aristotle's letter to Olympias telling her to arrange a banquet for all the women who do not mourn the loss of a loved one; the precepts that Alexander gives unto his disciples in a long address at the time of his death; an account of God's dealings with Adam, Cain, Enoch, Noah, Abraham, Jacob, Job, David and Solomon, as well as the overthrow of Sődom; Alexander writes to his mother recapitulating his military triumphs; Alexander is poisoned by Antipater; Alexander's testament and dying commands; and finally, a listing of the cities he conquered. Notwithstanding the expected variance in proper names, the end of the Ethiopic coincides in many respects with the *Historia de Preliis*, the Syriac and the PC. Of these final episodes, only the letter to Olympias with instructions for a banquet that will serve to console her upon her son's death is present in QDh. Even though the letters show a similar content, there is a distinction. In the Ethiopic, it is from Aristotle to Olympias, while in QDh it is from Alexander to his mother.

From the above comparison of QDh with the Ethiopic Life of Alexander, it is clear that the Ethiopic text was not translated from an Arabic work near in filiation to QDh. Not even the most complete Christian reworking of the source material could account for the distinctions that separate the two texts, especially towards the beginning and end of Alexander's career. The similarities between the Ethiopic and earlier texts such as the PC, the Syriac and to some extent the *Historia de preliis*, suggest that the Ethiopic may indeed have been based on an Arabic text very close to the original Arabic translation of the Syriac, as Budge, García Gómez, and Nykl have determined. This would imply that QDh, which contains much material that is not common to the Syriac, the PC and *Historia de Preliis*, is either a significantly later recension of the Arabic text used for the Ethiopic with much interpolation, or a work belonging to an altogether different branch of Arabic Alexander romances. This distinct branch would have had to stem from a recension made of the Arabic translation of the Syriac preceding the one used for the Ethiopic.

Comparison of *Qiṣṣat Dhulqarnayn* with 'Umāra's Version of the Alexander Legend

'Umāra's version of the Alexander legend is contained in manuscript Add. 5928 of the British Museum in a compilation of narrative material commenting on Quranic and other personages. The text spans 80 folios including recto and verso with about 25 lines per page, and is the first narrative in a series of stories of the ancient kings.

The title page in the manuscript begins:

مجموع فيه قصة الاسكندر وما فيها من الامر العجيب وقصة اهل الكهف و[...][79] النبي وتواريخ الخلفا
والوزرا والملوك والسلاطين وحكآيا وشعار وفوايد

[79] There is a word (perhaps, two) that is illegible.

The Alexander story begins on folio 3r:

بسم الله الرحمن الرحيم الله ربي وصلى الله على سيدنا محمد اله وصحبه [...][80] حديـــث ذي القرنـــين
واخباره وعجايبه على اختلاف الروايا ومن جمعنا اخبارهم وذكرنا احسنها وذكرنا ما يوافق كتـــاب الله
تعالى منها والناس مختلفون في ذي القرنين منهم من يقول هو من اليمن ومنهم من يقول هو من الفـــرس
ومنهم من يقول هو من بني اسرايل ومنهم من يقول هو من الاشبان ومنهم من يقول كان نبيا ومنهم مـــن
يقول كان ملكا ومنهم من يقول كان [روميا] ومنهم من يقول كان من ولد العيص ابن اسحاق [...]
صلى الله عليه وسلم وكان ملكه بعد المسيح ومنهم من يقول كان روميا من ولد الروم الاول من ولـــد
يونس ابن سام ابن نوح وكان ملكه بعد نمرود ومنهم من يقول كان من العماليق من ولد عملاق ابـــن
سام ابن نوح وكلهم دون خبرا قال [ياسر ؟] حدثنا عمارة ابن زيد عن محمد ابن اسحاق وعـــن مـــن
حدثه ان ذو القرنين من قيصر القياصر و ...

'Umāra summarizes in the passage cited the great difference of opinion with regards to Alexander's roots and the era in which he lived. As a transmitter, 'Umāra has not been positively identified.[81] The scribe states on the first folio of text,[82] and again in the penultimate line of the Alexander romance, that the writer whose work he is copying is 'Umāra b. Zayd, and in the rest of the manuscript he refers to him as simply 'Umāra. Friedlaender (p. 139) conjectures that 'Umāra must have been a younger contemporary of Muqātil b. Sulaymān, which would place him in the eighth century. The scribe copying the manuscript identifies himself at the end of the story of Dhulqarnayn before beginning the next narrative in the compilation.[83] The passage is translated as follows:

> This is the end of what we have recounted accurately and completely of the story [of Dhulqarnayn]. We fear God for any addition or omission. Thank God, the Beholder of the Worlds, and his prophet Muhammed, and all the Companions. God forgive the scribes and the listener. Written by 'Ubayd Allah Muḥammad b. 'Abd al-Man'am b. Muḥammad al-Anṣarī al-Khazrajī al Malikī. God forgive him and forgive his parents, forgive the writer, the reader, and the listener as well as all Muslims. Have mercy on us all. The scribe finished writing on blessed Friday the 24 of the month of Muḥarram in the year 910 H [=1504 A.D.]. (f. 81v; trans. mine).

From this we know that 'Umāra wrote his text before 1504 A.D. While an in-depth discussion of the identity of 'Umāra is beyond the scope of this introduction, it is convenient to say a few words on the subject. It is possible that he is 'Umāra b. Wathīma b. Mūsa b. al-Furāt al-Misrī (died 902 A.D.), mentioned as a transmitter of stories concerning the prophets and the beginning of creation in al-Mas'ūdī's *Murūj al-dhahab.*[84] Wathīma b. Mūsa, possibly 'Umāra's father, is mentioned on ff. 268 and 275 of QDh. This hypothesis is supported by the fact that Wathīma b. Mūsa wrote in the same genre as 'Umāra, i.e., the stories of the

---

[80] One or two words written near the edge of the folio are illegible.

[81] A brief summary of 'Umāra's text may be found in Friedlaender, 1913, pp. 158-59.

[82] The folios in the British Library manuscript are not numbered.

[83] The next narrative is one that deals with the Boys of the Cave mentioned before Dhulqarnayn in Sura 18 of the Qur'ān.

[84] Ed. Barbier de Meynard and Pavet de Courteille. Beirut: 1979. 7: 521.

prophets. Also, the epoch in which Wathīma b. Mūsa lived coincided with a period of active study and reworkings of the legend of Alexander in Islam. On the other hand, a strong point of contention for the hypothesis is that the scribe above gives the name as 'Umāra b. Zayd, which can hardly be a corruption of Wathīma b. Mūsa. It is hoped that the question raised again here regarding 'Umāra's identity, pending since Friedlaender's book in 1913, will be resolved soon.

'Umāra includes elaborate renditions of most of the major episodes in the PC. Present is an account of Alexander's youth, the building of Alexandria, the campaigns against Persia, India, Samira (governed by Queen Candace), the Amazon women, China. To this material from the PC tradition, the work adds features from the Arabic tradition, such as the frequent use of the name Dhulqarnayn as opposed to Alexander, the hero's Islamic nature, the episodes relating Alexander's journey into the darkness, his conquest of Jābarṣā and Jābalqā, his building of the barrier containing Gog and Magog, among other events.

'Umāra's text and QDh share a considerable amount of narrative material: Dhulqarnayn's visit to the king of the Jinn and his gathering of sulphur and five candles from the royal chamber there; Dhulqarnayn's encounter with the inflating and deflating bird; Dhulqarnayn's conversation with the Hornblower and the grave lesson he learns from a smooth rock the Hornblower gives him; his visit to the pool of mud in which the sun sets every evening; his presence at a hearing in which a judge gives a striking sentence to an unusual dispute dealing with a man who complains that another has sold him real estate that contained a treasure which was not specified in their agreement; Alexander's mother's request for her son to send her treasures. For some passages, including the last mentioned here, 'Umāra provides details that help to clarify QDh.[85]

Yet, there are several details that prohibit us from saying that QDh's author directly used 'Umāra's text or that 'Umāra directly used QDh. The proper names are substantially and consistently different. Consider the following forms given in 'Umāra and QDh, respectively: Dārā vs. Dārius, Qūr vs. Labūr, Rūqīa[86] vs. al-Ghayda, Fāris and Māris vs. Tārish and Bārish, Elias[87] vs. al-Khiḍr. Even Alexander's name differs: in 'Umāra he is Alexander b. al-Qīlaqūs b. Qaṣīr b. [Nuwākl b. Nunin?][88] b. Sām b. Noah (f. 3v), while QDh starts by saying, "Now we begin the story of Dhulqarnayn b. Asās, who is also called Ibn Nabbāsh b. Qālūsh" (f. 14). There are also important omissions of proper names within common episodes: Brahmans in 'Umāra vs. omission in QDh, Afshakhīr in QDh vs. omission in 'Umāra. In contrast to QDh, 'Umāra includes Candace's episode together with the Amazon women, as well as the campaign into China.

---

[85] For instance, see f. 268 of QDh.

[86] 'Umāra must have confused the names of Alexander's wife and mother, as Rūqīa resembles Rashīqa, common form of his wife's name.

[87] The Prophet Elias also appears in a story told by al-Khiḍr in the Persian Alexander Romance *Iskandarnāma*. See the Afshār's edition (pp. 17-20.) This story is also found in Nīshābūrī's 12th Century (A.D.) compilation of stories of the prophets, *Qiṣāṣ al-Anbiyā'*, edited in 1961, pp. 338-342.

[88] The diacritical marks are difficult to identify here.

Additionally, the fantastic episode in 'Umāra relating Alexander's death is nowhere present in QDh. According to 'Umāra, the Macedon's last days involved much interpretation of dreams, Indian magic, and a personified strain of consumption called 'sulāl' that actually spoke to Dhulqarnayn, as it invaded his body, made him ill and eventually took his life.[89] 'Umāra lacks much of the material dealing with Arabian mythology, such as the stories of Hūd, Ṣāliḥ, the origin of the Jābalqāns and the Jābarṣāns, the Tārish and Bārish, the Mārib Barrier and the episodes of the Yāwil, Tāwil and Banī Mansik. One also notes a significant difference in the sources cited in the two texts: 'Umara's *isnāds* most often reach back to Ibn 'Abbās and Ibn Isḥāq, while the author of QDh tends to cite 'Abd al-Malik al-Malshūnī, Muqātil b. Sulaymān and Ka'b al-Aḥbār.

On the basis of the much shared material, and, in particular, the material they share which is not present elsewhere, one may conclude that QDh and 'Umāra's text ultimately derive from a near source. At the same time, from the significant variations in proper names, together with the addition and omission of episodes, one must also recognize that between their common source and the versions of 'Umāra's text and QDh that have come down to us, considerable time must have elapsed during which a great deal of material entered the legend. The long interpolations concerning the Arabian prophets, present in a more limited way in other Alexander legends, suggest that the author of QDh was familiar with Arabian mythology. The relative importance attributed to the episode in which Alexander reaches Spain points to the possibility that the transmitter of this episode may have been in some way attached to al-Andalus.

Comparison of *Qiṣṣat Dhulqarnayn* and Mubashshir's *Akhbār Alexander*

The life of Alexander by physician Mubashshir b. Fātik (d. 1053-4), edited in Arabic by Bruno Meissner in 1895, is an epitome of a larger work by the same author, as the author himself tells. To justify an abridgement, he writes in reference to Alexander's letter to his mother, "this letter is long and I mentioned it and other letters of his in my larger and complete history" (p. 601). Again, after abridging the sayings of the wise men at Alexander's coffin, we read, "and I have mentioned these things and more in my larger and complete history" (p. 602). While Mubashshir's full history is not extant, his epitome provides valuable details of what the larger work must have included.[90]

Akhbār Alexander begins similarly to 'Umāra's text, that is, without the *hadīth* introduction found in the *Rrekontamiento* and QDh, and without the adulterous affair of Alexander's mother with Nectanebus, as related in the PC, the Syriac and the Ethiopic texts. Alexander's father's name is given as Filibūs, and his mother is Rūfiyā, both matching 'Umāra's Qīlaqūs and Rūqiyā, if we allow for

---

[89] For the purpose of comparison, the ending to 'Umāra's text is provided in Appendix I. There is a similar account of Dhulqarnayn's adventure with an Indian sage in al-Mas'ūdī's *Murūj al-dhahab.* Cf. edition from 1861, 2, pp. 260-74.

[90] Our observations regarding Mubashshir's version of the Alexander story will also apply to the version of Muṭahhir b. Ṭāhir al-Muqdisī, contained in chapter three of his *Kitāb al-bida' wa al-tarīkh* (Paris 1913), as Ibn Ṭāhir's work is nearly identical to Mubashshir.

a minor reallocation of diacritical marks.[91] Darius is Dārā, as in 'Umāra, and Darius' daughter, whom Dhulqarnayn marries, is Rūshniq in Mubashshir similar to 'Umāra, as opposed to Rashīq in QDh.

The first episode Mubashshir narrates in his *Akhbār* is that of Fāwis' assassination of Philip. This is followed by Darius' messengers who come to collect the golden egg Alexander's father traditionally paid the Persians. Neither of these episodes figures in QDh. Nearly half of Mubashshir's text is then dedicated to the Persian campaign, which he narrates in considerable detail. He includes versions of the campaign against India, and Dhulqarnayn's visit to the Brahmans that have been substantially abridged. He refers to the well-known and extensive letter Alexander writes to Aristotle relating the wonders of India, but omits its contents. Upon Alexander's death Mubashshir includes some of the sayings of the wise men who congregate at Alexander's coffin, not mentioned in QDh. As we said above, Mubashshir makes reference to the letters Alexander writes to his mother when he is near death, but he omits them here.

Conspicuously missing from Mubashshir's epitome is the mention of the episode into the darkness, or of the peoples of Jābarsā and Jābalqā living at the ends of the earth, or of the building of the barrier of Gog and Magog, mentioned in the Qur'ān. One might infer from the complete omission in the epitome that none of this material is included in his 'larger and more complete work.' It would seem that Mubashshir, as historian, was sufficiently knowledgeable of the Arabic Alexander romance to know that the interpolated material stemming from the Quranic *tafsīr* did not fit in the same tradition as the Greek Alexander legend, familiar to historiographers.[92] Thus, in his *Akhbār*, and also likely in his *tarīkh* 'history' to which he refers, he was careful to distinguish between the prophetic figure of Dhulqarnayn of the Qur'ān and the Macedon conqueror of the PC. Such a distinction coincides with the sentiment among erudites of Mubashshir's epoch that there were two Dhulqarnayns: one, the pious Quranic saint, and another, the ambitious Macedon conqueror.[93] Indeed, as discussed below, other important writers of medieval Arabic histories such as al-Ṭabarī and al-Mas'ūdī also ignore the legendary material dealing with the prophetic Dhulqarnayn--abounding in QDh--that had become attached to the Arabic Alexander romance chiefly through Judeo-Christian interpretation.

In light of the differences in proper names and in content, one must assume that the physician Mubashshir and the author of QDh used sources possessing no immediate relation.

---

[91] In fact, if one of the scribes had confused Moroccan script with the traditional one, we can account for all differences.

[92] Cf. García Gómez, Intro. p. 39.

[93] Cf. García Gómez, Intro. p. 40.

Comparison of *Qiṣṣat Dhulqarnayn* with al-Tha'labī's[94] *Qiṣaṣ al-Anbiyā'*

Al-Tha'labī's wrote his *Qiṣaṣ al-Anbiyā'* in the eleventh century A.D. The chapter he dedicates to Dhulqarnayn comes after the one dealing with Balūqīyā, an imam of the Israelites said to have foreknowledge of Muhammed from the Torah,[95] and before the chapters on Zakaria, John the Baptist, Mary and Jesus. He selects and organizes the episodes he relates by citing a verse from the Qur'ān and then offering the episode as commentary or *tafsīr*.[96] Al-Tha'labī begins with Alexander's lineage. His father's name is Fīlbash b. Baṭriyūs, and his ancestral line goes back to Abraham. In contrast, according to QDh, the first in Dhulqarnayn's ancestral line is 'Arūm ("He is al-Askandar b. Asās and he was called Ibn Nabbāsh b. Qālūsh , b. Fastiyātīr b. Nijāwī, b. Yādūn b. al-Arzī b. Ḥirān b. 'Arūm" f. 31). Both texts have corrupted Philip's name on acccount of misplaced or illegible diacritical marks. Al-Tha'labī goes on to explain that the name Alexander is taken from an incident in his mother's life,[97] and that Alexander is the brother of the very Darius he fights in the romance.[98] The exploits of Alexander begin with the story of the golden egg that was tribute Philip used to pay to Persia annually, as is the case in the Syriac and the *Historia de Preliis*,[99] but not in the PC[100] or in QDh. Given the structure of al-Tha'labī's work, being a compilation of brief stories of the prophets, the subsequent material has the form of an epitome. He refers to the letters exchanged between Darius and Alexander without reproducing the text. He narrates in full the context for those details most well known such as the symbolic gifts Darius sends Alexander: a scepter, a ball, and a handful of sesame seeds. The latter two are perfectly

---

[94] This is Aḥmad b. Muḥammad b. Ibrāhīm Abū Isḥāq al-Nīsābūrī al-Tha'labī, born 427/1035. Cf. EI, 4, 735-6.

[95] "وكان قد عرف نعت النبي صلى الله عليه وسلم وامته في التوراة" (p. 353).

[96] Regarding al-Tha'labī's *Tafsīr*, I. Goldfeld says that it "has been acclaimed by a long line of biographer-critics as being very thorough and trustworthy. The critics outdo each other in lavishing more complementary epithets on the author. None of this seems to mind that *Al-Kashf wa'l Bayān* refers to ostracized works of *tafsīr*, like the books of al-Kalbī and Muqātil b. Sulaymān [...] The explanation seems to be at hand: Al-Tha'labī handled his *asānīd* (i.e., chains of authority) extremely carefully and introduced each work he used by the required chain of authorities. The material reached al-Tha'labī by the best of the methods discussed by the critics, namely *Samā'* and *Qirā'a*: al-Tha'labī had each of the commentaries he used dictated to him by an authority" (p. 134).

[97] According to the story, Alexander's father, Darius Senior, father of Darius Junior, King of Persian during Alexander's time, married the daughter of the King of Rūm who he discovered had about her a foul odor. Darius convoked with his wisest men to determine how to remove that smell from her so that he could consummate the marriage. They suggested the leaves of the *sandarūs* tree ("sandarac" in English). She tried this, but was unable to rid herself completely of the smell. Darius slept with her and then sent her back to her people. A son was born to her and she named him after the tree. Dīnawarī relates a similar story, with the variation that the *sandarūs* is an herb rather than a tree. He adds that the bride was a gift from Philip, whom the Persian king had defeated in battle. See Dīnawarī pp. 29-30.

[98] "وزعم بعض القدماء أن الاسكندر هو أخو دارا ابن دارا" (p. 359).

[99] "... Say to your lord Darius: When Philip had no children, his hens used to lay golden eggs, but from the time that his son Alexander has been born, they have become barren, and do not lay eggs any longer." Syriac p. 31; *Historia de Preliis* is similar, p. 24.

[100] At least, the golden egg is not found in the Armenian version of the PC edited by Wolohojian.

common among Alexander romances; the first is not one of the usual gifts.[101] QDh has somewhat different gifts: sesame seeds, a pearl, a jewel, and a chest filled with gold. Al-Tha'labī skips over the bulk of the Persian campaign and focuses on the dramatic scene showing Darius about to die, reclining his head on Alexander's lap. It is of interest that Darius' daughter whom Dhulqarnayn will marry is called Rūshnak as in the Syriac, but different from the Ethiopic and QDh where her name is Rashīk and Rashīqā, respectively.[102]

On the central issue of whether Dhulqarnayn was a prophet or a saint, al-Tha'labī says there are different opinions, of which the most correct is that he had not been sent to earth as a prophet but rather that he attained the status of prophet during his lifetime (والصحيح ان شاء الله أنه كان نبيا غير مرسل p. 361). In other words, he was a pious servant of God who had built his kingdom before God came to him with inspiration and a prophetic mission to carry His message to the seven peoples distributed throughout the earth who are said to be mankind (الإنس): the jinn, the barbarous Gog and Magog, Nāsak, Mansik, Hāwīl, Tāwīl (p. 362). QDh differs in that God delivers his inspiration to Dhulqarnayn somewhat earlier in the prince's life (for instance, God widens his intellect when as a youth he was subject to the examination of the Rūm elders) and communication is always through the angel Zayāqīl, never direct.[103] As far as the destinations laid out for Dhulqarnayn, the hero's itinerary in QDh take him to all of the peoples mentioned, except that the name Hāwīl has been corrupted and appears as Yāwīl in QDh. There would seem to be the omission in al-Tha'labī of the Tārish and Bārish who receive considerable attention in QDh. Dhulqarnayn feels overburdened and inadequate upon receiving word about the mission he is destined to carry out, and these feelings he expresses in a monologue (to Zayāqīl in QDh and to God directly in al-Tha'labī) common to many Alexander legends.[104]

Dhulqarnayn's next move in *Qiṣaṣ al-Anbiyā'* is to build a giant mosque, whose construction is described in great detail, similar to that of the building of the barrier of Gog and Magog. It would seem that medieval Arabic scholars had a fascination with the technicalities of metallurgy and structure. Although there are many anachronistic episodes in QDh, such as Dhulqarnayn uttering words from the Qur'ān and his meeting with Abraham at the Ka'b, there is no mention of him

---

[101] PC: a leather thong, a ball, a chest of gold (Wolohojian p. 58); Syriac: ball, whip, chest of gold, sesame seeds (p. 46); *Historia de Preliis*: ball, whip, chest of gold (p. 32).

[102] The translators of the PC and the *Historia de Preliis* call her Roxana.

[103] God speaks directly to Alexander in the Syriac text edited by Wallis Budge and titled, "A Christian Legend Concerning Alexander": "The Lord came to Alexander and found him asleep, and He called him and said to him, 'Rise up from there.' And the king arose and knelt down and did reverence to the Lord; and the Lord said to him, 'Behold, I have magnified thee above all kingdoms, and I have made horns of iron to grow on thy head that thou mayest thrust down the kingdoms of the earth with them; and upon me thou didst rely when thou wentest forth to war and to see the countries. But lo, a multitude of kings and their armies are coming against thee to slay thee; call upon me that I may come to aid thee, for I am the Lord, and I help all those that call upon me'" (*The History of Alexander the Great Being the Syriac Version* (p. 156).

[104] The division of the earth among the seven nations and Alexander's modest reaction to his mission appear in Ibn al-Jawzī almost verbatim. Ibn al-Jawzī cites al-Tha'labī as his source (f. 82).

building a mosque. Al-Tha'labī follows the mention of the mosque with a digression that gives us insight into the way Arabs of the first years after the Prophet consulted with Jewish scholars to understand the Qur'ān. He relates that one day Ibn 'Abbās and Mu'āwīya were quarreling over the meaning of Quranic verse 18:86 which says that Dhulqarnayn found that the sun set in a spring of murky water. To resolve their dispute they called Ka'b al-Aḥbār, a Yemenite Jew converted to Islam, to ask what the Torah says about the verse in question.[105] Ka'b says modestly that "You Arabs are wiser than I" and then goes on to explain that in the Torah it says "the sun sets in a spring filled with black mud."[106] K'ab finishes explaining word by word the Quranic verse. The dependency of Quranic scholarship on Judeo-Christian interpretation, as is evident in the passage referred to here, came to be reprehensible after the first two centuries of Islam. Texts citing Judeo-Christian authorities (such as is the case in much of the Alexander legendary material and the genre of the *qiṣaṣ al-anbiyā'*) were cut from the canon and ignored by serious Arab-Islamic scholars. The presence of this passage in al-Tha'labī may imply that the sources he used to compose his text were relatively early, i.e., from the first two centuries after the prophet, or at least one hundred years before the writing of *Qiṣaṣ al-Anbiyā'*.

Among the arms of war at the disposal of the Macedonian king is the very darkness itself, says al-Tha'labī in a passage reminiscent of the Ethiopic text: "He made the darkness to enter upon them [the people living near the sun set]. And it went in their mouths, in their noses, in their ears, and penetrated their insides. It entered their houses and homes, and enveloped them from above and below, and from every side" (p. 363; trans. mine). Even with the help of his guardian angel, Zayāqīl, the Dhulqarnayn of QDh does not have such powers.

Al-Tha'labī has his hero travel about the remaining parts of the earth in boats constructed by his own men. When traversing land, they disassemble the boat and each man carries one of the boards without a complaint.[107] In QDh, Dhulqarnayn is a great sailor, but there is never any mention of where he got his boats or what type of boats he used, or what he did with the boats when marching across land. The Hāwīl and Tāwīl are mentioned only briefly in *Qiṣaṣ al-Anbiyā'* and are said to have submitted to him as did the others. In contrast, their civilization and history receive considerable attention in QDh. Al-Tha'labī then takes Dhulqarnayn to visit the Mansik, who live near the rising sun. He relates anecdotal material about how the Mansik have adapted their lifestyle to bear the heat of the sun: they enter the sea when the sun comes up; they cover themselves with their ears which are large enough to wrap over their entire bodies; the bones of those who did not escape the rising sun littered the landscape.[108] QDh gives a

---

[105] Ibn al-Jawzī transmits this passage almost word for word (f. 79r).

[106] "فرأى مغيب الشمس عند غروبها في عين ذو خُلُب وثَأط حَرْمَـــد" where خلب and ثأط both mean 'mud' and حرمد means 'black' (p. 363).

[107] Ibn Isḥāq also reports that when Alexander's army "came to a sea or a ford, he would build ships from small boards, like sandals, and put them all together at once. Then he would put on them all of those people and those armies who were with him. When he had crossed the rivers and the seas, he would take them apart. Then he would give a board to each person, so that carrying them was no burden" (Newby, *Making of the Last Prophet*, p. 196).

[108] This passage is reproduced nearly verbatim in Ibn al-Jawzī (f. 79r-v).

similar description not for the Mansik, but for the people called Bārish. In contrast, the Mansik, as described in QDh, live on an island in the sea, and the dominant motif of Dhulqarnayn's encounter with them is the canal he builds to aid them in their eternal battles with the serpents.

Al-Tha'labī sets apart in a chapter the episode of the building of the barrier of Gog and Magog, so emphasizing its importance relative to the conglomerate episodes of Hāwīl, Tāwīl and Mansik. This is, of course, because the barrier is mentioned in the Qur'ān. As Dhulqarnayn marches along a road near the land of the Turks, the people come to him and complain that their barbaric neighbors will not let them live in peace. They offer to collect a *kharaj* tax to pay him to build a barrier to keep back the Gog and Magog. What follows is a description of the barrier, much the same as found in other authors that comment on this Quranic passage. One distinguishing feature of al-Tha'labī's text is a *hadīth* related on the authority of Qatāda, regarding a dream the Prophet had in which an expedition of fifty men travel to the barrier of Gog and Magog. This would be foresight of the historical mission sent out by the 'Abbāsid Caliph Wāthiq (842-846 A.D.), to search for the Barrier of Gog and Magog. This was reported by the tenth-century Arab traveller and geographer Muqaddasī.[109] A similar story is told in Ibn al-Jawzī (80v).

Al-Tha'labī transmits the episode of Dhulqarnayn's journey into the darkness[110] on the authority of Alī b. Abī Ṭālib, who is nowhere mentioned in QDh. Dhulqarnayn first learns of the darkness from his friend, the angel Rafā'īl. This appears to be the uncorrupted form for Zayāqīl, as the angel is called in QDh. During their conversation, Rafā'īl tells Dhulqarnayn to be sympathetic towards angels because they spend eternity in one position, some kneeling, others prostrating, all praising the Almighty God. When he hears this, Dhulqarnayn feels that his worship of the Lord has been insufficient, and he wishes to live forever to spend eternity in prayer, and to be present for the advent of Islam. The angel hints that this may be possible by informing him of the Fountain of Life, hidden in a darkness on earth, where he can drink and bathe in water that will permit him eternal life, until such a time as he asks God to end his life. This passage is different in QDh where he learns of the darkness in passing conversation with the people of Jābarṣā.[111] To inform himself further of the nature of the darkness, Dhulqarnayn asks one of his wisemen, who informs his king according to what he read in a book called Waṣīa Adam, i.e., Adam's Testament or advice. In QDh, the wise man Arfshakhīr cites as his source the knowledge Adam passed on to his son Seth. One infers that Arfshakhīr also got it from a book. Dhulqarnayn wants to know which beasts see best at night; both texts concurr in that virgin horses would be best in the darkness. Both texts also relate that the troops left behind should wait twelve years for him before returning home. Their parallel continues as Dhulqarnayn assigns al-Khiḍr a battalion of

---

[109] Cf. EI, 3, p. 708.

[110] Pp. 367-370.

[111] Nöldeke gives another interesting reason for Dhulqarnayn's search for the Fountain of Life, as told in the Syriac Alexander legend of Jacques de Sarūğ (died 521 A.D.), where Dhulqarnayn wishes to attain eternal life so he may live long enough to see Christ. *Beiträge*, p. 30.

troops and asks him to lead the expedition into the darkness. As an aid, the king gives al-Khiḍr a red bead that when thrown on the ground makes a noise loud enough for the troops to orient themselves and return if they go astray. However, in QDh, the bead is said to be white and emits enough light to illuminate the darkness.[112] After al-Khiḍr has bathed in the Fountain of Life, they enter a region of the darkness in which there is a light unlike the light of the sun and find a castle containing a talking bird hanging upside down from one of the beams inside: The bird poses questions to Dhulqarnayn and according to the responses first expands and then shrinks back to original size. Dhulqarnayn is directed to a lofty balcony, high above the castle, and meets the angel poised to blow the horn on Judgment Day, who after a brief conversation gives him a mysterious stone and a parable. All this coincides perfectly between the two texts, as does al-Khiḍr's interpretation of the parable and the lesson Dhulqarnayn receives. To demonstrate his newly acquired abstinence from worldly riches, both authors have him pass through a riverbed full of precious gems without stopping to pick up a single jewel. In fact, the only substantial difference between the two authors regarding the expedition into the darkness is that in al-Tha'labī, the angel of the horn does not give Dhulqarnayn a bunch of miraculous grapes to feed his troops, a detail which one suspects has been lost in the abridgement.

At this point, al-Tha'labī concludes his short history of Dhulqarnayn. He says that he returned to his home in Dūma al-Jandal, where he remained till his death at the age of thirty-seven. The abridged nature of al-Tha'labī's work has obliged him to cut material central to the romance, such as the expedition against the king of India, the episodes related in his letter to Aristotle concerning the wonders of India, and the letters of consolation he writes to his mother upon his death, among other things.

Al-Tha'labī and QDh show interesting similarities, especially regarding the outline of the conqueror's itinerary, the expedition into the darkness, and Dhulqarnayn's friendship with the angel Raphael. On the other hand, the differences with respect to the Alexander's background, youth, and the Persian campaign are substantial. It is likely that al-Tha'labī had at his disposal several versions of the Alexander romance, from which he selected material for his chapter on Alexander. The material he includes from *isrā'īlīyāt* authors such as Ka'b al-Aḥbār coincides with QDh, while that which he takes from elsewhere (sources unnamed in his text) is very different. In any case, one cannot conclude that they share an immediate source.

[112] In the Ethiopic text, Alexander gives his companion a "stone" to illuminate the darkness. This distinction might be a result of the Ethiopic scribe mistaking the Arabic خرز for حجر .

Comparison of QDh with the Version of Ibn al-Jawzī,[113] as Contained in His *Mir'āt al-zamān*.

Ibn al-Jawzī's version of Alexander's story is in his work entitled *Mir'āt al-zamān* cataloged as Or. 4215 in the British Library's collection. Within *Mir'āt al-zamān*, the chapter on Alexander appears on ff. 77-85, after the story of Lot.

The character of the work is decidedly oriented toward Quranic *tafsīr* and begins with an explanation of Qur'ān 18:83 ('وَيَسْئَلُونَكَ عَن ذِى ٱلْقَرْنَيْنِ'). Ibn Al-Jawzī says on the authority of Ibn Ma'ud that the subject of the verb يسئلونك , an ambiguous "they," who approach Muhammed to ask about Dhulqarnayn, is the Jews. This contradicts QDh, where it is Christians who pose questions to Muhammed. Ibn al-Jawzī continues with four variations on Dhulqarnayn's name: he is 'Alī Karam (according to al-Ḍaḥḥak), Alexander (according to Wahb b. al-Munabbih), 'Abbās b. Qaysar (i.e., son of caesar) where his father was the first of the caesars (according to Muhammed b.'Alī b. al-Ḥussayn b. Zayn al-'Abadīn), and finally S'ab b. al-Qalmis (according to Ibn Abī Haythim).[114] Of these, only Wahb's version of his name, Alexander, appears in our text. There is no mention of the name Ibn Nabbāsh often cited in QDh. Al-Jawzī continues in his meticulous scrutiny of the Quranic personage by listing twelve reasons for the nickname 'Dhulqarnayn.'[115] 1.) He called his people to be among the righteous and they hit him on the head (ضربوه على قرنه)[116] and he perished. Then God sent him as messenger to another people and they also hit him on the head, and he died.[117] So he is called 'the one of two heads.' This is told on the authority of 'Alī. 2.) He reached both the rising and the setting of the sun, according to Abū Ṣāliḥ who transmits on the authority of Ibn 'Abbās. 3.) He had two sides (صفحتي) of his head made of copper, according to Mujāhid. 4.) He had a dream in which his body grew till it extended from the earth to the heavens and he grabbed the sun by its two horns (فاخذ بقرني الشمس) and he told this to his people and they started to call him Dhulqarnayn.[118] 5.) He was king of the Rūm and of the Persians, according to Muqātil. 6.) He had something similar to two horns on his head, according to Wahb. 7.) There were two braids of hair on his head, according to al-Ḥassan and Ibn al-Anbārī. 8.) His lineage was noble on both sides of his family, according to al-Sha'bī. 9.) Two different nations were eliminated from the face of the earth during his time, and yet he lived on, according to Ibn al-Musayyab. 10.) He

---

[113] The complete name is Ibn al-Jawzī, Sibṭ, Shams al-Dīn Abu-l-Muẓaffar Yūsuf b. Qizoghlū. He was born in 582/1186 in Baghdad and died in Damascus in 684/1257. He was a preacher and author of *Mir'āt al-zamān fī ta'rīkh al-a'yān*, a universal history not yet printed. Cf. EI, 2, 372.

[114] f. 77v

[115] Given on f. 77v.

[116] See Dozy's Supplement for idiomatic use of '*qarn*' as 'head.'

[117] He was subsequently resuscitated.

[118] Source's name is not legible, perhaps we could read "عكرمه".

traveled in the darkness and the light. 11.) When he was in combat he struck with his hand and his knee at the same time.[119] 12.) His knowledge spanned that which is apparent and that which is hidden (الظاهر والباطن), according to al-Tha'labī.

The next point Ibn al-Jawzī discusses is the era in which Dhulqarnayn lived. He cites 'Alī saying that it was during the first century after Yāfith b. Noah. Al-Ḥassan says it was after Nimrod. According to Muqātil, Dhulqarnayn came after Isḥaq from the line of al-'Ayṣ. Al-Jawzī states, without citing a source, that there were those that said he lived between the time of Moses and Jesus, and others who believed he was between Jesus and Muhammed. On the authority of Abū al-Ḥasayn b. al-Munādī, he says Dhulqarnayn descended from Yūnān b. Moses and lived during the days of Abraham (الخليل). Regarding the last possibility, he says "and this is the most correct" (وهو الاصح). Muqātil also passed on an anecdote in which Abraham was sitting in Palestine, when he heard the noise of an approaching army and asked who it was. Upon learning that it was Dhulqarnayn, he sent his greetings. When Dhulqarnayn heard that he had taken his army through the lands of Abraham, he went to ask to be forgiven. The Macedon dismounted in front of Abraham, and the two talked and Abraham gave Dhulqarnayn advice and guidance, as well as a cow and a lamb. Despite his favoring Muqātil's opinion, Ibn al-Jawzī (f. 78r) seems to recognize the anachronism of such an encounter, and says that their meeting would contradict the fact that Dhulqarnayn lived four hundred years after Nimrod and Nimrod lived during the time of Abraham.[120]

Ibn al-Jawzī (f. 78r-v) addresses the question as to whether or not Dhulqarnayn was a prophet. He tells us that, according to al-Ḍaḥḥak and Abdullah b. 'Umar, he was indeed a prophet. The second opinion is that of al-Jidī, in his *al-Tabaṣṣura*, affirming that he was neither prophet nor king, but rather a pious servant of God. A third opinion, on the authority of 'Alī and Ibn 'Abbās, states that he was a king and pious servant who followed the religion of Abraham, and who was blessed with God's favor. The last of these opinions coincides with QDh,[121] although the work's author does not cite his source. Ibn al-Jawzī (f. 78v) suggests that the light of day and darkness of night were subject to him to use as weapons against his enemies. Such power is not granted the hero of QDh.[122]

Alexander's first deed as a young man, related on authority of Ibn 'Abbās, was to go to Egypt and build Alexandria. This effectively coincides with the first chapter in QDh after the introductory *hadīth*. Ibn al-Jawzī follows this episode immediately with Dhulqarnayn's meeting with an angel, during which he receives the mission God has designed for him, that is to preach His word to the ignorant (i.e., الجاهل). The sequence is identical to that of QDh, as well as to the Aljamiado *Rrekontamiento*.

---

[119] Source not cited.

[120] Cf. B. Chapira, "Légendes bibliques attribuée a Ka'b el-Aḥbar" (96-100) for an excellent summary of a Judeo-Arabic story of Abraham and Nimrod.

[121] See QDh translation, f. 22.

[122] In Ibn Isḥāq, God says to Dhulqarnayn, "I will make light and darkness subservient to you, and I will make the two of them as armies of your armies, the light to guide in front of you and the darkness to conceal behind you" (Newby, *Making of the Last Prophet*, p. 195).

Following Alexandria, Ibn al-Jawzī cites various opinions as to where and how the sun sets. The presentation is in the manner of Quranic *tafsīr* quite similar to al-Tha'labī. The point of contention is whether the pool in which the sun sets is of water, mud, clay, tar, or milk (!) with different scholars (Ka'b, Hassan al-Baṣrī, Ibn 'Abbās, al-Tha'labī), each supporting a position. In QDh, the spring is said to be of mud; other points of view are surpressed. Ibn al-Jawzī then cites al-Tha'labī and relates several anecdotes (listed above in our discussion of al-Tha'labī) regarding the nature and customs of the people that live near the setting sun. None of this discussion is particularly pertinent to QDh, where the emphasis is on the elaboration and development of Dhulqarnayn's encounter with the people of Jābalqā, said to live nearby. As well informed as Ibn al-Jawzī seems to be, he does not mention the Jābalqāns, who, together with the people of Jābarṣā, are central figures in QDh, as well as in the *Rrekontamiento.* Perhaps he thought their fantastic city surrounded by walls, containing ten thousand doors, was too farfetched to be included in a serious *tafsīr,* or he did not have at his disposal geographic encyclopedias from which the Jābalqān material seems to have been taken.

As the Quranic episode takes Dhulqarnayn from the setting sun to the rising sun, al-Jawzī comments on the meaning of Qur'ān 18:90 ("*Until, when he came to the rising of the sun, he found it rising on a people for whom we had provided no covering against the sun.*"). According to al-Kalbī, the region of the rising sun is inhabited by the Tāris, the Mansik and the Tāwīl. The author of QDh, not only mentions each of these peoples, but also, by means of long dialogues between Dhulqarnayn and their kings, narrates their histories.

Continuing to follow the Qur'ān (18:93-101), al-Jawzī describes the people of Gog and Magog. He transmits an interesting anecdote that he read in al-Tha'labī who had taken it from Ka'b. According to legend, Gog and Magog were the descendants of Adam, but not through Eve. One night, Adam had a wet dream and his sperm mixed with the earth and the Gog and Magog were the resultant offspring (80r).[123] Al-Jawzī's subsequent description of the construction of the barrier to retain the hordes of Gog and Magog from swarming the earth is perfectly common. He transmits another anecdote that he took from a chapter entitled "Sīrat Dhulqarnayn" in Jidī's *al-Ṭabassura.* It describes an expedition of messengers of the commander of the faithful (امير المؤمنين) in search of the barrier. Having passed through the Sudan, they travel on until they come to the barrier, where they discover people who speak Arabic. They are Muslims. They read the Qur'ān and worship in a mosque (80v).[124] No explanation of their presence is given, but perhaps we are to understand that they had been left there by Dhulqarnayn. These Muslims show the Amīr's expedition the great wall spanning a valley near Mount Amlas.[125] Al-Jawzī describes its dimensions, its locks, chains and bars in detail, and says that this portion of his narration is an abridgement of material he took from Sirāt Dhulqarnayn in Jidī's *al-Ṭabassura* (f. 81r). He

---

[123] Al-Jawzī may have taken this account of the origin of Gog and Magog from al-Ṭabarī, who mentions it in his *Tafsīr,* 15, p. 494.

[124] This refers to the expedition of the Caliph Wāthim. See above **Comparison with al-Tha'labī.**

[125] Al-Jawzī also transmits that Qatāda says the wall is near Mount Radam (f. 81r).

finishes the chapter on the Gog and Magog by providing the opinions of other authorities (Muqātil, Qatāda, and again Jidī in his book *al-Mawḍu'āt*), and by placing particular emphasis on prophecy regarding how and when the barrier will come down, thus allowing the Gog and Magog to swarm the earth.

Having finished his commentary of the Quranic material concerning Dhulqarnayn, Ibn al-Jawzī narrates the expedition into the darkness, followed by Alexander's visit to the Brahmans, and ends with his letter to his mother and an account of his death. Similar to al-Tha'labī, in Ibn al-Jawzī Dhulqarnayn learns of the darkness from an angel, called here Rabāyīl,[126] who points him toward a means to achieve his wish to worship the Lord like the angels, which for a mortal could only be through attaining immortality.[127] For this *hadīth*, both authors consulted Jidī's history entitled "*al-Muntaẓẓim*"[128] where the author cites, as authority for the *hadīth*, an *isnād* reaching back to 'Alī b. Abī Ṭālib (f. 81v). This *isnād* is apparently intended to be valid for the entire account of the expedition into the darkness, as no other is mentioned until after its conclusion. After learning from the angel about the darkness, Dhulqarnayn confirms his knowledge with the wise man Afshakhīr, the only one of his company to know what the darkness contains. This is identical to QDh. Leading the troops is al-Khiḍr who receives from Dhulqarnayn a red bead similar to the one mentioned in al-Tha'labī, that is, one that emits a sound when thrown on the ground. Both, al-Jawzī and al-Tha'labī, must have consulted sources different from QDh, where, as we've said, the bead is white and emits light rather than sound. From beginning to end, al-Jawzī's text is nearly identical to al-Tha'labī (including the toponym Dūma al-Jandal to where Dhulqarnayn returns after the expedition into the darkness), and need not be repeated here.[129]

Upon leaving the darkness, Alexander visits the Hāwīl, the Tāwīl, the Mansik and the Nāsik, and then receives word from the angel regarding the mission God has set for him, or so al-Jawzī relates on the authority of al-Tha'labī, except that in the latter this material precedes the expedition into the darkness.[130]

Al-Tha'labī, as we saw, concludes his abridged version of Alexander's story with the episode into the darkness. However, Ibn al-Jawzī goes farther and includes Alexander's visit to the people vaguely resembling the Gymnosophists from the PC. His text is similar to QDh in that Dhulqarnayn marches ostentatiously into a city (Jābalqā in QDh, name not given in al-Jawzī) and comes upon an old man who pays the pompous leader no attention. He dismounts to talk to the man. In their conversation, Dhulqarnayn learns they are the most pious of people and that their society is utopian. Missing from al-Jawzī are the questions involving how the man spends the little money he earns. From QDh we know that one third is put away for retirement, one third goes towards the debt he has with his parents for taking care of him as a child, and one third he uses to live. This distinction between the two texts may be because al-Jawzī cites Wahb b. al-

[126] The name is clearly a corruption of Raphael found in al-Tha'labī.

[127] See al-Tha'labī above.

[128] The dot has been left off the ẓ.

[129] See al-Tha'labī above.

[130] See al-Tha'labī above.

Munabbih as his source, while the author of QDh cites Ka'b al-Aḥbār, or maybe the omission is simply to save space.

The following chapter related on authority of al-Suddī transmits Alexander's correspondence with his discreet and discerning mother, written 'Rūfia,' but the author tells us that her name is pronounced with a *qāf* (وقيل بالقاف), i.e., Rūqīa, just as in QDh. Her letter warns him to rule justly and not to swell with pride, for he has risen to power very quickly and is inexperienced in governance. In many respects the content and even wording is identical.[131] Without doubt they derive from sources in close proximity. Additionally, in both Ibn al-Jawzī and QDh, Dhulqarnayn gathers his ministers and has them make a list of every item in the treasury to send to his mother with a man on horseback.

Ibn al-Jawzī's second to last chapter is his "mention of the cities he built." On the authority of first the Prophet, then al-Kalbī, Ibn 'Abbās and al-Suddī, he only tells us that Dhulqarnayn built the city of Marūfāna, and then on his return from the darkness, he passed through Khurāsān, but was unable to cross a deep river there,[132] so he built a bridge and was finally able to cross. From there he heads to the land of Rūm, where he counts and has a talisman drawn on each item in his treasury (f. 84r-v).

His death as told by the "wise men who transmitted his heroic deeds" (علمـــآ الســـير) came as the fulfillment of a prophecy: he would die on a floor of iron beneath a sky of wood. This odd situation arose when he fell off his horse on top of a metal shield. As he lay there recovering, his men shaded him from the sun with a piece of wood. He recognized it immediately as the sign of his near death and called for his scribe to write a letter to his mother. The *isnād* given for the letter is "Abū al-Yaman Zayd al-Hasn al-Kandī, bless him, on the authority of 'Abd Allah b. Muḥammad b.'Ubayd b. Abī al-Dunyā al-Qurshī from the book [titled] *al-'Atbār wa 'Aqāb al-Surūr wa al-Aḥzān*, where he says: Abū Yūsif 'Aqūb b.'Ubayd told us, on the authority of 'Abd Allah b. Ziyād al-Mudnī, on the authority of someone who read books that said..."(f. 84). The *isnād* given in QDh is: 'Abd Allah b. Abī Bakr, on the authority of 'Abd Allah b. Ziyād,[133] who related, on the authority of Abī Ṣāliḥ, who related on the authority of Qitāda, who said..." (f. 272). The only name in common is 'Abd Allah b. Ziyād. The text of the two letters shows some similarities, pointing ultimately towards the same original source, however, clearly both authors used an immediate source that was not identical.

Compare the beginning of both letters:

---

[131] Compare the following selections from QDh (f. 270):

واعلم انّك عن قليل تحول عمّا انت عليه يا بُنَيّ أيّاك و الشُحُ فان الشُحَّ يوذيك وأيّاك والطَمعُ فان الطَمعُ يوذيك وقد وصلني كتابك بجميع ما كتبتَ فيه بعدّة كنوزك

and Ibn al-Jawzī (f. 85r):

واعلم انك عن قليل محول عما انت فيه كما تحول من غيرك اليك واياك والشح فانه برديك وعليك بنور العدل فانه يهديك وانظر ما جمعت من الاموال وكثرت من الكنوز

[132] The name of the river is not clearly legible, it may be جَنْجُون referring to the Gangis River.

[133] The same source is mentioned in Ibn al-Jawzī, except that he adds that he is the Mudnī (f. 84v).

QDh:

بسم الله الرحمان الرحيم من عبد الله ذي القرنين ابن نبّاش ابن الضّحاك ابن عويلم ابن سام ابن نوح عليه السّلام الى امّي اعزّها الله اما بعد فان هذا [كتابي] اليكِ رفيق اهل الارض ببدَنهِ قليلا ورفيق الملايكة بروحه كثيرا الى الام ذاتِ الصّفا التى لم تُمتّع ثمرتها في دار الخراب وهى بمجاورة عمّا قليل في دار البُعْد .

Ibn al-Jawzī:

بسم الله الرحمان الرحيم من الاسكندر بن قيصر رفيق اهل الرض بجسده قليلا ورفيق اهل السما بروحِه طويلا الى امه روفيه ذات الصلا التي لم تمتع ثمرتها في ذات القرب وَهى بمَجاورته في دار البَعد

The remaining portions of the letter follow a similar pattern of occasional common phrases.

Ibn al-Jawzī also includes a second letter from Dhulqarnayn to his mother, written when he felt death was near. Related on the authority of Ibn Abī al-Dunyā, it is the well-known letter telling his mother to make a banquet for the women who do not grieve the loss of a loved one. This letter also appears in QDh, except it is attributed to Abū ʻAbd al-Mālik, and shows a variance similar to the preceding letter.

Ibn al-Jawzī says they differed as to where Alexander died. Some say it was in Dūma al-Jandal, others in Shahrazūr, and the third opinion is that he died in Babel, having withdrawn from the world and become an ascetic. Al-Jawzī believes that the last opinion is the 'most correct' and that the one who died in Shahrazūr was the second Alexander (الاسكندر الثاني). There is no *isnād* given for these opinions.

Regarding how long Alexander lived, al-Jawzī says they differed regarding his age. Jidī in his *Kitāb ʻAmār al-Aʻyān* says Dhulqarnayn lived 2600 years. The people of the book (اهل الكتاب) claimed it was closer to 3000 years, saying this was not preposterous since Noah was believed to have lived 3600 years. A third opinion is that of Mujāhid, who said that he lived 1000 years, as did Adam. In QDh, the author tells us only that "Several of the transmitters say that Dhulqarnayn kept the strength, Blessed and Almighty God bestowed on him, until he was thirty two years old" (f. 278).

The last bit of news al-Jawzī passes on with regards to Dhulqarnayn is the sayings pronounced by the wise men over his coffin. The *isnād* is Ibn Abī al-Dunyā, on the authority of Mubārik b. Faḍāla, on the authority of al-Hasan. According to the story, when Alexander felt death coming upon him, he summoned his eldest son and told him to bring the wisest men in his reign to his coffin and to have them say what they learned from their experience with Alexander. None of this is found in QDh.

Comparison of *Qiṣṣat Dhulqarnayn* with the *Rrekontamiento del rrey Alisandre*

The anonymous Aljamiado-Morisco legend of Alexander entitled *Rrekontamiento del rrey Alisandre* was edited in 1929 by A.R. Nykl. In the same year, and likely unbeknownst to Nykl, Emilio García Gómez, in the introduction to *Un texto árabe occidental de la leyenda de Alejandro Magno*, reviewed the Aljamiado Alexander romance and compared it to the Arabic text he was editing.[134] The work has received scant attention since then;[135] its author has remained anonymous and the date of the work is still largely unknown. One of the most interesting aspects of the *Rrekontamiento* is the preservation of the captions to some 32 miniatures that preceded the headings to each chapter. The miniatures themselves are not reproduced. Their inclusion in the Arabic original for the *Rrekontamiento* indicates that that manuscript must have been quite valuable and elegant.

Of all the Arabic Alexander romances that I have examined, the *Rrekontamiento* and our text show the most similarity in the initial episodic sequence. Both begin by citing the same source, 'Abd al-Rahmān b. Ziyād as transmitter, although in the Aljamiado text the name is written 'Abd Raḥmānī b. Ziyādī b. An'umin. It is noteworthy that this transmitter is not mentioned in other Arabic Alexander romances. Both texts frame the Alexander story as a *hadīth* in which non-Muslims come to pose queries to Muhammad to verify the authenticity of his messengership, and the Prophet responds by telling the story of Alexander. Both follow the introduction with Alexander's youth and upbringing, his flight into the air beneath the angel's wing, the construction of Alexandria, and his journey to the land of the setting sun. Subsequently, the two texts diverge as QDh digresses to narrate long passages on the history of Arabian legendary figures, such as Ḥūd, Ṣāliḥ, and the Thamūd, before continuing with the Persian, Indian campaigns, etc. The *Rrekontamiento* alludes only very briefly to these figures, but includes largely intact versions of Alexander's visit to Candace, Queen of Samira, to Bawāris, Queen of the Amazons, and to China, all three of which have been cut from QDh. With respect to proper names, Darius, Al-Ghayda (Darius' mother), Rashiqa (Darius' daughter), Alexander's advisors –Afshakhīr, Leṭaqun and Baṭlamis—the 'Anqā' (Phoenix), al-Andalus (visited by Dhulqarnayn), and Abū 'Abd al-Malik[136] (a major source), are common to these two texts with only slight and expected variations.

In short, there are enough similarities between the two to ensure that they derive from a common source, perhaps the very 'Abd al-Raḥmān b. Ziyād, cited at the beginning of the work, and yet, their considerable differences indicate that there were one or more recensions intervening. Although Nykl (p. 447) conjectures that the author of the *Rrekontamiento* likely used 'Umāra's recension itself, the Aljamiado work's episodic sequence, together with the proper names would seem to suggest that the *Rrekontamiento* is much closer to QDh than to 'Umāra.

---

[134] Cf. *Un texto árabe occidental de la leyenda de Alejandro Magno*, Introduction, pp. 99-113.

[135] There is Pablo Roza Candás' thesis (Trabajo de Investigación del Tercer Ciclo), *Vocabulario Completo del* Recontamiento del rrey *Ališandre*, presented to the Dept. de Filología Clásica y Románica of the Universidad de Oviedo, Sept. 1999. Cf. also the dissertation of Z. Zuwiyya, *Western and Oriental Aspects of the Rrekontamiento del rrey Ališandre* (1995), which contains a more extensive comparison of the *Rrekontamiento* and QDh in the "Source Study," pp. 86-260.

[136] See Proper Names below for this transmitter's complete name.

Comparison of *Qiṣṣat Dhulqarnayn* with *Un texto árabe occidental de la leyenda de Alejandro Magno*

Another of the Arabic Alexander romances was edited and translated into Spanish in 1929 by Emilio García Gómez. Preceding the text is an excellent study of the history of the Alexander legend in Islam, as well as an investigation of the manuscript's sources. This introductory study is without doubt the best point of departure for the study of the Alexander legend in Arabic literature. A subsequent study of A.R. Anderson sought to show that version of the Alexander romance contained in *Un texto árabe occidental de la leyenda de Alejandro Magno* is a thirteenth-century copy of the original Arabic Alexander romance made from the Syriac in the ninth century.[137] As the first two folios of the manuscript are missing, García Gómez has given the work the title *Hadith Dhuqarnayn*, and in Spanish, *Historia de Dulcarnain* (HD).

HD is similar to QDh in its Islamic theme and in the episodes universally present in the Alexander legend, but the discrepancies are such that any relation between the two works is at best remote. Nearly the first half of QDh is not found in HD: missing is the introductory *hadīth*, the construction of Alexandria, Dhulqarnayn's flight into the air with his guardian angel, Zayāqīl, Alexander's march across the face of the water as if he were on land, his expedition to the spring in which the sun sets, his expeditions to Jābalqā and Jābarsā, and to the land of the snakes. García Gómez says that the material found in these episodes is from Islamic *hadīths* born from glosses made of the Quranic figure of Dhulqarnayn, and that they have nothing to do with the Greek sources, rightly implying that HD is close in some respects to the PC.[138]

A comparison of the HD and QDh, with respect to the central episodes, reveals further variations in detail. For example, in HD Darius does not send the symbolic gifts, nor does he make a peace proposal upon his defeat. There is also an important distinction at the end of HD where the hero dies, poisoned by the queen of the Amazon women, as opposed to the death by illnesss in fulfillment of prophecy found in QDh.

Another important distinguishing feature of HD is that it makes almost no attempt to give sources for the different episodes. Whereas QDh, 'Umāra and to some extent the *Rrekontamiento* regularly cite sources, be they invented or authentic, HD cites sources on less than a handful of occasions, as can be verified by a quick review of García Gómez' glossary. Nowhere in HD are the omnipresent authorities Muqātil b. Sulaymān, Ka'b al-Aḥbār, and Ibn 'Abbas

---

[137] A.R. Anderson used as a method for proving this assertion a comparison of García Gómez's text with the Ethiopic. In light of the fact that many episodes coincide, he concludes that *Un texto árabe occidental* is the original for the Ethiopic. Unfortunately, this method is faulty in that, had he considered other Arabic Alexander legends, as well as the Aljamiado version, he would have found that much of their material also coincides with the Ethiopic. For example, he attributes undue importance to the fact that in García Gómez' text the hero is called Dhulqarnayn, as in the Ethiopic, and says that nowhere else does this name replace Alexander. However, nearly all Arabic versions of Alexander's story use the name Dhulqarnayn in place of Alexander. Cf. "The Arabic History of Dulcarnain and the Ethiopian History of Alexander" (pp. 438-445).

[138] *Un texto árabe occidental*, p. 104.

named. In this sense, and in its somewhat abridged form, HD would seem to be a less scholarly endeavor than the other Arabic Alexander romances cited. As has been stated above, the Aljamiado *Rrekontamiento* and QDh share a lot of material. At the same time, García Gómez correctly recognized that HD is fundamentally distinct from the *Rrekontamiento*. He says:

> "no existe entre ambos textos relación inmediata alguna (es decir, que la redacción árabe no es el original de la versión aljamiada), e incluso puede sostenerse que la relación mediata que entre ellos existe es bastante remota, a través de diversas recensiones perdidas, cuya filiación es imposible conjeturar" (113).

In this light, it comes as no surprise that HD and QDh are so different.

Towards the Dating and Identification of Sources for *Qiṣṣat Dhulqarnyan*

The only version of the Arabic Alexander legend for which a source has been identified is that of the Qur'ān. Nöldeke in his *Beiträge* showed definitively that Muhammad's news on Alexander derives from the Syriac legend.[139] The Arabic legends of 'Umāra and al-Ṣūrī both bear these transmitters' names on the title pages and in frequent references throughout the manuscripts. Beyond this, nothing is known of their sources. The work accompanied by the most extensive study of the sources is HD. Yet García Gómez admits to being unable to determine the filiation of his text within the convoluted branches of the Alexander romance in Arabic.[140] *Qiṣṣat Dhulqarnayn* bears the name of the last transmitter, 'Abd al-Raḥmān b. Ziyād, on the title page: "This book contains the story of Dhulqarnayn, [...], which is transmitted by 'Abd al-Raḥmān b. Ziyād." His name appears again on folio 4:

> 'Abd al-Wāḥid said: Muqātil b. Sulaymān said: I told 'Abd al-Rahmān b. Ziyād that I wanted to hear from him the story of Dhulqarnayn, God bless him. He said: Yes, I'll tell you in the same way that Sa'īd b. al-Musayyab told me on the authority of Sa'd b. Abī Waqqāṣ.

However, he is nowhere else mentioned in the rest of the manuscript, which is disconcerting because it casts doubt on how much of the recension was actually transmitted by him. One could more safely identify him as the transmitter of the whole manuscript if his name appeared periodically throughout the text, as is the case in 'Umāra and al-Ṣūrī. The same may be said for the *Rrekontamiento del rrey Ališandre*.

The comparison of QDh with a number of Arabic Alexander legends has shown that the text edited here is closest to the *Rrekontamiento* and to 'Umāra's text with the former showing most similarity. However, neither of these texts is an immediate source.

In following the clue given on the title page (f. 1 of manuscript A) written by an unknown hand, first in Castilian and then in Arabic, informing that *Qiṣṣat Dhulqarnayn* was copied from *Kitāb al-jumān fī Akhbār al-zamān*, one finds no

[139] p. 32.
[140] pp. 116-17.

record in Brockelmann's G.A.L., or anywhere else that I am aware, of a work by that title. The handwriting on the title page of Ms. A and the handwriting of the texts of both A and B show signs of being late, probably no earlier than the eighteenth or nineteenth century, indicating the surviving copy was made at that time, perhaps made by any one of the Arab scholars working in the Escorial, or even by a nineteenth-century Spanish Arabist.[141] A perusal of Brockelmann's index does turn up a work entitled *Kitāb al-jumān fī mukhtaṣar Akhbār al-zamān.* Is it possible that these two works are one and the same? In either case, one does recognize that both works are abridgements of al-Mas'ūdī's ambitious thirty-volume universal history, *Kitāb akhbār al-zamān,* no longer extant except for the first volume. It was with great surprise that the present author learned that *Qiṣṣat Dhulqarnayn* may have been taken from this famous universal history. It has been mentioned above that al-Mas'ūdī referred on several occasions in his *Murūj al-dhahab* to the more extensive account that he gave of Alexander/Dhulqarnayn's life and exploits in his *Akhbār al-zamān* as well as in his *Kitāb al-awsaṭ* (also lost). The abridgement, *Kitāb al-jumān fī mukhtaṣar Akhbār al-zamān,* was composed by Abū 'Abd Allah Muḥammad b. 'Alī al-Shāṭibī of Tāza, Morocco sometime after 1248 A.D.,[142] and is said to contain material from al-Mas'ūdī's *Murūj al-dhahab,* and possibly also from *Akhbār al-zamān* and *Kitāb al-awsaṭ.*

As a world traveller, al-Mas'ūdī's tenth-century history likely gathered material concerning Alexander/ Dhulqarnayn from the most diverse sources reaching back for three hundred years to the early period of Islam. As a historian who accepted legendary material without criticism,[143] he would have certainly collected tales from Persia and Arabia that sought to claim the Quranic personage as one of their own, as has been mentioned above, and included them in *Akhbār al-zamān.* While one may be tempted to look for the content of the two lost works in the surviving work, *Murūj al-dhahab,* one must consider that the author tells the reader that he does not repeat in *Murūj al-dhahab* what he has written elsewhere:

> Nous n'en dirons rien ici pour ne pas être trop long, et pour rester fidèle au plan de cet ouvrage, qui est un abrégé; [...]. On raconte encore une foule d'autres détails sur les expéditions d'Alexandre, sur son séjour au milieu des provinces, sur ses marches à travers toutes les régions connues, sur les peuples qu'il observa, sur les sages qui eurent des entrevues avec lui en dépit des distances et de l'éloignement de leur patrie, et malgré la diversité de leur langage, l'étrangeté de leurs coutumes; la différence de leurs qualités et de leur caractère; sur les guerres, les stratagèmes; sur les procédés ingénieux mis en pratique par le conquérant, sur les monuments qu'il a fondés. Nous en avons traité au long dans ceux de nos ouvrages que nous avons nommés, sans parler d'autres particularités que nous passons sous silence. Nous n'avons consigné ici le peu qui précède que pour ne pas laisser ce livre entièrement dénué des légendes qui

---

[141] The analysis of the handwriting I owe to my friend Juan Pedro Monferrer Sala, Arabist at the Universidad de Córdoba. I, of course, assume full responsibility for any error in interpreting his much appreciated comments.

[142] EI, 3, p. 403 (Brockelmann). One should note that name "al-Shāṭibī," referring to Játiva in Andalusia may imply this man had some family relationship across the Mediterranean in Spain.

[143] Ibid.

se rapportent à Alexandre; en même temps que nous racontions ses expéditions et les détails de sa mort. (ed. 1861, 2, p. 277-8)

It would seem likely that the account of Alexander's life al-Mas'ūdī refers to here must have been a full-length romance. By the last remark in the passage cited, one might infer from the disproportionate number of pages al-Mas'ūdī dedicates to Alexander's encounter with the Indian sage Kand, and to the gathering of wise men at his funeral, that precisely this material is not found in the earlier lost works. This hypothesis has a bearing on the study of the sources for QDh because none of the sayings of the thirty sages at Alexander's funeral,[144] nor the long account of Alexander's final days in India,[145] appears in QDh. And yet, the Indian material is very much present in 'Umāra's text.[146]

K.F. Weymann in his study of the Ethiopic Alexander romance determined that the romance in Arabic must have passed through three stages before being translated into Ethiopic.[147] In the first stage, the Arabic truly reflected the Syriac from which it was translated, except for the beginning portion narrating Alexander's supernatural birth. In the second stage, the material dealing with Greek culture and paganism was removed and/or transformed in order to make the book more accessible to Muslims. The ending of the PC in which Alexander is poisoned was cut and replaced by Alexander's death by illness. This stage already included the developed adventure of Alexander's journey into the darkness. In the final stage, the novel must have come into the hands of an Arab author, probably in Egypt, who had knowledge of the PC. He removed the beginning he found in the Arabic text before him and reinserted the beginning found in the Ethiopic, which is very similar to the PC. Since the Arab author wanted to produce a readable novel, he undertook the necessary changes in the body of the text that followed from the new beginning. With the ending he was more conservative and left intact the letter of consolation from Alexander to his mother, because it already reflected his taste. He did, however, reinsert the ending from the PC without attempting to tie it in with what preceded. This is the state of the romance, as it is found in the Ethiopic text edited by Budge (1896).

A.R. Anderson, upon reviewing this argument, believes that Weymann was correct in identifying the first and second stages, but, regarding the final stage, he says: "It may be gravely doubted whether (3) ever existed in Arabic as a form from which the Ethiopian redactor translated it into Ethiopian [...] for it must be borne in mind that the Ethiopian redactor knew of versions of the Alexander Romance in other languages."[148] One would have to agree. Viewing the Arabic Alexander romance from this perspective, QDh would be situated in the second stage, for it has been shown above that it bears little resemblance to the Syriac text, nor does it show a close relationship to the Ethiopic. At the same time, the text has been sufficiently Islamicized to satisfy a Muslim public.

---

[144] Ed. from 1861, pp. 251-57

[145] Ed. from 1861, pp. 260-78

[146] See Appendix I.

[147] Weymann's explanation of the three stages, found on pp. 81-83 of his *Die aethiopische und arabische*, is summarized here.

[148] A.R. Anderson, "The Arabic History of Dulcarnain and the Ethiopian History of Alexander," p. 444.

At this point, an outline is provided representing a proposed genealogy for the branch of the Alexander romance to which QDh belongs. In light of the fact that both García Gómez and Nykl have situated the Arabic Alexander legend in a genealogical tree including other languages (Latin, Greek, Ethiopic, Armenian, etc.),[149] the outline below is intended just for the genealogy of QDh within Arabic. An attempt has been made to include select references from QDh to illustrate what each transmitter may have contributed to the legend at each stage in its evolution. The attribution of episodes to specific transmitters, while based on logic and on an intuition acquired from the reading of much Alexander material, is not intended to be definitive proof, nor could it be, since the work of many of the scholars cited has been lost.

[149] See *Un texto árabe occidental* p. 32; *Rrekontamiento*, p. 445.

Model for the Evolution of *Qiṣṣat Dhulqarnayn*

Syriac version of the PC and the Quranic episodes (Arabia; 7th century A.D.; probably circulated in oral tradition).

↓

Ka'b al-Aḥbār (version in his *Qiṣaṣ al-anbiyā'*, Arabia; 7th century; may have added material of Hebrew origin, such as the episode of Dhulqarnayn overhearing a judge give a novel sentence to an unusual case, ff. 270-72); **Ibn 'Abbās** (Arabia; 7th century) is also cited as authority of the episode of Dhulqarnayn riding the *al-burāq*, and an account of the history of the people of Ṣūd 170-73).

↓

Wahb b. Munabbih, Ibn Isḥāq, (both men were authors of a *Qiṣaṣ al-anbiyā'* ; Arabia for the former, the latter moved from Arabia to Egypt and then to Iraq; 8th century; were disciples of Ka'b; may have contributed material of Arabian origin, for example, the interpolated stories of Thamūd, Ṣāliḥ, and the Ḥūd, ff. 61-66 and 170-73); **Muqātil b. Sulaymān** (Mecca and Medina and Baṣra, Iraq; 8th century; cited as source for Dhulqarnayn's march across the surface of the sea, ff. 39-40; Mount Qāf and comments about the geography of the earth, ff. 135-36).

↓

'Abd al-Malik al-Malshūnī (North Africa; probably 8th century; important source, cited as transmitter for many episodes throughout QDh; besides transmitting material collected from Muqātil and others, he may have interpolated the episodes relating Dhulqarnayn's trip to al-Maghrib and al-Andalus, ff. 236-45).

↓

'Abd al-Raḥmān b. Ziyād (Qāḍī from North Africa; 8th century; probably knew 'Abd al-Malik al-Malshūnī; may have heard the frame story from Muqātil b. Sulaymān, ff. 4-14).

↓

al-Mas'ūdī (included a version in his Akhbār al-zamān and Kitāb al-awsat; said to be from Baghdad, traveled in Persia, Baṣra and Egypt, among other places; 10th century; may have interpolated material on the origin of Yūnān (ff. 36-38), as he refers briefly to this in Murūj al-dhahab, ed. from 1861, pp. 242-44; other additions of al-Mas'ūdī are nearly certain, but cannot be determined due to loss of texts).

↓

Abū 'Abd Allah Muḥammad b. 'Alī al-Shāṭibī (included a version in his Kitāb al-jumān fī mukhtaṣar akhbār al-zamān; Morocco; post mid-13th century; probably interpolated material referring to Crusades, ff. 85, 261; linguistic analysis suggests that this work may have been copied by an Andalusian scribe).

↓

Copy of the Alexander version contained in Kitāb al-jumān fī akhbār al-zamān (Morocco or Spain; 18th or 19th century; not likely that material is added at this point)

The degree to which this genealogical model for QDh may be applied to 'Umāra's text, the *Rrekontamiento* and al-Ṣūrī's text (to a lesser extent) remains to be shown. A closer analysis of their sources would be required and this is beyond the scope of this introduction. The reader is referred to García Gómez's excellent study of the sources for HD that is still valid for episodes in this edition as well as in the *Rrekontamiento* that coincide with HD.[150] Ultimately, our knowledge of the evolution of the Arabic Alexander romance will only significantly advance once the texts have been published with indices and studies. This edition of *Qiṣṣat Dhulqarnayn* seeks to begin to fill this void. It is hoped that by drawing attention to the Arabic Alexander romance, the extensive romances of 'Umāra and al-Ṣūrī might also, someday soon, be edited and published.

The Manuscripts and Their Language. Criteria Used in the Edition and in the Translation.

Description of the Manuscripts

The text edited here is found in two manuscripts in Madrid. The first is in the Real Academia de la Historia, number 61. This is the version referred to as B. The second, version A, is in the Biblioteca Nacional, number 5379. The manuscript in the Biblioteca Nacional is without date, but the handwriting suggests that it was probably copied in the eighteenth or nineteenth century.[151] It consists of 140 parchment folios within a leather binding in good condition. There is no watermark. The size of the parchment is 14 cm. x 10 cm. The size of the box in which the text is written is 10 cm. x 7 cm, approximately. The recto and verso of each folio are numbered consecutively with Roman numerals so that it reads like a modern book with pages from 1 to 279. Thus, it has been convenient to use this numbering system (indicated, for example, as f. 7 or f. 223) in reference to the manuscript. The ink is black with some epigraphs in red. The script is Naskhī Maghribī, and appears to be written by two separate hands. The first scribe wrote pages 1-132. He is very neat and careful in his handwriting and provides occasional vocalization. The second scribe wrote pages 133-153. His handwriting is significantly worse. He is more careless with spelling and rarely vocalizes. After page 153 the two scribes alternate, each contributing ten or twenty pages at a time. The text is fit within a box traced on each page consisting of 15 to 17 lines leaving ample margins. On the first page of ms. A in the manner of a title, we find written in Spanish, "Vida de Alexandre Magno, llamado Du-l Cornain, cọpiada del libro intitulado Kitab al-chuman fi Ajbar e-zaman" and then in Arabic "كتاب الجمان في اخبار الزَّمَان".[152] It is not known who wrote this title.[153]

---

[150] *Un texto árabe occidental*, pp. 94-162.

[151] Cf. above, "Towards the Identification of the Sources and Dating of QDh," p. 56, for acknowledgments regarding the paleographic analysis of the manuscripts.

[152] In a literal translation, this title might be rendered: 'Book of the Pearls contained in the News of the Times.'

Ms. B of the Real Academia is also without date and consists of 109 parchment folios, each numbered on the verso. The binding is leather and in good condition. There is no watermark. The size of the parchment is 15 x 10 cm. There are several blank pages at the end of the manuscript, as if the book were left unfinished. The folios bear a stamped Roman numeral in the upper lefthand corner, the first being 2, as folio 1 is counted as the cover of the book. Reference to the work is given as B:*5r.* or B:*57v.* The title of the work is set apart on folio 2 recto and written in red and black ink with a simple Maghribī calligraphy reading:

بسْم الله الرحمان الرحيم صلى الله عَلَى مَولانا محمَّد وءاله
كِتَابٌ فيه قصّة ذي القَرْنينْ بنْ نبّاشٍ رضى الله تعلى عنهُ ونفعنا به
رواها عبْد الرحمَن بن زَيد رضى الله عنه عَن رسُل الله صلى الله عليه وسلم

The ink throughout the manuscript is black with occasional words and epigraphs in red. In contrast to manuscript A, the manuscript of the Real Academia appears to be written nearly entirely by a single scribe. The possible exception might be folios 7r. (bottom), 44r, 95r, where the handwriting takes on a different character, though this may just be due to a mood change in the scribe. The handwriting throughout is small but clear, with occasional vocalizations. The number of lines per page varies between 13 and 21. There are lacunas on folios 38r, 39v, 46v, 47r, 73r. The story of Alexander is left unfinished truncated in mid-page on folio 107, where the last line reads: قال فكتب , indicating the scribe intended to continue writing. After this, the manuscript begins on the following folio (f. 108) with a new text, two folios in length, barely legible, dealing with prophetic traditions unrelated to the Alexander story.

Criteria Used in the Edition.

The language of this Alexander legend may turn out to be useful for philological study of the state of Arabic in Morocco and/or Andalusia after the mid-thirteenth century. With this in mind, every effort has been made to preserve the integrity of the work from the linguistic perspective by limiting undocumented changes to the text. However, the carelessness of the scribe with respect to diacritical points, spelling, concordance, word order and repetition has necessitated some correction of his errors. Where possible, corrected forms were verified in Ms. B, and acknowledged in a footnote. Following is a substantial although not complete list of changes introduced into the text:

Corrected text	Text in Manuscript A	Folio
رقُودٌ	رفُودٌ	f. 12
جابرصا	حابرصا	f. 13
خبره...	فلما رءا هذا الرّويا بلغ خبرها	f. 16

153 See above, "Towards the Dating and Identification of the Sources of QDh," p. 79 and sq., for reference and discussion of this title.

f. 18	فولد له من اشرف نسآيه يقال له قاشورة	يقال لها...
f. 24	بغيظ	بغبط
f. 30	الا	ان لا
f. 36	في اخر النبيين	و اخر النبيين
f. 36	معقل	مقاتل
f. 44	بلغ فلما	فلما بلغ
f. 44	ضلحاً	صلحاً
f. 52	ان	عن
f. 53	فوّصت	فوّضت
f. 54	امر	امري
f. 59	قلبك	قبلك
f. 72	ما	مع
f. 73	ولاكفي	ولاكني
f. 78	هلكهما علي الصفة	خلقهما علي الصفة
f. 80	مجر	مجرا
f. 81	فاوّل من وف	فاوّل من لقي
f. 87	ما قالوا لهم وما قالوا لهم	ما قالوا لهم
f. 88	عن ما علي ما	علي ما
f. 95	عرافتها	غرافتها
f. 99	فنعم الملاد	فنعم الملاذ
f. 104	من اول النهار الى ارتفاعة	الى ارتفاعه...
f. 117	فقال لجدنا منسك نقدم انت واخوتك	...تقدم انت...
f. 118	حتى انتهبنا الى هذه الجزيرة	...انتهينا الى...
f. 119	بعضهم اطول من ذلك ومنهم قل من ذلك	...اقلّ من ذلك...
f. 121	نحن نحشوْ	نحن نخشوْ
f. 127	تتاعد	تتعاد
f. 140	السباع	السباخ
f. 142	ربّونيّة	ربّوبيّة
f. 147	يقوم عدوا	يا قوم عدوا
f. 147	حاصة	خاصّة
f. 147	حذوا	خذوا
f. 152	مقالتك	مقاتلتك
f. 153	من يوم هذا	من اليوم هذا
f. 154	فانا احوا	فانا ارجوا
f. 154	الى	الا
f. 155	ملكك	ملككم
f. 158	العتيد الجبار	العنيد الجبار

رعبهم	رعبهم رعبهم	f. 174
لَحّ عليه في المسئلة	لَجّ عليه في المسئلة	f. 178
لو [...] لابتغيت	لو [...] لا ابتغيت	f. 204
كان لي	هان في	f. 210
...امامه	بعضهم خلفه وبعضهم امن به	f. 212
جُنودَك	جُودَك	f. 217
فأيسوا	ماسبوا	f. 220
لازَاحَكَ	لارَاحَكَ	f. 222
ما اختار	ما ختار	f. 225
سراج	سراح	f. 225
مناخرها	متاخرها	f. 231
لمعان الاسنّة	ملعان الاسنّة	f. 231
صارت القتلي	صلوة القتلي	f. 232
للملوك	للملود	f. 233
فحقره	فحفره	f. 234
خلف	حلف	f. 235
عمل	علمل	f. 238
رِحلُ البحر	رجلُ البحر	f. 240
جنودى	جنود	f. 242
اختصّهم	احتصّهم	f. 245
الاعداء	العداد	f. 249
اليهم...	ما كرمهم واحسن اليه	f. 250
خرجت...	حرجت عليهم حيّاتٌ	f. 251
حية	حيه	f. 253
بساحة	بساحه	f. 255
خلت	خلقت	f. 266

Besides the above correction of errors, the editor has adhered to the following norms with regards to orthography:

a.) The *hamza* has been placed according to the rules of Classical Arabic:

اول > أوّل ; مومن > مؤمن .

b.) The scribe used the *shadda* very sporadically. Often, on the same line, he spelled the word once with *shadda* and again without it. The editor felt this inconsistency detracted from the clarity of the edition and has regularized use of the *shadda*. However, this does not imply that the reader will find a text replete with full Classical usage of the *shadda*. Without full vocalization, such an endeavor would be uncalled for. The *shadda* has been placed on the following words and (where applicable) on their derivatives:

Verbs: حدّث ، سلّم ، ردّ ، حقّق ، صلّى ، بشّر ، غمّ ، كثّر ، تحرّق ، اتّبع
اتّفق ، كنّا ، ظنّ ، تعجّب ، اتّباع ، حقّ ، شكّ ، تمّ ، حبّ ، تعلّق ، سمّى ،
مرّ ، فرّ ، قرّ ، استقرّ ، توفّي ، اتّصل ، اتّق ، ارتدّ ، اتّخذ ، تقدّم ، اشتدّ ،
توفّى ، فسّر ، مسّح ، تولّى ، جرّا ، حسّ ، خبّر

Nouns and pronouns: نبيّ ، أيّام ، ربّ ، أمّ ، معلّم ، فضّة ، نحّاس ، متّقين
دوابّ ، عمّ ، واليّ ، شدّة ، متّفق ، أقلّ ، مدّة ، الحظّ ، حيّ ، سرّ ، شرّ ،
قوّة ، ضدّ ، جنّ ، مشوّرة ، بدّ ، دبّ ، دابّة ، عدوّ ، سدّ ، مسدّد ، مقدّمة
برّ ، وحدانيّة ، شابّ ، ذرّيّة ، كافّة ، البوّاب ، درّة ، جبّار ، ناصريّ ، جدّ ،
قويّ ، عبوديّة ، فنّ ، عامّ ، كفّ ، قصّة ، حرّ ، سيّد ، كرسيّ ، ربوبيّة ،
كوّة ، غمّ

Proper Nouns: محمّد ، أسّاس ، عبّاس ، الصبّاح ، ذرّ ، آدميّين ، فضّالة

Toponyms: مكّة ، بيت المقدّس

Particles and Prepositions: أمّا ، حتّى ، ثمّ ، منّي ، عنّا ، إليّ ، عليّ ،
كلّ ، إنّ "وأخواتها" ، إنّما ، إلاّ ، لمّا ، ممّا ، منّا ، أيّها ، لعلّى ، لأنّ ، لكنّها ،
عمّا ، ممّن ، بلّى

Adverbs and Adjectives: ستّة ، وطيّة ، ضيّة ، غربيّ ، شرقيّ ، قبليّ ، عاليّ
مصوّرة ، مبنيّة ، عزّ وجلّ ، عاصيّ ، جفّة ، أوّل ، خاصّة

Adjectives of Place: الاسكندريّ ، الهمدانيّ ، الملشونيّ ، الهنديّ

c.) Quranic passages have been identified, set off with decorative brackets, and given full vocalization.

d.) The *madda* placed by the scribe consistently over *alif* before *hamza* has been removed: ابنآء > ابناء ; اشيآء > أشياء .

e.) Where the scribe replaces *ya'* for *hamza* in word-internal position, *hamza* is returned to its proper place: يوميذ > يومئذ ; سيل > سئل ; عشآيرنا > عشائرنا .

f.) *Hamza* is reinstated in word-final position where the scribe has omitted it:
شاطى > شاطيء ; عطا > عطاء .

g.) The appropriate diacritical marks are placed beneath the *ya'* in word-final position: هى > هي ; رضى > رضي .

h.) The grapheme ءا used in the manuscript is written as آ :
قرءان > قرآن ; ءاباينا > آبائنا.

i.) Misspellings arising from interference of the scribe's Middle Arabic linguistic orientation have been corrected and documented in a footnote:
جيهة > جهة ; دو > ذو ; اسثفتحوا > استفتحوا .

j.) The diacritical marks are placed on the *tā' marbūṭa*: حفنه > حفنة

k.) The epithet used upon invocation of the name of God has been changed throughout the edition as follows: تعلى > تعـالى . The manuscript form may represent a tendency to prefer form V over form VI. But one must ask why the scribe never places the *shadda* on this form V as he does occasionally (but not consistently) with other form V verbs, such as توفّى ، تولّى ، تخبّر .

It is believed that these criteria will not obstruct the linguist in his/her study of the text. The scribe's sporadic vocalization has not been modified, even when incorrect, nor have any short vowels been placed in the text. The graphemic norms introduced here are almost entirely predictable. The only loss the editor foresees would regard the study of the *shadda*, as it is impossible to distinguish between a *shadda* introduced into the text and one that was already present. It is hoped that the benefit of seeing the *shadda* and the other graphemes where they are habitually placed outweighs any incovenience.[154]

The Language of *Qiṣṣat Dhulqarnayn*

Below is a representative listing of lexicographical and morphological forms that serve to characterize the language of this text. In addition to the identification of the Andalusian Middle Arabic forms that constantly interfere in the scribe's attempt to produce a Classical Arabic text, the listing may also serve as a valuable tool in assessing the period to which the manuscript belongs. This

[154] I actually made what amounted to a paleographic edition of the manuscript before normalizing the orthography. However, the people kind enough to read the Arabic text for me found my insistence on maintaining manuscript forms in the edition to be cumbersome and an impediment to the reading of the text. Upon their urging, I was convinced to normalize the orthography to something more familiar to a reader today. While this process was very tedious and consumed many days, it was also enlightening as I discovered the orthographic patterns of the scribe. In the end, it became clear to me that I was not changing the text, but rather replacing medieval manuscript forms with the current set of spelling norms in an entirely predictable way. I was able to put my conscience at ease by documenting any deviation in footnotes.

study is intended for the reader unfamiliar with features of Andalusian Middle Arabic, and will help him/her to understand the relationship between the Classical Arabic forms placed in the text and the "misspellings" relegated to the footnotes. At the same time, this study does not pretend to be a rigorous linguistic analysis and will likely not satisfy the serious medieval Arabic linguist. Such an analysis is presently beyond the author's capabilities. The primary work consulted for the study of Hispano-Arabic is F. Corriente's *A Grammatical Sketch of the Spanish Arabic Dialect Bundle.* For the sake of placing the text in the larger context of Middle Arabic in general, Joshua Blau's *A Grammar of Christian Arabic,* based on South Palestinian texts of the first millennium, has been used. Where applicable, reference to these works is provided for each feature of the language discussed here for the benefit of the reader who wishes to further pursue the linguistic aspects of *Qiṣṣat Dhulqarnayn.*

Vowels

The lengthening of the short vowel *kasra* to *ya'*, called اشباع in Corriente (196), is common in the language of the scribe. The text did not show examples of the lengthening of *kasra* to *alif* or *ḍumma* to *waw*. Due to the number of occasions and the consistency with which the scribe substitutes the long vowel for the short one, this feature must have been common in Hispano-Arabic. However, whereas Blau discusses shortening of long vowels and the disappearance of short vowels (61-64), he does not mention lengthening of short vowels as being a general characteristic of the Middle Arabic texts he studies. Following are examples of this phenomenon and the Classical forms used to correct them. All such changes are documented in footnotes:

صفة < صيفة (117); يصل < يصيل (133); جهة < جيهة (33 and regularly); فيبسوا < فيبيسوا (65); دهسة < دهيسة (179); كصفة < كصيفة (265); بغض < بغيض (206); هم < هيم (207).

The case of the reduction of unstressed long vowels is found in at least two cases in the text and corrected as indicated: بالسيوف < بالسوف (162); ثم آته < ثم أتيه (33). Corriente (62) provides a number of examples to support this feature of Hispano-Arabic. Blau (66) only mentions that he is "inclined to assume" that long vowels were sometimes affected in unstressed open syllables.

The author was only able to find one instance of the Hispano-Arabic phenomenon described by Corriente (64) by which a long vowel shifts to a final syllable previously occupied by a short vowel: عامتهم < عماقم (165). The reverse is found in one case, present in both manuscripts A and B, and must remain, for now, unexplained, if it is not to be attributed to hypercorrection: جهاد <جاهد (142).

Consonants

The text shows that *ta'* and *tha'* often failed to contrast. Thus, the following forms were identified, rewritten in Classical Arabic as indicated, and documented in footnotes: (85) مُكَثُّهُ > مُكَتُّهُ; (68) تمار > ثمار; (21) ثَمَّ > تَمَّ; (257) متل > مثل; (186) ثوارثها > توارثها; (3) اسثفتحوا > استفتحوا; (45) ثرك > ترك. For the Hispano-Arabic trend *tha'* > *ta'*, see Corriente (44). Blau (106) says that he has "not noted instances of th > t." However, he does point out that this is a common feature in sedentary dialects. The reverse, i.e., *ta'* > *tha'*, also seen here, is likely a product of hypercorrection.

With regards to the spiral pair *ha'* and *ḥa'*, Corriente (57) points out that the latter was on occasion realized as the former. This would explain هروب which is corrected to حروب (147). There is also the curious rendition of خلقهما which has been corrupted to هلكهما, and is possibly explained as hypercorrection of *kha'* to *ḥa* (Corriente 57) and the mistaking of *ḥa'* for *ha'*.

Many are the examples of confusion between the *dāl* and *dhāl*. Blau (107-108) points to this trend as a general feature of Middle Arabic and Corriente (45) says there is "plenty of evidence" in Hispano-Arabic marking the shift *dhāl* to *dāl*. The following forms have been identified in *Qiṣṣat Dhulqarnayn* and corrected as indicated:

(72) دراوينا > ذرارينا; (71) باذروه > بادروه; (259) ادينه > اذينه; (68) مشيَّدَةٌ > مشيِّدَةٌ.

The instances of *dāl* to *dhāl* may be explained as hypercorrection.

The merger of the *ẓā'* and *ḍāḍ*, as discussed by Blau (114) regarding his selection of Middle Arabic texts, and Corriente (46-47) with respect to Hispano-Arabic is also patent in this Alexander romance and corrected as follows:

(194) عضيما > عظيما; (231) اضهرني > اظهرني.

Perhaps the most common nonstandard language feature of the work edited here is the confusion among the *sīn*, *ṣāḍ*, and *shīn*. Blau (109-11) has observed frequent shifts of the nature *sīn* > *ṣāḍ* and the reverse *ṣād* > *sīn*, as has Corriente (49-50) for Hispano-Arabic. Corriente (50) has additionally found several instances of *shīn* > *sīn*. The following forms were identified and corrected:

(257) اسجاره > اشجاره; (254) فاشرعوا > فاسرعوا; (78) تسهدوا > تشهدوا
(162) صور > سور; (238, 156) صور > سار; (225) سجاع > شجاع
(270) هرص > هرس; (269) صيَّرت > سيَّرت; (254) السحارى > الصحارى

.(159) يحاسروها > يحاصروها ;(153) قاسم > قاصم

The case of *sīn* to *shīn* is explained by hypercorrection.

According to Blau, "*ghayn* instead of Classical *'ayn* occurs quite frequently" (115) in his pool of Middle Arabic texts of South Palestine. Corriente (55) has observed the reverse trend in Hispano-Arabic, *'ayn* < *ghayn*. Our text shows instances of only the latter, rewritten in Classical Arabic as follows:

.(169) عيريَ > غيري ;(183) لا عني > لا اغني ;(151) عزوة > غزوة ;(151) عـــنى > غـــنى

Where the letters vary by only a dot, one must always consider the possibility that the scribe simply forgot to dot the *'ayn*.

Another noteworthy shift is *'ayn* > *zero*. This possible trend is not mentioned by Blau. Corriente (56) observes the disappearance of the *'ayn* in the low registers of Hispano-Arabic. The following examples were identified in QDh and corrected: موضا > موضعا (193); ما > مع (72); ان > عن (52).

The merger between *qāf* and *kāf* in Hispano-Arabic is well-documented, according to Corriente (54). Neither of these letters is discussed in Blau, so one assumes that their contrast in the Middle Arabic of South Palestine was maintained. The forms found in the text here together with their corrections are: مكفول > مقفـــول (B:66); مكفولة > مقفولة (178); هلكهما > خلقهما (78). This feature was apparently common in most registers of Hispano-Arabic.

Morpho-Syntax

There are several morpho-syntactical forms that serve to characterize the language of the text. To begin with, the first person singular verb sometimes appears with a *nūn* prefix. Although we indicate here the Classical Arabic form, this feature is not corrected in the text:

نسئله > اســـئله (125); فانا نفتح > فانا افتح (166); نضىء > اضيء (148). Corriente (100) identifies the use of *nūn* as the first person marker to be typical in the Arabic of Spain. Blau does not mention it.

Human broken plurals of a collective nature regularly take feminine singular verbal agreement when they follow the verb. This feature is occasionally found in Hispano-Arabic, according to Corriente (131), but not mentioned in Blau. The examples from our text and their contrast with the forms one might expect to find in Classical Arabic are indicated below. There was no correction made to the text in these cases:

(15) كانت علماء الروم > كان علماء الروم

(17) وركبت معه ملوك الروم > وركب معه ملوك الروم

(166) ما حوته ملوكهم > ما حويه ملوكهم

(18) كانت ابنآء الملوك >كان ابناء الملوك.

Negation in the language of *Qiṣṣat Dhulqarnayn* is obtained by means of any one the Classical Arabic particles: لن ، لا ، ليس (ليست ، ليسوا) ، لم ، ما. Not found is the negative form إش used in Hispano-Arabic, especially during the Granada period. The system of negation shows regular and proper usage of the لا ، ليـــس ، لم. The particle لن, signifying future negation as in لن تبلغ 'You will not attain,' appears twice. At the same time, ليس is used with the imperfect (ليس ينتهى and ليسوا يظاهرين and ليس يملو عينك and شـــــيء), and the perfect (ليس زالتا ان امسكهما). The particle لم may also precede the perfect as it does in لم سلكها احد (268) and لم قلـــت (9). The common Middle Arabic particle of negation , ما , which Blau (103) says "has become the 'basic' negative particle," and which Corriente (143) also sees in Hispano-Arabic is found in our text in negation of nominal sentences, ما اعظـــمَ شـــانه (2), in negation of the imperfect ما تدري نفس (14), and the perfect ما دخلـــها (99), but not to any greater extent than the other forms of negation. The negative reinforcer قـــطّ appears frequently in imperfect, perfect, and nominal constructions, typical of Hispano-Arabic as Corriente (145) points out. For instance, we find: ما رءا الرّاون مثله قط (57); ولا جنّيٌّ قط ولا ملك (179).

The language of *Qiṣṣat Dhulqarnayn* is much richer in its linguistic content than the few features pointed out here. Unfortunately, a more in-depth linguistic study is beyond the scope of this introduction. Even so, it is believed that the observations made demonstrate that, from a linguistic perspective, the text shares much with the language identified by Corriente as the "Spanish Arabic Dialect Bundle." To a lesser degree the work shows similarities to the Middle Arabic described by Blau based on South Palestinian texts of the first millenium, as one would expect. Ultimately, the language of the work edited here is Classical Arabic with facets and constant interference from the Middle Arabic of what must have been a Spanish Arabic scribe. The use of frequent vocalizations at a time when short vowels in determined contexts were disappearing from the spoken language,[155] the attempt at erudition in the use of an extensive system of negation, the maintenance of the dual, and the many errors resulting from

[155] Blau, 61-63.

hypercorrection, all point to a conscientious effort by the scribe(s) to write in Classical Arabic. However, his inability to maintain contrast between consonants, such as dāl and dhāl, ta' and tha', ḍāḍ and ẓā', sīn and ṣāḍ, and his tendency to shift vowels and stress within words, proved too difficult to overcome. Fortunately, the loss of integrity the text suffered from the Classical Arabic standpoint will likely be compensated by the tremendous linguistic value the work holds for the scholar of medieval Arabic.

Criteria Used in the Translation

The translation was done by chapters over a period of several years, and has since been revised and made uniform, as much as uniformity was attainable. As the reader will appreciate from the first page of the translation, the language of *Qiṣṣat Dhulqarnayn* is frequently Islamic in tone, especially in the epistolary correspondence between the hero and the peoples of the earth, whom the former admonishes to follow the religion of God. It has not been possible or even desirable to alter the Islamic nature of the text. The inclusion in the English translation of the many blessings conferred upon Muhammad and the other prophets (e.g., "May God bless him and grant him salvation") was at one point questioned, as it becomes cumbersome and repetitive in English, but in the end the decision was to maintain them, as they are an integral part of the narrative. The blessings and the Islamic language contribute to the sacred tone the transmitters wished to convey in Dhulqarnayn's story.

A related aspect is the extensive use of *isnāds* or chains of authority (e.g., "'Abd al-Wāḥid said: Muqātil b. Sulaymān said: I told 'Abd al-Rahmān b. Ziyād that I wanted to hear from him the story of Dhulqarnayn, God bless him. He said: Yes, I'll tell you in the same way that Sa'īd b. al-Musayyab told me, on the authority of Sa'd b. Abi Waqqāṣ, may God be satisfied with him). The temptation was to simplify these *isnāds* by reporting in indirect speech what the different authorities said. However, preference for the literal translation prevailed, as it was essential to preserve the exact wording of what each transmitter said. It is believed that the reader will quickly become accustomed to this fundamental feature of Islamic narratives. Dialogue on the level of the transmitters is not set apart in double quotes, as it was felt that this was a way to distinguish it from dialogue among characters in the story.

The Arabic scribe has an evident predilection for phrases of two verbs or adjectives when one sufficiently gets the idea across, i.e., "to weep and sob deeply," or "they raid us and harass us," "the One who is Matchless and Unequaled." In most cases, both verbs and/or adjectives are translated into English, so as to convey the effect of the Arabic original. The translator is aware that this device, while typically medieval, is not as common in modern English texts.

With respect to words like *isnād* and *hadīth* that are not found in my Webster's New English Dictionary, they are italicized. Other Arabic words like jihad, sura, sunna, now present in the dictionary, are spelled according to current

English usage and are not italicized.[156] Common toponyms and peoples' names are spelled in the English manner, i.e., Jerusalem, Rome, Morocco, Egypt; Noah, Aristotle, Jesus, Darius, Muhammad. Exceptions are Rūm and Ifrīqiyā. The translator felt Rūm was too broad a term in Arabic to be captured in a single word in English, while using Africa or Tunisia for the latter might be misleading. Names such as Dhu al-Qarnayn and Abū 'Abd Allah are never declined in the translation, i.e., always Dhulqarnayn and Abū, never Dhilqarnayn or Abā.

Quranic citations were taken from the edition of 'Abd Allah Yūsuf 'Alī and italicized. Epithets and formulas attributed to God and the prophets were also used in accordance with the same edition of the Qur'ān. When Islamic expressions were not locatable in the Qur'ān, the English equivalents given in Hans Wehr's Arabic – English Dictionary were used.

Several features of medieval Arabic were lost in the translation. Long blocks of Arabic narrative consisting of a string of sentences connected with *wa* ("and"), lacking any sort of punctuation, had to be dissected into English phrases, sentences and paragraphs. On occasion, the point at which the author moves from one idea to another is not obvious, and the translator has had to interpret the intention of the medieval Arabic scribe, placing paragraph breaks in a subjective manner. It is hoped that this process did not distort the Arabic text more than necessary. The medieval Arabic narrative may begin a segment with simply *qāla*, i.e., "He said." There were two or three occasions when the subject of this verb was ambiguous. In those cases, the translation reads, "[The narrator] said:" with a footnote explaining who is likely the narrator. With regards to verb tenses, medieval Arabic, as other medieval languages, may switch between the perfect and imperfect in the middle of a narrative segment, relying on the context to set the time frame. The change between perfect and imperfect in mid-paragraph or even in mid-sentence is unacceptable in English. Verb tenses have been rendered in a fashion as to convey consistency and stability, inasmuch as this was possible. The measurement of distance in *Qiṣṣat Dhulqarnayn* is given in temporal units, i.e., "the island was two months long and three months wide." Implied is that it would take two months to march across the length of the island and three to march its width. In these cases, the translation reads, "it would take a journey of two months to traverse the island's length, and three months to traverse its width." The reader is also advised that frequently the Arabic expression in its literal translation is not effective in English and has been substituted with a word or phrase that sounds better in English, such as "lo and behold," "in the blink of an eye," "take the Lord for granted."

On occasion there were passages in the Arabic text whose meaning was not entirely clear. This may be due to corruption the text suffered in the many recensions through which it passed before arriving in the twenty-first century. Alternatively, an obscure passage may be the result of the incredulity of its content. For example, where the writer attempts to describe a castle that goes into a spiraling motion when someone approaches it, the effectiveness of his description breaks down once he begins to describe the intricacies of its

---

[156] One wonders why "sunna" is in the dictionary, but "hadith" is not, since they carry similar weight in Islam.

mechanisms, because, in truth, there could be no clear explanation of it! In these cases, the translator has had to intuit the intended meaning.

Finally, when my understanding of Arabic had reached its limits, and I had exhausted my dictionaries, I consulted with experts, and Arabic natives, whenever possible. If something still remained unclear, which was sometimes the case, I made an educated guess. It is hoped that the reader will pardon any errors resulting from my non-native knowledge of the Arabic language. He/she ean be assured that every attempt was made to accurately reflect the meaning of the Arabic text.

ISLAMIC LEGENDS CONCERNING ALEXANDER THE GREAT

English Translation

In the Name of God, the Most Compassionate and Merciful, bless and grant salvation to our Lord and Master Muhammad along with his family and Companions.

This book contains the story of Dhulqarnayn, may God be satisfied with him and may we benefit from his example, which is transmitted by 'Abd al-Raḥmān b. Ziyād[1] from the Prophet, God bless him and grant him salvation. Praise be to God, who with his light brightens the darkness, whose omnipotence makes the noise of the pen as it moves across the page, who grants us abundant blessings, and who has bestowed on us the most generous Prophet, and favored us over other nations. Praise the Lord whose light brightens all the lights. He [exists in a space that] is beyond the ability of the eye to see. Both the darkness of night and the light of day bow before Him. He is the High-Elevated One whose knowledge encompasses those who have passed away and those who remain living. His knowledge extends to the heavens and the worlds. His command is faster than the blink of an eye, and his knowledge spans that which has been and that which will be. He is the Beneficent One in providing evidence to us, the Oldest in majesty [f. 2], and Greatest in his glory. He split open the abyss and made the climates; He made the light shine. He has given life to the dead and rendered the living dead. He created the heavens and raised them. He flattened the earth and smoothened it. He planted the mountains and erected them. He populated all these things for the magnificence of his lordship. He preached his Divine Oneness and his command existed before anything else and He will remain after all has passed. He was there when there was no place nor time nor age nor epoch. He was there when there was neither shade nor rainclouds, nor sky nor smoke, nor years nor ages except the One the Benefactor. He is the One and Only in whose kingdom there is no equal, the Resurrector of Souls and Sender of the Winds. He divides and restores. He gives life and provides sustenance. He promises and fulfills. How great is his stature and how powerful

---

1 This transmitter is 'Abd al-Raḥmān b. Ziyād b. An'um, called Abū Khālid al-Ifriqī al-Qāḍī. Ibn Ḥajar (*Tahdhīb al-Tahdhīb*, 6: 173-76) provides information on this eighth-century African *qāḍī*, which is summarized here. Through al-Muqrī, it is known that 'Abd al-Raḥmān said: "I was the first person to be born into Islam after the opening of Africa (i.e., modern day Tunisia)." His colleagues thought he was pleasant of speech and his traditions were said to be trustworthy. But others disagree. Ibn Mahdī said: "As for the African, it is not advisable to transmit *hadīth* on his authority." If a consensus were possible, it would seem to be that one must be skeptical of his *hadīth* because they are related on the authority of unknown personages. In so many words, this is what Abū Zar'a says, except that he remarks that 'Abd al-Raḥmān did transmit some *hadīth* on the authority of Sa'īd b. al-Musayyab, who was certainly well known. On the authority of Yaḥya b. Ma'īn, it is stated that " 'Abd al-Raḥmān transmitted *hadīth* of an extraordinary nature, which one should take care to censure." Abū al-'Arab said that "Ibn An'um belonged to the honorable Followers and that he was just and firm as *qāḍī*." Abū al-Ḥasan b. Qaṭṭān said: "He was a man of wisdom and asceticism who moved among the people without discord. There were those who backed him ... those who studied with him and others who thought the large majority of his stories reproachable and he himself an affliction to righteous men." He died in circa 156/778, having surpassed one hundred years of age, according to al-Muqrī. Some of his *hadīth* on the authority of the Prophet narrating the conquest of Africa are to be found in al-Bakrī, Abū 'Ubayd Allah, *Kitāb al-Mugrib*, p. 22 (Arabic text).

his dominance! His essence is beyond all boundaries; He is too holy to admit of being compared to the creatures in his attributes. His signs are evidence of his mightiness and his dazzling wisdom is evident in his traces [f. 3]. Everything other than Him withers away and perishes. He alone terminates life and revives it for He rules his creation as He wishes. He has known since the beginning that in the small and big creatures there is nothing like Him for He is the All-Hearing and All-Seeing. Verily, He knows what He has created! He is the Kind-One and the most Well-Informed. All words that do not begin with praise for Him are fruitless. Rarely will God assist man and grant him victory unless he says before his action, "There is no power nor strength save in God, the Almighty and Exalted." There is little divine aid or assistance to the performers of tasks unaccompanied by the saying, "There is no power nor strength save in God." Every prayer should contain a blessing for the Prophet, God bless him and grant him salvation. Very seldom will a prayer succeed and be succored that does not contain a blessing upon the Prophet. So begin your every word and act with thanks and praise to God. Depend on Him for aid and support. Be frequent in your prayer to Muhammad, his messenger and servant, God bless him and grant him salvation. Bless the Prophet, the chosen-one, the messenger who pleased God, the one sent with his mercy and guidance and saved from error and blindness [f. 4]. He was the seal of God's messengers, one of his creatures, leader of the believers, the one who unveiled God's commands and prohibitions. God bless him, his family and Companions and grant them salvation and deliver them from harm.

'Abd al-Wāḥid said: Muqātil b. Sulaymān[2] said: I told 'Abd al-Rahmān b. Ziyād that I wanted to hear from him the story of Dhulqarnayn, God bless him. He said: Yes, I'll tell you in the same way that Sa'īd b. al-Musayyab told me on the authority of Sa'd b. Abī Waqqāṣ, may God be satisfied with him:

One day I was visiting the Prophet at about the time mid-day prayer had ended. I had just left his house when, lo and behold, there were people sitting down waiting in front of the al-Khayzurān house. It was a group of elderly men, the most noble, handsome and virtuous of their people and they had a book with them. Now when I saw them and they saw me, they stood up and I stopped. I pretended not to notice them [f. 5] and didn't greet them. Suddenly, one of them stepped forward to speak to me. "What's your name, young man?" "I am Sa'd b. Abī Waqqāṣ." Then he asked, "By chance, are you one of Muhammad's

[2] Muqātil is said to have studied with Mujāhid and al-Daḥḥāk, among others, but some Islamic scholars cast doubt on his relationship to these two scholars. There is some difference with respect to opinion regarding Muqātil. His traditions are accepted in good faith by some, while for a great many others he is not to be trusted because his *isnāds* lack precision. In fact, most call him an outright liar and disregard his traditions. Ibn al-Mubārak says that " there would be no better interpretations than those of Muqātil if only they could be trusted" (Ibn Ḥajar, *Tahdhīb* 10:280; trans. mine). Indeed, some suspect that Muqātil gathered people's scholarly interpretations and commented on them without ever having actually studied personally with them (*Tahdhīb* 10:281). He is also accused of gathering material from the books of Jews and Christians regarding the Quran (*Tahdhīb* 10:284). Muqātil died in Basra in 150/757.

Companions?" "Yes, what do you want from Muhammad?" They responded together, "Ask for permission for us to go in and see your Prophet."[3]

Happy and full of joy, I turned and went back to his hut anxious to hear what they would say to him and to see how the Prophet of God would respond, God bless him and grant him salvation. When I saw the Prophet I said, "O Messenger of God, there are people at the door with books, and they would like to come in and ask you some questions." The Messenger of God turned white, God bless him and grant him salvation, and then began to weep and sob deeply. He said, "O Sa'd, they want to ask me about things I do not know. I am just a man like anyone of you, except that I receive revelation from God. But it hasn't come to me recently, and I won't say a word to them without [f. 6] revelation."

Sa'd continued: Then the Messenger of God, God bless him and grant him salvation, bowed his head, and I didn't dare say anything more to him after that. But then he called me and said, "O Sa'd, let them in." So I let them in.

The oldest, most respectable and most intelligent came forward and said, "Muhammad, we have come here to ask you about three things that we have found in our books and in the writings of our ancestors. By means of these questions we will know the authenticity of your messengership. Your task will be to instruct us in the answers to these questions, making them evident and interpreting them for us. If you are unable to do this, then you will not be welcome in our lands and we will not abandon our religion and the religion of our fathers. If and when you answer these questions we will believe in you and in the message you bring. This is what the kings of our tribes have sent us here for." To this the Messenger, God bless him and grant him salvation, responded, "What are your questions?" One of them said, "Muhammad, we ask you about men who are lost and who have died, but who are alive. What are their names and what is their story? Secondly, we ask you about a man who has travelled about [f. 7] the world, by land and by sea, to the East and to the West. Who is he? What are his ancestry and lineage? Thirdly, we ask you about the Hour of Resurrection: When will be its appointed time and when will it end? There you have our three questions, O Muhammad, with which we will know the truth of your prophecy. By way of your explanation of these things we will be certain that the revelation that comes down to you is from God. So explain the meaning of these things to us and in turn we will teach it to the leaders of our tribes, and we will believe in you and so will the descendants of our people. This is what we have come to you for, O Muhammad!"

Sa'd b. Abī Waqqāṣ said that the Prophet, God bless him and grant him salvation, would not utter a word or take any action except with revelation from

---

[3] A similar story is related in al-Ṭabarī, *Tafsīr*, 16, 6. A group of sages with scripture approach the Prophet to ask about Dhulqarnayn. The Prophet tells them that he does not know anything until God illuminates him. Then he takes some water and does the ritual ablutions. The expression in his face brightens and he tells the sages to come in together with his Companions. With all gathered before him he says: "If you like, you may pose your questions now: I will respond with what is written in your books." They say: "Tell us." He begins: "You have come here to ask me about Dhulqarnayn. You will find in your books that he was a young man from the Rūm. He came and built Alexandria in Egypt, and when he was finished, an angel came to him who lifted him and flew into the heavens ..."

God. So Muhammad said to his inquisitors, "I will explain the interpretation of your questions tomorrow." But he forgot to add, "God willing." Then they left and went to a house in the city to await the answers from the Messenger of God, God bless him and grant him salvation. They waited one night, and then the following day and night, and then till the morning after. In the end, they waited eight [f. 8] days during which the Prophet, God bless him and grant him salvation, came to be greatly distressed. The Christians[4] said, "Muhammad is unable to answer our questions. He promised to respond eight days ago and we've waited. Really, if he hasn't been able to do so until now, he'll never do it."

The Prophet was not able to reply and it seemed nearly certain that what they were saying was true.[5] This saddened his Companions and they became very worried. Indeed, revelation was slow in coming to Muhammad, God bless him and grant him salvation. It took fifteen days and on the fifteenth day Gabriel, bless him, came down from heaven and appeared to the Prophet, God bless him and grant him salvation. When Muhammad, God bless him and grant him salvation, saw him, his eyes swelled and filled with tears. Gabriel greeted him and Muhammad, God bless him and grant him salvation, returned his greeting, honored him and said, "Dear Gabriel! [f. 9] I thought that revelation had ceased for me when you no longer descended and appeared to me. Tell me, what does my Lord discern and command me to do with respect to my promise to the Christians?" Gabriel, peace be with him, said, "O Muhammad, your Lord is angry with you for what you said to the Christians. You dared to take the Lord for granted, hardly considering what His Will would be. O Muhammad, you said to the Christians when they posed those questions, 'I will instruct you in the interpretation of your questions,' but Muhammad, you didn't say, 'God willing.'"

Mujāhid said: And these are the words of God to his Prophet, Muhammad, God bless him and grant him salvation. Do not tell anybody that you will do something tomorrow without qualifying this by saying, "If God wishes." The Messenger of God cried when he brought upon himself the rebuke of his Lord by forgetting to consider his will.

Qatāda said: God scolded his prophet, God bless him and grant him salvation, in two versets in the Book of God, "Do not say you will do something tomorrow without adding '*God willing*'"[6] and "*Be not in haste with the Qur'ān before its revelation to thee is completed, but say, 'O my Lord! Advance me in knowledge.'*"[7] Now the first thing that brought on the Lord's reproval was that Muhammad forgot to say "if God wills" or "if God wishes" when he promised the Christians. The second thing was that Muhammad, God bless him and grant him salvation, was about to [f. 10] recite verses from the Qur'ān without them having been delivered to him yet. So God in his might and sublimity scolded him and forbade him from saying or doing anything until revelation had come down to

---

[4] In Ibn al-Jawzī, the ones who pose questions to Muhammed are the Jews (f. 77v), as is also the case in the *Rrekontamiento del rrey Ališandre*: "beos kon jentes kon ellos al-kitebes i-eskribturas, i ellos eran judios" (f. 1).

[5] The meaning of this clause in the Arabic (لأنّ من تمام صدقهم الوفاء بما قالوا) is not entirely clear to me.

[6] Qur'ān 18:23-24

[7] Qur'ān 20:114

him. And that is what He said to his friend, God bless him and grant him salvation.

Sa'd b. Abī Waqqāṣ said: At that point, Gabriel said, "Muhammad, recite!" Muhammad said, "My dear Gabriel, what should I recite?" Gabriel responded, "Say: 'Praise be to God the one who sends the Book down to his servant. Do not take words said in the straightest way and twist them, or else they will claim that the verses of the Qur'ān are untruthful.'"[8]

When the Lord had enlightened Muhammad, God bless him and grant him salvation, I saw his face and heart fill with joy and happiness. Then the good news appeared in his face and he called out, "O Sa'd!" I answered, "At your service, O Messenger of God, bless you." Then he said, "Tell my friends to gather around me, and have the Christians come in and sit with them. Rejoice my friends! My grief caused by the cessation of revelation has passed!"

Sa'd said: I saw the Messenger of God's face, God bless him and grant him salvation, fill with happiness and light and I knew that revelation had come to him [f. 11] from God, the Almighty and Exalted. The Prophet laughed as his heart filled with happiness, God bless him and grant him salvation. Sa'd said: I informed the Companions of the good news regarding the Prophet, God bless him and grant him salvation. This put an end to their sadness and made their hearts fill with happiness. They thanked and praised God, and came to the Prophet, God bless him and grant him salvation, formed a tight circle around him and said, "We are truly delighted." Muhammad said, "Rejoice, for God, the Almighty and Exalted, has revealed to me the answers to the Christians' queries. However, my Lord has scolded me for telling them that I would instruct them in the interpretation of their questions without saying 'God willing.' From this you should learn never to take for granted the will of God, the Almighty and Exalted. As for you, Christians, I will now answer your question about the lost men who were alive and dead at the same time.

"They are men from among you Christians who abandoned the religion of the unbelievers and the mistaken ones and fled to seek refuge in the Creator of Heaven and Earth. They believed in Him. There were seven of them and they were from the city of unbelievers called Daqyūs [f. 12]. God sealed their hearts with faith and left his mark there and they slept on. They are one of the wonders and signs that appeared among the Rūm people because they were companions, ministers and men intimate with King Daqyūs. The Lord revealed this information to me and told me to pass it on to you. He said, and how sublime are his words, '*Or dost thou reflect that the Companions of the Cave and of the Inscription were wonders among our Signs.*'[9] While they were sleeping, God closed their ears and they slept three hundred and nine years at which point God resurrected them in the middle of the day. Then they went back to their lives and they were not dead or alive. Verily, they are one of the wonders of the Almighty

---

[8] Refers to Qur'ān 18:2 and 98:3.

[9] Qur'ān 18:9. For a valuable study on how the legend of the Companions of the Cave is integrated thematically with the Quranic legend of Dhulqarnayn, as well as with other aspects of sura 18, see B. Scarcia Amoretti, "Nota a Corano XVIII, 94," pp. 13-14. See also L. Massignon, "Les sept dormants, apocalypse de l'Islam," p. 104 and sq.

God. The cave is the cavern in which they rested and the inscription is a lead tablet on which the people of their times wrote their names. Again, there were seven of them and the interpretation of their affair is quite lengthy.

"As for your question on the man who travelled around the world by land and by sea, east and west, he is Alexander b. Asās and in another account [f. 13] he is Ibn Nabbāsh[10] known as Dhulqarnayn, who was devout in his religion, one who knew his Lord and was submissive in his obedience. God gave him knowledge and worked through him. Scholars differ as to whether he was a prophet or a saint, but God knows best.[11] God made him a king and gave him wisdom. He reached Jābarqā and Jābarṣā and arrived at Sind and Hind. He built the barriers and traversed the darkness. He conquered the kings of Rūm and Persia, climbed Mt. Qāf and came to rule over a great kingdom. And that is the answer to your question on Dhulqarnayn. *Recite: I will rehearse to you something of his story. Verily We established his power on earth and We gave him the ways and the means to all ends. One such way he followed.*[12]

"Regarding your question about the Hour of Resurrection, and when is its appointed time, that knowledge is forbidden to man. The mystery of time is above all but the Almighty and Exalted One.[13] It is one of the five secrets unknown to man. No one has ever known or will ever know when time will come to its end. Neither kings who rule with God's favor nor prophets sent down from heaven are an exception! The five truths [f. 14] withheld from man belong to the realm of occult knowledge. The Lofty one in his loftiness said: Verily, God possesses the knowledge of time. He knows when to send down rain and what is in the womb. But you do not even know what you will gain tomorrow, or in what land you will die. Verily, God is the wisest of sages. Know that the Almighty and Exalted God sent to his Prophet Muhammad the Christians' queries regarding '*when will be the appointed time wherein art thou (concerned) with the declaration thereof? With thy Lord is the Limit fixed therefor. Thou art but a Warner for such as fear it. The Day they see it, (it will be) as if they had tarried but a single evening, or (at most 'till) the following morning!*'[14] No one knows when the Appointed Time will come except the One who sets the term until some

---

[10] Nabbāsh is a name not found in other Alexander romances of which I am aware. It is probably a corruption of the Arabic name for Alexander's father, Philip, which could be فِلبس Filibus or فيلبوس Fīlibūs, or فيلبس Fīlibus, all three forms appear in Mas'ūdī (1979), 7, p. 560. It would seem that the redactor mistook 'fil' or 'fīl' to be the Greek word for 'son' and rendered it 'ibn' From there, the corruption is understandable: ش for س was common in Andalusian Arabic. The reverse, س > ش , is typical hypercorrection. Also common was the tendency to elongate the vowel of the final syllable, which likely did not carry a diacritical mark. ابن بس < نبّس < نبّاش .

[11] See Ibn al-Jawzī in the above Introduction above for several opinions as to Dhulqarnayn's status as prophet or saint.

[12] Qur'ān 18:83-85.

[13] The reference is to the Qur'ān 7: 187: *They ask thee about the (final) Hour – when will be its appointed time? Say: "The knowledge thereof is with my Lord (alone): None but He can reveal as to when it will occur. Heavy were its burden through the heavens and the earth. Only, all of a sudden will it come to you." They ask thee as if thou wert eager in search thereof: Say: "The knowledge thereof is with Allah (alone), but most men know not."*

[14] Qur'ān 79:42-46.

predetermined later date. There you have the answer to your questions. Know that the full explanation of these matters is quite lengthy."

Now begins the story of Dhulqarnayn b. Asās, who is also called Ibn Nabbāsh b. Qālūsh. Ibn Isḥāq, on the authority of 'Abd al-Malik, who reported from [15] Muqātil b. Sulaymān, who said on the authority of al-Daḥḥāk b. Muzāḥim, [f. 15] who related on the authority of Ibn 'Abbās,[16] may God be satisfied with him, said: The Messenger of God, God bless him and grant him salvation, was asked about the story of Dhulqarnayn and what happened during his life. He responded: He was one of the emirs of the Rūm people. Rūm scholars found in their books and in the common knowledge of the Rūm people that God, the Almighty and Exalted, would send among them a man whose name was Dhulqarnayn, the Knowledgeable One, who would reach the ends of the earth, east and west. There were well-informed men familiar with his story that spoke of him and related his feats and deeds.

Now during those times, there was a great king who ruled over the lands and who knew the power of the Almighty God. Dhulqarnayn was one of the princes in the kingdom. There also lived in that day a pious man whom the Almighty God had endowed with great knowledge. His name was Aristotle. The Rūm had heard of him and knew his righteousness and the favor God bestowed on him. They spread word of his feats. It is said that Aristotle was prince Dhulqarnayn's uncle on his mother's side. Dhulqarnayn went to him to study [f. 16] as a boy. It was soon evident that he was an articulate scholar who had attained great achievements in his pursuit of knowledge. The Rūm scholars were amazed at his wisdom and at how well he spoke. For these talents Dhulqarnayn had the Almighty God to thank since it was He who had singled him out and raised him above other men. There is no God but Him. Some transmitters say that Dhulqarnayn was from an adulterous and shameless people.[17] But both Muqātil and al-Kalbī say that his people were good and honorable. They differ as to the consistency of his moral character. They exalted him for his great deeds, and relate in his story that he ruled over lands extending from sunrise to sunset, from east to west.

When news of the prodigious student reached the great king, the king had him summoned. Dhulqarnayn appeared at court with the Master of Goodness, Aristotle. The king commanded Aristotle to supervise Dhulqarnayn's education. Sometime later the king would summon him to evaluate the young prince's intelligence on the basis of his experience with the Master. Aristotle continued to

---

[15] Here the manuscript form بن i.e., 'ibn,' is a mistake for عن i.e., 'on the authority of.' The *isnād* 'Abd al-Malik from Muqātil appears elsewhere in the Ms. (see, for example, ff. 39, 61, 85, 92, 101, 103, 110, 130, 135, 142, 148, 222, 260), while nowhere else is the former said to be the latter's son. Since both manuscripts A and B make this mistake, it is further indication that Mss. A and B are copies of the same text, which must have contained this error.

[16] According to R.G. Khoury (1987), one must always be careful of *isnāds* citing Ibn 'Abbās. As a well-known first generation transmitter of *hadīth*, he came to figure in many forgeries, as very well may be the case here. Pp. 195-96.

[17] Probable reference to the tradition of the *Pseudo-Callisthenes* in which Alexander is born of the adulterous union of Olympias and Nectanebus. See PC (Wolohojian), pp. 23-35.

supervise him and to observe his intelligence. He asked him things from all the branches of knowledge and there was not a single question for which he did not have an answer that [f. 17] went beyond the objective of the question.[18] The Prophet, God bless him and grant him salvation, said: This inspiration was from God the Almighty who wanted to honor him by making him a man of great achievements.

Then the king brought Dhulqarnayn into his chambers, made him king, gave him sovereignty over his kingdom, freed him to do as he pleased and said to him, "You are a greater king than I. You have more right to rule over this kingdom than I." He commanded his advisors to listen to him and obey his orders. Finally, he took the crown off his head and put it on Dhulqarnayn's head. And so, still a young man, Dhulqarnayn was crowned.

Then Dhulqarnayn called the kings of the earth into submission and obedience, and told them to meet him in Egypt.

Concerning[19] Dhulqarnayn and the Building of Alexandria.

Soon Dhulqarnayn set out for Egypt along with the kings of Rūm in numbers known only to God, the Sublime and Blessed One. After a short while he arrived at the site where Alexandria would be built. Verily, it was he who built Alexandria.

In another text, Ibn Isḥāq said: 'Abd al-Malik b. Mas'ūd,[20] on the authority of Sa'd b. Abī Waqqāṣ, who spoke on the Prophet's authority, God bless him and grant him salvation, said: He was the noblest and greatest [f. 18] of the Rūm kings. His name was Asās b. Qālūsh b. Bisyātīn. A son was born to him by the most noble and honorable of his women whose name was Qāshūra. It is also said that he was the only son of an older woman.[21] From the time he was a young man, he spoke in words filled with wisdom and knowledge inspired by the Almighty God whose will it was to raise him above other men in honor. The princes of his day were his kinsfolk, and they praised him for the depth of his understanding and the wisdom of his words. By the time seven years had passed, news that the son of King Asās b. Nabbāsh was the most intelligent, strongest, and most learned man of his day had spread far and wide. His fame continued to grow as word of him traveled from one king to the next and from one noble to

---

[18] This is perhaps an abridgment of Alexander's dialogue with the ten sages, which I. Lévi provides in translation from Hebrew in his "La légende d'Alexandre dans le Talmud" (pp. 294-95).

[19] Here and throughout the word ذكر, i.e., 'the mention of' or 'chapter,' has been cut from the chapter heading.

[20] B: "bin Mas'ūda." This transmitter is unidentified. One suspects the *isnād* has been corrupted. Perhaps, it should read 'Abd Allah b. Mas'ūd or 'Abd al-Malik on the authority of (i.e., عن) Ibn Mas'ūd, the latter is quite plausible considering the graphical similarity of عن and بن. 'Abd Allah b. Mas'ūd was one of the companions of the Prophet, died circa 33/653. Cf. EI², 3, pp. 897-99.

[21] Al-Tha'labī on the authority of Wahb b. al-Munabbih also believes Alexander to be the son of an older woman who had no other children (p. 361). Al-Ṭabarī mentions this on the authority of Wahb in his *Tafsīr*, 16, pp. 6-7.

another. From the land of Rūm the news spread to all the kingdoms of the earth. Kings and governors alike hastened to pay him hommage.

The clergymen and monks from among the Rūm sages went to see him [f. 19]. When they were all present they examined him to determine how wise he was. They discovered that for every question they posed to him he had an answer that went beyond what was asked. He was indeed the most perceptive man of his time. His fame reached Aristotle, who was said to be his maternal uncle, and Aristotle was greatly impressed with the quality of young Dhulqarnayn's character. He arranged to give an exam in which he would ask questions and Dhulqarnayn would answer.

Their first inquiry was into knowledge itself. Aristotle asked, "With what does one search for knowledge?" He responded, "With one's mind." Aristotle continued, "What is the benefit of seeking out knowledge?" "Piety." "What is the essence of piety?" "Fear of the Almighty God for what is manifest and what is hidden from us." "And what is the brightest sign that one possesses the fear of God?" "Justice, which is in the hands of wisemen." "How does one rise in life?" "Through unfailing obedience." "How does one attempt to maintain order?" "By making sure people obey." "What will destroy a man's obedience?" "The proximity of disobedience. [f. 20] Since when one attempts to disobey he becomes closer to missing what he had hoped to achieve and what one had hoped to prevent arrives faster." Aristotle told Alexander, "You are the wisest man of your day." He recognized him as his equal and then said good-bye.

Once his fame had reached all the kings and nobles of Rūm, he began to search the kingdom for those rebels who refused to submit to him. In this he was helped by many kings and nobles. With great determination he rounded up the rebels and banished them to the land of Egypt, which in that day and age was a most celebrated country.

At that moment the Amalekites ruled Egypt. Dhulqarnayn traveled there with his army and went down the canal[22] to the mouth of the Nile, where God inspired him to build a city. His name in Greek was Alexander and in Arabic it was Aḥmad b. Asās[23]. The last name, Asās, meaning 'Abbās.[24] So he built the city and called it Alexandria according to his own name. After building it he fortified it. Upon seeing his might, all the Amalekites as well as the other peoples of Egypt obeyed him. [f. 21]

Concerning the Means Given to Dhulqarnayn and How He Achieved So Many Wondrous Things

Abū 'Abd al-Malik said: When Dhulqarnayn finished constructing and erecting the city and its lighthouse, he settled people there from the noblest tribes

---

[22] الخليج

[23] The use of the name Aḥmad, stemming from the same root as the Prophet's name, Muhammad, is an attempt to depict Dhulqarnayn as a prefiguration for Muhammad. The typological relationship between the Prophet and Alexander is studied in a forthcoming article: See Zuwiyya, "A Typological Interpretation of Aljamiado Morisco Texts" in *Qurṭuba*.

[24] That Asās is a corruption of 'Abbas is supported by al-Tha'labī (p. 361): وكان اسمه الاسكندر و يقال كان اسمه عباسا.

of the Rūm and ordered some of the Amalekite nobles to live there together with the Rūm. At this point in his life Dhulqarnayn was an obedient servant of his Lord, the Almighty and Exalted. The future lay before him and he wondered what he should do next. He thought deeply about this matter. Since he was not a man to act without first consulting with his advisors, he sought advice from the scholars of Rūmia, from the people of the Covenant, the clergymen and the monks. He also exchanged letters with his teacher, Aristotle, as always seeking counsel in his master's wisdom before his every endeavor.

The first thing for which he sought consultation was something that his father had never resolved up until his death: Should he go east or west? So he wrote a letter to Aristotle saying:

> In your name, Lord, to Aristotle the Wise and Master of Goodness,
> From Ibn Asās.
> May peace be upon you,
> We came to the land of Egypt [f. 22] and the Lofty One in his Loftiness inspired us to build a city that would be a shelter for the weak, for our friends, and also serve as a center of communications. The city was built from the resources remaining after we payed our soldiers.[25] Now it is completed and our goal accomplished. The Omnipotent One inspired us to build a lighthouse, which was promptly built and erected in the form of a spiral and they put it together with the required movement. All this work was done with the inspiration of God, praise be to Him.
>
> I wanted to inform the Master of Goodness of what I had done and also to consult his opinion as to whether I should at this point turn my attention to the east or the west. Master, how would you guide me in this matter?
> May we seek aid in God.

So he sealed the letter and gave it to his messenger who departed immediately.

When Aristotle received the letter he opened it, read it out loud and understood what Alexander meant, whereupon he answered with a letter that said:

> In the name of God the Most Compassionate and Merciful, and in the name of God the Magnificent the Most High One,
> To the one whose hand brings every endeavor to a prosperous end,
> To the one whom God aids in the fulfillment of his objectives,
> Dhulqarnayn b. Asās,
> From his teacher Aristotle [f. 23]
> I received your letter and I was gladdened to know that things are coming along well. Praise be to God for inspiring you to do good works. Ask Him to guide you to the highest level on the straight path for He is the one who inspired you to build the city. By turning to Him, soldiers and citizens alike will be well-guided. In Him seek counsel as to which direction, east or west, would be best to begin. That knowledge belongs to the One the Everlasting. Ask

[25] The meaning of the Arabic text here is not entirely clear, probably due to corruption.

Him and implore of Him to point out for you the road that will strengthen the integrity of your conduct. He is the One who aids.

Good-bye and may you go in peace.

He sealed the letter and handed it to his messenger who came with it straightaway. When the messenger delivered the letter, Dhulqarnayn opened it, read it and said, "The Master of Goodness is right!" He stood and went to perform the ritual ablutions. He prayed through the night and fasted during the day. He begged and implored God to show him which was the right road to take and to protect him from the road to destruction. At that moment in his life, he was in a place of prayer as a nine year-old, on his knees bowing in worship, humbling himself to the Almighty God. Then God sent him a powerful and righteous angel called [f. 24] Zayāqīl.[26]

God had ordered Zayāqīl to be a good friend to Dhulqarnayn.[27] The last time there were angels among man was during the era of Idrīs[28] and Noah, bless them. They befriended the children of Adam and taught them what was good. Zayāqīl was Dhulqarnayn's good friend. He came to him one day when he was sitting on his marble throne looking at the lighthouse he had built. The angel greeted him and he returned the greeting with great happiness. The angel Zayāqīl tucked him under his wing and flew with him into the air for an hour according to earthly time.[29] Then he pulled his head out from beneath the wing and said, "Look at the earth. What do you see?" Dhulqarnayn said, "I see my city and the cities around it." Then Zayāqīl flew again for as long as God willed until he stopped and pulled his head out and repeated, "Look at the earth. What do you see?" Dhulqarnayn said, "I see my city and other cities around it." Again,

---

[26] Al-Tha'labī's text has رفـــائيل, "Raphael," which is the likely spelling before the name became corrupted (p. 367). This angel is not listed among the four archangels God created according to Muslim tradition, who are Isrāfīl, Michael, Gabriel and 'Izrā'īl. In the Arabic spelling, perhaps the last, 'Izrā'īl, could be corrupted to read Zayāqīl, but this is the Angel of Death, and not likely Dhulqarnayn's "good friend." Cf. C. Castillo Castillo, "Algunos aspectos de la angelología islámica según Shihāb al-Dīn al-Ash'arī." p. 425. Also, EI^2, 4, 220-221 and 305-306 (A.J. Wensinck) for angels in Islam.

[27] That Raphael instead of Gabriel appears to Dhulqarnayn is an apparent indication that the Two-Horned One is not a true prophet. Regarding Dhulqarnayn's status, the *Rrekontamiento* says: "i si ubiese estado an-nabī abriale benido Jibrīl, i-esbiose del Jibrīl i binole Zayaqīl; enpero es de la kasa de lan-nubū'a" (f. 6). Also, see below f. 189. However, in al-Tha'labī's text, God speaks directly to Alexander without the intercession of an angel: فلما استحكم ملكه واجتمع أمره أوحى الله تعالى إليه : يا ذا القرنين إني قد بعثتك إلى جميع الخلائق ما بين الخافقين وجعلتك حجّتي عليهم وهذا تأويل رؤياك ، وإني باعثك إلى أمم الأرض كلهم وهم سبع أمم مختلفة ألسنتهم ... (p. 361).

[28] Idrīs is mentioned in Sura's 19:57 and 21:85. Nöldeke identifies him as Andreas, Alexander's cook who obtained immortality (*Zeitschr. Für Assyr.* 24, 84 sq.). Quranic exegetes identify him as Enoch from the Bible, who also obtained immortality or, as Jewish literature says, was taken alive to Paradise. Much of the material related to the Islamic legends of Idrīs comes from Apocryphal and Jewish sources. Cf. EI, 2, 449-450 (A. J. Wensinck).

[29] Regarding Alexander's ascension, A.R. Anderson (1927) says that "the symbolism of Alexander's identification with Mithras-Apollo-Helius as Alexander-Helias is held to be the dominant cause contributing to his being represented in some of the later versions of the Alexander Romance as making his celestial journey" (p. 100). The motif of an ascension into the heavens is common among prophets in Islam. Cf. C. Castillo Castillo, "El profeta Idrís y su 'viaje' al Más Allá" (pp. 132-35).

Zayāqīl flew for as long as God willed and then stopped and said, "Look at the earth and tell me what you see." [f. 25] He said, "I see my city alone with nothing around it except the seas." It was surrounded by the waters and looked like an island in the depths of a deep green sea. The angel said, "O Dhulqarnayn, what you see is not your city but the entire earth. It is surrounded by the sea. Know, Dhulqarnayn, that the earth is an island in the middle of the sea. You could compare it to a boat sailing on the high seas. The sea lifts the island just as ït lifts a boat. The force behind this lifting is the power of God. O Dhulqarnayn, verily, you should be amazed at the power of your Lord and Creator!"[30] Dhulqarnayn replied, "Dear Zayāqīl, certainly what I see with my own eyes amazes me! Indeed, after such a vision I testify that there is no God but Allah and that He is One without companion. Dear Zayāqīl, what do you command me to do?" The angel answered, "O Dhulqarnayn, the sea is wider than the land and the land is an island in the middle of the sea. Verily, God wants to work miracles through you, and He says to you, 'I have made you to dominate the people of the world and sent you to the children of Adam. I have empowered your soldiers so that they will be victorious [f. 26] and given your horse strength and I blessed them all for you. If some matter is beyond your cognitive power, ask the angel, Zayāqīl, who will teach you, for God is with him and aids him such that nothing is beyond him. I will provide whatever you need from me. Be one of those who are thankful for God's help.'"[31] Dhulqarnayn said, "Praise be to God the Lord of all worlds. I shall listen to and obey my Lord in all that He commands me. I am among those who are thankful.

"O God, you are the one who shows mercy on our kinsfolk. O God, You are the One who said, "*On no soul doth Allah place a burden greater than it can bear.*"[32] So why is it, my God, that you have asked me to do something which is beyond me? How could I ever accomplish all the things you require of me? How will I know how to speak to those whose tongue is different than my own? How will I interpret what the people of different nations say and how will I make war on them? How will I manage a journey across the seas and through the darkness? Could anyone ever do such a thing?"

So God sent the angel Zayāqīl and the angel said, "O Dhulqarnayn! The Most Compassionate of the Compassionate says to you: 'I am the Merciful King who pushes the spirit to its limits without [f. 27] overburdening it. I would never put you up to something that I wasn't sure you could accomplish. With my power I will broaden your intellect and the depth of your understanding. You shall understand the meaning of all words and comprehend the order of all things

---

[30] Alexander's ascension here recalls the Devil's temptation of Jesus in Mathew 4:8-9. " Again, the devil took him to a very high mountain and showed him all the kingdoms of the world and their splendors; and he said to him, 'All these I will give you, if you will fall down and worship me.' Jesus said to him, 'Away with you, Satan! ...'"

[31] In al-Tha'labī's text, God specifies for Dhulqarnayn that he will visit all the peoples of the earth namely: those of the center of the earth known as mankind (الإنس), the jinn, the barbarous Gog and Magog; at the western end of the earth are the Nāsik; at the eastern end are the Mansik; to the extreme "right" are the Hāwīl; to the extreme "left" are the Tāwīl (p. 362). A journey to each of these peoples would match fairly closely Dhulqarnayn's itinerary.

[32] Qur'ān 2:286

because my power extends to all things. I shall take possession of the lands for you and guide you along the path to integrity of conduct and teach you to grow intellectually so that you will have the strength for the journey to east and west, and will know the dimensions of the earth. Just as the moon only sets in determined places, you will spend the nights on your journey beneath my watchful eye. Know that I have power over all things so that with my guidance you will triumph. I will put the fear of God in you. You will come to know all that is hidden from man. We will give you a sufficiently large army, horses and plenty of men, and the people of the world will revere you. I will put love for you in the hearts of those around you. I am the Provider, the one with determination and strength. O Dhulqarnayn, collect a land tax from all the nations of the world and tribute from he who does not [f. 28] believe in Me, for you are their sovereign and I am your Lord. I want to empower you and create for you a kingdom above all others in which your sultanship will surpass that of other sultans. O Dhulqarnayn! Your Lord commands you to break the idols, and slay the idol-worshippers and work hard to promote God's word. Indeed, I order you to kill the people who speak in ungodly words. Kill them as they disobey me. I intended for you to be one of the miracles of this world and the Hereafter. So do what I have ordered, Dhulqarnayn, for I am aiding you against my enemies and your enemies alike. Praise God and be among the thankful."

At which point Dhulqarnayn said, "Praise be to God, Lord of the Worlds. To You we listen and obey. You are the best aid a man can have. Then the angel Zayāqīl turned back with his good friend, Dhulqarnayn, towards the city from which they had left. Verily, Dhulqarnayn had seen the whole world, its lands and seas. He now knew it inside and out. It was as if he had already traveled personally through all the lands of the earth. Promptly, he told his troops and his companions of what he had seen and what lay ahead, and they answered, "We hear and obey!" All of them, both young and old, were determined to depart on their journey [f. 29] with Dhulqarnayn.

Sa'd reports that the Prophet, God bless him and grant him salvation, said: It was He who honored and favored him. Later, when they were ready to leave, Dhulqarnayn said to his companions, "Place your faith in God and prepare yourselves for the journey." He gave his troops provisions and outfitted them in gear and weapons of war and ordered that they sound the horns. God commanded that their fear of Him would lead to success. Dhulqarnayn said to his group of advisors, "Tomorrow I will leave on a journey."

When the morning came, the horns sounded, which they had agreed would be a sign for them to depart or, if they were on the road, to stop and put up camp. So when the horns blew they left and after a time they arrived at the seashore. Since God had given him the means to all ends, he entered the water and walked on the surface of the water and his troops followed behind him. When they saw him walk on water they walked on water, with the will of God. When the sun went down, the horns blew indicating that they should stop and set up camp there. So the soldiers put down their things in that spot, in the depths of the seas. At night, the horses started to rock in a motion that spread from horse to horse until the whinnying and neighing became loud [f. 30]. The rocking waters and the noise reached the men and they were not able to sleep so they said, "O friend of

God, the horses are stirring up one another, and it keeps us awake. We can't sleep and we do not see a way to tie down the horses on the water. He said to them, "Erect your poles here. The one who made the Ocean receptive to your horses' hoofs will support the poles for your horses." Indeed, God commanded the sea that neither horse hoof nor human foot would penetrate it. Praise the Lord to whom the sea listens and obeys!

Abū 'Abd al-Malik reports that the Prophet, God bless him and grant him salvation, the one who sent us the Truth, said: They pounded their tent pegs into the surface of the water as if they were pounding into solid earth, such is the power of He who says 'Be' and there is. Praise be to the One and Only God. I hear and obey the Almighty and Exalted One. If the horns started to blow then they should depart, and if they were marching and the horns blew, then they should stop and make camp. The horns were a sign to either depart or to stop and make camp as well as a call to battle [f. 31] in all their wars and military campaigns. This is the story of Dhulqarnayn, how he achieved what he achieved, how he reached as far as he did, and the means by which he traveled to the lands of sunrise and sunset.[33]

With respect to what is known about his ancestry and lineage, I will tell you in the same way that my Lord, the Almighty and Exalted, told me. He is Alexander b. Asās and he was called Ibn Nabbāsh b. Qālūsh[34] b. Basṭīyātīn[35] b. Nijāwī b. Yādūn b. al-Arzī b. Ḥirān b. 'Arūm. He is the one who ruled all of Rūm as a young boy. His kingdom spread throughout the lands. He was the one who married more women than any other and did not die until forty male children were born to him. The Christians called them the Children of Rūm, and their Rūm name prevailed and this is how the Rūm came to be called the Rūm and he was the son of Farūm, a child named Khīl b. Maria b. 'Iṣū b. Isḥāq, bless him, Ibn Ibrahim, the friend of the Most Compassionate One. This is his ancestry and lineage.[36]

Ibn 'Abd Allah said: Ka'b al-Aḥbār tells us in his account and story of Alexander that when God commanded him, [f. 32] he walked on water in the wake of his friend, the angel Zayāqīl, with the power of the Almighty and Exalted One. Dhulqarnayn followed each step Zayāqīl took on water, and that is how he was able to walk on water. The Messenger of God, God bless him and grant him salvation, said: Each prophet that walked the earth had an angel from heaven who came to him with revelation from the Lord. Gabriel, blessings and peace be upon him, was generally the beloved friend of the prophets. But God assigned the

---

[33] At this point in the *Rrekontamiento*, the introductory frame story ends with the conversion of the question posers. See ff. 10v-11.

[34] Likely corruption of فيلقوس Fīlaqūs, a form of the name Philip, found, for instance, in the Persian *Sikandar Nāma*, ed. H. W. Clarke, 155.

[35] Byzantine

[36] The genealogy given, apparently fictitious and corrupt beyond recognition, is an attempt to give Alexander the lineage of a Prophet, that is, one descending directly from Abraham. Friedlander (276) suggests that the incomprehensible genealogies given in the Andalusian Alexander romances are an attempt to create for Alexander a Spanish origin. This does not seem to be the case here.

angel Zayāqīl to inform and command Dhulqarnayn. The young Rūm king was a pious servant who loved God and who was loved by the Almighty and Exalted God. He obeyed God's word and religion in all matters, small and large. In turn, God made him strong and made him an example for the people of the earth so that they would not say, "Nobody came to us as a herald of good tidings or warning us that You are our Lord." God the Almighty and Exalted meant for Dhulqarnayn to be evidence of Him among the people of the earth. God commanded him to go to the Children of Adam, by land and by sea, to the east and west, through level and rough terrain.

Over a period of twelve days Dhulqarnayn traveled by land the equivalent of what one would travel in twelve years, [f. 33] and he ended up on an island in the sea that was bleak and uninhabited. It was here that he decided to make his camp. He ordered some of his men to explore the island and its caves. They walked all day long without finding anything of interest until they managed to ask someone from the island. He led them to a castle made out of red, white and green marble. It was tall and there was no discernible way to climb the walls from any direction. If one wanted to enter, a spiral would move and the doors would revolve while the castle above remained still.

They observed the construction of the castle, which was plated in gold and silver such that they could find no way to get in. They returned to Dhulqarnayn and provided him with a full account of what they had seen. He was astonished and begged God to reveal to him the castle's secret. The angel Zayāqīl came to him and said, "Dhulqarnayn, the Almighty and Exalted God promised that you would be king of the whole world and ruler of all that is in it including this castle and all it contains. So, go and build a similar castle, except make yours out of wood. Construct it so that there are boards the length of a man's arm stretched out that protrude from the sides of the castle. Be sure to make your castle taller than [f. 34] the other one. Bring the two castles close together and attack. The revolving doors will be jammed by the boards extending out from the sides of your castle, and the castle will become vulnerable. The password to get in is the testimony, 'There is no God but Allah and Muhammad is the messenger of God.'"

Dhulqarnayn was able to do just what the angel explained much faster than it would have normally taken during that day and age. He moved quickly through the project because the time was right to begin the first raids of their military expeditions. He ordered twelve thousand craftsmen to come before him: three thousand were blacksmiths, three thousand were carpenters, and three thousand were craftsmen who made fittings for the horses. Beneath his command the carpenters and blacksmiths built his castle right away and drew it near to the other castle. Dhulqarnayn was able to move his castle because it was carried on a bed mounted on wheels. The wheels were turned by mules which were driven by both slaves and men of distinction alike. When the slaves came near the castle, which was revolving quickly on a pivoting coil spring, it moved in a circle around them. The castle was built on a bed of different species [f. 35] of marble. The pivoting coil spring spun on the marble bed. The castle was built on tall pivoting coil springs sitting in the center of a marble foundation, such that no wooden pole or board or man could get near it without those doors being set in motion. This, in turn, began to move the center pivoting coil spring, which propelled the castle to spin as well. The muleteers came near the castle and the ground below them collapsed, the doors began to revolve, and the castle to spin. The boards extending out from the walls of Dhulqarnayn's castle jammed the revolving doors and they stopped. Dhulqarnayn walked up to the castle and looked at the door and saw that on it was written, "I testifiy that there is no God but Allah and I testify that Muhammad is the Messenger of God." Then with the will of God Almighty, the castle opened up and Dhulqarnayn stepped inside. Lo and behold, there was a locked chest made out of red gold and studded with different sorts of gems. On the lock there was written, "There is no power nor strength save in God, the Almighty One, the Greatest." Dhulqarnayn said, [f. 36] "There is no power nor strength save in God, the Almighty One, the Greatest."

With the will of God he was able to open the chest and find a letter on the inside that said, "In the name of God the Most Compassionate and Merciful, God bless our master Muhammad, the Seal of the prophets, leader of all those who have received revelation, Messenger of the Lord of the Worlds to all people, and the last of the prophets. He is the one spoken of in the Book of those who have received revelation as the last of the prophets. God's aid remains with the well-intentioned. God is the Benefactor of those who fear Him." The signature at the bottom of this plaque read, "Sitrūn, the Yānūnī, the descendant of the Yānūn," who was with the prophet Noah b. Lāmak, bless him. Sitrūn believed in Noah and recorded on the plaque the names of those among his offspring who would be among the prophets and messengers of God: the first prophet was Noah and the last of them would be Muhammad, God bless him and grant him salvation. The first among the faithful to come upon the plaque was Dhulqarnayn. This was a sign that he would triumph against the people of Jābalqā and Jābarṣā and against all who lay between them. Praise be to God, Lord of the Worlds.

Abū 'Abd Allah said: When he read what was written he said, "Praise be to God, Lord of the Worlds, the One who [f. 37] created us to be thankful and to obey Him in our work. O Zayāqīl, who was the man who made the inscription on this plaque?" Zayāqīl answered that it was engraved by the Yānūn,[37] who were among the first people created on earth. They preceded Adam and did not descend from his ancestral line. They are people created by God the Almighty before Adam and they propagated and multiplied and overpopulated the earth. Among them was a man named Qāṭūr who knew God. He decided to separate from the rest of his people. So he left them and came to this island where he procreated until God destroyed all the Yānūn. He unleashed His wrath on them because they refused to believe the Truth and instead killed the prophet He sent to call them to the religion of God. They propagated at a tremendous rate until they crowded the island, at which point God sent fire from the sky to burn and destroy them down to the last of one them. Only Qāṭūr remained on this island and procreated until he became weak and died leaving behind his people. But soon they went astray from the religion of God in the same way as the great population

[37] Corruption of Yāwān b. Yāfith b. Noah (English, Javan), whose name became confused with Yūnān, i.e., the ancestor of the Greeks. Cf. Mas'ūdī (1979), 7, p. 762. In Daniel 8:21, Alexander is called the King of al-Yāwān. Mas'ūdī confirms that there were those who believed that Yūnān lived during the First Age of the earth (الزمان الاول). See edition from 1979, vol. 2, p. 5.

that preceded them and God destroyed them just as he had destroyed those that lived before Adam. They were four tribes: al-Yūnān [f. 38], al-Lahūn, al-Ṭumm and the Ṭumāṭīm. They were all tribes like the children of Adam, that is, God sent to all of them a prophet. Their survival or destruction was in their own hands, but they turned away from the Almighty Lord and He sent down from the heavens fire to burn and destroy them down to the last one of them. But before they were all destroyed He allowed the prophet among them to escape. When the peoples of the past had been destroyed, God created Adam and from him sprung the prophet Noah, Bless him. [During Noah's time,] God drowned the people of the earth, though some were saved. One of those chosen to be saved with Noah was Siṭrūn, a descendant of Qāṭūr. He was a pious servant who learned the knowledge that Noah possessed, Bless him, and lived on after Noah until prophecy was sent down to Sām b. Noah. Siṭrūn and Sām were neighbors. Siṭrūn found in the writings of Noah and of Sām b. Noah that prophecy would be successively inherited through the generations of their descendants until the last of the prophets so he recorded this on the plaque. Since he was a king he thought to build this castle to protect the chest containing the plaque. For additional protection he contrived the device of the pivoting spring coil so that [f. 39] no jinn or man would ever reach it. But God wanted to present Dhulqarnayn with the honor of finding it and He wanted him to know that it is a sign that he will triumph over all the world. Such is the story behind the castle and the plaque. Dhulqarnayn said, "Praise be to God the Lord of the Worlds."

The transmitter of the *hadīth* says that Dhulqarnayn returned to his camp and decided to leave. With the aid of God, he headed in the direction of Jābalqā, towards sunset. He would go alone without a leader to lead him or a driver to drive him.

Concerning Dhulqarnayn's Trip to the City of Jābalqā.

Abū 'Abd al-Malik al-Malshūnī said: Muqātil b. Sulaymān tells us that Dhulqarnayn sounded the horns and the people dismounted to traverse the waters and departed walking beside their horses. As before, they marched over the face of the water by the will of God Almighty. In their wake rose a dust cloud from the pounding of the horses' hoofs, the beasts, the mules and the men, as if they were crossing dry earth. Such is the power of the Most High and Honorable One! On they walked over the face of the water, following the path set out for them for one full day [f. 40]. However, by the end of the day they had covered a distance equivalent to the march of one full year. In front of them loomed a hill coming out of the sea with waves breaking against its shores spraying water high into the air. This hill atop an island looked down on a city with tall buildings and wide-open fields. The island was comparable to one of the Western Islands or perhaps smaller. Its buildings were simple constructions. The wall surrounding the city was made of petrified stone. Each stone in the wall was cut in the shape of a pillar with a breadth of 24 cubits and a height of sixty cubits. There were balconies made of pumice stone and a total of twelve thousand doors. Between each door there was a distance of three parasangs.[38] Twelve thousand men guarded each door every night, and they did not leave their posts except for personal necessities, to go to the market, or to attend to their stores.

At that time, Dhulqarnayn's army had three hundred thousand men not counting the craftsmen. When they descended on Jābalqā, and blew their horns and yelled louder and louder, fright gripped the hearts of the people of Jābalqā because they didn't know who it was and they thought it was their enemy, the people of Jābarṣā who had come to raid them. Only God in heaven could tell how many men stood in the ranks of the army before them. [f. 41] They deliberated among themselves about whether or not they should attack, not knowing that it was the army of Dhulqarnayn. Then they started to pour out of the doors in hoards. Some of the accounts of this episode say that one hundred thousand people came out through the doors.

When Dhulqarnayn saw how many people were charging towards him, he appointed his paternal first cousin, Qaṭlāmūs, one of the Rūm kings, as general to lead the cavalry brigade of one hundred thousand men. He also appointed as general his paternal first cousin, Antigonus, to lead the rear guard with one hundred thousand men. His order was to take the men and to circle around to the right of the city. Then he appointed a third general from among the Rūm kings whose name was Shaqārīsh and gave him one hundred thousand men. As his fourth general he chose a Rūm king named Shamāmīs and sent him around to the left of the city with one hundred thousand men. The Rūm king, Qawmash, was his fifth general and he took one hundred thousand men around the western end of the city. His sixth general [f. 42] was a Rūm noble called Qāṭūsh. His seventh general was a Rūm king named Nāhūsh who was given command of the brigade of swordsmen.

When the people of the city saw this, they were terrified. The guards at each of the doors around the city looked on with awe as the army of God approached. They felt the fear that God instilled in their hearts and were taken back by the wind He cast against them. They shuddered in fright at the enormous army, at their swords flashing white, and at the whipping of the banners in the wind atop long spears held by enemy warriors. "We are helpless against such an army," they said. When the horns began to blow and the towering clouds of dust to rise, they were struck with terror. The people, civilians and soldiers alike, rushed to look at the army, and then they all hastened to leave the city through the multitude of doors. They told Alexander, "O commander! The horsemen are asking for the commander of all soldiers. They are ready to surrender and obey you."

Abū 'Abd al-Malik said: They all remained silent awaiting the response. The soldiers from each brigade directed the people toward King Dhulqarnayn until they reached him and said, [f. 43] "Dhulqarnayn, teach us about your military campaign and your religion and share with us your knowledge. We will serve you on your military campaign and adopt your religion. Our army challenged you only because we thought that it was our enemy, the people of Jābarṣā, who had come to attack us. If we had known it was you standing before

[38] Three parasangs are the equivalent of approximately ten miles or sixteen kilometers.

us, we would not have deployed our forces for we heed your every command. We are the obedient servants of first God and then you. With all of this, we have learned to whom you are good and to whom you are bad."

Abū 'Abd al-Malik al-Malshūnī said: Dhulqarnayn listened to them cautiously as the conversation passed from one army to the other. After seeking counsel from his generals, it was decided that they would be spared war and safe from attack. The people of Jābalqā asked more questions, "Dhulqarnayn, who is it that you serve and who are those that you punish? For whom do you have sympathy and whom do you reward with protection from harm?" He responded, "I punish only those who refuse to believe in God. As for the believers, my intention is purely to further inform them and to offer my protection and that of those with me."

Their spokesmen went back to their people and their tribes and informed them of what Dhulqarnayn had said. Soon they appeared again before [f. 44] Dhulqarnayn and said, "We believe in your Lord, the One and Only, without equal." He honored and rewarded them graciously. They opened the doors for him and all together they entered the city and testified to the divine oneness of God.

Abū 'Abd al-Malik al-Malshūnī said: Those were the words of the Almighty One. *Until, when he reached The setting of the sun, He found it set in a spring of murky water: Near it he found a People: We said: "O Dhulqarnayn! (Thou hast authority,) either to punish them, or to treat them with kindness." He said: "Whoever doth wrong, him shall we punish; then shall he be sent back to his Lord; and He will punish him with a punishment unheard-of (before). But whoever believes, and works righteousness—he shall have a goodly reward, and easy will be his task as we order it by our command." Then followed he (another) way.*[39]

Abū 'Abd al-Malik al-Malshūnī said: With respect to the wrongdoer, he who resists placing faith in God in the presence of Dhulqarnayn will be tortured and have to endure the evils of the soldiers and suffer their terror, their shackles and be put to death. Verily, the Lofty One in his Loftiness sent this army so that those on earth would believe in Him. [f. 45] If one does not believe in Him, he will return to his Lord and be punished with torments unbeknown to man using fire that will cause unimaginable pain.

Abū 'Abd al-Malik al-Malshūnī reported on the authority of Abū Ayyūb, who related on the authority of Yurīd al-Khaṣmī, who said on the authority of Mālik b. Mu'ādh b. Jābar, may God be satisfied with him, that Dhulqarnayn departed to the city of Jābalqā. When he arrived at the main square of the city, he left his people behind to sleep and placed his crown on the head of his paternal first cousin, who had always been very loyal.[40] The matter at hand was that he was going to disappear, so he walked away into the night alone leaving behind his army.

---

[39] Qur'ān 18:86-89.

[40] According to Ibn al-Jawzī this would be al-Khidr (f. 82r).

He took a road never before traveled to a place nobody had ever been, riding on the Alborak.[41] This is the animal which the Almighty and Exalted God refers to in his revelation. According to Mujāhid and Ibn 'Abbās, may God be satisfied with the two of them, Dhulqarnayn followed an inaccessible road known only to the birds until he arrived at a city the likes of which had never been seen by human eyes [f. 46]. The area had been blessed and had more inhabitants than anyone but God the Almighty could count. He entered the city wearing the same clothes as the inhabitants and all day long walked through its narrow streets. He observed the people and the buildings and the layout of the city. He was struck by the awe-inspiring appearance of its noble citizens, and continued to explore until evening.

When the sun went down in the hot spring, Dhulqarnayn was able to see that it was a spring of black mud that boiled like a kettle on the fire. If anything comes within three hundred and sixty parasangs of that spring when the sun is setting, it will be consumed by fire. The city is quite a distance from the spring, because when the sun sets it makes a deafening noise. In fact, when Dhulqarnayn heard the roar of the boiling mud, he thought that all the people of the world would die from its loudness. However, there is a moment [f. 47] as the sun is setting when everyone in the city shouts, "There is no God but Allah" and "God is great," and they humble themselves before God Almighty. This is done to save the people of the earth from the tremendous noise the sun makes when it crashes into the mud. Dhulqarnayn was overwhelmed when he heard its roar.

Regarding this matter, Mujāhid said: If it were not for the clamor raised by the people of the city humbling themselves to God, and reciting the formula, "There is no God but Allah," the noise from the violent crash of setting sun would kill people living at the western end of the earth. Qatāda also said: If it were not for the remoteness of the hot spring in which the sun sets, the noise from the violent crash of the setting sun would kill people living at the western end of the earth. In another account by Qatāda, it says: The Prophet, God bless him and grant him salvation, said: God the Almighty and Exalted created two cities, one at sunrise called Jābarṣā and the other at sunset called Jābalqā. Each city has ten thousand doors with a guard on each door every night. Men serve their guard only once. He, [God] bless him and grant him salvation, said: "By God, who has my soul in his hand! [f. 48] If it were not for their shouting, people throughout the world would hear the thundering crash of the sun setting in the hot spring." Behind them live six nations whose populations are known only to God.

After witnessing the sun set, Dhulqarnayn went to Jābalqā alone and called together all their nobles and men of distinction and said to them, "I am the messenger of Dhulqarnayn. I have been sent to you to learn what you say and what is your position with respect to my king's religion and whether or not you

---

[41] From the PC, Bk. ii, chpt. 41 (Müller p. 91). Also mentioned in Budge (1896): "And [Alexander] made himself small, and flew through the air on the back of an eagle, and he arrived in the heights of the heavens and explored them, and he saw the east and the west thereof, and the beauties and the terrors thereof, and the stations of the birth and going forth of the stars, and he described thoroughly all these things in a great book which he called "The Book of the Works of the Whole World" (277-278). For the relationship between Alexander's flight into the air and the flight of Gilgamesh, see Budge (1896), p. 278, note 1.

are willing to believe in it." Among themselves they said to one another, "We have no chance against the army of Alexander. We shall become believers." Others said, "He is going to leave us and continue on his journey. Let us believe for as long as he is here with us, then as soon as he turns and walks away, we will go back to what we believed before." They differed as to what they should do so they came forward with a request, "O messenger of Dhulqarnayn, wait until tomorrow and we will let you know what agreement we have reached." He said, "Yes, I will wait because I would like for you to come to a unanimous and undivided decision." They said, "Dear messenger, we have among us an old sheikh who is one thousand years old [f. 49] and very wise. He is different from the rest of us. We will contact him and ask his advice in this matter and then we will get back to you." He answered, "I would like to meet him." They said, "If you are prepared to agree to what we decide and accept our collective determination, then we will arrange a meeting between you and him. If you were to meet him, you would think he is a marvel of wisdom, refinement, nobility and honor." He said to them, "It is my wish to meet him."

The narrator said:[42] They asked to be excused to go look for the sheikh. After eight days he came to them and they met with him and he offered his opinion concerning what they should do about Dhulqarnayn and his messenger. They said to him: "If you could see his messenger and what he possesses in the way of wisdom, refinement and patience, you would be amazed." The sheikh said, "Arrange a meeting between him and I where I will ask him about some linguistic puzzles which I happen to know. If he is a prophet we will accept him as our lord, but if he is just a king like any other king, our response to his aggression against us will be to make war against him." They agreed. Then they brought the sheikh and went back to Alexander. All along they thought that it was his messenger, as this is what he had told them. [f. 50]

Upon entering Alexander's tent, the sheikh said, "O messenger of Dhulqarnayn, what is your name?" " 'Abd Allah," he said. " 'Abd Allah, what religion should a king follow?" "Listening to and obeying the Creator of creation," said Dhulqarnayn. "What path in life should he follow?" asked the sheikh. "The pursuit of what is true and proper." "Of what should a king speak?" Dhulqarnyan responded, "Enforcing that which is good and just, while prohibiting that which is reprehensible." The sheikh asked, "What makes for a virtuous army?" Dhulqarnayn responded, "One which has an excess of soldiers and equipment, enjoys the grace of God, and abstains from that which is prohibited." The sheikh asked, "What three things should a king love and what three things should a king loathe?" "A king should love to hear the mention of God. He should love obedience of God's will. And he should love to hate those that disobey God. As for the three things that a king should loathe, they are those who disobey God, those who act immorally, and the polytheists." "On what three principles should a king build his kingdom?" asked the sheikh. "Fairness in one's

---

[42] There is no expressed subject for the verb here, قال. According to A.F.L. Beeston (p. 24), the use of قال in this context is a device used to mark a return to the narrative of "the author of the original text," after a digression of commentary. In the case here, the commentary would be that of Mujāhid and Qatada, and the return would be to the text of 'Abd al-Malik al-Malshūnī.

judgements, the speaking of the truth, and the fulfillment of one's commitments," answered Dhulqarnayn. "What will destroy his kingdom?" "Allowing the pursuit of worldly passions [f. 51], the breaking of oaths, and the issuing of judgements according to greed and personal desire." Then the sheikh asked, "O 'Abd Allah, how does one discover the truth of things?" "By being truthful oneself and by miracles," responded Dhulqarnayn. "How does one tell if others are being truthful?" "By the certainty with which they speak." The sheikh asked, "How does one distinguish a miracle?" "By the achievement of things never before achieved, by behavior never before exhibited, and by one who has the power to bring about the appearance of marvelous signs." The sheikh asked the messenger, "What are the distinguishing characteristics of Dhulqarnayn?" "He is a sincere man who speaks the truth and who requires the truth of others, one who makes fair judgements and is satisfied with them, one who hauls the swindler off to jail, one who exercises patience when someone makes a mistake, one who loves in the name of God and who loathes in the name of God, one who is not among those *of the reproaches of such as find fault* [f. 144] in the Lord."[43] Then the sheikh asked, "What are you in relation to Dhulqarnayn and what is he in relation to you?" "I am he and he is I." The sheikh asked, "Tell me how you spell the beginning and end of your name." "It begins with four and ends with fifty." Then the sheikh exclaimed, "You are Dhulqarnayn!" and to those around he said, "Come and kiss the hand of your lord, citizens of Jābalqā!" "Who told you this, sheikh? [f. 52] As I said, I am 'Abd Allah." He said, "We are all 'Abd Allah, as 'Abd Allah means servant of God!" "How did you arrive at the conclusion that I was Dhulqarnayn?" "I asked you about the spelling of the beginning of your name and you said it was four. That was how I learned that you were Dhulqarnayn." Dhulqarnayn asked, "How can you say that Dhulqarnayn, who is served by thousands of men, would leave behind his army and come before you like this? Don't you imagine he would have someone to do this for him?" "I have learned what nobody else except me knows about the tricks kings use. This is one of their most common stratagems. There is no doubt that you are Dhulqarnayn!" "So you think that Dhulqarnayn has come to you all alone. What are you, your companions and your people going to do about it?" The sheikh said, "Come now! Word reached me that Dhulqarnayn was one of the Rūm kings full of tricks and cunning.

"[According to one account,] he entered upon a king to trick him. As a visitor he requested to be admitted with the pretense that he had to discuss certain matters with the local king. The local king, in turn, proposed some quizzes. When their conversation had reached its end, the local king realized the trick of the visitor [f. 53]. The visitor said: 'If you were to bow before me and entrust me with your affairs, then I would put king so and so under your control, and deliver him to you.' By this he secretly intended to trick the other. He said: 'If you were to do that then my kingdom would be yours.' He shook his hand firmly and the joining of their hands brought the two of them into close accord. The visitor by this act intended to trick him, but the host king was taking his word as a king's word. When the agreement among them was concluded, he asked: 'Where would

[43] The meaning of the Arabic text is not entirely clear to me. It seems to refer to Qur'ān 5:54.

you like to meet with the king?' 'Right here in this court,' he responded. 'If I joined you two, what would you do with him?' 'I would forgive and pardon him.' He said: 'You promise by God?' 'Yes,' he responded. 'I am the king.' He shook his hand and embraced him and honored him and treated him kindly and he put him in command of his kingdom.

"And so, 'Abd Allah, if you are Dhulqarnayn, I hear and obey you. If you are not Dhulqarnayn, send him greetings from my part. The people of this city and I are ready to accept his religion. It has become apparent to me [f. 54] from what you have told me about him, and the responses you gave to the questions, that he is a pious king and a righteous prophet. Stand and go home in peace." Dhulqarnayn replied, "You are beyond doubt the most apt person to govern this city, and I'll appoint you governor for as long as you live." "Why so? I have seen kings, nobles, epochs, and fame. Nothing remains after the kings except the epochs. Nothing remains after the epochs except fame. All that remains of my life is an insignificant portion. In that little bit of time it would be difficult for me to change." Then Dhulqarnayn asked, "What is your name, sheikh?" "I am Jūdib b. Jūdib." "How old are you?" "One thousand one hundred and sixty three years old." "How many kings have you seen come and go?" "I saw King Yaqamṭīsh b. Rawīsh." "How long did his reign last?" "Two thousand less three hundred," answered the sheikh. "How many men were in his army?" "Two thousand less three hundred." "How large [f. 55] was his kingdom?" asked Dhulqarnayn. "It extended from Sind to Hind and from the Karadh Mountains to Egypt." "Who ousted him from the throne?" "Dārūm," responded the sheikh. "How long did he remain on the throne?" "One thousand years less one hundred. But he established a dynasty that spanned seven generations." "You deserve to live as long as you have. I am Dhulqarnayn, and I recognize you as the sovereign power here. I appoint you governor of this city."

Abū 'Abd al-Malik al-Malshūnī said: Abū al-Ṣabbāḥ reported on the authority of Hishām, who related on the authority of Ka'b, that Dhulqarnayn arrived with his army to the steppes of the mountain that surrounds the world. He ordered his men to tie their horses to the mountain and to hang their weapons from the Pleiades. Obediently, they did as they were told.

When he had finished what needed to be done, he went back to the place where his men had left their weapons, and they could not retrieve them because the Pleiades had rotated in its celestial orbit and the weapons were now hidden from view. [f. 56] By the time Dhulqarnayn had returned to the spot where the arms were, they had disappeared from their place. No one was able to figure out how to get the weapons back. So Dhulqarnayn went back to the sheikh and asked him about the particular circumstance of the Pleiades. The sheikh replied, "O Dhulqarnayn, you will not be able to retrieve the arms of your comrades until one full year has passed."

Dhulqarnayn dwelled in that place until the end of the year when the Pleiades moved along its path and returned to its place. Although people are ignorant of this matter, it is true that the skies revolve around the earth. They remained in that place until the Pleiades had returned to the place where it had been exactly one year before. Then they retrieved their arms.

Ka'b al-Aḥbār told me this *hadīth* which comes from Abū Dharr who sat with Ka'b. Abū Dharr said: Verily, God's word is truer than yours, Ka'b! The Almighty God speaks of this matter and He says that God holds the earth and skies together so that they do not vanish, and they have remained joined. Indeed, whatever holds them [f. 57] together never ceases its grip. Abū Dharr replied: If the two separated, no one would ever be able to bring them together again because of the great distance and they would float away. Ka'b al-Aḥbār answered: Abū Dharr! *Verily, God gave Dhulqarnayn things that He never gave to anyone else. Here is the word of the Almighty One: Verily, We established his power on earth, and We gave him the ways and the means to all ends.*[44] In other words, God gave him knowledge and power above all others.

Abū 'Abd al-Malik al-Malshūnī said: Every time I come across scholars, I ask them what is the meaning of the name "Dhulqarnayn," and each of them has something different to say and their own interpretation. Once I said: Truly he was a devout man. And the man I was with at the time told me that Hishām b. 'Urwa, on the authority of Ka'b, said that he had two horns made of flesh like two tufts of hair of the darkest black ever seen. The hair of those two tufts never grew in length beyond the tips of his [f. 58] ears. This was the sign by which knowledgeable people were able to distinguish him because he never wrapped a turban around his horns unless he needed to put on his crown. [Abū 'Abd al-Malik al-Malshūnī][45] said: I asked Muqātil why he was called Dhulqarnayn and he said: Some well informed people told me that it was because he had reached the highest point in the west and the highest point in the east. In the west he saw how the sun set in the hot spring and rose as a great sphere in the east. So God called him Dhulqarnayn. Abū 'Abd al-Malik said: I heard Abū Dhirr al-Hamadānī say: Mujāhid said that Dhulqarnayn was a valiant man who would go into battle himself and if the fighting got intense he would take charge. When his men saw him riding towards the enemy they were incited to follow. They could not let him ride into the face of the enemy alone. At those moments he could triumph in any endeavor. The narrator[46] said: In some of his battles [f. 59] he would strike a blow with his right horn and then another with his left horn and this is why he is called Dhulqarnayn.[47]

---

[44] Qur'ān 18:84

[45] There is no expressed subject for the verb, قال. It is assumed that Abū 'Abd al-Malik al-Malshūnī is still speaking. See note to f. 49 above.

[46] There is no expressed subject for the verb here, قال. Although it is not clear who is speaking, one must assume that it is Abū 'Abd al-Malish al-Malshūnī. See note to f. 49 above.

[47] Al-Tha'labī gives several different reasons for the name 'Dhulqarnayn':
اختلفوا بسبب تسميته بذلك ، فقال بعضهم: سمى بذلك لأنه ملك الروم وفارس ، وقيل لأنه كان فى مقدم رأسه شبه القرنين من لحم ، وقيل لأنه رأى فى المنام كأنه أخذ بقرنى الشمس ، وكان تأويل رؤياه أنه طاف المشرق والمغرب ، وقيل لأنه دعا قومه الى التوحيد فضربوه على قرنه الأيمن ، ثم دعاهم الى التوحيد فضربوه على قرنه الأيسر . وقيل لأنه كان له ذؤابتان حسنتان ، والذؤابة تسمى قرنا ، وقيل لأنه كان كريم الطرفين ، من أهل بيت شرف من قبل أبيه وأمه . وقيل لأنه كان انقرض فى وقته قرنان من الناس وهو حى ، وقيل لأنه كان اذا حارب قاتل بيديه وركابه جميعا ، وقيل لأنه أعطي علم الظاهر والباطن ، وقيل لأنه دخل النور والظلمة ، والله أعلم (f. 359-360). Perhaps the best study of the origin of the name Dhulqarnayn is "Alexander's Horns." In this study, A.R. Anderson shows how the motif of the horns associated with Alexander began first with his identification as Alexander Helius, and then as the son of the ram's-horned Ammon and later, as Moses.

Ka'b al-Aḥbār said: Dhulqarnayn entered Jābalqā with his army and their righteous companions. He ordered the trumpeteers to blow their horns and the sound of trumpets filled the air. The people of that town saw a spectacle the likes of which they had never before seen. In the whole of the city there was not an old lady, woman, virgin, or girl kept in seclusion that did not come out to see Dhulqarnayn and his army, except an old man sitting bent down over his work.[48] When Dhulqarnayn passed he did not even raise his head or turn to look. He was busy with his work. But there was not another man in the city with more knowledge of God than he. When Dhulqarnayn dismounted and the army came to a halt, he summoned the old man. They brought him and Dhulqarnayn said, "Sheikh! Can't you see that I have with me the army of God, embodying his strength, accompanied by the righteous? Why is it that you do not look at them?" The sheikh responded, "O Dhulqarnayn, I have seen many kings before you who were granted the same things you have been granted, [f. 60] and who bestowed on others the same things you have bestowed. But the things of this world betrayed them and they were dispossessed of all they had. They lost their kingdom and their money. All trace of them has disappeared except the fame they earned for their good works and their righteousness. If you work in the name of God, you will gain renown. But if you choose not to follow God, your name will be vilified. So look more closely at yourself and consider carefully the nature of your prosperity." Dhulqarnayn replied, "Sheikh, how much do you earn in a day for your work?" "One dirham." "What do you spend it on?" "One third goes for religious obligations, one third I loan, and with the remaining third I maintain my family." "How is that?" "My parents are old now and in my care. I pay one third of one dirham to them each day. This is what I owe them for what they spent on me in my upbringing and religious instruction. I loan one third to my children who will repay it by supporting and caring for me when I grow old and [f. 61] do not have money to support myself. With the remaining third, my family and I live." Dhulqarnayn said, "You are wise! I shall make you governor of this city and you shall be in charge of upholding God's law." So he gave the sheikh authority regarding the legal statutes of Islam, and the city was ruled by Dhulqarnayn, the sheikh, and the king. The people swore their allegiance and promised to listen to and to obey the three rulers.

Abū 'Abd al-Malik al-Malshūnī said that he asked Muqātil b. Sulaymān about the people of Jābalqā. He answered that Abū Rawāq had said that he heard Mujāhid say that the people of Jābalqā and the people of Jābarṣā were followers of the righteous prophet Hūd, Bless him.[49] God had destroyed some of his people

[48] This is perhaps an echo of Alexander's meeting with Diogenes or of his dialogue with the Gymnosophists. The contrast of the pompous entry of Dhulqarnayn and the humble but wise old man was a favored topic in many medieval Arabic gnomic works, for which the Arabic prototype was the work of the celebrated translator Hunayn b. Isḥaq, as shown by García Gómez in the preliminary study to *Un texto árabe occidental de la leyenda de Alejandro Magno* (pp. 151-154).

[49] Hūd is the prophet who, in Quranic tradition, appeared to the 'Ād. His genealogy thus coincides to some degree with that of 'Ād, the tribe's founder. He is also identified with 'Ābir (the biblical 'Eber, ancestor of the Hebrews). When God destroyed the disbelieving people of 'Ād, he saved Hūd and his followers. From a historical perspective, the existence of Hūd is doubtful, and

and saved others. Those of Jābalqā and Jābarṣā had been saved because Hūd had ordered them to flee to the ends of the seas. They emigrated [f. 62] and God killed those who didn't believe. But He saved Hūd and his followers. They were only a few and came to be known as the Muhājirīn, the Emigrants, who traveled to the farthest limits of the seas.

They were firm in their ways until the death of Hūd, Bless him. His people reproduced and their population grew tremendously. God did not send them a prophet after Hūd. So they continued to believe in the religion of Hūd, Bless him, until Ṣāliḥ, Bless him, arose from the tribe of Thamūd. They believed and trusted in him and prospered until a rebel appeared among the tribe of Thamūd named 'Ātiq b. 'Ūṣ b. 'Amalāq.[50] The rebel raided the villages and tyrannized people throughout the world. He destroyed villages and the pious people were dispersed. They left their homes, built ships and set sail on the seas. God sent a guardian angel to fly over the seas. He guided them and showed them the route [f. 63] to the island called Baṭāḥ. They sailed the seas and put their lives in God's hands, and they came to an island off the coast where many goats grazed in the mountains, with wide open fields, without a single building. It was an island never before known by man or jinn. They disembarked and lived there as long as God willed. They cultivated the land, but it soon became clear that nothing would grow there and that they would not be able to provide a means of subsistence for themselves. They met and decided that, "Since there is no way we can survive on this island, we should go back to our country." Some among them were of a different opinion and said, "We can't go back to the land of the unbelievers. Come with us back to our boats and we will sail the sea. Whoever brought us to this island has the power to guide us to another, better than this."

They agreed that this was the best choice and sailed [f. 64] the sea in their boats. God cast one group of them into the seas of the far east and the other into the far west. The two boats set sail availing themselves of the wind with which God intended to guide them to their destination.

Among the people were two men born of two sisters. The one was Jābal and the other Jābar. Their mothers were Balqā and Barṣā. While at sea they were split up and each party ended up where God willed. The boat of the son of Barṣā came upon a spacious island whose abundant waters and vast fertile plains God had blessed with good things beyond the power of human description. The island was enormous and would take six months to cover on foot. They settled on the island and enjoyed abundant supplies of wheat and barley and God's favor. They had come upon the island [f.65] during plowing season so they plowed and planted. The seeds sprouted and became beautiful plants and the trees quickly bloomed.

They stayed there for a year during which they were wholeheartedly devoted to the life of the communtiy. Time passed and the months turned into

---

appears to be a derivation of the Arabic verb h-w-d, meaning to profess Judaism. Cf. EI, 2, 328 (Wensinck).

[50] The leader of the opponents of Ṣāliḥ among the Thamūd is said to have been Junda' b. 'Amr. Cf. EI 4, 736 (H. H. Bräu). 'Ātiq is not one of the sons of 'Ūṣ given by al-Ṭabarī (2,13): "Then Uz b. Aram begat Gether b. Uz (and 'Ād b. Uz) and 'Ubayl b. Uz." 'Ātiq is probably a legendary figure who was named in this manner to mean 'ancient' as in عاتق .

years, and their treatment of one another remained amicable. One day Jābar rose up as a leader among them and then built a large house and called it by his name. The people called it the Dār Jābar b. Barṣā. His family grew and multiplied in that house. Eventually, the name Jābar b. Barṣā was shortened to Barṣā. The people joined the son's and the mother's names and called their community 'Jābarṣā,' and the consensus was to erect a city on the site of the house. They built and erected it. Afterwards they turned to one another and said, "Arên't we a strange people! We don't know who inhabits these lands. If we had built the fortress around our gardens and the pastures where our beasts feed, it would have been a stronger and [f. 66] more secure place for us to live out our exile. Also, the number of our livestock would be able to grow tremendously." So they expanded the fortress and built new walls before settling into their new city.

In much the same way, the people of Jābalqā settled into their new city and their population grew at a similar rate. Such things did Dhulqarnayn learn when he came to them. The Jābalqāns are also the descendants of Hūd, bless him.

Mujāhid said: The Prophet, God bless him and grant him salvation, was asked: To what tribe do the people of Jābalqā belong? He, God bless him and grant him salvation, responded: One of those two cities is located at sunset and the other at sunrise. Both of them are scared of one another and both of them are descendants of the tribe of Tārish b. Yāfit b. Noah, Bless him. Both of the two cities are populous and have so many people that only God the Almighty knows their number. This is the story of the two cities.

Concerning Dhulqarnayn's Trip from Jābalqā to the East

[f. 67] Abū 'Abd al-Malik al-Malshūnī said: Once Dhulqarnayn had finished what he had intended to do in the kingdom of Jābalqā, that is, when he had turned power over to the sheikh and ordered the people to obey him and to follow the judgements that he as ruler had made, and once he had preached to them, guided them down the path of righteousness, and obtained a promise from them to obey God, he started to make arrangements for his departure. He thought about where he would go next, and in which direction he would travel. As he considered his possibilities, the angel Zayāqīl came to him and brought him good tidings. He was ordered to seek out the people of Bārish. He left by noon that same day with Zayāqīl close behind. God had ordered the angel himself to watch over Dhulqarnayn at sea and to follow his tracks wherever he might go. This is what is meant in the Qur'ān when it says, "*We gave him the means,*"[51] and that is the word of God. Together they traveled until the will of God deposited them on the shore of an island in the Ocean unknown to man, whose width was one month in crossing. There were rivers and valleys, mountains, rugged cliffs [f. 68] and wide open plains. There were flatlands that would take ten days to cross whose fields were covered with saffron and *al-wars.*[52] A river flowed from its source at one end of the island. It's waters cut the island in half before emptying into the

---

[51] 18:84

[52] Yemenite, dye-yielding plant (Memecylon tinctorium; bot.).

sea. On its banks grew all kinds of food. Castles stood lofty against their surroundings with rooms perched high in the towers, all empty since the place was uninhabited.

When Dhulqarnayn approached the castle with his army, he was impressed by what he saw and decided to make camp and to send some soldiers to enter the castle. The exploration party spent a day and a night inside, but saw no sign of life or any indication that anybody lived there. They returned to their commander to inform him of what they had found. Puzzled, he turned to the Lord to ask about the island and the people that had built the castle. He also asked what his next move should be. The angel Zayāqīl descended and said, "O Dhulqarnayn, set sail again for ten days and you will find someone who will tell you about the island and the flatlands."

So Dhulqarnayn traveled for ten days until he came to another island nearby, very much like the island he had just left [f. 69]. He entered the harbor, set anchor and ordered some of his men to disembark and explore the island. They found it to be populated. So they went back and told Dhulqarnayn who dispatched a messenger with a letter he wrote that said:

> In your name, O God
> From the servant of God, the one commissioned to enforce the will of God, Dhulqarnayn,
> To the people of the island,
> Peace to those who obey God and follow his path. We have come to see whether you follow God's religion and are rightly guided or have gone astray down the path of error. If you believe in God we will leave you in peace and security, with honor and proof that you have chosen the right path. But if you are tyrants then prepare yourselves to suffer humiliation and defeat, for God has sent us to kill his enemies and He has promised us victory. Know that God never breaks his promise.

He sealed the letter and gave it to his messenger who departed immediately and delivered it to the inhabitants of that island. They gathered around him and he took out the letter and read it outloud to them. They were gladdened by the good words they heard and hastened [f. 70] to answer. They wrote a letter responding to his call:

> In the name of God, the One and Only God,
> To 'Abd Allah Dhulqarnayn,
> From all of the people of Bārish,
> We received your letter in which you mention the most powerful of all names, and the most worthy of all religions. You called us to obey the Benefactor. You spoke of the righteousness and truth in your mission as well as the promise God has made to you and the backing He will give you to fulfill that promise, for He is the one who brings triumph to the righteous and grants them power to defeat their enemies. You inquired if we were truthful. Indeed, we bring to fruition the word of truth and we obey those who obey God and help the righteous. You wondered if we were not truthful.

Verily, God has placed a barrier between us and the wrongdoers.

Peace be with you.

They sealed their letter and gave it to Dhulqarnayn's messenger who promptly delivered it to his lord. Upon receiving the letter he opened it, read it, and understood what the people of Bārish meant. He recalled for his companions that God the Almighty had mentioned to him previously that these would be the most pious of the earth's people. "I want to go to them, meet them and ask about the first island we were on [f. 71]. Who does it belong to and who lives on it?"

Thirteen thousand horses and men road out and made camp to the west of the city. Soon the young and old, the educated and the honorable met to go and welcome Dhulqarnayn. Once they had approached and greeted him, he asked, "Who are you?" "We are the Bārish," they answered. "And who are the Bārish?" he asked. "We are Adam's people." "From which tribe do you come?" "From the tribe of Thamūd who belonged to the prophets sent to the Israelites. They received five prophets during a single epoch. We had a king who was kind to both his subjects and visitors, and beneath whom the lower classes and the nobles alike lived prosperously in an equitable society. His name was Ḥazaqīl. But he perished and his throne was vacated and then claimed by one of his paternal first cousins. The new ruler was an oppressor who tyrannized his subjects and laid waste to their shelters. We gathered on the coast and fled far away from him. The prophets of the Israelites came to us and impressed us greatly so we believed and trusted in them. Each of the five prophets gave us their word [f. 72]. They told us that God the Lofty One had given them an order to attack a people called Abū Zuka'īl who are from the tribe of 'Ād. Their ancestral head was Abāwīl b. 'Āwīl b. 'Ūṣ b. Arūm b. 'Amalāq and Arūm b. Farkhashid b. Sām b. Noah, bless him. They once lived on the uninhabited island that you left behind before coming here. Their population was so great that nobody could keep track of their numbers. Only God the Almighty knows how many of them there were. A modest estimate might be that there were at least three hundred thousand men, all warriors. None of whom obeyed his Lord. God sent us the angel Zayāqīl who called upon one of the five prophets alive at that time to go after these people and destroy them with the help of the nation of Bārish. The angel ordered us to sail out to sea with as many of us as there were, with our children, and as much strength as we could muster. Together with the prophet we set out with five hundred thirty thousand warriors aboard a fleet of boats [f. 73] each following in the wake of the preceding one.

With the aid of God, we successfully reached the island, which was a miracle considering the frightful things that could happen to someone navigating the depths of the high seas. Accompanying us all the while was the prophet that God the Almighty had sent us. He was with us when we went into battle. The fighting raged on for six months and we were destroying one another other. But in the end, God gave victory to the righteous against His enemies. Only a few of them remained and they fled to take refugee in caves beneath the ground where they were temporarily safe from us because we returned to our country. However, before long the tribe of Bārish attacked them again and finished them off leaving no survivors. All that remains of them are the vestiges of their dwellings, which you saw empty and abandoned. Afterwards our prophet died and disappeared from among us. We have grown as a people and now we live in our own land. What is it you want from us, Dhulqarnayn?" "If I wanted to make war against you, I would be unable. So I wish nothing but to visit your lands and see what they contain in the same way as I have visited other lands before yours [f. 74]. This is something that God has commanded me to do."

So he traveled with them to their land. What he saw when he entered was a land like no other, with poor people content in their poverty, fortified hermitages, shining dinars, livestock that roamed without shepherds, men who were equal in their earnings, strength, and dress. He saw their tombs at the doors to their houses so that they couldn't enter or leave without contemplating their death. He observed a people who without doubt constituted the most pious of nations. There were no leaders or judges among them. There were no poor or rich. All of them lived in equality. None of them committed injustices, nor did they quarrel or bring lawsuits against one another.[53] Dhulqarnayn was amazed by these things and said to them, "You are the most pious of nations. My Lord told me about you. He said you obeyed Him. All you need to do is say: 'There is no God but Allah,'" to which they responded, "We have been saying those words from the time we were sent a prophet. We do not believe God has a partner in any form." "Why is it that I see your livestock wandering without pastors?" asked Dhulqarnayn. "There are no thieves or treacherous people among us" [f. 75]. "Why is it that your houses have no doors?" asked Dhulqarnayn. "There are no crooks or robbers among us. Locked doors and the greed associated with them are found in places where there is deceit and thievery." "Why is it that you have no governors or leaders?" he asked. "Governors and leaders are for those who swell with pride and flaunt their strength. God eliminated these things from our people and from our hearts. Our prophets and our forebears made a covenant to live honestly and to always honor the truth. They adhered to these principles and their descendants from one generation to the next have preserved this way of life, and it has continued in our ancestral line. Today, we are the living proof of the covenant our forebears entered into." "Why is it there are no judges among you?" asked Dhulqarnayn. "We live according to vows taken long ago stating that no one shall wrong his neighbor, so we have no need for judges." "Why is it that there are no rich nor poor among you?" asked Dhulqarnayn. "Our prophets and forebears agreed that the rich among us would give charity to the poor. So a rich man shares what he has with a poor man [f. 76]."

During this time, Dhulqarnayn was sitting on a donkey. When he heard the answer to the last question he turned to find a poor man among the people of Bārish. He dismounted and shared his money with a poor man because he was afraid he would come to covet wealth. He was afraid of falsehood because he knew that money corrupts and forces the rich to become false. The thought of

---

[53] Ibn al-Jawzī relates the same episode on the authority of Wahb b. Munabbih (f. 83r). Similar versions, also citing Wahb, are found in Ibn Hishām *Kitāb al-tighān* (Arabic text in Lidzbarski, 1893, 305-08) and in al-Ṭabarī (*Tafsīr*, 18, pp. 20-21) who uses Ibn Isḥāq's version. This episode and its evolution from the PC to the Persian Alexander legends, in as much as it reflects a Utopian City, has been studied by M. Casari, pp. 30-43.

failing to fulfill the covenant between the forefathers and their prophets further frightened him. The old man continued, "God does not favor one over another. The world is equal for all of us and all enjoy the same manner of living. For this reason there are no rich or poor among us." Then Dhulqarnayn asked, "Why is it that your graves are at the doors to your houses and your buildings?" They replied, "So as not to forget that one day we will die." "By God, I have not seen anyone like you anywhere in the world! There is no doubt that you are the most pious of nations. You have no need for anyone to look over you! May you go in peace and security and continue to live as you have up until now. Know that God provides the greatest aid and He will reckon with us and what a lawyer he is!" When he was ready to leave he said, "My friends, peace by with you." [f. 77] At noon he departed and headed west. In the company of more soldiers than can be counted, Dhulqarnayn led the march across the face of the water.

Al-Suddī said:[54] With the same one hundred thirty thousand soldiers that were with him when he spoke to the Bārish people, he now traversed the seas. The dust cloud that they lifted settled on the face of the water as if it were dry level ground. They walked for one day and one night, but God shortened the distance for them and in that time they traveled what would normally take six and a half complete days. They arrived to Mount al-Amlas,[55] which God pulled out from the depths of the right side of the earth. On the left side of the earth he created a similar mountain. They are two lofty high mountains that soar into the sky attaining an elevation that no bird, human being or jinn ever reached without dying from the sky's fierce cold. The two mountains stand facing one another and between them is a wide open plain that would take one day to cross.

When Dhulqarnayn approached the mountains, news of his arrival quickly spread among the local inhabitants [f. 78] and they went to gather around him. One of their leaders spoke out and said, "O Dhulqarnayn, God created these two mountains and made them to look as they do. Then He settled us here to live. The right mountain is called Mount al-Ayqāf, and the left one is called Mount al-Iskāf.[56] The plain that stretches between them is the Ma'rib Plain. Behind the two mountains you will find tribes with long necks and bodies, and extremely long lives. In fact, some of them live to be one thousand two hundred and others live to be one thousand five hundred years old. They never utter the name of God, and they refuse to profess the truth. They kill people unjustly. We are believers in God, and they make it impossible for us to live peacebly. Our religion is the approved one, the one of the Maker of the earth and heavens, the one of He who is Matchless and Unequaled, his Lordship to whom we are obedient. They raid us each year during the most profitable part of the year and harass us, bear down on

---

[54] Ms. B has the Prophet as the narrator here.

[55] i.e., the smooth mountain. Also mentioned in al-Tha'labī, who explains that by smooth we are to understand without vegetation (p. 365). Could this be the lofty Mount Jardā, which Idrīsī (9th part of the 5th Clime) says "is so smooth on all sides that it cannot be ascended"? Cf. C.E. Wilson, p. 586.

[56] According to A. Grohmann, the two hills enclosing the Mārib barrier are called Balaq al-Qiblī and Balaq al-Awsaṭ (EI, 3, p. 286). Yaqūt says that the village of Iskāf is between Baghdad and Wāsṭ (1, p. 181), which would indicate that it bears no relation to the Mārib barrier. The toponym al-Ayqāf has not been located.

us and abuse us. There is no way for us to live beside them in peace [f. 79]." On and on they listed their grievances against their neighbors. They said, "No one can get near them except by crossing the plain between the two mountains, which we call the 'Barrier of Ma'rib.' God has not forbidden us from reaching them, except by way of the mountain." Dhulqarnayn asked, "Who are you?" "We are from the tribe of Shūd from the people of Madīn b. Abraham, bless him. Our people grew numerous in the land of Madīn until discord erupted one day between us and the tribe of Madīn. We fled with our people and came to these two mountains and decided to settle here where we have lived ever-since. But these people attack us." "Who are they?" asked Dhulqarnayn. "It is said that they are the from the tribe of Bārish b. Yāfit b. Noah. They are an evil people, warlike and insolent against whom we are helpless. We cannot live with them as neighbors." Dhulqarnayn replied, "Do not let this matter worry you further. I will protect you from them."

The people were happy to hear this and they rejoiced. Some were anxious to see what he would do, while others were wary. So Dhulqarnayn set out for the pass [f. 80] between the two mountains. Upon reaching the far side of the mountains, he was so high that he looked down on heights that exist nowhere else in the world. Beneath him the side of the mountain dropped off tremendously. There was a trail that wound up the side of the mountain and was visible from the people's village below, but it was so steep and treacherous that no one dared to set foot on it or to contemplate ascending it. From the top one could see the Ocean from any direction. This pass over the mountain was the only way to get to the barrier of Mārib. When Dhulqarnayn was able to look down the other side at the people below, he dispatched a messenger with a letter that said:

> In the name of God, the Initiator and Dispatcher in these matters,[57] the One and Only Lord, the One for whom there is no deity equal to Him,
> From Dhulqarnayn,
> To the people of Tārish, the ones who unjustly tyrannize the Believers with insolent behavior,
> Peace to those who are rightly guided and follow God, the Almighty and Exalted, and fear the consequences [f. 81] they shall bear for their actions.
>
> O People of Tārish, save yourselves from the punishment that lies ahead for those who do evil, act tyrannically and worship idols! Believe in God the One and Only Lord, the One for whom there is no deity equal. If you choose to believe and obey, you will have what we have and live as we live. But if you persist in your evil ways and refuse to believe, then the army of God will bear down on you with innumerable soldiers. No one can stand up

[57] Formula from the Qur'ān 11:41. In the Quranic story of Noah and his ark this formula is translated by 'Abdullah Yūsuf 'Alī as "In the Name of Allah, Whether it move or be at rest," and refers to the ark. Throughout *Qiṣṣat Dhulqarnayn*, this expression is used to begin many of Dhulqarnayn's letters. It has been necessary to find another expression with which to translate it.

against them in battle. You will be disgraced and your kingdom lost. God provides the greatest of aid.

He sealed the letter and his messenger delivered it promptly to the people of Tārish. When the messenger approached them he saw more people than the eye could count. It struck him immediately that they had human features except that their faces were like the faces of dogs and their bodies were like great geese. He handed the letter to their reader who read it outloud for them. They were amazed by the beauty of his wording and the way in which he humbled himself to God Almighty. The reader then admonished his people, "O people of Tārish, believe in God, [f. 82] who created the heavens and the earth, and in them made you, giving you the form he wished." Another of them stood up and said, "O people of Tārish, there stands before you a very brave army. Call the people together and when you gather, come to a unanimous decision. If it is war, then it will be with those who sent the letter. If it is surrender, then send a message to inform him." They agreed. So he convened a meeting at which everyone, from the highest noble to the lowest peasant, was present. Together they reached an accord to submit to Dhulqarnayn and to obey him rather than to go into battle against him. To communicate this they wrote a letter that said:

In the name of God, the Initiator and Dispatcher in these matters,
From the people of Tārish b. Yāfit b. Noah, bless him,
To Dhulqarnayn Nabbāsh,
Greetings to he who bears the word of all those who submit to the word of the Maker of Creation. We received your letter and understand your demands upon us, and we obey he who is obedient. We have no need or desire to make war against you. Even if there were to exist an army with as many soldiers as we have, there could be no one capable of defeating us in battle. We know what it takes to win. Indeed we have demonstrated [f. 83] to other kings *that Kings, when they enter a country, despoil it, and make the noblest of its people its meanest thus do they behave,*[58] O Dhulqarnayn. If you leave us in peace in our homeland, and do not force things upon us, with the exception of your request for aid for matters outside our kingdom, then we will obey you and support your decisions. On the other hand, if you were to enter our country and try to force us into submission and exact tribute from us, then you would stand no chance against us. Peace be with you.

They sealed the letter and handed it to the messenger of Dhulqarnayn. When he received their letter, he opened it, read it and understood their position. He consulted with his men regarding how to respond to the people of Tārish. They gave him their opinion and their counsel, and he said to the people of Tārish, "I have no choice but to enter your land."

Dhulqarnayn ordered [his men] to depart and march until they came to the center of their city. As the people rushed to see him he was able to see their faces

---

[58] Qur'ān 27:34

and their bodies. There were some as tall [f. 84] and as wide as a bear. Some would wrap themselves with one ear and use the other as a coat. Some were as tall as the great cedar.[59] Their faces, we might say, were the faces of dogs, but their bodies were human. Once they had gathered around him they spoke to him in their customary way and in their languages. He called them to God and they believed in Him, but in their hearts they concealed deceit as it was their custom to act dishonestly. They said they believed because they were afraid of him, but in their hearts they concealed faithlessness. When Dhulqarnayn heard this from them, he ordered his men to depart from there and he told the people of Tārish that he would accept the terms they had layed out in their letter to him.

Ibn 'Abbās, on the authority of the Prophet, May God bless and grant him salvation, reported in another narration concerning the same matter that Muhammad said that before him there had never been a prophet who did not warn his people against he who is missing his right eye, and who says to the people that "I am your lord" and who has a paradise and a hell. But his paradise is hell and his hell is paradise. A line is written across his forehead, which all believers in God can read, "May God protect from this man's temptations whomever He chooses by defending him with divine aid" [f. 85]. He crushed beneath his foot the Western Islands, but God liberated from him the cities of Mecca, Medina and Jerusalem as well as Mount Sinai. When the enemy of God tried to enter the city of Jidda, God sent an angel with a sharp sword in his hand and he drove them back. His time on earth will last forty days. Then Jesus, bless him, will set upon him with a spear made of light. When he sees it he will melt like lead and he will kill him and his companions until even the stones cry out, "O believers! Here beneath me is an enemy of God who does not believe in God Almighty! Kill him!"

'Abd al-Malik said: I heard Muqātil say that the Tārish were the same as the Gog and Magog,[60] and that their shortest man measures eighty cubits and the tallest measures one hundred cubits. Dhulqarnayn came upon them and saw they were living the most pleasant life: how excellent it was and how great were their numbers! How long were their lives! The males do not die until they have born one thousand male offspring [f. 86]. Once their offspring number one thousand, death comes upon them, and they are prepared for it.[61] They lived that way without knowing God and without professing the true religion.

---

[59] Ibn al-Jawzī says the same about the Gog and Magog on the authority of al-Tha'labī who took it from 'Abd Allah who took it from the Prophet (f. 81r).

[60] The Gog and Magog belong to Muslim and Biblical eschatology. They are mentioned in the Qur'ān 18:94, and in the OT Ez 38,39, and Gen. 10. Magog in Gen. 10 is placed among the offspring of Japheth. Both Biblical and Islamic sources state that these are the barbarians who will break through the barrier Dhulqarnayn built to contain them and swarm the earth on Judgment Day. Cf. EI, 4, 1142 (Wensinck). According to C.E. Wilson, they first came to be associated with the Alexander legend in manuscript C of the PC (Müller's edition Bk. 3, chpt. 26), "The Wall of Alexander Against Gog and Magog" (pp. 575-76). See also the excellent study of A.R. Anderson, *Alexander's Gate, Gog and Magog, and the Inclosed Nations.*

[61] Ibn al-Jawzī says the same about the Gog and Magog on the authority of Qatāda (f. 81).

Abū 'Abd al-Malik said: I heard Muhammad b. al-Sāyb[62] say: One of our companions in whom I have full confidence said that the height of a man from Tārish is between eighty and one hundred cubits.

When Dhulqarnayn was getting ready to leave that land, they came to him and said, "Dhulqarnayn, you know that the People of Tārish will break their agreements with you and turn away from the truth. Once you set off with your troops to other lands in the Far East, they will go back to practicing idolatry as they did before you, during the reign of their last king, 'Ālaj b. 'Ūs. He was a tyrant and his people suffered many injustices. His propensity to exceed the proper bounds of kingly conduct was never more flagrant than when he attacked the walls of the city of Mārib and killed one million eighty thousand people, most of whom were from the tribe of Yāfit b. Noah, and some from the tribe of Kūsh b. Noah.[63] King Ibn 'Ūs defeated them and they submitted to him [f. 87]. He made peace with them on the condition that they stop attacking the people of Bārish, and they agreed to honor their treaty. But when he departed, they broke the treaty and raided the people of Bārish and killed as many of them as they wished and took many prisoners. And now you have left them without building the Mārib barrier between the two of us. [Such a barrier is the only means by which] they will stop attacking us as they attacked the people of Bārish, and cease to say things they do not mean." "What did they say?" asked Dhulqarnayn. "When 'Ālaj left, they said to them: 'You are the ones who helped him and brought him to our lands.' From there war broke out and the Bārish were conquered. In the end they abandoned the island and left its houses uninhabited. That is the place you traveled through on your way here." Dhulqarnayn asked, "What do you want us to build for you?" "We would like to offer you the accumulated proceeds from a *kharaj* tax that has been collected here over the last forty years so that you can use the money to hire people to build a barrier between us and them" [f. 88]. Dhulqarnayn understood their offer and said, "Come forth with the *kharaj* tax as you have described to me, immediately, because I must leave you soon and travel elsewhere."

At that time Dhulqarnayn was leading a huge army. There were one hundred thousand soldiers present at these negotiations, in addition to those who were serving in other regions. He had one hundred sixty-two thousand soldiers all together, many of whom were metal workers. Blacksmiths numbered twenty two thousand and coppersmiths twelve thousand. He ordered these men to work on this project in the same manner as in their shops when they work for pay. And they set out to work. He told the people to measure the distance between the two mountains, and they measured it. Then he appointed one thousand supervisors from his engineers and metal workers to lead groups of twenty thousand men. Each work unit was assigned a piece of the terrain on which they were to build the

---

[62] Muhammad b. al-Musayyab

[63] Kūsh, written Cush in English, is the son of Ham b. Noah and is mentioned in Ezequiel 29:17, 30:4, 5 & 9, and in Jeremiah 46:9. In the Bible it is a name for the Nubians. Godbey places them on the West Coast of the Red Sea in Ethiopia (*The Lost Tribes a Myth*, pp. 94, 95). According to al-Ṭabarī (*History*, 2, p. 15), Nimrod was the son of Cush. The fact that Nimrod was thought to be one of the four kings who ruled the whole world may explain why Kūsh below (f. 251) is given the title, King of the World. For more on Nimrod, see EI, 3, pp. 842-843.

barrier. In the interest of completion of the project, Dhulqarnayn delayed his departure thirty days and he ordered the workers to [f. 89] use their craft to make each brick from copper and iron and to bore them out uniformly. They obeyed and worked together, each craftsman taking orders from the next. Its foundation was twenty-four cubits high and one cubit thick, using their standard of measurement. In another narration its breadth is said to be three hundred cubits. From bottom to top, it was six hundred fifty cubits, using a long arm as measure. According to others, it was eighty-five cubits.[64]

The Gog and Magog are a relatively short people, their height usually being no more than one and two hand spans. They copulate and multiply like animals. Neither their men nor women die until they have had one thousand offspring. Some say that beyond them on the seashore there is another tribe like the Gog and Magog, who populate the lands like locusts. They are the Tārish and Bārish. God created them for Hell. Some are as tall as a cedar and some of them [f. 90] wrap themselves with one ear and wear the other as a coat. Neither their males nor females die until they have had one thousand offspring. Once they have one thousand children then they know that their time has come and they begin to prepare.

Whenever a structure was to be built, Dhulqarnayn ordered them to bring copper, to melt it, and to pour it into holes like a shaft so that it would run down from the top of the structure to the bottom. Bit by bit it would strenghten all of its parts until the construction is complete. Then he ordered them to heat more copper until it was red hot and pour it over the surface of the barrier that faces the people of Tārish. Then they poured copper inside the barrier again and it ran down the structure. The Barrier of Mārib is composed of iron and copper bricks. It is built and constructed in such a way that no one can climb over it, go around it or penetrate it. These are the words of the Almighty One, "*Until, when he reached (a tract) between two mountains,*[65] *He found, beneath them, a people who scarcely understood a word.*"[66] It is said that these are the people of Tārish, who are [f. 91] on this side of the two mountains. On the other hand, those that said, "*The Gog and Magog (people) do great mischief on earth: Shall we then render thee tribute in order that thou mightest erect a barrier between us and them?*"[67] are the people of Bārish. Dhulqarnayn built and erected their barrier, so that it stretched across the divide between the two mountains.[68] Then they poured copper over it. To this day the barrier stands as Dhulqarnayn built it[69] and it will

---

[64] The barrier Alexander built to reign in the tribe of Gog and Magog recalls the one mentioned in *Jeremiah* 1:14-18.

[65] 'Abd Allah Yūsuf 'Alī translates the word *saddayn* as two mountains. Although Hans Wehr gives 'barrier,' 'rampart,' 'dam,' the Quranic translation is used here and throughout.

[66] Qur'ān 18:93

[67] Qur'ān 18:94

[68] Ibn al-Jawzī relates on the authority of Qatāda that the barrier is at Mount al-Radam (f. 81r). According to the EI (3, p. 288), at Mārib there was a great barrier of a dam between the two Balaq mountains.

[69] Al-Tha'labī relates on the authority of Qatāda that the location of the wall of Gog and Magog is as follows: موضع وراء زخرد بقرب مشرق الأرض ، بينه وبين الخزر مسيرة اثنين وسبعين يوما (p. 365). For more theories about the location of this legendary wall see 'Abdullah Yūsuf Alī's appendix to Sura 18 of the Qur'ān.

remain in this state until the day arrives for which God designated its purpose. In this way, God protected them from the Gog and Magog, and they are the descendants of Tārish b. Yāfit b. Noah, bless him.

On the authority of Ka'b al-Aḥbār it was reported that both the peoples of Tārish and Bārish come from the line of Yāfit b. Noah, bless him. They are tribes scattered throughout the lands, and no one knows how far and wide they are dispersed, nor how many of them there are, save God Almighty, the One and Only, the All-powerful.

When Dhulqarnayn left these people they reneged and returned to their [f. 92] godlessness. They violated their covenant with Dhulqarnayn and, again, wanted to attack the people of Bārish and Thamūd. But because of the smoothness of the copper on the face of the barrier they were unable. Instead, they turned to boring through the barrier. Yet however much they bored, seawater came out of the hole. Until Judgment Day they will continue in their attempts to penetrate the barrier.

Concerning Dhulqarnayn's Trip to the Country Called Yāwīl.

Abū 'Abd al-Malik al-Malshūnī said: I heard Muqātil say: When they finished building the barrier, Dhulqarnayn moved on to a people called the Yāwīl. He departed with his army wholly intact. None of them had died. Then he sailed the seas letting God determine his route. The angel Zayāqīl descended and guided him to an island in the sea after a trip of one day and one night, which otherwise would have taken a year and a half. When he anchored in front of a field near the seashore, lofty castles with elevated balconies appeared to him on the island [f. 93]. He stepped onto the island and summoned his advisors for consultation, "I've devised a plan for which I seek your approval before carrying it out. I think that this island is the one my Lord promised I would arrive at. Its people are high-bred, mighty, powerful, and courageous. I don't want to risk sending anyone to them except myself alone. What do you think?" "O Servant of God, we have no opinion except to follow the will of God, and then you. Look after yourself, for what is good for you is best for all of us. Go ahead with your plan" said the advisors. "I'm going alone, counting on God's blessing." "Who among us should follow?" "None of you move from this place until I've returned." "Dhulqarnayn, we're concerned about you and afraid for your safety." He replied, "I'm going to trick them with a ruse" [f. 94]. They will never discover my trick, unless I desire it so. I'm going to write them a letter, for which I myself will be the messenger." They said, "Go ahead with your plan and be sure you are counting on the will of God." Dhulqarnayn wrote the letter saying:

> In the name of God, the Initiator and Dispatcher in these matters,
> From the Servant of God, Dhulqarnayn b. Nabbāsh,
> To the people of Yāwīl,
> Peace to those who follow the true religion and fear the consequences of evil, and to those who feel shame in front of their Lord, He who sees and is not seen. We write knowing the

> splendor of uttering God's loftiness, and the fear of His truth. May this be a warning to you! Our Creator has commanded us to come to you. If you are among the believers, and are thankful for our Lord's blessing, and praise his beneficence, then you are faithful and we are here only as visitors, and we shall treat your lands with great reverence. But if you are a demonic and tyrannical people who serve idols, and who delight in depravity and vileness, then we have dispatched our messenger to you with the divine order to inform you [f. 95], as these words specify, of our good conduct for those who obey God, and of our bad deeds against those who do not obey. The Lord never overlooks recompense for a good deed.
> Peace be with you.

He sealed the letter and folded it. At night he went on foot to the doors of the city they had seen. Its lofty balconies, buildings and castles suggested the radiance of the rooms situated therein. In the meantime, the city's lighthouse had appeared in the distance to Dhulqarnayn's army at sea. It would take them six days to reach the city.

When Dhulqarnayn stood in front of the door to the city, the watchman asked, "Who are you? I don't recall seeing you on this island in any of its cities." Dhulqarnayn asked, "Are there cities here besides this one?" The watchman responded, "Yes, there are four cities of which this is the fourth. In each of them there are twenty five [f. 96] thousand archers with long bows, and another twenty five thousand that alternate guard duty. There are twenty thousand warriors, and twelve thousand craftsmen, all of whom make swords, armor, spears and lances for war. Each craftsman is paid by the king out of the treasury." "In which of the cities is the main king?" asked Dhulqarnayn. "In this city." "What is his name?" "Nawwāsh b. 'Amlāq," answered the watchman before repeating his question, "Who are you?" "I am the messenger of the servant of God, Dhulqarnayn b. Nabbāsh, carrying a letter for the king of this city. I would like to go in and see him. Perhaps you could help me. I would inform Dhulqarnayn of your cooperation when I return to him." "Give me a moment, I will let the king know you are here." The watchman entered the king's chambers, and saluted him in their accustomed manner, with the most proper etiquette. He informed the king of the presence of Dhulqarnayn's messenger. Nawwāsh ordered the watchman to bring him in [f. 97]. So he entered and was seated next to the king. The king then asked him, "Who are you? Where do you come from? What is your name?" "I have been sent by the servant of God, 'Abd Allah Dhulqarnayn. I'm a soldier in Dhulqarnayn's Army of God, and my name is 'Abd Allah. I've come to you as a visitor seeking refuge. I've decided to come to you and inform you about Dhulqarnayn. He approached me and asked me to meet with you. But I feel grateful to you and would warn you of his intrigues and evil doings. If you heed my warning you could save yourself from great misfortune." King 'Amlāq said to him, "O 'Abd Allah, when kings enter villages they ruin them. They reduce the most honorable people in the village to vileness, among other terrible things. No king has ever entered this village who was not from the people here. It is well protected from the dangers of the world. In it there are twelve thousand longbow archers and twelve [f. 98] thousand more who alternate with them. In each of the city's four towers there are marksmen. There is a span of one mile between the towers. In the area surrounding the towers there are other cities like this one. On this island each of the cities is equally protected with similar numbers of horses, marksmen, men and arms.

In the center city's fortifications there is a cave with three hundred steps for those wishing to enter or leave the cave. Upon entering, one finds inside caverns beneath the ground like nothing imaginable. The water there is more abundant and sweeter than can be found anywhere. In this cave there are so many chambers with stairs leading to other caves, each with its own attraction, that to describe it would take forever. If we were to enter this cave, it would serve us as sufficient protection from Dhulqarnayn for as long as he might stay in our lands. However, we have learned that when people come to your lands they do irreparable harm. So we are going to send you back to Dhulqarnayn in peace so that you can give him our warmest greetings. I will write him a letter swearing to listen to him and [f. 99] obey him if he leaves us alone to manage our own affairs. We will pay him tribute in the form of military support, arms of warfare, men, for as long as need be, and in whatever form he wants, without having to go to war and wreak havoc in the lands and kill one another.

When Dhulqarnayn heard him say this he exclaimed, "If you do as you say, what an excellent king you would be! What good sense and good judgment, and what a benefit to your subjects!" King Nawwāsh b. 'Amlāq wrote:

> In the name of God, the Initiator and Dispatcher in these matters,
> To Dhulqarnayn b. Nabbāsh,
> From Nawwāsh b. 'Amlāq, leader of the Yāwīl tribe,
> Peace be to you followed by thanks and wishes for happiness, splendor, and light, for the views you expressed in your brilliant letter to us, delivered by your noble messenger. We received it welcomely, and considered it with reverence. We understood its contents with a discerning understanding; you mention in it the promise to God, and the safety and security one derives from such a commitment. You warned us of the punishments that await in the Hereafter. We are fearful of His wrath unleashed through the hands of His [f. 100] servants. We are believers, obeying His commands, and those of the servants in whom God has entrusted the imposition of His will. If you were to order us to come out to you, we would do so obediently for we fear the Lord and we are afraid of you. Consider our words as an example and deem our letter a success. For God does not forsake the rewards of those who act well.
> Peace be upon you.

He folded the letter and gave it to Dhulqarnayn without knowing that the messenger was Dhulqarnayn. Nawwāsh b. 'Amlāq was a friend to his subjects, and a man of judgment and deliberation.

Dhulqarnayn went back to his companions and informed them of what Nawwāsh b. 'Amlāq had written. He gave them the letter and briefed them on the strength of the city and what it looked like. He described for them the cave of which 'Amlāq had spoken. Seeking advice he asked their opinion.

They responded, "O Dhulqarnayn, write to Nawwāsh [asking him] to pay you a tax gathered from his people with an increase for all that is in India [sic]. Promise them that they will be able to continue to live as they have been living. Verily Nawwāsh's letter [f. 101] is one of sincere surrender. Surely, he will do as you command." He replied, "You're right." He sent for Nawwāsh to come out and meet him. When they met he honored him and treated him well. Nawwāsh learned that the messenger had been Dhulqarnayn himself and that the whole affair had been a ruse. Dhulqarnayn praised the king's insight and intellect. Then Nawwāsh gave tribute that included twelve thousand rotls in gold and the equivalent in silver, and he said, "Spend it for the cause of God. Give it to your army to strengthen them. Here are twelve thousand suits of armor and the same in swords and helmets, saddled horses, shields. It is all from my wealth and comes with my blessing as aid to you and support to your Army of God. His cause rests in your hands, Dhulqarnayn. Take also twenty five thousand soldiers that will go on the road with you and fight for God as you command."

Abū 'Abd al-Malik al-Malshūnī said: I heard Muqātil say that [f. 102] Dhulqarnayn stayed with the Yāwīl. They are a people whose opinion is on the mark and whose king is well guided, and Dhulqarnayn played a trick against him. God demonstrated to him what it means to conduct oneself with integrity and to use sound judgment. The Macedonian army did not traverse his kingdom and his subjects prospered during his reign. Dhulqarnayn supported his kingship and appointed his nephew, Rawwāsh b. Hurmar, to be head of the division of the army that Nawwāsh contributed to Dhulqarnayn's army of God. He equipped them, bestowed favors upon them, honored them, and supplied them with provisions. He conferred upon Rawwāsh his rise in rank to division leader, decreed it publicly and commended them all to God, the One and Only. Then Dhulqarnayn turned to Nawwāsh and said, "Nawwāsh, the best thing you have given this army is this man, Rawwāsh, whose service to us as officer will be invaluable." And so the king's nephew assumed his post at the head of the Yāwīl and Dhulqarnayn kept him close to him, which perpetuated the memory of his uncle Nawwāsh, and his honorable conduct. Then Dhulqarnayn resolved to depart from that land.

Concerning Dhulqarnayn's Journey to the Country of Tāwīl [f. 103]

Abū 'Abd al-Malik al-Malshūnī said: I heard Muqātil say: Dhulqarnayn departed from the people of Yāwīl and headed towards the people of Tāwīl, who were a tribe descending from Yāfit b. Noah. He traveled by sea abandoning himself to the will of the Almighty God. Soon God sent down to him his angel, Zayāqīl, bless him. They were on the sea only one day and one night, but actually covered a distance equivalent to a trip of one and a half years. During their voyage, whenever they wanted to stop to rest, they would sound the horns. Then the troops would stop and put down on the very face of the water; they pounded in the stakes to tie the horses and beasts, and the stakes went into the water as if it were land, such was God's command. God also made Dhulqarnayn able to cover great distances quickly, as if the distances were shorter. When dawn broke and the troops gazed out at the horizon and looked into the depths of the sea, they were in awe at the Almighty God's power. Suddenly they noticed an island in the sea at a distance of [f. 104] twelve miles. They looked more carefully and saw the island was green with vegetation. They walked towards it until they came near the coast. Some of them remained while others went ashore. The sea off the coast was firm as if it were a level stretch of land. Dhulqarnayn summoned all those that went ashore to meet. When they were all gathered, Dhulqarnayn selected ten men who on their horses would go into the city on the island. They assessed the mission on which they were to embark and entered the city at the first light of day and remained until sunset. At one point when they were in among the ruins of buildings, they spotted a man walking on a nearby road. They grabbed him to ask him questions. But they quickly discovered that he did not understand a word they said nor did they know his language. So they brought him before Dhulqarnayn and the king said, "What tribe do you belong to?" The man replied, "We are the people of Tāwīl." "Who do the Tāwīl descend from?" asked Dhulqarnayn. "We come from the people of [f. 105] Yāfit b. Noah, bless him. There are sixty three different tribes in all," said the man. "How many are in each tribe?" asked Dhulqarnayn. "Somewhere between eighty and one hundred thousand." "How many are in the tribe of Tārish b. Yāfit?" "Count them." "Are they God fearing people?" "Some of them are believers, while others disbelieve." Dhulqarnayn said, "You are the Tāwīl. How many of you are there?" "We are comprised of forty tribes, each with a population of about forty or fifty thousand." "Do these tribes have kings?" asked Dhulqarnayn. "Each of the tribes has two chiefs each of whom answers to a greater king." "What is his name?" asked Dhulqarnayn. "Shūrish b. Sharīsh," said the man. "What religion does he practice?" "The one that recognizes the monotheistic nature of the Lord." "Where does he live?" "In the middle of one of our cities." "Which one?" "Taḥlaba." Dhulqarnayn said, "I want to write your king [f. 106] a letter of praise and advise him of the mission God has given us and let him know of our arrival to his lands. You will be a messenger for us." "As you please," said the man. Dhulqarnayn wrote:

> In the name of God, the Initiator and Dispatcher in these matters,
> To King Shūrash b. Sharīsh,
> From 'Abd Allah Dhulqarnayn,
> Peace be upon those who are rightly guided and know to fear the ruin and destruction of God's punishment, and those who know enough to feel shame before the Creator of the earth and the heavens. We write to you with the most pious of intentions graciously seeking to call you to your Creator, the One and Only Lord of the Worlds, the One to whom no other godhead is equal. If you answer God's call and confess his oneness, you will have safety and security throughout the world and into the Hereafter.

> But if you are accustomed to stray from the right path in disobedience and sin, then you can expect war from God and his messenger. For your sins you will receive torment and ruin which will cause you to greatly regret your error. Then you will return to the invisible world and find proof. Prepare yourself in word and action. God is not unaware of what you are doing [f. 107].

He sealed the letter and gave it to the man and said, "We'll wait two days for the answer."

Off the man went to bring the letter to their king, Shūrash b. Sharīsh. When the king received it, he summoned the people of his kingdom, and his counselors, and asked for their advice. One of them said, "What a difference there is between a band of men who have left their native country and gone abroad, and an established nation endowed with great strength and power! What could be, O Shūrash, the destiny of a nation without stability, strength and aid? God, unique in his power, taught us without it being necessary for this man to warn us in his letter. We are in our country, on your island, with so many horses and men that one cannot count them all." He commanded the army to gather, and had their numbers and troops assessed. He ordered them to get ready to go into battle against Dhulqarnayn. This was all done in accordance with the ministers' view of the situation, which was not the king's view. In truth, their king, Shūrash, tried his best to warn them. But they refused anything but war. He appraised their situation and ordered them [f. 108] to come together and meet and be resolved to go forward with their plans. So they came out in numbers so great they could not be counted. There must have been more than one hundred and sixty thousand. Their islands were laid out close together so that they could look at each other from one island to the next. They joined together and determined to go to war. They endured the hardships of war for a day and a half; there was great loss of life and the dead appeared everywhere.

When King Shūrash saw so much death around him, it saddened him greatly, to the point that he threw himself between the opposing armies and cried out, "O people of Dhulqarnayn, enough killing! I shall ask Dhulqarnayn to order an end to this senseless slaughter of our troops." The men ceased their attack, and Shūrash continued, "Who will take me to Dhulqarnayn?" One of Dhulqarnayn's companions led him to Dhulqarnayn. They found him sitting among a group of people. The Tāwīl king greeted Dhulqarnayn by saying "Peace be upon you." [f. 109] "Who are you?" asked Dhulqarnayn. "I am Shūrash b. Sharīsh." "Why do you come and see me now, Shūrāsh, after so many men have perished?" "O most obedient and attentive Amir! I came as your supporter, against the opinion of those who strive to make war against you so that men are destroyed and heroes are lost, and righteousness is set apart from error. Anyone who possesses discretion knows the consequences of holding to a particular opinion. I feared the destruction of the nation, the splitting up of my people, and the corruption that would result. I've come to you as your obedient servant. Do as you see fit, now that I've come here to put my fate in your hands." Dhulqarnayn asked, "What would you like to do now?" "Call upon me and my kingdom, and we will collect a *kharaj* tax from the islanders, for as much as we can afford to pay. I shall be among those who listen to God's commands, and who obey his messenger." "O Shūrash! Rejoice! [f. 110] The affair has turned out in such a way as to fulfill your word and command, and the opinion of those who are in the city has been delegated to you. If you had come to me sooner there would not have been this war and so much slaughter. But God's promises must be fulfilled and His sentence is now complete." Dhulqarnayn gave an order to his troops and they retreated.

He treated Shūrash well and honored him, and then asked him to contribute soldiers and provisions to his army. Shūrash gave him hōrses and a contingent of twelve thousand combatants, among whom three thousand were archers, and nine thousand were soldiers. All went on horseback and were armed. In the end, his people were thankful that Shūrash had taken the action that he did, and regretful of their decision to fight. Before Dhulqarnayn said good bye, he preached to them, attested to their merits as a people, and honored those among them who had conducted themselves honorably. Then he left and traveled towards a people called the Banī Mansik.

Concerning Dhulqarnayn's Journey to the Land of the Banī Mansik

Abū 'Abd al-Malik said: I heard Muqātil say: Dhulqarnayn left the Tāwīl and headed for the lands of the Banī [f. 111] Mansik. He sailed the seas in his usual way until his companions saw a great island with mountains and thick vegetation. The land was surrounded on three sides by water and on the fourth connected to another body of land, so making it a peninsula. The coast was dominated by bluffs, and facing the peninsula was a similar body of land. The first peninsula would take one month to cross in its width and two months in its length, while the second one would take two complete months to cross in both length and width. Dhulqarnayn set anchor in the sea between the two peninsulas. He sent a messenger with a letter to the people of the second peninsula that read:

> In the name of God, the Initiator and Dispatcher in these matters,
> From 'Abd Allah Dhulqarnayn,
> To the people of these isolated lands, in the middle of the sea,
> Peace be upon those who are rightly guided and know to fear the ruin and destruction of God's punishment, and who feel shame before the One who sees but is not seen. Peace be upon he who answers the call [f. 112] of the Creator of creation in its entirety and more.
>
> We have written to you out of a desire to learn more about you. We have called you to join us in obedience to the Creator of creation, the Supreme Giver of sustenance, and to join us in professing his oneness. If to this you answer affirmatively, then you will have all that we have, and you will benefit from God's gifts as we do. On the other hand, if you arrogantly reject these principles, and if your hearts are set in ways that err and anger the

> Lord, then be on your guard because we have come to you with an army whose numbers are beyond counting. We are aided by God. Your defeat is near since there is no way to be victorious against him. He is the greatest of aid to those who obey him. He brings death to the unbelievers. Peace to you.

He sealed the letter and gave it to his messenger. When the messenger reached them with Dhulqarnayn's letter, they hastened to gather and surround the messenger. There was much discussion but the messenger could not understand a word. They took him to their king, and he entered and found the king sitting [f. 113] on a golden throne, adorned with different kinds of jewels. He was a boy more beautiful than anyone had ever seen before. He was different than his people in looks. They would only have as their king one whose face God had endowed with beauty and perfection, and who was the most graceful of men. All of them had man-like bodies, but their faces were elongated and their eyes ran vertically down their faces. The men's skin was bare and they were beardless. The women were normal in both their faces and the shape of their bodies.

When the king saw him, he honored him, had him seated next to him and treated him in a friendly way. The king asked, "How is it that you came upon this place? We've been living here since our Lord commanded us to settle on this peninsula, and we've never seen anyone before you. Where are you from?" "O king! I am Dhulqarnayn's messenger [f. 114]. He is a king like you. God has gifted him with eloquence of speech and the ability to communicate in all languages." "Who is this king who has sent you to us?" "Dhulqarnayn." "What are his roots?" "He comes from the Rūm." "From whom do the Rūm descend?" "From the tribe of Adam." "From the line of Noah?" "Yes." "From which of Noah's children?" "Sam b. Noah." "Verily, our people and his are from the same tribal branch. All of us descend from the same person. " He continued, "Why did he send you to us?" "He sent me with a letter for you and the people of this island." "Let me see the letter." He broke the seal, opened and read it. Then he exclaimed, "We extend a warm welcome to he who brought this letter, and to the one who sent it." The messenger said, "O king! I've been sent to you with one day and one night to return with an answer. If you and your people agree to submit to Dhulqarnayn, then bring forward to me the most authoritive figure among you, [f. 115] the most knowledgeable and the most respectable, and I will take him to Dhulqarnayn. He will be informed as to the details of the affair, and Dhulqarnayn will give him orders concerning what he should do, and notify him of what is prohibited." Their king stepped forward and said, "I myself will go, since I alone can satisfy him in all his questions. I'll go to honor him, entertain him, and to stay with him all night long until God brings upon the new day." Then the king rode among a gathering of his people and ordered his advisors and other people of understanding and discretion to meet him at Dhulqarnayn's camp, and then the king went ahead to meet Dhulqarnayn, whom he honored and treated in the friendliest manner. In the morning a contingent of the king's advisors and counselors arrived. Dhulqarnayn asked him, "Who are you and what is your name?" "I am Dahqān b. ʻĀlaj b. Khawlān b. Jadʻān b. Mansik b. Arfakhshad b.

Sām b. Noah, bless him." "What is it [f. 116] that separated you from the tribes of Adam and brought you to this peninsula?" He answered, "Our grandfather, and your grandfather, Noah, bless him, who sailed the seas, brought a group of eighty men with their wives and children to a mountain. This group of eighty human beings got off the boat at Mount Jūdī. The spot where they landed became a meeting place for these men, women and children from among the believers of the Banī Adam, and they called it Sūq Thamānīn.[70] Their lifespans were long: an individual lived to be eleven hundred or twelve hundred years old and he or she would not die without first giving birth to one thousand male offspring, each of whose descendants multiplied.

One day our forefather Sām said to his father, our most illustrious grandfather, Noah, 'O father! Next to Adam, you are God's successor on earth. Show us where each one of us should go to establish our ancestral line so that our people [f. 117] will multiply after you.' Mansik said to our grandfather, 'We shall send you and your brothers with the aid of God into the sea till you reach an island called Ṭaḥūla, and there you will live, with those accompanying you and your brothers, Bārish and Tārish.' They said, 'O Father! Let us stay and live here with our brothers on this island.' He responded, 'God gave you orders regarding what to do.' But they refused and our grandfather Noah got mad and said to them, 'May God transform you into animals in the same way as he has done to others.' He transformed the faces of our men into the shape in which you see them, but the women remained as they were initially. One would not know who among us is the king if it were not for the fact that God has chosen him and created him to look as we first did. Abū 'Ālaj was born with a very handsome appearance. He had one thousand children, some of whom died and some of whom lived. But none of them looked like their father except me. With respect to what you asked regarding our arrival at this island, well, it was by order of the [f. 118] leader of the Banī Adam who, as governor of our previous island of residence, had ordered us to leave. We made boats just as he wished and sailed the seas in them, with the wind carrying us to wherever God desired, until we ended up on this island. We've been living ever since with our brothers Bārish and Tārish in the same manner as you see now. It's a good life, except that we are in a terrible war." Dhulqarnayn asked, "Which war are you referring to?" Dahqān replied, "Near us there is an island that would take two months to cross in both its length and width, which is inhabited by serpents."[71] Dhulqarnayn asked, "How do you manage to combat the serpents?" "There is no way except with large trenches of fire. No people on earth are without knowledge of the boundaries within which they live. That is to say that each nation knows the limits of its land. So they dig many trenches. When the time draws near [f. 119] for the serpents to attack, the people pile firewood and grass in their trenches and valleys until they are full. When they attack us we set fire to the wood and grasses, so that whatsoever moves across them burns up and dies. They no longer attack us except in the summer. Each serpent measures around one mile stretched

---

[70] i.e, Marketplace of Eighty.

[71] Dhulqarnayn's visit to a land inhabited by serpents located near Sijistān is mentioned in Mas'ūdī (1979), 1, p. 235.

out on land, while there are some that are longer and some shorter. Other serpents have managed to grow in size tremendously. But our men are only as big as you have seen: some are eighty cubits tall, their faces are elongated as you saw, and I told you about their lifespans. We will continue to inhabit this land, and to practice the religion of our forefather Noah, until Judgment Day." Dhulqarnayn asked, "O Dahqān! Where do most of these serpents live?" "In the open country on this [f. 120] island, where the earth is sandy." He asked, "Is their anything behind you?" "Mount Qāf." "Has anyone ever seen it or traveled there?" "A group of men from our people set out to sea some time ago. They were navigating through currents and their boat became lost at sea. They stayed afloat nine months. We thought they would never return to us. At times we were hopeful and at times we felt hopeless, until one day a boat appeared in the sea. The people rushed to meet it, and lo and behold, it was the men who had been gone. The people gathered around them and asked them about what happened. [Here is what they told us][72]:

'We went out to sea to go fishing for food when the wind picked up. We became caught in it and could not get back to shore. We got off the boat as we were nearing a group of islands that were close to one another. Some were large and others small. We sought a respite [f. 121] from the fear that had gripped us during our voyage at sea, and so we went ashore on one of the islands. The wind never let up and we feared for our boat that was moored off the coast. We stayed on the island for as long as God wanted us to be there, then the wind quieted and we returned to our boat and slept in it. We passed the night without incident until a bird flew down and lifted the boat with us inside up into the air. He flew with us until we came to an island in the sea. We no longer knew what sea we were in. The bird dropped us on the shore of the island. We spoke to the bird, but it was frightened of our words and flew away when hearing them. But soon it landed and stayed not too far away, quietly watching us. It wanted to pounce on us, but we started to yell at it, wave our banners, and startle it with our horns. Then it flew away and left us on the island to which it had brought us.

We climbed a mountain [f. 122] whose long and winding paths led us high above the sea. But again the bird appeared, so we kindled and started a fire. When it saw the flames it gave up and abandoned us, and we felt relieved it was gone. The fire had brought the bird to the point of despair. We lived off creatures from the sea during the two full months we stayed on that island.

One day a man and a woman came out of the sea. All afternoon they looked at us in amazement and we looked at them in wonder. As evening approached, the two of them disappeared into the sea. Then in the morning they came back to us. None of us attempted to speak to them nor did they speak to us. This continued for several days until there appeared another woman in addition to the first. Their faces were the same as human faces; and their only unique feature was their hair. They treated us in a friendly way without saying a word. But when they wanted to [f. 123] take leave of us they were able to express themselves in a very precise language. We got along well together for a full four

[72] The text has here just قالوا . The translator felt the need for a stronger marker for the new narrative about to be intercalated.

months during which time their numbers as a group continued to grow. There were nearly thirty of them, when one day they came with a sheikh and an old man who looked like the sheikh. They must have been the oldest in their tribe. They looked at us and made a gesture with their fingers as if to say, "Where are you from?" We answered with a hand motion that said, "From wherever the Almighty God wishes." They spoke amongst themselves and then left without returning until three days had passed. When they came back there was an old woman with them whose age and chronic illness had caused her to move about with a hunch. She approached us and uttered, "In the name of God Almighty," and then she went on, "O people! Who are you and how did you come to us?" "We came by the will of God, which brought us to an island among the islands of a sea we did not know [f. 124]. We stayed there until a giant bird lifted our boat and flew with us until it landed on this island, where we have been ever since. We have no idea what will become of us." "How terrible! Don't you know that bird?" "We have never seen or heard of such a bird. We don't have them in our country." The old woman said, "That bird brings ruin to us; it is called the 'Anqā.[73] It alone has been responsible for the destruction of our islands such that the only remaining inhabitants are those whom the Almighty God saved by having them enter the sea. We are the sole survivors." We asked her, "From which among God's creatures do you come?" She said, "We are the Yānūn, and we are not from Banī Adam." "Is there anyone else as old as you are?" "No." "How old are you?" "One thousand nine hundred years old." "Can you see under water?" "Any animal that can see on land can also see [f. 125] in the sea." "Do you mate and reproduce?" "Yes. Our progeny live in the sea for an hour, and they become habituated to the water." We asked her, "Is there another sea beyond this one?"

She began, "Once there lived among us a sheikh from the Yānūn. He lived in a cave for six hundred and eighty years out of fear of the 'Anqā. We all continued to live on land because we were terrified of the sea. One day the loneliness, desolation, and misery of the cave became too much for the sheikh and he took up residence in the sea. He stayed in the sea for one thousand years not including the years he spent on land. He was submerged in the water, and absent from us for ten years and we assumed he was dead. But he returned after that and we asked him about his absence. He told us he was in the sea and that a man appeared to him there. I wanted a companion and friend, [said the sheikh,] so I followed him and all the while he wanted me to follow him. We came to [f. 126] the seashore and he walked out of the sea and I walked out with him and we met and carried on in a friendly way for quite some time. We wandered from West to East, about the shores of the seas, sometimes on land and sometimes in the water, and came to know the whole world. We looked down upon the curtain that separates the skies and the earth and nothing else appeared to us except the darkness. I stayed with him as friends, he asking me questions and I asking him. We fed ourselves from the sea like other sea creatures. I asked him things about his personal life, 'Which people do you come from?' 'From the remaining

[73] A legendary bird named for its long neck, or perhaps a white collar on its neck. Related to the 'Anaqim of the Bible. There is some disagreement as to whether it is the griffin or the phoenix. Cf. EI, 1, 356.

members of the Yānūn.' 'Which Yānūn?' 'From the family of 'Ājūn.' 'Which 'Ājūn?' 'From the tribe of 'Āhūn.' I continued to question him in this manner until I learned that he was one of my forefathers. We were friends until he died. Then I returned to you. There is nothing beyond this sea except the darkness."

We said to her, "Old woman! Can you devise a way for us to return to our country and our families?" She said, "If you were patient [f. 127] then we could provide with you with a better way. But you are not patient. So you will need to fish a lot. Put the catch on the deck of your boat and do not light a fire. The 'Anqā comes to check on this island once a month. It has no shelter anywhere but here and on the island from which it captured you. Now if it gets used to seeing the fish, then it will dive and carry away the boat with you hidden inside it. It won't be able to reach you or the meat you will have stored away beneath the deck, and at the same time it won't give up trying to get at the meat, and will always keep the boat nearby. So when he goes to his other shelter on the island you desire to return to, he'll fly with the boat thinking to get the meat inside. Just do as I say."

We did as the old woman said and gathered large quantities of meat in the hold beneath the deck of the boat. Then we hid ourselves beneath the most protected boards of our boat, and soon enough the 'Anqā attacked us [f. 128] and carried the boat with us inside to the island from which we had come. We spoke to the bird and our words scared it and it fled. Then we sailed in our boat and made it back to you. This is the reason for our absence. After that experience, we never thought we would see anyone again.'"

When Dahqān finished speaking and relating the story of these people, Dhulqarnayn said to him, "Now, how would you like to resolve the matter of the serpents?" "O Dhulqarnayn! We are a people residing on this island dependent on our Creator who brought us to settle here. All of us belong to the peoples of Mansikīn, Bārish and Tārish, and we are all of one kind. We support one another and together we fight the serpents with fire. There may be one, two or three battles a year. We take turns fighting: the first time we fight, the next they fight. We would appreciate it if you left us alone in our country to fight our enemy, as God has so desired. In exchange, we will give you tribute. Dhulqarnayn replied, [f. 129] "I will let you continue to live as you have lived and I will also build you a tunnel with the aid of God that will allow you to reach the island of the serpents by crossing the sea, and at the same time restrain your enemy." Their king, Dahqān, reacted favorably to this. Then the crowd separated to make way for Dhulqarnayn to pass through and he rode on horse around the island for some time. Then he elaborated a plan, surveyed the island, and found two places close to each other. He commanded them to dig there until water was exposed on both sides. Between the two sides he built a canal protecting the people from the serpents. When he was done, he reassured them it would be sufficient protection. The king praised him and thanked him. Dhulqarnayn walked around the island so that he would know its length and width from one end to the other. He discovered that most of the island was sand. Then he returned to his camp and ordered the Tārish, the Bārish, and the Mansik to gather. He looked at them and was amazed at the enormity of their bodies and their towering height [f. 130]. Some of them were eighty cubits tall and ten cubits wide. Others were one hundred cubits tall and twenty five cubits wide. Some of them were not that big, but the faces of all the men were elongated like the muzzle of a mule, and their eyes ran down the length of their faces. Dhulqarnayn preached to them and taught them that God was their Creator, and that there is no lord except Him, and that none of his servants is his equal. They believed in him and trusted him.

Abū 'Abd al-Malik al-Malshūnī said: I heard Muqātil say: Dhulqarnayn walked about the island stopping where and when he pleased until he came to the far end. The serpents he saw there were absolutely indescribable. This was the place from which the serpents attacked. The islanders were fighting them with fire. The serpents would attack crowds of people who were throwing fire at them. Some of the serpents managed to escape the fire, while others burned up. Many people [f. 131] fainted from the attacks and perished.

Dhulqarnayn gave orders to dig the canal. He also ordered them to use arrows to fight the serpents. Excavations were to be done at two different spots on the island so that the waves would crash in the canal and the people would have a break from the serpent attacks. Then Dhulqarnayn asked the angel Zayāqīl about those peoples and the angel responded, "They are exactly as their king, Dahqān b. 'Ālaj described them to you. They are scattered peoples. Each tribe among them is more numerous than the Banī Adam." Zayāqīl informed him that those people would be believers as long as he was present. But as soon as he left, they would go back to being idolaters. Dhulqarnayn said, "O dear Zayāqīl! What are these serpents, and why are they here?" "O Dhulqarnayn! These serpents are all that remains of the vermin of the sea from which God created the skies and the land. Its waters dried up and left the serpents on solid land, which came to be these islands. They've stayed here ever since. One of those serpents [f. 132] can measure one hundred cubits, or eighty cubits, or even reach sizes ranging from two to fifty miles long. Their fangs are like great pieces of wood. Dhulqarnayn exclaimed, "My God! Give me a ways and means, and guide me so that I do good in all you have destined for me, for You are able to do anything." The angel Zayāqīl, who used to come to him with revelation from his Lord, said, "God commanded me to teach you all aspects of knowledge and reason, so that nothing is beyond your comprehension. So I'll tell you. Dhulqarnayn, know that no one before you had ever seen these serpents, and no one after you will see them, except the peoples that live here to whom God has given the ways and means to live near them. Know that they are scattered peoples, and that God has restrained them from mixing with those who believe in Him. These people will always persist in their customary beliefs that they keep concealed in their hearts. If you left them, they would go back to their idolatrous practices."

Abū [f. 133] 'Abd al-Malik said: Ka'b al-Aḥbār told me that in some of the books of the Banī Isrā'īl[74] it states that God sent Adam and the serpent down to earth on the same day. God gave Adam a portion of the earth that would take one hundred years to cross on foot, and placed him in a land called Hind. God put the serpent in a land called Sind. The serpent was a giant: it would take one hundred years to walk from its head to tail. The serpents that Dhulqarnayn has

---

[74] The narrator tells us that the source material comes from the the Jewish *isrā'īlīyāt*, considered by Muslim scholars after the second century of Islam to be untrustworthy.

been fighting are the descendants of this serpent, but they are not nearly as large as their progenitor, in the same way that men today are not as large as in ancient times. That serpent lived seven hundred years after Adam died, God bless him. Due to its enormous size, the serpent never left or even moved from the spot in which it lived. It procreated, and its offspring lived on the ground, and sustained themselves by eating earth [f. 134]. The large ones died because of their weight and their stationary lives. All of them found their sustenance in the earth. The Banī Adam were capable of fighting only those that measured around one hundred cubits. These are the snakes the angels carry and throw into Hell to bite the unbelievers, while the people look on.[75] They are the descendants of those serpents, as Illustrious God himself mentions. They are about one hundred miles long or less. From them come the snakes' stench and poison. They are the descendants of those birds. He gave the ways and means to the birds to gather the offspring of those serpents. Then he said that the snakes are from the ancestral line of the eagle, which is the bird mentioned above, but God knows best. God gave the ways and means [f. 135] to those peoples to fight those serpents on those islands. The Banī Adam and the snakes will be together on those islands until the Day of Judgment. Since Dhulqarnayn's visit,[76] combatting the snakes has not been a difficult task. They trusted him and to this day have never gone back on their word. They are waiting for Islam, as Dhulqarnayn promised them, and God knows best.

'Abū 'Abd [al-Malik] al-Malshūnī said: I said to Muqātil b. Sulaymān: Tell me some of the narratives you know that are based on authority and concern the wonders of the world and its islands. How long and how wide is the earth? He responded: Someone who was not one of the Prophet's Companions, God bless him and grant him salvation, told me that when one goes from the western summit of Mount Qāf to the eastern summit, and from the southern summit to the northern one, there is a total distance equivalent to what a man would cross on foot in five hundred years. Surrounding these [f. 136] islands on all sides, in the shape of a ring, is the sea. Mount Qāf encircles the entire world and the Ocean is behind Mount Qāf. There are people who have extensively studied the seas, but nobody knows what is behind Mount Qāf except the High and Almighty God. I asked Muqātil, "Who inhabits this portion of the earth equivalent to a five hundred year journey?"

He said, "God divided the part equivalent to the first three hundred year journey into thirds: the land transversed in a one hundred year journey is inhabited by the serpents, the land transversed in a second hundred year journey by the seas, and the land transversed in a third hundred year journey is uninhabited. Of the land remaining, equivalent to a two hundred year journey, one hundred goes to the Abyssinians and Gog and Magog, ninety nine goes to the Rūm people, and the land equivalent to a one year journey is for these people."

---

[75] The same snakes are mentioned in the story of Balūqīyā from al-Tha'labī's *Qiṣṣa al-anbiyā'*. See p. 353.

[76] Dhulqarnayn's visit to the land of the snakes is related in al-Mas'ūdī's *Murūj al-dhahab* wherein we learn that the snakes were contained by mounds of wood and sugar cane which Dhulqarnayn had erected around the perimeter of their sandy habitat. Cf. 1979 edition, 1, p. 235.

Abū 'Abd Allah said: I heard Muqātil say that Gog and Magog and [f. 137] the Abyssinians got land equivalent to a journey of one hundred twenty years. The Rūm and their islands got land equivalent to a journey of ninety nine years and Islam got land equivalent to a journey of one year. A group of people descending from the Gog and Magog are the Turks, who were named by Dhulqarnayn. He called them the Turks, for what he said to them, "tarakahum," which means, leave them alone.

The Prophet, God bless him and grant him salvation, said that "It is certain that between now and when they rally in their lands, and escape through a hole in the barrier to destroy the world there is but little time. Also on that day the Anti-Christ[77] will come forth, and Jesus son of Mary, bless him, will descend on earth, the sun will rise in the west." Know these things. Verily God has transmitted them to us in his Book when he says, "*But when the promise of my Lord comes to pass, He will make it into dust; and the promise of My Lord is true.*"[78] When my Lord's promise comes true, it will mean destruction. My Lord's promise was true. The Prophet, God bless him and grant him salvation, said, "All who are on the other side of the barrier are from God's first creatures, born before Adam. Their lifespans are long, their bodies [f. 138] are wide, and their beasts and livestock are similar in that respect. On the other hand, everything on this side of the barrier has a short lifespan, and their bodies, their beasts, their livestock, and their birds are proportionately smaller in size." Then the Prophet, God bless him and grant him salvation, said, "A man during the time of Solomon, bless him, measured twelve cubits. A lifetime lasted one hundred years or somewhere thereabouts. Back in that time, the ant was the size of the jackal, and the jackal used to be bigger than it is now."

At that point Dhulqarnayn said goodbye to the people of Mansik and made a covenant with them concerning their practice of God's religion, and their obedience to His commands. Then he prepared for the trip. He begged God to indicate to him the route he should follow through the seas. The angel Zayāqīl came down to him [f. 139] and said, "Your Lord orders you to go to the people of al-Naghāsh, who descend from the children of Adam, from the line of Luwā b. Sām b. Noah, bless him. He arrived at their islands in the sea to the right, which is the one that faces the setting sun in winter.

Concerning Dhulqarnayn's Journey to the Lands of the al-Naghāsh

'Abd al-Malik said: Dhulqarnayn disembarked and traveled on land for eight days, which was the equivalent of a journey of eight years. Then he rode the

---

[77] In Arabic, *al-Dajjāl.* According to prophecy transmitted in al-Ṭabari's chronicle, al-Dajjāl's real name is 'Abd Allah al-Ṣayātīd, and he is to appear mounted on an ass when the Gog and Magog break through the wall. His reign will last forty days and his power will dominate the world. However, Jesus and the Mahdī will humble him and the latter will slay him. Al-Ṭabarī, Persian synopsis, ed. Zotenberg, i, 67 *et. seq.*, as cited in EI, 1, 886-7. Reference to the coming of the Anti-Christ is also found in the *Rrekontamiento*, f. 39v and "The History of Alexander: A Christian Romance" translated from Ethiopic to English in Budge (1896), p. 453.

[78] Qur'ān 18:98

seas for one hour during the day and came upon an island that had abundant waters, meadows and predatory animals. Their buildings kept the animals out. The people there did not see well. As he approached them, he saw they were fighting cranes in the summer time; they were a menace because they destroyed the fruits of the land, ate the seeds and left nothing for the people to eat [f. 140]. In winter the cranes left and the storks arrived, but they were easier to fight than the cranes.

Dhulqarnayn asked the angel Zayāqīl, "Why are these people fighting with the birds?" "God is afflicting them, by weakening them in mind and body. They are a strong people prone to riot among themselves. When they start to fight one another, God sends the cranes to keep them occupied. They worry about their crop and are afraid it will be ruined." Dhulqarnayn asked the angel Zayāqīl, "Is there an emir among them?" "They have no emir or sheikh to judge among them. Everyone judges as he sees fit." Then Dhulqarnayn sent a messenger to them with a letter that said:

> In the name of God, the Initiator and Dispatcher in these matters,
> From 'Abd Allah Dhulqarnayn,
> To all of the people of al-Naghāsh,
> Peace be to those who follow the righteous path, place their faith in God, and obey His messenger. From us to you, all of you without exception, the common people [f. 141]. If you believe in God and his messenger, and profess his oneness, and that there is no Lord except Him, and that none of his servants are his equal, and that He is the One who created you, gave you shape, and provides your sustenance, and the One who gives you life, then death, and brings you back to life, then you will return to Him. Believe in Him and save yourselves from the disaster that our strength will unleash on you. God has commanded us to fight those who do not believe in Him, and to treat amicably those who have faith in Him. If you obey God, who is the One and Only, then from us you can expect peace and security. But if you refuse to believe in Him, and your will is to go to war against God and his messenger, then you will come to regret your decision.

Then he sealed the letter and gave it to his messenger. When they received the letter, they were quick to profess the oneness of God. They believed in God, and came to an agreement with Dhulqarnayn regarding the tribute they would pay, the alms they would give to the poor, and a promise not [to cheat one another any more][79], or to turn back on their faith. After drawing up this pact, he left them [f. 142] and came to another place where the angel Zayāqīl told him that God ordered him to return to the House of the King of Rūm. So he traveled until he returned to the city of Rome.

'Abd al-Malik al-Malshūnī said: I heard Muqātil say: Dhulqarnayn reached the setting sun and the rising sun. He traveled through the sea of

[79] B: f. 49v

darkness, and went to Mount Qāf with the aid of God. I[80] heard Muhammad b. al-Musayyab say the same thing. He said:

When he stopped at the city of Rome, the angel descended upon him and said, "O Dhulqarnayn! Your Lord orders you to break the idols and fight all men who worship them. He commands you to wage holy war against them wherever they may be until they say, 'There is no God but Allah,' and profess His oneness and divinity."

Then he sent his letter to all the tribes of the Rūm, and they met and acknowledged that he was the immaculate leader sent to the Rūm kings [f. 143]. They answered him and hurried with their answer to him. In his letter to the Rūm, Dhulqarnayn said:

> In the name of God, the Initiator and Dispatcher in these matters,
> From 'Abd Allah b. Nabbāsh,
> To all the people of the kings of Rūm, including nobles and great ones,
> Verily, God gave preference to your forefathers, he chose you and set you above the rest of his creatures. He made your grandfather, Abraham, his friend. He chose your grandfather, Isaac, for you. From Isaac's ancestral line, he selected your grandfather Esau, from whom you descend. You became his most favored creatures. He sent his holiness among you to cleanse you of your sins. He established you in power, strengthened you on earth, and made you rule all the world. So thank Him for favoring you. If he was gracious to you, and gave preference to your noble fathers, answer Him with obedience and hurry to accept his calling. Know that He is your Lord, the One who created you, shaped you, and gave you sustenance, according to his will. Listen to his command, and obey Him. Never be among those *of the reproaches of such as find fault* [f. 144] in the Lord.[81] Verily, I have admonished you. Know that God has no mercy for those who do not believe in Him, Creator of the earth and skies. He commanded me to break the idols and kill the idol worshippers. God aids he who seeks aid, and guides he who seeks guidance to the path of the righteous. There is no power save in the Almighty and All-powerful God.

Then he wrote a letter to Jerusalem stating:

> In the name of God, the most Compassionate and Merciful,
> From 'Abd Allah Dhulqarnayn b. Nabbāsh,
> To the noblest of the Rūm, who dwell in Jerusalem, a place safeguarded by God that has been a shelter of guidance for those who live there, and a place of elucidation for those who follow his rightly guided friend Abraham.

---

[80] Not clear if "I" refers to 'Abd al-Malik or to Muqātil.

[81] The meaning of the Arabic text is not entirely clear to me. It seems to refer to Qur'ān 5:54.

I have sent you a letter to lead you down the path of righteousness and remind you of the favors your Lord bestows. Remember God's threats, beware of his punishments. Know that He alone holds the treasures of the skies and the earth and that He alone is their Sovereign. He made a covenant with you in which He stated you are to make good on your promise, be obedient to his demands, guard his statutes, and, in accordance with his command, be kind and good and abstain from what is abominable to Him [f. 145]. I testify that there is no god but Allah and I am committed to fulfill all that is specified here.

The Master of Goodness, Aristotle, is present, and in my eye he is God's noblest subject. As you may have heard, in his scientific studies he found that God would send upon the kings and their citizens a purified holy man, one who is invincible and who will not be vanquished. The giants of the earth will surrender to him and the kings will bow before him. I hope that God, the One and Only Lord, who has no equal among his servants, has bestowed his blessings on me, and that I am that righteous person. Our people's wisest men --Aristotle, Afshakhīr[82], and al-Khiḍr b. 'Āmal, bless him-- proved this, and they attest to it. May God suffice you as witness; He is our Accountant, the Beneficent Trustee. There is no power save in God.

He sealed the letter and dispatched it to the Rūm people, to both commoners and nobility. Whenever his letter reached a noble, the noble hastened to accept its conditions [f. 146] and whenever he came upon a people, they hastened to bow before him. Soon he had gathered a Rūm army whose numbers reached one hundred fifty thousand and included their most valiant, noble and brave men. When they were before him, he honored them and treated them well in both word and action. They stayed with him for as long as God wished. They discussed matters amongst themselves and their consensus was to back Dhulqarnayn. Together they would undertake the jihad and fight. Dhulqarnayn sent for Aristotle, al-Khiḍr and Afshakhīr, and asked their advice. They advised him to set out on a campaign to wage holy war on Jerusalem.

'Abd al-Malik said that the first king Dhulqarnayn declared war against was Darius, King of Persia. The land of Persia was east of the capital city of the Rūm. Darius received news that Dhulqarnayn planned to attack the kings of the earth one by one, so he ordered the Persians to gather, and they were quick to obey [f. 147]. He asked their advice concerning the threat of Dhulqarnayn. An orator stood up among the crowd and said, "People! A Rūm boy has united men to attack us, but they are nothing but a bunch of thieves. What do you think we should do when he attacks?" They responded, "This is not an urgent affair, since

---

[82] Corruption of Arpachshad, son of Aram, son of Shem, son of Noah (*Genesis* 10:21). See Friedlaender 165, 175. Al-Ṭabarī states that "from the descendants of Arpachshad came the prophets and apostles and the Best of Mankind [i.e., Muhammad] and all the Pharoahs of Egypt" 2, 14.

he hasn't got the strength to fight us. We are the most powerful and the strongest. We will certainly fight him and our army will outnumber his."

When Darius heard them say this he said, "People! Prepare yourselves and get the supplies ready. When you meet them, attack. Be determined to win and grab the boy alone and bring him to me. You are warriors, clever, brave and strong. There is no excuse for you to be scared and run away from a small Rūm boy with no combat experience and no knowledge of how to run these affairs. So be on the lookout for him, and let all of you be of one mind." They answered, "Yes, sire. You are the one with power in these lands. A person like you cannot remain behind his soldiers, because soldiers have no valour except when they are led by their king. [f. 148]. Your capacity to cut down the enemy in battle is unrivaled among the Persian people. So get ready to sally forth with your nobles."

'Abd al-Malik al-Malshūnī said: I heard Muqātil say that Darius marched forward with all of his people until he came to a river called the Biṣwariṣ. Their numbers reached two hundred twenty thousand. When they had settled on the banks of the Biṣwariṣ, he wrote a letter to Dhulqarnayn:

> From Darius, King of Persia,
>
> To the thief Dhulqarnayn, and his companion thieves,
>
> God made me the guardian of his creation. He named me with his name and gave me the title of king and the highest status and nobility. I am the one who shines like the sun and the moon in the world. I see you have dominated countries and seas, traveled through mountains, and traversed the deserts and dry lands. You have even dared come to our country to destroy its lands and rule its people. I learned that you crowned yourself with a king's crown, and that you declared yourself to be independent, standing on your own two feet. Then you mobilized [f. 149] troops and came to destroy us. Go back to your country with your people and companions. I am above punishing you for this reckless act and I have forgiven you your error. Otherwise I will grab you for the insolence of having come here with a little band of men to challenge an army of uncountable numbers who cannot be defeated. O ye people of Rūm! Think about what you are up against, and the shame and humility you face. Act reasonably and look to save yourselves. You have come here with the intent to make war on us, but now you have seen what lies before you, which is the greatest sight of our age. I've warned you with my letter; let this be sufficient warning.
>
> God gives the best aid.

He sealed the letter and gave it to his messenger. He gave him a bag of sesame seeds, a pearl, a jewel, and a chest filled with gold [f. 150].

Once the letter reached Dhulqarnayn and he read it, he told them to detain the messenger and those with him. They removed their clothes, and shackled their hands behind their backs as if they were going to kill them. Then he said to them, "Don't blame me! Blame your companion who called me a thief. I'd like to do with you as a typical thief might do to someone he met by chance." Then one of the messengers said, "O Dhulqarnayn! Before we didn't know you and we didn't know what you stood for. But now we have learned how powerful you are, and what you stand for. You are distinguished in knowledge and magnificent in your power. Be liberal with your favor and grace and do not kill us. We'll go back to our people and our lands and inform Darius of what we have seen of your honor and kindness. We could be the best mediators between the two of you. It could be that the One who chose you will guide us all into your hands."

Dhulqarnayn was a compassionate man at heart. When he heard them begging him in such eloquent language, he said, "Rejoice! I agree with what you said about treating fairly all those who implore their Lord. At first I wanted to kill you [f. 151], but then I learned that messengers are not killed, so I pardoned you from being put to death. I wanted to demonstrate the graciousness and honor of the Rūm as opposed to the Persians. Now honor them, treat them well, and let them go on their way." When they were about to leave they wanted to tell Dhulqarnayn the way to attack Darius, and to inform him of how he could trick Darius, but he prohibited them from saying anything and responded, "I won't hear a word from you or receive any of your advice, for as good as it may be, because you plan on going back to your families and your king. Nobody is trying to harm us with a trick [sic]. By the grace of God, I can do without your words and your opinions."

When they heard that of him they were amazed and said, "O master! No woman has given birth to another like you. God has blessed you over all the rest of creation." Then he wrote a letter stating:

> In the name of God the most Compassionate and Merciful,
> From 'Abd Allah Dhulqarnayn b. Nabbāsh, king of the Rūm,
> [To the king of Persia],[83]
> [f. 152] I received your letter in which you mention bad words, because your soul has moved you to adorn language and to pursue the falseness of those that are lost, but the truth is you yourself possess all that you have mentioned. I heard that you believe that the armies of heaven are backing you and that the armies of the earth are afraid of your kingdom, and tremble with fear when they read your words. But you are the most vile and despicable of men, and the Blessed One is the Most Sublime and the Greatest, and He is far above helping his enemies against his supporters! I am not afraid of your numerous army, because God aids those who obey Him and humbles those who do not believe in Him. Verily, his aid is the best. For your tyranny and lies, you will not be triumphant in what you endeavor. I am not going to retreat from your lands, and we are not afraid to meet you in combat. I have with me God's army, the obedient ones from the honorable sons of the Rūm. They are quick to respond to calls for the higher cause, and triumphant over those who speak of only the lowest aspects of life. God endorses with his help whomever He wants [f. 153] and God is All-Powerful. You dared to call yourself by his name. He

[83] B:53r

> destroys all those who swell with pride. He withholds his gracious gifts and humbles the kingdoms and undermines the power of those who refuse to believe in his divine beneficence. God willing, I am coming to you on this very day with God's army consisting of the bravest, most noble sons of the Rūm people to attack you with an army that you cannot possibly defeat. I will not allow you to continue in your blindness. You seem to think that your death is not written. Understand my words so that you will know he who will finish you off. God is my backer against you. He is the greatest aid to those who obey Him.
>
> There is no power nor strength save in the Almighty God.

Upon finishing the letter, he grabbed a handful of the sesame seeds and threw them in his mouth and chewed them in front of the messengers. Then he wrote a second letter:

> I have seen everything that you have sent me and I have scorned it in the way one puts to flight a troublesome bird. As for the pearl, it is the whip of God's punishment for He has sent me to you as a sample of valor. He has appointed me to be [f. 154] your king, in accordance with his command and promise. As for the jewel, I hope that my deeds will shine as it shines. As for the coffer, I requested of my Lord that He bring together for me the best parts of the world and its kingdoms, just as the coffer holds this money. As for the sesame seeds, I looked at them, chewed them up and spit them out,[84] which, I swear, is just what I will do to your army: they are numerous but they have no fierceness or spice inside and they lack cleverness in battle. I will destroy you and your army as I've done with the sesame seeds. You sent the sesame to me so that I would know how numerous your army is, but the truth is that the greater their numbers the lesser the fervor of each soldier. You sent the jewel so as to show that your army is so strong there is no way to fight against it, and to show how your kingship shines, but ignorance will never shine in the presence of wisdom. You sent the jewel and likened it to your kingdom, which you claim encloses wisdom within it. But the key that opens the lock of ignorance is knowledge. God helps me against all those like you. With his support we will conquer your numerous army.

Then he called the messengers and gave them the gold [f. 155] that their tyrannical emir, Darius, had sent with them. Dhulqarnayn said to them, "Go knowing that God has become your friend."

After the messengers had seen what Dhulqarnayn had done with the sesame seeds, they thought he was a man of knowledge and conviction and they tried to bow before him to honor him before leaving. But he said to them, "Bow

---

[84] Both mss. A&B are corrupt here as they literally read "He chewed them up, spit them out and swallowed them."

before God. He is the One who created me and who created you and He is the One who raised me above your king."

When the messengers reached Darius and gave him the letter, he read it and found the bag of mustard seeds that Dhulqarnayn had sent along. Angrily, he grabbed a handful of mustard seeds and threw them in his mouth. When he chewed them, his mouth started to burn up from their spiciness and he spit it out and gulped water. He said, "Verily, Dhulqarnayn's army is numerous and they fight with a furor like the fire in the mustard seeds. But I am focusing all my attention on this matter, and I am determined to meet him in battle." Then he ordered his army to get ready for battle against Dhulqarnayn.

This news reached Dhulqarnayn, and he determined to attack Darius. Darius, in turn, learned that Dhulqarnayn was coming towards him. Both of them marched on until the two sides met in Iraq.

When the two armies were facing one another, Dhulqarnayn ordered the horns to be blown, and they blew the horns and the army marched faster. War broke out. The combat was so fierce that every soldier thought they were going to die there and then. Troops on both sides died from the wounds of lances and arrows. They fought all day long and called a ceasefire at night because they could no longer tell themselves apart. The battle lasted seven days and nobody on either side fled. The tremendous heroic acts and widespread death brought destruction on the people. On the last day, God's army with the power of the Almighty One managed to cut down the Persians from the rear. They charged them and their swords fell upon Darius' men from every which way and they were put to flight by the will of God. The sword chased them and the slaughter continued until they reached the land of Persia in retreat. There were so many killed that their numbers were uncountable.

When it was all over, Dhulqarnayn ordered that the dead [f. 157] among his men be properly buried. Then he ordered that the fallen Persians also be buried. He said, "Cover them with dirt." When this was done, Dhulqarnayn went out and collected the spoils of war in unimaginable quantities and divided it among his troops.

In the meanwhile, Darius had escaped with a band of his followers and together they safely reached the lands of Persia.

Concerning Dhulqarnayn's Journey to the Land of Katāba[85]

Dhulqarnayn determined to leave. He first entered the region of Mount Sinai. This is east of Mount al-Jūdi, when approaching it from the Karam mountains. He made camp there and captured many cities and came to an agreement with each of them to pay tribute for as much as was necessary to carry on the Holy War. So every year they paid him a tax. He made a pact with them and then left.

After leaving the land of Katāba and Mount Sinai, he headed to the land called Fadūma,[86] where he found a people unlike anything seen before with

[85] See Introduction, note 51.

regards to their physiognomy and the size of their bodies. They were called the Naqrūn [f. 158]. He wanted to fight them, but his policy was not to attack anyone without first calling them to the Almighty God's religion. If they surrendered without having to be forced, then he made an agreement with them to pay him tribute and taxes each year for the amount needed to carry on the holy war. The Fadūma made such an agreement.

Then he departed from there and came to a people called the al-Qaylūn[87] in the land of al-Qablī. They claim that from these people originates the human trait of wisdom. Dhulqarnayn called them to the religion of the Almighty God and they responded to his call so he made a pact with them to pay him tribute and tax every year.

When he left them he came to a land called Qadūmā,[88] which is towards where the Rūm people have their roots. They have a king there called Falaṣ, who is a stubborn, tyrannical, oppressive ruler. When the news of the approaching army reached the city, they closed the doors in fear of Dhulqarnayn, who ordered that the city be surrounded and that a seige be initiated. [f. 159] He also gave the order to kill any citizens of the city whom they should come upon. When they saw this, they said, "O Dhulqarnayn! We didn't close the doors because we wanted to fight you. Rather, we closed them because we were afraid of Darius. If we opened them for you, every last one of us would be annihilated."

Dhulqarnayn said, "Go ahead and open the doors to the city. I will not enter until God has helped me to triumph over Darius and your land becomes part of my kingdom. Do not be afraid of me. I have informed you and you know that I keep my promise to those who make a pact with me. My Lord would not have raised and exalted me above his other servants, and made me a leader, if I hadn't passed his tests to uphold the truth and fulfill my obligations to Him as king and sultan, always being thankful and a keeper of promises."

They opened the doors to the city and brought the markets out to his soldiers. He did not enter their city, as they had made a pact with him to uphold the truth. Then he left them and traveled to a city called Qasamṭīna [f. 160] in the land of Majrān on the border between the land of Sind and Persia. Soon thereafter the troops began to starve from lack of food. Their hunger was so severe it was killing all of his companions. So they ate their beasts, at which point Dhulqarnayn said to them, "Do not let this frighten you. Bear your hunger with patience; this is the work of God." After hearing this, they went back to eating their beasts. The shortage of food brought on great inflation. A loaf of bread that weighed sixteen ounces cost one dirham, which was the equivalent to a *dānaq*[89] of Dhulqarnayn's dirhams. Ten ounces of flour cost one dirham. Fifteen ounces of meat cost one dirham. A horse's head reached the price of one dinar. Due to these exorbitant prices, the troops and their horses suffered a terrible hunger.

Then Dhulqarnayn spoke to his men and said, "O people! I am aware of what you are experiencing, for I am experiencing the same. Let us travel behind

---

86 "Fīlā'm" in Mubashshir (p. 592).
87 "Faraq Ayliyūn" in Mubashshir (p. 592).
88 "Māqadhūniyā" in Mubashshir (p. 592)
89 a *dānaq*=1/6 of a dirham

this mountain, perhaps God will help us to find success [in our search for food]. Verily, He is the best help in finding a way out of difficult situation. Then he left that place [f. 161] and traveled to a city that they called Taṭūsh, where he found a temple. He asked the keeper of the temple to foretell what would become of him and the response was, "I will not tell you anything." Dhulqarnayn told him, "By God, if you don't tell me, we will burn down this temple and you will never again wear the vestments and robes of your priesthood."

His men quickly went to carry out his orders, when they heard a voice from the temple saying, "O Dhulqarnayn! Do not do this for you are from the Holy Land. Your deeds will be great. You will conquer all people throughout the world, and you will be remembered until Judgment Day."

When Dhulqarnayn heard this, his anger subsided and he ordered his men to give back what they had taken from the temple. Then he left there and traveled to the land of Amānīsh.

The Amānīsh were strong and powerful. They had eighty thousand soldiers. When news of Dhulqarnayn [f. 162] and his advent reached them, they closed the doors to their city and climbed the walls to the battlements and cried out, "O people of Dhulqarnayn! By God, you'll get nothing from us except fierce fighting, like nothing you've seen since you left your kingdom. So leave our city." Dhulqarnayn laughed and said, "If you only knew what would happen to you if you came out against us!"

He ordered his men to encircle the entire city. The archers stood ready with their arrows, and the cavalry with their lances and swords. When they saw that they came out with one hundred thousand soldiers and war broke out between the two armies. Men charged one another and there rang out a great clamor. The battle was fierce and many lost their lives. Dhulqarnayn encircled the enemy army. As his men fought with great bravery the seige grew tighter. When they saw this they were certain that he would soon crush them, and they knew that there was nothing they could do to stop Dhulqarnayn.

Since they were [f. 163] beneath the crown of Darius, King of Persia, they hastened to send a letter saying, "Come and meet Dhulqarnayn in battle, or we will surrender our lands to him, and open the doors to our city."

That city was in the kingdom of Persia, so that when the news reached Darius he had no choice but to meet Dhulqarnayn in battle. He ordered the troops to gather and seven hundred thousand horsemen came out to him and about the same number of infantry. News of this reached Dhulqarnayn, and he went out to meet the Persians. The battle was fierce and the number of dead multiplied on both sides.

Darius was knowledgeable of military strategems, but Dhulqarnayn was more knowledgeable. If it seemed that one of them would be victorious, the other would come forward with a trick. Whenever Dhulqarnayn charged with a squadron of horses, Darius met him with the same number of horses. The killing spread and the battle continued [f. 164]. The combat intensified and the perdition increased on both sides. Bones were cut by the edge of the sword and a cloud of death descended upon the field. The fighting went on from sunrise to sunset and blood flowed like a river from both lines. By the end of the day, the Persian soldiers were defeated as well as their notables. One after another they ran them through with the sword until the Persians were finished.

When Darius saw the battle had claimed the lives of all his mighty warriors, on whom he depended, he was very frightened and fled into the wilderness with a group made up of nobles from his tribe and Persia. He escaped scared and fearful of Dhulqarnayn and his companions. Dhulqarnayn did not concern himself with looting until the Persian king and his followers were killed. They proceeded in that manner. He said, "Kill them and you may take all you want from them." And they pursued them with the sword. Darius persisted in his escape until he reached [f. 165] the Ṭīrqān River, which is a great river that comes down from the city of Rome. Its banks are steep and there are few paths to access the river. Darius could not find a safe passage and the Rūm horses were quickly drawing near. The Persians threw themselves into the river and the common people, wounded and dying, sank. Dhulqarnayn reached there. He and his men stood on one bank of the river, and Darius on the other. Dhulqarnayn called to him, "O misguided, lost and ignorant king! Look at the state you are in: your army has perished and your kingdom has been devastated by your own hand. O you of the vile mind! Believe in God, the One who created you. Surrender yourself to Him. Save yourself from the trickery of the world and the Hereafter."

Darius replied, "O obedient one and invincible opponent in battle! Turn back your soldiers and cease your brave assault against us. I have no choice after this but to surrender to you, so let your kindness and generosity be upon us, and in your wisdom accept my proposal. Withdraw your troops and I myself will come to you [f. 166] with the Persian nobles that are here with me."

Dhulqarnayn accepted these terms and turned his troops back, and Darius escaped to his royal palaces. He entered a temple, and locked the doors behind him. All alone, he wept for the ruin of his kingdom. Remembering how exalted and powerful he had been, he wept bitterly. Then he thought about what he was going to do and he warned himself. He said, "I'll never save myself from Dhulqarnayn unless I believe in his Lord and agree to be his slave for the rest of his life, which is a judgment that God has granted to us kings. But then he is generous when it comes to granting favors, and possesses a great capacity to forgive; certainly he'll be one to keep his word." He determined to surrender and wrote a letter to Dhulqarnayn:

> In the name of God the most Compassionate and Merciful,
> To the powerful king,
> From his servant Darius,
> God the Almighty has given you victory, made you triumphant, provided you with a kingdom and made you leader over all the kings of the world. So return to me my family with my daughter and my brother and send them back to me assuring their safety and I will open for you the Persia treasures of Nabūrān [f. 167] amassed by the Persian kings. I'll give you their treasures and all that my grandfathers, my father, and I have accumulated. You will have me beneath your watch, in your power, to guard you against your enemies. Peace be to you.

Then he folded the letter and gave it to his messengers and they delivered it to Dhulqarnayn. Dhulqarnayn read the letter and understood its purpose. On the day of the defeat, he had captured Darius' brother, and now he was returning him along with his daughter, his wife, and his mother. When he finished reading the letter, he wanted to honor Darius' requests and faithfully comply with all that Darius had mentioned. Dhulqarnayn wrote to him:

> Verily, you should have told me these things before war broke out. You would have saved yourself the deception. Come here and you will find safety and protection.

The messengers said to him, "You speak the truth, Dhulqarnayn!" He ordered a proper burial for those Persians that had not been buried, and to the prisoners he promised to be charitable and set them free.

Then [f. 168] Darius wrote a letter to Labūr, King of India, to ask for assistance against Dhulqarnayn:

> In the name of God, to Labūr, the Greatest of Kings,
>
> I am writing to you at a time when my days have come to an end, and my kingdom has ceased to exist, and another king has taken my lands. Be kind to me and come to my aid. Dhulqarnayn has conquered and defeated me. He has killed my men and defeated my bravest warriors. I assailed him from every angle possible and threatened him with every war strategem I know,[90] but he entered our land only to destroy us. I beg of you to help me with your awesome power so that together we can demolish him and drive his army back out of my lands. I have no choice but to go out and meet him in battle again, because death is preferable to me than to live through what has befallen me. Show your kindness to me and come to my aid with a huge army and attack he who is treating me unjustly. Hurry, I'm already waiting for you. I have set up camp along the border of your land and I'll go out to attack him with your army and [f. 169] what army I have left. I'm waiting. Whichever of your troops arrive here will become wealthy. If I defeat him, you will get half of the spoils I take from him and the land tax. But if he is victorious, I fear that what has befallen me will soon be heading your way. Be sure of that. Peace be upon you.

He sealed the letter, gave it to his messenger and sent him off with a present. When Darius's letter reached Labūr, King of India, Dhulqarnayn was at that time to the east of the lands of the Mansik tribe, from whom come the most powerful Persian nobles and kings.

Abū 'Abd al-Malik al-Malshūni said: Once Dhulqarnayn had wiped out the king of Persia he determined to leave there. He departed east towards Jābarṣā.

---

[90] The meaning of two or three words in Arabic here is not clear to me.

Concerning Dhulqarnayn's Journey to the City of Jābarṣā

Abū 'Abd al-Malik al-Malshūnī said: Dhulqarnayn departed from the islands of the Mansik and the Bārish tribes [f. 170] and left behind the islands of the snakes. Traveling through the seas, he stayed his course towards whatever lay ahead. As he marched over the waters, God shortened the distances for him and made it easier for him to come near his destination. He traveled ten days and nights and traversed a distance equal to a journey of ten years. In the depths of the sea he drew near the city of Jābarṣā. As he approached he saw it was one of the largest cities in the world. It was located in open country on an island like the Western Islands. The city had ten thousand doors with a distance between each door of three parasangs. Some knowledgeable people will accent the third syllable of the word instead of the first. Each door had seventy thousand soldiers; half of the archers carried crossbows and the other half had simple bows. From each door one hundred thousand people exited to conduct their business and the same number entered to attend to whatever they needed to do and to go to the markets.

In the narrative of Ibn 'Abbās, may God be satisfied with him, it says that when Ṣāliḥ [f. 171], bless him, settled in the town of al-Ḥaram he found a fertile land. He ordered his people, who believed as he did, to claim for themselves a place to live. They built houses and planted trees, and made rivers to run. They erected buildings and more buildings and castles, and held firmly to the religion of Islam. Then he left with his people to Mecca, where he stayed for some time. Ṣāliḥ would come preaching and calling upon them to be compassionate and forgiving, and he would sit with them, firm in his religion. Nearby there were the remaining followers of Ḥūd, bless him. When God destroyed the people of 'Ād with a terrible wind,[91] he spared a group of Ḥūd's people. Seventy men, all believers, left with Ḥūd, bless him. When Ḥūd died, bless him, they left for the land of Palestine. They stopped near al-Ḥijāz, and became Ṣāliḥ's neighbors, bless him [f. 172]. Ṣāliḥ used to come to them in the morning, and they would pray with him and strictly follow his religion. When Ṣāliḥ passed away, bless him, some people from Ḥūd's tribe went to see Ṣāliḥ's tribe, and they spoke to one another, "The prophet of God, Ḥūd, has died and Ṣāliḥ too, bless them. It is not advisable for us to stay in a land without a prophet to guide us and show us the path of the righteous. We are scared that we will disobey God the Almighty and that what happened to those who preceded us will befall us as well."

So the believers in Ḥūd left there and went west and settled where the city of Jābalqā is located. Once they were established, the Almighty God made their progeny grow. They built the city, erected it, and gave it ten thousand doors. Between each of the doors there was a distance of three parasangs, although some

---

[91] Al-Ṭabarī also mentions this wind: "God employed it against them for seven long nights and eight days. It left no one alive of 'Ād, whereas Hūd and those believers who were with him hid themselves in an enclosure." *The History of al-Ṭabarī*, 2, 36. The destruction of 'Ād by the wind is also in the Qur'ān 69:7.

put the accent on the third syllable instead of the first. Ten thousand men guard each of these doors, and each man serves his duty only once. They built the houses and the castles, and made rivers to flow, and planted trees [f. 173] and led a devout life. These people were the Nāsik, and they were the progeny of seventy men from among the believers in Ḥūd, bless him. When Ṣāliḥ's people saw that Ḥūd's people had gone west, they said, "The only thing left for us to do is to depart to the far east, where there is a city they call Jābarṣā." Ṣāliḥ's people amounted to eighty men. When they settled there, they stayed for some time and the Almighty God made their progeny grow and their offspring multiply. They built on that spot a city called Barṣā. They made it with ten thousand doors, with a distance of three parasangs between each door, although some knowledgeable people put the accent on the third syllable instead of the second. They built houses, planted trees, and made rivers to flow. These were the Mansik, and they are the people of these two cities, whose numbers exceed those of the Gog and Magog. When God sent the Prophet, God bless him and grant him salvation, and he came forth, they believed in him, and he called them to Islam [f. 174]. They received him favorably, believed in him and placed their faith in him. The faithful among them were with the faithful in Muhammad's tribe and the polytheists among them were with the polytheists in Muhammad's tribe. But God knows best!

Let us return to the narration of 'Abd al-Malik al-Malshūnī. 'Abd al-Malik al-Malshūnī said: When Dhulqarnayn's army came upon them and they heard the horns and saw the banners, they hastened to gather and lock the doors thinking that it was their enemy, the people of Jābalqā, attacking them. They were so scared of the people of Jābalqā that they were unable to sleep. Terror set in their hearts from the thought of their ferocity. But they rushed out to meet them bearing arms and ballasts. When Dhulqarnayn saw this he ordered his men to stay put and he sent ahead a letter saying:

> In the name of God the most Compassionate and Merciful,
> From 'Abd Allah Dhulqarnayn,
> To the people of the city of Jābarṣā,
> Peace [f. 175] be to those who follow the path of the righteous, fear the consequences of what is to come, and readily obey He who is the Highest of the High.
>
> We write to you calling you to obey your Creator, to make his laws your laws, and to confess his divine oneness. If you obey Him, you will be like us and have the things we have. But if you are rebellious, and try to tyrannize us, and follow the path of error, and persist in your evil practices, then you will know the war of God and his messenger, for we are coming to you with an army so large their numbers are unimaginable. God aids he who He wants, and He gives guidance to those who repent.

He sealed the letter and gave it to a group of his soldiers, who took it straight away to where the opposing army was. When they reached there, the people quickly gathered around and there was a great clamor of voices. The soldiers delivered the letter, and they took it to their king and nobles. They opened the letter and found that it began, "In the name of God, the most Compassionate and Merciful." They knew immediately that it was not from their Jābalqān enemies. The messengers, who were well received, were asked whether [f. 176] Dhulqarnayn was a king or a prophet. They said, "He is a just king and a saintly prophet who carries the will of the Almighty God. He will not do injustice to anyone. Dhulqarnayn will not wage war before demanding first obedience of God's word. For that reason we have been sent to ask you to obey and to believe in God. If you choose not to, then war will fall upon you which you cannot sustain." The king of the people said, "Go back to Dhulqarnayn and ask him if he will see me. I would like to meet him." This was done and the king went to see Dhulqarnayn.

Both parties greeted each other warmly. After the exchange of proper greetings, Dhulqarnayn asked the people of Jābarṣā which tribes they descended from. They replied that they were of Tārish descent, through the son of Yāfit, b. Noah, may peace be upon him. Dhulqarnayn asked them why they live on the island. They answered [f. 177], "It was the will of God." Dhulqarnayn asked if they recognized their Creator and Benefactor? They replied. "How could we not? He saved us from our enemies, the people of Jābalqā. He granted us evidence regarding the path of the righteous, and we maintained the religion of our grandfather, Noah, bless him. He led us from the darkness unto the light by sending you to us. When you arrived we were frightened and in despair. Your army came through the Ocean and we thought you were our enemy, the people of Jābalqā. News of your advent did not reach us until your letter arrived. As for your question regarding how we came to this island, we sailed the seas by God's command with our brothers from the tribe of Yāfit b. Noah. We stayed our course and, eventually, without ever intending to, ended up on this island. It was our forefathers who came here, and waited for their brothers, first for one year, then two, and soon it was twenty years. They [f. 178] waited and waited to be reunited[92] *with our brothers. Everything we planted in the earth, as if by some miracle, grew and multiplied. Our forefathers continued in this manner until they finally gave up all hope for [B: f. 64r] their brothers." They were all descendants of Yāfit b. Noah. From them, Dhulqarnayn learned of all that their forefathers wrote and did in the city: how they built it, inhabited it and lived there.*

Dhulqarnayn asked the total number of their population. They replied that they have thousands of warriors. Every gate to the city is guarded every night by a thousand guards. Once the guards complete their turn, they never again serve guard duty. Dhulqarnayn asked, "How do you manage to keep track of that?" They replied, "Each gate has an administrator who writes down everyone's name when it is their turn to guard the gates. So they know." Dhulqarnayn asked them about their king. "It was Jalaṣ b. Falaṣ," they replied. "How old are you?" Dhulqarnayn asked him. "One thousand and eighty years," he replied. "What is your religion?" "I believe in the oneness of God the Almighty." "How are you governed?" They replied that their governor is concise in speech, just in government, [f. 64v] and is merciful to the poor and righteous; our people also

[92] The scribe of A has inadvertently omitted here a substantial passage. The text marked in italics is from Ms. B.

rely on God who never dies. "How do you live in this city?" Dhulqarnayn asked. "We live comfortably and are content. We have enough fruit and enough food. Our bodies are covered by leaves from the trees." "What are your houses like?" Dhulqarnayn asked. "We live in castles, in caves, boxes, and vessels." "Why?" Dhulqarnayn asked. "Because of the sun. When it is hot, we enter the caves to avoid the heat. We then move to higher residences and decorative rooms until the sunset when we re-enter the caves and boxes." "Why do your faces and heads have no hair?" "It fell out from the heat," the king replied. "How long do you live?" Dhulqarnayn asked. "Some of us are one thousand years old, some two thousand, and others in between." [f. 65r] Dhulqarnayn then asked them about their belief in God. They believed and were truthful in their belief. Dhulqarnayn asked, "From where does the sun rise?" "From behind that mountain." Dhulqarnayn walked and stood on the mountain looking down at the city. Two thirds of the city spread over the mountainside and was very well protected. Dhulqarnayn stood on the edge of the mountain and looked at the sun and how it rose over them. There was nothing between him and the sun to protect the people of the city from the heat. In this respect, God the Almighty has said, "Until, when he came to the rising of the sun, he found it rising on a people for whom We had provided no covering protection against the sun."[93] *Dhulqarnayn asked about the neighboring lands, and they responded, "Dhulqarnayn, God sent our fathers to this island across the seas just as He guided you to us. We do not know anything about the world except that which we have seen. [f. 65v] There is in this part of the world, near the setting sun, a darkness.[94] We have seen it but we haven't traveled there or ever come near."*

Dhulqarnayn said goodbye to them and departed for he wanted to see the darkness which they had mentioned to him.

Concerning Dhulqarnayn's [Preparations for the] Journey to the Darkness[95]

'Abd al-Malik said: When Dhulqarnayn heard the news of the darkness, he was impressed, and determined to see it. So he departed from the people of Jābarṣā and walked on land until he stopped at a place that God the Almighty had designated for him. He implored God to inform him about the darkness. Soon thereafter, as he stood alone, the angel Zayāqīl came down and greeted him. He returned the greeting and said, "My beloved Zayāqīl! You promised me that God would aid me with things as long as I serve him devoutly and obey him rightfully. This darkness that the people of Jābarṣā mentioned to me, and that I see ahead, what wonders does it contain?" The angel Zayāqīl said, "O Dhulqarnayn! I was in the company of God's angels [B: f. 66r] in heaven and one of them said that the Almighty One possesses a darkness that no king, however pious, or prophet sent

---

[93] Qur'ān 18:90

[94] Probably the land of the darkness referred to in the PC, book ii, chap. 37 (Müller, p. 88).

[95] According to an Ethiopic Alexander legend, the darkness is in Arabia. In addition to veiling the Fountain of Life, the darkness is said to be "the blackness of thick darkness wherein is hidden the storehouse of His knowledge." Cf. Budge (1896), p. 261.

upon the earth, has ever traveled through. In it is the Fountain of Life. Another of the angels then asked if this darkness containing the Fountain of Life was the one in the east or the west. Another responded that between the eastern and western ends of the earth there is only one darkness, which is located near sunrise. An angel observed that the darkness takes forty years to pass through. Within it there is a stream of running water that is the Fountain of Life—anyone that drinks its water or performs the ritual ablutions in it will be granted immortality by God until Judgment Day."

So Dhulqarnayn left that place and traveled until he came near the darkness. He saw that it extended from the heavens down to the earth, and he was unable to discern an end to the darkness lengthwise or widthwise. It was an intense [96] [f. 178] black like nothing he had seen on earth, if not a tightly locked house or dungeon. Dhulqarnayn stopped nearby and his soldiers made camp in a land that was cultivated, sandy, hospitable and vaster than the region of Jābarṣā. He knew that between him and the darkness there were no people from the Banī Adam, except those who were in the city of Jābarṣā.

He asked and implored his Lord to send down to him Zayāqīl, the one who would come to him with revelation. So God sent the angel Zayāqīl. Dhulqarnayn said to him, "O Zayāqīl! Does God possess a darkness on earth that is hidden from his creatures?" "Yes." "Is it what I see in front of me?" "Yes." "What is the distance between me and it?" "It would take twelve years to walk there from the place from which you are now looking at it." "Do any of the Banī Adam live between here and there?" "No, this is the end [f. 179] of civilization. From here in the direction of Jābarṣā to the end of the world it would take fifty years to walk: forty years would be in the darkness and ten in the light. This is the most remote settlement of the children of Adam." Dhulqarnayn asked him, "Has anyone ever conquered it?" "No man or jinn, nor king nor demon, has ever conquered it, and the only one who knows what it contains within is the One the All-Powerful." Dhulqarnayn asked, "Why did God hide it from his creatures?" "Because it contains the Fountain of Life, which I mentioned to you." Dhulqarnayn asked, "Where is it located in the darkness and how do we get there?" "It is in the middle. You walk the first half, which takes twenty years, and then you also walk the second half, which also takes twenty years." Dhulqarnayn said, "Are there mountains in it?" "There are no mountains or sea or trees. It is nothing but white sandy flat land consisting of an arable reddish soil." He asked [f. 180], "How wide is the land?" "The land extends to Mount Qāf, the one that surrounds the world." Dhulqarnayn said, "If I crossed through the darkness and came out the other side, would that land be in the darkness or in the light?" "It borders the sea of darkness and is actually in the light but with a veil of shadow." "Is there sunlight?" The angel Zayāqīl said to him, "There is no sunlight." "How is it that there is daylight but no sun?" "It is not in the path of the sun; the mountain God used to anchor the earth is a very high mountain and blocks the sun from reaching that land. So there is daylight but no sun." Dhulqarnayn said to the angel, "Go, may God reward you on behalf of a friend."

---

[96] We return here to Ms. A, line 1.

The angel left and Dhulqarnayn went back to his army and said, "Bring me the wisemen," and one thousand Rūm wise men gathered before him. He asked them, "Do any of you know what is between us and the end of the world?" They responded, "We know nothing of this" [f. 181]. But one of them, who was called Afshakhīr said, "Sire! From what I know, between you and the end of the world is a distance walked in twelve years, a fact which I am able to pass on to you because Adam, bless him, mentioned to his son, Seth,[97] bless him, that God has a darkness that He concealed from his creatures, whose length would take forty years to walk. Between it and the Banī Adam is a distance equivalent to a journey of twelve years. No man or jinn has ever entered it." Dhulqarnayn said to him, "O Afshakhīr! Is it like the night or like smoke?" "Not like night nor like smoke. But rather it is a darker black than that. Nobody could enter any part of it without dying from the intensity of that darkness." Dhulqarnayn said to him, "What is behind it?" "A white sandy land from which no mountains rise." "Does the sun shine there?" "No. There is no sun. Rather, God has concealed it from his creatures." "Around the perimeter are there mountains?" "Yes. [f. 182] There are high and elevated mountains that surround the earth, just like a ring or a circle. With those mountains, God anchored the earth. They are so high that even when the sun reaches its peak, the mountaintops come between the earth and the sun. He said, "Why did God veil it from his creatures?" "Because the Fountain of Life is in it." Dhulqarnayn asked, "Who mentions this Fountain of Life?" "Seth, bless him, said that the fountain is in the middle of that darkness." Dhulqarnayn said to him, "What did he say about the water of that fountain?" "It is whiter than yogurt, sweeter than honey, and its aroma is more pleasant than musk."

'Abd al-Malik al-Malshūnī said: [In his answers] he coincided with what the angel Zayāqīl had said, without adding or taking away anything. Dhulqarnayn said [f. 183], "O Afshakhīr! You are the most knowledgeable person on earth! And you are the most knowledgeable person of your time since what you say is comparable to what the angels say. Truly, you are of tremendous worth to us. Give me your opinion." Afshakhīr said to him, "Tell me what you want to know?" "I want to ask you about the darkness, and what wonders it contains, so that I might write about them in a book that people in later ages will marvel about."[98] Afshakhīr said, "You will not be able to do that." "Why?" "It is of a blackness so intense that you cannot even see the palm of your hand in it. I am afraid that your entering it will not please God. I am afraid that it is something God veiled from his creatures and their eyes. I am afraid it will make God mad." Dhulqarnayn said, "I must do this." Afshakhīr said, "Fear God, O Dhulqarnayn!

---

[97] From Budge (1896): "O Matun, hast thou any knowledge of this darkness and of the Well of the water of Life?" And he replied, "Yea, I will tell thee truly the history thereof." And the Two-horned said to him, "Tell it to me." And Matun said unto him, "I have read in the 'Book of Life,' that is to say, the 'Book of Creation,' which is called 'El-Musika,' that is to say, the 'Book of the Law of the Histories of Books," that God Almighty hath a place of darkness on earth, the knowledge of which is hidden" (p. 264). Al-Tha'labī (p. 367) relates that this knowledge comes from a book called 'Adam's Commandments' or 'Adam's Testament': قرأت وصية أدم عليه السلام فوجدت فيها أن الله خلق فى الأرض ظلمة.

[98] This would be Alexander's "The Book of the Works of the Whole World" mentioned in Budge (1896), p. 288. See above note to f. 181.

I am afraid [f. 184] that you and your soldiers, and all the people who accompany you will be destroyed, and God will use your transgression of his law as a lesson to the people of the world and they will suffer great affliction." But Dhulqarnayn said, "I must enter it."

Muqātil said: Dhulqarnayn was a brave man who was not scared of anything. Dhulqarnayn continued to question the wise man, "O Afshakhīr! Which beasts see best in the darkness?" "Horses." "Which type of horse is strongest and most powerful?" "Mares which have not copulated with stallions."

Dhulqarnayn gave the order to gather them and this was done. Then he chose from them five thousand horses, all of them virgins, twelve thousand from the region of Jābarṣā, none of which had copulated with stallions. From the rest of the regions of the world he chose six thousand. He also summoned the noblest people among his hosts to accompany him. From the region of Jābarṣā he chose six thousand men of the strongest, bravest, most determined, valiant, and powerful Jābarṣāns. From the remaining regions of the world he chose another six thousand of the same class of noble and brave men. Dhulqarnayn desired for them [f. 185] to live forever just as he would upon drinking from the fountain's water. He would rule the earth with them for the rest of his life. So he said, "Prepare to leave for the darkness, with God's blessing. Let us wish for the best of his help towards our success." Afshakhīr complained, "O king! We'll go in there but how will we get out? I swear by God that if we enter we will never come out." Dhulqarnayn replied, "Bring al-Khiḍr to me."

Al-Khiḍr was a very knowledgeable, righteous and noble man, one who did good among the Rūm people. So they summoned him and Dhulqarnayn said to him, "You will lead us throughout our expedition. Now go to the head of the column, with the Almighty God's blessing." "Where are we going?" He said, "I want to go into this darkness." "Fear God, Dhulqarnayn! Do not go places that God has forbidden. I am afraid we will all die by following you." "I must enter. Look. I've got something that will guide us [f. 186] on our way out, God willing." He took out a jeweled white bead that lit up like a star shining in the heavens.

'Abd al-Malik al-Malshūnī said that he asked Muqātil b. Sulaymān what this bead was, and what it was made of, and Muqātil told him that it was the one Adam brought down from heaven, which prophets inherit. It was passed down to Aristotle and he gave it to Dhulqarnayn when he became king saying, 'Take this bead and if you need it, it will light up the darkness and guide you on land and sea through the darkness.' Muqātil continued by saying that one of the knowledgeable people he had met said, "It is the bead which was given to Noah, bless him, so that he would know the prayer times, and it was passed down until it reached Ismael, after Abraham. Then it came down to Esau, and it remained through the reign of his son [f. 187], and was passed from one generation to the next, down through the ages, until it reached Dhulqarnayn."

Dhulqarnayn said to al-Khiḍr, "Take this bead; it will light up the darkness, God willing. Use it to guide me." Al-Khiḍr had no choice but to obey Dhulqarnayn. Al-Khiḍr led with six thousand horses, and Dhulqarnayn followed with another six thousand. Others say that the party that accompanied him into the darkness consisted of six thousand led by al-Khiḍr including two thousand horses, and Dhulqarnayn followed with four thousand horses. The first figure is the more accurate. Dhulqarnayn ordered the soldiers that stayed behind to "hold your position until twelve years have passed." If he had not returned by then, he added, "Go back to your countries. Your leader will be Laṭīqūn, so listen to him and obey him, for he is the most judicious among God's creatures. He will return you to your countries with the will of God, who is the One who disposes of matters as He pleases [f. 188]. There is no God but He, the Creator of all things."

He left his army in inhabited and cultivated lands with abundant waters, enjoying many comforts. He departed from there with one of the two figures mentioned above. God knows which of the horses was the oldest and best.

Concerning Dhulqarnayn's Journey to the Island of the Darkness

Abū 'Abd al-Malik said: Dhulqarnayn and al-Khiḍr entered the darkness at the head of the cavalry and marched quickly. In twelve days they traversed a distance equivalent to a journey of twelve years. When they were almost there, and his companions began to see the darkness, they got scared and became frightened. The darkness rose before them like high mountains. Al-Khiḍr, bless him, was leading them when Dhulqarnayn came to him. Al-Khiḍr said, "What should I do, great king? It is our duty to obey the imam, as God has commanded [f. 189]." "Put the bead on the tip of your lance and raise it up high so that the soldiers can see it. It will guide us like a star in the heavens." Al-Khiḍr, bless him, did as he was told and led the men as they gathered around. Thus al-Khiḍr overcame the darkness and the soldiers followed behind him, able to watch the bead in the midst of darkness. They followed him and the light split open the darkness like the stars the heavens. They marched on in this way through the darkness for twenty days without sleeping or stopping. But God shortened the way for them, and in a journey of twenty days they covered a distance equal to a journey of twenty years. When he had gone twenty days, God sent revelation to al-Khiḍr, bless him. This was because he was an honorable prophet. Gabriel came to him, bless him, and said, "O Khiḍr! In the darkness there is only one river and you are close to it [f. 190]. In the river there is a well. It is the only water there, since the riverbed is dry and filled with sand and gravel."

At this time, the people were behind him at a distance of about one half mile. Nobody was with him. He walked until he came to the river. The bead had now disappeared from sight, and the people had stopped in their tracks, thinking that something had happened to him. He was gone. Dhulqarnayn and his companions were lost, and they stood waiting for the bead to appear. They were terrified of the darkness. Al-Khiḍr had said, "Stay put until I return." He walked and stopped at the well. He did the ritual ablutions and drank from it, beneath the light of the bead. Meanwhile, the people peered into the darkness, hoping the bead would appear, as time passed slowly.

In another narration, Dhulqarnayn and his companions stood looking for the bead for a long time [f. 191] until they said to him, "O Dhulqarnayn! Al-Khiḍr is gone and we are afraid we are going to die." He replied, "People, be strong and do not be afraid. What is keeping him away is certainly only some current in the river. Stay put so that you do not get lost." Meanwhile, al-Khiḍr found the water and did the ritual ablutions. When he kneeled and drank, he found the water to be just as Gabriel,[99] bless him, told him it would be. Then he took the bead and walked with it through the current in the river until he reached his horse. He put the bead back on the tip of his lance, rode, and left the bank of the river. Soon the bead appeared to the people and they followed it. Then the people said to Dhulqarnayn, "Great friend of God! We hope that al-Khiḍr, God willing, will guide us." Dhulqarnayn looked at the light of the bead and said, "The light is coming from the riverbed and it is moving away from us." So they went after it, and marched quickly in pursuit until they came to the riverbed. Word spread among them and they said, "There is no doubt that al-Khiḍr, when he left [f. 192] us, was at this riverbed. Certainly, Dhulqarnayn, this is the middle of the darkness that the angel Zāyāqīl and Afshakhīr referred to when they said that there was only one river in the darkness." Dhulqarnayn said to his companions, "Hurry, let's get out of this darkness."

Al-Khiḍr passed by them, having fulfilled the purpose that God had intended for him throughout his life. Indeed, it had been written in God's Book that he and no other would bathe in the Fountain of Life. Al-Khiḍr moved to the front and the troops were guided by the light of the bead. They walked for another twenty days. Upon leaving the darkness they had spent forty days within.

When they came out they found themselves in a sandy white land, with no elevation in the terrain or visible topographical deviations. They walked in the daylight twelve days and walked on. By the end of their twentieth day they saw a castle built tall with a light shining from an opening in the ground near to which there were no buildings. They walked towards it until they came to the castle's grounds. There the soldiers stopped and Dhulqarnayn ordered them to stay put until he returned [f. 193].

Concerning the Wonders Dhulqarnayn Saw in the Castle

Abū 'Abd al-Malik said: Then Dhulqarnayn marched on until he approached the castle. He assessed its width to be three parasangs and its length to be the same. The building itself was one of the best he had ever seen. He kept circling the castle until he found the door and entered. Inside he found an iron beam circling the entire castle, from one end to the other. And there was a bird similar to a sort of swallow hanging from the iron beam by its legs with its head suspended close to the ground. When Dhulqarnayn came up to it, the bird said, "O Dhulqarnayn! Wasn't it enough to see all the wonders you've seen and all the countries through which you have passed? Now you have to enter a place which no man or jinn has ever seen, as it is reserved for angels? What is it that has brought you here?" Dhulqarnayn looked at it, with its nose wrinkled and its long head, and it was blacker [f. 194] than [any bird] anybody had ever seen in the

[99] Note that Gabriel is the angel who intercedes between al-Khiḍr and God. It is an indication that al-Khiḍr was a true prophet. Raphael appears to Dhulqarnayn because he is not prophet but 'friend of God,' ولي الله .

world. Its head was underneath the iron beam. Dhulqarnayn responded, "My Lord brought me here because He wanted someone to fulfill his command, and for that purpose I came, and He is the One whose dictums are carried out." He continued, "Great bird, imprisoned by God's command, tell me your story." The bird said to him, "O Dhulqarnayn! Are there many sinners among the Israelites?" He answered, "Yes." And the bird swelled and filled a third of the castle. Then the bird turned to him and said, "O Dhulqarnayn! Are there many adulterers, suicides, and people of libertine practices?" "Yes." And the bird swelled a second time and filled another third of the castle and asked, "Do people of the tribe of Israel attest to falsehood and stone chaste woman?" "Yes." And the bird swelled a third time and filled the entire castle, leaving no place for Dhulqarnayn to stand. He got scared and a great fear filled him. The bird said to him, "The Promised Day is near, have Adam's people built mosques?" "Yes." "Do they do the principal ablutions to cleanse themselves from ritual impurity?" [f. 195] "Yes." And the bird shrunk by one third. The bird asked, "Do they make the hajj and the minor pilgrimage and utter the name of God in the houses?" "Yes." "Do they take the most sacred oath by swearing against their children's Muslim upbringing and against their protection from what is sinful?" "Yes." And then it shrunk again and filled one third of the castle and said, "O Dhulqarnayn! Is there usury and the taking of illicit profits?" ["Yes."] And then it swelled and filled another third of the castle and said, "Do they violate their pacts and do they spill blood?" "Yes." And then it swelled and filled the entire castle to such an extent that it became visible to people standing outside. The bird said, "O Dhulqarnayn! Tell me about what I am going to ask you." Dhulqarnayn said, "Ask me about whatever you want." He said, "Have people stopped saying 'There is no God but Allah'?" "No. With this testimony I have entered many countries and come to this place, and for the sake of this testimony [f. 196] I have killed and will continue to kill the people of the earth." The bird said, "Have people abandoned the prescribed prayer?" "No." Then the bird shrank one third and asked, "Have people abandoned the ablutions against ritual impurities?" "No." Then the bird got smaller and shrank until it was again its original size and it said, "O Dhulqarnayn! Go up the stairs, for waiting at the top is something very good for you and something that will save you from what you are pursuing."

Dhulqarnayn looked and there were stairs leading from the bottom to the top of the castle. He ascended the stairs until he reached the top of the castle. There was a large terrace above the castle, high in the sky, as if it was equal in elevation to tall mountains, like the ones God used to anchor the earth. It was such that it commanded a view of nearly all the countries in the world. He looked out upon the terrace and saw a boy whose beauty surpassed that of all men. He was wearing white clothes. His stance was with one foot forward and the other behind [f. 197]. He was looking at a horn that he had placed in his mouth. Then with one eye he fixed his gaze on Dhulqarnayn, and with the other he looked out up into the sky, without ever blinking. He was waiting for the command to be given to blow the horn. When he realized Dhulqarnayn[100] was standing there he said, "Who is it?" "It is Dhulqarnayn." "O Dhulqarnayn, wasn't what you've

[100] The text is in the first person here, i.e., "when he realized I was standing there..."

seen of the world till now enough? You had to come here to see me?" Dhulqarnayn replied, "Who are you?" "I am an angel. If you want to see what the horn blower looks like, then look at me, for I am he. I stand waiting for the order to be given to blow the trumpet.[101] What do you want from this land? Is it that you would like to extend your kingdom to the angels of heaven, whom God, with his blessing, has veiled from the view of his chosen creatures?" Dhulqarnayn said to him, "God forbid, great angel!" The angel asked, "Is there anything you need?" "Yes. Our provisions have run out and we are weak and afraid that we will die in this darkness." He said, "Take this and thank your Lord [f. 198]. It will feed you and all those with you until you leave the darkness and reach your army. It is a bunch of grapes."[102] Dhulqarnayn asked, "Will it be sufficient provision for everyone?" "Yes, by the power of the Almighty God." Dhulqarnayn said, "This is truly something great!" Then he took a grape and ate it. He felt full and his appetite was satiated. In place of the grape another appeared. At that point Dhulqarnayn knew that the grapes would never run out and he was greatly satisfied. The angel gave him a smooth stone about the size of the palm of his hand and said, "Take this. God made it to be like you. If it is sated, then you will be sated. If it is never sated, then you will never be sated."[103] He continued, "O Dhulqarnayn! Do you know who the bird is?" "No." "He was one of mankind whom God transformed into a bird. He is a trial for those who come after you. He is the Anti-Christ, whom God transformed into the bird-like image you observed. When he appears on earth, my Lord promised that he will come as a one-eyed man and will be a trial for those whom God wants to test [f. 199]." This astonished Dhulqarnayn.

He left the castle and came to his companions. Having exhausted all their energies, they were unable to carry on further. Dhulqarnayn said to himself, "If I tell them about the provision that I have brought for them, they will never believe it. They'll get mad and in their fury the stronger of them will kill the weaker." So he said to them, "Come here to me, I want to count you." To each man that came to him, he gave a grape. This way the following man never knew what the person in front of him was getting. And he did this until all had passed by him. Then he said, "Line up again so that I can give you the provision for your horses." Each man that passed received a grape, and was told, "Give it to your horse." And the man placed it in the mouth of his horse, and it served as both food and drink for the horse. Each time a grape was broken off, by the power, will, and generosity

---

[101] According to Muslim tradition, this would be the angel Isrāfīl, who is charged with the specific mission of blowing the trumpet on Judgment Day. Cf. Concepción Castillo Castillo's "Algunos aspectos de la angelología según Shihāb al-Dīn al-Ash'arī." pp. 425-426. Cf. also, EI, 3, 189-91; and Chapira for the frequent intervention of an angel in the life of Arabaham (p. 90).

[102] The motif of the bunch of grapes that are sufficient provision to feed an army is also found in the Arabic Life of Alexander published by Lidzbarski (Bezold's *Zeitschrift*, Bd. VIII, p. 303). According to Mas'udi, the miraculous grapes appear in a story told of 'Amran, the son of Jabir, who had gone up the Nile to its source and crossed the sea on the back of an enormous monster near to where the Nile flowed from Paradise. The king of that region gave 'Amran the grapes to sustain him on his return trip down the Nile. Cf. edition from 1861, 1, p. 268.

[103] In al-Tha'labī the message is: إن شبع هذا شبعت ، وإن جاع هذا جعت . 'If it is satiated you will be satiated, and if it is hungry you will be hungry' (p. 369).

of the Almighty God, another one grew in its place [f. 200]. When Dhulqarnayn and his companions saw this, they knew that this provision would never run out.

"Bring me the wisemen," said Dhulqarnayn. When they had gathered before him he showed them the stone and said, "This was made to be an example for me, and I do not know how to interpret it. It resembles nothing else [I've ever seen.] I would like to know what its meaning is."[104]

So the wisemen took the stone and weighed it with another the same size and found that the first weighed more. Then they added another stone, and the balance again tipped in favor of the first stone. With three stones on the balance, the smooth stone that the angel had given him still weighed more. They tried again with four and five, then ten and twenty, then fifty and one hundred, but the smooth stone weighed more than all of them together. They could not find anything to match its weight. They tried with one thousand stones, but the balance tipped in favor of the smooth stone. They tried weighing it against copper, iron and lead, but they were unable to find anything to match its weight. They were astonished, and the matter caused great [f. 201] concern among them. They said, "We've never seen anything more astonishing than this. The only one to explain this would be God Almighty. We fear that it is some sort of magic with which God intends to put us to the test."

At this point, Dhulqarnayn said, "Bring me al-Khiḍr b. 'Āmal." And he came forth. "Great Khiḍr! Look into the matter of this stone, which seems to have been given to us as a test. We do not know its interpretation or meaning." Al-Khiḍr stayed quiet observing them and what they had done. God inspired him with insight and knowledge in the form of revelation sent down to him. Then he said to Dhulqarnayn, "O Dhulqarnayn! Yes, I have knowledge regarding the meaning and interpretation of the matter in question. Give me the stone." And it was given to him. He took it and placed it on the plate of the balance, and then he grabbed a handful of dirt and placed it on the other plate. By the power of the Almighty God they balanced perfectly. The wise man Afshakhīr said, "Praise be to God, O Khiḍr! We weighed it with one stone after another, and with iron, lead and copper [f. 202], and we were unable to determine its weight. But you have weighed it with a handful of dirt. This is truly amazing. We have never heard anything similar!" Then Dhulqarnayn said to him, "Explain to us the meaning of the stone and the dirt, O Khiḍr, and may God bless you! I swear it is the most astonishing thing we have ever seen."

He said to them, "People! This is Divine knowledge. It is one of the wonders He divulges among his creatures, and is something that He has ordered, sentenced and decreed to be in effect among his creatures. God All-Powerful and

[104] This episode recalls Alexander's arrival to paradise, which he finds surrounded by a great smooth wall. Circling the wall, he comes upon a window and knocks. When they answer, he demands something of the inhabitants inside. They give him a stone (sometimes called the 'wonderstone') that they say will impart on him an important lesson, which is nearly identical to the one will learn here shortly. This episode is related in a Hebrew text described by I. Lévi antedating the fifth century, as well as in a Latin work (12th century) titled *Alexandri magni iter ad Paradisum*, published by Julius Zacher in 1859. Cf. I. Lévi, "La legende de Alexandre dans le Talmud," p. 299. See also G. Cary (19-21) for a synopsis of the story and reference to several European versions of this legend.

Magestic made creation and preferred some of his creatures to others. He tested the wise with the ignorant, and made you to test me and me to test you, O Dhulqarnayn![105] I am here to advise you in your actions, yet I cannot dissuade you, as you refuse to abandon your position. You seek my consultation, but then you act contrary to the advice I give you because of your desire to achieve that which you hope for."

Dhulqarnayn wept and said, "Explain it to me, Khiḍr" and his weeping intensified. Al-Khiḍr continued, "God made this stone as an example for you, since God, may we glorify Him by mentioning his name, gave you [f. 203] a kingdom and commanded you to spread his word and his religion and made you to see the angels veiled from the eyes of mankind. He guided you so that you would reach all the world from the western peak of mount Qāf to the eastern one. He placed in your hands the governance of the world and chose you over the rest of mankind. He made you to march over the face of the waters with your soldiers. He taught you things you did not know. Verily, the preference He shows for you is great. With his might He empowered you to enter the darkness, and with his generosity He showed you the way out. You turned your eye toward men who live in countries known only to angels. He let you see so many wonders that I am unable to describe them all for you now. He gave you the stone that would serve as an example and warning for what lies ahead for you in the future. He has given you the world with all that it holds within. But you were not satisfied and dared to enter the darkness, which no one had ever entered before you. You have treaded upon lands that have never before been treaded upon, except by angels. Yes Dhulqarnayn! This stone was meant to be an example for you: if you were given the entire world [f. 204] and everything in it you would not be satisfied and you would continue to desire the world that lay ahead of you. The stone is Adam's son's eye. If you were to dominate the whole world, you would avidly desire something else. This is the nature of the children of Adam. However, upon death, you and the poor and weak will have nothing but a tattered cloth with which to be enshrouded and a place in the ground for a grave. Nothing but dirt and worms will fill your eye. Similarly, God made the stone as an example for you, O Dhulqarnayn. Nothing will fill your eye except dirt. From your great kingdom, you will have bread, water and a tattered piece of cloth to enshroud yourself, and a grave, which all men will also have, be they rich or poor, free or enslaved. Do not exhaust yourself, O Dhulqarnayn, dominating the world, for you will die and leave it behind, as did the ones before you."[106]

Dhulqarnayn wept and wept until he was about to faint. Then God commanded his companions to depart from there. He inspired al-Khiḍr to guide them down a road [that would not lead them to the well] [f. 205]. God did not want to grant Dhulqarnayn his wish [to drink from the fountain], because what

---

[105] In al-Tha'labī, this passage is rendered more completely: ان الله ابتلى خلقه بعضهم ببعض ، فابتلى العالم بالعالم ، والجاهل بالجاهل ، والجاهل بالعالم ، والعالم بالجاهل ، وإنه ابتلاني بك وابتلاك بي. 'Verily, the Lord has his creatures test one another, and so the wise test the wise, the ignorant test the ignorant, the ignorant test the wise, and the wise test the ignorant. And He is testing you with me just as He is testing me with you' (p. 369).

[106] This story is also found in the Arabic Life of Alexander edited by Lidzbarski (Bezold's *Zeitschrift*, Bd. VIII, p. 303).

drove him was uncontrolled ambition. Neither God nor al-Khiḍr informed Dhulqarnayn that he was being led away from the fountain that he sought. Al-Khiḍr went to the front of the troops and cavalry. They had no provisions other than bunches of grapes, which served them as both food and drink. They walked along a riverbed filled with many stones, and pebbles that gave off a great light beneath the horses' hoofs. The people were astonished at this and said to Dhulqarnayn, "Great friend of God! What is this?" "Stones. Whosoever takes some will be regretful and whosoever chooses not to take any will also be regretful." Some people gathered stones and others decided not to, but all of them regretted their choice. When they left there and came into the light of day, lo and behold, some found that what they had collected was naturally transparent green topaz, and others said they had red rubies. This is why the light there was so bright. The Prophet, God bless him and grant him salvation, said, "Whoever came upon the stones was full of regret, [f. 206] some regretted that they didn't take any, while others regretted that they didn't take more. All of them were full of regret."

Abū 'Abd al-Malik said: The Prophet, God bless him and grant him salvation, the one who has my soul in his hand, said: Dhuqarnayn marched into the valley with a feeling of ascetism after what he had heard from al-Khiḍr. He walked away from the temptations of the world. After learning from the example of the stone, he now detested material wealth. God had given him a lesson by way of al-Khiḍr's words, bless him. Had he entered the river before that, he would not have left anything in the riverbed. But now he hated wealth.

He left the darkness and walked until he returned to his army. He ordered them to go and they departed. He marched on until he came to the two mountains mentioned above.[107] The people of the two mountains rushed out to present him with gifts from all over the world. Then they asked him for help. "O Dhulqarnayn! Gog and Magog attack us in the spring since our lands are better [f. 207] than their lands. They graze in our lands and take our herds and our money, leaving nothing. They kill those of us who try to stop them. We have no way to fight against them. We believed in your God, and in you, and your religion. We will collect a tax for you to build a barrier between us."[108]

Abū 'Abd al-Malik said: The commentators differ as to whether he built it before or after entering the darkness. God knows best which of the two opinions is right.

Abū 'Abd al-Malik said: When Dhulqarnayn built the barrier, and events developed as mentioned above in the beginning of this book, the people of the two mountains came to him and complained about the iniquitous behavior of Gog and Magog and said, "Keep them away from us." Dhulqarnayn sent word to them and a group of their leaders gathered and went before Dhulqarnayn, who warned them and prohibited them from evil acts, and ordered them to obey, and to behave more properly with the people around them [f. 208]. They said, "We hear and obey." He said to them, "Leave them[109] to rebuild their country." And so he

---

[107] The reference is to the two mountains and the barrier of Gog and Magog. See above, f. 90.

[108] This passage is related by Ibn al-Jawzī on authority of al-Kalbī (f. 80r).

[109] The verb t-r-k in Arabic, meaning 'to leave,' is given to be the origin of the 'Turk.'

named them the "People of Turk" [i.e., the Turks]. Now they live in eastern India to the right of the land of Sind.

In the meantime, the people of Hind were heeding Darius' request. Dhulqarnayn and his party marched on their return until they stopped in the lands east of Persia. There he learned that Darius had sought the aid of the king of India, Labūr, against him. Upon receiving the news, he ordered his men to find Darius, wherever he might be. Elsewhere, Labūr, King of India, had read Darius' letter and ordered his army to get ready and to join him with three million soldiers. Labūr together with his nephew, Habār b. Labār, led them with three hundred million men. He appointed as general another of his nephews, Shanān b. Anān, at the head of ten million soldiers. Then he appointed a third general, who was his cousin called Dād b. Kaydād, who led thirty million men. He ordered them to sally forth to help Darius. He stayed behind to prepare the soldiers and strengthen the city's defenses, as a precaution [f. 209] in case Dhulqarnayn attacked. Labūr continued to prepare for war until news reached him of Darius' death. This news he kept to himself, afraid that with Darius' death the country would be destroyed.

At about the same time, Dhulqarnayn was off looking for Darius, who, when he had learned that Dhulqarnayn was after him, hastened to flee. Just when Dhulqarnayn's pursuit was quickly closing in on Darius, Darius' ministers betrayed their sovereign and slaughtered him treacherously. As Dhulqarnayn's party arrived on the scene, the assassins ran away, leaving him lying on the ground. Then they called out, "Companions of Dhulqarnayn! We have killed your king's enemy. Inform him of this." Dhulqarnayn ordered his men to stop pursuing Darius' ministers, and he made it known that whosoever would come back and turn himself in would be safe and that the people of Persia would elevate them and the seven ministers that treacherously killed Darius. Dhulqarnayn saw him lying wounded and wept over his head. He was merciful at heart, and generously forgiving. He lifted his head and put it in his lap, and wiped the dirt from his face. He found him to still be alive and said to him, "O Darius! If you do not die, I will give you a place among the best of my people [f. 210]. If you get up from this spot, we will add another country to your lands, and another reign to your kingdom, just as I gave you your wife, your brother and your son. You will be most dear to me and I will not take anything away from you. Tell me who killed you, and I swear, that if you die from these wounds we will kill him in the worst way, whoever it is, Rūmī or Persian."

Then Darius wept, and took Dhulqarnayn's hand and placed it on his chest. He turned his head and said, "O Dhulqarnayn! Do not aspire for more than can rightfully be yours. If you wanted everything, think of the consequences that would await you. Look at what I have attained, how I was yesterday, and where I stand today. By force I conquered the land of the king of kings. The kings of Nūbad I have subdued, but now I've become [f. 211] afraid of everyone around me. I've had to hide from the powerful Persians, their leaders, and abandon my numerous armies and my great sultanship and all that I had in the world. And now, O Dhulqarnayn, the Highest of the High has set you apart and has been generous in giving you aid. I repent to God and I believe in your Lord, who is the One and Only. He is the one who appointed me King of Persia and other countries. He ordained for me the life that I lived. You are one of those who testify that there is no God but Allah and Muhammed is the prophet of God. When I die you will be in charge of washing me for my burial and enshrouding me. Be good to the Persians for they are brave, strong and full of valour. Let my mother stay with your mother, my wife with your sister, my brother with your brother, and I will marry you to my daughter, Rashīq.[110] She is the noblest of women, and she will be very sweet with you. With her be content and generous. I am about to depart from you."

Then God took Darius and he died. Dhulqarnayn ordered that they bring musk, amber and camphor. They washed him for burial and enshrouded him in the clothes [f. 212] of a king, woven with threads of gold. He treated Darius as he would treat one of the kings that were obedient to him. He wrapped him in a shroud and felt compassion for him and cried. When he had finished shrouding him, he called the Persian soldiers to meet and they gathered. He ordered twelve thousand soldiers with their arms to march beneath Darius' coffin brandishing their weapons. On the right of the coffin six thousand soldiers marched and on the left the same. All of them brandished their swords. Some were behind and others marched in front. With them marched the Rūm princes and leaders and the heroes of Persia. The procession ended at his grave. Dhulqarnayn, al-Khiḍr and Afshakhīr came to a halt and gave Darius a good burial. Afterwards, Dhulqarnayn said to the artisans, "Build him a mausoleum with a dome and by his head place a golden plaque engraved with his family backround and lineage, and what happened to him on account of his treacherous ministers." [f. 213] Then the armies and their leaders went before Dhulqarnayn and paid hommage to him and joined his forces. Impressed by how Darius' death saddened their new leader, they became attentive and obedient soldiers. In time, Dhulqarnayn wrote a letter to the cities of Persia and their kings to draw them to him with his benevolence:

> In the name of God the most Compassionate and Merciful,
> From Dhulqarnayn b. Nabbāsh,
> To the people living in the land of Persia and their kings, wherever they may be, on the plain or up in the mountains, near or far,
> It is my desire to rebuild your country. I abhor seeing its damage and destruction. God declared me to be victorious over your country. Any praise goes to Him for the benevolence he has shown me in the way of favors both manifest and hidden. He has raised the word of righteousness above the word of baseness, made me triumphant and humbled you. But you as a people and an army were noble, very brave, strong and powerful, and a tremendous help to Darius until God took him away from us by the treacherous act of his ministers. These were the same ministers to whom he had shown his kindness. Do not let this concern you, for this was preordained in God's wisdom, the One who preordains. I will stand in his place [f. 214]. If you listen and obey, and stick to the

[110] The scribe is not consistent in the spelling of her name. Elsewhere in the Ms. she is *Rashīqā* and *Rashīqa*.

> truth, then I will oblige no one to change religions. Whoever wants may convert to Islam, and who ever pleases, may remain in his current religion. In the latter case, you will pay the tithe from your money in accordance with the rules of your religion. With me you will have the same arrangement as you had with Darius. I am not going to evict anybody from his house. If you obey, then collect your arms and gather your horses and place your trust in my command. Soon my messenger will come to you and with him I'll send horses to whoever is in need of a horse. Understand my words, and do not be carried away by the zeal of ignorance. Repent for your errors of the past and tomorrow begin anew.

Then he sealed the letter and gave it to his messenger to deliver to Persians throughout the kingdom. The messenger departed immediately.

Dhulqarnayn convened his soldiers and stood among them as an orator and said, "Dear people. It is incumbent on us now and is truly our duty to be generous to the group that committed treason against Darius. We shall honor their houses and promote their ranks [f. 215] since they killed our enemy as a service to us out of respect for our kingdom."

When the people of Persia heard him say this they turned color, looked at one another and said amongst themselves, "People of Persia! Do not let the words of the king fool you. He just wants to test you to see what you will say." They spoke in Persian so as not to divulge what they were saying. When Dhulqarnayn heard them talking in this way, he said, "Have faith in me and do not be frightened. We want to find Darius' assassin and pay him recompense for what he did. I will honor him in the same way that one honors another who has performed a commendable service, whether he be Rūmī or Persian. I swear by God to raise Darius' assassins above the whole of my army. I'll put them at the head of my troops and honor them." When the Persians heard this, the nobles wept for the destruction of their kingdom. Then the seven ministers that had killed Darius came forward and stopped in front of Dhulqarnayn and said, "Sire. Do as you have said for we are the seven men you are looking for [f. 216]. We plotted to assassinate Darius and then we killed him because we saw that he was deceiving you. He made another agreement that directly contradicted the one he made with you, and we feared the destruction of Persia. He violated your pact. So we killed him, content to give you our loyalty and to convert to your religion." He asked again to make sure, "It was you who killed Darius?" "Yes." "Is there anyone else besides you?" "There is no one but us."

He ordered them to be crucified high above the ground on a wooden cross overlooking Darius' grave. They said, "What about what you promised us?" "I have fulfilled my promise to the letter. I have raised you above the heads of even the noblest Rūm and Persians just as one should do with those who betray their lord after he has done them favors." Then he looked at the Rūm and Persian soldiers, and the nobles and said, "People, this is the reward for those who kill their Lord after he has done them favors." Then Dhulqarnayn summoned the archers and they shot them with arrows.

After this he wrote to Darius' mother and brother:

In the name of God the most Compassionate and Merciful, in the name of God, the Sacred One,
To the mother of Darius,
We sought out Darius [f. 217] since he was our enemy, and when we reached him he was on the verge of death. If he had not died we would have restored him to his throne. After giving him a fitting burial, I caught the ministers that betrayed him. Before dying he asked me to care for you, along with his brother and son. Then he departed from the world. Don't worry about what is in God's hands, for He and his will always prevail. Now I will take Darius' place and treat you as he treated you, as I would have done even if he had not entrusted you to me. Peace be upon you.

Darius' mother wrote back to Dhulqarnayn:

I asked God [why] He took the crown from Darius' head and snatched away his kingdom and his sultanship, even as Sultan of Persia, and made you king and head of state, triumphant and victorious. We learned that your reign will be one of glory for us. To us you are like Darius and we thank you for what you have done. We will spread your goodness among the people of Nūbarān and their group. I will prepare your wife for you and she will pray for your safety. She was chosen for you by the will of God. [f. 218] Peace be upon you.

Then the letter arrived, and Dhulqarnayn read it and said, "I am God's servant and my soul is in God's hand. He is the one who brought me to power and gave me all of this."

The next letter Dhulqarnayn wrote was to his mother, al-Ghaydā',[111] with news of what happened in the campaign against Persia and how Darius died:

With the messenger who delivered this letter to you, I also sent a gift of some money. I send it so that you will understand God's blessing, and prepare the trousseau of Darius' daughter, Rashīq.

His mother arrived and he consummated the marriage in the presence of his mother. Here ends the story of Darius, praise God the Lord of the Worlds.

Concerning Dhulqarnayn's Attack against Labūr, King of India.

When Labūr b. Labūr the Hindi learned of Darius, the King of Persia's death, he brought his soldiers back. Dhulqarnayn wrote to him saying:

Great Labūr, I look upon you as I look to myself [f. 219]. So do not force me to spill your blood, pillage your wealth, destroy your kingdom and enter your land. God aids me over all the kings and provides me with the means to follow all roads. He granted me the

---

[111] Corruption of Olympiada. In the *Rrekontamiento*, her name is Algaide (f. 9) and al-'Īde (f. 121v), the latter form because of a missing diacritical mark for the غ .

kingship of the land of Persia and now I am intent on becoming lord of your land. If you do not obey and listen to me, then my Lord will aid me to triumph over you and I will appoint the most hateful governor to rule over you. However, if you were to obey and be loyal, I would permit you to remain as king in your land, and I would add to the good things you now enjoy. I shall not enter your land as a combatant and spill your blood except if you seek to attack me and spill my blood. So hurry to answer. Be smart and take advantage of this opportunity. Embrace God's oneness and you will gain, or else destruction will fall upon you. For I swore to the Lord of the Heavens that if you do not recognize God's oneness and bow before the truth, by converting to God's religion, I am coming to you with soldiers who triumph by the will of God. Do yourself well. Verily, I have given you good advice [f. 220]. There is no power nor strength save in the Almighty God the Most Powerful.

He sent the letter and Labūr, King of India, answered with a letter that stated:

To Dhulqarnayn,

Your letter reached me with your messenger and I read it and I understood what it says. You mention that you want to come to our land along with the Rūm and Persians that are with you. Haven't you heard that people cease to covet our lands once they learn how brave and unbeatable we are in our own country? How many were there before you in past centuries, both kings and pharoahs? Yet they gave up hope of conquering us and retreated, afraid of meeting us in battle. Your victory against the king of Persia was decided by the fact that when you entered Khardhala, Darius' ministers betrayed their Lord, which left the Persians without leadership and they lost unity of purpose. You desire our kingdom but you will not enter it, nor will you take possession of any part of it. Do not think that you can be successful in this ambition. The Indian warriors and their nobles and the most valiant of us number three hundred million, all of whom are courageous and noble [f. 221]. If the Indian warriors meet the soldiers serving in the Rūm army, souls will be annihilated, and there will be much lamentation and wailing. But in the end, the two kingdoms will become one beneath me. It is my hope that, as they say, the greedy one is defeated and the content one is victorious. Go back to your country and save your soldiers. Be content with what you have obtained in the way of a kingdom, and do not desire more. The desire to rule another's kingdom has its consequences: the ruin of one of the two pretenders, the fractioning of the soldiers, and the pillaging of the treasuries. This is my good advice to you,

> Dhulqarnayn. If you do not turn back, then I will be the one coming to you with my soldiers and my elite forces, my elephants and wild animals, and a multitude of supporters. In my kingdom there are a thousand elephants and one thousand lions, all of them hungry to fight with mankind and their weapons. If you attack we will kill all of your soldiers. You are a little boy, without many years under your belt, without ever having slept with a woman, who has never led an army into war. You have risen above yourself, and pretend to be something you are not. You were pleased by your conquest of Persia, [f. 222] but you have risked your life and now your pride has become arrogance. Respect my country, and look out for yourself and those with you. If Darius' companions had not killed him dishonestly and deceitfully, he would have killed you. Do not be among the negligent. Peace be upon you.

He put his stamp on the letter and gave it to his messenger who delivered it to its destination. When the letter reached Dhulqarnayn, he opened it, read it and understood what Labūr demanded of him. He ordered his troops to depart immediately for Labūr's lands and to begin the invasion.

Concerning Dhulqarnayn's Campaign against Labūr, King of India, and What Happened Therein.

Abū 'Abd al-Malik said: Muqātil b. Sulaymān said: Dhulqarnayn left the land of Persia after consummating his marriage to Darius' daughter, and meeting his [own] mother al-Ghaydā'. He traveled until he came to a river valley called al-Mukhaḍib. There were fields of pepper plants, cinammon trees, and clove trees growing on the sides of the mountains and in the al-Mukhaḍib river valley [f. 223]. When the crops bloom and ripen, they fall on the ground. With the coming of heavy rain showers, the water carries the fallen pepper, cinammon and clove produced high in the Indian mountains. These floodwaters cover the flatlands for a distance equal to what one would walk in ten days. When Dhulqarnayn came to the valley, a party of his men went to explore and to hunt and they encountered two Indian men. They captured one of them and the other fled. They brought him to Dhulqarnayn. He informed Dhulqarnayn that their livelihood is the food that grows in the valley. They gather the pepper during the valley's harvest season in the winter and the spring. They throw the pepper in an iron kettle and boil it like wheat and barley. Then they put it in bowls. If they did not cook it in this way the intense spiciness of the pepper would prevent anyone from picking the bowls up.

Dhulqarnayn asked them, "How can you do this work, live this way, and bear the spiciness of the pepper and the heat of the fire?" They said, "O Dhulqarnayn! Those who live off something are the best producers of that thing. [f. 224] When we gathered the pepper we wore leather gloves made extra thick.

We used the leather to make masks for our faces and we stirred the kettles with long iron laddles. There were long wooden boards on which we set the pepper, and we moved it from one place to another with the ladle. We protect ourselves from the heat and spiciness with the leather gloves. We protect ourselves from the fire by using the long ladles. Every one knows his trade." He asked, "What does King Labūr look like?" He answered, "He wears a tightly-wrapped veil. Despite his strength and his secrecy, he is concerned about the people's well-being. He is a friend of the weak, who welcomes strangers in his lands, and aids those in need. He gives to all what they deserve. He follows the religion of his forefathers." Dhulqarnayn asked, "What is the religion of his forefathers?" "His forefathers' religion was good, *enjoining what is right, And forbidding what is wrong.*[112] He testifies that God is the Creator of the land and the heavens and that He is the Victorious One at the time of one's death." "Do you give alms to the poor?" "No." "Do you pay the *kharaj* tax?" "No." "What are his soldiers like?" He said, [f. 225] "A group of his soldiers aided Darius, King of Persia, all of whom were valiant, heroic and brave. We heard that the numbers in his army were around three million. To them you add one thousand elephants and one thousand lions, all of them hungry to fight with mankind." Dhulqarnayn said, "Knowing we have God's aid, we are determined to meet Labūr in battle, and this would be the case even if his army were bigger than what you mentioned."

After Dhulqarnayn had consummated his marriage with Rashīqā, the daughter of King Darius, he expanded his army by recruiting eighty thousand knights and eighty thousand infantry men from Persia, and one hundred [thousand] knights and infantrymen from the Rūm. There were also men from the Kurd mountains, from Turkey and al-Daylam, and one hundred thousand in the way of elephants and men --from the islands and the cities-- together with another group of eighty thousand men and elephants. Artisans from every trade numbered one hundred thousand, among them saddlers and tailors [f. 226], blacksmiths and carpenters. These artisans were the ones necessary to undertake a journey, and they were all the most skilled in their trade.

When Dhulqarnayn heard these things from the Indian man he summoned his soldiers and honored them in front of the Indian man. Dhulqarnayn's companions marveled at what Labūr said in his letter and they got scared. Dhulqarnayn looked at them and said, "Do not worry yourselves over what he says in his letter and what they have told you." He marched them out to see face to face the army of Labūr and said, "Upon seeing them, our reverence for their size and strength only diminishes. Their intention is for us to see an intimidatingly large army, when, in fact, the bodies before us are without minds and without strength." When he had said this to them, they became eager to fight Labūr and he said, "I am going to write a letter to him in an attempt to counsel him to choose the right path and avoid war." They said, "Go ahead and write him." Dhulqarnayn wrote to Labūr the following:

From 'Abd Allah Dhulqarnayn to Labūr,

I received your missive, [f. 227] from which it is clear that you attribute little importance to my mission. Your answer has served

---

[112] Qur'ān 3:104

only to augment my desire to kill you. You mentioned that your country does not contain the worldly delights that kings require. We do not desire the pleasures of the world, but rather what we want is for you to enter our religion, and to dismember your kingdom. I hope to defeat you as I have defeated others. I am eager to meet you and I am coming at you today. God is the Helper and the Victorious One.

When Dhulqarnayn's letter reached Labūr, he ordered his troops to prepare to go into battle. He ordered the elephants to be brought out together with the wild hungry man-eating beasts. The two armies met at the lowest of the valleys of India called the Valley of al-Nahrān, which has at the bottom a wide open field that measures the equivalent of a ten day walk in both its length and width. This was where the two armies met. The first to sally forth was Labūr with elephants [f. 228] and their riders. They wore armor so complete that one could only see the pupils of their eyes. In front of the elephants were men; others marched behind driving them on. Hungry wild beasts came forth in the same manner. Between every two elephants there was a lion and another two lions in a cage. On top of the cages there were men in closed cabs driving the carts. On the carts were the cages and in the cages were the wild beasts guided by the men who wanted to wage war with them. Whenever anyone came near they opened the cages and the lions ran out and attacked whomever they found in their path. In this manner Labūr's forces were most prepared for battle.

When Dhulqarnayn saw how the enemy was deployed, he prepared his men and told them to dig great big trenches that nobody could cross, so separating the two armies. He ordered his men to get the elephants and wild beasts ready, whose number reached [f. 229] twenty-four thousand of every type. Then he ordered his men to lay down their arms for twenty four hours. During this time he made twenty four thousand statues that looked like elephants and lions. This was the number that he had produced to use against the people of Jābarṣā to devastate them. He had left them behind in the city of Jābarṣā when he conquered them and departed from there. Now he was using the same technique against Labūr. Whenever he passed through a city he would recruit all the craftsmen to work for him in their trade. He had them put faces of lions, elephants and men on the statues, and hollow out their insides so they remained empty. He ordered them to fill the space with tar, pitch and sulphur. Next they brought a flame and set fire to the insides. What was inside burned until it became like hot coals. At the front of the statues he had them attach iron wheels. He assigned a man to each statue and had them carry an iron pole with two horns on top.

When all was ready he said to them, "Go and [f. 230] fight Labūr's people. He will attack us first with his elephants and lions. When they come towards us, each one of you will push his statue forward." He ordered his companions with the metal poles in their hands to guide the carts with the statues and the iron rams on top. Three hundred thousand men with javelins followed the men with the statues. He made a group of statues to uniformly look like warriors. Some were made of iron and others of copper, but most were made of wood. He put them in different houses like tents. The men marched behind the warrior images in an army that extended for a half mile. In front of the warrior images were the statues of elephants and lions, with Philon[113] advancing to the right of the warrior images with three hundred fifty thousand men, all of whom [f. 231] were the noblest and bravest of Rūm soldiers. Dhulqarnayn led the rest of the army. He ordered them to sound the horns and prepare for battle. They came in the darkness making a great clamor. Flames lashed out and blazed from the mouths and noses of those statues.

When Labūr and his people heard the sounding of the horns, and the noise the burning statues made as they advanced, and he saw the great cloud of dust, and the ardor of the elephants' tusks and lions' fangs and the flames, and he heard the panting of the horses and the wailing of the Rūm as they advanced professing God's oneness, they charged into battle from all sides. They joined hands and cried out to each other, "Hey there soldier, hey there brave tribe! What was it you were saying before? Now it seems you have been pretending and deep inside lack courage. Will Labūr favor you with recompense if you do not fight bravely today?" This brought on the fervor to go into battle. Ahead of the frontline of soldiers, they sent the elephants and wild animals, just as Dhulqarnayn had done.

Finally, the two sides met. [Dhulqarnayn's] men carried statues of men, the elephants carried [f. 232] statues of elephants, and the lions statues of lions. Each species of combatant carried a statue of its own likeness. Every time someone attacked one of those statues, the flames burned him and he turned to flee the intense heat. Each time one of Labūr's beasts took them in its mouth, it was burned from the inside. And so the hellish burns inflicted by the heat of the fire beat back their advance. Next men entered into combat with men, and horses with horses. All soon realized that the battle would be a long one so they took recourse in their patience. Many perished on that day. The Indian men said, "This is the last day we will ever see." They took off their cotton and silk clothing, and put on armor made in India, brandished Indian swords, and Indian crossbows. How many heroic warriors died! How many brave heroes were lost! The slaughter between the two adversaries lasted twenty days. No one was winning. It was dragging on so long that all of them grew tired of the great pain, and the screaming of the horses as they were slaughtered. But the men stood firm as mountains.

The loss of life continued to increase throughout [f. 233] the battle. The fighting intensified to the point that all of Dhulqarnayn's men were being crushed. The number of wounded multiplied such that they considered surrendering to the Persians and turning Dhulqarnayn over to Labūr. Then they remembered what Dhulqarnayn had done to those who had betrayed Darius. News of this reached Dhulqarnayn and he said to his people,
"People! I see a vision in which there is confrontation and then peace for both sides." People came to a halt and the fighting stopped. Dhulqarnayn stepped forward from among his troops into the area between the two armies and called out, "Labūr!" He said, "What?" Dhulqarnayn answered, "Come here to me."

---

[113] In Arabic, افلاطون. The author has confused Philon (افليون) with Plato (افلاطون) who was not one of Alexander's companions. According to al-Mas'ūdī, افلاطون was the student of سُقراط Socrates. Cf. edition from 1979, 2, p. 9.

"Who are you?" "I am Dhulqarnayn." "What do you want?" "O Labūr! It is not fit for kings to bring death upon themselves. If one kills all of his soldiers then what good is life? What we are doing is terribly wrong. Soldiers are dying on both sides on our account. It is the duty of he who is free and generous, as are kings, to personally watch over [f. 234] his companion's well-being. What would you say to the following: You command your lines of soldiers on all sides to stop fighting and you and I will step forward and fight alone and whoever wins will be the lord of the kingdom?" Labūr liked the idea since he was of huge stature, experienced in battle, strong and powerful. In contrast, Dhulqarnayn was a handsome young man, with little experience in battle. So Labūr disdained him and was eager to fight. He gave the order to his soldiers and they stopped fighting. The two of them came forward and attacked each other with blows for an hour. Then Labūr heard a terrible noise that made his hair stand on end, and he turned to see where the noise was coming from. At that precise moment, Dhulqarnayn lunged at him and dealt him a great blow that hit its mark; he slit his throat and his head fell from his body and his body was thrown from his mount. When Labūr's soldiers saw this they rushed to attack and a group of them carried away their king's body. Dhulqarnayn cried out, "People! Whoever puts down his arms will be in God's protection. God will vouch [f. 235] for this."

The Indian men came to him and joined his army at that very moment. He left them and set about appropriating the treasures and arms that Labūr and his army possessed. He stored it all with the other treasures he had amassed. Then he ordered Labūr to be buried, and he was given a proper burial in a shroud, as was fit for a king. Then he went up into the Indian mountains and took as many prisoners as he wished, burned whatever he desired, and broke the idols. In his wake, there did not remain a single idol worshipper to offend the Almighty God. They believed in God and made a pact with Dhulqarnayn to pay a *kharaj* tax and to aid God's religion. He appointed one of Labūr's people to rule over the Indian people. Then he wrote a letter to his teacher Aristotle, sealed it and sent it with a group of his servants. It said:

> In the name of God the most Compassionate and Merciful,
> From Dhulqarnayn b. Nabbāsh,
> To his teacher, Aristotle,
> I am writing you [f. 236] to inform you of the wonders of the earth as I have seen them. You mentioned that you would like me to explain everything to you exactly as I see it and so I will. Regarding what happened with Darius, King of Persia, my Lord assisted me and I was able to defeat him. His kingship passed into our kingship and his soldiers now serve beneath our soldiers. He married me to his daughter, Rashīq. After burying him and showing my favor to his brother and his mother, I left his lands and traveled to India, which God conquered for us, after the deaths of many men, horses and other creatures. You should know that I have not reached the kingdom of Syria, nor the kingdom of

China[114] nor the Turjamānīn. But I am heading there, God the Almighty willing. I am heading west, peace be with you.

Abū 'Abd al-Malik said: Then Dhulqarnayn departed and went west looking to kill those who did not believe in God. He came to a land where the people scoffed at lions and rode them as if they were meek animals. They considered men to be their enemies and they would throw their heads into the sea [f. 237]. He sought the counsel of his companions and asked them, "What is your view regarding these wizard-like people who cannot be fought by the sword?"

Abū 'Abd al-Malik said: I asked al-Mubārak b. Fuḍḍāla about these people and he said that they are called the Berbers, but in that era they were called Libyans. They are located in the west between Egypt and Ifrīqīyā. Then he moved on until he reached the farthest region of the country up in the mountains. Dhulqarnayn called them to Islam and he called upon his Lord to save him from their magic. God answered his prayers. His angel friend said, "March on, I bring glad tidings for you. God has informed me that he will help you to conquer whatever land you set your eye upon. In front of you, these are the strongest of God's creatures, and they are disbelievers so be tough on them." [Dhulqarnayn] gave the order to fight and they went into battle and the fighting was thick. With the help of the Almighty God, he defeated them. When they saw how many of their own were being killed, they sought peace from Dhulqarnayn and he accepted the request. They paid him tribute and a *kharaj* tax [f. 238]. They are a Berber tribe from the Berbers of Ifrīqīyā. They believed in him and made a pact with him to be honest and loyal. So he left there and went on his way towards the lands of Ifrīqīyā.

Concerning Dhulqarnayn's Campaign to the Lands of Ifrīqīyā.

Abū 'Abd al-Malik said: Then Dhulqarnayn left the land of Libya and traveled over the water until he came upon the land of Ifrīqīyā. There he found several tribes each of whom was aware of what the others were doing. The tribes consisted of many clans, among them were the Kutāma and the Muzāta, and others that belonged to these clans. Dhulqarnayn called upon them to become Muslims. Some believed and others refused. He killed those that refused and claimed victory with the help of God. Their peace accord was based on religion, the keeping of an agreement, a *kharaj* tax and tribute. Then he left Ifrīqīyā and went west along the coast until he came to a people called the Hajyasa, whom he called to his religion [f. 239]. They hurried to accept the terms when they saw it was the Rūm who were threatening them.

Then he left and traveled until he came to a mountain on the al-Dara called Jarjara, where he found a people called the Zawāwa. They fought him for one

[114] The episode of Dhulqarnayn's arrival to China, which does not appear further along in this text, is present in the Syriac *Life and Exploits of Alexander the Great* (Budge, pp. 109-113), in the Ethiopic *History of Alexander the Great* (Budge, pp. 172-180), in the Aljamiado *Rrekontamiento* (ff. 116v-120), and in the Arabic *Hadith Dhulqarnayn* (in García Gómez, pp. 24-30, Spanish text) and the Alexander legend of 'Umāra (ff. 50v-52v). It has likely been abridged here.

day and made peace with him on the second day on the basis of tribute and the *kharaj* tax. From there he traveled until he came to the Kutāma tribe, who were governed by a man named Khīdād b. Kīdād Senior from whom descends Kīdād Junior who lived during the time of Islam. They too made peace with him on the basis of the *kharaj* tax and tribute. He left them and went down to the coast to a place called Nakara, whose name he changed to Naldar. Here live people who are of Rūm lineage called the al-Zarāhunah,[115] after whom the mountain is named. They too made peace on the basis of the *kharaj* tax and tribute. From there he came to a place on the coast, and looking around, he saw that it was only a short way across the sea. He found a people living there who were called the Nafzah. He fought them, forcing them into submission after a number of them died [f. 240]. He made peace with them on the basis of the *kharaj* tax and tribute. Then he sailed along the coast and conquered Kafāl b. Ghawwāṣ, who had settled there with his people during the time of Ba'ṭīsh. Ba'ṭīsh was the one who had led them from their homeland in the Kurd mountains. After he had conquered them he called that place Mount al-Fataḥa. He stayed there for a year and three months, until he conquered the inhabitants of the Moroccan mountains, which at that time were sparsely populated with primitive hostile tribes. These were concentrated in the city of Aylān and the surrounding area. When he conquered them, he had the idea to build the al-Anfajār route, which is the maritime route on which Alexandria is built. Its waters issue forth from the Great Sea. He wanted to build that route, but he encountered resistance and was unable to attain what he desired. The Aylān region was also coveted by the Greek and al-Ṣumm kings who also thought to build there. Then he left and sought to cross the sea [f. 241] and disembark on the distant island's shore.

Concerning Dhulqarnayn's Campaign into al-Andalūs

Abū 'Abd al-Malik al-Malshūnī said: Then Dhulqarnayn left North Africa and sailed the seas until he came to the shores of Mount al-Fataḥa. Once ashore, he found there to be many tribes in the area. The words they used sounded like birdcalls, and their languages were so different that nobody could understand a word they said. They are a people called the al-Andalus, though some knowledgeable people call them the al-Anbār.[116] He made camp between the mountains and their buildings. Soon a great wind came upon them and kept them there for a few days.

When he was ready to leave that place, Zayāqīl came down to him and commanded him to order the soldiers led by Ghaydāf b. Māzin b. Arūm to leave behind the stakes in the ground just as they were. The stakes of Dhulqarnayn's horses were made from the wood of the olive [f. 242]. So they left them, and all of them by the will of God took root. The olive stakes of the soldier Ibn Sharaf b.

[115] The translator is aware of the redundance of 'the' and 'al-' here and elsewhere but finds this preferable to referring to a group of people without the required definite article in English.

[116] For an explanation of why the people of Spain are called the Anbār see the Index of Proper Names.

Ghaydāf grew and the place was named after this noble military commander, and will remain with this name until the end of the world.

When the al-Anbār learned that Dhulqarnayn had entered their lands, they came to him and said, "O Dhulqarnayn! There is no way we can fight you since God the Almighty has granted you victory over all the people of the earth, so conduct yourself righteously with what He has given you. We are a small tribe in these lands, so be kind to us and do not destroy us. We are obedient to you and believe in your Lord." He said to them, "Do not worry. None of my soldiers will hurt you. I have no intention to invade your lands. But you will pay tribute to me and you may live peacefully in your land." They agreed and then he asked them, "From what people do you come?" They said, "We are the descendants of Shu'ayb." "What brought you to these lands?" "One of the kings of Persia expelled us from our lands. Our people are small in number, we adhere to the religious pact of the tribe, bless him [f. 243]. We originated in Abraham's cities. Then 'Amītīs expelled us and we went by land from Jerusalem to the city of Constantinople. They told us: 'Beware of a sea monster with a long neck that comes out of the sea each year to the west of this mountain and eats anything that passes nearby, including those beasts you saw on your way here. If it did not eat them, then life on the island would be unbearable. Get into your boats and go straight, stay your course for six days and there will appear to you a tall mountain in the sea. Bear left and you will come upon scattered islands with great meadows, inhabited only by the jinn and ghouls. To your right you will find the island of al-Anbār. Go to their people and inform them about your situation.' So we did and they showed us where they lived and described to us their way of life, just as we have told you." When they had finished their story, Dhulqarnayn [f. 244] asked if there was anyone else living in those parts. They replied, "Yes. There are a people called the Zawābira. They are bald and blue with no hair on their bodies. Nobody knows how many of them there are except God Almighty. They are one of God's creatures. They look like people but they are not. The waters of the sea surround them from all sides except one, which is in the direction of Mount Shāmakh. It is a tall mountain with two peaks both of them high in the heavens." Dhulqarnayn asked them, "Is there any way for me to climb to the top of the mountain?" "There is no way up." "Why is that?" "It would take two months to climb." "If I climbed it would I see the Zawābra islands?" "There is no way you can climb it because no one has ever climbed it without winds blowing him to his death." He said to them, "God grants his aid to whomever He wishes, and He will facilitate [f. 245] the ascent for me."

He left them and climbed the mountain and God came to him and made it easier for him. Their ascent to the peak took two days. When they reached the top, the wind blew from above and all of them fell down the other side of the mountain. One hundred of his best men had made the climb with him and that was the end for them. Dhulqarnayn fell to his knees and prayed to God to save him, and the winds quieted by the power of the Almighty God. He went back to his companions and informed them of what happened and he told them that God had divided the world at that mountain and that whoever climbed it perished. Then he ordered his troops to set sail. He stopped to see those peoples before continuing on his voyage.

'Abd al-Malik al-Malshūnī said: When Dhulqarnayn wanted to set sail, Philon stood up before him and said, "Great king! Do not precipitate us into the high seas, for I [f. 246] have an idea. You stay on land and I'll take some people with me and sail into the sea. If we see something of interest, we will return to get you so we can go look at it together. If we do not find anything we will be content to demonstrate our absolute loyalty to you." He agreed to this proposition. So Philon and one hundred men sailed into the sea for a day and a night. In the sea they saw an island with a city. They headed towards it in their boat, but when they came near to it they saw that it moved and walked over the face of the sea. They followed in its wake until it stopped, then they approached it and saw that it was a city built on boards, and the boards were on a ship, and the ship floated on the sea.[117] They marveled at the way it was built, with its balconies, towers and castles and asked the people of the city if they could enter. They refused and said, "Out of our fear of mankind, and people like you, we fled and built this city in the sea." "How many of you are there?" [f. 247] "We are four thousand men not counting those that have not reached the age of maturity or those who are unable to participate if we give the call to gather for war." Philon said, "People! We are only a few men and you have far greater numbers than we do. How is it that you are scared of us and will not invite us into the city to stay for a day and a night? Afterwards, we will leave you." They responded, "Why is it that you want to enter our city?" "We want to know who you are and what you are like. We are Dhulqarnayn's messengers." "Who is Dhulqarnayn?" "He is one whose advent God foretold. God gave him the means to all ends." "Can he walk on water?" "Yes." "Does he need a boat or can he do it without one?" Philon said, "God gave him the power to walk on water without the need of a boat." They said, "We would like you to meet our king."

They brought them into the king's chambers. When they saw him they found that he was a boy scant in years [f. 248], among the most beautiful people they had ever seen. He was seated on a golden throne adorned with all sorts of jewels. On his head was a crown encrusted with pearls and saphire. They greeted him and he returned their greeting. His companions said to him, "These men claim to be the companions of Dhulqarnayn, so ask them about their king and his present situation." He asked, "Are you Dhulqarnayn's companions?" "Yes." "What is his religion?" "Islam, whose Lord is the Greatest One in his oneness. Declare Him to be your Lord." "How much of the earth has he seen?" Philon said, "He reached the setting sun and the rising sun." "Did he reach Persia?" "Yes." "Did he reach India?" "Yes." "What did he send you into the seas for?" They said, "To learn what is in the sea." "Did you see anything in the sea worth reporting to Dhulqarnayn?" Philon said, "We haven't seen anything more surprising than a city that moves across the surface of the sea." [The king's companions] said, "This city dates back to the time of our ancestors [f. 249]." Philon said, "Who are your ancestors?" They said, "The people of 'Alqama b. Luwāda b. Sām b. Noah, bless him." "How is that so?" [The king answered], "'Alqama was one of the great kings of his day. He traveled through the world

[117] The floating city recalls the city built on reeds described in the letter relating the Wonders of India in the PC (Wolohojian, p. 125).

until the people of 'Ād became his slaves. They then became known as the 'Amālqa. He stayed in power as king until the people of 'Ūs rebelled against him. The 'Ūs belong to the 'Amālqa people. He fled to the sea and made ships and inhabited them, and stayed in them at a safe distance from his enemies. But he never felt secure from the people on land until he made up his mind to build this city. He built it and erected it as you see. Ever since then their work has been its maintenance and repair. News of Dhulqarnayn has reached us here, and we are afraid for our safety. Our flight from him has carried us all over the seas, both in the east and the west. Now we ask of you to swear by Great God that you will not hurt us and will not follow us when we depart [f. 250]. All of us believe in his Lord, who has no partners, for believing otherwise would bring us no good. No king in his kingdom surpasses God in His."

The king honored them and treated them kindly, and together with Philon's guidance they came to an agreement. Then Philon returned to Dhulqarnayn and fulfilled his obligations as stipulated in their agreement. Afterwards they set sail into a great sea flowing into the Ocean towards the land of Taqlīs, which is in the eastern part of the lands of the Rūm on the coast.

They came to a great city surrounded by many islands with no water on them:[118] We were at the point of dying of thirst.[119] From there we turned back towards an island populated with many tigers, beasts, and hungry wild animals. There were large hungry lions, as hostile towards us as they were towards other creatures. We made camp there and found water sweeter than honey. A group of soldiers left the camp and took a walk along the seashore [f. 251]. Soon they found themselves in an enormous cave near the shore. In it was a spring. They entered the cave, drank from the water, looked around and saw a massive column made of green marble. On top of it was a statue of a man, whose features were more beautiful than one could imagine, with a brilliant face, eyes painted with kohl, a beautiful beard, and an engraving across his chest that read,

> "This is a likeness of Kūsh, King of Persia, King of the World.[120] His kingdom and his knowledge spread from this place to al-Shūs in the West and to China in the East. They camped on this island. When night fell, Kūsh slept on a bed of gold. Once a third of the night had passed, wild beasts came out from the surrounding jungle. They charged and attacked [the men].[121] Then it was snakes and black, green and white scorpions [f. 252] with horns. They were such that each time they attacked a lion they killed it, so the lions fled to the seashore. Then indescribable beasts like elephants attacked. The wild animals lashed out and fought with one another. Fire spread with the flames shooting out from the snakes' mouths. It burnt all of those wild animals including the elephant-like beasts. Then it charged whistling and puffing and

---

[118] Abrupt change to first person is in Arabic text.

[119] From the letter relating the Wonders of India in the PC (Wolohojian, p. 125).

[120] From the letter relating the Wonders of India in the PC (Wolohojian, p. 126).

[121] The Arabic text slips into the first person pl. here (i.e., "attacked us"), apparently from interference of the external narrative which is related in the first person.

encircled everyone and all who went down to the lake were burned. The only one who did not die from the fire was Kūsh, who died of fright. The one writing this is his nephew who was absent when this happened. When he reached here he wrote this letter on the chest of his uncle's statue. The one who carried the column was the young man, Kūsh's nephew, who moved it to a castle in the land of Taqlīs, and then built a building over it in the Rūm mosque."

From there we settled in to make camp in the vicinity of a similar lake with heavy winds and a harsh climate. When [f. 253] night fell, a beast larger than an elephant charged us. Immediately people rushed towards it to come between the beast and the camp. Dhulqarnayn[122] ordered them to kill it. So they lit a torch and set fire all around the beast to keep it away till morning. When the fire went out and day broke, the beast attacked and killed forty men. Then the people fought on horseback using weapons made of iron and they managed to kill it. Once it had been slaughtered, Dhulqarnayn ordered his men to split open its belly, and this was done. It was a giant serpent. Inside there was a snake ten cubits in length, according to their understanding of the cubit. It had swallowed the snake whole. It was such a terrible beast that no one could reach that island without ending up dead in the mouth of the serpent. By nature it was a nocturnal creature, as it could see best during the night. The only thing that stopped the beast from killing them all that night was the fires they had set which burned until morning.

Then we left the island on which there were the snakes [f. 254] and headed towards another. We sailed into the seas for a day and night until we landed in an area with great deserts and dry lands along the coast. We made camp there and found a people with fangs and faces like dogs and whose color was black like the crow. The strong among them eats the weak. They wear skins and are more numerous than any other creature. They do not know what is permissible and what is forbidden according to God's law, and they are not Muslims.

When Dhulqarnayn had settled into his camp on the outskirts of where they lived, they hurried to make war against him. Most of them are men that do not know the horse. The soil in their lands is sandy, so they live off the plants that grow wild. They also eat one another as well as the beasts that roam the deserts without cooking them first. As soon as they attacked us, we surrounded them with our horses. As soon as they saw our men riding horses, they got scared and became terribly frightened. Their defeat was easy and quick and a great many of them were killed [f. 255], both male and female in equal numbers. Dhulqarnayn's soldiers captured some of them and brought them to their king, who asked them about their origins. They said, "We are the Abyssinians from Kūsh." Dhulqarnayn asked, "What brought you to this island?" "Our people came here during the time of our grandfather, Kūsh, whom Noah ordered to live here. We are their descendants. Until you arrived, we had never before seen men that differ from us with respect to appearance and skin color. Who are you?" "We are

---

[122] Again, the Arabic text changes narrative person haphazardly from the first to the third person.

from the Rūm. God ordered us to make war on mankind until they acknowledge Him as their Lord and testify to his oneness." They agreed to his terms and became believers. Then he asked them, "Do you bury your dead?" "We eat them." "You are an atrocious people." He ordered them to bury their dead and departed from there.

He came to a river valley with great cliffs, many rocks, and treacherous mountain paths. There were no sowed fields or buildings. But fruit grew abundantly. We made camp in the valley beside the riverbed and we ate dates and fruits. People talked a great deal, and in the midst of conversation, we found ourselves face to face with a beast larger than an elephant [f. 256]. It had hair like a pig and attacked our people and carried away a woman from the army and killed her. In an instant she was in its mouth, and he ate as much of her as he pleased. Then the people attacked and slaughtered it. Before departing, Dhulqarnayn ordered his men to burn the mountainous paths from which the beast had come. Marching on we came to a great body of land up in the mountains, with many river valleys and springs. Inhabiting those lands is a people that belong to mankind, but their bodies are covered with feet from top to bottom and they are black in color, with no visible nose. Their language is incomprehensible. They do not live in houses, but in the fields in the highlands like wild animals. When we arrived there and they saw us, they attacked by throwing rocks at us, killing a number of our soldiers. They had no weapons of war. So we attacked them and caused great loss of life. They entered caves and caverns, where they remained in impregnable underground shelters. We saw the footprints [f. 257] they left behind and they all differed: some matched those of donkeys, mules, and horses. Some were human except they were very long.

Then we departed and marched till we came to a land without any trees, rocks or mountains. There were many wide open fields and river valleys. We found a people whose heads and faces were like beasts. Their bodies were hairy like pigs. They bore semblance to humans only in their legs and hands. When they saw us they fled, and we turned and left them.

We came to another land where there was a great river valley with many trees. The trees were such that as long as the day was getting longer they grew higher into the air. When the daylight began to wane, the trees started getting smaller, and when the sun disappeared altogether [f. 258] the trees disappeared too. This cycle never ceased. The aroma of those trees was like musk. When the people saw that they were amazed and informed Dhulqarnayn. He told them, "Bring me a piece of fruit that grows on those trees and one of its leaves." They went back to the trees to bring back what he wanted. Suddenly, rocks began to fall on them, but they could not tell from where they were coming. They heard a voice saying, "Do not cut anything off those trees. Whoever cuts anything off the trees will be destroyed." Then we looked up into those trees and saw a bird of great beauty and grace.[123] In the river we were amazed to find black rocks that turned white when we took them out of the water.

---

[123] These trees are a substantially different rendition of the Trees of the Sun and Moon from the PC. The graceful and beautiful bird is the phoenix and the temple Alexander will soon enter is

Then we left there and came upon a people who looked like humans, except that they had no beard or hair on their bodies, and they were red [f. 259]. They live on the coast of the great Ocean that surrounds the world. We landed in plain view of them and a group attacked us. They took some of our people, and drowned them in the sea. The only trace they left behind were their cries and the crash of their disappearing into the waves. We never learned who they were. We left there and came to a wide open and spacious land, inhabited by a short bald people with ears like shields. When one of them wanted to sleep he would lay down one of his ears like a cushion and cover himself with the other. They had no brains and we thought they were not human.

We left them and went west to the land of Babel, which was a land of great mountains and valleys, without any buildings. We remained there exploring until we came to a high mountain with a giant temple on top. It was painted in every color. It was one hundred cubits in height and fifty in width. Written on the door in gold was an inscription. Inside was a chair that had one hundred arms each adorned with a golden statue. The chamber was filled with silver and golden leaflets [f. 260]. There were piles of pearls, saphires and jewels. In the middle of the room was a bed crowned with pearls and saphires. That room might be compared to a golden vineyard. The temple scintillated and shined in all directions. What we saw astonished us. Then we went to see what was in the bed, and we saw someone laid out, covered with a cloth woven of gold and silver threads. Dhulqarnayn walked over to uncover his face and then he heard a voice calling out, "O Dhulqarnayn! Didn't your Lord forbid you from trying to uncover the secrets? And didn't He tell you that not everything would fall within your domain? The man on the bed adorned with jewels is the king of the Jinn.[124] Go back from where you came in peace."

Abū 'Abd al-Malik said: Muqātil said that when Dhulqarnayn approached the bed he saw a pile of red sulphur and he used it to light a fire. Before leaving he gathered some and took it to show to his companions and they marvelled at it.[125] When he returned [to Jerusalem] [f. 261], he put some of it in his mouth and discovered that it was medicine for leprosy. They found that it was very beneficial for people. When the Rūm took Jerusalem and pillaged objects of value, they took it back to Rome and placed it in their churches.

Abū 'Abd al-Malik said: I heard Muqātil saying: Ka'b reported that another of the Rūm wisemen told him the story of Dhulqarnayn. According to him, when Dhulqarnayn reached the temple of the king of the Jinn, and looked at all the statues and images captured in gold and silver, encrusted with different types of jewels and saphires, he continued to pray for God to inform him about what he was seeing. God sent the angel Zayāqīl down to him and he said, "O Dhulqarnayn! This is all the work of the jinn who rebeled against God. This temple belongs to the king of the Jinn, whom God, may we exalt Him by

---

that of Dionysius. The three elements together in sequence suggest that this material ultimately derives from the PC (Müller), bk. 3, chpt. 17.

[124] The man lying on the bed is Dionysius in the Syriac (p. 102) and the PC, cited by Budge (1889) without page number, and is called Enoch in the Ethiopic, Budge (1896), p. 158.

[125] In the PC, Alexander wishes to carry away the candlesticks standing near the bed.

mentioning his name, ordered to fight against the jinn and the rebels. Every time he fights them and triumphs, he carries away booty and brings it [f. 262] to this temple which you see. And the one you see lying on the bed covered with a cloth of silver and gold is the son of the God-fearing jinn. He was hurt and his father laid him out in that place and said to him: 'If you heal and live, I will give you my throne. If you die you will rest forever in this temple.' And you, Dhulqarnayn, continue your journey in the western seas for you will see more of the marvels the world contains."

He sailed the seas for two days and nights and in that time covered a distance equal to two complete months. Then he came to a long island stretching out between two seas. If waves from the seas on each side of the island met and crashed above the island, a coconut was created, except that it was like a goose's egg just before hatching. The waves only crashed over the island for a period in the morning and a period in the afternoon. When the shell of that coconut broke, a maid more beautiful than any maiden one could imagine emerged from the egg [f. 263]. When the waves retreated back into the waters from which they came in the late afternoon, then a second egg was created, and from it a bird was born that resembled a vulture. It would sweep down on that maiden, pick her up and fly away with her over the sea. After that no one would ever know what would become of the two of them. When Dhulqarnayn saw that, he prayed insistently to God to inform him of what the bird did with the maiden. The angel Zayāqīl came down to him and said, "Continue your journey on the seas and you will marvel at the wonders the world contains."

So he sailed the sea until he reached its end, where a mountain rose high into the sky. There he encountered an angel sitting in a chair.[126] On each of the four legs of the chair there was a snake fastened to the chair by four stakes. The angel was watching how some of the snakes pulled on the stakes until [their bodies] were stretched out taut and others snakes [loosened their grip on the stakes]. He was on the peak of a tall mountain high above the world. When Dhulqarnayn reached him, he felt that he was in heaven because of the great elevation of the mountain. Dhulqarnayn greeted him and the angel returned his greetings, then said to him [f. 264], "O Dhulqarnayn! You astonish me. You want to rule over the lands of angels, and to participate with God in the ruling of His kingdom." Dhulqarnayn said to him, "May God deliver me from such accusations! Great angel, I am a commissioned and obedient servant of my Lord. I have come to you only with the desire to ask you about certain wondrous things that I've come across on my journey recently." "What things?" "About the snakes that run between your hand and these stakes." He said, "O Dhulqarnayn! If God had not permitted me to speak with you about these things, I could not say a word to you. Know that to these stakes are tied the roots to the entire world. With them God can put fear in the hearts of the people on earth. Or when he

---

[126] This angel recalls the angel that Alexander meets in the Ethiopic text during his journey into the darkness. Who says: "And I tell thee that, when God desireth to destroy the earth, together with those which are therein, He will pluck up this mountain by the roots, and when He doeth this the earth will be shaken, and those that are therein will perish..." (p. 252). The mountain is the one that surrounds the world, i.e., Mt. Qāf.

wants to be nice to them he orders me to release the snakes, and so remove tension from the roots of the whole world. This is all by God's omnipotence and judgment." He said, "What is this tall mountain?" "Did you see what it looks like?" "Yes." "What does it look like to you?" "I saw its slopes rising high into the air, and its base so wide that if I was below looking at it [f. 265] I would not be able to encompass its sides with my gaze." The angel said, "That's right, Dhulqarnayn, you have described it correctly. It is Mount Qāf, the mountain that surrounds the world. To the eye its two peaks seem nearby. The sides of the mountain are so enormous that the eye cannot encompass their totality. But, O Dhulqarnayn, they are nothing more than a little boat anchored in the midst of the waters. This is what the whole world is like, an island in the sea with this mountain surrounding the island. Now ask me about something else." Dhulqarnayn said to him, "Great angel! What is the story of the maiden who grew out of the coconut and the bird that carried her away?" "Only Powerful and Exalted God knows the story of the maiden and the bird, but the angels talk about them and say that the bird comes to paradise and stays there by the command of God. The people of paradise eat it and it gives them life. Similarly, the maiden is one of the houries of paradise. But God knows best and we have no other news concerning them."

Then we departed [f. 266] and came to a land of many good things. It had fertile lands where fruits and plants grew in abundance. When Dhulqarnayn saw its beauty and discovered that there was no one living there, he ordered some of the Persians, Rūm and Turks to settle and to live there until Judgment Day.

Then he left there and came to a land of abundant fruits and dates, with many caves and caverns. When he saw how pleasant and beautiful a place it was, and how abundant its comforts, without any inhabitants, he asked the Almighty God to inform him about that land, and to tell him what he should do with it. God sent down the angel Zayāqīl, who used to come down to him, and he told Dhulqarnayn that that land had been disinhabited due to great injustices committed there. The people used to live in caves until God unleashed his punishment upon them, and all of them to the last disappeared. There remained only their ruins, in which Dhulqarnayn made his camp from the beginning to the end of the summer [f. 267]. They ate the dates and fruits, and when they had finished eating they moved on to another land similar to this one in the abundance of date groves. The ground was always covered with snow there and it was very cold. Dhulqarnayn wanted to survey the area so that some of his armies might live there. When he saw how cold the region was, while still able to produce an abundance of fruits, he said, "No one would be able to endure living in this land except the Rūm." So he ordered a division of the Rūm forces to inhabit the lands, and they will be there until Judgment Day. Dhulqarnayn said: Then we left and came to a similar land without buildings, and uninhabited except for the jinn. Dhulqarnayn went for a walk there by himself and saw vestiges and roads, but they were not from buildings or roads that men make. They had markets and shops and cities and vineyards, except there was nobody visible. He asked the Almighty God to inform him about their state and condition. Soon the angel Zayāqīl came down and said to him, "O Dhulqarnayn! These are the lands of the jinn. No man has ever set foot here [f. 268]. Behind it there are only the seas.

Behind the seas there is nothing but the darkness. God has made it easier for you to traverse the east, west, north and south. No one has ever set foot here, except you and your soldiers. God was benevolent with you and gave you his preference over others. So it is incumbent upon you to thank him and to praise him. He is the One who helped you attain your desires in life. Ask him to help you attain your goal in the afterlife."

Then Dhulqarnayn ordered his men to gather the treasures.[127] He wrote his name on each item in the treasury and counted them and made note of their place in the treasury. He stamped his name on it. Then he made an inventory of all the treasure and put it in a book and went with the book towards his homeland.

Wathīma b. Musā tells us that Dhulqarnayn wrote his name on all the treasure and sent it to his mother in Alexandria. With the treasure he sent a letter that read:

> In the name of God the most Compassionate and Merciful,
> From your son, 'Abd Allah, whom God has aided against his enemies, and who in turn obeys God,
> I have enumerated all the treasures and written on each of them how many there are. Then I put my seal with my name on each of the treasures, and recorded everything in a book. Afterwards I wrote this letter to you including in it the quantities of each treasure I managed to amass. I dispatched the letter to you with a single man on horseback.
> Peace be upon you together with His mercy and blessings.

Then his soldiers continued their journey until they penetrated deep into the lands of China. There he received his mother's letter in which she explained to him the proper way to live one's life, provided him with advice, gave him guidance and her approval of what he was doing. Her letter read:

> In the name of God the most Compassionate and Merciful,
> From the mother of 'Abd Allah Alexander, God's servant, who has no power except in God, who fulfills God's orders, who by the power of God is invincible, who is enriched by the riches of the Lord, and who is guided by the Lord,
> My dear son,
> Do not become vain [f. 270], for vanity is one of your vices, and vanity will bring harm to you. Do not hasten to achieve things, for haste will afflict you. Do not let happiness be your objective, and do not eat gluttonously. Know that fame and power are still very new to you. Beware of avarice for avarice will bring you harm.

[127] The text has either been poorly abridged or corrupted here, for it is upon request of his mother that Dhulqarnayn gathers the treasures, makes a note of each item in a letter that he sends with a lone man on horseback to his mother. So reads Mubashshir (p. 595) and 'Omara (f. 74r). In Ibn al-Jawzī (f. 84r), the letter from his mother is almost identical to the one related here with one important difference: Rūqīa's letter with the request for the treasures *precedes* Alexander's dispatching the list of the treasures he has amassed, which is the more logical chronology of events.

Beware of ambition for ambition will bring you harm. Your letter enumerating your treasures was delivered to me by the hand of a single soldier on horseback. May God guide you, show you the right path, and make you successful in what you endeavor. Peace be upon you.

On one of his journeys, he entered the lands disguised so that no one would recognize him. He would sit with the wisemen and judges there and if there were a dispute he would judge in the matter. He did this in all the cities of that land. In one particular city, he was sitting as a judge without anybody knowing who he was, when two men came in disputing. One of them said [f. 271] to the judges, "Listen to what I have to say, and may God make you successful in whatever you endeavor." The judge said, "Speak." "I bought one of this man's houses. When I went to live in it I found a lot of money. I called him to come and get it, but he refused and I was unable to convince him otherwise. He insisted that he had no money in the house." The judge said to the other disputant, "What do you have to say in this matter?" "Yes, that house was mine and I sold it to this man but, I swear, I left no treasure or money in it." The judge said to the two of them, "Do you have children?" The first man said he had a boy and the second man said he had a girl, so the judge said, "Marry your son to the daughter of your disputant, and let the money be theirs." When Dhulqarnayn heard the sentence from the judge he was amazed and said, "Who would ever think that a judge would deliver such a sentence, and who would ever believe that two men like these two would dispute over this." The judge asked, "Is there anyone on earth who would judge otherwise?" [f. 272] Dhulqarnayn said, "Yes." Then he left them.[128]

'Abd Allah b. Abū Bakr, on the authority of 'Abd Allah b. Ziyād,[129] who transmitted on the authority of Abū Ṣāliḥ, who transmitted on the authority of Qatāda, said: Following Alexander's conquest of China, and upon his return, he felt ill and so complained. When he lay down to sleep a sign came to him in his dreams. It said, "May God take pity on you, for you will die upon new ground above which is green." When he awoke in the morning[130] he said to his scribe, "Write a letter for me to my mother that will console her in my death. Then return here and read it back to me."[131]

The letter began:

---

[128] In Mubashshir, the conversation continues with: "And the qadī asked if it rains in his country. This astonished Dhulqarnayn and he answered that the heavens and the earth are the same there as here" (p. 600). M. Casari (p. 36, n. 102) points out that this episode is of Hebrew origin and cites Fraenkel, 1891, p. 329.

[129] The same source is mentioned in Ibn al-Jawzī, except that he adds that he is 'Abd Allah b. Ziyād al-Mudnī (f. 84v).

[130] According to Ibn al-Jawzī, he feared for his life and felt too weak to write so he summoned his scribe (f. 84v).

[131] In the Ethiopic, Alexander tells Raḥāmān his scribe: "And now, O my beloved, hasten thee to bring me paper, whereupon I may write a letter to my mother, which may console her upon my death, and which may also tell her what hath befallen me" (p. 302). Preceding this request, Alexander gives an exceptionally long speech to Raḥāmān explaining his Christian faith and rationalizing his death.

In the name of God the most merciful and compassionate.
From ‘Abd Allah Dhulqarnayn b. Nabbāsh b. al-Ḍaḥāq b. ‘Uwīlm b. Sām b. Noah, bless him,
To my mother, may God love her,
This letter of mine comes to you from one who, in body, is a companion to the people on earth for a short time, but whose soul shall be a companion of the angels for a long time. To my mother [f. 273] who has not enjoyed her offspring in this world of destruction. I will soon transfer to the distant world.

Mother, have you ever seen a giver that does not take? A believer that does not get? Mother, I ask for your mercy and your love of my birth. Have you ever seen a creature that remains constant over time? Mother, haven't you seen the trees with their green leaves, their fruits, and their branches, how they blossom and then the leaves will fall, the fruits would also disappear, and the branches become bare? Mother, haven't you seen the green plants and enjoyed looking at them but soon they too will fade. Mother, haven't you seen the light of the day and the darkness that follows in the night? Mother, haven't you seen how the fresh water flows into the salty seas?[132] Mother, haven't you seen the people and how deceived they are in this world? How many children die at birth [f. 274], and how many sheikhs indulge excessively in their sins! All those of God's creation shall perish. Mother, have you seen a custodian that does not return the custody?

Mother, if any one has the right to cry, let the sky cry over the stars, the earth over its rulers, and the human over himself. Mother, you have to learn and to recognize that what I am heading toward is better than the manner in which I now exist. I am exiting the world of sunset, worry and grief, tiredness, sickness, and death, to the world of eternity and gratitude. May peace and God's mercy and blessing fall upon you from this vanishing world to eternity.

After showing the letter to Dhulqarnayn, he folded it and sent it [f. 275] to Alexander's mother. When it reached her, she read it and began to cry. Then she anointed it with amber and put it away in a safe place.

The second account was according to Wathīma b. Musā as told by Sufyān b. ‘Uyayna.

Abraham and Ismael made pilgrimages to the Ka‘ba on foot. So Dhulqarnayn desired and prayed for the Almighty God to allow him to meet Abraham so he could ask him about it. When this was granted, Abraham said to him, "O Dhulqarnayn! The Holy Ka‘ba is being desecrated." Dhulqarnayn denied this and said, "O Friend of God! Its desecration is not my doing. Nobody ever told me this before." Then Dhulqarnayn stepped forward, set down his arms,

---

[132] As the meaning of the Arabic text is not clear here, I intuit the meaning from the corresponding passage in Ibn al-Jawzī: " "الم ترَ الى عذب المياه الصّافية ما اعذبها اسرعها الى البحور المغيرة" (f. 84).

and performed the circumambulation of the Ka'ba. Abraham gave him cows and sheep.[133]

Soon Dhulqarnayn realized that he was dying. He summoned his wisemen, his ministers and all the residents of his kingdom and distributed among them his gold, silver, and precious clothing. To his soldiers he also gave generously money and horses. [f. 276] Then he appointed a benevolent leader and ordered all soldiers to return to their homes. He soon died and was placed on an iron shield that was covered with a green cloth and sweet basil. Then he was laid to rest and buried, may God have mercy on him.

[In a third account] Abū 'Abd al-Malik said: Ibn al-Musayyab and al-Kalbī tell us that Dhulqarnayn arrived to Jerusalem and set up camp in a place that is known as Darmatu al-Jandal[134] where he died. May God have mercy on him.

[In a fourth account] Abū Isḥāq said: Abū 'Abd al-Malik transmitted to us on the authority of Razq al-Hamdānī, who related on the authority of Mujāhid, that Dhulqarnayn did not die until he reached Jerusalem. He added: I heard Abū 'Abd Allah[135] say: Muqātil told us on the authority of Wahb b. Munabbih that Dhulqarnayn did not die until he arrived in [f. 277] Jerusalem. This was also re-iterated by Isḥāq on the authority of Abū 'Abd al-Malik, who reported on the authority of 'Abd Allah b. al-Mubārak b. Faḍāla, who transmitted on the authority of al-Ḥasan.

Several of the transmitters say that Dhulqarnayn kept the strength the Blessed and Almighty God had bestowed on him until he was thirty-two years old.

Abū 'Abd al-Malik said: Someone who knew told him that when death was upon Dhulqarnayn, he wrote a letter to his mother saying:

> This is Dhulqarnayn's letter to his mother:
>
> Dear Mother,
>
> I wish for you to throw a party in which there is an abundance of food. Invite all of the women to the party. No one will sit with you and eat your food except those women who are not grieving the loss of someone. [f. 278]

The letter reached his mother and she arranged a party such as there had never been before. She sent word for the women of the kingdom to come to her palace. As they were arriving from all directions, she sat on her throne. Then she said to them, "Not one of you will enter my house and eat my food unless you are a woman who is not carrying the burden of grief for the loss of someone." As each woman approached Alexander's mother, she was asked, "Are you grieving the loss of someone?" And they would say, "Yes, I bereave the loss of my son." Then she would ask another, "Are you grieving the loss of someone?" And she

---

133 According to Ibn al-Jawzī, on the authority of Ibn 'Abbās, Alexander not only met Abraham in Mecca, but was the first to do the pilgrimage to the Ka'ba on foot: اول من حجّ ماشيا ذو القرنين (f. 78r).

134 Said to be Dawma al-Jandal in al-Jawzī on authority of al-Kalbī (f. 82).

135 If the Abū Isḥāq mentioned above is 'Abd Allah al-Hamadānī, known as Abū Isḥāq (according to Ibn Ḥibbān, *Majrūḥīn*, 28, 29), then Abū 'Abd Allah may be the same Abū Isḥāq. The substitution of Abū Isḥāq by Abū 'Abd Allah as initiator of the *isnād* for the passage about to be related would suggest that this identification is correct.

would respond, “Yes.” Then she would ask another, “Are you grieving the loss of someone?” And she would respond, “I’m grieving the loss of my father.” In the end, she asked all of the women to see if any of them were not grieving, and she found that all of them answered that they were grieving the loss of their father, or their husband or their son or their brother. When she saw this [f. 279] she felt pain herself, and resigned to accept the will of God, the Almighty and Blessed, who would take care of her son in the Hereafter. Then he died after that, God bless him. This is what has come down to us regarding Dhulqarnayn.

Muqātil said that someone knowledgeable told him that Dhulqarnayn was not admitted to the ranks of prophethood because he did not come from the House of Prophecy. But rather he was sent to the East and West of the earth. They said to him, “O Abū al-Ḥasan,” referring to Muqātil, “Where is the House of Prophecy and Messengership?” He said, “God never sends a prophet unless he is from Mecca, may God hold it dear, or from Jerusalem. From there comes the root of prophecy.” The House of Prophecy has always lain between these two spots, and scholars have a lot to say regarding whether Dhulqarnayn was a prophet or a saint! May God bless our master Muhammad, and his people! Praise to the Lord of the Worlds. Peace and Amen.

APPENDIX I

A First Translation of the Ending of 'Umāra's *Life of Alexander*, as Found in the British Library's Manuscript Add. 5928 on ff. 74-81.

It was said that when Dhulqarnayn's time of death approached, there was a king of India called Qaydar. He ruled in a land that had many marvels. He performed magic and was able to abstain from food and drink for a long time. As a magician he could make himself disappear in addition to other mysterious doings. He drank poison without getting harmed and lived for four hundred years. This mysterious king was mentioned in the Indian Books recounting fantastic stories of his magical powers. According to 'Umāra, the king had a dream that saddened and frightened him. He summoned his friends, assistants and his philosophers to interpret the dream and asked them to be truthful. They replied that he was wiser than they, but that they would promise to speak to him truthfully. They said there are a number of things that could happen. Part of it is troublesome and unclear and the other part is clear. When the king said he dreamed of his demise and the end of his kingdom, the Brahman philosophers' interpretation was favorable and good. The king then remarked that a human cannot deny what comes from Heaven. We should not be greedy and hang on to life and its material wealth. The words of the philosophers were neither right nor truthful. They spoke like ordinary people. Another of his dreams involved a calf nursing a cow: how can a big cow nurse from a small calf? He dreamed of blind people in a city buying and selling, eating and drinking, and fighting. He dreamed of people obliging a huge man with two heads to eat everything in his path. He dreamed of an elephant enclosed in a small space that managed to get out except for its tail. He was surprised to see that the elephant's head and body were able to come out but not the small tail. He said he dreamed of a thirsty man dying from thirst while drowning in the water [...].

These dreams, the wise men said, have frightened and worried us to the utmost. Our advice to you is to seek our spiritual leader for interpretation. He lives without food or drink. He can meet with the angels and the devil whether they be in the heavens or the ocean or on earth. If this king wishes, he can meet with him and listen to his interpretation of these dreams. The king, curious to learn, traveled to meet their spiritual leader. When he saw him, he knelt in front of him. The spiritual leader asked the king what brought him. He told him about his dreams. His reply was not to fear. Your rule will extend for five hundred and fifty three years. At the end of this period, a king from the west named Dhulqarnayn will enter the Eastern countries. He shall be obeyed and the people will rally around him. Dhulqarnayn will be victorious and will spread his knowledge and wisdom throughout the region. Concerning the interpretation of your dreams, 1. The white elephant that left the small space in the house except for his tail symbolizes a king who abandoned his religious beliefs and worshipped material things. 2. The person who was sitting on the king's bed means that the kings will become the lower class and the latter will become kings who will prostrate themselves to the slaves and honor their subjects. 3. About the thirsty man who ignored the water that surrounded him, this means that the people are ignorant of life and knowledge. What you have seen regarding the two-headed man means that the people in your city are greedy. They take everything and do not give anything. The cow that was milking a calf means that the people who usually feed the calf will be fed by the others. With respect to the Three Jars the middle one of which was empty, this means that the people will die at the hands of the rich and will receive nothing from their fortune. The water you saw flowing dry means that things will move in the wrong direction and the kings of those countries will become slaves. Except for you and your kingdom, I see what I have described as the defeat and destruction of all Indian kings. Their spiritual leader confirmed the correctness of what he had seen. He asked the king's permission to leave and he advised him not to fight Dhulqarnayn, but rather to offer him the gem as well as his beautiful daughter. Offer also your doctors and your philosophers. Then you will succeed and remain in power until death. The king then returned to his country pleased with what he had learned and remained in power after most of his people had died. His black hair turned white.

After Alexander's campaign succeeded in the conquest of Iraq, he moved to India and fought its rulers and kings. He caused a lot of destruction, subjugating the nobles, using them as slaves, and collecting their fortunes. Dhulqarnayn then wrote a letter to King Qaydar, which began: "In the name of God the Most Compassionate and the Merciful. Peace be upon you. When you receive my letter I would like you to join me and not to be afraid. Otherwise, I will destroy you and destroy your country, as I destroyed all of your friends." Qaydar wrote back and thanked Dhulqarnayn for his generosity. In return, he offered him four gifts. The first was his most beautiful daughter, the second a precious stone to be filled with water and used for drinking by the soldiers so that they would never get sick. Third, he offered him his philosopher who would answer any questions he might have about the earth, the heavens, the stars, the body, and the spirits. Alexander read his letter and was pleased. He then wrote Qaydar and sent seven older men to see and describe the daughter. If she was as beautiful as described then he would marry her. If Dhulqarnayn was also satisfied with the philosopher, the doctor, and the precious stone, then the Indian king would enjoy peace and be saved from destruction.

When the seven men arrived and saw the girl, they were amazed by her beauty. They described her to Dhulqarnayn. He wrote Qaydar and asked him to speed up delivery of the four things that he had offered. Qaydar then sent the slave-girl. She was well received and extremely well taken care of. The philosopher, when he arrived, was asked to remain in a quiet pleasant place to rest his mind and body. When dinnertime arrived, Dhulqarnayn sent him a jar of butter and asked him to relax and use it to rub his body and his feet. This butter was brought from an Indian country. When the philosopher saw the jar, he opened it and examined the butter. He asked for one thousand needles and stuck them in the jar with the butter, sealed it, and returned it to Dhulqarnayn. Dhulqarnayn next sent him an iron that spoke. When it was submerged in water, it sank. The philosopher kept hitting it until it was flattened. After this, when he submerged it, it floated. Dhulqarnayn was impressed by the Indian philosopher and his actions, so he summoned him to his presence. When he entered, Dhulqarnayn noticed that he was a very tall man. Commenting on his size, he said that one of out of a thousand tall men is a man of science. The philosopher put his finger on his nose. Dhulqarnayn, bewildered, asked him why he tapped his nose with his finger. He replied, "When you looked at me, you said only one out of a thousand tall men has wisdom or science. I am that one."

Dhulqarnayn asked the philosopher why he put the needles in the jar of butter. He said, "I interpreted this to mean that your heart is full of wisdom, if I added more butter, there would be no more room in the jar, so I added one thousand needles instead. Regarding the iron, it meant that your heart is stressed from killing all these people. I have flattened and polished it once. By virtue of its sinking and submergence, I mean to show how you can extend your life when the time of death is near." The philosopher did more work on the iron and flattened it enough to float. This, he explained, meant only that he would diligently strive to extend the kingdom and the life of Dhulqarnayn.

Dhulqarnayn was impressed by the philosopher and offered him gifts. However, the philosopher refused the gifts saying, "If I loved money, then I would not love science. Money is the enemy of science and they are never in one heart. All I want is to go back home and I will send you the physician."

The physician arrived. Dhulqarnayn asked him what is most painful and how it is treated. The doctor replied indigestion is the cause of every pain. Dhulqarnayn then said, "I have experienced indigestion and pain, but can anyone die from it?" "You, the people of the west," the doctor said, "are ruthless and merciless. You do not even care about yourselves or your own health." Dhulqarnayn answered, "There now you started to show the rudeness of your mind and words." The doctor then said, "You do not need a doctor. You already know about indigestion and have endured it. But, there is no sickness worse than torture by fire. You indulge yourself in your desires more than you should." Dhulqarnayn reassured the doctor and said, "Tell me, why did you say this?" He replied, "I said it because I know you as a man of science and a wise man and one who is not afraid of wisdom or the scientist regardless of how rude they speak. Their interest is to offer advice even when spoken to rudely." Dhulqarnayn let the doctor go. He then distributed a fortune among the people and was very generous to the land of India and its people.

A few days later, DQ began to see visions of a disease known as *sulāl*[136] entering his body. According to these visions, the disease would enter and stay for four years and gradually weaken him until death. If Dhulqarnayn were to resist the entry of the disease into his body, then it would force itself upon him and kill him in one hour.

Two days later, the doctor came. Dhulqarnayn told him about his visions. The doctor replied, "I can see *sulāl* by looking at you." "But, I feel no pain," Dhulqarnayn said. "Before pain there are signs that I can see," the doctor replied. "Since you know so much about it, start preparing medications," Dhulqarnayn said. The doctor sent for his medications.

---

[136] Hans Wehr lists *sull* as meaning "consumption" or "tuberculosis."

Before drinking the medicine, Dhulqarnayn had to go to relieve himself. While in the bathroom, the vision came back to him and said: "I am the *sulāl* that was planning to stay inside of you for four years. However, I saw the medicine the doctor prepared and decided to leave you instead of being tortured by his medicine." Dhulqarnayn then left and asked the doctor for his medicine to drink. When he saw him, the doctor threw the medicine on the ground. Dhulqarnayn asked, "Why did you do that?" The doctor replied, "You entered [the bathroom] sick and came out healthy. Whatever was ailing you has left you. You do not need medicine any more." Dhulqarnayn was very pleased and very surprised by the Indian's level of knowledge in science and medicine. Then he asked for the precious stone, filled it with water and had all his soldiers drink from it. Dhulqarnayn was impressed with the Indian people and promised them peace and prosperity in return for their obedience and sincerity. He then returned to Iraq. However, the vision reappeared to him, and he became worried. He wrote to the doctor in India. The vision appeared again and spoke to Dhulqarnayn saying it would take one month for the message to reach the doctor and another month for the doctor to come. It continued, "I shall hurry to torture you before his arrival. O Dhulqarnayn! I shall make you weep as you cause the weeping of all the mothers and fathers over the deaths of their children. You cannot overcome your fate." Soon afterward Dhulqarnayn felt fire burning in his body, his sickness became more severe until he died in Babel. Dhulqarnayn realized his doctor would not arrive in time to save him.

Dhulqarnayn summoned his scribes and asked them to write his mother and to get help from the wise men of Persia. His letter read: "O Mother, if crying helps to alleviate the pain of things we miss, then let the sky cry for its stars, the oceans for its whales, the earth for its children, the birds for their nests, and the human for himself. Every hour somebody's fate arrives and brings upon death. Mother, I shall depart this earth, but the place I will go to is better than the one I am leaving. Mother, my memory will be forgotten by the people of the earth who had known me and my kingdom. Mother, there is no peace on this earth, but in eternity there will be eternal peace."

When Dhulqarnayn's sickness had worsened, he asked God for peace and forgiveness for himself and his soldiers. He also asked his companions to spread camphor on his body and to wrap it in cotton. Dhulqarnayn died, God have mercy on him. His body was washed. Roses and camphor were placed on it as he had wished. Some of his students said: "If power, wealth, gold, and silver can help defend against death then so be it." Others commented saying: "Today you have seen the most respected among you humbled, the plentiful made scarce, the powerful weakened, and the speaker silenced." Dhulqarnayn's coffin was taken to Alexandria where his mother saw it. She ordered the coffin opened to see his face and said: "You have provided to others more than for yourself. You have built many cities and helped many people in your life. You are now in the hands of God, the Almighty. Your wisdom has reached Heaven and all the regions of the earth. You are now forever asleep and can no longer advise. Bless you in death as you were blessed in your life." She asked al-Khiḍr to pray for him. When his body was placed in the earth, his companions remained at his grave for five years crying and praying for him. May God have mercy on him.

INDEX OF PROPER NAMES

Note: Names beginning with the prefix *al-* are indexed under the capital letter immediately following.
Note: The asterisk next to a folio number (i.e., f. 55*) indicates that there is more information to be found in a footnote in the text at that location.
Note: Folio number only is given for unidentified people and places.

Al-Anbār, ff. 241, 242, 243. The town of al-Anbār is on the left bank of the Eurphrates. However, any relation with the inhabitants of Spain seems unlikely. Al-Anbār is more likely a corruption of Banū al-Aṣfar. In Andalusian Arabic this might have been rendered الاصفار. With the diacritical point of the *fā'* written beneath, as in Andalusian script, the mistaken transcription is understandable. The Banū al-Aṣfar, meaning the sons of the yellow/blond one, were equated in the Medieval period with the Christians of Rūm, and later with the Christians of Europe, especially Spain. Thus, a medieval history of Spain called *Tarīkh al-Ṣufr*. Cf. EI, 1, p. 477 (Goldziher). Alternatively, Anbār may be a corruption of Ishbān or Ispān=Spain (found, for instance, in 'Umāra, f. 3r), where the *shīn* becomes *nūn* and the final *nūn* becomes *rā'*, both mistakes very plausible. Finally, according to Blachère, *Dictionnare*, I, p. 126, an Iranian colony from Iṣfahān established itself in North Africa and Spain. The corruption of Iṣfahān to Anbār would be more difficult to explain but not impossible.

Al-Andalūs, 241. Medieval Arabic name for Spain.

Anti-Christ, ff. 137*, 198. Fabulous personaje from Muslim eschatology whose advent will bring on the Messiah.

Antigonus, f. 41. One of Alexander's generals, died at the Battle of Ipsus 301 B.C.

Aristotle, ff. 15, 16, 19-22, 145, 146, 186, 236. Alexander's teacher.

Arūm b. Farkhashid b. Sām b. Noah, f. 72. Corruption of Iram of the Quran, Aram of the Bible.

'Ātiq b. 'Ūs b. 'Amlāq, f. 62*. Legendary son of Uz.

Berber, ff. 237, 238. People settled in N. Africa since remote antiquity.

Bārīsh, ff. 67, 70, 71, 72, 73, 76, 77, 79, 87, 89, 91, 117, 118, 128, 129, 170.

Ba'ṭīsh, f. 240.

Barṣā, ff. 64, 65. Mother of Jābar, the legendary founder of Jābarṣa.

Balqā, f. 64. Mother of Jābal, legendary founder of Jābalqā.

Dād b. Kaydād, f. 208. Unable to identify. Cousin of Labūr, King of India.

Al-Ḍaḥḥāk b. Muzāhim, f. 14. Al-Ḍaḥḥāk b. Muzāhim al-Khurasānī. Traditionist died in 97/715. Cf. Ibn Ḥajar, *Tahdhīb* 4, pp. 453-4; Dhahabī, *Mīzān* 2, pp. 325-26.

Dahqān b. 'Ālaj b. Khūlān b. Jada'ān b. Mansik b. Artakhad b. Sām b. Noah, ff. 115, 118, 119, 128, 129, 131.

Daqyūs, ff. 11, 12. Daqyānus, the Roman Emperor Decius who ruled from 249-251 A.D., and was a violent persecutor of Christians. Cf. 'Abd Allah Yūsuf 'Alī's commentary to Surā 18:10 of the Quran. See also EI, 1, pp. 478-479.

Dārūm, f. 55.

Darius, King of Persia, ff. 147-151, 155-159, 163-169, 208-218, 220, 222, 225, 233, 236.

Dhulqarnayn. The 'two-horned' one, most commonly believed to refer to Alexander the Great. For an excellent study on his name, Cf. Andrew R. Anderson, "Alexander's Horns" in *Transactions of the American Philological Association* 58 (1927): 100-122.

Eagle, f. 134. In Arabic: al-'Uqāb=(fishing) eagle

Esau, f. 187. Firstborn of Isaac, twin of Jacob, according to Gen 25:21-26. Also, in al-Ṭabari, 2, pp. 133, 134.

Falaṣ (ms. B: Falaḍ), f. 158. Unidentified ruler of the city of Aqlabia, which is mentioned in the *Rrekontamiento*, f. 56.

Gabriel, ff. 8, 9, 10, 32, 189, 191. According to Muslim tradition, the angel who intercedes between God and all honorable prophets.

Ghamṭīs (Ms. B: 'Amīṭīs), f. 243. One of the kings of Persia.

Al-Ghaydā', f. 218*. Alexander's mother. Olympias in the PC. Her name in the text, الغيداء, means 'young and delicate woman.'

Ghaydāf b. Māzin b. Arūm, ff. 241, 242.

Gog and Magog, ff. 85*, 89, 91, 136, 137, 173, 206, 207. Two peoples from Biblical and Islamic tradition who will swarm the earth from the north during the Last Days. Al-Ṭabarī says that these two peoples are situated beyond Sind, i.e., Pakistan, and that their impurity is due to their cannibalism. Cf. al-Ṭabarī, *Tafsīr*, 16, p. 12.

Habār b. Labār, f. 208.

Hajyasa, f. 238.

Al-Ḥasan, f. 277. Probably refers to al-Ḥasan al-Baṣrī also mentioned in the *Rrekontamiento* (f. 101) whose full name is Abū Sa'īd al-Ḥasan b. Abī al-Ḥasan b. Yasār al-Baṣrī. Traditionist born in 21/642 and died in 110/728. Cf. EI[2], 3, pp. 254-255 (H. Ritter); G. Dugat, *Histoire des philosophes*, pp. 245-250; H. Heinrich Schaeder, "Ḥasan al-Basrī, Studien zur Frügeschichte des Islam," *Der Islam*, 14 (1925): 1-75.

Ḥazaqīl, f. 71.
Hishām, f. 55. Refers to Hishām b. ʻUrwa. See below.
Hishām b. ʻUrwa, f. 57. Hishām b. ʻUrwa b. al-Zubayr. Traditionist from Medina died in 146/763-4. Cf. Ibn Ḥajar. *Tahdhīb*, 40, 48-51.
Hūd, ff. 61*, 62, 66, 79, 172. Prophet that appeared among the tribe of ʻĀd.
Ibn ʻAbbās, ff. 15, 45, 84, 170. Refers to ʻAbd Allah b. ʻAbbās died 68/687-8. Greatly admired for his knowledge of profane and sacred tradition, of jurisprudence and Quranic exegesis. He was also a transmitter of Judeo-Christian lore. Cf. EI, 1, p. 20 (F. Buhl).
Ibn Isḥāq, ff. 14, 17, 31. Refers to Abū ʻAbd Allah Muḥammad b. Isḥāq, author of *Kitāb Sīrat Rasūl Allah*, an early biography of Muḥammad, died 767 A.D. Accused by his contemporaries and posterity of transmitting legendary material of the Christians and Jews. Cf. *EI*, 2, pp. 389-90 (Brockelmann).
Ibn Nabbāsh b. Qālūsh, b. Fasṭīyāṭīr b. Nijāwī, b. Yādūn b. al-Arzī b. Ḥirān b. ʻArūm. See Dhulqarnayn.
Idrīs, f. 24*. Enoch.
Isḥāq, f. 277. Probably Ibn Isḥāq or Abū Isḥāq, see above.
Israelites, ff. 71, 133, 194. Tribes of Israel from the Bible.
Ismael, ff. 186, 275. Son of Abraham. Several Muslim theologians, among them Ibn Abbās and Mujāhid, say Ismael was the son Abraham intended to sacrifice. Cf. EI, 2, p. 544 (Wensinck).
Jābal, f. 64. Legendary founder of Jābalqā.
Jābar, ff. 64, 65. Legendary founder of Jābarṣā.
Jalaṣ b. Falaṣ, f. B: 64r. Righteous king of Jābarṣā during Dhulqarnayn's time.
Jesus, ff. 85, 137. In Arabic, written, عيسى. Son of Mary. According to Islam, the prophet Jesus will return to earth on Judgment Day. Cf. EI, 2, pp. 524-526 (D. B. MacDonald).
Jinn, ff. 39, 63, 77, 179, 181, 193, 243, 260, 261, 262, 267. Considered by Muslims to possess airy, fiery bodies, and to be intelligent and imperceptible beings. Some confusion exists as to their relation to angels. In folklore, they often perform mischievous deeds of a magic. Cf. EI, 2, pp. 1045-46 (D. B. MacDonald).
Jūdib b. Jūdib, f. 54. Legendary sheikh of Jābalqā.
Kaʻb al-Aḥbār, ff. 31, 56, 57, 59, 91, 133. Abū Isḥāq b. Māti' Haysū' or Haynū'. Yemenite Jew converted to Islam. Kaʻb was well known as an authority on the *isrā'īlīyāt*, and is said to have transmitted a great number of Rabbinic traditions to Islam. He died circa 32/652-53. Cf. EI[2], 4, pp. 330-331 (M. Schmitz). See also, B. Chàpira, "Légendes bibliques attribuées a Kaʻb al-Aḥbār", *Revue des Études Juives* 69 (1919): 86-107 and 70 (1920): 37-43.
Kafāl b. Ghawwāṣ, f. 240 Unidentified leader in North Africa.
Kaydād al-Aṣghar, f. 239.
Khaydān b. Kaydād al-Akbar, f. 239.
Al-Khiḍir. See below al-Khiḍir b. ʻĀmal.
Al-Khiḍir b. ʻĀmal, ff. 145,146, 185, 187-192, 201, 202, 204-206, 212. Refers to al-Khaḍir, a legendary figure whose name means 'the green one'. Al-Khiḍir is mentioned in the Qur'ān 18:59-81, where he is Moses' servant who loses a fish in the Fountain of Life and when he tries to retrieve it attains immortality. In addition to the Alexander romance, the immortal green one figures in the Gilgamesh epic and a Jewish legend. Cf. EI, 2, pp. 861-5 (A. J. Wensinck); Friedlaender, *Die Chadhirlegende*, 1913; and Piemontese, 1995, p. 178.
Kūsh, ff. 86*, 251, 252, 255. Son of Ham b. Noah.
Kutāma, f. 238. Mentioned in Idrīsī as being one of the Berber tribes of Maghrib, inhabiting Mount Ansharīs and Mount Aykjān. Cf. *Description*, pp. 57, 85, 98-99.
Al-Lahūn, f. 38.
Labūr, ff. 168, 169, 209, 218, 220, 222, 224-227, 229-236. King of India. In the PC his name is Poros. Nöldeke says the Arabic versions of the name Poros (Būr, Liyūn, Fūr) derive from a corruption of Pūl, Nöldeke, *Beiträge*, p. 32, n. 2.
Luwā' b. Sām b. Noah, f. 139. Corruption of Luwd b. Sam b. Noah.
Madīn b. Abraham, f. 79. Refers to Madyān, son of Abraham, from whom descended the people of Midian. Cf. al-Ṭabarī, *History*, 2, pp. 127, 143.
Magog. See Gog and Magog.
Mālik b. Muʻādh b. Jābar, f. 45.
Mansik, ff. 110, 111, 115, 117, 128, 129, 138, 169, 173. According to Ibn Isḥāq, the Mansik inhabited the lands near the place of the rising sun. Cf. Newby, *Making of the Last Prophet*, p. 195. In *Kitāb al-buldān* of Ibn Faqīh, de Goeje identifies the Mansik as Meshech (p. 299). Meshech (also spelled

Meshach) in Biblical maps is located in Transcaucasia. Cf. Bible, *Dan* 1:6, 8-20; *Dan* 3:1-18, 19-30. In Arabic, *mansik* means 'hermitage, place of asceticism.'

Al-Mubārak b. Fuḍḍāla, f. 237. Traditionist died in 164/780. Cf. Ibn Ḥajar, *Tahdhīb*, 10, pp. 28-31.

Mujāhid, ff. 9, 45, 47, 58, 61, 66, 276. Refers to Abū al-Hajjāj Mujāhid b. Jabayr. Celebrated *imām*, *tābi'*, and traditionist from Medina, student of Ibn 'Abbās, died circa 103/722. Cf. Ibn Ḥajar, *Tahdhīb*, 10, pp. 42-44 and Huart, 1, p. 137.

Muḥammad, ff. 1, 3-10, 14, 34-36, 84, 174, 279. Refers to the Prophet of Islam.

Muhammad b. al-Musayyīb, ff. 4, 142. See below Sa'īd b. al-Musayyab.

Muqātil b. Sulaymān, ff. 4*, 14, 16, 39, 58, 61, 85, 93, 101, 103, 110, 130, 135, 136, 142, 148, 184, 186, 222, 260, 261, 276, 279. Quranic commentator and traditionist.

Muzāna, f. 238. Probably refers to Muzāta, mentioned along with Kutāma in Idrīsī. One of the Berber tribes of Maghrib, inhabiting Mount Ansharīs and Mount Aykjān. Cf. Idrīsī, pp. 57, 85, 98-99.

Nabūrān, f. 166. Ancient Persian King.

Nafza, f. 239. One of the Berber tribes. Cf. Idrīsī, p. 57. In Tunisia (نفزاوة).

Nāhūsh, f. 43. Perhaps, Neokles, one of Alexander's companions mentioned in Budge (1896), p. 163, n. 3.

Al-Naghāsh, f. 139. Legendary descendants of Lud, son of Shem, son of Noah. Lud and his descendants would have lived on the lower west coast of the Red Sea, according to A.H. Godbey, p. 95.

Naldar, f. 239. Possible corruption of the Nūkubards (Lombards) mentioned in al-Mas'ūdī's version of the Alexander legend in *Les Prairies d'or* (1861), 2, p. 246.

Naqrūn, f. 158.

Noah b. Lāmak, f. 36. Noah of the Bible.

Nuwwāsh b. 'Amalāq, ff. 96-103. Legendary ancient king of the Amalekites. Perhaps, related to the Noachian Yahū-worshippers. Cf. Godbey, pp. 480, 525, 573, 580, 582.

Nāsik, f. 173. According to Ibn Ishāq, the Nāsik were a community inhabiting the land near the setting place of the sun. Cp. Newby, *Making of the Last Prophet*, p. 195. The Arabic term *nāsik* means 'hermit, recluse, ascetic, pious man.'

Persians, ff. 146, 148, 151, 156, 157, 163-169, 210-220, 233, 266. Of the Persian Empire during Alexander's time.

Philon, ff. 230, 245-250. One of Alexander's companions. Also mentioned in the Syriac (95) and the Ethiopian (143) Alexander legends.

Qāshūra, f. 18.

Qāṭūr, ff. 37, 38. Legendary ancestor of the Greeks. Al-Ṭabarī mentions a Qaḥṭān b. Eber b. Shelah B. Arpachshad b. Shem b. Noah, also known as Joktan. Qaḥṭān inherited prophecy, scripture and beauty from his ancestor Shem. Cf. al-Ṭabarī, *History*, 2, pp. 17-19. Considering that the *nūn* of Qaḥṭān can easily be mistaken for the *rā'* of Qāṭūr, the corruption is plausible.

Qāṭūsh, f. 42. Unidentified companion of Alexander.

Al-Qaylūn, f. 158. Given in Mubashshir as "Faraq Ayliyūn" (592). City Alexander takes during the Persian Campaign.

Qatāda, f. 272. Qatāda b. al-Nu'mān. Companion of the Prophet who took part in various Islamic military campaigns, including that of *Badr*. He died circa 23-24/ 643-644. Cf. EI², 4, p. 778 (C. Pellat).

Qawmash, f. 41. Legendary companion of Alexander.

Rashīq(a), ff. 211, 218, 225, 236. Darius' daughter given to Alexander in marriage. Roxiane in the PC, Rôshnâq in Syriac p. 118, Rasīk in Ethiopian, 2, 102, Rrashīqa in the *Rrekontamiento* f. 62v.

Rawwāsh b. Hurmar, f. 102. Nawwāsh's nephew.

Razq al-Hamdānī, f. 276. Corruption of Abū Zirr al-Hamdhānī. See above.

Al-Rūm, ff. 12-21, 31, 32, 41, 42, 52, 114, 136, 137, 142-153, 158, 165, 180, 185, 210, 212, 215, 216, 220, 221, 225, 231, 239, 241, 250, 252, 255, 261, 266, 267. Byzantium, Asia Minor. Also may refer to the Christians of Europe. Cf. EI, 3, pp. 1174-75 (Franz Babinger). Yāqūt gives several genealogies for the people of Rūm, one of which links them to Abraham, and another to Noah (*Mu'jam al-buldān*, 3, pp. 97-100).

Rome, f. 142, 165.

Sa'īd b. al-Musayyab, ff. 4, 142. Refers to Abū Muhammad Sa'īd b. al-Musayyab, who was a member of the tribe of Quraysh and a native of Medina, and one of the great legal authorities and traditionists of that city. He studied with Sa'ad b. Abī Waqqāṣ and Abū Hurayra. He died circa 91/709-710. Cf. Ibn Khallikan, 1, p. 568; Huart, 2, p. 146.

Sufyān b. 'Uyayna. f. 275. Traditionist from Kūfa, died in 198/813. Cf. Ibn Ḥajar, *Tahdhīb*, 4, pp. 119-20.

Sām b. Noah, ff. 38, 72, 115, 116, 139, 249, 272. Shem, son of Noah, father of all the Semitic peoples. "Father of the Arabs, the Persians and the Greeks" says al-Ṭabarī, *History*, 2, p. 11.

Ṣāliḥ, ff. 62, 170-173. Prophet to the people of Thamūd. He called them to obey God. Only the weak among the Thamūd became followers, and the rest scoffed at him. God sent a sign, a she-camel, but they killed it. The disbelievers were then destroyed by a tremendous storm, in some accounts an earthquake. Cf. EI, pp. 4, 107, 108 (Fr. Buhl). See also J. Stetkevych, pp. 17-29.

Siṭrūn al-Yunānī, f. 38.

Seth, f. 181. Son of Adam

Shamāmīs, f. 41. Legendary companion of Alexander.

Shanān b. Anān, f. 208.

Shaqārīsh, f. 41. One of the Rūm kings.

Shu'ayb, f. 242. Shu'ayb, prophet to the Madyan people (the Midianites), mentioned in the Qur'an 7:93. Shu'ayb is the Arabic name for Jethro (F. Corriente, *Relatos Píos y Profanos*, p. 317.)

Shūrish b. Shurīsh, f. 105. King of the forty tribes of Tāwīl.

Snakes, ff. 134, 135, 170, 251-253, 263, 264.

Solomon, f. 138. King of the Old Testament

Al-Suddī, f. 77. Refers to Muḥammad b. Marwān al-Suddī, identified by Isaiah Goldfeld (129) as being a model of unreliable transmitters of *hadīth* and *tafsīr* material (d. circa 800 A.D.). Also mentioned in al-Ṭabarī, *History*, 4, p. 118.

Al-Ṣumm, f. 240.

Sulaymān. See Muqātil b. Sulaymān above.

Tārīsh, ff. 66, 80-87, 89, 90, 91, 105, 117, 118, 128, 129, 176. Inhabitants of the Biblical Tharshish (*Isa.* 60:8-9, *Jer.* 10:9, *1 Kings* 10:22), being the Tarshish of Sardinia or the Tartessus of Southern Spain. Alternatively, in Ibn Faqīh's *Kitāb al-buldān*, de Goege identifies them as the Transcaucasian people, Tirās (p. 299).

Tāwīl, ff. 102-105, 108, 110. According to Ibn Isḥāq, the Tāwīl inhabited the northern quarter of the earth. Cf. Newby, *Making of the Last Prophet*, p. 195. Nykl says they are the Transcaucasian tribes related to the Yāwīl, sometimes written Māwīl and Hāwīl (see *Rrekontamiento*, p. 584). In Ibn Faqīh's relation (from 903 A.D.), in the de Goeje edition (p. 298) the Tāwīl are identified as Tubāl (See *Ezek* 38:1-8, 15). Huart admits the possibility that they are equivalent to the Tibarenians mentioned in Herodotus and Xenophon. With a minor change in the diacritical points, they may be the same as the Nūyāl and Yūāl mentioned in Budge (1896), 2, p. 231. Another possibility is that they are descendants of Japheth, ancestor of the Gog and Magog. Al-Ṭabarī in his *History* (2, p. 11) mentions Japheth's sons as: Mariḥu, Wā'il, Ḥawwān, Tubal, Hawshil, and Tiras (whose son was Batāwīl). The last name mentioned here could easily be corrupted to Tāwīl.

Thamūd, ff. 62, 71, 92. The Thamūd people, frequently mentioned in the Qur'an (for instance, see 7:73-79, 11:61-68), were the successors to the tribes of 'Ād. They were cousins to the 'Ād, apparently a younger branch of the same race. Their story belongs to Arabian tradition, which relates that their eponymous ancestor Thamūd was a son of 'Abir (a brother of Aram), son of Sām, son of Noah. They inhabited northwestern Arabia. Cf. *The Holy Qur'ān*, sura 7:73 n. 1043, 1044 and Appendix VII to sura 26 in the edition and trans. of 'Abdullah Yūsuf Alī. See also EI, 4, p. 736 (H. H. Bräu).

Al-Ṭumāṭīm, f. 38.

Al-Ṭumm, f. 38.

Al-Turk, ff. 137, 208, 225, 266. The Turks.

'Ūṣ, ff. 62, 72. Uz, son of Aram, son of Shem, son of Noah from the Bible (Gen 10:21). In the Muslim tradition: 'Ūṣ b. Irām b. Sām b. Nūḥ, *EI*, 2, p. 519 (A. J. Wensinck).

Wahb b. Munabbih, f. 276. Jew converted to Islam, well known transmitter of the *isrā'īlīyāt* and author of compilatory works. Died circa 110-14/728-32. Cf. EI^2, 4, pp. 1142-43 (J. Horovitz); R.G. Khoury. *Wahb b. Munabbih.* Wiesbaden, 1972; N. Abbott, "Wahb b. Munabbih: A Review Article," *Journal of Near Eastern Studies* 36 (1977): 103-112.

Wathīma b. Mūsā, ff. 269, 275. Perhaps he is Wathīma b. Mūsā b. al-Farāt al-Fārsī al-Fūsī Abū Yazīd al-Washā'. Author of *Kitāb al-Rada* as well as a book of history. Cf. al-Mas'ūdī (1979), 6, p. 99.

Al-Yānūn, ff. 36*-38, 124-126, 240. Ancestor of the Greeks.

Yaqamṭīsh b. Rawīsh, f. 54.

Yāwīl, ff. 92, 94, 99, 102, 103. According to Ibn Isḥāq, the Yāwīl are the inhabitants of the southern quarter of the earth. Cf. Newby, *Making of the Last Prophet*, p. 195. See also, Tāwīl, above.

Yurīd al-Khaṣmī, f. 45. Ms. B has Sa'īd al-Khaṣmī.

Al-Zarāhunah, f. 240. Named after a mountain of the same name (زرهون), located near Fez today.

Zawāwah, Zawāwa, f. 239. (B: Zawāra) People from village of the same name in central N. Africa east of Morocco. Cf. Yaqūt 3, p. 155.

Al-Zawābira, f. 244. Ms. B has Zawākīra. Apparent corruption. Perhaps refers to the inhabitants of the region of al-Zawābī containing the four rivers called Zāb near Baghdad. Cf. al-Ṭabarī (*History*, 2, p. 49).

Zayāqīl. Corruption of the angel Raphael, ff. 24, 25, 26, 28, 32, 33, 37, 67, 68, 72, 92, 103, 131, 132, 138, 140, 142, 178, 180, 183, 241, 261, 263, 266, 267.

INDEX OF PLACE NAMES

Mount al-Amlas, f. 77*.
Mount al-Ayqāf, f. 78*.
Mount al-Fataḥa, f. 241. i.e., Mount Conquest. Possible reference to Gibraltar?
Mount al-Iskāf, f. 78*.
Mount Jūdī, f. 116. Lofty mountain in the district of Bohtān, near Djazīrat ibn 'Umar at the confluence of modern Turkey, modern Iraq and modern Syria. According to Muslim tradition, it is where Noah's ark came to rest. Cf. EI, 1, pp. 1058-59.
Mount Qāf, ff. 13, 78, 120, 135, 136, 142, 180, 203, 265. Mountain that surrounds the world in medieval Islamic geography.
Mount Sinai, f. 85. Where Moses received the Law.
Al-Mukhaḍib, f. 222.
Muzāta, f. 238. Village located near the Berber valley near Kutāma according to al-Mas'ūdī (1979), 2, p. 244. Al-Idrīsī (p. 57 Arabic text) says it is in Western Maghrib.
Nakarah, f. 239.
Naldar, f. 239.
Al-Nahrān, f. 228. Refers to the river and town by the name of al-Nahrawān between Wāsṭ and Baghdad. Cf. al-Mas'ūdī (1979), 7, p. 732.
Nile River, f. 20.
Palestine, f. 171.
Persia, ff. 13, 146, 148, 151, 156-169, 208-225, 233, 236, 242, 248, 251, 266.
Qāf, ff. 13, 120, 135, 142, 180, 203, 265. See Mount Qāf above.
Qadūmā, f. 158. Possible corruption of Farmā, town in N. Egypt ? Cf. al-Mas'ūdī (1979), 7, p. 556 and Yaqūt, 6, p. 637.
Sea of Darkness, ff. 142, 180. Also called the Baḥr al-Muḥīṭ, or Surrounding Sea. By "foreigners" it is called the Okeanos or Atlant, according to Ibn Khaldūn. Cf. "Maghrib" in EI, 3, pp. 108-109.
Sind, ff. 13, 55, 134, 160, 208. Pakistan.
Al-Shūs, f. 251. Possible corruption of 'Shūsh ? Cf. Yaqūt, 7, p. 593. Or may be Sūs in Morocco.
Sūq Thamānīn, f. 116. Where Noah's children lived before migrating and building Babylon. Ṭabarī, *History*, 2, p. 12.
Ṭaḥlaba, 105. (B: Talḥibah)
Ṭaḥūla, f. 117.
al-Ṭirqān River, f. 165.
Taqlīs, ff. 250, 252.
Taṭūsh, f. 161.

١٢٩
٣٦:٢٢ [ثم]
٣٧:٣ [يجب] يجب عليه ; [الادب] ادبهم ; [فامر] فامر الملك
٣٤،٢٠ [جند ذي القرنين] جنده

www.ingramcontent.com/pod-product-compliance
Lightning Source LLC
Chambersburg PA
CBHW081355090726
47908CB00011B/2683

* 9 7 8 1 5 8 6 8 4 1 3 2 4 *

From Manuscript B

بسم الله الرحمن الرحيم، صلى الله على سيدنا محمد وآله

كتاب

فيه ... [illegible]

رضي الله تعالى عنه ونفعنا به

رواه ... [illegible]

محمد رسول الله صلى الله عليه وسلم

الحمد لله الذي أشرق فتابنور القلم.
وأسمع بغير تدبير القلم. وأسبغ علينا من فضله جزيل النعم
ومنّ علينا سبحانه بالنبي الأكرم. محمد سيد العرب والعجم صلى
الله عليه وسلم. وفضلنا على سائر الأمم من فات منهم ومن تقدم
الذي أشرق فتابنور الأنوار وتعالى عن إدراك الأبصار
وتجبر بوحدته ستر الليل وضياء النهار لم ينفع الذي علمه في
الأموات الغابرين كعلمه في الأحياء الباقين وعلمه في
السموات كعلمه في الأرضين سبحان من أدرك شيء العيون وعلم
ما كان وما لم يكن فهو الله الكريم في آلائه والقديم في جلاله
والعظيم في كبريائه. بنى السموات وجرى النجوم وأضاء الضياء
وأحيا ... [illegible] وأمات الأحياء خلق السماوات بعضها فوق بعضها
الأرض بعدها ونصب الجبال أوتادها فسكن ذلك

جسا ١١

From Manuscript A

1

بسم الله الرحمن الرحيم صلى الله على
سيدنا ومولانا محمد وءاله وصحبه وسلم تسليما

كتاب فيه قصة تميم الداري

رضي الله عنه ونفعنا به رواية عبد الرحمن
بن زياد عن رسول الله صلى الله عليه
وسلم الحمد لله الذي اشرقت بنوره
الظلم واجرى بقدرته صرير القلم واسبغ
علينا جزيل النعم ومن علينا بالنبي الاكرم
وفضلنا على سائر الامم والحمد لله الذي
اشرقت بنوره الانوار وتعلى عن ادراك
الابصار وسجد لوجهه ظلام الليل وضياء
النهار المرتفع الذي علمه في الاموات
الغابرين كعلمه في الاحياء الباقين وعلمه
في السموات كعلمه في الارضين سبق امره
لمح العيون وعلم ما كان وما يكون فهو
الكريم في الابد والقديم في جلاله والعظيم

قصّة ذي القرنين

رواية

عبد الرحمان بن زياد

تحقيق

الدكتور داوود زويّا

بسم الله الرحمان الرحيم صلى الله على سيّدنا ومولانا محمّد وآله وصحبه وسلّم تسليما

كتاب فيه قِصّة ذي القرنين رضى الله عنه ونفعنا به
رواية عبد الرحمان بن زياد
عن رسول الله صلى الله عليه وسلّم[١]

الحمد لله الذي أشرقت بنوره الظّلم وأجرى بقدرته صرير القلم و[أسبغ][٢] علينا جزيل النعم و[مَنَّ][٣] علينا بالنبيّ الأكرم وفَضّلنا على سائر الأمَم والحمد لله الذي أشرقت بنوره الأنوار وتعالى عن إدراك الأبصار وسجد لوجهه ظلام [الليل][٤] وضياءُ النّهار المرتفع الذي علمه في الأموات الغابرين كعلمه في الأحياء الباقين وعلمه في السّموات كعلمه في الأرضين سبق أمره لمح العيون وعلم ما كان وما يكون فهو الكريم في الآية والقديم في جَلاله والعظيم [f. 2] في كبرائه[٥] فتق الهوى وجَو الأجوا[ء] وأضاء الضياء وأحيا الموتى وهو يميت الأحياء خلق السّموات فرفعها ودحا الأرض فمهّدها ونصب الجبال فأوتدها فسكن كلّ ذالك جلالا لربوبيّته أعظاما لوحدانيّته له الأمر من قبل كلّ شيء كان ولا مكان ولاحين ولا أوان ولا وقتا[٦] ولا زمان ولا ظِلّ ولا غمام ولا سماء ولا دخان ولا عام ولا عمرا[٧] إلاّ الواحد المنّان واحد واحْداني ليس له في الملك ثاني[٨] باعث الأرواح ومرسل الرِّياح فتق ورتق وأحيا ورزق ووعد فصدق ما أعظمَ شأنه وأعز سلطانه تنزّهت عن الحدود ذاته وتقدست عن تشبيه الخلائق صفاته ودلّت على قدرته إياته وبهرت عن حكمته علامته [f. 3] كلّ شيء غيره يفنا ويبيد

---

[١] The eulogy following the Prophet's name is abbreviated صلعم

[٢] في الاصل "اصبغ"

[٣] في الاصل "منّ"

[٤] في الاصل "اليل"

[٥] كبريائه

[٦] وقت

[٧] عمران

[٨] ثانٍ

وهو يبدى الخلق ويعيد ويحكم فيهم بما يشاء وما يريد علم ذلك في الأول من الصغير والكبير ﴿ لَيْسَ كَمِثْلِهِ شَيْءٌ وَهُوَ السَّمِيعُ البَصِيرُ ﴾ [٩] إلاّ يعلم من خلق وهو اللّطيف الخير [١٠]

كلُّ كلام لا يُبْتَدَؤُ فِيه [١١] بالحمد لله فهو إبتر وكلّ فعل لا يقال فيه لا حول ولا قوّة إلاّ بالله العلى العظيم فقلّ ما يعانُ صاحبه ويُنْصَرْ وكلُّ دعاء لا يصلّى فيه على النبيّ صلعم فقلّ ما ينجح صاحبه ويظفر [فاستفتحوا] [١٢] كلامكم وأوّل أموركم بشكره وحمده وعولوا على عونه ورفده واكثروا من الصّلاة على محمّد صلعم نبيّه وعبده صلّوا على النبيّ المصطفا والرسول [المرتضى] [١٣] الذي أرسل بالرحمة و[الهدى] [١٤] [وأنقذ] [١٥] من الضّلالة [f. 4] والعما خاتم أنبيائه وواحدُ خلقه وأمام [المؤمنين] [١٦] المبين عن أمره نهيه صلّى الله عليه وعلى آله وصحبه وسلّم تسليما كثيرا

قال عبد الواحد حدّثنا مقاتل ابن سليمان قال قلت لعبد الرحمان ابن زياد أريد أن أسمع منك حديث ذي القرنين يرحمك الله قال نعم أُحدِثُك كما حدّثني سعيد ابن المسيّب عن سعد ابن أبي وقّاص رضى الله عنه قال كنتُ يوما عند رسول الله صلعم عند فراغه صلاة الظُّهُر فخرجت من عنده فإذا بقوم جلوس وهم على باب الخيزران وهم جماعة رجال كهول من أشراف قومهم وأحسنهم صفاتا ومعهم كتاب فلمّا رأيتهم ورأوني قاموا ووقفت أنا فانكرتهم [f. 5] فلم أسلّم عليهم فبادرني أحدُهُم بالكلام وقالوا لي «ما اسمك يا فتاى ؟» فقلتُ أنا «سعد ابن أبي وقّاص» قال لي «لعلّك من أصحاب محمّد ؟» فقلتُ له «نعم وما تريدون من محمّد [صلعم] ؟» فقالوا لي «استأذن لنا على نبيّكم فإنّا نريد الدخول عليه»

فرجعت إليه فرحا مسرُوراً أريد ان أسمع ما يكون من كلامهم وما يقول لهم رسول الله صلعم في جوابه لهم قال فدخلتُ عليه وقلتُ «يا رسول الله إن قوما بالباب معهم مصاحف وكتب يريدون الدخول عليك يسئلونك» فتغيّر لون رسول الله عليه السلام ثمّ بكا بكاء طويلا قال «يا سعد وما

---

[٩] Qur'ān 14:11

[١٠] الخبير

[١١] In margin لا يُبْتَدَؤُ فِيه

[١٢] في الاصل "فاستفتحوا"

[١٣] في الاصل "المرتضاى"

[١٤] في الاصل "الهداى"

[١٥] في الاصل "وانقد"

[١٦] في الاصل "مومنين"

يريدون ان يسئلونني عمّا لا علم لي به ﴿ إِنَّمَآ أَنَا بَشَرٌ مِثْلُكُمْ يُوحَى إِلَيَّ ﴾ [١٧] وقد غاب عنّى الوحي وأنا لا أقول لهم قولا [f. 6] إلاّ بالوحي» قال سعيد فاطرق رسول الله صلعم وشقّ عليّ ان أكلّمتهُ بعد ذلك فقال «يا سعد مُرْهُم بالدخول» فأدخلتهم فَبَادَر أكْبَرُهُم سنّا وأعظمهم قدراً وأبلغهم فهما فقال «يا محمّد أتيناك نسئلك عن ثلاثة أشياء وجدها في كتبنا وإثار آبائنا وبها نعلم صدق رسالتك إنّ أعلمتنا بها وبَيَّنتَها[١٨] وأشرحت[١٩] لنا قصصها وبيّنتَ لنا أمور كلّ مسئلة منها وإلاّ فلا سبيل لك إلى بلادنا ونحن لا نترك ديننا ولا دين آبائنا إلاّ أن تبين لنا هذه المسائل فحينئذ [٢٠] [نؤمن][٢١] بك وبما جئْيت به وبهذا بعثنا ملوك عشائرنا» فقال لهم رسول الله صلعم« اذكروا مسائلكم» فقال له بعضهم «يا محمّد نسئلك عن رجال فقدوا وماتوا وهم أحيَاءٌ وما قصّتهم وما اسماؤهم ؟ ونسئلك عن رجل طاف [f. 7] الدنيا برّها وبحرها شرقها وغربها ما هو وما أصله وما نسبه ؟ ونسئلك عن الساعة إيان مرساها ومتى منتهاها ؟ فهذه الثلاثة مسائل يا محمّد نعلموا به صدقك وصدق نبوّتك وبشرحها نتيقّنُ نزول الوحي عليك من عند الله فاعلمنا بها واشرح لنا معانيها لنُعلّمُوا بها ملوك عشائرنا ونؤمن بك نحن ومن خلفنا من جملة قبائلنا ولذالك أتيناك يا محمّد»

قال سعد ابن أبي وقّاص كان رسول الله صلعم لم يقل قولا و لم يفعل فعلا إلاّ بالوحي فقال لهم «أنا أُنبّئُكم بتفسير مسائلكم غدا» و لم يقل 'إن شاء الله' فانصرفوا عنه ومضوا إلى دار في المدينة ينتظرون جوابهم من عند رسول الله صلعم تلك الليلة وغُدُوّها[٢٢] إلى [الليل][٢٣] ثمّ إلى الصبح ثمّ إلى ثمانية [f. 8] أيّام فاغتمّ رسول الله صلعم غمّاً شديداً وقالت النصارى «عجز محمّد عن جوابنا وقد انتظرناه بعد وعده إلى ثمانية أيّام فما لم يكن فيها لم يكن بعدها»

والرسول [ليعجز][٢٤] عن ردّ الجواب لأنّ من تمام صدقهم الوفاء بما قالوا فاغتمّوا أصحاب رسول الله صلعم غمًّا شديدا واهتمّوا غاية الاهتمام وأبطأ نزول الوحي على رسول الله صلعم إلى خمسة عشر يوما ورسول الله صلعم في غَمٍّ شديد فلمّا كان فى اليوم الخامس عشر نزل جبريل عليه

---

[١٧] Qur'ān 18:110

[١٨] نفهم "بيّنتَها"

[١٩] شرحت

[٢٠] في الاصل "فحينيذ"

[٢١] في الاصل "نومن"

[٢٢] نفهم "غُدَوّها"

[٢٣] في الاصل "الّيل"

[٢٤] في الاصل "لا يعجز"

السّلام على رسول الله صلعم من عند الله عزّ وجلّ فلمّا رآه رسول الله صلعم ذرفت عيناه وامتلأت دموعا فسلّم عليه جبريل عليه السّلام فردّ عليه صلعم بالتّحيّة والإكرام فقال له صلعم «يا حبيبي يا جبريل [f. 9] ظننت بانقطاع الوحي عنّي لانقطاع نزولك عليّ ما رآ ربّي [و]ما أمرني به في [وعدي][٢٥] للنصارى ؟» فقال له جبريل عليه السّلام«يا محمّد عاتبك ربُّك بقولك الذي رتّبته لنفسك دون أرادت[٢٦] ربّك يا محمّد لم قلت للنصارى في سؤالهم أنا أُعلمكم بتفسير مسائلكم و لم تقل إن شاء الله»

قال مجاهد وذالك قوله عزّ وجلّ لنبيّه صلعم[٢٧] لمّا حقق على نفسه العتاب لنسيانه لمشيئة الله قال قتادة عاتب الله نبيّه صلعم بأيتين[٢٨] في كتاب الله قوله ﴿ وَلَا تَقُولَنَّ لِشَاْيءٍ إِنِّي فَاعِلٌ ذَالِكَ غَداً إِلاَّ أَن يَشَآءَ اللهُ﴾[٢٩] وفي قوله لا تعجل بالقرآن من قبل أن [يقضى][٣٠] إليك وحيه ﴿ وَقُل رَّبِّ زِدْنِي عِلْماً﴾[٣١] فالأولى معاتبته في نسيانه ذكر الأرادة والأشاءة في وعده للنصارى والثانية أنّه كان صلعم كاد أن [f. 10] ينطق[٣٢] بالقرآن قبل أن ينزل عليه فعاتبه الله عزّ وجلّ على ذلك وكأنّه نهاه أن لا يقول قولا ولا يفعل فعلا ألاّ بعد نزول الوحي عليه وذالك قوله لتصديقه صلعم

وقال سَعْدُ ابن أبي وقّاص فعند ذالك قال جبريل «يا محمّد إقْرَأ» قال «وما أقرأ يا حبيبي يا جبريل ؟» قال إقرأ «الحمد لله الذي أنزل على عبده الكتاب و لم يجعل له عوجا قيماً» إلى قوله «ان يقولون ألاّ كذابا الأية»[٣٣] فلمّا أعلمه صلعم أنا رأيت وجهه وأمتلا قلبه فرحا وسرورا ثمّ ظهرت [البشرى][٣٤] في وجهه فنادا «يا سعد !» قلتُ «لبيّك يا رسول الله صلّى الله عليك» قال «اعلم أصحابي أن يجتمعوا إليّ وأمر النصارى أن يدخلوا مع الدّاخلين وبشّر أصحابي بذهاب ما نزل في من غمّ بانقطاع الوحي» قال سعد فرأيت وجه رسول الله صلعم قد امتلأ سُرُوراً وضياءً فعلمتُ أن الوحي قد أتاه [f. 11] من عند الله عزّ وجلّ فضحك رسول الله صلعم وامتلا قلبُهُ سُرُوراً قال سعد

---

[٢٥] من B في الاصل "وعد"

[٢٦] أرادة

[٢٧] Between the lines: "ولا تقولين لشاي اني فاعل ذلك غدا الا ان شاء الله فبكا رسول الله"

[٢٨] في الاصل "بأيثين"

[٢٩] Qur'ān 18:23

[٣٠] في الاصل "يقضاى"

[٣١] Qur'ān 20:114

[٣٢] B: "كان ينطق"

[٣٣] This sentence is not found in the Qur'ān. However, the allusion is to Suras 98:3 & 18:2.

[٣٤] في الاصل "البشراي"

فعلمتُ الصّحابة وبشّرتهم بما كان من رسول الله صلعم فامتلأت قلوبهم سُرُوراً وذهب ما كان بهم من الغَمِّ وحمدوا الله وشكروه وأقبلوا إلى رسول الله صلعم وأحدقُوا به وقالوا «يا رسول الله بشِّرنا حقّـا» فقال لهم «ابشروا أن الله عزّ وجلّ أعلمني بمسائل النصارى وعاتبني ربّي بقولي لهم 'أنا أعلمكم بتفسير مسائلكمْ' ولم نقل[35] 'إن شاء الله' وأنا أعلمتكم بالعتابِ على قول لم يستثنا عليه بإرادة الله عزّ وجلّ

وأنتمِ أيّها النصارى سؤالكم عن رجال فُقِدوا وهم أحياءٌ وأمواتٌ [وهمْ][36] رجـال منكـم من جملة النصارى خرجوا من دين الكفر والضلالة وهربوا ألى خالق الأرض والسموات وآمنوا به وهم من مدينة الكافر دقيوس وهم سبعة [f. 12] رجال ختم الله على قلوبهم بالإيمان وطبع على قلوبهم فناموا وهم من عجائب الله تعالى عند جملة الرّوم ومن إياته وهم من أصحاب الملك دقيوس ووزرائه وقرابتـه وأعلمني ربّي بهم وأمرني أن أعلمكم بهم فقال جلّ ذكره﴿ أَم حَسِبْتَ أَنَّ أَصْحَابَ الكَهَفِ وَالرَّقِيـمِ كَانُوا مِنْ ءَايَاتِنَا عَجَبَاً ﴾[37] وهم في الكهف رُقودٌ[38] ضرب الله على آذانهم فناموا ثلاثة مِائة سـنين وأزدادوا تسعا فبعثهم الله بالحياة جزءا من النهار ثمّ أعادوا إلى ما هم فيه وليسوا بأموات ولا بأحيـاء وهم من آية الله تعالى والكهف الغار الذي هم فيه والرّقيم لوح من رَصَاص كتب أهل زمـانهم فيـه أسماؤهم وهم سبعة وتأويلهم يطول

وأمّا سؤالكم عن الرجل الذي طاف الدّنيا برّها وبحرها شرقها وغربها فهو الإسـكندر ابـن أسّاس وفي رواية أُخرَى [f. 13] ابن نّباش المعروف بذي القرنين وهو رجل من الـروم صالح في دينـه عارف بربّه مطاع طائع أعطاه الله العلم والعمل به ويقال أنّه نبيّ أوّ وليّ لاختلاف العلماء والله اعلـم أعطاه الله الملك والحكمة ووصل جابرقا و[جابرصا][39] وبلغ السِّنَدَ والهند وبنا السُّدُودَ ودخل الظّلمـة وقهر [مملكة][40] الرّوم والفرس ودخل جبل قاف فانتها ملكه ملكا عظيمـا وذالـك معـني قولـه ﴿وَيَسْئَلُونَكَ عَن ذِي القَرْنَيْنِ قُلْ سَأَتْلُواْ عَلَيْكُم مِّنْهُ ذِكْراً إِنَّا مَكَّنَّا لَهُ فِي الأَرْضِ وَءَاتَيْناهُ مِن كُلِّ شَيْءٍ سَبَباً فَأَتْبَعَ سَبَباً ﴾[41] الأية

٣٥ نفهم "لم اقل"

٣٦ من B

٣٧ Qur'ān 18:9

٣٨ في الاصل "رُفودٌ"

٣٩ في الاصل "حابرصا" : جابرسا Note in Mss. this city is sometimes spelled

٤٠ في الاصل "مملكته"

٤١ Qur'ān 18:83-85

وأمّا سؤالكم عن الساعة متى هي ومتى مرساها ومنتهاها فما المسئوُل عنها بأعلم من السّائل لا يعلمها إلاّ ربّي عزّ وجلّ وهي من الخمسة المحجوبات عن الخلق لا أحد يعلم متى هي من الأوّلين والأخرين ولا يعلمها ملك مقرّب ولا نبيٌّ مرسلٌ وذكر الخمسة [f. 14] المحجوبات في علم الغيب قال فيهم الجليل جلّ جَلاَلُهُ أن الله عنده علم السّاعة وينزل الغيث ويعلم ما في الأرحام وما تدري نفس ماذا تكسب غدا وما تدري نفس بأيّ أرض تموت أن الله عليم خبيرٌ وذالك أن الله عزّ وجلّ انبأ نبيّه سؤال النصارى ﴿ عَنِ السّاعَةِ أَيّانَ مُرْسَاهَا فِيمَ أَنتَ مِن ذِكْرَاهآ إِلَى رَبِّكَ مُنتَهَاها إِنَّمآ أَنتَ مُنذِرُ مَن يَخْشَاها كَأَنَّهُمْ يَوْمَ يَرَوْنَهَا لَمْ [٤٢] يَلْبَثُوا إِلاّ عَشِيَّةً أَوْ ضُحاهَا ﴾[٤٣] [الاية ان][٤٤] لا يعلم أجلها إلاّ الذي أجَّلها إلى أجل معلوم وذالك معاني مسائلكم وذكر شرحها يطول فاعلموه»

ذكر قِصَّة ذي القرنين ابن أسّاس وقيل ابن نّباس ابن قالوش

قال ابن اسحاق حدّثنا عبد الملك ابن مقاتل ابن سليمان عن الضحّاك ابن مزاحم [f. 15] عن ابن عبّاس رضى الله عنه قال سئل رسول الله صلعم عن ذي القرنين وما كان من شأنه وقصّته وما جرا له قال لنا رسول الله صلعم كان أميرا من أمراء الروم وكانت علماء الروم يجدون في كتبهم وفي علمهم أن الله عزّ وجلّ سوف يبعث فيهم رجلا يسمّى بذي القرنين [العالم][٤٥] الذي يبلغ مشارق الأرض ومغاربها وكانت علماءوهم يجدونه ويذكرونه ويصفونه وكان يملكهم في ذلك الزمان ملكاً عظيماً[٤٦] قدره عارفا بالله تعالى قال وكان ذو القرنين من أبناء الملوك وكان في زمانهم رجلا قد أعطاه الله تعالى علما عظيما وكان يقال له أرسطاطاليس وكان عبداً صالحا وكانت الرّوم يعرفونه ويعرفون حقّه وفضله ويعظمون شأنه ويروا أنه خاله أخي أمّه فقُصِدَ [f. 16] ذو القرنين بالحكمة مبلغا عظيما وكانت علماء الروم تتعجّب منه ومن كلامه وحكمته كلُّ ذالك الهاما من الله تعالى الذي خصّه بذالك لا إله إلاّ هو وقال بعض الروات[٤٧] يقولون أن ذا القرنين من أهل الزّنية والمواجّنة[٤٨] فقال مقاتل والكلبيّ أنّه كان من أهل الخير والشرف وكان يتخلّق بمكارم الأخلاق ويسموا إلى الأمور العظام وقد

---

[٤٢] في الاصل "لهم"

[٤٣] Qur'ān 79:42-46

[٤٤] من B في الاصل "اي"

[٤٥] من B في الاصل "العامل"

[٤٦] ملكٌ عظيمٌ

[٤٧] الرواة

[٤٨] نفهم "الزنا والمجون" ، B المراجعة

رآ رَؤْيَا أنّه وَلّي من مطلع الشمس إلىمغربها في شرقها وغربها قال فلمّا رآ هذا الرّويا بلغ خبره إلى الملك الأعظم فبعث إليه الملك فاستقدمه معه ورجع معه معلّم الخير أرسطاطاليس قال فأمر الملك أرسطاطاليس أن يفتّش عليه وعلى أخباره ويختبره لّما يرا ويسمع من كلامه فما زال أرسطاطاليس يَفتّش عليه وعلى أخباره ويسئله عن جميع العلوم فما سأله عن شيءٍ إلاّ وأجابه عليه [f. 17] بأكثر ما سأله عنه قال النبيّ صلعم وذالك الهاما من الله تعالى [حيث][٤٩] أراد أن يكرمه وأن يبلغه ما أكرمه به ثمّ إنّ الملك قرّب ذا القرنين وأدناه من نفسه وتولاّه وقلّده أمر الملك وبرا إليه منه[٥٠] وقال « أنت أولّ[٥١] بالملك منّي وأحَقَّ فيه» ثمّ أن الملك أمر العلماء الروم بأن يسمعوا له ويطيعوا ثمّ أن الملك نزع التّاج عن رأسه وجعله على رأس ذي القرنين وهو شابٌّ صغير وأمر ملوك الأرض بالسّمِع والطّاعة له وأن يّهبطوا[٥٢] معه إلى أرض مصر

قِصّة ذي القرنين حين بنا الإسكندرية

قال فركب ذو القرنين وركبت معه ملوك الرّوم في عدّة لا يعلمها إلاّ الله تبارك وتعالى قال فنزل يومئذ بموضع الإسكندريّة قبل بنائها وهو الذي بناها وفي رواية أخرى قال ابن اسحاق حدّثنا عبد الملك ابن[٥٣] مسعود عن سعد بن أبي وقّاص عن النبيّ صلعم أنّه قال كان ملكاً [f. 18] من ملوك الرّوم وأشرفهم وعظمائهم اسمه أسّاس ابن قالوش ابن بسياطين فولد له ولد من أشرف نسائه[٥٤] يقال لها قاشورة وقيل كان ابن عجوز ولم يكن لها ولد غيره فلمّا نشأ الولد في الكلام تعلق كلامه بالحكمة والمعرفة من صغره الهاما من الله تعالى ألهمه لذالك لّما أراد الله به من الكرامة وكانت ابناء الملوك من عشيرته يُهنُّونه لفهمه ونطقه بالحكمة فشاع خبره في سبعة أعوام أن ولد الملك أسّاس ابن تّباش ولَداً أفهم أهل زمانه وأعظمهم قدراً وأبلغهم معرفة فلم يزل خبره يرتفع من ملك إلى ملك ومن شريف إلى شريف بين الرّوم حتى شاع في جميع الملوك وبعثت إليه الملوك والأشراف وساروا يزورونه القسيسون والرُّهبان من علماء الرّوم [f. 19] كلّها ورهبانها وكلُّهم يسئلونه عن الحكمة فكلٌّ من سأله عنه[٥٥] شيء

---

[٤٩] من B

[٥٠] نفهم "تخلى له عنة"

[٥١] أوّلى

[٥٢] sic

[٥٣] Perhaps we should read here: عن See note to f. 17 in Trans.

[٥٤] "فولد له ولد من اشرف نسآيه" This line is written twice

[٥٥] عن

أجابه بعلم أكثر ممّا أجابه وكان أعلم الرُّوميّة كلّها في ذالك الزمان حتى انتها إلى ارسطاطاليس وفيما يقال أنّه خاله القريب لامّه وكان يرا له الشأن شأن عظيمٌ وكان يسئله ويجيبه فأوّل ما سأله أرسطاطاليس عن طلب العلم عن مسائل فكلُّ ما سأله من مسئلة أجابه عنها

فقال له أرسطاطاليس «بما يطلب العلم ؟» قال له ذو القرنين «بالعقل» قال له «فما ثمرة العلم ؟» قال له «الورع» قال له «فما جوهرة الورع ؟» قال له «خشية الله تعالى في السرّ والعلانية» قال له «وما نور الخشية ؟» قال له «العدل وهو قوام العلم» قال «فيما تنال الدّرجات ؟» قال «بيقين الطاعات» قال «فيما يحاول ثبوت الأمر ؟» قال «بتحقيق الطاعة» قال «فيما تهدم الطاعة ؟» قال « بمقاربة المعصيّة لأنّه متى حاول أمر المعصيّة كان [f. 20] أقرب بفوات ما رجى وأسرع لمجيءَ ما اتّقى» فقال له أرسطاطاليس «أنت أعلم أهل زمانك» فاستقربه واستذناه من نفسه

فلمّا شاع خبره وظهر أمره للملوك والأشراف من جميع الرّوم وأنّه يطلب المراد في جميع البلاد وأن يكونوا أعوانه على طلبهم فأمرهم بالعزم والْقُدُوم إلى أرض مِصْرَ وأنظارها وهي حينئذ من أشرف البلاد وفيها ملوك العمالقة

فارتحل بجنوده حتّى نزل بالخليج على ناحية مضرب النّيل من حيث يقع في البحر فَمُثِّلَ ذالك له ببنيان مدينة ألهمه الله إليها وكان اسمه بالرُّوميّة إسكندر وبالعربيّة أحمد وهو أحمد ابن أسّاس ومعنا أسّاس عبّاس فبنا المدينة وسمّاها على اسمه بمدينة الإسكندرية وبناها وشدّها واسمع له وأطاع له كلّ من بمصر من العمالقة وغيرهم من النّاس

ذكر سبب ذو[٥٦] القرنين [f. 21] كيف بلغ ما بلغ من العجائب

قال أبو عبد الملك لمّا [تَمَّ][٥٧] ذو القرنين بنيان المدينة ومنارها على نحو ما تقدّم من ذكر بنيانها وتشيدها وأسكنها أشرف القبائل من الرّوم وأمر لبعض أشراف العمالقة أن يسكنوا مع الرّوم فسكنوا وأقبل يحاول الأمر وطلبه وهو في ذالك طائع لربّه عزّ وجلّ لا يعمل عملا حتّى يشاور فيه أهل المعرفة من الروميّة وأهل الطاعة من القسيسين والرّهبان ويكاتب معلّمه أرسطاطاليس بالمشورة على كلّ ما يحاوله من الحركة وغيرها فأوّل ما كان شاوره عليه وعلى ما يبدأ به من الطلب هل إلى المغرب أم إلى المشرق فكتب إليه كتابا فذكر فيه:

---

٥٦ ذي

٥٧ في الاصل "تَمّ"

باسمك اللهم الى معلّم الخير أرسطاطاليس الحكيم من ذي القرنين ابن أسّاس سلام عليك قد انتهينا إلى الأرض مِصر فألهمنا [f. 22] الجليل جلّ جلاله إلى بنيان مدينة تكون لنا مأوى للمقيم من ضعفائنا[٥٨] وأصحابنا ومقصدا لِلمراسلة و[حصنا افضل][٥٩] ما يُتبعًا على العطا من نّفقة جنودنا فبنيت وشُيِّدت و[تمّ][٦٠] المراد فيها ثمّ ألهمنا الجبار إلى بنيان المنار فبني وشُيِّد ولَوْلب وركّبتُ فيه حركات المراد ألهاما من الله سبحانه إلى جميع ما صنعت وأردتُ أن أُعْلِمَ معلّم الخير بذالك واستشاره على أيّ الجهتين أبدا بالقدوم عليها هل بمغرب الأرض أو بمشرقها ففي رأيك الرّشاد والله المستعان

فختم الكتاب ودفعه إلى رسوله وانصرف به حتّى بلغ أرسطاطاليس ففكّه وقرأه وفهم غرضه فأجاب به مجاوبا له

بسم الله الرحمان الرحيم بسم الله العظيم الجليل إلى المويّد بالتوفيق المنصور بالتحقيق ذو[٦١] القرنين ابن أسّاس من مُعلّمه أرسطاطاليس [f. 23] وصلني كتابك وسرّني بلوغك مرادك وحمدت الله تعالى الذي ألهمك فعل الخيرات وأسئله ان يُبلّغك أعْلَى الدّرجات والذي ألهمك إليه من بنيان المدينة ففي ذالك رُشْداً لِلْجُند والرّعيّة والذي ذكرت من المشورة على أيّ الجهتين يكون إليها القدوم فذالك في علم الواحد القيم وأسئله وأُلحّ عليه في المسئلة يُدلّك إلى طريق الرّشاد وهو المعين والسّلام

فختم الكتاب ودفعه للرسول فأتاه إلى ذي القرنين ففكّه وقرأه وقال صدق معلّم بالخير[٦٢] ثمّ أنّه قام وتوضّا وصلّى وقام ليلاً وصام نهاراً ولَحّ في المسئلة ورغب إلى الله أن يُدلّه على طريق الهدى ويُجنبه سبيل الرّدا فهو في مكان مُصلاّه وهو ابن تسع سنين ساجدا وراكعا ومتضرّعا الله تعالى ثمّ بعث الله إليه ملكاً عظيما مطيعا يقال له [f. 24] زياقيل وكان زياقيل أمره الله أن يتّخذ ذا القرنين خليلا وقد كانت الملائكة في الزّمان المتقدّم في عهد إدريس ونوح عليهما السّلام يصاحبون بنى آدم ويعلّمُونهم الخير وكانِ زياقيل خليل ذي القرنين فأتاه يوما وهو على كرسي من رُخام جالس ينظر في المنار الذي بنا

---

[٥٨] Word not clear in either A or B

[٥٩] من B . في الاصل "كتبنا وحضنا الفضل" ; Meaning not clear here

[٦٠] في الاصل "ثمّ"

[٦١] ذي

[٦٢] sic

فسلّم عليه فردّ عليه السّلام [بغبط] عليه[٦٣] وأدخله الملك زياقيل تحت جناحه ثمّ طار به في الهوا ساعة زمانيّة فأخرج رأسه من تحت جناحه فقال له الملك«انظر إلى الدّنيا وماذا ترا منها ؟» فقال ذو القرنين «أرى مدينتي ومدائِن حولها» ثمّ طار به ما شاء الله ثمّ أخرج رأسه من تحت الجناح فقال له «انظر إلى الأرض وماذا ترا منها ؟» قال له«أرى مدينتي ومدائِن حولها» ثمّ طار به ايضا ما شاء الله ثمّ أخرج رأسه من تحت الجناح ثمّ قال له«انظر إلى الأرض وماذا ترى [f. 25] منها ؟» قال له «أرى مدينتي وحدها وليس حولها إلاّ البحار وهي محدقة بها وهي في لجّة خضراء» قال له الملك «يا ذا القرنين ليست تلك مدينتك إنّما ذالك الدنيا كلّها وقد احاط بها البحر والدّنيا يا ذا القرنين كلّها جزيرة في لجج البحر ومثلها كمثل سفينة في وسط البحر والبحر حمل الجزيرة والبحر حملته القُدْرَة يا ذا القرنين أفلا تتعجّب من قدرة ربّك وخالقك» فقال ذو القرنين «حبيبي زياقيل وكيف لا أتعجّب من أمر رأيته بعيني بلا بعد النظر ؟ أشهد أن لا الله إلاّ الله وحده لا شريك له حبيبي زياقيل بماذا أمرت أن تفعل فيّ؟» قال له الملك«يا ذا القرنين البحر اوسع من الجزيرة والجزيرة في وسط البحر وإن الله أراد بك الكرامات ويقول لك ' قد سلّطتك على أهل الدنيا وبعثتك إلى جملة بنى آدم وأقوي جُنُودك وأنصرهم [f. 26] وأُقوّي خيلك وأبارك لك فيهم وإذا خَفِيَ عليك أَمْرٌ فأَسْئَل عليه الملك زياقيل فإنّه يُعلّمُكَ فإنّه من كان الله معه وناصره فلا غالب له فامض إلى ما أُمرتَ وكن من الشاكرين' » قال ذو القرنين «الحمد لله ربّ العالمين وإنّي سميع مطيع لربّي في كلّ ما أمرني به وأنا من الشاكرين» ثمّ قال «يا [الإهي][٦٤] أنت أرحم الرّاحمين وأنت الذي قلت ﴿ لاَ يُكَلِّفُ اللهُ نَفْساً إِلاَّ وُسْعَهَا ﴾ [٦٥] فكيف الإهي تكلّفني ما لا أطيق ؟ الإهي وكيف أقدر على هذا كلّه ؟ وكيف أعرف من خالق لغتي والأمم التي ذكرتهم لا علم لي بتأويلهم وحربهم ؟ وكيف أقدر على المسير في البحار والظلمات ؟ فهل يطيق ذالك أحد ؟» فبعث الله له الملك زياقيل فقال له الملك زياقيل«يا ذا القرنين يقول لك أرحم الراحمين ' أنا الملك الرَّؤفُ الذي لا أُكلّفُ [f. 27] نفسا إلاّ وسعها ودون طاقتها وجهدها وأنا لا أُحمِّلك أمرا إلاّ وأنا موعدك بتمامه وأوسع لك بقدرتي في عقلك وفهمك فتعرف معاني كلّ كلام وتعقل كلّ نظام وأنا على كِلّ شيء قدير يا ذا القرنين أنا أطوي لك البلاد وأهديك إلى سبيل الرّشاد وألقي في عقلك تقدير المراحل التي تبلغ بها مشارق الأرض ومغاربها وتعرفها بقياسك ولا تبيتُ على مراحل بقدرتي كالقمر

[٦٣] في الاصل "بغيظ عليه"

[٦٤] في الاصل "للهي" Here and following

[٦٥] Qur'ān 2:286

[و]لا ينزل إلاّ في منازل التّقدير وأنا القادر على كلّ شيء وأعطيك النصر وألقى في ذِكْرِكَ الرّعبَ خليلك أن يُعلمك كلّما خفا عليك من الأمور أكثر من الجنود ما استطعت ومن الخيل والرّجال ما استطعت فإن ذالك هيبة لك وأنا ألقي في قلوب أصحابك محبّتك وأنا الرَّزاق ذو القوة المتين يا ذا القرنين خذ الخراج من جميع البلاد وخذ الجزية ممّن [f. 28] كفر بي فأنت المسلط عليهم وأنا ربّك الذي أريد أن أعِزّك وأجعل لك ملكاً فوق الملوك ويفوق سلطانك على كل سلطان ' يا ذا القرنين يقول لك ربّك 'اكسر الأصنام وأقتل عبدة الأوثان وجاهد على الكلمة العليا' وقد أمرتك بقتل أهل الكلمة السّفلى فاقتلهم كما عصوني وإنّما أردتُ بك كرامة الدنيا والأخرة فافعل ما أمرتك به يا ذا القرنين وأنا ناصرك على أعدائي وأعدائك فأحمد الله وكن من الشّاكرين» فقال ذو القرنين عند ذالك «الحمد لله ربّ العالمين لك السّمْعُ والطّاعة يا خير النّاصرين» قال فتولّى الملك زياقيل بخليله ذو[٦٦] القرنين إلى المدينة وقد أراه جميع الدنيا برّها وبحرها وعرّفه مداخلها ومَخارِجَها حتّى كاد كأنّه دخلها قبل ذالك ثمّ أعلم بذالك جميع جنوده وأصحابه فاجَابُوه سَمْعاً وطاعةً وعزم الكبير منهم والصّغير على المسير [f.29] مع ذي القرنين

قال سعد قال رسول الله صلعم والذي كرّمه وفضّله أنّه كان لمّا عزم على المسير قال لأصحابه «توكّلوا على الله وأعزموا على السّفر» وميّن جنوده وألقي عليهم العدّة والسّلاح الحربيّة وأمر بكثرة الأبواق وألقى الله تعالى في توفيقهم الرّعب وقال لأهل مشورته «أنا من الغد على سَفَرٍ» فلمّا أصبح ضربت الأبواق وكانت عَلاَمة رحيلهم ونزوهم فلمّا ضربت الأبواق ارتحلوا ومشوا ساعة فوقف بهم على شاطيء البحر فسبّب الله له سببا فدخل في البحر فمشا على ظهر الماء فدخلت الجنود خلفه بإذن الله لّما رأوه دخل في البحر فمشا ومشوا خلفه على الماء بقدرة الله تعالى فإذا غربت الشّمسُ ضربت الأبواق للنزول فنزلوا العاسكير في لجج البحر فتناهز الخيل بعضها على بعض فيشدّ تصهيلها وتنحنحها [f. 30] وتوديهم فلا يقدرون على المنام فيقولون «يا وليّ الله [آذت][٦٧] الخيل بَعْضُها بعضاً ولا يكاد النّوم يَقْرُبُنا ولا ننامُوا ولا نجد كيف نربطها على الماء فقال لهم «أضربوا أوتادكم فإنّ الذي سخّر البحر لحوافر خيلكم سيسخرُ الأوتاد لخيلكم» وقد أمر الله سبحانه البحر [أن لا][٦٨] يدع حافر فرس ولا قدم رجل أن يدخل فيه فسمع البحر لله وأطاعه قال ابو عبد الملك قال رسول الله صلعم والذي بعثني بالحقّ ما كانوا يضربُون أوتادهم على ظهر الماء الاكما كانوا يضربونها على ظهر الأرض

---

[٦٦] ذي

[٦٧] في الاصل "ادت"

[٦٨] في الاصل "الا"

بقدرة من يقول للشيء كن فيكون سبحانه لا إله إلاّ هو سمعا وطاعة لله عزّ وجلّ فأذا أصبح ضربت الأبواق ورحلوا وإذا أمشوا ضربت الأبواق فنزلوا وكانت الأبواق علامة للرّحيل وللنزول وهيبة للقتال [f. 31] في حينه في جميع حروبهم ومغازيهم وهذا ما كان من قصّة ذي القرنين وكيف نال ما نال وبلغ ما بلغ والسّبب الذي بلغ به مطلع الشّمس ومغربها

وأمّا ما ذكرتُ من حسبه ونسبه فأنا أُعْلِمُكُم كما أعلمني ربّي عزّ وجلّ هو الإسكندر ابن أسّاس وقيل ابن نّباش ابن قالوش ابن فسطياطير ابن نحاوي ابن يادون ابن الأرزي ابن حيران[٦٩] ابن عَرُوم وهو الذي مَلَكَ الروم كُلّهَا وهو شابٌّ حَدَث السِّنّ فنال ملكا عظيما وأكثر من تزويج النِّساء فما مات حتّى ولد له أربعون ولداً ذكورا فكانوا النصارى يسمُّونَهم أولاد الروم فغلب عليهم اسم الروم سُمِّيت الرُّوم رُومٌ وهو ابن فَرُوم ابن سما بخيل ابن مريا ابن عيصوا ابن اسحاق عليه السلام [ابن ابرحيم][٧٠] حليل الرّحمان وهذا حَسَبُهُ ونَسَبُهُ

قال ابن عبد الله حَدَّثَنَا كعب الأحبار عن الإسكندر بقِصَّتِهِ وأخباره وأنّه لّما أمره [f. 32] الله تعالى بما أمره مشا على الماء بقُدْرَةِ الله عزّ وجلّ وأنّه متبّعٌ لِلْمَلَكِ الذي كان خليلُهُ وهو زياقيل فكُلّما مشا زياقيل على الماء مشا ذو القرنين على أثرِهِ وهو السَّبب الذي كان يتّبعُهُ وقال رسول الله صلعم لِكِلّ نبيّى[٧١] من الأنبياء ملك من الملائكة يأتيه بالوحي من عند ربّه وكان جبريل صلوات الله عليه وسلامه حبيب الأنبياء عَامَّةً وكان ذو القرنين وكّل الله به الملك زياقيل يُعلّمُهُ ويأمره وكان عبدا صالحا أحبّ الله فأحبّه الله عزّ وجلّ وأطاع الله فأطاعه كل شيء و[عزّ][٧٢] دين الله وكلماته فأعزّه الله وجعله حجّة على أهل الأرض حتّى يقولوا ' ما جاءنا من بشير ولا نذير يخبرنا بانك ربُّنَا' فأراد الله تبارك وتعالى بأن[٧٣] يقطع به الحجّة على أهل الأرض فأمره الله أن يأتي بني آدم في البرّ والبحر مغرباً ومشرقاً وسهلا ووعْراً فمشا في البِرّ اثنا عشر يوما مقدار ما يمشي اثنا عشر عامّاً [f 33] حتّى انتها إلى جزيرة في البحر مُقْفِرة لا عمارة فيها

فنزل بها وأمر بعض من معه يمشون في الجزيرة وكهوفها فمشا فيها إلى آخر النّهار فلم يجد فيها شِيّا يكون لهم عجبا أو [رجلا ؟] يسئلونه عن الجزيرة فوجدوا فيها قصرا مبنيًّا بأصناف الرّخام

---

[٦٩] يمكن نقرأ "حبران"

[٧٠] من B

[٧١] نبيّ

[٧٢] من B ، في الاصل "عن"

[٧٣] أن

الأخضر والأحمر والأبيض عالي[٧٤] لا يكاد يوجد إليه مصعدا من كلّ جيهة منه فحيث إذا أراد أحد الدُّخُولَ فيه والصعود إليه [تحركت الأبواب ودارت اللوالب][٧٥] والقصْرُ ثابت من أعلائه[٧٦] ونظروا إلى بنيان ذالك القصر [فإذا هو بصفاح[٧٧] الذهب والفضّة ظاهيرة[٧٨] لهمْ ولم يجدوا حيلة يصلون بها إلى ذلك القصر][٧٩] فرجعوا إلى ذي القرنين فأعلموه بما رأوْا فتعجّب من ذلك غاية التعجّب ورغب إلى الله أن يعلمه خبر القصر

قال فأتاه الملك زياقيل فقال له «يا ذا القرنين إن الله عزّ وجلّ وعدك ملك الدنيا وما فيها ووعدك القصْر وما فيها ثمّ أته وأصنع قصراً مثله من عود وأجعل له الواحا من جوانب قصرك ظاهرا منه كمثل ذراع الرّجُل إذا مدّها وأجعل قصرك أعلا من [f. 34] القصر وأقدم بالقصر على القصر وأهجم به عليه فإنّ اللواليب يقفوا بالألواح الممدودة الخارجة من أجنابات[٨٠] قصرك ويقف القصر ومفتاح قفله شهادة أن لا إله إلاّ الله محمّد رسول الله» ففعل ذو القرنين ذلك في يومه أسرع ممّا كان ذالك أنه كان حين نهوضه إلى الخروج إلى الغزوات أمر لأهل كلّ صناعة أن يخرجوا معه باثني عشر ألفا ثلاثة آلاف منها[٨١] في صنعة الحديد وثلاثة آلاف منها[٨٢] في صنعة العود وثلاثة آلاف منها[٨٣] في صنعة صلاح الخيل فأمر أهل صنعة الحديد والعود فصنعوا له القصر من يومه وأقبل على القصر فلمّا قرب منه وكان قصره محمولا على الأسرّة والأسرّة حُمِلت على العجلات والعجلات يحركها الأبغال يقودهم الرِّجال والعبيد فلمّا قرب العبيد من القصر وله حركات في لواليب كثيرة دارت بهم والقصر مبنيٌّ على سرير مستعمل من أصناف [f. 35] الرُّخام ودارت اللّواليب بالسرير والقصر مبنيّ على لواليب عاليات مستعملة على وسط السّرير فلا يقرب من السّرير لوح ولا نفس إلاّ تحركت تلك الأبواب فتتحرّك اللواليب الوسط ويدور القصر لتحريكها فلمّا قرّبَتِ العبيد الأبغال تدكدكت الأرض

[٧٤] عالٍ Here and following
[٧٥] من B. في الاصل "تتحرك الابواب وداروا"
[٧٦] اعلاة
[٧٧] بصفائح
[٧٨] ظاهرة
[٧٩] من B.
[٨٠] جوانب
[٨١] منهم
[٨٢] منهم
[٨٣] منهم

وتحرّكوا[٨٤] الأبواب ودار القصر لتحريكها فمسكته الألواح الممتدّة من قصر ذي القرنين فوقف القصر فدنا منه ذو القرنين فنظر إلى بابه فإذا عليها مكتوب ' أشهد أن لا إله إلاّ الله وأشهد أن محمّداً رسول الله ' فقال ذو القرنين «أشهد أن لا إله إلاّ الله أشهد أن محمّداً رسول الله» فانفتح القصر بإذن الله تعالى

فلمّا دخل فيه ذو القرنين فإذا فيه تابوت مقفول مصنوع من الذهب الأحمر مرصّع بأصناف الجواهر على قفله مكتوب ' لا حول ولا قوّة إلاّ بالله العليّ العظيم ' فقال ذو القرنين [f. 36] «لا حول ولا قوّة إلاّ بالله العليّ العظيم» فانفتح التابوت بإذن الله تعالى فإذا في التابوت مكتوب ' بسم الله الرّحمان الرّحيم صلّى الله على سيّدنا محمّد خاتم النبيّين وإمام المرسلين ورسول ربّ العالمين إلى الخلق أجمعين [و] [٨٥] آخر النبيّين وهو الموجود في كتب المرسلين ونصر الله قريب من الحسنين والله ولى المتّقين ' [وفي آخر] [٨٦] هذا [اللوح][٨٧] ' سطرون اليناني بقيّة من اليانون كان مع النبيّ نوح عليه السّلام ابن لامك فأمر به و[أرّخ][٨٨] في لوحه من بعده من ذرّيته الأنبياء والرّسل الذين أوّلهم نوح وآخرهم محمّداً صلعم ' وأوّل من يقف على اللوح من أهل الصّدق ذو القرنين ويكون له علامة نصره على أهل جابلقا وعلى أهل جابرسا وما بينهما والحمد لله رب العالمين

قال أبو عبد الله لمّا قرأ ما فيه قال «الحمد لله ربّ العالمين الذي [f. 37] جعلني لأمرِهِ من الشاكرين ولطاعته من العاملين يا حبيبي يا زياقيل ما يكون هذا الرّجل الذي كتب هذا اللوح ؟» قال «يا ذا القرنين كان سِطْرٌ من اليانون وهم من الخلق الأوّل الذين هم قبل آدم وليس هم من نّسله وإنّما هم قوم وخلقهم الله تعالى قبل آدم فكثّروا وتنسلوا[٨٩] وطغوا في الأرض فاعتزل رجل منهم عارف بالله تعالى يقال له قاطور فاعتزل في هذا الجزيرة فتنسّل[٩٠] بها نسلا حتّى أهلك الله اليانون كُلّهم بعد أن بعث الله فيهم نبيّاً فدعاهم إلى دين الله فقتلوه كفرا منهم وطغيانا فبعث الله عليهم نارا من السّماءِ فاحرقتهم عن آخرهم فبقا قاطورُ في هذه الجزيرة فتنسّل بها حتّى هلك ومات وبقى نسله في هذه الجزيرة فعدوا فيها على دين الله كما كانوا الذين طغوا قبلهم فأهلكهم الله كما أهلك الذين كانوا قبل آدم وهم أربعة أمم اليانون [f. 38] واللهون والطُّمّ والطّماطيم وهم أمم كبني آدم كلّ أمّة يبعث الله فيها

---

[٨٤] تتحرّكت

[٨٥] في الاصل "في" :Due to interference with following line

[٨٦] من B.

[٨٧] في الاصل "الوح"

[٨٨] في الاصل "ورّخ"

[٨٩] تناسلوا

[٩٠] فتناسل

نبيّاً فيكون سبب هلاكها على يديه فيدعوا ربّه تعالى فيبعث على الأمّة نارا من السّماءِ فتحرّق الأمة على آخرها ولا يحرقهم حتّى يخرج نبيُّهم منهم فلمّا هلكت القرون الماضية خلق آدم وتنسّل نبيّه نوحٌ عليه السّلام فأغرقهم الله ونجا من نّجا وممّن نّجا مع نوح من ذرّيّة قاطور ومن نسله سطرون وكان عبداً صالحاً تَعَلّم العلم من نوح عليه السّلام وبقى بعد نوح حتّى نزلت النّبوّة على سام ابن نوح وكان سطرون من جواريه ووجد في صحب نوح وصُحُب سام ابن نوح المنزلة عليهم أن الانبياء يتوارثوا من نسلهم إلى آخر الانبياء فكتب في اللوح ذالك وكان ذا[٩١] ملك وشأن فبنا هذا القصر وجعل اللوح في تابوت في القصر وحفظ باللواليب كي لا يصل [f. 39] إليه جنٌّ ولا إنس وإنّما أراد الله أن يُكرِمَه به ويعلمك بأنه علامة نصرك على أهل الدنيا وهذا ما كان من القصر واللوح» فقال ذو القرنين «الحمد لله ربّ العالمين» قال صاحب الحديث فرجع ذو القرنين إلى محلّته وعزم على الرحيل بعون الله إلى جهة جابلقا من جهة مغرب الشمس من غير قائد يقوده ولا سائق يسوقه

ذكر مسير ذي القرنين إلى مدينة جابلقا

قال أبو عبد الملك الملشوني حدّثنا [مقاتل] [٩٢] ابن سليمان أن ذا القرنين ضرب الأبواق فنزل القوم على وجه الماء ثمّ ارتحل فسار على نحو ما تقدّم من المسير على وجه الماء بإذن الله تعالى يقوم منه غُبَارٌ كما يقوم من التراب من شدّة حوافر الخيل والدوّاب والبغال والرّجال بقدرة ذي الجلال والإكرام ومشا بجنوده على الماء يتبّع السبب يوماً كاملاً [f. 40] فقطع فيه مسيرة سنة كاملة حتّى انتها إلى تَلّ عالي في البحر أمواجه تلْتَطِمُ[٩٣] في الهوى فأشرق على مدينة عالية البنيان واسعة الميدان في جزيرة كجزيرة الغرب أو دونها يسير مبنيّة حيطانها من حجر الجلمود المصنوع كُلّ حجر كالسّاريّة عرض الحجر أربعة وعشرون ذراعا وطولها ستّون ذراعا وشرافاتها[٩٤] من الكذّان ولها اثنا عشر ألف باب بين كلّ باب ثلاثة فراسخ وكلّ باب يحرس عليه كلّ ليلة اثنا عشرة ألف رجل ولا يعودون إلاّ في حوائفهم وأسواقهم وتجارتهم وجنود ذي القرنين يومئذ ثلاثمائة ألف رُجِل[٩٥] دون أهل الصّنائع فلمّا أشرفت

---

[٩١] ذو

[٩٢] في الاصل "معقل"

[٩٣] تلْتَطَم

[٩٤] شرفاتها

[٩٥] sic، نفهم "رَجْل" أو "رُجلان" ؟

جنود ذو[٩٦] القرنين على أهل جابلقا ضربت الأبواق وعلت أصواتهم[٩٧] ونزل الرُّعب في قلوب أهل جابلقا من صوت الأبواق و لم يكونوا يَعْلَمُونها وظَنّوا أن أعدائهم أهل جابَرْسا أقبلوا عليهم وكانوا في عِدّةٍ لا يعلم منتهاها [f. 41] إلاّ الله فتوامَرُوا[٩٨] فيما بينهم بالخروج للقاء الجنود من غير أن يعلموا أن ذالك ذو القرنين فأقبلوا إلى الأبواب يَنْدفعُونَ فيها ويَخرُجُون أفواجاً من كلّ باب مائة ألف

فلمّا نظر ذو القرنين إلى كثرة عَدَدِهِم أمر ابن عمّ له من ملوك الرّوم يقال له [قطلاميس عَلى الخيل فعقد لهُ] [٩٩] لِواء بماية ألف وأمر أيضا ابن عمّ له يقال له لَاطيقون على ساقة الجنود في مائة ألف فأمره أن يخرج بمن مّعُهُ على يمين المدينة ثمّ عقد لواء[١٠٠] ثالثا لملك من ملوك الرّوم يقال له شقاريش بمائة ألف ثمّ عقد لواء رابعا لملك من ملوك الروم يقال له شماميس بمائة ألف على [يسار][١٠١] المدينة ثمّ عقد لِواء خامسا لملك من ملوك الروم يقال له قَوْمَشْ بمائة ألف وأمره أن يمرّ من غرب المدينة ثمّ عقد لواء سادسا للملك [f. 42] كبير من أبناء الرّوم يقال له قاطوش ثمّ عقد لواء سابعا لملك من ملوك الرّوم يقال له ناهوش فأمره بمبارزة القوم

فلمّا رَأوه أهل المدينة قد فرّق عليهم القبائل ونظر أهل كلّ باب وأهل كلّ جهة إلى ما يقابلها من جنود الله ألقى الله في قلوبهم الرُّعب وبعث إليهم الرّيح وأظهر لهم العدد وبروق الأسِنّة ولمعان البيض وتَفَرْقَعَتْ الألوية بالريح على الأقنيّة الطِوال في أيد الرِّجال فأرعبوا وقال «لا طاقة لنا بهذه الجنود» وارتعبواْ لّما سمعوا من ضرب الأبواق وشدّة الغبرات فبادرواْ[١٠٢] مسرعين فأشرف رجالهم وخرجوا إلى كلّ جهة يقولون «يا قائد العِنّة يسئلونه عن الوالي الذي يلي الجنود كلّها وأنهم إلى السمع والطاعة» قال أبو عبد الملك فسكتوا عن أجابتهم فكلّ طائفة من العساكير يدلونهم على الملك ذو القرنين حتّى إذا بلغوا له قالوا له[f. 43] «يا ذا القرنين اعلمنا بسيرتك وحكمك ودينك فإنّا عاملون بسيرتك مُتّبعون لدينك وما كان خروجنا بجنودنا إلاّ ظنّنا أن أعداءنا أهل جابرسا قدموا علينا ولو

---

[٩٦] ذي

[٩٧] أصواتها

[٩٨] فتأمر

[٩٩] من B

[١٠٠] لواءً

[١٠١] في الاصل "سيّار"

[١٠٢] sic

علمنا أنّك القادم علينا لأتيناك قبل تفريق جنودنا و[لاكن][١٠٣] نحن الآن سامعون لأمرك طـائعون لله ثمّ لك ومع هذا كله تعلمنا من تحسن إليه ومن تسوء إليه»

قال أبو عبد الملك الملشوني وذو القرنين مع ذالك على حذر من الجنود والجنود كفّـوا عـن الحرب والضرب فعادوه في السّؤال فقالوا «يا ذا القرنين اعلمنا من تعبد ومن تعاقب ومن تحسن إليـه ومن تجازيه بالأمان من شرّك [١٠٤]؟» قال لهم « إنّي لا أعاقب إلاّ من كفر بالله وأمّا من آمن بالله فـلا سبيل لي إليه إلاّ بالخير والأمان مني ومن معي» فرجعوا إلى أهاهيم[١٠٥] وقبائلهم وأعلموهم بمقالـة ذي القرنين فرجعوا [f. 44] إليه فقالوا له «آمنا بربّك أنّه لا ربّ غيره ولا تشرك بـه شـيئا» فاكرمـهم وجزائهم خيرا وفتحوا له الأبواب ودخلوا المدينة وشهدوا الله بالوحدانيّة قال أبو عبد الملك الملشـوني وذلك قوله تعالى [فلمّا بلغ][١٠٦] ﴿ مَغْرِبَ الشَّمْسِ وَجَدَهَا تَغْرُبُ فِي عَيْنٍ حَمِئَةٍ وَوَجَدَ عِندَهَا قَوْماً قُلْنَا ياذَا الْقَرْنَيْنِ إِمَّآ أَن تُعَذِّبَ وَإِمَّآ أَن تَتَّخِذَ فِيهِمْ حُسْناً قَالَ أَمَّا مَن ظَلَمَ فَسَوْفَ نُعَذِّبُهُ ثُمَّ يُرَدُّ إِلَى رَبِّـهِ فَيُعَذِّبُهُ عَذَاباً نُّكْراً وَأَمَّا مَنْ ءَامَنَ وَعَمِلَ صالِحاً فَلَهُ جَزَآءً الْحُسْنَى وَسَنَقُولُ لَهُ مِنْ أَمْرِنَا يُسْراً ثُمَّ أَتْبَعَ سَبَباً ﴾[١٠٧] قال أبو عبد الملك الملشوني يعني من ظلم من أمتنع من الإيمان بالله على يـد ذي القرنـين فسَوْفَ يعذّبُ وَيلْقَا الشرّ من سطوات عذاب الجنود وشرّها وهو لها وانكالها والرُّعب منها والسّـبب الذي أمره الله جلّ جلالَهُ بها من يُؤمن به في الدنيا ثمّ [f. 45] يُردُّ إلى ربّه فيعذّبه عذابا نكرا بالنار عذابا شديدا لا يقدرون على وصفه

قال أبو عبد الملك الملشوني عن أبي أيُّوب عن يريد الخصمي[١٠٨] عن مالك ابن معاذ ابن جـلبر رضى الله عنه أن ذا القرنين مضا إلى مدينة جابلقا فلمّا نزل بساحتها [ترك][١٠٩] الناس حتّى ناموا جعل التاج[١١٠] على رأس ابن امه وكان من [ثقاته][١١١] وأمره أن يخفى أمره ومضـى [بـالليل][١١٢] وحـده وخلف عسكره ومضى على طريق غير معروف لا يسلكه أحد وركب إليه البراق وهى السّبب الذي

---

١٠٣ في الاصل "للكن"

١٠٤ sic

١٠٥ أهاليهم

١٠٦ في الاصل "بلغ فلما"

١٠٧ Qur'ān 18:86-89

١٠٨ B: سعيد الخصَمي

١٠٩ في الاصل "ثرك"

١١٠ نفهم "وضع التاج"

١١١ في الاصل "تقاته"

١١٢ في الاصل "بالّيل"

ذكر الله عزّ وجلّ بقوله جلّ ذكره ﴿ ثُمَّ أَتْبَعَ سَبَباً ﴾[١١٣] وهى البراق وفي قول مجاهد وابن عبّاس رضى الله عنهم اجمعين والله أعلم أنّه قال تحمّل ذو القرنين على طريق واعرة حتّى وصل إليهم على طريق لا يسلُكَها إلاّ الطّيرُ فوصل إلى مدينة لم يري[١١٤] الرأون [f. 46] مثلها وهى بلد ناعمة لا يعلم عَدَدَ ما فيها من الخلق إلاّ الله تعالى فدخل المدينة في زيّ أهلها ومشا في ازقتها نهاراً فنظر إلى ما فيها من الخلق والبنيان والترتيب والهيبة في أشرافها وهو في كلّ ذلك لا يعرفه أحدٌ إلى [أن وصل][١١٥] الليل فلمّا غربت الشمس في عين حمّاية وهي عين طينها أسود يفور ماؤها ويغلى كَغِلْيَانِ[١١٦] القِدْرِ على النار فإذا غربت الشمس في تلك العين على مقدار ثلاث مائة وستّين فرسخا فلا تمرّ بشيء إلاّ وأحرقته وهي في غرب المدينة بفراسيخ كثيرة لاكنّها إذا غربت تكون بها جَلَبَة عظيمة فلمّا غربت الشمس سمع ذو القرنين تلك الجلبة فظنّ أن أهل الدنيا[١١٧] قد ماتوا كلّهم من شدّتها وأهل المدينة لهم وقتٌ أبدا [f. 47] عند غروبها يضَجّون بالتهليل والتكبير والتضرُّع إلى الله تعالى من شدّة الجلبة وقوتها وسقوطها في العين فغشى على ذي القرنين شدّة الجلبة وقَال مجاهدلولا صوت للهدَّة من تضرُّع أهل المدينة وتهليلهم لمات من بأطَراف الدنيا ممّن في المغرب من حلبة شِدّة سُقُوطِ الشمس وقال قتادة لولا بعد المغرب وبعد المَشْرِق وقوع الشمس في العين الحمايّة وفي رواية أخري عن قتادة أنّه قال قال رسول الله صلعم أن الله عزّ وجلّ خلق مدينتين أحداهما بالمشرق يقال لها جابرصا والأخرى بالمغرب يقال لها جابلقا لِكلّ مدينة عشر آلاف باب يحرسونها كلّ ليلة عشر آلاف رّجُلٍ فلا يعودون يحرسون أبدا قال صلعم والذي نفسي [بيده][١١٨] [f. 48] لولا كثرة أصواتهم لسمع أهل الدنيا سقوط الشمس حين تسقط في العين الحمّاية ومن ورأيهم[١١٩] ستّة أمم لا يعلم عدَدُهم إلاّ الله ثمّ أن ذا القرنين جاء لجابَلقا وحده وجمّع أشرافهم وعظمائَهم وقال لهم «أنا رسول ذي القرنين أرسلني اليكم لنعلم ما تقولون وما رأيكم في دينه والإيمان به» قال بعضهم لبعض «لا طاقة لنا بجنود الإسكندريّ ونحن به مؤمنون» وقال بعضهم «هو ملك زائرٌ لايقيمُ ببلدنا نؤمن به مدّة أقامته فإذا أظعن رحل عن بلدنا عدنا على ما كُنّا عليه» فاختلف رأيهم وقالوا «يا رسول ذي القرنين اصبر علينا إلى غدٍ حتّى نعلم منتها أتّفاقنا» قال لهم «نعم أنا أصبر

---

١١٣ Qur'ān 18:89

١١٤ ير

١١٥ من B

١١٦ كَغَلَيان

١١٧ Here and throughout the manuscript: يكتب الكاتب "دنيا" مع ثلاثة نقاط تحت الياء

١١٨ في الاصل "يده"

١١٩ ورائهم

عليكم ولا أريد منكم إلاّ رأيّ واحد وقول متّفق[١٢٠]» فقالوا له يا رسول ذي القرنين عندنا شيخ زَمِن قد عمّر ألف سنّة [f. 49] وعرف الأمور وهو مختلف عن جمعنا فأنا نبعث إليه ونشاوروه في أمرنا ونجاوبك» قال لهم «أردْتُ الاجتماع معه» فقال له «إذا اتّفق رأينا وعزم جمعنا على رأيّ واحد فأنا نجمع بينك وبينه وهو يا رسول ذي القرنين لو رأيته عظيما من علم وأدبٍ وشرف وكرم» فقال لهم «رغبتي في الاجتماع معه» قال فانصرفوا من مجلسهم ذالك وبعثوا إلى الشيخ فأتاهم في اليوم الثامن فاجتمعوا به وأعلموه بخبرِ ذي القرنين ورسوله وقالوا له «لو رأيت رسولَه وما رُكّبَ فيه من علم وأدبٍ وصبرٍ لرأيت عظيماً» قال لهم الشيخ «اجمعوا بيني وبينه أسئله عن أمور ليّ بها معرفة بالغة فإن كان نبيّا آمنا بربّه وأن كان ملكا من الملوك ورأينا رأياً في حربه حاربناه» فقالوا له «نعم» فمضوا بالشيخ حتّى وصلوا به إلى الإسكندريّ وظنّ أنّه رسول [f. 50] كما ذكِر له فلمّا دخل عليه الشيخ قال له «يا رسول ذي القرنين ما اسمك ؟» قال «عبد الله» قال له «يا عبد الله ما دين الملك ؟» قال له «السَّمْعُ والطاعة لخالق الخلق» قال له «وما سيرته ؟» قال له «الصِّدْقُ واتّبَاع الحقّ» قال له «وما كلام الملك ؟» قال له «الأمر بالمعروف والنهّيُ عن المنكر» قال «وما عفّةُ الجند عنده ؟» قال له «الفَضْلُ والعفّةُ عن الحرام» قال له «وما ثلاثة يحبُّهُنّ وما ثلاثة يبغضُهُنّ الملك؟» قال له «يحبُّه الذّكر لله والطاعة لله والبغض فيمن عصى الله وأما الثلاثة التي يبغضُهُنّ الملك» قال «يبغض المعاصي والفجور والشِّرْك بالله» قال «وما ثلاثة يُقِمن مُلْكَهُ ؟» قال له «أقامة ملكه بثلاثة أشياء بالعدل في الأحكام والصِّدق في الاقوال والوفاء بالعهود» قال فيما يُهْدَمُ عِزّ مُلُكِهِ ؟» قال «باتّبَاع الهواء[١٢١] [f. 51] والنقض لِلْعَهْدِ والحكم بالشهوات» قال الشيخ «يا عبد الله بما يُعْرفُ صِدق الأشياء ؟» قال «بالصِّدق والمُعْجَزَات» قال «فيما يعلم صِدقُهُم» قال «بثبوت أقوالهم» قال «فيما تعرف معجزاتهم ؟» قال «ببلوغ ما لم يُبْلَغْ وسلوك ما لم يُسْلَكْ وظهور الأيات على أيديهم» قال «فما علامة ذي القرنين ؟» قال له «رجل صادق يقول الحقّ ويقضى به ويحكم بالعدل ويرضا به ويحتمل المكارة[١٢٢] ويصبر على الهفوات ويحبُّ في الله ويبغض في الله ولا تأخذه في الله لومة لائم» قال الشيخ «فمن أنت منه وما هو منك ؟» قال «أنا مِنه وهو منّي ؟» قال له الشيخ «فاهج لي أوّل اسمك وآخره» «أوّل اسمي أربعةٌ وآخره خمسين» قال له الشيخ «أنت ذو القرنين فخذوا على يَدِ سيّدكم يا أهل المدينة» قال له ذو القرنين «ومَن أعلمك بهذا [f. 52] يا شيخ واسمي عبد الله ؟» قال «وكلّنا عباد الله» قال «فيما استَدْلَلْتَ على اسمى إنّي ذو

---

[١٢٠] رأياً واحداً وقولاً متّفقً

[١٢١] الهوى

[١٢٢] المكاره

القرنين ؟» قال «لأنّي سألت عن أوّل اسمك في هجاية فقُلْتَ لي أوّله أربعة والدّال [اربعة نقصات[١٢٣] وآخر اسمك خمسُون فعلمت أن النُّون آخر اسمك خمسُون][١٢٤] فعلمتُ أن اسمك ذو القرنين» [قال:] «كيف يميل إليكم ويترك جنوده وهو في خلق كثير ولا عنده من [يُحرّيه][١٢٥] عن هذا؟» قال له الشيخ «عَلِمْتُ من مكائد الملوك ما لم يَعْلَمُهُ أحد غيري وهذا من أعظم فعالهم ولا شكٌّ أنّك ذو القرنين» قال له «أ رأيت أن بلغك ذو القرنين وحده ما أنت صانعٌ أنت وأصحابك وقومك ؟» قال «هيهات هيهات بلغني أنه كان ملكاً من ملوك الرّوم ذو كيودٍ وحِيَالٍ ودخل على ملك يكيده فسئله الدّاخلُ [على][١٢٦] أمور فاجابه المقيمُ بأمور فلمّا كان في آخر حديثهم عرف المقيم مكيدة [f. 53] الداخل عليه فقال له الدَّاخِلُ [لو] صَغَيْتَ إليّ وفوّضت[١٢٧] أمرك إليّ لجعلت فلان الملك في تحكمك ويده في يدك وأراد به مكيدة بنفسه» فقال له «إن فعلت كذالك كان ملكي بيدك» فصَافَحَه بيده عَضُداً فترابطا بايديهما يدا بيد والدّاخلُ يريد به المكيدة والمقيم على نيّة الملك يأخذه فلمّا [تمّ][١٢٨] عقدهم فيما بينهم قال له «وأين تريد أن اجمع بينك وبين الملك ؟» قال «في مجلسي هذا» قال «فإن جمعت بينكما ما أنت صانعٌ به ؟» قال «[أعفو][١٢٩] عنه واصفح» قال له «الله عليك» قال «نعم» قال له «أنا هو الملك» فصافحه وعناقه وأكرمه وأحسن إليه وفوّضه أمر ملكه

«فكذالك يا عبد الله إن كنت ذو القرنين بالسّمعُ والطاعة لك وإن كنت لست ذو القرنين فاقرأه منّي السّلام أنا وأهل المدينة في دينه فإنّي ظهر لي فيه لسبب [f. 54] أخبارك عنه وأجابتك السّوال عنه انه ملك صالح ونبيّ صالح فقم وأرجع إلى موطنك» فقال له ذو القرنين «لا يصلح أن يكون في هذه المدينة والي غيرك مُدّة حياتك» قال «ما لي وذالك وقد رأيتُ ملوكاً وأشرافاً ودهورا وأوصافا فلم يبق من بعد الملوك إلاّ الدهور ولم يبق من بعد الدهور إلاّ الأوصاف ولم يبق من [أمري][١٣٠] إلاّ اليسير فأكون في اليسير على صفة التغيير» فقال له ذو القرنين «ما اسمك يا شيخ ؟» فقال له «أنا جودب ابن جودب» قال له «وكم مضا عنك من السّنين ؟» قال له «ألف ومائة وثلاثة وستّون عامّا» قال «كم

---

١٢٣ This word is not clear.

١٢٤ من B

١٢٥ في الاصل "يُحزّيه"

١٢٦ من B. في الاصل "ان"

١٢٧ في الاصل "فوّصت"

١٢٨ في الاصل "ثمّ"

١٢٩ في الاصل "اعف"

١٣٠ في الاصل "امر"

رأيت من الملوك ؟» قال له رأيت الملك يقمطيش ابن رويش » قال «كم قام في ملكه ؟» قال له «ألفَان غير ثلاثة مائة» قال له «كم بلغ جنده ؟» قال له «ألفان غير ثلاثة مائة» قال «كم بلغ [f. 55] ملكه ؟» قال «بلغ من السِّند إلى الهند إلى جَبال الكرد[١٣١] إلى مصر» قال «ومن أخرجه من ملكه ؟» قال له «داروم» قال «وكم مكث في الملك؟» قال له «ألف وأقلٌ مائة وفي نسله يتوارثوا إلى سبع ملوك» قال له «حقّ عليك العُمُر ولك الولاية وأنا ذو القرنين وقد ولّيتك أمر هذه المدينة»

قال أبو عبد الملك الملشونيّ حدّثنا أبو الصبّاح عن هشام عن كعب أن ذو[١٣٢] القرنين وصل إليهم بالجنود ونزل بعسكره إلى جانب الجبل المحيط بالدنيا [١٣٣] وأمر أصحابه أن يربطوا خيلهم إلى الجبل وأن يعلقوا أسلحتهم إلى الثريّا فأصابها عند وجوها فلمّا قضى ما يريد أتا إلى موضع السلاح أصحابه فلم يقدروا عليها وكانت الثريا حين علّقت السلاح فيها حُنَي إليها في الحجاب وهي في الفَلَكِ [f. 56] مسجّةٌ[١٣٤] فلم يرجع ذو القرنين إليها الأ وقد ارتفعت من مكانها ولم يقدروا على الوصول إلى شيء مما تعلّق إليها من سلاحهم فرجع ذو القرنين إلى الشيخ فسأله عن حول الثريّا فقال له الشيخ «يا ذا القرنين أنّك لن تبلغ إلى ما تريد من سلاح أصحابك إلاّ إلى عام كامل» فأقام ذو القرنين إلى تمام الحول فرجعت الثريّا إلى طريقها وعادت إلى موضعها وإن السّماء تدور على الدنيا والناس لا يعلمون بذالك فأقاموا إلى رأس الحول حتّى عادت الثريّا إلى مكانها في ذالك اليوم بعينه فأخذوا سلاحهم وحدّثني كعب الاحبار بهذا الحديث وأبو ذَرّ جالس عنده فقال أبو ذرٍّ قول الله أصْدَق من قولك يا كعب لأنّ الله جلّ ذكره يقول أن الله يمسك السّموات والأرض أن تزولا وليس زالتا أن أمسكهما [f. 57] من أحد من بعده قال أبو ذرٍّ ولا زالتا ما أمسكها أحدا من بعده أبدا ولذهبتا قال كعب الاحبار يا أبا ذرّ أنّ الله عطا لذي القرنين ما لم يعط أحدا من الناس وذالك قوله تعالى ﴿ إِنَّا مَكَّنَّا لَهُ فِي الأَرْضِ وَءَاتَيْنَاهُ مِن كُلِّ شَيْءٍ سَبَباً ﴾[١٣٥] يعني من كلّ شيء عِلماً وقدراً إلاّ يقدر عليها أحد غيره قال أبو عبد الملك الملشوني ولم أدع من لقيته من العلماء إلاّ وسألتهم أن ذو القرنين لّما سُمي بذالك فكلّ واحد يقول فيه قول وتفسير[١٣٦] لا يُجابه الأخر قُلتُ لأبي صالح لّما سُمي ذو القرنين قال لي

[١٣١] الكرد

[١٣٢] ذا

[١٣٣] يكتب "دنيا" مع ثلاثة نقطة تحت الياء

[١٣٤] يمكن نفهم "مُسَجّاة" أو "مسجةٌ" ؟

[١٣٥] Qur'ān 18:84

[١٣٦] قولا وتفسيرا

حدّثني هشام بن عروة عن كعب أنّه قال كان له قرنان من لَحم مثل دَوّابتان[١٣٧] عليهما الشعَرَ بأشدِ سواد ما رآ الرّأون مثله قطُّ وشَعَرُ تلك الدوّابتان لا يطول أبدا وكان مبلغ تلك الدّوّابتان إلى أطراف أذنيه وكان لا يربط عليهما عمامة إلاّ أنّه كان يضع على رأسه التاج فكانت تلك علامته إلتي [f. 58] يعرفونه بها أهل العلم قال وسألت مقاتل لمّا سُمي ذو القرنين ؟ فقال لي حدّثنا بعض أهل العلم أنّه بلغ من الدنيا إلى قِرن المغرب وبلغ منها إلى قرن المشرق فلمّا بلغ إلى المغرب رآ كيف تغرب الشمس في عين الحماية ثمّ رآ كيف تطلع من فلكها من المشرق فسماه الله ذو[١٣٨] القرنين

قال أبو عبد الملك وسمعتُ أبا ذرّ[١٣٩] الهمداني يقول حدّثنا مجاهد أنّه قال كان ذو القرنين رجلا شجاعا وكان يلاقي القِتال بنفسه إذا اشتدّ تولاه فإذا نظروا أصحابه إلى ذالك تقدموا معه ولم يقدروا أن يفرّ[وا] عنه فحينئذ يظفر بما يريد قال فضُرِبَ في بعض حروبه [f. 59] بضربةٍ في قرنه الأيمن وضربة في قرنه الأيسر فسُمّي بذالك ذو القرنين

قال كعب الاحبار بل دخل جابلقا بجنوده ومن معه وأمر أصحاب الأبواق يَضْرِبُوا أبواقهم فرأوا أمرا لم يروا مثله قطّ فلم يبق في تلك المدينة عجوز ولا إمراة ولا بكر ولا مخدّرة إلاّ خرجوا ينظرون إلى ذي القرنين وإلى جنوده فمرّ ذو القرنين برحل سكّاف قاعدٍ على عمله لا يرفع إليهم رأسه ولا ينظر إليهم وهو قاعد على شغله ولم يكن في تلك المدينة أعرف بالله منه فلمّا نزل ذو القرنين بجنوده واستقرّ بهم النزول أمر أن يأتوه بذالك الرجل فأتوه به فقال له ذو القرنين «يا شيخ إنّ هذه الجنود التي معي هي جنود الله وحيله وأولياؤه فما لك لا تنظر إليهم ؟» فقال له الشيخ «يا ذا القرنين قد رأيت [قبلك][١٤٠] ملوكاً كثيرة أُعْطُوا مثل الذي أُعْطِيتَ [f. 60] ونالوا مثل الذي نلْتَ و[لاكنّها][١٤١] غدرَتهم وسُلبتْ عنهم فذهب ملكهم وذهبت أموالُهُم وقُطِعَت آثارهم فلم يبق منهم إلاّ الأخبار فَخَيْرُهُم عند الله أعدلهم فإن عملتَ لله فسَوْف تُصيبُ خيرا وإن عمِلت لغير الله فقد فَسَدَ خَيْرك فأنظر لنفسك بأَوْفَرَ النظر وأوفر الحظّ» قال له ذو القرنين «يا شيخ كم تُصِيبُ كلّ يوم من عَمَلك ؟» قال له «دِرْهَم» قال له «[فماذا][١٤٢] تُنْفَقَه ؟» قال له «ثَلْثٌ أقضي به ديني وثلثٌ أُسَلّفُهُ وثلْثٌ أعيش به أنا وعيالي» قال له «كيف ذالك يا شيخ ؟» قال له «كان لي أبوان شيخان كبيران قد

---

[١٣٧] نفهم "ذُوَابتين"

[١٣٨] ذا

[١٣٩] An alternative reading of this not clearly legible name is "أبا زرّ" as we find written in B, f. 61.

[١٤٠] في الاصل "قلبك"

[١٤١] في الاصل "للكنّها"

[١٤٢] في الاصل "فيماذا"

أدركهما عندي الكبر فلهما عليّ في كلّ يوم ثلث درهم أقضيهما دَيْنَهُمَا الذي كأنا يُنفقان عليّ من مالِهما وثلث أُنفقُه على أولادي وهو الذي أُسَلِّفُهُ فإن طال عُمري بينهُم [f. 61] واحتجتُ إليهم ردّوا عليّ سلفي والثلث الباقى أعيش به أنا وعيالي» قال له ذو القرنين «أنّك [العليم][١٤٣] وأُحِبُّ أن أوليك على هذه المدينة وإنّي أظنّك أن تقيم بها حدود الله فولاه أمرها هو والشيخ وملكهم عليها وأمر أهل المدينة بالسمع والطاعة فسَمعُوا [له][١٤٤] وأطاعوا»

قال أبو عبد الملك الملشونيّ قلت لمقاتل ابن سليمان أخبرني على أهل جابلقا من يكونوا قال أبو رَوْقٍ سمعتُ مجاهداً يقول أهل جابلقا وأهل جابرسا من قوم هود النبيّ عليه السّلام الذين آمنوا معه فهم منه فهلك الله منهم من هَلَك ونجا من قوم هود فهم من الناجين وذالك أنّه أمرهم هود أن يخرجوا إلى أطراف البحار مهاجرين من قومهم [f. 62] حتّى أهلك الله الكفار ونجا هودا ومن آمن معه و لم يأمن معه إلاّ قليل وهم المهاجرون إلى أطراف البحار فهم في ذلك حتّى مات هود عليه السلام وكثر القوم وتنسّلوا وكثُرَ عَدَدُهم و لم يبعث فيهم نَبيّاً بعْدَ هُودٍ وَهُم على دين هُودٍ عليه السّلام فأقاموا على دينهم حتّى أقام في آل ثمود صَالِحاً عليه السّلام فآمنوا به وصدّقُوهُ فهم على صِحّةٍ من صَالح النّبيّ حتّى قام قَائِمٌ في آل [ثَمُودَ][١٤٥] وهو عاتق ابن عوص ابن عملاق [فثار][١٤٦] في البلاد وجار في الدنيا وهلك البلاد وانجلت العباد فقام القوم من مواضعهم واستعملوا السُّفُن فدخلوا البحار فأمر الله الملك المُوكّل بالسّراب في البحار أن يريهم نفسه على صفة راكب يدلُّهُم على طريق من [f. 63] الطّرف التي تهديهم إلى مسلك الجزيرة التي تُسمّى جزيرة البطاح فمشت بهم السُّفُن بأمر الله حتّى خرجوا في جزائر في سواحل البحر كثيرة الشعاري[١٤٧] في جبال واسِعَةِ البَراري لا عمارة فيها و لم يسكنها قبلهم جنيٌّ ولا إنْسِيٌّ فَدَخَلُوهَا فسكنوا فيها ما شاء الله وغرسوها فلم يروا فيها شيئا يُمْسِكُهُم ويُهْنِيهِم للمعاش فرجعوا إلى أنفسهم وقالوا «ما لنا ولهذه الجزيرة لا بقاء لنا فيها أرجعوا لنا إلى بلدنا» فقال بعْضهم لبعض لا رجوع لنا إلى بلاد الكفر قوموا بنا إلى سفوننا[١٤٨] فنركب البحر فإنّ الذي أخرجَنا إلى هذا [المكان][١٤٩] قادر أن يخرج بنا إلى غيره فعسى يوصِّلُنَا إلى بلاد يُرْضِيها لنا» فاتّفق رأْيُهُم على ذالك

---

١٤٣ من B في الاصل "الحيم"

١٤٤ في الاصل "لهم"

١٤٥ في الاصل "ثَمُوذَ"

١٤٦ في الاصل "فتار"

١٤٧ i.e., goats

١٤٨ سفننا

١٤٩ في الاصل "الملكان"

فركبوا [f. 64] السّفن فألقا الله بعضهم في أقصا المشرق وبعضهم في أقصا المغرب فركبوا السّفن حتّى انتهت كلّ فرقة من الفرقتين الريح حيث شاء الله وكان في القوم رجلين شريفين ابناء الأختين أحدهما يُسمّى جابل والأخر جابر واسماء أمهاتهم أحدهما تُسمّى بلقا والأخرى برْصا وكان ركوبهم في البحر مفترقات فانتهت كلّ فُرْقةٍ حيث شاء الله

فخرجوا في جزائر واسعة وبلاد منعمة لا يصفها الواصفون مما خصّها الله من طيب الأرض وكثرة مائِها وسهلها [و] وَسْعِهَا[١٥٠] ليس منها جزيرة إلاّ وفي وسعها مسيرة ستّة أشهرٍ ومثلها فلمّا استقرّوا بتلك الأرض واستقرّوا الفريقين[١٥١] في هذه الجزائر ومعهم فضل من أزودتهم من القمح والشعير وقد خرجوا [f. 65] في زمان الحرث فزرعوا من بعض ما معهم ونبت على أحسن نبات وغرسوا الأشجار فنبتوا على أحسن شجرٍ رأوْها وأقاموا فيها سنّة وقلوبهم متعلّقة بالاجتماع بعضهم إلى بَعْضٍ وطال بهم الأمد [فيبسوا][١٥٢] من الاجتماع بينهم فقام جابرٌ فبنا داراً وشيّدها وسمّاها على اسمه فكان القوم يُسَمُّونَها دار جابر بن برسا فكَثُر نسله بها وترك اسم جابر ابن برسا وسمّوها برسا فجمعوا بين اسم للرّجل وبين اسم أُمه فاتّفق رأيُ القوم أي بنيان المدينة في موضع الدار فبنوها وشيدوها فقال بعضهم لبعضٍ أنا قوم غرباء لا علم لنا بمن في هذا الأرض فلو عملنا في داخل حِصْنِنا في موضع حرثنا ومراعي دوّابنا لكان أقوا [f. 66] وأحصن لغربتنا وأوفر لدوّابنا ووسّعوا وشيدوا وأقاموا في مدينتهم وكذالك عملوا أهل جابلقا فأقاموا في مدينتهم وكثُر نسلهم حتّى بلغوهم ذو القرنين وهم من قوم هَوْدٍ عليه السّلام وقال مجاهد سئل[١٥٣] رسول الله صلعم ممن أهل جابلقا من أيّ الأمم هم ؟ فقال صلعم تلك المدينتين أحدهما بمغرب الشمس والأخرى بمطلعها فكلتاهما تخاف من الأخرى وأهلهما من آل تاريش ابن يافت ابن نوح عليه السّلام وهما في الكثرة والعدد فيما لا يعلمه إلاّ الله تعالى وهذه قِصَّة المدينتين والله أعلم

---

[١٥٠] وسِعِها

[١٥١] واستقر الفريقان

[١٥٢] في الاصل "فيبيسوا"

[١٥٣] نفهم "سائل"

ذِكْر مسير ذو[١٥٤] القرنين من جابلقا إلى المشرق [f. 67]

قال أبو عبد الملك الملشونيّ فلمّا انتها ملك ذو القرنين إلى ما انتها من ملك جابلقا وأهلها ووكّل عليها الشيخ وأمر بطاعته واتّباع رأيه ومن ولاه عليهم الشيخ فهو الوالي وأمرهم بطاعة الله ووَعَظَهُم وأرشدهم إلى دين الله وعزم على الرحيل منها وبات على الرّحيل وأقبل يتفكّر إلى أين تسوقه تمادير من نَواحي الأرض فأتاه الملك زياقيل وعلّمه الخير وأمره أن يرحل إلى أمّة يقال لها باريش فأصبح على ظهر ورحل ووكّل الله به للملك زياقيل يريه نفسه في البحر ويقصّ أثره أي يتبعه وهو السّبب الذي ذكر الله عزّ وجلّ وهو قوله تعالى ﴿ ثُمَّ أَتْبَعَ سَبَباً ﴾[١٥٥] حتّى انتها بأمر الله إلى جزيرة في البحر المحيط وُسْعُهَا مسيرة شهر ولا سلَكَها آدميٌّ قطُّ وفيها انهارٌ وأوديةٌ وجبال وأوعارٌ [f. 68] وسهولٌ وفيها بطحة وُسْعها عشرة أيّام حشيشها الزّعفران وأشجارها [الورس][١٥٦] وفيها وادٌ[١٥٧] يجري خرج من طرف الجزيرة وشقّ في وسطها حتّى انتها إلى البحر عليها [ثمار][١٥٨] مختلفات الألوان والطُّعْمِ وقصورٌ [مشَيَّدَةٌ][١٥٩] وغرفات عاليات مقفرات لا أحداً يسكنها فلمّا وصل ذو القرنين بجنوده ونظر إليها نزل بمن هناك بقربها وأمر بعضهم فدخلوها فأقاموا بها يوماً وليلةً ولا يجد فيها أثر حيّ ولا عمارة ثمّ رجعوا فأعلموه فرغب إلى الله أن يعلمه ما تلك الجزيرة وما أهلها وكيف ذهبوا منها فأتاه الملك زياقيل فقال له «يا ذا القرنين سرّ أمامك عشرة أيّام تلقا من يُعْلِمُكَ خبر الجزيرة والبطحاء» فمشا ذو القرنين عشرة أيّام فانتها إلى جزيرة مثل الجزيرة الأوّلى حافاتها [f. 69] واحدة فأتى إلى مرساها فنزل فأمر بعض رجاله يدخلوها فوجَدُوها عامِرَةً فدخلوا عليه فأعلموه بخبر الجزيرة فإنّها عامرة فبعث إليهم رسوله وكتابه فكتب إليهم:

> باسمك اللّهم من عبد الله المأمور بأمرِ الله ذو القرنين إلى أهل الجزيرة سلام على من أطاع الله وأتبع سبيله فأنا أتيناكم على علم من دينكم وما أنتم عليه من الهدى ومن الضلالة فإن كنتم بالله مؤمنين فلكم الأمن والأمان والعزّة والبرهان وإن كنتم

---

[١٥٤] ذي

[١٥٥] Qur'ān 18:89

[١٥٦] في الاصل "الورش"

[١٥٧] واد

[١٥٨] في الاصل "تمار"

[١٥٩] في الاصل "مشَيَّدةٌ"

من أهل الطغيان فابشروا بالذّل والخسران فإنّ الله أمرنا بقتال أعدائه ووعدنا بالنصر والظفر والله لا يخلف الميعاد

فختم الكتاب ودفعه إلى رسوله فانصرف حتّى أتاهم به فاجتمعوا إليه فألقى إليه الكتاب وقرأوه وسرّهم ما رأوا من حسن كلامه وبادروا [f. 70] بجوابه فكتبوا كتابا مجيبا لدعَوته:

بسم الله الذي لا إله إلاّ هو إلى عبد الله ذو القرنين من أهل باريش كافّة فإنّا وصلنا كتابك تذكر فيه أعزّ الاسماءِ وأطيب الأديان وتذكر فيه طاعة الرّحمان وما أنتم عليه من الصدق والحقّ وتذكر فيه وعد الله وإنّ الله لا يخلف الميعاد وإنّه ناصر لأوليائه ومسلّطُهم على أعدائه فإن كنتم صاديقين[١٦٠] فنحن على التحقيق بكلمة التصديق ومطيعون لمن أطاع الله وناصرون أولياء الله وإن كنتم غير صادقين بالله يحول بيننا وبين القوم والظالمين والسّلام

وختموا كتابهم ودفعوه إلى رسول ذي القرنين فلمّا أتاه الكتاب فكّه وقرأه وفهم قول باريش ثمّ قال لأصحابه «إنّ الله جلّ ذكره جعل هذه الأمة خير أمّة وأنا أريد الوصول إليهم والاجتماع بهم وأسئلهم عن الجزيرة الأولى [f. 71] لمن هي ومن يسكنها»

فركب في ثلاثين ألفا من الفرسان من أجناد عسكره حتّى نزل بالقرب منهم [فبادروه][١٦١] أعيالهم وكهولهم وشبّانُهُم وعلماؤهم وأهل المعرفة منهم فأتوه فسلموا عليه فقال لهم «من أيّ الناس أنتم ؟» قالوا له «نحن بارش» قال له «من يكون بارش ؟» قالوا له «من بني آدم» قال «ومن أيّ الأمم أنتم ؟» قالوا «نحن من آل ثمود من الانبياء الذين كانوا بعثوا في بني إسرائيل وكانوا خمسة انبياء في عصر واحد وكان لنا ملك رفيق بالرّعيّة رفيق بالضعيف ويعرف حقّ الشريف والوضيع يقال له حزقيل فهلك وفقد مكانه ورجع مكانه ابن عمٍّ له فجار على الرّعيّة وهتك الأستار فاجتمعنا إلى سواحل البحر فتباعدنا عنه وأقبلت انبياء بني إسرائيل يأتوا إلينا ويعظمُونا فآمنا بهم وصدّقناهم ووعد إلينا [f. 72] أحد الأنبياء وذكروا [لأبائِنا][١٦٢] أن الله جلّ ذكره أمرهم أن يغزوا أمّة يقال لها أبا زُكائلٍ وهم من آل عاد وأبوهم اباويل ابن عاويل ابن عوص ابن اروم ابن عملاق واروم ابن فرخشد ابن سام ابن نوح عليه السّلام وسكناهم في الجزيرة إلتي خرجتَ منها وارتحلت منها وهي خالية ومنها أتيت إلينا وهي أمّة لا تحصى ولا تعد ولا يعلم عدّهم إلاّ الله تعالى فيها ثلاثة مائة ألف الرحل كلّهم أهل

---

[١٦٠] صادقين

[١٦١] في الاصل "فباذروه"

[١٦٢] في الاصل "لأياثنا"

حرب ليس منهم واحد مطيعٌ لربّه فأمر الله الملك زياقيل أن يأمر نبيّاً من الخمسة أنبياء الذين كانوا في عصره أن يخرج لقتال تلك الأمة بأمّة بارش فأمرنا الملك فخرجنا في البحار في عَدَدِنا و[ذرارينا][١٦٣] وما نحن عليه من القوّة وخرجنا [مع][١٦٤] ذالك النبيّ في خمس مائة ألف وثلاثون ألف مقاتل متتابعين في السُفُن [f. 73] في البحر بعضنا في أثر بعض فتكامل القوم في هذه الجزيرة بأمر الله و لم نعرفوا كيف انتهينا إليها من أهوال البحار ولججها ونحن مع النبيّ الذي أمره الملك بأمر الله تعالى فخرج بنا إلى قتال القوم فحاربناهم ستّة أشهر حتّى تفانت الفئتان فنصر الله أولياءه على أعدائه فلم يبق منهم إلاّ القليل فدَخل الباقون منهم في كهوف تحت الأرض فنجو فيها منّا حتّى رجعنا إلى بلدنا هذه فخرج عليهم آل بارش من بعضنا فهلكوا عن آخرهم وبقيت آثارهم وديارهم كما رأيتها خالية وتُوُفّي ذالك النبيّ بين أظهرنا وكثر نسلنا ونحن الان في بلدنا هذه وما لك منّا يا ذو القرنين ؟» قال لهم ذو القرنين « أمّا حربكم فلا سبيل لي إليه ولاكنّي أدخل أرضكم حتّى أراها كما رأيت غيرها من سائر البلاد [f. 74] وقد أمرني ربّي بذالك»

قال ورحل معهم حتّى وصل إلى أرضهم ودخلها [فرآ][١٦٥] أرضا ليس مثلها أرض ومساكين مرضيّة وصوامع محصّنة ودينار ضيّة ومواشي لا رعاة لها وأناس مستوية في الكسب والقوّة واللباس ورآ قبورا على باب دورهم لا يدخلون ولا يخرجون إلاّ نظروا إليها ونظر إلى أمّة لا شكّ أنّها خير أمّة لا ولات فيها ولا قضات ولا فيهم فقير ولا غنيّ كلّهم على السّويّة ولا جَوْرَ بينهم ولا مخاصمة ولا مداعية فتعجّب من ذلك وقال لهم «أنتم خير أمّة أعلمني بكم ربّي بأنّكم مطيعون لله لأمره ولاكنّكم قولوا ' لا إله إلاّ الله' » فقالوا له نحن على تلك الكلمة من عهد أنبيائنا ولا نشرك بالله شيئا» قال لهم ذو القرنين «ما لي أراكم ليس لمواشيكم رعاة ؟» قالوا «ليس عندنا سارقٌ ولا مُخَاينٌ[١٦٦] » [f. 75] قال «فما بال بيوتكم ليس لها أبواب تغلق بها ؟» قالوا «ليس عندنا خدّاعٌ ولا لصوص والحرز والحرصُ إنّما يكون لمن عندهم المكر والخداع» قال «فما بالكم ليس عندكم ولات والحُكّامٌ ؟» قالوا «الولات[١٦٧] والحُكّامُ على أهل التكبُر والتجبُر ونحن قد قطع الله ذلك من قومنا وقلوبنا وقد عاهدت أنبياؤنا آباؤنا[١٦٨] على الصّدق والوفاء بالحق فكانت آباؤنا يتعاهدون ذالك ويتوارثون سلفا بعد سلف

---

[١٦٣] في الاصل "دراوينا"

[١٦٤] في الاصل "ما"

[١٦٥] في الاصل "فراء"

[١٦٦] خائن

[١٦٧] الولاة

[١٦٨] آباءَنا

وأثرا بعد أثر ونحن على ذالك» قال لهم «فما بالكم ليس عليكم قضات[١٦٩]؟» قالوا «كنّا على العهد القديم لا يظلم بعضا[١٧٠] بعضا فما لنا والقضات» قال «فما بالكم لا غنيّ فيكم ولا فقيرٌ ؟» قالوا «عهدت أنبياؤنا آباؤنا على مواساة أغنيائنا للفقراء بنا فكان الغنيّ منا يقاسم الفقير [f. 76] فيما عنده» فكان ذو القرنين يركب حماراً ويمشي في آل بارش حتّى يجد الفقير فيقاسم فيما عنده خوفاً من الحساب بالمال وخوفا من التحبُّور به لأنّ التحبُّور لا يخلفه في القلب إلاّ كثرت المال وخوفاً من نقض العهد المعهود بين آبائنا وأنبيائهم «وإنّه لا فضل لأحد منّا على الأخر فاستوت بنا الدنيا واعتدل بنا المعاش فلا فقير فينا ولا غنيّ» فقال لهم ذو القرنين «فما بالكم جعلتم قبوركم عند باب دوركم وبيوتكم ؟» قالوا ذالك كي لا ننسى الموت من قلوبنا» قال لهم ذو القرنين «ما رأيت مثلكم في الدنيا ولا شكّ أنّكم خير أمّة وأنتم لا تحتاجون إلى من يكون عليكم كونوا على أمن وأمان على ما أنتم عليه والله المعين وهو حسبنا ونعم الوكيل وعليكم السّلام»

وانصرف [f. 77] وأصبح على ظهر وارتحل إلى جهة المشرق وسار على الماء بجنود لا تحصى قال السّديُّ كانت جنود ذي القرنين مائة ألف وثلاثون ألفا فتلك العدّةُ التي نزل بها على أهل بارش وارتحل عنهم ومضا على الماء والغبار يقوم على وجه الماء كما يقوم من الصّعيد اليابس فصاروا يوما وليلة وقد طوّى الله لهم البعيد ومشا في ذالك اليوم والليلة مسيرة سنة كاملة ونصف حتّى انتها إلى الجبل الأملس الذي أخرجه الله من قُطر الأرض الأيمن وأخرج من القُطر الأيسر جبلٌ مثلهُ وهما جبلان شامخان طويلان قد ذهبا في السّماء بطول ارتفاعهما لا يعلوها طير ولا إنس ولا جنٌّ إلاّ هلك من شدّة بردِ السّماء وهما ضدّان متقابلان وبينهما مسيرة يوم في الأرض مستوية لا جبل بينهما

فلمّا انتها ذو القرنين وقرب منهما واتّصل خبره إلى [f. 78] أهل الجبلين فتبادروا إليه واجتمعوا عنده فقالوا له علماؤهم «يا ذا القرنين هذان جبلين [خلقهما][١٧١] الله تعالى على الصّفة الذي خلقهما عليها وأسكننا فيهما والأيمن منهم[١٧٢] يقال له جبل الأيقاف والأيسر يقال له جبل الاسكاب والسّهل الذي بينهما يقال له سهل مأرب وخلفهما أقوام طوال الأعناق طوال الأجسام طوال الأعمار يعمر أحدهم ألف [سنة][١٧٣] ومائتان وألف وخمسة مائة لا يذكرون الله ولا يدينون بالحقّ يقتلون الناس بغير

---

[١٦٩] قضاة

[١٧٠] بعضنا

[١٧١] جبلان . في الاصل "هلكهما"

[١٧٢] منهما

[١٧٣] في الاصل "ستة"

حقّ لا راحة لنا معهم ونحن قوم مؤمنون بالله وديننا دين الارتضى [نشهدوا][١٧٤] الخلّـــاق[١٧٥] الأرض والسّموات بالوحدانيّة والربُوبيّة ونحن طائعون فكانوا يخرجون إلينا في كلّ عام في وقت منافع عامنــا فيعتون [ ][١٧٦] علينا ويسبّونا وما لنا معهم معيشة» [f. 79] فأكثروا بالشكيّة بالقوم وقالوا «لا يقــدر احد ان يّصل إليهم إلاّ من ذالك السّهل الذي بين الجبلين وهو يسمّى عندنا سُدُّ مأرب ولا طريق للقوم إلاّ مِنْهُ وما منعنا الله منه ألاّ بعُلُوِّ الجبل» قال لهم «وأنتم ممن أنتم ؟» قالوا «نحن من آل شود من قــوم مدين ابن إبراهيم عليه السّلام كثُر نسلُنا بأرض مدين فوقعت فتنة في آل مدين ففررنا بأهلنا إلى هذين الجبلين فسكناهما إلى الآن وقد ضربنا القوم» قال «ومن يكون هؤلاء القوم ؟» قالوا «يذكرون أنّــهم من آل بارش[١٧٧] أبي يافت ابن نوح وهم أهل شرٍّ وحرب وعُتُوٍ لا طاقة لنا بهم ولا بالسّكنى بجواريهم» قال لهم ذو القرنين «لا يهمُّكم أمرهم فأنا نكفيكم أمرهم» ففرح القوم لذالك وتباشر به النّاس فكانوا منه على حذر واستعداد ثمّ أنّه مضا على ذلك [f. 80] الباب الذي بين الجبلين فوصل إلى مــا خلــف الجبلين فأشرف على أشراف لم يرا مثله في الدنيا وقد أشرف على هبوط من جهة الجبلين وهي عقبــة من جهة القوم مكوّرة لا يكاد يستقرّ لمعودها عليه قدمٌ ولا يحيط بصعوده بصرٌ والبحر محيط ببلاد القوم من كلّ جهة ولا مسلك لأهلها ولا لأحد بين الجبلين ممّا يلى تلك العقبة إلى سدّ مأرب فلمّا أشــرف ذو القرنين على القوم بعث إليهم رسوله فكتب إليهم كتابا يقول فيه:

بسم الله مجرا هذه الأمور ومرساها[١٧٨] الحمد لله الذي لا ربّ غيره ولا معبود سواه من عبد الله ذو القرنين إلى أهل تاريش[١٧٩] الذين طَغَوْا وعَتَوْا على عباد الله وبــلاده بغَيْر حقّ سلام على من أتبع الهدى وأطاع الله عزّ وجلّ وخشي عواقب [f. 81] الرّدا يا أهل تاريش كفوا أنفسكم عن الظّلم والطّغيان وعن عبادة الأوثان وآمِنُوا بــالله الذي لا ربّ غيره ولا معبود سواه فإن آمنتم وأطعتم فلكم ما لنا وعليكم ما علينــا وإن تَماديتم على ما أنتم عليه من الضّلالة والكبْر والكفر فإنّا مقبلون عليكم بجنود الله التي لا يُحصَى عَدَدُهَا ولا يقوم أحد لحربها فيكون عزّكم ذلٌّ وملككم خاســرٌ والله المستعان

---

[١٧٤] في الاصل "نسهدوا"

[١٧٥] خالق

[١٧٦] في الاصل "فكانوا"

[١٧٧] Spelling in Mss. is often باريش

[١٧٨] Formula taken from Qur'ān 11:41

[١٧٩] Spelling in Mss. is often تارش

فختم الكتاب ودفعه إلى رسوله فأتا ألى أهل تاريش فوصل إلى أمّة لها عدد لا يُحصى فأوّل من [لقي][١٨٠] رسوله أُمّةً صفاتهم كصفات الآدميّين ووجههم كوجوه الكلاب أجسادهم كالأرز العظام فدفع لهم كتاب ذو القرنين فقرأه قاريهم فتعجّب من حسن الفاظه وتواضعه لله تعالى وقال لهم «يئال تاريش آمنوا بالله الذي [f. 82] خلق السّموات والأرض وأنشأكم فيها وصوّركم كيف شاء» فقال بعضهم لبعض «يئال تاريش أنتم أولوا بأس شديد ولاكنّكم أبعثوا إلى آل تارش بالجمع فإذا احتمعتم فاجتمعوا على رأيٍ واحدٍ فإن كان حربا كان لصاحب الكتاب فإن كان طوعا فلرسوله» فقالوا «نعم» فأمروا بالجمع فاجتمع أوّلهم وآخرهم فاتّفق رأيهم على أن لا يُقَاتَلُوهُ وأن يسمعوا له وأن يُطيعوه فكتبوا كتابا فيه:

بسم الله مجراها وبأمر الله مرساها من آل تارش ابن يافت ابن نوح عليه السّلام إلى ذي القرنين نّباش سلام على جملة الطيعين لخالق الخلق اجمعين أنا وصلنا كتابك وفهمنا مقتضاه ونحن مطيعون لمن أمَرْت بالطاعة والسّمع والإجابة ولا حاجة لنا لحربك وأن كنّا عَدَداً أنتها لعدِدنا ولا أحد يطيق حربنا كنّا نعلم وعملنا [f. 83] ﴿إِنَّ الْمُلُوكَ إِذَا دَخَلُواْ قَرْيَةً أَفْسَدُوهَا وَجَعَلُواْ أَعِزَّةَ أَهْلِهَآ أَذِلَّةً وَكَذَالِكَ يَفْعَلُونَ﴾[١٨١] يا ذا القرنين إن كنت تاركنا في بلادنا من غير داخلها ولا تسئل منّا قوّة من شيء إلاّ ما كان من خارج الأرض فنحن مطيعون لك ولرأيك وإن كنت تدخل بلادنا وتأخذ منّا الخراج والقوّة من الرّجال فلا سبيل لك إلى ذالك والسّلام

وختم الكتاب ودفعوه إلى رسول ذي القرنين فلمّا وصل الكتاب فكّه وقرأهُ وفهم مقتضاه استشار ذوي الرأي من أصحابه على مقالة أهل تارش فردّوا عليه الرأي والمشوّرة وقال لهم «لا بُدَّ لي من أرضكم ودخولها» قال فأمر ذو القرنين بالرحيل حتّى نزل بساحة القوم فتبادروا إليه بالجموع [فرآ][١٨٢] صفة القوم وأجسامهم فمنهم من هو طُولُهُ [f. 84] وعرضُهُ كالدُّبّ ومنهم من يلتحف بإذنه ويتّزرُ بالأخرى ومنهم من هو كالأرز العظام وجوههم على جملة كوجوه الكلاب وأجسامهم كلُّهُم أجساد الآدميّين فلمّا احتمعوا إليه كلّموه بالسنتهم ولغاتِهم فدعاهم إلى الإسلام فآمنوا بالله بالسنتهم وقلوبُهم غاشة فآمنوا خوفا منه وأضمروا الغشّ في قلوبهم فلمّا سمع منهم ذالك أمر بالرّحيل عنهم وإن يدَعَهُم في بلادِهِم على ما كتبوا به إليه

---

[١٨٠] من B. في الاصل "وفى"

[١٨١] Qur'ān 27:34

[١٨٢] في الاصل "راء"

وفي رواية عن [ا]بن عبّاس عنه عن النبيّ صلعم أنّه قال لم يكن نبيّ قبله إلاّ وقد حذّر قومه من ممسوج العين اليمنى يقول للناس أنا ربّكم ومعه جنّةٌ ونارٌ فجنّتُهُ ناراً وناره جنّةٌ مكتوب على جبهتـــه سطر يقرؤه كلّ مؤمن بالله فليعصمَن الله من فتنته من عَصَمَ بتوفيقه [f. 85] يطا برجله جزائر الغـــرب ويعصمُ الله مكّة والمدينة وبيت المقدس وطور سيناء فلمّا أراد عَدُوّ الله أن يدخل واحدة بعث الله إليـــه ملكا بيده سيفا مرهفا[١٨٣] فيردّه عنها يدُوم [مُكْثُهُ][١٨٤] في الأرض أربعين يوما ثمّ ينزل عليـــه عيســى عليه السّلام بيده حربةً من نُور فإذا رآه [ذاب][١٨٥] كما [يذوب][١٨٦] الرّصاص فيقتله ويقتل أصحابـــه حتّى أن الحجر لينادي ' يا مؤمن هذا عدُوُّ الله من دوني كافرُ بالله تعالى فاقتله '

قال عبد الملك سَمِعْتُ مقاتلا يقول أن أدنى رجلا من أهل تاريش وهم يـــاجوج ومـــاجوج يكون طوله ثمانون ذراعاً وأعلاهم مائة ذراع وأصاهم ذو القرنين في [الذّ][١٨٧] عيش ما أحلّه وفي عـدَدِ ما أكثره وهم في ذالك لا يعرفون الله ولا يدينون بدين الحقّ أعمارهم طويلة لا يموت أحدهم حتّـــى يولد له ألف ولد ذكورا دون الإناث [f. 86] من صُلْبِه فإذا أولد له ألف ولد يقرب [١٨٨] بالموت واستعد له قال أبو عبد الملك سمعت محمّد ابن [المسيِّب][١٨٩] يقول حدّثنا بعض أصحابنا ممـــن اتّق[١٩٠] بـــه أن الرّجل من أهل باريش في طوله مائة ذراع وأقلُّهم ثمانون ذراعا فلمّا أراد ذو القرنين الرّحيل عنهم أتوه فقالوا له «يا ذا القرنين أنّ آل تارش قومٌ ضالين العَهْدَ ناقضين عن الحقّ وإنّهم إذا خرجت من البـــلاد وارتحلت عنّا إلى أقصا المشرق [سيعودون][١٩١] إلى ما كانوا عليه قبل هذا في عهد ملكٍ يقال له عـــالج ابن عوص كان ملكا جائراً اجار في البلاد وطغى على العباد» ووصل إلى سدّ مأرب وقـــاتل أهل[١٩٢] تاريش بألف ألف وثمانون ألفاً كلّهم من ولد يافت ابن نوح وبعضهم من بني كوش ابن نوح فغلـــب عليهم فأطاعوه [f. 87] وعاهدهم عهد على الوفاء أن يكُفُّوا عن قتال أهل باريش وعاهدوه على ذالـــك فلمّا ارتحل منهم نقضوا العهد وخرجوا عليهم وقتلوا منهم من قتلوا وسبَوْا من سبَوْا فإنّ ارتحلت عنهم

---

[١٨٣] سيفٌ مرهفٌ

[١٨٤] في الاصل "مُكْثُهُ"

[١٨٥] في الاصل "داب"

[١٨٦] في الاصل "يدوب"

[١٨٧] في الاصل "الد"

[١٨٨] Scratched out "ايقز"

[١٨٩] في الاصل "السّايب"

[١٩٠] أثق

[١٩١] في الاصل "سيعوذون"

[١٩٢] Written twice: "اهل"

قبل أن تَبْني لنا سُدّ مأرب يكوَن بيننا وبينهم لكي [لا][١٩٣] يخرجوا علينا كما خرجوا على أهل باريش ويقولون مثل ما قالوا لهم لمّا ارتحل عنهم عالج قالوا لهم ' أنتم الذين أخذتم بيده وسقتموه[١٩٤] إلى بلدنا' فقاتَلُوهُم وغلبوا عليهم وأخلُوا ديارهم وجزيرتهم التي سلكتُموهَا حين قدمتم إلينا قال لهم ذو القرنين «وما تريدون أن [أ]صنعه لكم ؟» قالوا له «نريد أن نجمعوا لك خراجَ أربعين عامّاً كان قد جُمِعَ عندنا موفوراً فيكون قوّة لك لأهل الصّنائع فتبني لنا بنيانا [f. 88] يكون بيننا وبينهم» قال لهم «نعم أجعلوا خراجكم

[عزما][١٩٥] على ما وصفتم فإنّي أريد الرّحيل إلى غيركم» قال وكان في القوم عدد كثير يجمع جمعهم مائة ألف مقاتل غير من لم يحضروه إذا احتاجوا إلى حضرته وفي جنود ذي القرنين حينئذٍ مائة ألف وأثنين وستّين ألفاً من المقاتلين وفيهم من أهل الصّنائع صنعة الحديد أثنا عشر ألفا ومن صنعة النحاس أثنا عشر ألفا

فأمرهم بالعمل في الحديد والنحّاس أن يصنعوا كما يصنع الدكان وهو الأحور[١٩٦] المصنوع فصنعوا ما أمرهم وأمر القوم أنّ يقيسوا ما بين الجبلين فقاسوه فأعطا لكلّ عشرين ألفا من الرّجال ألفا من أهل الصّناعة وأعطا لكلّ جزء من القوم حظّه من الأرض فأجّل لهم في ذالك ثلاثين يوما فأمر الصّنّاع [f. 89] أن يصنعوا في صنعتهم كُلّ [طوبة][١٩٧] من حديد ونحّاس أن يثقبوها ثقبا مستويّا فطبعوا وأمر البنائين بالبنيان فبنوا فكان في سعة الأسّاس أربعة وعشرين ذراعا بذراع أحدهم وفي رواية أخرى عرض الرّدم ثلاثة مائة ذراع وارتفاعه من أسفله إلى أعلاه ستّمائة وخمسون ذراعا بالذّراع الكبير وقيل خمسٌ وثمانون ذراعا ويا جوج وماجوج قوم قِصَارٌ من الشبر إلى الشبرين يتراكبون كما تتراكب الدوّابٌ لا يموت أحدهم حتّى لا يكون له ألف وَلد ومن روّايهم على ساحل البحر قبائل اخرى مثل الجراد المنتشر يقال لهم تاريش وبارش قدّ [ذوى][١٩٨] الشّبر والشّبرين خلقهم الله إلى النار ومنهم من هو طوله كالأرز ومنهم من هو [f. 90] يلتحف بإذنيه و[يتّزر][١٩٩] بالأخرى لا يموت الذكور منهم ولا الإناث حتّى يخلّف ألف ولد فإذا ولد ألف ولد حينئذ يعلم أنّ أجله قد قرب فيستعدُّ له فكلّما بنا بنيانا

---

[١٩٣] من B

[١٩٤] من الفعل "ساق"

[١٩٥] من B

[١٩٦] Unfamiliar word.

[١٩٧] في الاصل "طوية"

[١٩٨] من B

[١٩٩] من B في الاصل "يتّر"

أمر بالنحّاس فيُذَوّب ويفرغ في الثقب فيجري من أعلا البنيان إلى أسفله كالوتد فيشدُّ ذالك بعضه بعضا حتّى تَمّ البنيان فلمّا تمّ أمر بالنحّاس فأحمي عليه وأفرغ أي على وجهه السُّدّ مما يلقا وجوه آل تاريش فَيُفَرَّغ ويجري على البنيان من داخل السُّدِّ وما يلي سُدّ مأرب لبنة من حديد ولبنة من نحّاس فبنا وشيّد لا أحد [يستطيع][٢٠٠] طوله ولا عرضهُ ولا ثقبه وذالك قوله تعالى﴿ حَتَّى إِذَا بَلَغَ بَيْنَ السَّدَّيْنِ وَجَدَ مِن دُونِهِما قَوْماً لا يَكَادُونَ يَفْقَهُونَ قَوْلاً ﴾[٢٠١] يعني اهل تاريش من الذين هُم [f. 91] دون الجبلين والذين ﴿ قَالُواْ يَا ذَا القَرْنَيْنِ إِنَّ يَأْجُوجَ وَمَأْجُوجَ مُفْسِدُونَ فِي الأَرْضِ فَهَل نَجْعَلُ لَكَ خَرْجاً عَلَى أَن تَجْعَلَ بَيْنَنَا وَبَيْنَهُمْ سَدّاً ﴾.[٢٠٢] هم أهل بارش فبني وشيّد حتّى استوي البنيان بالصدفين فأفرغ عليه قطرا وهو النحّاس وهو الآن في الحال الذي بناه ذو القرنين وهو ثابت حتّى يأتي الأجل الذي أجل الله له وبذالك منعهم الله من ياجوج وماجوج وهم من آل تاريش ابن يافت ابن نوح عليه السّلام روي عن كعب الاحبار أنّه قال أن أهل تاريش وباريش كلّهم من يافت ابن نوح عليه السّلام وهم قبائل شتّى لا يعلم منتهاهم ولا منتهى عددهم إلاّ الله تعالى الواحد القهارُ وإنّهم لمّا رحل عنهم ذو القرنين ارتدّوا وكفروا [f. 92] بالله ونقضوا عهود ذو القرنين وأرادوا الهجوم على أهل بلويش وإلى ثمود فلم يقدروا على الصعود لملاسة النحّاس فنقبوا فلم يظهروا على أظهار ما نقبوا لأظهار ماء البحر ليخرج عليهم من الثقب بهم كذالك الى يوم القيامة

ذكر مسيرة ذي القرنين إلى أمّة يقال لها ياويل

قال أبو عبد الملك الملشونيّ سَمِعتُ مقاتلاً يقول لمّا تمّ بنيان السّدّ ومضى ذو القرنين إلى أمّة يقال لها ياويل ارتحل بجنوده و لم يمت منهم أحد ثمّ ركب البحر على ما كان من امر الله ونزل الملك زياقيل وأتبعه إلى جزيرة في البحر بعد يوم وليلة فقطع في ذالك مسيرة سنة ونصف فلمّا نزل بساحة الجزيرة في ساحل البحر ظهر[ت] له من تلك [f. 93] الجزيرة قصورٌ مشرقاتٌ وشرافات[٢٠٣] عاليات فنزل بشاطيء البحر وقال لأهل المشورة من أصحابه «إنّي أرا أمر[اً] دبّرته في نفسي ولا أريد أنفاذَهُ إلاّ بمشورتكم وإنّي لا ظنّ أن هذه الجزيرة هي التي وعدنا ربّنا بالوصول إليها وإن أهلها أهلُ شرفٍ وعزّة وأهلُ قوّة وبأسٍ ولا أريد أن أرسل إليهم غيري بل السير إليهم بنفسي فما ترون في ذالك ؟» فقالوا له

---

[٢٠٠] في الاصل "يسطيع"

[٢٠١] Qur'ān 18:93

[٢٠٢] Qur'ān 18:94

[٢٠٣] شرفات

أهل المشورة «يا عبد الله ما لنا ولرأيك ولا حكم إلاّ بأمر الله ثمّ بأمرك فانظر لنفسك ما يصلح للجميع فافعله» قال «أنا أُريدهُم بنفسي دون غيري على بركة الله» قالوا له «ومن لنا بعدك ؟» قال «لا تبرحوا حتّى أرجع إليكم» فقالوا له أنا بك مشفقون وعليك خائفون» قال «أنا أكيدهم بكيدٍ [f. 94] لا يصلوا به إليّ إلاّ على خير فأنا أكتب لهم كتابا فأكون فيه رسول» فقالوا له «افعل واعزم على بركـــة الله» فكتب إليهم كتابا يذكر فيه:

بسم الله مجراها وبأمر الله مرساها من عبد الله ذو[٢٠٤] القرنين ابن نّباش إلى أهل تاويل سلام على من اتّبع الهدى وخشي عواقب الرّدا واستحيا من ربّ يَرا ولا يُــرَا إنّــا كتبناه إليكم [...][٢٠٥] بأمر الله الذي خلقنا وخلقكم فإن كنتم بالله مؤمنين ولنعمته شاكرين وللالاه[٢٠٦] ذاكرين فأنتم الأمنون ونحن لكم زائرون وعن أرضكم مُوَسِّعُوَن وإن كنتم من أهل المردة والطغيان وعبادة الأوثان فابشروا بالذّلّ والخسران وقــد وجّهنا إليكم رسولنا بأمر الله يُنبئُكم [f. 95] بما خصّه اللفظ من فعلنا بإحْسَان لمــن أطاع الله وسوءِ فعْلنا لمن عصى الله وأنّه لا يضيع أجر من أحسن عملا والسّلام

وختم الكتاب وطواه وأقام إلى الليل ومشا على قدميه حتّى وصل إلى باب المدينة الظــاهرة شــرافتها عاليات بنيانها وقصورها إلتي دلت على موضعها بإشراق غرافتها وذالك أن جنود ذي القرنين ظـــهر إليهم منارها وهم في البحر مقدار ستة أيّام في إقبالهم إليها

فلمّا وقف ذو القرنين على باب قال له البوّاب «من أنت الذي لم نراك قبل هــذا في هــذه الجزيرة ولا في مدائنها ؟» قال له «فهل لها مدائن غير هذه ؟» قال له «نعم فيها أربع مدائـــن وهــذه الرّابعة وفي كلّ واحدة منها خمسة وعشرين [f. 96] ألف رامي بالقوس العاتق وخمسة وعشرون ألــف رامي بالقوس العاقب وخمسون ألف مقاتل واثنا عشر ألف صانع كلّهم يصنعون السّيوف والــدُّرُوع والرِّماح وآلة الحرب وأجرة كلّ صانع على الملك من بيت المال» قال ذو القرنين «وأيّ مدينة فيـــها الملك الأكبر من [ملوكهم][٢٠٧] ؟» قال «هو في هذه المدينة» قال «وما اسمه ؟» قــال «نــواش ابــن عملاق» ثمّ قال له البوّاب «و من أنت ؟» قال له «أنا رسول عبد الله ذي القرنين ابن نّباش [أتيت][٢٠٨]

---

٢٠٤ ذي

٢٠٥ The following corrupt passage has been cut: " من حلال بذكر ومراعات بحقوق الله وهيتالكم انّا قدمنا اليكم "

٢٠٦ لله

٢٠٧ في الاصل "الملوكهم"

٢٠٨ من B

إلى ملك هذه الجزيرة بكتاب وأريد الدخول عليه وعسى أن يكون ذالك على يديك وأُعْلِمُ بأمرك ذو القرنين إذا أرجعتُ إليه» قال «نعم أنا أشاورُهُ عليك» فدخل البوّاب على الملك نوّاش ابن عملاق فسلّم عليه كما يجب عندهم بحسن الأدب فخبره بخبر رسول ذي القرنين قال فأمر نوّاش بدخوله [f.97] فدخل فأجلسه بجواره فقال له الملك «من أنت ومن أين أقبلت وما اسمك ؟» قال له «أقبلت من عند عبدِ الله ذو[٢٠٩] القرنين وأنا من جند الله جند ذي القرنين واسمي عبد الله وأنا أتيت إليك زائرا ومستجيرا وأردت القرب إليك ومنك وأعلمك بسيرة ذي القرنين وأنّه كان استقربني من نفسه ثمّ سألني في قرابتي وأنا رأيت لمكاني عندك فضل ما زلتُ من جوارك وأعلّمك من مكائد ما تنجوا به من شرّه» قال له الملك نوّاش ابن عملاق «يا عبد الله إنّ الملوك إذا أدخلوا قرية أفسدوها وجعلوا أعزّة أهلها أذلة وكذالك يفعلون وقريتنا هذه قرية ما دخلها قط أحدا ملكا من غير أهلها وأنّها لمصونة من دوائر الدنيا وفيها أثنا عشر ألف رامي بالقوس العاتق واثنا [f. 98] عشر ألف رمي بالقوس العاقب على كلّ برج من أبراجها الرُّمات وفيها أربعة أبراج وكل برج وسعه ميلٌ وفي أقطاها مدائن مثلها في هذه الجزيرة في كلّ مدينة منّها مثل ما في الأخرى من الخيل والرّمات[٢١٠] والرّجال والعدد والسّلاح وفي هذه المدينة كهفاً في وَسَطِ حِصْنٍ فيه ثلاث مائة مدارج لمن أراد دخوله أو الخروج منه فإذا دخل الداخل فيه وجد فيه كهوفا لا توصف تحت الأرض فيه[٢١١] من الماء ما يقوم به وبأهله أبدا وفيه[٢١٢] غُرَفٌ وإدراج وكهوف وأمور لا منتها إلى وصفها ولو دخلنا فيها لكانت تحصننا على طول أقامة ذي القرنين على بلدنا ولاكنّنا علمنا أنّ القوم إذا حضروا فسد عليهم ما لم يصلح ولاكنّك ترجع إلى ذي القرنين سلاح وتقرأه منّا[٢١٣] السّلام وأنا أكتب إليه كتاباً بالطّوع [f. 99] والسّمع له وإنّ يتركنا على ما نحن فيه وعليه من امور بلدنا ونعطيه خراجها ونُمِدُّه بما إحتاج اليه من العدد والسّلاح وقوّة الرّجال دون حربه وفساد بعضنا على بعض» فلمّا سمع ذو القرنين منه ما سمع سرّه ذالك فقال له «افعل ما بذالك أيّها الملك فنعم [الملاذ][٢١٤] أنت والرّأي والرشاد لرعيتك» فكتب نوّاش ابن عملاق

---

[٢٠٩] ذي

[٢١٠] والرّماة

[٢١١] فيها

[٢١٢] فيها

[٢١٣] نفهم "تقرأ عليه منّا"

[٢١٤] في الاصل "الملاد" . "الملك" :B

بسم الله مجراها وبأمر الله مرساها إلى عبد الله ذو[٢١٥] القرنين ابن نّباش من نوّاش ابن عملاق مقدّمُ بني ياويل سلام عليكم من بعد الشُكر والسُرور والبهجة والنُور بالنظر في كتابك المنير ورد علينا بيد رسولك الأثير فأخذناه بيد القبول ونظرنا فيه بعين القبول وقرأناه بأفهم العقول تذكرُ فيه وعد الله والإيمان به وتحذّرنا من عذابه في الأخرة وتخوفنا فيه من نقمته على يد [f. 100] عباده فأنا به مؤمنون ولأمره سامعون ولمن ولاّه من عباده [طائعون][٢١٦] أمرتنا بالخروج أليك أتيناك بالسّمع والطاعة وإن رأيت غير ذالك فأنا من الله خائفون ومنك وجِلُون ومثل مقالتنا وأفلج رسالتنا فإنّ الله لا يضيع أجر من أحسن عَمَلاً والسّلام

و طوي الكتاب ودفعه ألى ذي القرنين وهو لا يعلم أنّه ذو القرنين وكان نوّاش ابن عملاق رفيق بالرّعيّة ذو رُأي ومشورة فمشا ذو القرنين وأتا أصحابه وأعلمهم بمقالة نوّاش ابن عملاق ودفع إليهم الكتاب وأعلمهم بما في المدينة من القوّة وأنظارها ووصف لهم ما وصف له نوّاش في الكهف والقوّة وشاورهم في الرّأي فقالوا له «يا ذا القرنين أبعث إلى نوّاش يعطيك خراج أهله ويُقوّيك بزيادة ما في الهند ودعهم على ما هم فيه فإنّ خطاب [f. 101] نوّاش خطاب طائع» قال لهم «نعم» فبعث إلى نوّاش فأخرج إليه وأكرمه وأحسن إليه وأعلمه أنّه هو الذي دخل عليه , وأنّ الذي كان منه كلُّهُ مكيدة منه عليه فشكره لثبوت عقله ثمّ أنّ نوّاش أعطاه الأموال من جملة ما أعطاه اثنا عشر ألف رطل من الذهب ومثلها من الفضّة وقال له «هذا انتفقه[٢١٧] في سبيل الله على جندك قوّةً لك وهذه اثنا عشر ألفا من [الدروع][٢١٨] ومثلها سيوف ومثلها بيضات ومثلها خيول بسروجها وتُرُوسِها معاونة مني إليك كلّ ذالك من مالي وإحساني إليك وعونا للجند في سبيل الله على يديك يا ذا القرنين وهذه خمسة وعشرين[٢١٩] ألف مقاتل يمرُّون معك ويتجاهدون[٢٢٠] بين يديك

قال أبو عبد الملك الملشونيّ سمعتُ مقاتلا يقول [f. 102] نزل ذو القرنين على ياويل وهم أُمَمٌ مسدّدٌ رأيهم وملكهم مرشدٌ كائده ذو القرنين بثبت الله على الرُّشْدِ وحسن الرّأي فلم [يجاوبه][٢٢١] و لم

---

[٢١٥] ذي

[٢١٦] في الاصل "لمآيعون"

[٢١٧] انفقه

[٢١٨] في الاصل "الذروع"

[٢١٩] عشرون

[٢٢٠] يجاهدون

[٢٢١] من B. في الاصل "يحاوبه"

تملك الرّعيّة على يديه وثبّته على ملكه وقدم على الجيش الذي سيّره ذو القرنين ابنُ عمّ له يقال له رواّش ابن هُرْمَزْ فجهَّزهم وأفضل عليهم وأكرمهم وزوّدهم وأفضل بالزيادة على رواّش وواعدهم الله الذي لا إله إلاّ هو ثمّ أوصى عليه ذو القرنين فقال له ذو القرنين «يا نوّاش إحسانك إلينا وإلى الجند أعظم الوصايا لا يكون عندنا أفضل من رواّش» ثمّ توادعوا وانصرف وبقى رواّش على مقدّمة عسكر آل ياويل فاستقربه ذو القرنين من نفسه لمكان فعل نوّاش وإحسانه ثمّ عزم على الرحيل

ذِكر مسيرة ذو[222] القرنين إلى أمّة [f. 103] يقال لها تاويل

قال أبو عبد الملك الملشوني سمعتُ مقاتلا يقول ارتحل ذو القرنين عن آل ياويل إلى أمّة يقال لها تاويل وكان الأمم من نسل يافت ابن نوح فارتحل وركب البحر على ما كان من أمر الله تعالى فبعث الله إليه ملكه زياقيل عليه السّلام فسار على البحر يوما وليلة قطع فيها مسيرة عام و[نصف][223] وكان إذا أراد النزول ضرب الأبواق ونزل القوم على وجه الماءِ فكانوا يضربون أوتاد الخيل والدوّاب والاخبية على وجه الماءِ كما تُضرب على وجه التُّراب بأمر الله تعالى فطوا الله له البعيد وقصّر له المسافة

فلمّا أصبح لهم شخصوْا بأبصارهم في اللُّجج ووُسْعِ البحر وتعجّبوا من قدرة الله تعالى إذ لاحت لهم جزيرة في البحر بينها وبين [f. 104] البحر اثنا عشر ميلاً فنظروا إلى الجزيرة في اللُّجج وهى جَزيرة خضراء فاعتمدوا نحوها حتّى نزلوا بالقرب منها على ساحتها فنزلوا بعضهم في البرّ وبعضهم في البحر وهم على السّوية فيما بينهم فيه من البرِّ والبحر فلمّا نزلوا واستقرّ بهم النُّزول أمر ذو القرنين بالجمع في الناس فاجتمعوا إليه فبعث منهم عشرة رجال على خيولهم فدخلوا الجزيرة وقاسوها فمشوْا فيها من أوّل النهار إلى ارتفاعه فإذا هم بأثَرِ العمارة فنظروا فراوا رجلاً ماشياً في طريق من طرق الجزيرة [فبادروه][224] فاخذوه فسَأَلُوه فلم يعرف له كلامٌ ولا عرفوا لغته فأتوا به إلى ذي القرنين فقال له ذو القرنين «من أنتم من الأمم ؟» فقال له «نحن من آل تاويل» قال «ومن يكون تاويل ؟» قال «من [f. 105] آل يافت ابن نوح عليه السّلام وهم ثلاثة وستّون قبيلة ؟» قال «وكم في كلّ قبيلة ؟» قال «ما بين الثمانين والمائة ألف» قال «وكم في أهل تارش ابن يافت ؟» «قال ضدّها[225]» قال «فهل يذكرون الله تعالى ؟» قال «منهم من آمن بالله تعالى ومنهم من كفر به» قال له «وأنتم أهل تاويل فكم

---

[222] ذي

[223] في الاصل "نسف"

[224] في الاصل "فبادروه"

[225] Maybe one could understand: "عدّها"

أنتم ؟» قال «نحن أربعين قبيلة ما بين الأربعين والخمسين ألفا» قال له ذو القرنين «وهل لكم ملوك ؟» قال «نعم ملك واثنان في كلّ قبيلة قائدها ولنا ملك إليه يرجع كلّ الأمراء منا» قال «وما اسمه ؟» قال «شورش ابن شريش» قال «ما دينُهُ ؟» قال «يدين بالوحدانيّة لله» قال «وأين مسكنُهُ ؟» قال «في قرية في وسط المدينة» قال «وما اسم مدينته ؟» قال طحْلبه» قال «أريد أن أكتب إلى ملككم [f. 106] كتابا وأعظمه فيه وأنبيئه بمكاننا من الله تعالى وبقدومنا على أرضه وتكون لنا رسولاً» قال «افعل» فكتب ذو القرنين

بسم الله مجراها وبأمر الله مرساها إلى الملك شورش ابن شريش من عبد الله ذو القرنين سلام على من اتّبع الهدى وخشي عواقب الرّدا واستحيا من خالق الأرض والسّموات فأنّا كتبْناه إليك من صالح رأي وفضل قول يدعوكم إلى خالقكم الذي لا ربّ غيره ولا معبود سواه فإنّ أجبتم الدّعوة وأقررتم لله بالوحدانيّة فلكم الأمن والأمان من الله في الدنيا والآخرة وإن كنتم متعادين على الضّلالة والمعصيّة والغواية فإذنوا بحرب من الله ورسوله فسيأتكم العذاب والنّدامة والخراب ثمّ تُرَدُونَ إلى عالم الغيب والشّهادة فيجازيكم بقولكم وفعلكم وما الله بغافل عما تعملون

[f. 107] فختم الكتاب ودفعه إلى الرّجل وقال له «أنّا منتظرون لجوابكم إلى يؤمين» فانصرف الرجل وأتا إلى ملكهم شورش ابن شريش فدفع له الكتاب فقرأه فدعا أهل مملكته ومشورته فاستشارهم فقال لهم «هيهات فإذ طارت من موطنها وسارت غريبة في غير بلدها و[نحن] أمة ثابتة ذو[٢٢٦] قوّةٍ وبأسٍ شديد وما عسا يا شورش أن يكون من أمة لا قرار لها ولا قوّة ولا مدد علمنا الله واحد في ملكه من غير أن يُنبهَنَا هذا الرجل في كتابه ونحن في بلدنا هذه[٢٢٧] وفي جزيرتك ما لا يحصا من الخيل والرجال فأمر بجمع الجنود وتقويم العدد والبنود وعزم على حرب ذي القرنين برأي وزراءه لا برائه فوعظهم ملكهم شورش جهده فابوا إلاّ الحرب وتقويم حالهم فأمرهم [f. 108] بالقدوم والجمع والعزم على ما هم عِليه عازمين فخرجوا في عدد لا يُحصى يزيد عَدَدُهم على مائة وستّون ألفا وجزائرهم متقاربة العمارة يناظر بعضهم بعضاً فاجتمعوا وثبت الحرب وصبر القوم على شدّة الحرب يوم ونصف يوم فكثر الفنا وبرز القتلى فلمّا نظر شورش إلى ذالك من كثرة الموت في الخلق غمه ذالك فرمَا بنفسه بين

---

[٢٢٦] ذات

[٢٢٧] هذا

الفريقين وقال[٢٢٨] برفيع صوته «يئال[٢٢٩] ذي القرنين كفّوْا عن القتال فإنّي استشير ذي القرنين على أمر أن يكون رشدا للفريقين» فمسك الناس عن القتال «من يَدُلُّني على ذي القرنين ؟» فمشا معه بعض من أصحاب ذي القرنين حتّى أتاه فوجده جالسا في ملأ من الناس فسلّم عليه وإذّا حقّ السّلام فقال له ذو [f. 109] القرنين «من أنت ؟» قال له «أنا شورش ابن شريش» قال له ذو القرنين «وفيماذا[٢٣٠] جئت يا شريش من بعد فناء الناس ؟» فقال له «أيُّها الأمير المطيع السّميع جيئت ناصرك ومخالف لرأي من اجتهد في حربك حتّى فنيت الرجال وفقدت الأبطال وتبيّن الرّشْدُ من الغيُ[٢٣١] وعرف كلّ ذى رأيٍ منتها رأيه فخفت على خراب البلاد والتشتيت والفساد وأتيتك مطيعاً ولأمرِك سميعاً فأفعل ما أنت أهله بعد قدومي عليك ووقوفي بين يديك» فقال له ذو القرنين «و[ما][٢٣٢] تريد الآن ؟» قال له «تدعني في بلادي وأمدُّك بما استطعت من خراج جزيرتي وأنا لأمر الله من السّامعين ولرسوله من الطائعين» قال له ذو القرنين «يا شورش أبشر فإن الأمر [f. 110] قد حلّ [بقولك][٢٣٣] وأمرك ورأي من فيها مفوّضٌ أليك فلو كان وصولك قبل هذا لا كان من الحرب والقتال ما كان ولاكن وعْدُ الله [نافذُ][٢٣٤] وحكمُه تامٌّ» فأمر ذو القرنين الجنود فكفّت عن الحرب وأحسن إلى شورش فأكرمه وسأله القوّة من الخيل والرجال فأمر له باثنا عشر ألف مقاتل منها ثلاثة آلاف رامي وتسعة آلاف مقاتل كلّهم على خيلهم واسلحتهم فشكروا[٢٣٥] القوم رأي شورش وندموا على ما فعلوا وودعهم ذو القرنين ووعظهم واوصاهم وأكرم من [وجبت][٢٣٦] له الكرامة وارتحل ألى أمة يقال لها بني منسك

---

[٢٢٨] Begin lacuna in B

[٢٢٩] نفهم "يا آل"

[٢٣٠] Meaning: لماذا

[٢٣١] End lacuna in B

[٢٣٢] من B

[٢٣٣] في الاصل "بقومك"

[٢٣٤] في الاصل "نافدُ"

[٢٣٥] فشكر

[٢٣٦] في الاصل "وجبته"

ذِكر مسير ذو[٢٣٧] القرنين إلى أمة يقال لها بني منسك

قال أبو عبد الملك سمعتُ مقاتلا يقول ارتحل ذو القرنين من آل تاويل إلى أرض بـني [f. 111] منسك فركب البحر على عدته فنظروا أصحابه إلى جزيرة عظيمة الجبال كثيرة الشّعار أحاط ها البحر من كلّ جهة إلاّ [جهة][٢٣٨] واحده مما يلي الجرف في البحر وثلاثة أرباع الجزيرة في البحر وربعـها في البرّ مناظرة لجزيرة مثلها أوسع منها والجزيرة التي تلي البحر وسعها شهرا وطولها شهران والتي تناظرها وسعها وطولها شهران كاملان فنزل ذو القرنين مما يلي بينهما نحو التي في البحر فبعث إلى أهلها رسولاً بكتابه يذكر فيه

باسم الله مجراها وبأمر الله مرساها من عبد الله ذو القرنين إلى أهل الجزيرة المعتزلة من الديار المنفردة في لجج البحر سلام على من اتّبع الهدا وخشي عواقب الردّا واستحيا من ربٍّ يَرَا ولاَ يُرَا و[استجاب][٢٣٩] لدعوة [f. 112] الخالق الخلق أجمعين و[أمّا] بعد فإنّا كتبناه إليكم عن قلّة معرفتنا بكم فقد دعوناكم لنكونوا أجميعا[٢٤٠] مطيعين لخالق الخلق وباسط الرِّزق وتقرّوا له بالوحدانيّة فإن أجبتم فلكم ما لنا وعليكم ما علينـا وإن تمرّدتُّم عن الإجابة وركنت قلوبكم إلى الضلالة بتبـوّء وبغضب[٢٤١] مـن الله وخذوا على حذركم فإنّا عليكم قادمون بجنود لا يحصى عددها ونصر من الله وفتح قريب فلا غالب لأمره وهو الناصر لمن أطاعه ويقطع دابر الكافرين والسّلام

وختم الكتاب ودفعه إلى رسوله فلمّا وصلهم الرسول بكتاب ذي القرنين [بادروا][٢٤٢] بالاجتماع إلى الرسول فأحاطوا به وكثُر كلامهم والرسول لا يعرف لغتهم فأقبلوا به إلى ملكهم فدخلوا عليه فوجدوه على [f. 113] سرير من ذهب مرصع بأصناف الجواهر وهو شابٌّ جميل أجمل ما رأ الرأي من بـني آدم وهو مخالف لقومه في الصِّفة لأنّه لا يكون عليهم مَلِكٌ إلاّ من يكون على صفتهم قد خلقه الله وفضّله بالجمال والكمال على صفة أملح[٢٤٣] ما يكون من بني آدم وصفاتهم كلّهم أجسادهم كأجساد بني آدم

---

[٢٣٧] ذي

[٢٣٨] في الاصل "حيهة"

[٢٣٩] في الاصل "استحاب"

[٢٤٠] اجمعين

[٢٤١] An alternative reading might be: "فتبوّء بغضب"

[٢٤٢] في الاصل "باذروا"

[٢٤٣] An alternative reading might be: اصلح

ووجوههم مستطيلة وأعينهم على طول[٢٤٤] وجوههم ورجالهم بلى[٢٤٥] لحاء مرد جُرْدٌ ونساؤهم كنساء بني آدم في الخلق والصِّفة فلما رآه الملك أكرمه وأحسن إليه وقرّبه من مجلسه فقال له «من أين كان أقبالك إلى بلدنا ونحن فيها منذ أمرنا ربّنا فسكنّا فيها فما رأينا أحدا من الخلق غيرك من أنت ومن أين أتيت ؟» فقال له «أيُّها الملك أنا رسول ذي [f. 114] القرنين مثلك وكان ذالك الملك أعطاه الله الفصاحة ويعلم كلّ لُغَةٍ» فقال له الملكومن يكون هذا الملك الذي ارسلك إلينا ؟» قال له «ذو القرنين» قال «وما أصْلُه ؟» قال «من الرُّوم» قال «وأيّ الخلق كان منه الرُّوم ؟» قال له «من بني آدم» قال له «هل من ذرّيّة نوح ؟» قال له «نعم[٢٤٦]» قال له «من أيّ أولاد نوح ؟» قال «من سام ابن نوح» قال «أجل قوم نحن وآباؤهم من فرع واحد وأب واحد» قال وفيما أرسلك إلينا ؟» قال له «بعثني بكتابه إليك وإلى أهل الجزيرة» قال له«هات الكتاب» ففكّه وقرأه ثمّ قال «أهلا وسهلا ومرحبا بمن جاء بالكتاب ومن أرسله إلينا» فقال له الرسول«أيُّها الملك أن ذو[٢٤٧] القرنين بعثني إليكم وأجّل لي يوما واحدا وليلة فإن كنتم لأمره طائعين فأعطوني منكم أعْرَفُكُم [f. 115] وأفْهَمُكُم وأعْظَمُكُم قَدْراً فيصلون معي إلى ذي القرنين يخبرهم فصائل أمره ويأمرهم بما يفعلون وينَبِّئُهم بما عنه ينتهون» قال له الملك «نعم أنا أسير بنفسي فأنّي لا يكفيني في السُّؤال إلاّ نفسي» فأكرمه وضيّفه وبات عنده حتّى أصبح الله خير الصّباح وركب الملك في ملا من قومه وأمر بمن في المدينة أن يجتمعوا إليه كلّ من أهل المشوّرة والرأي والفهم وأن يلحقوا به عند ذي القرنين فلحق الملك بذي القرنين فأكرمه وأحسن إليه فلمّا أصبح احتمع عليه [ذو][٢٤٨] الرأي والمشوّرة من أصحابه فقال له ذو القرنين «من أنت وما اسمك ؟» قال «أنا دهقان ابن عالج ابن خولان ابن جدعان ابن منسك ابن ارتخشد ابن سام ابن نوح عليه السّلام» قال له «فما [f. 116] الذي بلّغكم إلى هذه الجزيرة وأخرجكم من بين بني آدم ؟» قال له «كان جدنا وجدُّك نُوحٌ عليه السّلام نزل في السّفينة بثمانين رجلاً بنسائهم وأولادهم ويجمع جمعهم في ثمانين آدميا فنزلت به السّفينة على جبل الجودي وكان للقوم موضع يجتمعون فيه يوم ميعادهم فيسمُّونه بسوق ثمانين فكانوا فيه أولاد نوح ونسائهم ومن آمن مع نوح من بني آدم وكانت

---

[٢٤٤] Begin lacuna in B

[٢٤٥] نفهم "بلا"

[٢٤٦] End lacuna in B

[٢٤٧] ذا

[٢٤٨] في الاصل "دوى"

أعمارُهم طويلة يعمّر أحدهم الفان[٢٤٩] ومائة وألف وثمان مائة ولا يموت أحدهم حتّى يخرج من صلبه ألف رجل فكثُرَ نسلهم فلمّا قرب أجل جدّنا نوح قال له جدّنا سام: ' يا أبانا أنت خليفة الله من بعد آدم في أرضه فبيّن لنا حيث يكون نسلٌ كل واحدٍ منّا فان النّسل [f. 117] يكثر بعدك' فقال لجدنا منسكـ' تقدّم أنت وأخوتك بعون الله في البحر على جزيرة تسمّى طحولة وتسكنها أنت ومن معك من أخوتك باريش وتاريش ' فقالوا' يا أبانا دعنا نسكن مع أخواتنا في هذه الجزيرة' فقال لهم 'الله أمركم بذالك' فامتنعوا فأغتاظ جدّنا نُوحٌ فقال لهم ' بدّلكم الله كما بدّل غيركم' فرجعت وجوه رجالنا كما ترا وبقيت النساء على حالاتها أوّل مرّةٍ فكان الملك لا يُعرفُ فينا إلاّ بما فضّله الله به ويخلقه على الصّفة الأوّلى فكان أبي[٢٥٠] عالج على حسن [صفة] [٢٥١] فولد له ألف ولد منهم من مات ومنهم من عاش و لم يخرج على صيفته[٢٥٢] إلاّ أنا وأخذ القوم بيدي وأمّا ما سألت عنه من أمر وصولنا إلى هذه الجزيرة كان [f. 118] من أمر جزيرتنا إليّ فيها بنو آدم الآن وأمرنا بالخروج منها فصنعت السُّفُن على عينه [فركبنا][٢٥٣] البحر فيها فكانت الرّيح منّا حيث شاء الله حتّى انتهينا إلى هذه [الجزيرة][٢٥٤] ونحن فيها على الصّفة التي تراها من حالنا نحن وأخواننا آل باريش وآل تاريش ونحن في عيش رغد غير أنّنا في حرب شديد» قال له ذو القرنين «وأيّ حرب أنتم فيه ؟» قال له دهقان «كانت بجوارنا جزيرة وسعها وطولها مسيرة شهران[٢٥٥] سُكّانها الحيّات» قال له ذو القرنين «كيف قتالكم معهم ؟» قالوا له «لا طاقة لنا بقتالهم إلاّ بسُرادِق[٢٥٦] النيران وما منّا من أمّة إلاّ لها قِيَاسٌ معروف في الأرض كلّ أمة تعرف قياسها ويحفرون في ذالك سرادق[٢٥٧] كثيرة فإذا كان وقتُ [f. 119] خروج الحيّات جمّع الناس في أوديتهم وحفيرهم من الحطب والحشيش ما يملا ذلك فإذا خرجوا علينا ألقينا النار في الحطب المجموع فكلّما وطيهُ أحد من الحيّات احترق ومات ولا يخرجون إلينا إلاّ في زمان الحرّ وإنّ كلّ حيّة من تلك الحيّات منهم ما يكون طولها في الأرض مقدار ميلٌ وبعضهم أطول من ذالك ومنهم أقلّ من

---

[٢٤٩] الفين

[٢٥٠] ابو

[٢٥١] في الاصل "صيفة"

[٢٥٢] صفته

[٢٥٣] في الاصل "فركبن"

[٢٥٤] في الاصل "حزيره"

[٢٥٥] شهرين

[٢٥٦] نفهم "سَراديب"

[٢٥٧] نفهم "سَراديب"

ذلك ومنهم أكثر واجسامهم عظيمة ورجالنا كما ترا منهم من يكون لهم في الطُّول ثمانون ذراعا ومنهم من له مائةُ ذِرَاعٍ وصفاهم على مثل ما ترا وأعمارهم كما ذكرت لك ونحن في بلادنا هذه إلى يوم القيامة على دين أبينا نوح» قال له ذو القرنين «يا دهقان أين أكثر سكناها ؟» قال «في فلوات هذه [f. 120] الجزيرة في أرض مرملة» قال «هل وراكم شيْءٌ ؟» قال «جبل قاف» قال «هل منكم من رآه أو سلكه ؟» قالِ يا ذا القرنين ركب منّنا أناس قبل هذا في البحر فذهبُوا في مجاريها وانقلبوا[٢٥٨] في البحر فأقاموا فيه ذاهبين حتّى تمّ لهم تسعة أشهر وظننّا أنّهم لا يرجعون إلينا أبدا فنحن بين الأياس[٢٥٩] منهم والرّجاء حتّى [لاح][٢٦٠] لنا مركب في البحر فذهب الناس إليه فإذا هم الرّجال الذاهبون فأقبل الناس يسئلونهم فقالوا 'خرجنا في البحر نصطاد للمعيشة فهبّتْ علينا ريحٌ فمرّت بنا في البحر فلم نقدروا على الرّجوع حتّى خرج بنا زورقنا في جزائر متقاربات بعضها من بعض وبعضها أوسع من بعض فخرجنا لنجد راحة في أنفسنا [f. 121] مما حلّ بنا من هول البحر فنزلنا في الجزيرة الواحدة من الجزائر فبينما نحن فيها والرّيحُ لا يُهْنَا والزّورُق موقوف ونحن نخشو[٢٦١] عليه الكسر فأقمنا في الجزيرة ما شاء الله فسكن الرّيح فرجعنا في زورقنا وبتنا فيه فلم نشعروا بشيْء حتّى هبّ علينا طير فرفع الزّوَرُق ونحن فيه فطار بنا في الهوا ونحن فيه حتّى انتها بنا إلى جزيرة في البحر ولا نعرف أيّ البحار هي فانتها بنا إلى ساحل البحر فنزل بنا فكلمناه كلاما فنفر من الكلام لّما سمعه وطار عنّا ونزل بالقرب منّا وسكن قليلا وأراد الهجمة علينا فعلّينا بالأصوات وأشهرنا الألوية ونفّرنا بالأبواق فطار وتركنا في الجزيرة التي نزل بنا فيها فعلونا الجبل [f. 122] قد بلغت أسبابه للهوا طُولاً وعُلُوّاً ثمّ ارتحل عنّا واوقدناها النار و[أججناها][٢٦٢] فلمّا رآها كفّ عنّا وقفر منّا ووجدنا منه راحة لوقد النار حتّى أيس[٢٦٣] منّا وكان عَيْشُنَا من هوامِ البحر فنحن في تلك الجزيرة إلى تمام شهرين فظهر لنا في البحر رجل وإمراة فأقبلوا يتعجّبون[٢٦٤] منّا ونتعجّب منهم[٢٦٥] طول النّهار فلمّا كان في آخر النّهار دخلا البحر فإذا أصبح رجعا إلينا وينظران فينا ولا تكلّم أحدٌ منّا إليهم ولا أحد منهم إلينا مدّة أيّام ثمّ أزدادت معهما إمراة دون

---

[٢٥٨] B: "اختلفوا" Word not legible in A. Perhaps one could read "انتلفوا" أو "اتنلفوا"

[٢٥٩] نفهم "اليأس"

[٢٦٠] في الاصل "لاحو"

[٢٦١] نخشى

[٢٦٢] من B. في الاصل "اوقدنا النار واوقدناها"

[٢٦٣] نفهم "يأس"

[٢٦٤] فأقبلا يتعجبان

[٢٦٥] منهما

الأخرى وصفاهم كصفات الآدميين لم يستتروا إلاّ بشعورهم فأنِسُوا إلينا من غير كلام إلاّ [أن][٢٦٦] هم ضبطة في أصواهم إذا أرادوا [f. 123] الانصراف عنّا فأنِسْنَا بهم وأنِسُوا بنا إلى تمام أربعة أشهر وهم في الزيادة إلينا عنهم إلى أن بلغوا نحو الثلاثين أنسياً فأتوا يوما وبينهم شيخ وعَجُوزٌ يشبه أن يكون من قدمائهم فنظروا إلينا فأشاروا بأصابعهم كأنّهم يقولون من أين أنتم فأشرنا إليهم بأيدينا من حيث شاء الله تعالى فطنطنوا في كلامهم وانصرفوا فأقاموا عنّا ثلاثة أيّام فرجعوا إلينا ومعهم إمراة زمينة قد احتنت فوقفت إلينا ونطقت بالله تعالى وقالت يا هؤلاء من أين أقبلتم ومن أنتم ؟ قلنا لها كان من أمرنا ما كان من قدرة الله تعالى حتّى سرنا إلى جزيرة من جزائر البحر بحرُ كذا [f. 124] وكذا وأقمنا فيها حتّى التقمنا طيرٌ كبير في زورقنا وطار بنا حتّى نزل بنا في هذه الجزيرة ونحن فيها إلى الآن ولا نعلم ما يكون من أمرنا قالت يا هؤلاء أمّا تعرفون ذلك الطير ؟ قالوا لها لا علم لنا به وليس في بلادنا مثله قالتْ ذلك طير زوال يقال له العنقا وهو الذي خرّب الجزائر كلّها و لم يبق من جميع سكّانها إلاّ من نجّاه الله تعالى في البحر ونحن ممن انجينا منه لدخولنا في البحر فقلنا لها ومن تكونوا من الخلق ؟ قالت لهم نحن اليانون ولسنا من بني آدم قلنا لها وهل لكم مثلك في السِّنّ ؟ قالت لا قلنا لها وكم لك من السّنّ ؟ قالت ألفان أقلّ مائة قلنا لها هل في البحر لك أنظار ؟ قالت ما من دابّة في البرّ إلاّ ولها [f. 125] نظير في البحر قلنا وهل تتناكحون وهل تتناسلون ؟ قالت نعم ونسانا يعيش في البحر ساعة واحدة قد أنسنا بالبحر قلنا لها وهذا البحر هل له بحر آخر من خلفه ؟

قالت كان شيخ من اليانون عُمّر في البرّ ساكنٌ يسكن في الكهوف خوفا من العنقا ثمانين وستُّ مائة وعاقبنا في البرّ هيبة للبحر حتّى اشتدّ به الوحش والشِّدّة والوحدة فجلّ نفسه على البحر فعاش إلى تمام ألف سنة في البحر دون ما عمر في البرّ فغاص في البحر وغاب عنّا عشرة أعوام فظنّنّاه ميّتٌ[٢٦٧] ورجع بعد ذالك فسألناه عن غيبته قال لنا في البحر فقال لنا خُيِّلَ لي أنسيّاً[٢٦٨] في البحر فأردّتُ صحبته وموانسته وذهبتُ خلفه فطمعني في نفسه حتّى انتها بي إلى [f. 126] ساحل البحر فخرج وخرجتُ معه فأنّسني وأنّسته مُدّة طويلة صحبته على سواحل البحار مرّة في الماء ومرّة في البرّ حتّى أحطنا بالدنيا من جهة مغرب الشمس إلى جهة مشرقها فأشرفنا على الحجاب الذي بين السّماء والأرض فلم يظهر لنا إلاّ الظلمة فأقمتُ معه موانسان[٢٦٩] يسئلني ونسئله وعشنا من البحر كسائر

---

[٢٦٦] في الاصل "انّ"

[٢٦٧] ميتاً

[٢٦٨] انسيٌّ

[٢٦٩] مؤانساً

هوامّه فسألته من نفسه من أيّ الأمم هو قال من بقيّة اليانون قلتُ له وأيّ اليانون أنت ؟ قال من آل عاجون قلتُ وأيّ عاجون ؟ قال من بني عاهون فأتبعته بالسُّوال حتّى وجدته أبي[٢٧٠] فصحبته حتّى مات ورجعت إليكم وليس بعد هذا البحر إلاّ الظلمة

قلنا لها يا عجوز هل تجد[ينَ] لنا حيلة نرجع بها إلى بلدنا وأهالينا ؟ قالتْ لو أنّكم تصبرون [f. 127] لكان أرفق بكم ولاكنّكم لا تصبرون أمّا ما تصنعون إنّكم تكثرون من الصيد وتلقونه على وجه الزورق ولا تُوقِدُوا نارا فإن العنقا [تتعاد الى][٢٧١] الجزيرة في كلّ شهر مرّة ولا لها ماوي إلاّ في جزيرتها هذه إلى الجزيرة التي حملتم منها فإنّها إذا اعتادتكم ونظرت إلى الصَّيَدِ فإنّها تنكبُّ عليه وتحمل الزورق وتكونوا أنتم في خفاءٍ من لوح في الزورق فإذا حملت الزورق فإنّها لا تصل إلى اللحم في بطن الزورق ولا[٢٧٢] تئيس منه لنظرها فيه حتّى تضعه حيث كانت [تعود اليه][٢٧٣] قبل هذا ولا تضعه إلاّ في جزيرتها فأفعلوا ذالك فأنتم ترجعون إلى بلدكم

ففعلنا ذلك وجمعنا لحما كثيرا في بطن الزورق واستخفينا في أسفل لوح من زورقنا فهبّت علينا [f. 128] العنقا فحملتنا بزورقنا حتّى وضعتنا من حيث حملتنا فتكلّمنا فنفرت منّا بالكلام وركبنا زورقنا فخرجنا إليكم وهذا أصلُ غيبتنا عنكم ومَا ظنّنا أن نرا أحدا من الخلق بعد هذا ،

فلمّا [أ]تمّ دهقان كلامَهُ وحديث القوم قال لهم ذو القرنين «فما تريد الآن أن يكون من أمركم مع الحيّات ؟» قال له يا ذا القرنين نحن قوم معتزلون في هذه الجزيرة متوكلون على خالقنا الذي أوصلنا إليها وأسكننا فيها وكلّنا إهل منسكٍ وباريش وتاريش صِنَفٌ واحد يشدّ بعضهم بعضا ونحن في جزيرة واحدة نقاتل الحيّات بالنار في كل عام مرّة أو مرّتين وثلاث مرّات فمرّةً علينا ومرّةً عليهم فلعلّك تَتْرُكُنا في بلادنا لقتال عدُونا كيف شاء الله ونُعْدُوك خراج بلادنا» قال لهم ذو [f 129] القرنين «أنا أترُكُكم فيما أنتم فيه وأُعيّنكم أيضا بعون الله وأجعل بينكم وبين جزيرة الحيّات سربا يدخل فيه البحر فيُرُدّ عنكم عدُوّكُم» فأجابوه لذالك

فقام وركب في ملاءٍ من قومه فمشا في الجزيرة ما شاء الله ثمّ دبّرها ورآ فيها موضعين قريبين

---

[٢٧٠] ابا

[٢٧١] في الاصل "تتعاهد"

[٢٧٢] B: "والا"

[٢٧٣] في الاصل "تتاعده"

بعضهما من بعض فأمر بالحفير[٢٧٤] في ذالك المكان حتّى استظهر الماء من الجهيتين[٢٧٥] وسار بينهما سربا واحداً بين القوم والحيّات فلمّا تمّ ذالك حمدوه وشكروه وأمّنهم ومشا في الجزيرة حتّى عرف منتهاها وسعها من أطراف البحر فوجد كثرتها رملا عالجا فرجع إلى محلّة فأمر بجمع آل تاريش وآل باريش وآل منسك فاجتمعوا عنده ونظرهم تعجّب من عظم أجسامهم وطولهم [f. 130] منهم من له ثمانون ذراعا طولا وعشرة أذرع عرضا ومنهم من له مائة ذراع طولا وخمسة وعشرون ذراعا عِرْضا ومنهم من دون ذلك إلاّ أن وجوه الرجال كلّهم مستديلة كوجوه البغال وأعينهم مستطيلة على طول وجوههم فوعظهم ذو القرنين وأعلمهم أن الله الذي خلقهم لا ربّ غيره ولا معبود سواه فآمنوا به وصدّقوه

قال أبو عبد الملك الملشونيّ سمعتُ مقاتلا يقول مشا ذو القرنين في الجزيرة فجال فيها حتّى انتها إلى أطرافها فرآ بعض الحيّات لا توصف ولا يرا مثلها وذلك في حين[٢٧٦] خروج الحيّات وكانوا أهل الجزيرة يقاتلونهم بالنار فإذا هجموا[٢٧٧] الحيّات على الناس وهجموا في ملاءٍ من الناس فكم من ميّت بها وكم من محترق بالنار يخرج من فيها وكم من واقع يقع [f. 131] مغشياً عليه فتهلك القوم فأمرهم بحفير الخليج وإن يكون قتالهم للحيّات بالنشاب وأمر لهم بالحفير في موضعين في الجزيرة حتّى التطم الموج في ذلك الحفير فوجد القوم راحة من تلك الحيّات

ثمّ سأل ذو القرنين الملك زياقيل عن تلك الأمم فقال له زياقيل «هم كما ذكر لك ملكهم دهقان ابن عالج وإنّهم أممٌ شتّى وكلّ أُمّةٍ منهم أكثر نسلا من بني آدم» وأعلمه زياقيل أن القوم يآمنوا به في حضوره فإذا رحل عنهم رجعوا إلى كفرهم فقال له ذو القرنين «يا حبيبى يا زياقيل ما هذه الحيّات وما سَبَبُهم[٢٧٨]؟» قال «يا ذا القرنين هذه الحيّات بقيّة من هوامّ البحر الذي خلق الله منه السموات والأرض فجفّ الماء وبقيت الحيّات في تلك الجزائر إلى الآن من ذلك الزّمان وإن أحد تلك الحيّات من [f. 132] في طولها مائة ذراع ومنهم[٢٧٩] من في طولها ثمانون ذراعا ومنهم من في طولها خمسة أميال ومنهم من هي على ميلين وأنياهم[٢٨٠] كالخشب العظام» فقال ذو القرنين «اللّهمّ أجعل لي من

---

[٢٧٤] بالحفر

[٢٧٥] الجهتين

[٢٧٦] Perhaps one could read here "في حيز"

[٢٧٧] هجمت

[٢٧٨] سببها

[٢٧٩] Here and following منها

[٢٨٠] انيابها

أمري فرجا ومخرجا وأجعل لي في كلّ ما مكّنتني فيه خيراً أنك على كلّ شيء قدير» فقال له الملك زياقيل الذي كان يأتيه بالوحي من عند ربّه «إن الله لأمرني أن أخبرك بكلّ سبب حتّى لا يشكل عليك خبر وذلك يا ذا القرنين أن هذه الحيّات لم يراها أحد من بني آدم قبلك ولا يراها أحدا بعدك إلاّ هذه الأمم إلتي سبّب الله القرب بينهما وإنّهما قوم[٢٨١] شتّى وإنّ الله تعالى الجمهما عن من صدّق بالإيمان به وإنّ هذه الأمم مؤمنون[ة] بالسنتهم[٢٨٢] غاشّين بقلوبهم فلو ارتحلت عنهم لكفروا

قال أبو [f. 133] عبد الملك حدّثني كعب الاحبار أن في بعض الكتب من كتب بني إسرائيل أن الله أنزل آدم والحيّة في يوم واحد فأعطى الله لآدم من أرض مسيرة مائة عام وأنزل الله آدم في أرض الهند والحيّة في أرض السند وكانت الحيّة التي أنزلت مع آدم طولها مسيرة عام وهذه الحيّات من نسلها ولاكن ليس ينتهى شيء من عدمها[٢٨٣] في نسلها كبني آدم قليل منهم من [يصل][٢٨٤] إليهم وعاشت تلك الحيّة بعد موت آدم عليه السلام سبعماية عام والعظام من تلك الحيّة لا تترك ولا تزل من حيث خلقت وولدت ورزقها في التراب تعيش به وتأكله وأن كلّ كبيرة لا تُدى[٢٨٥] أحدا لثقلها وقلّة حركتها وإنّما يقاتل بني آدم منهن من كانت على قدر مائة [ذراع][٢٨٦] ونحوها [f. 134] ورزق الجميع[٢٨٧] في التراب وإنّما جعل الله السبب في القتال للحيّات الصغار ولو سبب للكبار لمات كلّ من كان منهم وترميهم في جهنّم تلدغ فيه من كفر بالله وهم بقدر مائة ميل إلى ما بين دونها فتنشى رائِحة الحيّات وسمّها ومنهن التعابين[٢٨٨] التي تحملهم الملائكة وترميهم في جهنم تلدغ فيه من كفر بالله ويروهم الناس وهم من نسل تلك الحيّات وذالك أن جَل ذكره يسبب سببا كيف يشاء لبعض تلك الحيّات حتّى يلدن في بعض تلك الجزائر بسبب بعض الطيور يلتقطن أولاد تلك الحيّات فيأكلون التعابين نسل تلك الطيور ويقال والله أعلم أن التعابن من نسل العقاب وهو ذالك الطير المذكور وأن الله تعالى سبب لتلك [f. 135] الأمم في قتال تلك الحيّات في تلك الجزائر وهم فيها جميعا إلى يوم القيامة وأن قتالهم خفيف على تلك الأمم من [عهد][٢٨٩] ذي القرنين وإنّهم آمنوا به و لم يرتدوا عن أيامّم إلى الآن وهم

---

[٢٨١] أقوَام

[٢٨٢] بالسنتها Fem. sing. agreement here and following

[٢٨٣] من B

[٢٨٤] في الاصل "يصيل"

[٢٨٥] توذي

[٢٨٦] في الاصل "دراع"

[٢٨٧] Line drawn through "في رزق"

[٢٨٨] التعابين Here and following

تلك الأمم من [عهد][٢٨٩] ذي القرنين وإنّهم آمنوا به و لم يرتدوا عن أيامّم إلى الآن وهم ينتظرون دين الإسلام وعليه عاهدهم ذو القرنين وهم له منتظرون والله أعلم

قال أبو عبد الملك الملشونيّ قلت لمقاتل ابن سُليمان حدّثنا بعض [ما رويتَهُ عن الثقات من غرائب الدنيا وجزائرها و][٢٩٠] كم فيها طولا وعرضا ؟ قال حدّثني غير واحد من أصحاب رسول الله صلعم أن في جزيرة في الدنيا من قرن جبل قاف الغربيّ إلى قرنه الشرقيّ ومن قرنه القبليّ إلى قرنه الجوفي كلّ ذالك مسيرة خمسمائة عام وقد أحاطت بهذه [f. 136] الجزائر البحار من كلّ جانب كالحلقة وجبل قاف محيط بالدنيا كلّها والبحر المحيط خلف جبل قاف ومنهم [من] يتبحّر جميع هذه الأبحار ولا يعلم ما خلف المحيط إلاّ الله الواحد القهار قلت لمقاتل فما هذه الخمسمائة عام من سكنها من الخلق ؟ قال أمّا ثلاثمائة عام منها جعلها الله جل ذكره على ثلاثة أثلاث ثلة أسكن الله فيه الحيّات وثلث جعله الله بحار وثلث جعله الله تعالى قفارا لا عمارة فيها والمأتان الباقيتان مائة منها عمارة للحباش وجزائر [ياجوج][٢٩١] وماجوج وتسعة وتسعون عامّا للروم وسنة واحدة عمارة لهذه الأمّة

قال أبو عبد الملك بالملشونيّ][٢٩٢] سمعت مقاتلا يقول عمارة ياجوج وماجوج [f. 137] والحبشة مائة وعشرون سنة وعمارة الروم وجزائرها تسعة وتسعون سنة وللإسلام سنة واحدة وبقيّة ياجوج وماجوج منهم الترك وقد سماهم ذو القرنين الترك لقوله ' أتركوهم ' قال رسول الله صلعم لا بدّ والله من اظهارهم إلى البلاد ومن تقب[٢٩٣] السدّ والخروج منه حتّى يهلكوا أهل الدنيا وليس بينكم وبين خروجهم إلاّ قليل وخروج الدجال ونزول عيسى ابن مريم عليه السلام وطلوع الشمس من مغربها[٢٩٤] فأعلموا ذالك وقد نبانا الله في كتابه حيث قال ﴿فَإِذَا جَآءَ وَعْدُ رَبِّي جَعَلَهُ دَكَّآءَ وَكَانَ وَعْدَ رَبِّي حَقّاً﴾ [٢٩٥] قال النبيّ صلعم كلّ من كان خلف السدّ [٢٩٦] فهو من الخلق الأوّل من من ولد آدم [أ]عمارهم طويلة وأبدانهم [f. 138] عريضة ومواشيهم ودوّابهم مثل ذالك وكلّ من كان دون السدّ من هذه الناحية أعمارهم قصيرة وأجسامهم ودوّابهم مواشيهم وَطُيورهم كذالك يكون كلّ شيء علـى

---

[٢٨٩] في الاصل "اهد" أو يمكن "احد"

[٢٩٠] من B . الغرائب أن التقات في الدنيا وعجائبها وجزائرها :A

[٢٩١] في الاصل " يجوج "

[٢٩٢] في الاصل "المسونى"

[٢٩٣] ثقب

[٢٩٤] These words attributed to the Prophet are not documented in HE.

[٢٩٥] Qur'ān 18:98

[٢٩٦] Reference to the Qur'ān 36:9

قدرهم[٢٩٧] ثم قال النبيّ صلعم كان رجل في زمان سليمان عليه السلام طوله اثنا عشر ذراعا وأعمار[ه][٢٩٨] مائة سنة إلى مثل ذالك وأذنا[ه] عشرة أذروع[٢٩٩] وكانت النمل في ذالك الزمان مثل الذيب والذيب أكبر ممّا هو اليوم

قال ثمّ أن ذو[٣٠٠] القرنين وادع أهل السدّ وعاهدهم على دين الله وعلى طاعته والسمع للأمر وعزم على الرحيل ورغب إلى الله في المسئلة أن يدلّه على طريق الخير فنَزَل عليه الملك زياقيل [f. 139] وقال له قد أمرك ربّك بالقدوم على أمّة النغاش وهم من ولد آدم من نسل لواء ابن سام ابن نوح عليه السلام فأقام على جزائرهم في البحر الأيمن الذي هو ممّا في[٣٠١] مرجع الشمس في الشتاء

ذكر مسيرة ذي القرنين إلى بلد النغاش

قال أبو عبد الملك [فرحل][٣٠٢] ذو القرنين على وجه الأرض فمشى ثمانية أيّام على الأرض قطع فيها ثمانية أعوام ثمّ أنّه أشرف على البحر فمشى فيه ساعة من النهار ثم أنّه خرج إلى جزيرة كثيرة المياه والمروج والسباع وقد أحاطت السباع بعمائرها وأهلها قوم ضعاف الأبصار فوجدهم ذو القرنين يقاتلون الغرانيق في زمان الصيف لأنّهم في بلادهم تصيف الغرانيق وفي بلادهم تشتى البراريج[٣٠٣] فإذا كان زمان الصيف فسدوا عليهم ثمار بلدهم وزرعهم لا يتركون لهم من معائشهم إلاّ اليسير فإذا جاءهم [f. 140] الشتاء ارتحل الغرانيق منهم وراجع[٣٠٤] إليهم البراريج وهو أهون عليهم من الغرانيق قال ذو القرنين للملك زياقيل «ذالك ما لهؤلاء القوم يقاتلون هذه الطيور ؟» قال له قد ابتلاهم الله بهم وذالك أنّهم على ضعفهم وضعف أجسامهم وهم قوم شداد البأس والفتن بينهم فإذا أراد بعضهم فتنة بعض بعث الله إليهم الغرانيق يشغلونهم عن ذالك فيشتغلون بمعاشهم خوفا من فسادها» قال فسأل ذو

---

[٢٩٧] Not in HE

[٢٩٨] في الاصل "هم" Masc. Sing. agreement here and following

[٢٩٩] أذرع

[٣٠٠] ذا

[٣٠١] "هو مما في مرجع الشمس" Not clearly legible. "مقابل الشمس" :B

[٣٠٢] في الاصل "فرخل"

[٣٠٣] نفهم "بلارج"

[٣٠٤] ورجعت

القرنين الملك زياقيل «هل كان لهم أمير أم لا ؟» قال له «لا أمير لهم ولا شيخ يحكم بينهم وكلّ واحد يحكم برأيه» ثمّ أن ذا القرنين [عَمَدَ][٣٠٥] بكتابه فكاتب إليهم :

بسم الله مجريها وبأمر الله مرسيها من عبد الله ذو القرنين ابن نّباش إلى جميع النغاش سلام على من أتبع الهدى وآمن بالله وأطاع رسوله منا إليكم كافّة وجمعكم عامة أن [f. 141] تأمنوا بالله ورسوله وتقروا لله بالواحدانيّة وأنّه لا ربّ غيره ولا معبود سواه الذي خلقكم وصوركم وأعطاكم ورزقكم وهو الذي أحياكم ثمّ يميتكم ثمّ يحييكم ثمّ إليه ترجعون فآمنوا بالله وكونوا على حذر من [شدّتنا][٣٠٦] وبأسنا فإنّ الله أمرنا بقتال من كفر به والإحسان لمن آمن به فإنّ أطعتم الله الذي لا إله إلاّ هو فلكم منّا الأمن والأمان وإن أنتم امتنعتم من الإيمان به فأذنوا بحرب من الله ورسوله فتُصبحوا على ما فعلتم نادمين والسلام

فختم الكتاب ودفعه إلى رسوله فلمّا أتاه أسرعوا بالأقرار لله بالوحدانيّة فآمنوا بالله ووعدهم ذو القرنين على خراج بلادهم وزكاتهم يؤَدونها لفقرائهم على أن لا يخادعوا بعضهم بعضا ولا يرتدوا بعد إيمانهم فعاهدوه على ذالك وارتحل عنهم [f. 142] حتّى أتا موضعا فأتاه الملك زياقيل فقال له يا ذا القرنين أمرك ربّك أن ترجع إلى دار ملك الروم فارتحل حتّى أتا إلى مدينة رُومَة فنزل بها

قال أبو عبد الملك الملشونيّ سمعتُ مقاتلا يقول كان ذو القرنين بلغ مغرب الشمس ومطلعها وطاف البحار و[الظُّلْمة][٣٠٧] وجبل قاف بنصره وعونه وسمعت محمّد ابن [المسيّب][٣٠٨] يقول مثل ذلك بقدرة الله عزّ وجلّ ثمّ رجع الحديث إلى دار ملكه برومة فنزل عليه الملك زياقيل «يا ذا القرنين إن ربّك يأمرك بكسر الأصنام وقتل من عبدها من جميع الأنام وأمرك [بجهاد][٣٠٩] ولد آدم حيث كانوا حتّى يقولوا لا الله إلاّ الله ويقرّوا له بالوحدانيّة والربوبيّة ثمّ بعث ذو القرنين كتابه على البلاد وجميع القبائل وقبائل الروم فاجتمعوا إليه وأقرّوا أنّه المقدّس المطهَّر المبعوث على ملوك الرّوم [f. 143] فأجابوه وأسرعوا بالإجابة إليه وكان قد كتب إلى ملوك الرّوم:

---

[٣٠٥] B: "بعث". This word is not clearly legible.

[٣٠٦] في الاصل "شدنا"

[٣٠٧] في الاصل "الضُّلْمة"

[٣٠٨] في الاصل "السايب". Probably refers to Saʿīd b. al-Musayyab.

[٣٠٩] في الاصل "بجاهد"

بسم الله مجراها وبأمر الله مرساها من عبد الله ذو القرنين ابن نّباش إلى ملوك الرّوم أشرافهم وعظمائهم وجملتهم أمّا بعد فإن الله الذي فضلكم واصطفاكم واختاركم من جملة خلقه فقد اتخذ جدّكم إبراهيم خليلا واصطفاكم جدّكم إسحاق واختاره ونشا من صلبه جدّكم عيصوا ونسلكم منه وجعلكم أفضل خلقٍ وطهّركم بالمقدّس المبعوث فيكم يُطهركم من [ذنوبكم][310] ويمكّن لكم في الأرض وبما لكم بمن فيها فأشكروه فيما خصّكم به إذ فضلكم بفضل أبائكم الكرام فأجيبوه وأطيعوه أمره وأسرعوا بالإجابة لدعوته وأعلم أنّه ربّكم الذي خلقكم وصوركم ورزقكم كيف يشاء فأسمعوا أمره وأطيعوا ولا تأخذكم [f. 144] في الله لومة لائم فتنقلبوا على أدباركم خاسرين فإنّي نصحت لكم فأعلموا أنّه ليس عندي رحمة لمن كفر بالله خالق الأرض والسموات فقد أمرني بكسر الأصنام وقتل من عبدها والله ينصر من يشاء ويهديه إلى صراط مستقيم ولا حول ولا قوّة إلاّ بالله العلى العظيم

ثمّ كتب كتابا إلى أهل بيت المقدّس

بسم الله الرحمان الرحيم من عبد الله ذي القرنين ابن نّباش إلى أشراف أبناء الروم إلى من [مكث][311] بيت المقدّس الذي أمن الله فيه وجعله ماوى للهدى وبيانا لمن أتبع خليله المهتدى فإنّي بعثت إليكم كتابا أرشدكم فيه وأذكّركم [الاء][312] عند ربكم فتذكروا وعيد الله وكونوا من عذابه على حذر وأعلموا أن بيده خزائن السموات والأرض ولا يمكنها إلاّ هو وقد عهد إليكم عهدا بما مدّ الله به من أوفي بالعهد والطوع لله والأمر بالمعروف والنهى عن المنكر والحفظ لحدود الله [f. 145] وأشهدت أن الله الذي لا إله إلاّ هو على الوفاء منّي بجميع ذالك

ومعلّم الخير ارْسَطَاطِلِيسْ حاضر وهو أكرم خلق الله لدىّ وقد وجد في علمه كما بلغكم أن الله جلّ ذكره سيبعث على ملوك الأرض و[رعيتهم][313] مقدّسا مطهرا لا يغلب ولا يقهر من تخضع له الجبابرة ويدين له الملوك ورجوت من الله الذي لا ربّ غيره ولا معبود سواه أنّه منّ عليّ أنّي ذالك الطاهر وقد ثبت ذالك

---

[310] في الاصل "دنوبكم"

[311] في الاصل "مكن"

[312] من B. من فعل "الو" i.e., "favor"

[313] من B. في الاصل "رعيائهم"

من علماء الأمّة والذّين [هم][٣١٤] ارسَطَطَالِيْس وافشخير والخضر ابن عامل عليه السلام فيشهدون بالصدق عهدته إليكم وكفى بالله شهيدا وهو حسبنا ونعم الوكيل ولا حول ولا قوّة إلاّ بالله العلى العظيم

ثمّ طوىَ [الكتاب][٣١٥] وختمه ودفعه إلى عامة الروم وعظمائِهم وكلّ ما وصل كتابه إلى الشريف وأسرع بالإجابة وكلّ [f. 146] ما مرّ بقوم أسرعوا بالإجابة إليه حتّى اجتمعوا له جنود الروم كلّها في عدد مبلغه مائة ألف وخمسون ألفا من صناديدها وأشرافها وشجعانها فلمّا اجتمعوا إليه وَواعَظَهُمْ وأكرمهم وأحسن القول والأفعال إليهم فأقاموا عنده مدّة ما شاء الله ثمّ أن القوم استشار بعضهم بعضا ورفعوا إليه الرأى واتّفق رأيهم على الجهاد والخروج إليه فبعث إليه ارسططاليس والخضر وافشخير فاستشارهم في الخروج فكلّهم أمره بالجهاد إلى أرض بيت المقدّس

قال أبو عبد الملك الملشونيّ أوّل ملك بدأ ذى القرنين بالحرب داريوس ملك فارس وكانت أرض الفرس شرقا من مدينة مملكة الروم وكان داريوس بلغه الخبر أن ذا القرنين عزم على قتال ملوك الأرض ملكا بعد ملك فأمر داريوس بجمع الفرس فأجابوه مسرعين [f. 147] فاستشارهم على أمر ذى القرنين وقام فيهم خطيبا وقال «يا قوم قد اتصل في خروج هذا الغلام الرُّوميِّ وما جمع من اللصوص فماذا ترون إذ قدم عليكم ؟» فقالوا له «لا يهمك أمر من لا طاقة له بحرابنا نحن أولوا قوّة وأوّلوا بأس شديد ولا بدّ لنا من حربه وأن كثر جمعه» فلمّا سمع ذالك منهم قال «[يا] قوم[٣١٦] عدوا واستعدوا وعولوا على لقائِه فإذا لاقيتم القوم فاقتلوا وأعزموا و[خذوا][٣١٧] الغلام بنفسه [خاصّة][٣١٨] وأتونيّ به فإنّكم أصحاب حرب ومكيدة وشدّة وشجاعة ولا لكم عندنا عذر[٣١٩] أن فررتم من غلام الرّوميّ[٣٢٠] صغير غير مجرب في [الحروب][٣٢١] ولا مقاسي في الأمور وأن تلقوا بايديكم إليه فيكون رأيكم عليه واحد» فقالوا له «نعم أيّها الملك أنت الشديد في قبائِلك وليس لمثلك البقاء بعد جنودك لأنّ الجنود لا

---

[٣١٤] من B

[٣١٥] في الاصل "الكتب"

[٣١٦] في الاصل "يقوم"

[٣١٧] في الاصل "حذوا"

[٣١٨] في الاصل "حاصة"

[٣١٩] في الاصل "عدر"

[٣٢٠] ممكن "الرّوميّ"

[٣٢١] في الاصل "الهروب"

يقف[٣٢٢] إلاّ بالملك [f. 148] فإنّ [مضرّتك][٣٢٣] أشدّ على القوم من جميع أهل الفرس فعول على الخروج بين أشراف قومك»

قال أبو عبد الملك الملشونيّ سمعت مقاتلا يقول خرج داريوس مع جميع قومه حتّى نزل بنهر يقال له بِصُوَرِصْ فنزل بعدة مبلغها ماتان ألف وعشرون ألفا فلمّا نزل واد بِصُوَرِصْ كتب كتابا ذي القرنين:

> من داريوس ملك الفرس إلى ذي القرنين اللصّ وأصحابه اللصوص أمّا بعد فإنّ الله جعلني أمينا على جميع خلقه وسماني باسمه وأعطاني الملك والرفعة والشرف وأنا الذي نضيء[٣٢٤] كما تضيء الشمس والقمر في الدنيا وأراك ملكت البلاد والبحار وسلكت الجبال وقطعت الفيافي والقفار حتّى أتيت إلى بلادنا لتهلكنا وقد اخبُرنا أنّك توجت بتاج الملك وقمت بنفسك على قدميك ثمّ جمعت الجموع وحشدت الحشود وجئت إلينا لتهلكنا وتملكنا ونكون تحت يديك فأرجع إلى بلدك [f. 149] [باهلك][٣٢٥] وأصحابك فإنّي قد كبرت نفسي عن جرءتك بفعل كفعلك وقد عفوت عن زلتك وغير آخذٍ عليك بما أجريت علينا بسفهك من قدومك [بشرذمة][٣٢٦] قليلة على عدد لا يحصى ولا يستطاع حربها يا معشر الروم تفكروا فيما أقبلتم وفيما تلقون من الهوان وكونوا على رشد بعقولكم ونجات[٣٢٧] لانفسكم لأنّكم جرّبتم حربنا ورأيتم هولنا فيما تقدم عليكم من حوادث الزمان وقد نصحت إليكم بكتابي نصيحة منّي إليكم والله المستعان

وختم الكتاب ودفعه إلى رسوله ودفع مع رسوله جِرَاباً مَمْلُوّاً سَمسَماً ودرّة وياقوتة و[تابُوتا][٣٢٨] مَمْلُوّاً [ذَهَباً][٣٢٩] وبعث معه الكتاب [f. 150] فلمّا وصل الرسول إلى ذو[٣٣٠] القرنين أمر بالرسل فنزعت عنهم

---

[٣٢٢] تقف

[٣٢٣] منَ B. في الاصل "مصرتك"

[٣٢٤] نفهم "أضيء"

[٣٢٥] من B

[٣٢٦] في الاصل "بشردمة"

[٣٢٧] نجاة

[٣٢٨] في الاصل "ثابُوتا"

[٣٢٩] في الاصل "دَهَباً"

[٣٣٠] ذي

[ثيابهم][٣٣١] وكتفت أيديهم إلى وراء ظهورهم كأنّهم يريدون قتالهم فقال لهم «لا تلوموني ولوموا صاحبكم الذي سمّاني لِصّاً فأنا أريد أن أفعل بكم فعل اللصوص بمن [صَادَفُوهُ][٣٣٢]» فقال له أحد الرسل «يا ذو[٣٣٣] القرنين أنا [لا][٣٣٤] نعرفك ولا ندري ما أنت عليه ولاكننا علمنا الآن مكانك وما أنت فيه وعليه فأنت فاضل العلم جليل القدر فجد إلينا بفضلك وإحسانك ولا تقتلنا وردنا إلى أهلنا وبلادنا حتّى يخبروا داريوس بما رأينا من كرامك [و إحسانك ونكونوا واسطة الخير فيما بينك وبينه فلعل الذي اصطفاك يهدينا][٣٣٥] جميعا على يديك» قال وكان ذو القرنين رجلا رحيم القلب فلمّا سمع تضرعهم وحسّ الفاظهم قال لهم «أبشروا فأنا على ما ذكرتم من الإحسان إلى كلّ متضرعين[٣٣٦] لله وقد أردت قتلكم [f. 151] أوّل مرّة ثمّ علمت أن الرسل لا يقتلون فعفوت عنكم من الموت وأردت [ان] أعلمكم فضل الروم وكرمهم على الفرس فخل سبيلهم وأكرمهم وأحسن إليهم» فلمّا أرادوا الإنصراف أرادوا أن يعلموا ذو[٣٣٧] القرنين طريق [غزوة][٣٣٨] بلاد داريوس ويخبرونه كيف يُكَايِدُهُم فمنعهم عن ذالك فقال لهم «لا أخذ لكم قولا ولا أقبل منكم نصيحة لأنّكم تريدون الرجوع إلى مجائركم[٣٣٩] وملككم ولا أحد يريد ضرنا بحيلة ولنا بعون الله [غني][٣٤٠] عنكم وعن قولكم ورأيكم» فلما سمعوا الرسل منه ذالك تعجّبوا منه وقالوا «يا سيّدنا ما ولد المرأة مثلك ولقد فضلك الله على كثير من خلقه ثمّ كتب كتابا يذكر فيه

بسم الله الرحمان الرحيم من عبد الله ذى القرنين ابن نّباش ملك الروم أمّا [f. 152] بعد بلغني كتابك [تذكر][٣٤١] فيه سوْء مقالاتك لمّا دعتك إليه نفسك من زخرف المقالة وبهتان الضلالة ولك ما قلت ولقد علمت أن جنود [السموات][٣٤٢] لك معينة

---

[٣٣١] في الاصل " تيابهم "

[٣٣٢] من B . في الاصل "صَادَقُوهُ"

[٣٣٣] ذا

[٣٣٤] من B. في الاصل "ان"

[٣٣٥] من B. Scribe of A inadvertently omitted a line

[٣٣٦] متضرع

[٣٣٧] ذي

[٣٣٨] في الاصل "عزوة"

[٣٣٩] B: "عشائركم" Perhaps this word is a plural for *mujīr* meaning, 'Protector or patron.'

[٣٤٠] في الاصل "عنى"

[٣٤١] في الاصل "تدكر"

[٣٤٢] في الاصل "السموت"

وجنود الأرض يهابون ملكك ويخافون [مقاتلتك][٣٤٣] بل أنت [أذل][٣٤٤] وأهــون تبارك هو أجل وأعظم من أن يعين أعداءه على أولياءه وأنا لا أهـــابك لكـثرت جنودك والله ينصر من أطاعه و[يذل] [٣٤٥] من كفر به وهو خير الناصرين ولســت بمنصور على ما أنت عليه من الطغيان وسبيل البهتان فأنا لست براجع عنك ولا عن أرضِك ولا نخاف من لقائك ومعي جنود الله المطيعون من أبناء الروم الكرام المجيبين لدعوة الكلمة العليا وهم المنصورون على أهل الكلمة السفلى والله يؤيد بنصره من يشاء [f. 153] ولله العزة جميعا وأنت تسميت باسمه وهو [قاصم][٣٤٦] كل جبار عنيد بل يسلبك نعمته ويذل ملكك وعزك بكفرك بنعمه وأنا إن شاء الله سائر إليك من [اليوم][٣٤٧] هذا بجنود الله وصناديد أبناء الروم الكرام وأهجــم عليــك بجنــود لا [طاقة][٣٤٨] لك بها وأنا لا أدعوك في أعمائك فأنك ظننــت أن لا كتــب عليــك الموت فتفهم قولي وتعرف من خالص نفسك والله معنى[٣٤٩] عنك وهو المعين لمــن أطاعه ولا حول ولا قوة إلا بالله العلى العظيم

ثم أخذ حفنة من ذالك السمسم وجعلها في فائه و[مضغها] [٣٥٠] وبلعها بين يدى الرسل

ثم كتب نسخة ثانية

أما بعد فإنى رأيت جميع ما بعثت به إلي وزجدته زجد الطير[٣٥١] فأما الــدرة فــهو سوط العذاب بعثني الله عليكم لاذيقكم بأسه وأولى [f. 154] ملككم بأمره ووعــده وأما الياقوتة فأنا [أرجوا][٣٥٢] أن يضيء أمري كضيائها وأما التابوت فرجوت ربي أن يجمع لي خير الدنيا وملكها كما جمع التابوت هذا المال وأما السمسم فقد رأيتــه

---

[٣٤٣] في الاصل "مقالتك"

[٣٤٤] في الاصل " ادل "

[٣٤٥] في الاصل "يدل"

[٣٤٦] في الاصل "قاسم" "قاسف" :B

[٣٤٧] في الاصل "يوم"

[٣٤٨] في الاصل "صاقة"

[٣٤٩] معيني . يعيني :B

[٣٥٠] في الاصل "مدغها"

[٣٥١] sic . يمكن نفهم: "ووجدته وجد الطير" ؟

[٣٥٢] في الاصل "اجوا"

و[مضغتّه][٣٥٣] وطحنتُه وبلعتُه ولعمري أن جنودك لكثيرة لاكنّهم لا حَدَت[٣٥٤] لهم ولا حرارة ولا مكيدة وأنا أطحنك وجنودك كما طحنتُ السَّمْسَم فلعمري ما بعثتَ به إلاّ لتعلمني بكثرة جنودك فما أكثرهم وأقلّ حرارتَهم وبعثتَ بالياقوتة زعَما أن مُلْكَكَ قَوِيٌّ لا يطاق على حربه وأنّك تضيء كما تُضَيء الياقوتة ولا ضياء للجهل مع بين العلِم وبعثتَ بالياقوت مثلا لملكك يقفل الحكم عليه بل مفتاح قَفْلُ الجهل مفتاح العلم والله ناصريّ على جميع أمثالك ومؤيدي على كثرة جنودك والله خير الناصرين

ثمّ دعا بالرّسل فأعطاهم الذهب [f. 155] الذي بعث به أميرهم داريوش جائرة لهم فقال لهم [ذو][٣٥٥] القرنين «إذهبوا فقد أذهب الله صاحبكم» فلمّا أرادوا أن يُدعوه سجدوا بين يديه لمّا رأوا من علمه ويقينه ولمّا قال لهم ولمّا صنع بالسَمْسَم فقال لهم«لا تسجدوا لي واسجدوا لله الذي خلقني وخلقكم وشرّفني على [ملككم][٣٥٦] »

فلمّا بلغت الرسل داريوش دفعوا إليه الكتاب فقرأه وكان ذو القرنين [قد بعث][٣٥٧] إليه جرابا مَمْلُوًا بحبّ [الخَرِدَل][٣٥٨] فأخذ داريوش حفنةً من ذلك [الخردل][٣٥٩] وهو غَضْبَانٌ فألقاها في فِيهِ فلمّا مَدَغَهُ وجَدَه حَرًّ في فيهِ [فبصقه][٣٦٠] من فيهِ وألقاه فقال«اذهبوا فان جنود ذي القرنين لكثيرةً وإن حربهم لشديدٌ وشوكتهم مثل حرارة [الخردل][٣٦١] ولكنّي ناظرٌ في أمره بالخروج والعزم» ثمّ أمر جنوده بالاستعداد لحرب ذي القرنين واتّصل الخبر بذو[٣٦٢] القرنين فرجع معولاً على القدوم على داريوش واتّصل [f. 156] الخبر أيضا بداريوش أن ذو[٣٦٣] القرنين مقبلا[٣٦٤] إليه [فسار][٣٦٥] كلّ واحد منهم حتّى

---

[٣٥٣] في الاصل "مظغتّه"

[٣٥٤] حِدّة

[٣٥٥] في الاصل "دوّ"

[٣٥٦] في الاصل "ملكك"

[٣٥٧] منَ B

[٣٥٨] في الاصل "الخزدَل" "الخردَل" :B

[٣٥٩] في الاصل "الخزدل"

[٣٦٠] في الاصل "فيسقه"

[٣٦١] في الاصل "الخزدل"

[٣٦٢] ذي

[٣٦٣] ذا

[٣٦٤] مقبل

تراه الفئتان بجهة العراق فلمّا ترأت الفئتان أمر ذو القرنين بضرب الأبواق فضربت وأسرعت الجنود فوقع الحرب في الميدان فاقتتلوا قتالاً شديداً حتّى ظنّ الناس أنّه ألفنا[ء] ونزل الفريقان للموت بالقنا والنشاب كِلْتَا الفرقتين في يومهما إلى [الليل][٣٦٦] ثمّ عهدهم إلى الليل فصبرت الفرقتان و لم يُعرف أحدٌ من أحدٍ فبقى قتالهم سبعة أيّام لا فرار لفرقةٍ من فرقةٍ حتّى هلك الناس من عظيم البلاءِ وكَثُرَ الموت في آخر اليوم السّابعِ فقطع الله دابر جنود آل فارس بقدرته ووقعت فيهم السُّيُوف من كلّ مكان وانهزموا بأذن الله السّيف فيهم والقتل حتى انتهوا الى ارض فارس وقتل منهم ما لا عَدَدَ له ثم امْر ذو القرنين بمن مات [f. 157] من أصحابه أن يُدفنوا جميعا ثمّ أمر بدفن من مات من الفرس وقال «استروهم بـالتراب» فدفنوا وصدر ذو القرنين وأصحابه وأخذوا من الغنائم ما لا يوصف ففرّق الغنيمة على أصحابه ونجا داريوش في جملة من بقى من أصحابه فبلغ أرض فارس

ذكر مسير ذي القرنين إلى أرض كتابة[٣٦٧]

فعزم [ذو][٣٦٨] القرنين على الرحيل فدخل إلى جبل طور سيناء وهو ينظر شرق جبل الجوديّ من نظر جبال الكرم فنزل بها وافتتح منه مدائن كثيرة وصالحهم على الخراج يودُونه إليه فيما يصلح للجهاد والجزية أن يُودُّوها إليه في كلّ عام فعاهدوه على ذلك وتركهم

ثمّ ارتحل من أرض كتابة وجبل طور سيناء إلى أرض يقال لها فدومة فوجد فيها أمّة من الناس لم يرا مثلهم لِعِظْمِ خِلْقَتِهِم وكبر أجسامهم يقال لها النقرون [٣٦٩] [f. 158] فأراد قتالهم وكان من شأنه أنّه لا يقاتل أمّة من الامَمِ حتّى يدعوها إلى دين الله تعالى فأجابوه [بلا ضرب][٣٧٠] ولا قتال فصالحهم على الجزية والخراج يؤدُّونها إليه في كلّ عام لّما يصلح للجهاد فصالحوه

ثمّ ارتحل عنهم إلى أمّة يقال لها القيلون في أرض يقال لها القبلى وهي التي يزعمون أن الخصال التي منها الحكمة [و]منها خرجت ثمّ دعاهم إلى دين الله تعالى فأجابوه وصالحوه على الخراج والجزية أن يؤدُّونها إليه في كلّ عام فصَالَحهم على ذلك

---

٣٦٥ في الاصل "صار"

٣٦٦ في الاصل "اليل" Here and following

٣٦٧ Mss. A&B sic . يمكن نفهم "كنانة" بمعنة "مصر" ؟

٣٦٨ في الاصل "دو"

٣٦٩ An alternative reading could be "النغرون"

٣٧٠ من B . في الاصل "بلى ضر"

ثمّ ارتحل عنهم إلى أرض يقال لها قَدومَا وهي من نحو الأرض التي منها أصول الروم وفيها ملك يقال له فلص وهو الملك العنيد الجبّار الطّاغي فلمّا بلغ أهل المدينة خَبَرُ ذو[٣٧١] القرنين غلقوا الأبواب خوفا منه فأمر ذو القرنين [f. 159] أن يحيطوا بالمدينة و[يحارصوها][٣٧٢] وأمرهم أن يقتلوا كلّ من لقوا من أهل المدينة فلمّا رأوا ذلك قالوا «يا ذو[٣٧٣] القرنين إنّا لم نغلقوا أبوابنا على إنّا نريد قتالك لاكنّا غلقناها خوفا من داريوش وإن نحن فتحناها لك افنيتنا عن آخرنا» قال لهم ذو القرنين «افتحوا أبواب مدينتكم فأنّا غير داخلها عليكم حتّى ينصرني ربّي على داريوش ويفتح لي أرضكم فلا تخافوا منّي فقد عرفتكم وعرفتم وفاء لمن عاهدوني وإنّما أعطاني ربّي الرفعة والشرف على عباده والرياسة لمّا قد علم منّي من الوفا[ء] من حقّه مع ما ابتلاني ربّي من ملكه وسلطانه ما وجب عليّ الشكر والوفا[ء] بحقّه» قال ففتحوا له أبواب المدينة وخرجوا إلى جنوده بالأسواق ولم يدخلها وعاهدهم على الحقّ وتركهم

ثمّ ارتحل عنهم إلى مدينة قسمطينة [f. 160] وهي كلها على أرض مجران من تخُوم[٣٧٤] أرض السند وأرض فارس فأصابه بها جوع شديد حتّى هلك عامة من أصحابه فأكلوا دوّابهم إلاّ قليلا فقال لهم ذو القرنين «لا يهولكم هذا فاصبروا لأمر الله» فرجعوا على دوّابهم فأكلوها فبلغ فيهم الجهد العظيم حتّى أن رغيفا من ستّة عشر أوقية بدرهم و[دانق][٣٧٥] من دراهم ذى القرنين وإن عشرة أوقية من الدقيق بدرهم وإن خمسة عشر أوقية من الّحم[٣٧٦] بدرهم ورأس الفرس والبغل بلغ عندهم دينار ووجدوا ذالك جوع شديد[٣٧٧] من شدّة ما بهم وعلى خيولهم ثمّ أن ذى[٣٧٨] القرنين قال لهم «يا قوم قد علمت [ماذا][٣٧٩] حل بكم ولقد حل بنا [مثل][٣٨٠] الذي حل بكم ولاكن ارتحلوا بنا إلى خلف هذا الجبل لعلّى[٣٨١] الله يعيننا ويفتح علينا وهو خير الفاتحين

---

[٣٧١] ذي

[٣٧٢] في الاصل "يحاسروها"

[٣٧٣] ذا

[٣٧٤] تحوم ؟. The word is not legible. The context suggests 'on the border between'.

[٣٧٥] في الاصل "ذانق"

[٣٧٦] اللحم

[٣٧٧] الجوع الشديد

[٣٧٨] ذا

[٣٧٩] في الاصل "مادا"

[٣٨٠] في الاصل "متل"

[٣٨١] لعلّ

ثمّ ارتحل من ذالك [الموضع][٣٨٢] [f. 161] إلى مدينة يقال لها تطوش فوجد فيها هيكلا فسئل أهل الهيكال[٣٨٣] أن [ينظروا][٣٨٤] في أمره فقال لهم القائم بالهيكل« أما أنا مخبرك بشيء » فقال له ذو القرنين «والله لئِن[٣٨٥] لم تخبرني لأحرقنا هذا الهيكل ولا ترجعن[٣٨٦] حلله وكسوته فأمر ذو القرنين عند ذالك بالخَرَاب للهيكل فبادروا إليه رجاله فَسَمِعُوا صوتا من ذالك الهيكل وهو يقول «يا ذا القرنين لا تفعل فإنّك من الأرض المقدّسة وأمرك عظيم وسوف تظهر على أهل الأرض وأهل الدنيا ويبقا ذِكرك إلى يوم القيامة» فلمّا سمع ذو القرنين ذالك سكن غضبه وأمر بتركه وبرد ما أخذ منه

ثمّ ارتحل إلى أرض يقال لها أرض أمانيش وأهلها أهل قوّة وشدّة وعدتهم ثمانون ألف مقاتل فلمّا اتّصل بهم خبر ذى القرنين [f. 162] وقدومه أغلقوا الأبواب وصعدوا على [سور][٣٨٧] مدينتهم وأعلوا أشرافتهم ونادوا «يا [أ]هل ذى القرنين هلموا إلى القتال فوالله ترون منا الحرب الشديد والبأس والحديد ما لا رأيتم [مُنْذُ][٣٨٨] خرجتم من دار ملككم أو ترحلوا من مَدِينَتَنَا» فضحك ذى القرنين وقال «لو تعلمون أن برزتم إلينا» ثمّ أمر بالجنود أن [يحدقوا][٣٨٩] بالمدينة كلّها وقامت الرمات[٣٩٠] بنبل والفرسان بالقنا و[بالسيوف][٣٩١] فلما رأوا أهل المدينة ذالك خرجوا إليه في مائة ألف مقاتل فانتشب بينهم وبينه الحرب واقتحم الرجال بالرجال وكثر الوغا[ء] واشتدّ الحرب وكثر الفنا[ء] وحاصرهم[٣٩٢] ذو القرنين واشتدّ بهم البلاء والحصار فلمّا رأوا ذالك أيقنوا بالهلاك وأيقنوا أن لا طاقة لهم [بذى][٣٩٣] القرنين وكانوا [f. 163] على ملك داريوش ملك الفرس فأرسلوا مسرعين إلى داريوس ملك الفرس:

أمّا بعد فإنّك تلقى ذو[٣٩٤] القرنين وإلاّ اسلمنا له البلاد وفتحنا له أبواب المدينة

---

[٣٨٢] من B

[٣٨٣] الهيكل

[٣٨٤] من B . في الاصل "ينتظروا"

[٣٨٥] ل + إنّ

[٣٨٦] Word is not entirely legible. يمكن نفهم "ولأخذن"؟

[٣٨٧] من B . في الاصل "صور"

[٣٨٨] في الاصل " مُنْذُ "

[٣٨٩] في الاصل "يحذقوا"

[٣٩٠] رماة

[٣٩١] في الاصل "بالسِوف"

[٣٩٢] "حاصرهم" مكتوب فوق "حارسهم" على نفس السطر

[٣٩٣] في الاصل "بذو"

[٣٩٤] ذا

وكانت تلك المدينة لداريوش ملك الفرس فلمّا بلغه الخبر لم يجد بدا من الخروج إلى لقاء ذى القرنين فأمر بالجموع فاجتمعت إليه الفرس في سبعمائة ألف فارس ومن الرجال مثل ذالك وخرج للقاء ذو القرنين فبلغ ذالك لذى القرنين وخرج إلى لقائه فالتقيا بالفرس واقتتلوا قتالا شديدا ووقع الموت في الفرقين[٣٩٥] وكان داريوش عارفا بمكائدة[٣٩٦] الحروب وذو القرنين أعرف منه وكلّ واحد منهم لا يفتح بالحرب إلاّ وظهر له صاحبه مثله من مكائدة الحرب وخداعها فكلّما خرج ذى[٣٩٧] القرنين طائفة من الخيل أعطاه داريوش مثلها فكثر القتل وطال الوغا [f. 164] واشتدّ الحرب وكثر الفنا[ء] في الجهتين وقطعت العظام بحدّ السيوف [فثارت][٣٩٨] عجاجة الموت فلم يزل ذالك بينهم من وقت اشراق الشمس إلى آخر النهار وسالت الدما[ء] مثل الأودية من كلتا الفرقين[٣٩٩] في يومهم هذا فلمّا كان آخر النهار انهزمت جنود فارس وقيادها[٤٠٠] وأشرافها ووقعُوا فيهم السيف حتّى فنيت الفرس فلمّا رآ داريوش ذالك من موت صناديده المعول عليهم في الحرب جزع جزعا شديدا ورما بنفسه في البرية مع جملة من أشراف قومه وأشراف الفرس وهرب ورعب وخاف من أمر ذي القرنين وأصحابه [فأمر ذو القرنين][٤٠١] أن لا يشتغل بشيء من الغنائم حتّى يفنا ملك الفرس وجنوده يفعلوا ذالك وقال «اقتلوهم ولكم كلّما أردتم»

قال فأتبعوهم بالقتل وجدّ داريوش في الهروب حتّى بلغ [f. 165] نهر الطيرقان وهو واد عظيم يهبط من مدينة رومة وهو واد عظيم الأجراف قليل المسالك فلم يجد داريوش مسلك يسلكه حتّى أشرفت عليه خيل الروم فحملوا أنفسهم على الأجراف و[ذهبت] [٤٠٢] [عامتهم][٤٠٣] كسرا وموتا [فأدركهما][٤٠٤] ذو القرنين ووقفوا في عدوة الوادي ووقف داريوش على جرف الواد[ي] من العدوة الأخرى فقال له ذو القرنين «أيّها الملك الضال الجاهل القويّ ما لك أفنيت جندك وخربت مملكك[٤٠٥]

---

[٣٩٥] الفريقين

[٣٩٦] مكائد Here and following

[٣٩٧] ذو

[٣٩٨] في الاصل "فتارت"

[٣٩٩] فرقتين

[٤٠٠] وقوادها

[٤٠١] من B

[٤٠٢] في الاصل "دهبت"

[٤٠٣] في الاصل "عماهم"

[٤٠٤] في الاصل "فاذركهما"

[٤٠٥] مملك

بيدك ؟ يا خسير العقل آمن بالله الذي خلقك وأسلم نفسك لأمره تنجوا من مكائد الدنيا والآخرة» فقال له داريوش «أيّها الملك المطاع والقرن عن[٤٠٦] المناع رد عنا جنودك وأمسك علينا بأسك وأنا لا بدّ لي بعد هذا من الوصول إليك [فبكراماتك][٤٠٧] علينا وبعلمك الأ صبرت علينا ورجعت عنا حتّى أتيك [f. 166] بنفسي ومن معي بأشراف الفرس» فاجابه ذو القرنين إلى ذالك ورجع عنه وانصرف داريوش إلى دار ملكه ودخل الهيكل ودار ملكه وأغلق الأبواب عن نفسه وبكا على خراب ملكه بكاء عظيما وذكر ما كان فيه من الشرف والعزّة ثمّ أنّه دبّر أمره ووعظ نفسه ثمّ قال «لا ينجيني من ذو[٤٠٨] القرنين إلاّ أن آمن بربه وأقرّ له بالعبوديّة في أيّامه التي وهبها الله حكمها فإنّه كريم القدر عظيم العفو وفى العهد» فعزم على ذالك فكتب إلى ذو القرنين كتابا يقول فيه:

بسم الله الرحمان الرحيم إلى الملك المؤيد من عبده داريوش أمّا بعد فإنّ الله تعالى عطاك الظفر والنصر والغلبة والملك والرياسة على جميع ملوك الدنيا فمن عليّ وارجعني وردّ عليّ أهلي وابنتي وأخي وابعث إلي بهم على أمان منك وأنا نفتح لك كنوز فارس من نبوران وما حوته [f. 167] ملوكهم وما جمعوا وأعطيك خزائنها وما جمعت أنا وأبي وأجدادي وأكون تحت يديك وأعينك على عدوك والسلام

ثمّ طوى الكتاب ودفعه إلى رُسُلِهِ فأتوا به إلى ذى القرنين وقرأه وفهم غرضه وكان يوم الهزيمة قد أسرّ لداريوس أخاه [...][٤٠٩] وابنته وزوجته وأمّه فلمّا قرأ الكتاب أراد أن يجيبه عن سؤاله على الوفا[ء] على كلّ ما ذكره داريوش فردّ عليه ذو القرنين أخاه وابنته وأمّه وكتب إليه [ذو][٤١٠] القرنين

حقّا عليك هذا الكتاب قبل انتشاب الحرب وتنجوا من المكروهات وتلقى الأمن والأمان

فقالوا[٤١١] له الرسل «صدقت يا ذا القرنين» ثمّ أمر بمن لم يدفن من الفرس فدفنوا بالأمان لمن بقا منهم وواعدهم بالإحسان وحلّ سراح من أُسِرَ ثمّ [f. 168] أن داريوس كتب كتابا إلى لبور ملك الهند يستنصر به على ذو[٤١٢] القرنين فكتب

---

[٤٠٦] Perhaps we should read here: "القرعن"

[٤٠٧] في الاصل "فبكاراماتك"

[٤٠٨] ذي Here and following

[٤٠٩] Scribal error. This has been cut as it appears to have been miscopied from the following line: "فرد علي ذو القرنين اخاه".

[٤١٠] في الاصل "دو"

[٤١١] فقال

[٤١٢] ذي

بسم الله إلى الملك الأعظم لبور أمّا بعد فإنّي كتبت كتابا حين غلبت عليّ أيّامي وزال ملكي ونصر على ملكي ملكا[٤١٣] آخر [غيري][٤١٤] فأحسن إلي وأنصرني أن ذو[٤١٥] القرنين غلبني وقهرني وقتل رجالي وجدل أبطالي وقد أتيته من كلّ باب ورعدته فنّ من الحرب [وابى ولج][٤١٦] إلاّ أن يأتي أرضنا هلكنا فاستعنت بك وبعزّتك وراعدة نفسي[٤١٧] بقوتك وأهدم عزّه وأردّ بك عن أرضي جنوده وإنّما حملني على ذالك [ما][٤١٨] عهدته من شدّة الشجاع وإنّي لا بدّ لي من لقائه لأنّ الموت أهون علي ممّا حلّ بي فأحسن إلي وانصرني بجيش عَرَمْرَمٍ أهجم به على من ظلمني وعجل عليّ فإنّي منتظر لذالك من قِبَلكَ وأنا نازل بتخوم أرضك وألقاه بجنودك مع [f. 169] ما بقى عندي من الجيش وأنا منتظر إلى من يأتي من قبالك وموسع عليهم فإنّ نصرت عليه فلك نصف ما أخذت منه ومن خراج أرض وأن نَصر عليّ فخوفي أن يصلك ما وصلني فأعلمه والسلام

وختم الكتاب ودفعه إلى رسوله واحسن إليه فلمّا بلغ إلى لبور ملك أرض الهند كتاب داريوس وذو القرنين الآن في ناحية من نواح شرق آل منسك ومنها [غزا][٤١٩] فارس وملكهم

قال أبو عبد الملك الملشونيّ لمّا عفا ذو القرنين عن ملك الفرس وهو داريوس عزم على الرحيل فارتحل مشرقا نحو جابرصا

ذكر مسيرة ذو[٤٢٠] القرنين إلى مدينة جابرصا

قال أبو عبد الملك الملشونيّ ثمّ أن ذا القرنين عزم على الرحيل فارتحل من جزائر آل منسك وآل [f. 170] باريش وجزائر الحيّات فركب البحر على نحو ما تقدم متبعا للسبب فمشى على البحر وطوى الله له البعيد ويسر له القريب فمشى عشرة أيّام بلياليه قطع فيها مسيرة عشر سنين ثمّ أشرف

---

[٤١٣] ملك

[٤١٤] في الاصل "عيرى"

[٤١٥] ذا

[٤١٦] "وابى ولج" من B . في الاصل "وياولج ؟" (Not legible) . يمكن نفهم [وألحّ] ؟

[٤١٧] Meaning of these two words not clear. They are not present in B.

[٤١٨] في الاصل "انى" ، لازم ان نقرأ "ما"

[٤١٩] من B . في الاصل "عزا"

[٤٢٠] ذي

على مدينة جَابَرصًا فلمّا أشرف عليها وهو في اللجاج أشرف على مدينة عظيمة من أعظم عظائم الدنيا وهي مدينة في فلات[٤٢١] جزيرة مثل جزائر الغرب أو دونها لها عشرة ألاف باب بين كلّ باب و[باب][٤٢٢] ثلاثة فراسخ ومن أهل العلم من يقول فرسخان على كلّ باب سبعون ألف حربي نصف الرمات[٤٢٣] بقوس العاقب والنصف الآخر بقوس العتيق يخرج من كلّ باب في حوائجهم مائة ألف ويدخلون كلّ يوم مثل ذالك في أسواقهم وحوائجهم

وفي رواية ابن عبّاس رضي الله عنه لمّا نزل صالح عليه [f. 171] السلام بقرية الحرم ووجد أرضا خصيبة أمر قومه الذين آمنوا معه أن يتخذوا لأنفسهم مساكين[٤٢٤] يسكنوها فبنوا الديار وغرسوا الأشجار وجروا الأنهار وعمروا العمار وشيدوا البُنيان والقصور متمسكين بدين الإسلام ثمّ خرج بأهله إلى مكّة فأقام بها ما شاء الله فكان يأتي إليهم ويُذكّرهم ويدعوا لهم بالرحمة والمغفرة ويجلس عندهم متمسكين بدينه وكان بقربهم بقية مِمَّن كان آمن بهود عليه السلام لمّا أَهْلَكَ الله قوم عاد بالريح وترك بقية من قوم هود خرج معهم في سبعين رجلا كانوا قد آمنوا بهود عليه السلام فلمّا توفّى هود عليه السلام خرجوا إلى ارض فِلَسْطِيْن فنزلوا بأرض بقرب من الحجاز فكانوا مجاورين لصالح عليه السلام [f. 172] فكان يصبح عندهم صالح ويصلّون بصلاته متمسكين بدينه فلمّا توفّى صالح عليه السلام جاء قوم من بني هود إلى قوم من بني صالح فقال بعضهم لبعض أنّه قد توفّى نبيّ الله هود وتوفّى صالح عليه السلام ولاكن لا ينبغى لنا أن نقيموا ببلاد لا يكون فيها نبي يرشدنا ويهدنا إلى صراط مستقيم فأنا نخشي أن نعصى الله تعالى فيصيبنا مثل ما أصاب قومنا وقومكم من قبل فارتحل القوم من بني هود إلى المغرب ونزلوا بموضع مدينة جابلقا فأقاموا ونشر الله تعالى درياهم[٤٢٥] فبنوا المدينة وشيدوها وجعلوا لها عشرة [آلاف][٤٢٦] باب ما بين الباب والباب ثلاثة فراسخ ويقال فرسخان فحرس كلّ باب من هذه الأبواب ألف رجل ولا تعود إليهم نوبتهم أبدا وبنوا الديار والقصور وأجروا الأنهار وغرسوا الأشجار [f. 173] فهؤلاء ناسك وهم من درّية[٤٢٧] سبعين رجلا من مؤمني قوم هود عليه السلام فلمّا رآ قوم صالح أن قوم هود قد ارتحلوا إلى المغرب قالوالا بقاء لنا ارتحلوا بنا إلى أقصا المشرق إلى موضع

---

[٤٢١] فلاة

[٤٢٢] من B . في الاصل "بات"

[٤٢٣] الرماة

[٤٢٤] مساكن

[٤٢٥] ذرياتهم ، i.e., progeny

[٤٢٦] في الاصل "ءالف"

[٤٢٧] ذرّية

مدينة يقال لها جابرصا وكان قوم صالح ثمانون[٤٢٨] رجلا فلمّا نزلوا أقاموا فيها ما شاء الله فنشر الله تعالى ما في أصلابهم وكثر نسلهم فبنوا فيها مدينة يقال لها بَرصا وجعلوا لها عشرة آلاف باب ما بين الباب والباب ثلاثة فراسخ ومن أهل العلم من يقول فرسخين وبنوا الديار وغرسوا الأشجار وأجروا الأنهار فيها فهؤلاء منسك وهم أهل هاتين المدينتين أكثر خلقا من ياجوج وما جوج فلمّا بعث النبي صلعم و[أُرسل آمنوا به][٤٢٩] فدعاهم إلى الإسلام [f. 174] فأجابوه وآمنوا به وصدقوه فمؤمنهم مع مؤمن أمّة محمّد صلعم والله أعلم إلي ذالك ثمّ نرجع إلى رواية عبد الملك الملشونيّ

قال أبو عبد الملك فلمّا أشرف عليهم ذو القرنين وسمعوا الأبواق وظهرت الرايات بادروا بالجمع وغلقوا الأبواب و[ظنّوا][٤٣٠] أن أعداءهم أهل جابلقا أقبلوا إليهم وكانوا لا يامَنون خوفا من أهل جابلقا وقد ظهر رعبهم في قلوبهم خوفا من بأسهم [فبادروا][٤٣١] إليهم بالخروج والعرد[٤٣٢] والسلاح فلمّا رآهم ذو القرنين أمر بالنزول وبعث إليهم كتابا يذكر فيه

> بسم الله الرحمان الرحيم من عبد الله ذى القرنين إلى أهل مدينة جابرصا السلام [f. 175] على من اتّبع الهدى وخشى عواقب الدهر وأرضي بطاعة العلي الأعلى فإنّا كتبناه إليكم ندعوكم إلى طاعة خالقكم والإنابة إلى شرَائِعه والإقرار بوحدانيّته فإنّ اطعتموه فلكم ما لنا وعليكم ما علينا وأن تمردتم وطغيتم واتّبعتُم الغواية وتماديتم على الضلالة فأدنوا[٤٣٣] بحرب من الله ورسوله فأنّا قادمون عليكم بجنود الله التي لا تحصى والله ينصر من يشاء ويهدى إليه من ينيب

وختم الكتاب ودفعه إلى نفر من قومه فمضوا به حتّى وصلوا القوم فبادروا إليهم بالجميع وارتفع الكلام فالقوا إليهم الكتاب فأخذوه وساروا به إلى ملكهم وأشرافهم فلمّا دخلوا عليه وفتح الكتاب وجدوا فيه ' بسم الله الرحمان الرحيم ' في أوّل [الكتاب][٤٣٤] وأنّه من غير عدوهم أهل جابلقا [فأمروا][٤٣٥] بالرسل فدخلوا عليهم [f. 176] فأكرمهم وسألهم عن ذى القرنين أملك هو أم نبيّ

---

[٤٢٨] ثمانين

[٤٢٩] من B. The text for A is not legible here.

[٤٣٠] في الاصل "طنوا"

[٤٣١] في الاصل "فباذروا"

[٤٣٢] يمكن "العرّادة" Corriente "balista, catapulta"

[٤٣٣] فأذنوا

[٤٣٤] في الاصل "الكتب"

[٤٣٥] "ف" من B

[فقالوا][٤٣٦] له «ملك عدل ونبيّ صالح لا يعمل عملا إلاّ [بإذن][٤٣٧] الله جلّ ذكره وأنّه لا يظلم أحدا وأنّه لا يحارب إلاّ من حاربه ولا يقرر من قتال أحد حتّى يستدانه[٤٣٨] على طاعة الله الواحد القهار فبذالك بعثنا إليكم فإن أنتم آمنتم لكم الأمن والأمان وإن لم تؤمنوا فخذوا على حربه ولا طاقة لكم بحربه» قال لهم ملك القوم «ارجعوا إلى ذى القرنين فاستأذنوا له علينا نقدموا عليه» ففعلوا فأتوا إلى ذى القرنين فإذا كلّ طائفة ودت حقّ السلام وكان بدأ الكلام بعد السَلام من ذى القرنين ثمّ قال «يا [أ]هل جابرصا من أيّ الأمم أنتم ؟» قالوا «يا ذا القرنين نحن آل تاريش ابن يافت ابن نوح عليه السلام» قال «وكيف كان سكناكم في هذه الجزيرة ؟» قالوا له [f. 177] «كيف شاء خالقنا» قال «وهل عرفتم [أن] لكم خالقا ورازقا ؟» قالوا له «وكيف لا نعلم بذالك وقد نجينا من عدونا أهل جابلقا ومن علينا ببيان لهدى وثبّتنا على دين جدنا نوح وخرجنا من الظلمات إلى النور بقدومك علينا ونحن في غمّ ورعب لمّا رأينا من شدّة ما ظهر لنا من [الرعب][٤٣٩] من جنودك حين أشرفتْ علينا في لجج البحر و[ظنّنا][٤٤٠] أنّكم أهل جابلقا فلم يكشف لنا خبر ذالك إلاّ كتابك الذي وصل إلينا وسؤالك عن وصولنا إلى هذه الجزيرة , وأنا وصلناها بأمر الله كنا ركبنا البحر مع إخواننا آل يافت ابْن نوح وقدمنا السبب حتّى خرجنا إلى هذه الجزيرة من غير قصدنا إليها فكانوا آباؤنا الذين وصلوها نظروا إخوانهم إلى سنة وسنتين وعشرين سنة وهم [f. 178] في ذالك على النظر[٤٤١] *[B f. 63v] و[الرجَاء][٤٤٢] للاجتماع بإخواننا فحرثنا وقبلنا ببركة ما زرعنا وكلّما صنعنا في الأرض نما وكثر فلم يزل آباؤنا عَلى ذلك حتّى ييسُوا [B f. 64r] من إخوانهم وأنّهم إخوة كلّهم من يافت بن نوح فأعلموا ذا القرنين كلما كتبوا آباؤهمْ وصنعوا في المدينة وَكيف بنوها وكيف صاروا فيها وانتها بهم إليها وأعلموه بجميع ذلك قالَ لهم ذو القرنين «كمْ أنتم في العَدد ؟» قالوا له «آلاف حربي وَلنا في كلّ ليلة على كلّ باب ألف حَارس يحرسنا فمن أدّى نوبته لا يعود للحرس أبدا» قَال لهم «وكيف تعلمُون ذلك ؟» قالوا لهُ « لكلّ باب من الأبواب أمينا يكتب كلّ طائفة باسمها وأنّهم ليلتها في كلّ شطر مسمّى فَيكون ذلك عَلامة لهم قال لهم «ومَن هو منكم الملك ؟» قالوا له «هذا» قال لهُ ذو القرنين «فما اسمك؟» [قال] «حلص بن فلص» قالَ لهُ «كمْ عمرك ؟» قال «ألف مضت وثمانون» قال لهُ «وما*

[٤٣٦] في الاصل "فقال"

[٤٣٧] في الاصل "بادن"

[٤٣٨] أستأذنه

[٤٣٩] في الاصل "الرغب"

[٤٤٠] في الاصل "ظنناكم"

[٤٤١] Begin Lacuna in A. Text is taken from B.

[٤٤٢] في الاصل "الرجَا"

اسمك؟» [قال] «حلص بن فلص» قال لَهُ «كَمْ عمرك ؟» قال «ألف مضت وثمانون» قال لَهُ «وما دينك في الماضي ؟» قال لَهُ «دين الله الوَاحد القهار» قال له «ومَا سيرتك ؟» قال «الصرف في القول والعدل في الحكم [f. 64v] والرفق بالضعيف والانابة عَلى الحقّ والتوكّل عَلى الحيّ [٤٤٣] الدائِم الذي لا يموت» قال لَهُ «وكَيفَ عيشتكمْ في هذه المدينة ؟» قَالَ «عيش رغد وقناعة ولنا من الثمار كفاء ومن الطّعام شفاء وَمن الثمار ما نوارى به [عريتنا] [٤٤٤]» قال «وكيف سكناكم ؟» قال «قصور في كهوف وبيوت في رفوف وصناديق في [ظروف] [٤٤٥]» قال «ولَم ذلك ؟» قال «إنّ الشمس تطلع من الحجاب عَلى حافته فإذا طلعت كان لّما دوى لا يستطيع الخلق دويها ولا صبر لهم على شدّة حرها فلا نجد لذلك راحة من حرها إلاّ بالدخول في الكهوف حتّى تعلوا عَلينا وَنخرج حين تعلوا إلى مساكين عاليّة في المدينة وغرفات مشيدات فإذا غربت الشمسْ في مغربها دخلنا في الكهوف والسّراديق ونكونوا فيها حتّى تطلع الشمس وتعلوا في السماءِ» قال لَهُ ذو القرنين «وما بَال رؤسكم ووجوهكمْ لا شعور فيها ؟» قال «سقطت الشعور من أجل الحرور» قال لهم «وكَم أعمَاركم ؟» قال لَهُ «ألف سنة ومنّا من لَهُ الفان وما بينهمَا» [B f. 65r] فدعاهم إلى الإيمان فآمنوا بالله تعالى وصدقوا في إيمانهم ثمّ قال ذو القرنين «من اين طلوع الشمس ؟» قال له «من خلف هذا الجبل ؟» فانطلق حتّى وقف عَلى الجبل من حافة المدينة والجبل عَلى شاطيء المدينة ثلثاه فيها وهو مكان تمام حصنها وبنيانها فوقف ذو القرنين بطرق الجبل ونظر إلى الشمس كيف تطلع عليهم ليس بينها وبينهم شيء يسترهم من حرها إذا طلعت على المدينة وذلك قوله تعالى ﴿حَتَّى إِذَا بَلَغَ مَطْلِعَ الشَّمْسِ وَجَدَهَا تَطْلُعُ عَلَى قَوْمٍ لَّمْ نَجْعَل لَّهُم مِّن دُونِهَا سِتْراً ﴾ [٤٤٦] كذلك فسألهم ذو القرنين عن البلاد ممّا يلي الدنيا قالوا «يا ذا القرنين سبب الله تعالى لآبائنا وحولهم إلى هذه الجزيرَة في البحار كما سبب لك في الوصُول إلينا فوصلوها وتركونا فيها وَلم نعلموا كيف هي الدنيا إلاّ أنّهُ ظهر لنا [f. 65v] وبين البلاد ممّا يلي مغرب الشمس ظلمة نروها ولم نسلكوها ولا قربنا منها قط فودعهم ذو القرنين وانصرف عنهم يريد الظلمة التي ذكروها له فارتحل عنهمْ وتركهم

---

٤٤٣ Perhaps we should read here: "الحقّ"

٤٤٤ في الاصل "عورتنا"

٤٤٥ في الاصل "ضروف"

٤٤٦ Qur'ān 18:90

ذكر مَسيرة ذا القرنين إلى الظُّلْمَة

قال عبْد الملك لما سمعَ ذو القرنين خَبر الظلمة وقف في نفسه أن يسلكها وينظر كيف هي ثمّ ارتحل عن أهل جابرصا ومشى في البرّ حتّى نزل بموضع أراد اللّٰه تعالى نزوله فيه ورغب إلى الله تعالى يعلمه أين الظلمة فنزل عليه الملك زياقيل فسلم عليه فردّ عليه السلام فخلا به فقال لهُ «يا حبيبي يا زياقيل وددت أن الله تعالى يمدّ لي في العمر حتّى أعبده حقّ عبادته وَأطاعهُ هذه الظلمة التي ذكرها لي أهل جابرصا وَأرى ما فيها من عجائب الدنيا ؟» قالَ لهُ الملك زياقيل «يا ذا القرنين صحبت بعض ملائِكة الله [B f. 66r] في السّماءِ فقال بعضهمُ [أن] لله ظلمة لم يسلكها ملك مغرب ولا نبيّ مرسل وفيها عيْن الحياة فَقال بعضهم أن الظلمة التي بها تلك العين هل هي ظلمة المشرق أو ظلمة المغرب ؟ فقال بعضهم ليس بين قرن المشرق وقرن المغرب إلاّ ظلمة واحدة في جهة مشرق الشمس فَقال بعضهم مقدار هذه الظلمة مَسيرة أربعين سنة ومن دخل هذه الظلمة فانّهُ يجد فيها عيْناً من مَاء وهيَ عين الحياة من شرب منها أو توضا منها أعطاه اللّٰه الخلود إلى يوم القيامة»

قال فَرحل ذو القرنين من ذلك المكان حتّى قرب من الظلمة فرأها قد أخذت من السماء إلى الأرض لا يدرك منتهاها لا طولا ولاَ عرضا وَهي شديدة [f. 178] [٤٤٧] السواد لا يرى مثلها في الدنيا إلا بيت مقفول أو مطمورة [مقفولة][٤٤٨] فمثل ذالك سواد تلك الظلمة فنزل ذى القرنين بجوارهم ونزلت جنوده في أرض معمورة كثيرة الرمال رفيقة لمن فيها واسعة من إقليم جابرصا وأعلم أن ليس بينه وبين الظلمة أحد من بني آدم إلاّ من كان بمدينة جابرصا فسأل ربه و[ألحّ][٤٤٩] عليه في المسئلة أن يبعثَ إليه زياقيل الذي يأتيهم بالوحي فبعث الله الملك زياقيل فقال له ذو القرنين «يا زياقيل هل لله من ظلمت في الأرض حجبت عن الخلق ؟» قال «نعم» قال «أ هي التي نرا أمامي ؟» قال «نعم» قال «كم بيني وبنيها؟» قال «مسيرة اثنا عشر سنة من هذا الموضع التي ظهرت منه» قال له ذو القرنين «هل بيني وبيننها أحد من بني آدم ؟» قال «لا هذا منتهى [f. 179] ولد آدم ومن [هاهنا][٤٥٠] على ناحية جابرصا إلى طرف الدنيا مسيرة [خمسين][٤٥١] عامّا منها في الظلمات أربعين عامّا وعشرة في الضّيا وهذا أقصا

---

[٤٤٧] End lacuna. Return to A.

[٤٤٨] في الاصل "مكفولة"

[٤٤٩] في الاصل "لحّ"

[٤٥٠] في الاصل "منهنا"

[٤٥١] من B

سكني ولد آدم» قال له ذو القرنين «هل ملكها أحد قط ؟» قال «ما ملكها نبيّ ولا جنّيٌّ قط ولا ملك ولا شيطان ولا يعلم ما فيها إلاّ الواحد القهار» قال له ذو القرنين «ولم حجبها الله عن الخلق ؟» قال «لأنّ فيها عين الحياة التي ذكرت لك» قال له ذو القرنين «وفي أيّ موضع هي في الظلمات وأين نقع منها ؟» قال «هي في النصف منها تمشى في النصف الأوّل عشرين سنة تمشى منها أيضا في النصف الثاني عشرينِ سنة» قال له ذو القرنين «هل لها جبال ؟» قال له«ما فيها جبال ولا حجر ولا شجر ولا هي إلاّ أرض وطيّة سهلة بيضا مرمّلة سَلْمَةٌ [دهسة][٤٥٢]» قال [f. 180] «كم وسع تلك الأرض ؟» قال «هي أرض متصلة بجبل قاف المحيط بالدنيا» قال له ذو القرنين «إذا خرجت تلك الظلمات ودخلت تلك الأرض هل هي في الظلمات متِّصلَت[٤٥٣] أم هي في الضياء ؟» قال «بل هي في الضياء متِّصلة بالحجاب على طرف بحر الظلمات» قال له ذو القرنين «هل بينها شمس ؟ قال له الملك زياقيل «ليس فيها شمس» قال «ولم تكن فيها شمس وعليها ضوء النهار ؟» قال «لأنّ الشمس تزّاور[٤٥٤] عنها وتستظل تلك الأرض بجبل [شامخ][٤٥٥] وهي تلك الجبال ثقل الله بها الأرض فالنهار يصل إليها ولا تصل إليها الشمس» قال ذو القرنين للملك«انصرف جزاك الله خيرا من خليل»

فانصرف الملك ومضى ذو القرنين إلى عسكره فقال«عليّ بالعلماء» فاجتمع إليه ألف عالم من علماء الروم ومائة عالم كلّهم من علماء الروم فقال لهم«هل تعلمون ما بيننا وبين آخر الدنيا ؟» قالوا «لا علم لنا بذالك» [f. 181] فقال له عالم منهم يقال له افشخير «أنا أيّها الملك أعلمك أن ما بينك وبين آخر الدنيا مسيرة اثنا عشر عامًا وذالك أن آدم عليه السلام ذكر لابنه شيت عليه السلام أن لله في الأرض ظلمة حجبها عن خلقه طولها أربعين سنة بينها وبين بني آدم اثنا عشر سنة ما دخلها إنسي ولا جنّي» قال له ذو القرنين «يا افشخير مثل [الليل][٤٥٦] أو مثل الدخان ؟» قال «ليست مثل ليل ولا مثل دخان إنّما هي ظلمة لا تشبه الليل ولا دخان بل هي أشدّ سوادا من ذالك كلّه لا يدخلها أحد إلاّ مات من شدّة الظلمات» قال لهُ ذو القرنين «فما ورآها ؟» قال «أرض بيضاء ورمال لا ترى فيها جبل ولا مرتفع» قال له«هل فيها شمسٌ ؟» قال «لا ليس فيها شمس بل حجبها الله عن خلقه» قال «وهل في أطرافها جبال ؟» قال «نعم [f. 182] فيها [جبال][٤٥٧] شوامخ عاليات تبلغ عنان السماء

---

[٤٥٢] في الاصل "دهيسة"

[٤٥٣] متصلة

[٤٥٤] sic Corriente: "apartarse, desviarse." يمكن نفهم "تزول" ؟

[٤٥٥] في الاصل "سامخ"

[٤٥٦] في الاصل "اليل" Here and following

[٤٥٧] في الاصل "جِبَل"

محيطة بالأرض كالخاتم أو كالحلقة الدائرة وبتلك الجبال ثقّل الله الأرض وهي شوامخ تطلع الشمس إلى سمتها ولا تصل إلى رُؤْيَتها وقد حالت رؤوس الجبال بين تلك الأرض وبينها» قال له ذو القرنين «ولم حجبها الله عن خلقه ؟» قال «لأن فيها عين الحيّات» قال له ذو القرنين «وأين ذكرت تلك العين فيها؟» قال «روى في مصحف شيْت عليه السلام أن تلك العين في وسط تلك الظلمة» قال له ذو القرنين «وكيف ذكر ماء تلك العين ؟» قال له «ما هذه العين أشدّ بياضا من اللبن وأحلى من الشهد وأطيب رائحة من المسك» قال أبو عبد الملك الملشونيّ فوافق قول افشخير قول الملك ما زاد ولا نقص منه قال له [f. 183] ذو القرنين «إنّك لأعلم أهل الأرض وأنت أعلم أهل زمانك يا افشخير إذا اتّفق قولك وقول الملائكة» قال له «لا [غنا] [٤٥٨] لي عنك فأشرّ علي برأيك» قال له افشخير «اخبرني عن ما تريد» قال له «أريد أن أسئلك عن هذه الظلمات وأريد أن أسلكها وأدخلها لعلّى أرا ما فيها من العجائب فأكتبها في كتاب يكون عجبا لأهل الزمان بعدنا» قال له افشخير «لا تقدر على ذالك» قال له «ولم ؟» قال «لأنّها ظلمة شديدة السواد لا يرا فيها أحد[٤٥٩] كفّه وأخاف أن يكون دخولك إليها لغير رضا الله واخاف أن يكون أمرا أحجبه الله عن خلقه وعن أعيُنِهم وأخاف أن يغضب الله [لذالك][٤٦٠]» قال له ذو القرنين «لا بدّ لي من ذالك» قال افشخير «اتّق الله تعالى يا ذا القرنين أنا نخاف[٤٦١] [f. 184] أن تهلك أنت وجنودك وجميع من دخلها من قومك فتكون [عظة][٤٦٢] لأهل الدنيا» قال ذو القرنين «لا بدّ لي من دخُولِهَا» قال مقاتل وكان ذو القرنين شجاعا لا يملأ قلبه من شيء قال له ذو القرنين «يا افشخير أيّ الدوّاب أقو[ى] لي على النظر في الظلمة ؟» قال «الخيل» قال «أيّهما في الألوان أقوى وأشدّ ؟» قال «الأبكار التي لا يثقها الأمهار»

فأمر ذو القرنين فاجتمعت إليه واختار منها خمسين ألف فارس كلّها أبكار فاختار منها اثنا عشر ألفا من إقليم جابرصا كلّها لم يثقها أمهار ومن سائر الأقاليم ستّة آلاف فاجتمع إليه من أشراف من معه ستّة آلاف من إقليم جابرصا من أشدّهم بأسا وأقواهم عزما وجلدا وأعظمهم قدرا ومن سائر الأقاليم ستّة آلاف مثلها من آل الشرف والشجاعة فطمع ذو القرنين [f. 185] أن يخلدوا معه في الدنيا إذا [شرب][٤٦٣] من تلك العين ويملك معهم الأرض أيّام حياته فقال لهم ذو القرنين «استعدوا

[٤٥٨] في الاصل "لا عنى"

[٤٥٩] Written twice: "احد"

[٤٦٠] في الاصل "لدالك"

[٤٦١] نفهم "انا اخاف"

[٤٦٢] في الاصل "عضة"

[٤٦٣] في الاصل "اشرب"

الخُرُوج إلى هذه الظّلمة على بركة الله وحسن عونه وتوفيقه» قال له افشخير «أيُّها الملك إنّا [ضَلَلْنَا][٤٦٤] فيها فكيف لنا بالخروج منها ؟ والله إنّ ضَلَلْنَا فيها لا خرجنا منها أبدا» قال ذو القرنين «علي بالخضر» وكان الخضر من أهل العلم والشرف والفضل والورع[٤٦٥] في جملة الرّوم فأوتى به فقال له «إنّك مُقَدَّم الأعنّة طول[٤٦٦] غزواتِنَا والآن خذ على مقدّمة الخيل على بركة الله تعالى» قال له «إلى أين تريد ؟» قال له «أريد الدخول إلى هذه الظلمة» قال له الخضر «اتّق الله يا ذا القرنين ولا تتعرّض لشيءْ حجبه الله عن خلقه فإنّا نخاف الهلاك على يديك» قال له «لاَ بُدَّ لِي من الدخول فإنّ معي أمر نهتدي به إن شاء [f. 186] الله على الخروج منها» فأخرج لهم خرزة بيضاء مجوهرة تتّقد كأنّها نجم وقّادٌ في السّماء

قال أبو عبد الملك الملشونيّ قلتُ لمقاتل ابن سليمان ما هذه الخرزة وما تكون ؟ قال هي التي نزل بها آدم عليه السّلام من الجنّة [فتوارثها][٤٦٧] الأنبياء ووصلت إلى ارسطَاطَالِيس فدفعها إلى ذي القرنين حين بعث وقال له «خذ هذه الخرزة تكون معك فإنِ احْتَجْت إليها فإنّها تجلوا الظلمة و[تهتدي][٤٦٨] بها أن شاء الله في ظلمات البرّ والبحر» وقال بعض من لَقَيْنَا من أهل العلم هي الخرزة التي [أعطاها][٤٦٩] الله لنوح عليه السّلام ليعرف بها أوقات الصّلاة حتّى انتهت إلى إسماعيل بعد إبراهيم ثمّ انتهْت إلى عَيْصُوا فصارت في ملك ولده [f. 187] حتّى انتهت إلى ذي القرنين سَلَفٍ بعد سَلَفٍ وأثر بعد أثر

وقال ذو القرنين للخضر «خذ هذه الخرزة إليك فإنّها تجلى الظلمة إن شاء الله فتهتدي بها» فلم يكن للخضر بُدٌّ من مطاوعة ذي القرنين فتقدّم الخضر في ستّة آلاف فارس وتأخّر ذو القرنين في ستّة آلاف فارس وقيل أن جملة ما مشا به ذو القرنين في الظلمة ستّة آلاف تقدّم الخضر في الفين فارس وتأخّر ذو القرنين في أربعة آلاف فارس والقول الأوّل أصحُّ ثمّ قال ذو القرنين لمن بقي من العسكر «اسكنوا [مكانكم][٤٧٠] حتّى يتمّ لكم اثنا عشر سنة فإنّ خرجت لكم وإلاّ رجعتم إلى بلادكم والوالي

---

[٤٦٤] في الاصل "ظَلَلْنَا" Here and following

[٤٦٥] Written twice: "العلم"

[٤٦٦] طوال

[٤٦٧] في الاصل "فتَوارثها"

[٤٦٨] في الاصل "تمندى"

[٤٦٩] في الاصل "اعطى"

[٤٧٠] في الاصل "مكانهم"

لأموركم لاطيقون فاسمعوا له واطيعوا فهو أشبه الخلق بالحكم وهو يرُدكم إلى بلادكم بإذن الله الـــذي [يُدَبِّر][٤٧١] الأمور كيف شاء [f. 188] لا الله إلاّ هو خالق كلّ شيء»

قال فترك عسكره في أرض [معمورة][٤٧٢] كثيرة المنافع والمياه ومضى هو في أحد [عدتين][٤٧٣] المذكورتين والله أعلم أيُّهما كان من عتاق الخيل وأجودها

ذكر دخول ذي القرنين إلى جزيرة الظلمة

قال أبو عبد الملك فدخل ذو القرنين والخضر بمقدّمة الأعنة فجدوا في السّـــير فســـاروا اثنـــا عشر يوما قطع فيها مسيرة اثنا عشر سنة حتّى أشرفوا على الظلمة فلمّا رأوها أصحابه رُعِبُوا وفزعـــوا منها فزعا عظيما والظلمة واقفة مثل الجبال الشوامخ فنزل الخضر عليه السّلام في أوّل الناس حتّى قـــدم عليه ذو القرنين قال له «ما أصنع أيُّها الملك ؟ فإن طوعَ الإمام علينا واجبٌ وفرض أمرنـــا [f. 189] الله به» قال له ذو القرنين «اجعل الخرزة على سِنّ رُمْحِك وارفعها حتّى تنظر[٤٧٤] إليها الجنود فإنّا نهتدي بها مثل الكوكب في السِّماء» قال ففعل الخضر عليه السّلام ذالك وتقدّم في نصف القوم وأفتح[٤٧٥] الخضـــر الظّلمة ودخلت الجنود ورآه وجعلوا ينظرون إلى الخرزة في لجج الظلمة فيتبعونها وقد فتق نورها الظلمة مثل الكوكب في السّماء فساروا كذالك في الظلمة مثل عشرين يوما لا ينامون ولا ينزلون فطـــوي الله لهم الطّريق فساروا في العشرين يوما مسيرة عشرين سنة فلمّا تمت له عشرين يوما أوحى الله إلى الخضر عليه السّلام وذالك أنّه نبيّ كريم فأتاه جبريل عليه السّلام وقال له «يا خضر إنّ في هذه الظلمة وادٍ وهو بالقرب منك [f. 190] وليس في هذه الظلمة وَادٍ غيْره وفيه عين من ماء وليس في ذالك الـــوادي مـــاءٌ وإنّما فيه الرّمل والحصاء والناس منه في بعد مثل نصف ميل لا ناس معه فمشا حتّى نـــزل بـــالوادي فغابت الخرزة عن الناس ووقفوا في مواضعهم وظُنّوا أنّه قد عرض له أمر في الظلمة لّما غـــاب عنـــهم فأمسكوا الناس كلّهم وفقدوا ذو القَرنين وأصحابه ينتظرون الخرزة ويهت[٤٧٦] الناس في أنفسهم معـــه وقال «امسكوا حتّى أرجع إليكم» ومشا حتّى وقف على العين فتوضّا منها وشرب وهـــو في نـــور

---

[٤٧١] في الاصل "يدبر"

[٤٧٢] من B. في الاصل "معموتى"

[٤٧٣] في الاصل "العدنين" "عددين" :B

[٤٧٤] ينظر

[٤٧٥] فتح

[٤٧٦] وتَهَتَ

الخرزة فبينما الناس ينظرون في ذلك ساعة زمانيّة إذ ظهرت إليهم الخرزة وفي رواية أخـــرى أن ذي[٤٧٧] القرنين وقف هو وجملة أصحابه ينظرون إلى الخرزة مدَّةً طويلةً [f. 191] يقالوا له «يا ذا القرنين غـــاب الخضر وخفنا الهلاك» فقال لهم ذو القرنين «يا قوم اصبروا على أنفسكم [ولا تخشوا فإنّه ما غاب][٤٧٨] عنّا إلاّ في بعض شعاب الوادي لاكنّكم قفوا [لئلاّ][٤٧٩] تضلُّوا» وأتا الخضر إلى الماء فتوضّـــا وشـــرب فوجد الماء على الصِّفة التي وصفها جبريل عليه السّلام

قال ثمّ أخذ الخرزة ومشا بها في شعاب الوادي حتّى أتا فرسه وردّ الخرزة على سِـــنّ رمحـــه وركب ومشا وخرج من عدوة الوادي وظهرت الخرزة لِلناس واتّبعوها وقالوا الناس لِذي القرنين «يـــا ولي الله رجونا أن الخضر قد اهتدا أن شاء الله فنظر ذو القرنين إلى ضوء الخرزة فقال «في الوادي غاب ضَوْءهَا» فمضوا خلفها واتّبعوه واسرعوا المشى حتّى نزلوا بالوادي فقال بعضهم لبعض «لا شـــكّ أن الخضر إنّما غاب [f. 192] عنّا في هذه الوادي» فأيقن ذو القرنين ذالك نصف الظلمة لمّا قال له الملـــك زياقيل وافشخير أن ليس في الظّلمة إلاّ واد واحد في نصفها فقال لأصحابه «اسرعوا بنا إلى الخروج من هذه الظلمة» فمضا الخضر وقد تمّ له المراد الذي أراد الله به من طول حياته وسَبَبُهُ الذي سبّب الله عليه دون غيره ومضت الجنود يهتدون بنور الخرزة إلى مقدار عشرين يوماً أخري فخرجوا من الظلمـــة في أربعين يوما ثمّ خرجوا إلى أرض بيضاء رمال لا ترا فيها عِوَجاً ولا أمتاً[٤٨٠] فمشوا في ضوء النهار اثنـــا عشر يوماً فلمّا أتوا إلى آخر عشرين يوما نظروا إلى قصر مشيّدٍ عالي يتلالا نورا في فلات من الأرض لم تقربه عمارة فأقبل إليه حتّى وصل بساحته فنزل بجنوده وأمرهم بالأقامة حتّى يرجع [f. 193] إليهم

ذكر القصر وما رآ فيه ذو القرنين من العجائب

قال أبو عبد الملك ثمّ مضا ذو القرنين حتّى قرب القصر فوجد عرضه ثلاثة فراســـخ وطولـــه ثلاثة فراسخ وبنيانه من أحسن ما يكون من البنيان فلم يزل يدور بالقصر حتّى وجد البـــاب فدخـــل فيه فإذا فيه خشبةٌ من حديد قد [أحدقت][٤٨١] من أوّل القصر إلى آخره فإذا بطائر كشبه الخطّافْ وهو معلّق برجله ورأسه منكس إلى الأرض وهو مشدود إلى تلك الخشبة فلمّا دَخل عليه ذو القرنين قال له

---

[٤٧٧] ذا

[٤٧٨] من B في الاصل "فانا نخشى ما غاب"

[٤٧٩] في الاصل "ليلا"

[٤٨٠] ولا امتنَ

[٤٨١] في الاصل "احذقت"

الطير «يا ذا القرنين أما كفاك ما رأيت من العجائب وما دَخلت من البلاد حتّى دخلت [موضعا][٤٨٢] ما دخله إنس ولا شيطان ولا يدخله إلا الملائكة فما الذي حملك على هذا وأدخلك هذا المكان ؟» فنظر ذو القرنين فإذا هو مزموم بأنفه [متدلاّ][٤٨٣] برأسه وهو أشدّ سوادا ما رآ [f. 194] الرأون قط في الدنيا-رأسه تحت الخشبة فقال له ذو القرنين «ربي أدخلني هذا الموضع لمّا أراد من تمام أمره وبه وصلت هذا الأرض وله أحكم فقال له ذو القرنين «أيّها الطير المَسْجُون بأمر الله ما قصتك ؟ فقال له الطائر «يا ذا القرنين هل كثر أولاد الحنث في بني إسرائيل ؟» قال له «نعم» قال فانتفض الطير فَمَلأ ثلث القصر ثمّ قال «يا ذو القرنين هل كثر الزنا[ء] والفسوق وقتل النفس ؟» قال له «نعم» فانتفض ثانية فملأ ثلثا القصر ثمّ قال له «يا ذا القرنين هل ظهرت شهادة الزور وقذف المحصنات في بني إسرائيل ؟» قال «نعم» فانتفض ثالثة فملأ القصر كلّه حتّى لم يجد موضعا ذو القرنين يقف فيه فَرُعِبَ رُعْباً [عظيما][٤٨٤] وفزع فزعا شديدا ثمّ قال الطائر «تقارب الوعد الموعود يا ذا القرنين هل تعمر المساجد في بني آدم ؟» قال له «نعم» قال له «و يغتسلون من الجنابة ؟» [f. 195] قال له «نعم» فانتفَض من الطير ثلثة ثمّ قال «هل يقام الحج والعمرة ويذكر الله في بيوته ؟» قال «نعم» فانتفض من الطير ثلثة الثاني ثمّ قال «يا ذا القرنين هل يحلفون الناس بالطلاق وَيَحْنِثُونَ و[يكون][٤٨٥] أولادهم في غير المساجد ويكنونهم بأولاد الحرام ؟» قال «نعم» ثمّ انتفضَ أيضا فملا ثلث القصر ثم قال «يا ذا القرنين هل يأكلون الناس السحت و[الربا][٤٨٦] ؟» قال «نعم» فانتفض وملأ ثلثي القصر ثمّ قال «يا ذا القرنين هل ينقضون العهد ويسفكون الدِّما ؟» قال «نعم» فانتفض فملأ القصر كلّه حتّى ظهر منه إلى من يراه من خارج القصر ثمّ قال له «يا ذا القرنين اخبرني عن شيء أسَلك عنه» قال له ذو القرنين «اسئل عمّا شئت وعن ما بَدَا لَكَ ؟» قال له «هل تَركَ الناس شهادة أن لا إلاه إلاّ الله ؟» قال له ذو القرنين لا وبها دخلت [البلاد][٤٨٧] ووصلت هذا المكان وبها [f. 196] أريد قتل أهل الأرض» قال له «هل ترك الناس الصلوة المفروضة ؟» قال له ذو القرنين «[لا][٤٨٨]» فضعف الطير ووقع فيه النقص حتّى رجع ثلثا ما فيه فقال له «يا ذا القرنين هل ترك الناس غسل الجنابة ؟» قال «لم يتركوها» فصغر وضعف حتّى رجع كما كان

---

[٤٨٢] في الاصل "موضا"

[٤٨٣] في الاصل "مدلأ"

[٤٨٤] في الاصل "عضيما"

[٤٨٥] في الاصل "ويكون"

[٤٨٦] في الاصل "الربى"

[٤٨٧] من B

[٤٨٨] من B

أوّل مرّة ثمّ قال «اصعد يا ذا القرنين إلى الدرج فإنّ لك في أعلائه خير كثير ونجاة ممّا أنت فيه» فنظر ذو القرنين فإذا هو بدرج من أسفل القصر [إلى][489] أعلاه

فصعد ذو القرنين على الدرج حتّى بلغ أعلى القصر فإذا هو بسَطْحٍ عظيم عالٍ على القصر كأنّه يساوى الجبال الشوامخ الذين ثقل الله بهم الأرض [كاد][490] ذالك السطح أن يشرف على جميع البلاد فنظر فإذا على ذالك السِّطح رجل شاب جميل من أحسن ما يكون من الرجال وعليه ثياب بيض وقد قدم قدما وأخر أخرى [f. 197] وهو ينظر إلى الصُّور وقد وضعه في فيه شاخص بعين ذي القرنين وعين في أعلاه لا تَطْرف منها عين ينتظر متى يؤمر بالنفخ في الصُّور قال ذو القرنين فلمّا أحسّ بي قال «من أنت» قلت «أنا ذو القرنين» قال «يا ذا القرنين أما كفاك ما رأيت من الدنيا حتّى وصلت إليّ ؟» قال له ذو القرنين «ومن أنت ؟» قال «أنا ملك من الملائكة أتريد أن أريك كيف صفة صاحب الصُّور فهو كما ترا ينتظر متى يؤمر بالنفخ في الصُّور فما تريد في هذه الأرض ؟ أتريد أن يجري سلطانك على ملائكة السَّماء المحجوبين عن خلقه المخصوصين برحمته ؟» قال له ذو القرنين «تعالى الله عن ذالك أيُّها الملك» فقال له الملك «هل لك من حاجة ؟» قال «نعم فرغت أزوادنا وضعفنا ونحن نخاف أن نهلكوا في هذه الظُّلمة» فقال له الملك «خُذْ هذا واشكر ربّك [f. 198] فهو زادك وزاد من معك حتّى تخرج من الظلمة وتصل إلى عسْكرك فإذا هو عنقود من عنب» فقال له ذو القرنين «هل يكون زاد العِدْةِ من الخلق ؟» قال «نعم بقدرة الله تعالى» قال له ذو القرنين «هذا أمر عظيم» فأكل منه حبّة فأشبعته ورَوا منها ونبتت حبّة أخرى في موضعها فعلم ذو القرنين أنّه شيْءٌ لا يفنى فجزاه خَيْراً ثمّ دفع إليه الملك حجراً املساً قدر ما يملأ كفّه فقال «خُذْ هذا فقد جعله الله لك مثلا فإنّ شبع هذا فأنّك تشبع وإن لم يشبع فإنّك لم تشبع أبدا» فقال له «يا ذا القرنين أتدري من الطَّيْر ؟» قال «لا» قال «ذالك رجل آدمي مسخ به وهو فتنة لمن يأت بعدك وهو المسيح الدّجَال مسخه الله فردّه كذالك فإذا جاء وعد ربّي خرج آدمي أعور يكون فتنة لمن أراد الله [فتنته][491]»

[f. 199] فتعجّب ذو القرنين من ذالك وخرج من القصر وأتا إلى أصحابه فوجدهم قد أجهدهم الجوع وبلغ فيهم كلّ مبلغ فقال ذو القرنين في نفسه «إنّ أنا أعلمتُ القوم بما عندي من هذا الزاد يزدحمون عليه فيقتل القويُّ منهم الضّعيف» فقال لهم «مُرُّوا بين يديّ أردتُ أن أَعَدَّكم» فمرُّوا بين يديه فكلّما مرّ عليه رجل منهم أعطاه حبّة من العنقود ولا يعلم من خلفه بذالك حتّى على آخرهم

[489] في الاصل "من اسفل القصر واعلاه" "الى" من B

[490] في الاصل "كاذ"

[491] في الاصل "فتمته"

فقال لهم «ارجعوا حتّى أدفع إليكم أزواد خيلكم» فكلّما مرّ عليه رجل أعطاه حبّة فيقول له «اعطها لفرسك» فيلقيها الرجل في فم فرسه فتكون له طعاما وشرابا وكلّما نزع من العنقود حبّة نبتت أخرى في موضعها بإذن الله [f. 200] تعالى وقدرته وكرمه وأعلم ذو القرنين ومن معه أن ذالك شيء لا يفنى

فقال ذو القرنين «عليّ بالعلماء» فاجتمعت إليه العلماء وأخرج لهم الحجر وقال لهم «إنّ هذا الحجر جعله لي مثلا ولا أعلم تأويل ذالك وليس مثلا غيري وأنا أحبّ أن أعرف ذالك» قال فأخذوا العلماء ذالك الحجر فوزنوه بمثله فرجح الحجر ثمّ زادوا إليه حجرا آخر فرجح به ثمّ زادوا ثالثا فرجح بهم الأملس الذي أعطاه ذالك الملك ثمّ أربعا ثمّ خمسا إلى عشرة إلى عشرين ثمّ إلى خمسين ثمّ إلى مائة فرجح الحجر الأملس بجميع ذالك فما وجدوا شيئا يزنوه به فوزنوه بألف حجر فرجح بهم الحجر الأملس فوزنوه بالنحّاس والحديد والرصاص فلم يقدروا على شيء يزنونه به ثمّ أنّه بلغ أعجابهم من ذالك ممّا استهمّوا منه غاية[٤٩٢] الاهتمام [f. 201] وقالوا «ما رأينا أعجب من ذالك لا يعلم ما هذا إلاّ الله الواحد القهار وإنّما نخاف أن يكون سحرا ابتلانا الله به» فعند ذالك قال ذو القرنين «عليّ بالخضر ابن عامل» فأتاه فقال له «يا خضر انظر في قصّة هذا الحجر وأمره وقد ابتلينا به ولا علم لنا بتأويله ولا معناه» وكان الخضر في ذالك ساكتا ينظر ما يكون في أمرهم مع الحجر وقد الهمه الله في ذالك معرفة وعلما بالوحي الذي ينزل عليه فقال له «يا ذا القرنين نعم عندي معنى ذالك وتأويله ناولني الحجر» فناوله له ثمّ أخذه وجعله في كفّة الميزان وأخذ حفنة من التراب ووضعه في الكفّة الأخرى فاعتدل الوزن بقدرة الله تعالى فقال العالم افشخير «[سبحان][٤٩٣] الله يا خضر أن وزناه بحجر بعد حجر وحديد ورصاص ونحّاس [f. 202] فلم نقدروا [على] وزنه ووزنته أنت [بحفنة][٤٩٤] من التراب إنّ هذا شيء عجيب ما سمعنا بمثله قط» ثمّ قال له ذو القرنين «فسِّر لنا معنى هذا التراب وهذا الحجر يا خضر يرحمك الله فهو والله أعجب ما رأينا» فقال لهم «يا قوم هذا من علم الله عجائبه في خلقه وذالك أن أمر الله وحكمه وقضائه [نافذ][٤٩٥] في خلقه وإن الله عزّ وجلّ خلق الخلق وفضّل بعضهم على بعض وأبلا العالم بالجاهل وأبلاني بك يا ذا القرنين وأبلاك بي وأنا لا أقدر أن أخالفك وأنت لا تترك رأيك فتشاورني في الرأي وتخالفني في الفعل رغبة منك في البلوغ الأمل» فبكَى ذو القرنين وقال «فسّرها لي يا خضر» واشتدّ بكاؤه قال له الخضر «يا ذا القرنين هذا الحجر فعله الله لك مثلا لأنّ الله تعالى جلّ

---

[٤٩٢] This word is written alone beneath the line.

[٤٩٣] في الاصل "سبحن"

[٤٩٤] في الاصل "حفنه"

[٤٩٥] في الاصل "نافد"

ذكره أعطاك [f. 203] الملك وأمرك بالنصيحةِ في الدّين وأراك الملائكة الذين حجبهم عن بني آدم وبلغك في الدنيا من قرن قاف الغربيّ إلى قرنها الشرقيّ وملْكك رقاب أهل الدنيا وفضّلك على سائر بني آدم وأمشاك على الماء بجنودك وسخّر لك البحر وعلمك ما لم تكن تعلم وكان فضل الله عليك عظيما وأدخلك في ظلماته بقدرته وأخرجك منها بكرامه وتعرضت أنت [لتلك][٤٩٦] العباد في بلاد لا يسْكنها إلاّ الملائكة وأراك من عجائبها ما لا أقدر أن أصفه لك وأعطاك الحجر يكون لك مثلا وتنبيها في مستقبل أمرك وإنه [أ]عطاك الدنيا بما فيها فلم تقنع حتّى دخلت الظلمات التي لم يدخلها أحد قبلك وسلكت موضعا لم يسلكه الا الملائيكة يا ذا القرنين وإن هذا الحجر جعله الله لك مثلا فلو [أ]عطاك الدنيا [f. 204] بما فيها ما تقنّعت[٤٩٧] ولا زالت رغِبة الدنيا من قبلك والحجر هو عين ابن آدم ولو ملكت الدنيا كلّها [لابتغيت][٤٩٨] غيرها رَغبةً من طبيعة ابن آدم و[ليس][٤٩٩] له منها إذا مات إلاّ ما للمسكين الضعيف خرقةً لكفنه وموضع قامت في الأرض لقبره ولا يملوا عينه إلاّ التراب والدود إذا مات وكذالك مثّل الله لك الحجر يا ذا القرنين ليس يملو عينك إلاّ التراب وليس لك من مملكك إلاّ خبزة وشربت ماء فليس لك الا كفنك وقبرك الذى يكون للغني والفقير والحرّ والعبد فلم تتعب نفسك يا ذا القرنين في ملك الدنيا وأنت تموت وتتركه ولا بدّ لك من مَصير من مضا قبلك» قال فبكا ذو القرنين حتّى كادت نفسه أن تزهق

ثمّ أمر الله أصحابه بالرحيل فأوحى الله إلى الخضر أن يأخذه على غير الطريق الذي [فيها العين][٥٠٠] [f. 205] و لم يَرد الله أن يعطى لذى القرنين منها ما أراد من ذالك وإنّما حمله على ذالك الطمع في [حياة][٥٠١] و لم يخبره بذالك أحَدا[٥٠٢] وأعلم الخضر ما أراد من ذالك فتقدّم الخضر على مقدمة الخيل وليس لهم زاد إلاّ ذالك العنقود فكان لهم طعاما وشرابا

فمرّوا بطريقهم بواد فيه حجارة كثيرة وحصات[٥٠٣] لها نور عظيم تنور بين حوافر خيلهم فتعجّب النّاس من ذالك وقالوا لذى القرنين «يا ولي الله ما هذا ؟» قال لهم «حجارة من أخذها ندم

---

[٤٩٦] في الاصل "تللك" او "تصلك" "تلك" من B

[٤٩٧] قنعت

[٤٩٨] في الاصل "لا ابتغيت"

[٤٩٩] من B

[٥٠٠] من B

[٥٠١] في الاصل "الحيّات"

[٥٠٢] أحدٌ

[٥٠٣] حصاة

ومن تركها ندم» قال فأخذ قوم منها وترك آخرون فكانوا كلّهم نادمين فلمّا خرجوا إلى ضوء النهار فإذا هم بالزبرجد الأخضر الخالص في [الصفاء][٥٠٤] ومن الرجال من قال «بل كانت اليواقيت الحَمْرَا فلذالك كان لهم نور عظيم قال النبيّ صلعم من أخذ [f. 206] ندم على قلّة ما أخذ ومن لم يأخذ ندم على ما لم يأخذ فكانوا كلّهم نادمين[٥٠٥]

قال [أبو] عبد[٥٠٦] الملك قال النبيّ صلعم والذي نفسي بيده لقد دخل ذو القرنين الوادي وهو زاهد في الدنيا قد مقّتها من أجل المثل الذي ضربه الله به على لسان الخضر عليه السلام فلو دخله قبل ذالك ما ترك فيه شيء ولاكنّه قد دخله وهو [بغض][٥٠٧] الدنيا[٥٠٨]

ثمّ مضا ذو القرنين حتّى خرج من الظلمات ومشى حتّى وصل إلى عسكره فأمر الناس بالرَّحيل فرحلوا ومشى على وجه الأرض حتّى بلغ السدّين المذكورين [فبادروه][٥٠٩] أهل السدين بالهداية من كلّ جيهة ومكان ثمّ استغاثوا به وقالوا له «يا ذا القرنين إنّ ياجوج وماجوج يخرجون علينا في أيّام الربيع وبلدنا أحسن [...][٥١٠] [f. 207] من بلادهم فيرعوا في بلدنا و لم يمرّ[وا] على شيء من مواشينا ولا أموالنا إلاّ ذهبوا به ومن عارَضهم منّا قتلوه ولا طاقة لنا [بهم][٥١١] وقد آمنا بربّك وبك وبدينك ونحن نجعل لك خَرْجاً على أن تجعل بيننا وبينهم سدّاً

قال أبو عبد الملك [اختلف][٥١٢] أهل التأويل على عمل السدّ فمنهم من قال صنعه قبل دخوله إلى الظلمة ومنهم من قال صنعه بعد خروجه من الظلمة والله يعلم أيّ القولين أصح قال أبو عبد الملك فلمّا نزل ذو القرنين بين السدّين وكان ما كان من أمر السدّ كما تقدم ذكره في أوّل الكتاب أتوه أهل السدّين فشكوا له بغية ياجوج وماجوج وقالوا له «اخرجهم عنّا» فأرسل إليهم ذو القرنين فاجتمعوا إليه نفرٌ من عظمائهم [فوعظهم][٥١٣] ونهاهُم عن الشرّ وأمرهم بالطوع وحُسن السيرة مع الناس [f.208]

---

[٥٠٤] في الاصل "الصفا"

[٥٠٥] Not found in HE.

[٥٠٦] في الاصل "ابوا عبد"

[٥٠٧] في الاصل "بغيض"

[٥٠٨] Not found in HE.

[٥٠٩] في الاصل "فباذروه"

[٥١٠] There is a word that is difficult to read. It is not found in B. Perhaps it is "احسّ الدرهم" ?

[٥١١] في الاصل "بيهم"

[٥١٢] في الاصل "اخلف"

[٥١٣] في الاصل "فوعضهم"

فقالوا «سمعنا وأطعنا» فقال لهم «اتركوهم يكون مع عمارة البلد» فسمّوهم[٥١٤] الناس التّرك وهم الآن بنظر مشرق الهند على يمين أرض السند وأهل الهند مجيبون لكتاب داريوش

فرجع ذو القرنين ومن معه حتّى نزل بمشرق أرض الفرس واتّصل به وبمن معه أن داريوش انتصر بلبُوَر ملك الهند على ذى القرنين فلمّا بلغ ذو القرنين ذالك أمر بطلب داريوش حيث كان وكان وصل الكتاب إلى لَبُورْ ملك الهند فأمر جنوده بالاستعداد وتجهّز إليه في ثلاثين ألف ألف وقدم لبور على مقدّمته عشر مائة ألف ألف مع ابن أخ له يقال له هَبَارَ ابن لَبَارْ ثمّ عقد لواء آخر على ابن أخ له يقال له شنان ابن انان في مقدّمته عشرة ألف ألف ثمّ عقد لواء ثالثا على ابن عمّ له يقال له داد ابن كَيْدَادْ فهذا ثلاثون ألف ألف وأمرهم بالخروج في نصرة داريوش وبقا هو للاستعداد جنود وإصلاح أمره وحُصونه [حذرا][٥١٥] ممّا يلاقيه [f. 209] من ذى القرنين فهو في جميع جنوده و[إصلاح][٥١٦] شأنه حتّى اتّصل به خبر موت داريُوس ثمّ اشتغل بنفسه خوفا من خراب البلاد

ثمّ أن ذا القرنين ركب في طلب داريوس فبلغ الخبر داريوش فولاَّ[٥١٧] هاربا وجَدَّ ذو القرنين في طلبه حتّى أدركه فتراموا عليه وزرائه فقتلوه غدرا ثمّ أدركهم [اصحاب][٥١٨] ذى القرنين ففرّوا عنه وتركوه مطروحا وقالوا وزراء داريوس «يا آل ذى القرنين إنّا قتلنا عدوه فاعلموه بذالك» ثمّ أمرهم ذو القرنين بالكفّ عن طلبهم وأن من رجع منهم فهو آمن قال فأشرفت عامّة الفرس والوزراء السبعة الذين غدروا داريوش وأبصره ذو القرنين مطروحا فبكا عند رأسه وكان رحيم القلب كريم الغفور ثمّ رفع [رأسه][٥١٩] فوضعه في حجره ومَسَحَ عن وجهه التراب فوجده بالروح ثمّ قال «يا دريوش إنّ نجوت من مقامك هذا لتكون من أهل الإحسان عندنا [f. 210] ولئن قمت من موضعك هذا لأزيدنّك بلاداً إلى بلادك وملكا إلى ملكك كما رددتُ عليك إمرأتك وأخاك وابنتك ولاعزّتك[٥٢٠] غاية العزّ وإنّي قد تحرّمتُ بطعامك وشرابك فاعلمني بقاتلك من هو فوالله لئن هلكت من جراحك لاقتلنّه أشدّ قتلة ولو كان من كان من الناس روميٌّ كان أو فارسيٌّ» قال فبكا داريوش وأخذ بيد ذي القرنين

---

[٥١٤] فسمّاهم

[٥١٥] في الاصل "حدرا"

[٥١٦] في الاصل "ااصلاح"

[٥١٧] فولى

[٥١٨] في الاصل "اصحب"

[٥١٩] في الاصل "رسه"

[٥٢٠] An alternative reading here might be ولاعزّنك

فوضعه على صدره ثمّ رفع رأسه وقال «يا ذا القرنين لا ترفع رأسك فوق قدرك فإنّك تريد أن تنال رفعة الأمور كلّها ففكّر في عاقبة ما أنت إليه [سائر][٥٢١] مع علمي أن المقادير التي بلغتني ما ترا من أمر الله انْظُر كيف كنت بالأمس وكيف أنا اليوم وَإنّا الذي استحوذت على الأرض بالجبرءوت وَ[كَانَ لي][٥٢٢] ملك الملوك وخضعت لي مُلُوك نوبد أن صرت [f. 211] اليوم مرعوبا من كلّ جانب بعد حجابي على جبارة[٥٢٣] الفرس ورؤوسائِها وكثرة جنودي وعظم سلطاني وما كنت عليه من أمر الدنيا ولاكن يا ذا القرنين [فضلك][٥٢٤] العليّ الأعلى وأكرمك بنصره وأنا تائب لله وآمِنٌ بربّك لا غيره وهو الذي ولأني ملك الفرس وغيرهم وهو الذي كتب عليّ ما أنا فيه وأنت من الشاهدين فإذا أنا مِتُ فأنت الذي تتولّى غسلي وكفني واستوصى بالفرس خيرا لانّهم ذو بأس وشدّة وشجاعة وأنزل أمّي بمنزلة أمّك وإمرأتي بمنزلة أختك وأخي بمنزلة أخيك وإنّي قد زوجتك ابنتي رشيق فإنّها من أكرم الخلق وهي وديعة إليك فكن لها رضيًّ مفضِّلاً وإنّي قريب الفراق منكم» ثمّ قبضه الله فمات داريوش

ثمّ أن ذي القرنين أمر بالِمسكِ والعَنْبَر والكافور فغسله وكفّنه في ثياب [f. 212] الملوك المنسوجة بالذهب وفعل به ما يفعل بالملك المطاع فكفّنه وتراحم عليه وبكا فلمّا فرغ ذو القرنين من كفنه أمر بالنداء في جنود فارس فاجتمعوا إليه فأمر منهم اثنا عشر ألفا كلّهم بالسِّلاح يمشون تحت سريره وأمرهم باشهار سلاحهم فمشا منهم عن يمين السرير ستّت[٥٢٥] آلاف وعن يساره مثلها كلّهم أشهر والسيوف في أيديهم وبعضهم خلفه وبعضهم [أمامه][٥٢٦] ومعهم سادات الرّوم وصناديدها وأبطال فارس حتّى انتهو إلى حفرته فنزل ذو القرنين مع الخضر وافشخير فدفنوه دفناً ناعماً

ثمّ قال ذو القرنين للبنّائين «ابنوا عليه قبّة وأجعلوا عند رأسه لوحا من ذَهبٍ فيه حسبه ونسبه وما جرّ له مع وزرائه وكيف غدروه» [f. 213] ثمّ انصرفت تلك الجيوش وقُيّادها[٥٢٧] [إلى][٥٢٨] ذي القرنين فبايعوه ودخلوا في عسكره فسَمِعُوا له وأطاعوا لمّا رأوْا من حزنه على داريوش ثمّ أن ذا القرنين كتب إلى مدائن الفُرْس وملوكها كتابا يجمعهم بلطفه:

---

[٥٢١] في الاصل "سير"

[٥٢٢] في الاصل "وهَانَ في"

[٥٢٣] جبابرة

[٥٢٤] في الاصل "فصلك"

[٥٢٥] ستّة

[٥٢٦] من B. في الاصل "امن به"

[٥٢٧] نفهم "قوادها"

[٥٢٨] من B. في الاصل "لذي القرنين"

بسم الله الرحمان الرحيم من ذي القرنين ابن نّباش إلى سُكّان أرض فارس وملوكها من أهل سَهْلِهَا وجبالها وأدناها وأقصاها أمَّا بعد فإنّي راغب في اصلاح بلادكم كارهٌ لفسادها وقد [أظهرني][٥٢٩] الله على بلادكم فله الحمد على ما [مَنَّ][٥٣٠] به عليَّ من جميع نعمائه ظاهرة وباطنة وقد رفع الكلمة العليا على الكلمة السّفلى ونصرني عليكم ووضعكم ولقد كنتم كراما ذو بأس شديد وشِدّة ومَنَعةٍ مع حسن مُوَازرتِكم لداريوش حتّى قبضه الله وباءَ باثمه وزراءه الذين جرأ عليهم إحسانُهُ فلا يهمُّكم ذالك فإنّه قد سبق في علم الله السّابق وإن لكم بمنزلته [f. 214] أن سمعتم واطعتم وأَدّيتم الحقّ المفروض عليكم وإنّي غير [مقهركم][٥٣١] على دينكم ومن شاء فليسلم أو ليقم على دينه وتكون زكاة أموالكم عن ما لكم على دينكم ويكون لكم عندي مثل الذي لكم على داريوش وَلسْتُ بمخروج[٥٣٢] أحدا من دياره فإنّ أطعتم فاجمعوا السِّلاح وأربطوا الخيل وعوّلوا على أمري حتّى يأتيكم رسولي بما يكون ومن كان منكم محتاجا إلى فرس حملناه على أعناق خيلنا فافهموا قولي ولا تأخذكم حمّية الجاهليّة فتصبحوا على ما فعلتم نادمين

ثمّ ختم الكتاب ودفعه إلى رسوله ليمرّ به على سائر الفرس فمضا رسوله

ثمّ أمر ذو القرنين بجنوده فاجتمعت ثمّ قام فيهم خطيبا فقال «أيُّها النّاس ينبغى لنا ونراه حقّاً واجبا علينا أن نكرموا العصابة الذين غدروا داريوش ونقربُوا منازلهم ونرفَعُ [f. 215] درجاتهم إذ قتلوا عَدُوَّنا [حرصاً][٥٣٣] على القائنا ورضائنا وتوقيرا لمُلْكِنَا» فلمّا سَمِعُوا الفُرْسَ ذالك تغيّرت الوانهم ونظر بعضهم إلى بعض وقال بعضهم لبعض «يا أهل فارس لا يغرّنكم[٥٣٤] قول الملك وإنّما أراد أن يجربكم حتّى يرا قولكم» وكان قولهم بلغات الفرس في خفًا فلمّا سمع عنهم ذالك قال «يا قوم آمنوا ولا تخافوا وإنّما نريد أن نعرف قاتل داريوش وأكافيه بفعله وأُقربه كما تقرّب لرضائنا روميّاً كان أو فارسيا فأقسم بالله لارفعنّ قاتل داريوش فوق عساكري كلّها ولاجعلنّه [أعلاهم][٥٣٥] وأكرمُهُم» فلمّا سمعت

[٥٢٩] في الاصل "اضهرني"

[٥٣٠] في الاصل "من"

[٥٣١] في الاصل "مقعركم"

[٥٣٢] بمخرج

[٥٣٣] في الاصل "خرصاً"

[٥٣٤] نفهم "يغرّكم"

[٥٣٥] في الاصل "علاهم"

الفُرْسَ بذلك بكت من أشرافهم على خراب ملكهم ثمّ أقبلوا الوزراء السّبعة الذيـن قتلـوا داريـوش حتّى وقفوا أمام ذي القرنين فقالوا «أيُّها الملك افعل ما بذلك فإنّا هَؤلاَء السّبعة الذين [f. 216] اتّفق رأينا على قتل داريوش فقتلناه لأنّا رأيناه مخادعك وبدّل عهدا بعهدك فخفنا على خراب الفارسيّة بنقض عهدك فقتلناه رضاءً لرُجُوعِنا إليك ودخولنا في دينك» فقال لهم «أنتم قتلتم داريوش ؟» قال «نعم» قال «هل معكم غيركم ؟» قالوا «لا غير معنا» قال فأمر بهم فصُلِّبُوا على أعلا خشبة محيطون[٥٣٦] بقبر داريوش فقالوا له «أين ما تحمّلت لنا من العهود ؟» قال «يا قوم [قد][٥٣٧] وفّيت لكم ورفعتكم على علا رؤس الرّوم والفرس كيف رأيتم من غدر سيّده بعد الإحسان» ثمّ نظر إلى جنود الرّوم وجنود الفرس وعظماء القوم فقال «يا قوم هذا جزاء من قتل سيّده بعد الإحسان» ثمّ أمر الرّمات[٥٣٨] فرشقوهُم بالسِّهام

ثمّ كتب كتاباً إلى أمّ داريوش وأخيه يذكر فيه

بسم الله الرّحمان الرحيم بسم الله القدُوس إلى أمّ دَارَيُوْش أمَّا بعد فإنّا طلبنا داريوش [f. 217] إذ كان معادياً لنا فلمّا ظفرنا به أكربنا موته ولو لم يمت لرددناه إلى ملكه وإنّ أصحابه الذين غدروه أدركتهم به بعد إحساني إليه في دَفْنِهِ بعد أن أوصَا إلينا بك وأخيه وابنته ثمّ فارق الدّنيا ولا يهمنّكم أمر الله فإنّه غالبٌ علينا وعليه فإنّا لكم .بمكانه ولو لم يوصي إليّ بغير ذالك والسّلام

ثمّ أن أمّ داريوش كتبت إلى ذي القرنين كتابا

أما بعد فأنا أسئل الله الذي وَضَعَ التاج من رَأس داريوش وسلبه ملكه وسلطانه من سلطان فَارِسَ أن يُعْطِيك المُلْكَ والرياسة والغلبة والقهرة وإنّا قد علمنا أن في بقائك عِزّاً لنا وأنت لنا بمنزلة داريُوشَ و[نحن] شاكرين فعلك وناشرين جُنودَك في آل نوبران وجُمْلَتِهِمْ وسوْفَ أُجهِّز لك زَوْجَتَك وهي تدعوا لك بالسلامة [f. 218] .بما أقسم الله لِهَا مِنْكَ [حين][٥٣٩] أخْتَرْتُهَا لك والسّلام

[٥٣٦] محيطين

[٥٣٧] في الاصل "قذ"

[٥٣٨] الرّماة

[٥٣٩] من B . في الاصل "خيرا"

ثمّ أتاه الكتاب فقرأه فقال «أنا عبدٌ لِلّه ونفسي بيد الله الذي ملّكني وأعطاني هذا كلّـــه» ثمّ أن ذي[٥٤٠] القرنين كتب إلى أُمّه الغيداء بخبر داريوش والذي كان من أمره وموته وهو يقول

أمّا بعد فقد أمرتُ لكِ بهديّة الذي معَكِ من الأموال وقد بعثت إليك لتعلم بركة الله ولتحضر جهاز رشيق ابنت داريوش

فَقَدمتْ أُمّه ودخل بزوجته بحضور أمّه وأنقضا حديث دَارَيُوشَ والحمد لله ربّ العالمين

ذِكْرُ غزوة ذي القرنين إلى لَبُورَ مَلك الهند

ثمّ أن لَبُور ابن لَبُورَ الهنديّ لّما علم بموت داريوش ملك الفرس رجعت جنوده إليـــه وكتـب إليه ذو القرنين

أمّا بعد يا لَبُورَ فإنّي نظرت إليك كنظري [f. 219] لنفسي فلا تسَلّطْني على أهــراق دمائك وانتهاب أموالك وخراب ملكك ودخول أرضك فإنّ الله ناصريّ على جميع الملوك ومُسبّبا لي في جميع السُّلوكِ وملّكني أرض فارس وأُريد مُلْكَ أرضك فـــإن لم تُطِعْ وتسمع فينصرني ربّي عليك ووَلّيْتُ عليك أبغض الخلق إليـــك وإن أطعـت وآمضنْتَ تَرَكْتُكَ مَلِكاً على أرضك وأُزيدك إحسانا وإنّـــي لســتُ بمحـاربك في أرضك ولا هارق دما إلاّ ممّن التمس ذالك منّي فعجّل بجوابي واعقـــل تنتفـع ولا تأخذك الحميّة وتُقِرُّ لله بالعبوديّة ولي أداء الخراب فإنّي أقْسَمْتُ بـــربّ السّـموات لئن لم تُقِرّ لله بالوحدانيّة وتصغا إلى الحقّ وتدين بدين الله لأسـيرنّ إليـك بجنـود منصورة بإذن الله فاحسن لنفسك فقد نصحتك [f. 220] ولا حول ولا قوّة إلاّ بـالله العلى العظيم

فبعث إليه الكتاب فأجابه لَبُورَ ملك الهند بكتاب كتب فيه

إلى ذي القرنين فإنّه أتاني كتابُك مع رسولك فقرأتُه وفهمتُ ما فيه فذكرتَ أنّـــك تريد الإقبال إلى أرضنا بمن معك من الرّوم والفرس فـــهل [بلغـك][٥٤١] أن أحـدا طمع في بلادنا وأرضنا لّما علم من شدّة بأسِنا وقوّة امتناعنا في بلادنا ؟ فكم كـــان قبلك من القرون الماضيّة والملوك والفراعنة [فأيسوا][٥٤٢] من ملكنا وهابوا التقاؤنا

---

[٥٤٠] ذا

[٥٤١] في الاصل "بلعك"

[٥٤٢] من B . في الاصل "ماسبوا"

لاكنّك لمّا غلبت على ملك الفُرْس إذ دَاخَلَتْهُم خرذلة فغَدَرُوا سيّدهم وتشتّت بذلك رأيهم طمعت في ملكنا لا تدخله داخلة ولا تتولّى فيه ولايت[٥٤٣] لا تَظُنّ بظنّك أن تكون في تلك الدّاخلة من أرضنا ومُلْكِنا وإن صناديد الهند وأشرافها وشُجْعَانهَا في ثلاثين مائة ألفٍ ألف كلّهم انجاداً وأشراف [f. 221] لئن التقيت صناديد الهند وعلُوج الرّوم لفنيت الأرواح ولكَثُر النّياح ولصار الملكان ملكاً واحداً ورجوت أن الرّاغب منهزِمٌ والمستَرَاح منصور[٥٤٤] فارجع إلى بلادك وأنج بجنودك واقنع بما نِلْتَ من الملك ولا تكن راغباً فإنّ الرغّبة في الملك عاقبتها فساد إحْدَي الوجهين تشتيت الجنود وانهاب بيوت الأموال فهذه نصيحة لك يا ذا القرنين فإنّ لم ترجع أنا القادم عليك بجنودي وصناديدي و[ا]فيالي وسباعي واضعف أنصاري فإنّ في ملكي ألف فيل وألف أسد كلّهم ضواري لحرب بني آدم وآلاته فإن قَدَمْتَ علينا هلكتْ جنودك لاكنّك غلامٌ حَدَثَ السِّنَّ لم تجرّب الاحور[٥٤٥] ولم تقم على الحروب وقد رفّعتَ نفسَك فوقَ قَدْرِكَ وأعجبَك فعلَك بدخول أرض فارس ولقد [f. 222] غرّرت بنفسك فوقّر بلادي وكن حذرا على نفسك وعلى من معك فإن داريوش لو لم يقتله أصحابه كيدا منهم ومكرا [لازَاحَكَ][٥٤٦] من الدنيا فلا تَكن من الغافلين والسّلام

وختم الكتاب ودفعه إلى رسوله وأتا به [إلى ذي][٥٤٧] القرنين فلمّا بلغ كتابه إلى ذي القرنين فكه وقرأه وعرف مقتضاه فأمر من ساعته بالرّحيل إليه والدخول إلى بلاده

ذِكْرُ مسير ذي القرنين إلى لَبُورَ ملك الهند وملاقاته معه

قال أبو عبد الملك قال مقاتل ابن سليمان إنّ ذي القرنين رحل من أرض الفُرْس بعد دخوله بابنت[٥٤٨] الملك داريوش واجتماعه مع أمّه الغَيْذَا فرحل حتّى انتها إلى وادٍ يقال له [وادي][٥٤٩] المخَضِب

---

[٥٤٣] ولاية

[٥٤٤] "ورجوت ان الرّاغب منهزِمٌ والمستَرَاح منصور" :Arabic refrain

[٥٤٥] ? الاعور Word written in between lines, not clearly legible. Might be

[٥٤٦] في الاصل "لاراَحَكَ"

[٥٤٧] من B

[٥٤٨] بابنة

[٥٤٩] في الاصل "واد"

فيه منابتُ أشجار الفلفل والقرفة والقرنفل ينبتون[٥٥٠] في أطراف الجبال وفي أجواف الوادي المخضب ويثمرون [f. 223] فإذا وقعوا في أيّام وقوعهم ونزل الغيث على الجبال فتسيل الأودية وتحملُ ذلك الموقوع من الفلفل وغيره من كلّ ما تسيل به جبال الهند ويرمونه في سهولها مقدار عشرة أيّام فلمّا نزل ذو القرنين بالوادي خرج من عسكره رجال يتنزّهون ويصطادون فصادفوا رجلان[٥٥١] من أهل الهند [فقبضوا علي أحدهم][٥٥٢] وانفلت منهم واحد

ثمّ أنّهم أتوا به إلى ذي القرنين وأخبره أن معاشهم من جميع ما يحمل به الوادي وإنّهم يجمعون الفلفل في أيّام حمل الأودية [في][٥٥٣] الشتاء والرّبيع فيلقون الفلفل في طواجين الحديد ويقلى كما يقلى القمح والشعير ويحملونه في الأوعيّة ولولا ذالك العمل الذي يعملونه على النار ما حمله وعاء من شدّة حرارته فقال لهم ذو القرنين «كيف كان عملكم وحالكم وصبركم على حرارة الفلفل وحرارة النار ؟» قالوا «يا ذا القرنين من عاش من شيء أحسن صنعته [f. 224] كُنّا نلبس عند جمعه الجلود القويّة المعمولة ونعمل منها براقعا لوجوهنا ولنا مغاريف من حديد طِوَالٍ والواح من عُودٍ طوالٍ فنجمعه بالألواح ونُنقّلوه بالمغارف ونتقى حرارته بلبس الجلود ونتقى النار لبعدها بالمغارف الطّوالٍ وكلّ عمل له صَنْعَةٌ تصلح به» قال له «كيف كان الملك لبور ؟» قال له «كان الملك لبور شديد الحجاب ومع شدّته واحتجابه [رئيف][٥٥٤] بالرّعية رفيق بالضّعيف وياوي الغريب وينصر الملهوف ويقضى لكلّ ذي حقٍّ حقّه ويدين بدين آبائه» قال لهم «وما دين آبائه ؟» قال له «دين آبائه معروف ﴿ يَأْمُرُونَ بِالْمَعْرُوفِ وَيَنْهُونَ عَنِ الْمُنكَرِ ﴾ [٥٥٥] ويشهدون لخالق الأرض والسّموات أنّه هو قاهرهم بالموت» قال له «وهل يؤدّون [الزكاة][٥٥٦] ؟» قال «لا» قال له «وهل يودّون الخراج ؟» قال «لا» قال له «وكيف جنوده ؟» قال له[f. 225] «كان جمْع من جنوده نصرة لِدَارِيُوشْ ملك الفرس ما [ا]ختار منها كلّ صنديد وبطل وسجاع[٥٥٧] فَبلغ أخبار عدته ثلاثون مائة ألف ألف ومعه ألف فيل وألف أسد كلّهم

---

[٥٥٠] تنبت

[٥٥١] رجلين

[٥٥٢] من B

[٥٥٣] في الاصل "فالشتآء"

[٥٥٤] في الاصل "رفيق"

[٥٥٥] Qur'ān 3:104

[٥٥٦] في الاصل "زكواة"

[٥٥٧] نفهم "شجاع"

ضوارى على حرب بني آدم» فقال لهم ذو القرنين «الله ناصرنا ونحن معوّلون على الالتقاء معه ولو كان في أكثر من ذالك عددا»

قال وكان عند ذى القرنين ممّن اجتمع الله بعد دخوله برشيقة ابنة الملك داريوش ثمانون ألف فارس من الفرس وثمانون ألف من الرجال ومن الروم مائة فارس ومائة راجل ومعه من جبال الكُرد ومن الترك وَالدِّيْلَمْ مائة ألف من الخيل والرجال ومن الجزائر والمدائن ثمانون ألف بين الخيل والرجال ومعه من أهل الصنائع من كلّ صنعة مائة ألف من [سرّاج][٥٥٨] وخياط [f. 226] وحدّادٍ ونجّارٍ وصاحب كلّ صنعة من هذه الصنايع التي تحتاج إلى السّفر وكلّ صنعة من الصّنائع اشتغل [بها أمهر][٥٥٩] أهلها

فلمّا سمع ذو القرنين من الرجل الهنديّ ذلك أمر بجمع جنوده وسيّرهم على عين الرجل الهندي وأصحاب ذي القرنين يتعجّبون بكلام لَبُوَر في كتابه وقد داخلهم الرُّعْبُ من قوله فنظر إليهم ذو القرنين وقال لهم «لا [يكفُّكُم][٥٦٠] ذالك من كلامه في كتابه وكلام رجاله» فخرج بهم على جهة لَبُوَر [فقال] «وما من أحد إلاّ ويصغر اجلالاً لنا ولعلّهم أجسام بلّى[٥٦١] عقول ولا خَيَل» فلمّا قال لهم ذالك نشطوا لحرب لبور ثمّ قال لهم «يا قوم أنا أكتب إليه كتابا أرشده فيه لَعَلّه يرشدُ» فقالوا له «افعل» فكتب ذو القرنين إلى لبور

> من عبد الله ذي القرنين إلى لبور أمّا بعد فانه وصلني ما كتبت به إليّ [f. 227] ممّا هان عليك من أمري فما زادني ذلك إلاّ حِرْصاً على قتالك وإنّك ذكرت أن بلادك ليس فيها ما يحتاج إليه الملوك من [لذّة][٥٦٢] الدنيا ليس لنا في [الذّهّا][٥٦٣] مراد ومرادنا دخولك في ديننا أو تشتيت مُلْكِكَ على أيدينا وإنّي رجوت النصر عليك كما نصرنا على غيرك وأعوِّلُ على لقائك فإنّي قادم عليك من يومي هذا والله المعين

فلمّا ورد كتاب ذو القرنين على لبور أمر بالاستعداد إلى لقائه وأمر بخروج الفِيَلَةِ والسِّباع الضّاريات الذين كانوا يأكلون[٥٦٤] بني آدم والتقا الجمعان في أسفل واد من أودية الهند يقال له وادي النَّهْرَان في أسفله بطحةٌ وسعها عشرة أيّام طولاً وعرضاً فالتقوا بها فأوّل من قدّم لبور للقتال بالفِيَلَةِ [f. 228]

---

[٥٥٨] في الاصل "سراح"

[٥٥٩] في الاصل "اهاص"

[٥٦٠] B: "يهمكم" ، في الاصل "يكفُمكُم" .Ms. A is not clearly legible here

[٥٦١] بلا

[٥٦٢] في الاصل "للذة"

[٥٦٣] في الاصل "للذّهّا"

[٥٦٤] التي تأكل

ورِجَالُها لبسوا الحديد لم يظهر من الرجال إلاّ أحداقُ أعينهم والرجال بمقدّمة الفيل وآخرون يسوقُونَهُم وكذلك السِّباع الضاريات بين كلّ فيلين أسد وأسدين في أقفاصها وعلى الأقفاص رجال في توابيتَ مغلوقةٍ يقودون العجلات وعلى العجلات الأقفاص وفي الأقفاص السِّباع يقودهم الرجال يريدون بهم الحرب وإنّهم إذا دَنَا القوم من القوم فتحوا الأقفاص فتخرّجَ الأسُود فتهْجَم على من يُلاَقيها وهو في أشدِّ عُدَّةٍ

فلمّا نظر ذو القرنين إلى ذلك وما تقدّم به إليه واستعداد رجاله قال لأصحابه «خندقوا خندقا» فخندقوا خندقا عظيما لا أحدٌ يقدر على جوازه وكفّ الناس عن الناس وأمَرَ بعدّة الفيل والسِّباع فإذا هي [f. 229] أربعة وعشرون ألفا من كلّ صنعة ثمّ منع القتال عندهم أربعة وعشرين يوما ثمّ صنع أربعة وعشرون ألفا بين [أ]فيال وأسُودٍ مِثلاً وتلك العدّة التي صنع إلى أهل جابرصا وبها أهلكهم وقد تركها بمدينة جابرصا حين فتحها وانصرف من عندهم وصنع مثلها لحرب لبور وكان لا يمرّ بمدينة إلاّ وأخذ منها كلّ صانعٍ في صنعته قال وجعل من كلّ التَّمَاثيل صفات الأسود وصفة الفِيَلَة وصفة الرجال وجعل أجوافها خاوية وأمر أن [تملأ][٥٦٥] أجوافها بالزّفت والقطران والكبريت ثمّ أمر بالنار فأضرمت في أجوافها حتّى صارت كالحجارة الموقودة ثمّ جعل في مقدّماها بُكّاراتٌ من حديد ووكّل بكلّ تمثال رجل بيده عمود من حديد له قرنان فقال لهم «تقدموا إلى [f. 230] حَرْب آل لبور وإنّهم أوّل ما يُقَربون إلينا فِيَلَتُهُم وأُسُودُهُم فإذا أقبلت نحونا فيدفع كلّ واحد منكم تمثاله» ثمّ أمر أصحابه التّماثيل الذين بأيديهم البُكَارات بمصنوعات يقودون [العجلات][٥٦٦] التي عليها التّماثيل وعليهم كباش الحديد وقدم ثلاث مائة رجل بأيديهم المزاريق فأردفهم خلف أصحاب التماثيل وجعل جملة التماثيل في صور واحد لها وجه واحد من مقابلة الحرب وجعلهم في بيوت مختلفة كالحوانيت بعضها من حديد وبعضها من نحّاس وأكثرها من العود ووجوه الصور من حديد والرجال خَلْفَ الصُّوَر وجعل في وسعه نصف ميلٍ والفِيَلَة والأسُود والرجال المصوّرة أمام تلك الصُّوَر وقدم قطلاَمس على يمين الصُّور في ثلاثة مائة ألف وخمسين ألفا كلّهم من [f. 231] صناديد الرّوم وأشرافها وأقبل هو في بقيّة الجيش وأمر بضرب الأبواق وميّزوا الناس للقتال وأقبل في [ظلمة][٥٦٧] وعجاجة وأقبلت النيران تلهم وتلمع من أفواه تلك التماثيل ومن [مناخرِها][٥٦٨]

---

[٥٦٥] في الاصل "تملا"

[٥٦٦] من B. في الاصل "العجيات"

[٥٦٧] في الاصل "طلمة"

[٥٦٨] من B. في الاصل "متاخرِها"

فلمّا سمع لبور ذالك وسمع الأبواق ودويها في الوهج وشدّة الغبرة و[لمعان][٥٦٩] الأسنّة وبروق النيران وهجمة الخيول وتهليل الرّوم لله بالوحدانيّة فلمّا سمعوا آل لبور ذالك تدافعوا للحرب من كلّ جانب ومكان وأخذ بعضهم بيد بعض وتداعوا بينهم بالشجاعة وناد كلّ واحد منهم «يا فلان يا بني فلان أين ما كنتم تقولون وتزعمون ؟» و«يئال قدرة هل يفضل لبور عليكم مُجَازَاتٌ في غير هذا اليوم؟» فداخلتهم الحميّة فقدّموا الفِيَلَة والسِّباع كما فعل ذو القرنين أمام الصُّفُوف حتّى التقت الفرقتان فحمَلت الرجال على تماثيل الرجال وحملت [f. 232] الفِيَلَة على تَمَاثيل الفِيَالَة والأسود على تماثيل الأسود وكلّ نوع حمل على نوعِهِ فلكلّما رمَا أحدٌ نفسه على تمثال من تلك التماثيل حرقته النار وولّى هارباً من حَرِّهَا وكلّما أخذ سبع بفيه احترق من جوف الأسود وانهزمت مقدّمتهم للقتال من حرارة النار والتقى الرجال بالرجال والخيل بالخيل فنزل الصّبر على الفرقتين وكَثُرَ الفناء يومهم ذالك ورجال أهل الهند يقولون «لا يوم بعد اليوم» قد جرّدوا نسِيجَ القُطْن والحَرير ولبسوا نسيج الحديد من نباط الهند وسيوف الهند ورماح الهند فكم من بطل شجاع قُتِلَ وكم من بطل منّاع فُقِدَ ومَكُثَت القتال بين الفرقتين عشرين يوما لم يفرّ أحدٌ من أحدٍ حتّى هلك الجمعان من عظيم الْبِلَا و[صارت][٥٧٠] القتلى من الخيل والرجال كالجبال الرّواسي وكَثُرَ الفناء من طول [f. 233] الوغا وأشدّ[٥٧١] الحرب حتّى هلك عامّة أصحاب ذي القرنين وكَثُرَ جراحاتُها حتّى هَمُّوا أن يأتوا بيديهم إلى لبور وإن يسلموا ذا القرنين

ثمّ ذكروا ما فعل ذو القرنين بأصحاب داريوش الذين غدروه فبلغ ذو القرنين ذالك وقال « يا قوم فإنّي أري رأياً فيه سدادٌ وصلاحٌ للفريقين» فمسك الناس أَعنّتَهُم وكفوا عن قتالهم فخرج ذو القرنين من عسكره إلى ما بين الفريقين ونادا «يا لبور» فقال له «نعم» فقال له ذو القرنين «اقدم عليَّ» فقال له «من أنت ؟» قال «أنا ذو القرنين» قال له «وما تريد ؟» قال له ذو القرنين «يا لبور ما ينبغي للملوك أن [توثِرَ][٥٧٢] بنفُوسِهَا عن أصحابها في الموت فإذا أهلكت الجنود فلا خير للحَيَاة للملوك هذا أمر عظيم فنيت الجنود من [الجهتين][٥٧٣] على أيدينا فالواجب للحرِّ الكريم أن يقي [f. 234] أصحابَه بنفسه هل لك أن تأمر الصُّفُوف من كلّ جيهة أن يكفُّوا عن القتال ويبرز بعضنا لبعض فأيُّنا قتل

---

[٥٦٩] من B في الاصل "ملعان"

[٥٧٠] في الاصل "صلوةِ"

[٥٧١] أشتدّ

[٥٧٢] في الاصل "توثِرَ"

[٥٧٣] في الاصل "الجيهتين"

صاحبَه كان له مُلْكُهُ» فأعجب لَبُورَ ذلك وكان جباراً في الأرض عارفاً بالحروب ذو شدَّة وقوّة وكان ذو القرنين شابّا جميلا حدث السِّنّ لم يجرب الحروب [فحقره][٥٧٤] لبور وطمع فيه

فأمر جنودها فكفّوا عن القتال وخرج كلّ واحد منهُمَا إلى صاحبه وتضاربا ساعة زمانية فسمع لَبُوَر جَلْبَةً عَظِيمَةً اقشعرّ منها جَلْدَه فالتفتَ لِيَرا ذلك فقام عليه ذو القرنين بضربةٍ عظيمة فأصاب فذبح فازال رأسَه عن جسده وطُرِحَ عن الجواد فلمّا رأتْ جنوده ذلك أقبلوا على القتال أسفا منهم على ملكهم فنادا ذو القرنين «أيُّها الناس من وضع السِّلاح فهو في أمان الله والله يشهد [f. 235] على ذالك فأشرَفَت إليه رجال الهند ودخلوا من ساعتهم في عسكره

فتركهم واستباحَ ما كان في عسكر لبور من الأموال والسِّلاح وأدخل ذالك كلّه في خزائنه وأمر بلبور [يُدفن][٥٧٥] وأحسن دفنه كما يُفْعَل بالملوك في أكفاهم ثمّ [سار][٥٧٦] حتّى دخل جبال الهند فسبا ما أراد وأحرق ما أراد وكسر الأصنام و[خلف][٥٧٧] لا يبقى منهم من يعبد صنماً من [دون][٥٧٨] الله تعالى فأمنوا بالله وعاهدوا ذو القرنين على أداء الخراج والنصر لدين الله وأمر عليهم رجلا من آل لبور وكتب إلى مُعَلّمه ارسطاطاليس كتابا وختم عليه وبعثه مع جملة عبيده يذكر فيه

بسم الله الرحمان الرحيم من ذي القرنين ابن نّباش إلى مُعَلِّمه ارسطاطاليس أمّا بعد فإنّي كتبت إليك [f. 236] أن أخبرك بعجائب الأرض وما رأيتُ فيها وذكَرْتَ لي أن أفسِّرَ لك ذالك حرفاً حرفاً وما لاقيتُ مع داريوش ملك الفُرس فقد نصرني عليه ربّي وصار مَلْكَه داخلا في ملكنا وجنوده ناظرة لجنودنا وزوّجني ابنتَهُ رشيق ثمّ ارتحلت من أرضه بعد دفنه وإحساني لأخيه وأمّه إلى أرض الهند ففتحها الله بعد موت خلقٍ كثيرٍ وخِيَلٌ وأمور وأعلم أنّي لم أبلغ إلى مِلِك الشام ولا إلى مِلِك الصِّين ولا التُرجَمانين وأنا إليهم سائر إن شاء الله تعالى وأنا متوجه للغرب والسّلام عليكم

قال أبو عبد الملك ثمّ ارتحل ذو القرنين قاصدا نحوا المغرب يطلب قتال من [كفر بربّه][٥٧٩] حتّى قدم على قوم يركبون الأسُود يسخِّرون بهم ويأخذون الرجال من عَدُوهم فيقذفون برؤسهم في البحر [f. 237] فاستشار فيهم أصحابه وقال «ما ترون من الرأي وهم قوم سحرة لا يقام السّيف لهم»

---

[٥٧٤] من B . في الاصل "فحفره"

[٥٧٥] من B . في الاصل "بدن"

[٥٧٦] في الاصل "صار"

[٥٧٧] في الاصل "حلف"

[٥٧٨] في الاصل "ذون"

[٥٧٩] من B

قال أبو عبد الملك سَأَلْتُ المُبَارَكُ ابن فُضَّالَةَ عن هؤلاَء القوم قال هم يقال لهم البربر وسَمُّون[٥٨٠] في ذالك الزمان لوبَيَا وهم في المغرب ما بين مصر وإفريقيّة ثم انطلق حتّى بلغ أقصاها من جبال أرضهم فدعاهم ذو القرنين إلى الإسلام ودعا ربّه أن يخلّصه من سحرهم فاستجاب الله له فقال لأصحابه «سيرُوا واستبشروا فإنّ الله أعلمني أنّه سيفتح لكم ما تريدون فإنّهم أشدُّ خلق الله كُفْراً وأقساهم قلباً» فسار إليهم وأمرهم بالقتال فاقتتلوا قتالا عظيما فهزمهم ذو القرنين بإذن الله تعالى ثمّ أنّهم لمّا كَثُرَ القَتْلُ فيهم طَلبوا من [ذي][٥٨١] القرنين الصّلحَ فأجابهم ورَدّوا له الجزية والخراج [f. 238] وهم قبائلٌ من البَرْبَر من برابر إفريقية فأمنوا به وعَاهَدُوه على الحقّ والوَفَاء وَتركَهُم وارتحل إلى بلاد إفريقية

ذِكْرُ غزوة ذي القرنين إلى بلاَد إفريقية

قال أبو عبد الملك ثمّ ارتحل عنهم من أرض لوبياً [فسار][٥٨٢] من عندهم حتّى انتها إلى البحر فركبه وسار حتّى خرج إلى أرض إفريقية فوجد فيها قبائل شتّى لا ينكر بعضهم [عمل][٥٨٣] بعض وهم [قرى][٥٨٤] كثيرة منهم مَنْ كُتامَة و[مُزاتَة][٥٨٥] وغيْرهم ممّن تعلّق إليهم فدعاهم إلى دين الله فامتنع بعضهم من الإيمان وآمن بعضُهم وقاتل من لم يُؤمن حتّى نصره الله عليهم فصالحوه على الدين والعهد والخراج والجزية

ثمّ ارتحل من إفريقية إلى جيهة المغرب على شاطيء البحر حتّى أتا قوماً يقال لهم هَجّيْسَه فدعاهم إلى دينه فأسرعوا [f. 239] بالأجابة لمّا تقارب من نسبة الرّوم إليهم

ثمّ ارتحل حتّى أتا جبلا على الدَّرَ يقال له جَرْجَرهْ فوجد فيه أمّة يقال لها زَوَاوَهْ فقاتلوه يوما وصالحوه في الثاني على الخراج والجزية

ثمّ ارتحل عنهم إلى قبيلة كُتَامَةَ وفيهم رجلا تولّى أمرهم يقال له خيدان ابن كيداد الأكبر من نسله كيداد الأصغر الذي كان في عهد الإسلام فصالحوه على الخراج والجزية

---

٥٨٠ وسموا

٥٨١ في الاصل "دي"

٥٨٢ في الاصل "فصار"

٥٨٣ في الاصل "علمل"

٥٨٤ في الاصل "قرون"

٥٨٥ في الاصل "مُزانَة"

ثمّ ارتحل عنهم وسار حتّى نزل على شاطيء البحر على موضع يقال له نكَره فبدّل اسمه إلى اسم نَلْدَرْ وفيه أُمّة من نسب الرّوم يقال لهم الزّراهيهْ[٥٨٦] ومنهم سُمِيَ جَبَلُهُم وصالحوه على الجزية والخراج

ثمّ ارتحل عنهم إلى موضع على شاطيء البحر فنظر فيه فإذا هو قريب المسلك إلى جواز البحر فوجد فيه لأمّة يقال لها نَفْزَهْ فقاتلهم فمات منهم علماً من الخلق ثمّ سألوه الصُّلْحَ [f. 240] فصالحهم على الجزية والخراج

ثمّ نزل بطرف البحر ففتح من منزله ذالك كفال ابن غوّاص وهم في تلك البلاد من عهد بعطيش وهو الذي أخرجهم من بلادهم من جبال الكرد ففتحهم من منزله ذالك فسمّاه جبل الفتح فأقام فيه عامّاً وثلاثَةُ أشْهُرِ حتّى فتح [جبال المغرب][٥٨٧] ومن سكنها وهي حينئذ قليلة السّكني ليس فيها إلاّ قبائل المصادِمَة[٥٨٨] وهي في مدينة ايلان وانظارها[٥٨٩]

فلمّا فتحهم وقع نظره في بنيان مسلك [الانفجار][٥٩٠] وهو الذي قام منه رحلُ البحر الذي بنيت عليه الإسكندرية خرج منفجرا من البحر الكبير فأراد بنيان ذالك المسلك فعانده فَلم يتمّ له مُرَادُهُ في ذالك وكان ذالك الموضع قد عاينوه ملوك اليانون وملوك الصُّمُّ ليَبْنُوا فيه بنياناً فلم يقدروا عليه فتركه وأراد جواز البحر [f. 241] إلى عدوة الجزيرة

ذكْرُ غزوة ذي القرنين إلى جزيرة الأندلوس

قال أبو عبد الملك الملشونيّ ثمّ رحل ذو القرنين وركب البحر حتّى انتها إلى برّ عدوة جبل الفتح فلمّا دخل البرّ إذا هو بقبائل كثيرة [فإذا][٥٩١] كلامهم ككلام الطُّيور ولغاتهم مختلفة لا يفقه أحدٌ كَلاَمَهُمْ وهم قوم يقال لهم الأندلوس وقال بعض أهل العِلْم [أن] يقال لهم الانبارُ ونزل بين جبالهم وعمارتهم وأخذه في ذالك الموضع هواءٌ عظيم فأقام فيه مُدَّةً ما سلكه أيّاماً وكانت أوتادُ خيل ذي القرنين من الزّيتون فلمّا أراد أن يرتحل من ذالك الموضع أتاه الملك زياقيل فأمره أن يأمر الجند الذي

---

[٥٨٦] بين الهأ والهأ بسكون خرفة بدون نقطة

[٥٨٧] من B. في الاصل "جبل المغر"

[٥٨٨] المصامدة

[٥٨٩] في الاصل "انضارها"

[٥٩٠] من B. في الاصل "الانفحار"

[٥٩١] في الاصل "فادا"

كان يقدّمُهُ غيداف ابن مازن ابن اروم أن يتركوا أوتادهم في الأرض على ما هم عليه [f. 242] [فتركوهم][٥٩٢] فنبتوا جميعا بإذن الله فكان من أوتاد [عسكر][٥٩٣] ابن شرف ابن غيداف الموضع المُشبع بزيتونه يسمّى باسم قائد العسكر بالشرف إلى آخر الدنيا

فلمّا سمعوا الانبار بدخول ذي القرنين إلى بلادهم أتوه فقالوا «يا ذا القرنين لا طاقة لنا بقتالك وإن الله تعالىٍ [أ]عطاك الظفر فأحسن فيما أعطاك وأنا قوم قلّة في هذه البلاد فأحسن إلينا ولا تهلكنا [ونحن][٥٩٤] طائعون لك مؤمنون بربّك» فقال لهم «نعم لا يعارضكم أحدا[٥٩٥] من [جنودي][٥٩٦] ولا سبيل لي إليكم ولاكن أخراج جزيتكم وبلادكم وأنتم على أرضكم» فأجابوه إلى ذالك فقال لهم «من أيّ الناس أنتم ؟» فقالوا «من نسل آل سبط شعيب» قال «وما بلغكم هذه البلاد ؟» قالوا «خرّجَنَا ملك من ملوك آل فارس من بلادنا نحن قوم قلّة معاهدين بدين شعيب عليه السلام [f. 243] من مدائن ابن إبراهيم فطردنا غمطيسٌ وطلعنا في البرّ من بيت المقدّس إلى مدينة قسمطينة[٥٩٧] فقالوا لنا ٬ كونوا على [حذر][٥٩٨] من دابت[٥٩٩] تخرج من البحر في كلّ عام على جيهة مغرب الشمس من هذا الجبل فتمد رقبتها فلا تمرّ بشيء من هذه البهائم التي رأيتموها إلاّ أكلتها ولَولا ضرها على تلك البهائم ما حملتها الجزيرة ولاكنكم ادْخلوا زورقكم واجعلوا الجبل بين أكتافكم ومرّوا على وجه واحدا[٦٠٠] ستّة أيّام يظهر لكم جبل عالي في البحر فاجعلوا على يساركم تخرجوا إلى جزائر مُتَفَرقة وأبطحات[٦٠١] واسعة لا يسكنها إلاّ الجنّ والغوال[٦٠٢] عن يمينك تخرجون إلى جزيرة الانبار وآتوا إلى أهاليها فاعلموهم لذالك٬ فعرِّفونا مسكن القوم وذكروا صفاتهم فأعلمناك بهم» قال لهم ذو [f. 244] القرنين «وهل دونهم أحد من الخلق ؟» قالوا «نعم دونهم قوم يقال لهم الزّوابرة وهم قوم صُلع زرق لا شعور في أجسامهم وهم خلق كثير لا يعلم منتها عددهم إلاّ الله تعالى وهم خلق من خلق الله يشبهون الناس في خلقهم وليس هم من الناس وقد أحاطت بهم الأمواج من كلّ جيهة [إلاّ][٦٠٣] جيهة واحدة وفي تلك الجيهة

---

[٥٩٢] في الاصل "فرتكوهم"

[٥٩٣] في الاصل "عسر"

[٥٩٤] من B

[٥٩٥] أحَدٌ

[٥٩٦] في الاصل "جنود"

[٥٩٧] قسطنطينية (Constantinople) or قسنطينة (Constantine in Algeria) Probably referring to

[٥٩٨] في الاصل "حدر"

[٥٩٩] دابة

[٦٠٠] واحدٍ

[٦٠١] وأبطح

[٦٠٢] الغول

الناس وقد أحاطت بهم الأمواج من كلّ جيهة [إلاّ][٦٠٣] جيهة واحدة وفي تلك الجيهة جبل شامخ عالي له رأسَانِ عاليان رؤوسهما في السماء» فقال لهم ذو القرنين «هل لي سبيل الى الصعود على رأس الجبل ؟» قالوا «لا مسلك له» قال «و لم ذالك ؟» قالوا «في ارتفاعه مسيرة شهرين» قال «فإذا أشرفت هل نرى[٦٠٤] جزائر القوم ؟» قالوا له «لا طاقة لك بالصعود إليه لأنّه ما صعده أحد قَط إلاّ هبت عليه الأرياح فأهلك» قال لهم «إنّ الله [يعوذ][٦٠٥] بنصره من يشاء ويسهّلُ [f.245] ذالك كلّه»

ثمّ ارتحل عنهم وقصد الجبل فأتاه فسَهّل الله له ذالك فصعدوا على رأسه في يومَيْن حتّى بلغ رأسه فهبت الرياح من فوقهم فوَقَعوا كلّهم من الجانب الأخر صعدت معه مائة رجل اختصّهم ممّن كان معه فخَرَّ ذو القرنين لله ساجدا ورغب إلى الله أن ينجيه من ذالك فطفت الأرياح بقدرة الله تعالى فرجع إلى أصحابه وأخبرهم بالخبر وقصّ عليهم الخبر أن الله تعالى قد قسم الدنيا [بذالك][٦٠٦] الجبل وأنّه لا يعلوه أحد من الخلق إلاّ هلك ثمّ أمر أصحابه بالركوب إلى البحر فركبوه ورجع عن تلك الأمم وتركهم

قال أبو عبد الملك الملشونيّ فلمّا أراد الركوب على البحر قام إليه افلاطون فقال له «أيّها الملك لا تقتحم بنا لجج البحار لاكنّي [f. 246] رأيت رُأْياً أن تقيم على البرّ فنركب أنا وأناس معي فندخل البحر فإنّ رأينا فيه شيئا نحتاجوا إليه رجعنا إليك ننظروه جميعا وإن لم نرى فيه شيئا يعجبنا فديناك بأنفسنا فأجابهم إلى ذالك ثمّ أن افلاطون ركب البحر في مائة رجل من قومه يوما وليلة فنظروا في البحر إلى جزيرة فيها مدينة فاعتمدوا عليها بالمركب الذي هم فيه فلمّا قربوا منها نظروا إليها قد تحركت ومشت على الماء فَتبّعوها فهم في أثرها حتّى وقفت وقصدوها فإذا هي مدينة على ألواح والألواح على السفون[٦٠٧] والسفون في البحر فنظروا إلى عجائب مبنيّة وشَرَافَات أبراج وقصور وسألوا الدخول إلى أهلها فأبوا لهم وقالوا لهم أهل المدينة «منكم هربنا وبنينا في البحر خوفا من بني آدم» قالوا لهم أهل افلاطُون ففيكم أنتم أهل المدينة ؟» [f. 247] قالوا لهم «نحن أربعة آلاف رجل غير من لم يبلغ الحلم ومَن لم يطق الحرب إذا اجتمعنا إليه» قال لهم افلاطون «يا قوم نحن قوم قلّة وأنتم أكثر منّا عددا فكيف تخافون منّا دعونا ندخل عليكم ونبيتوا يوما وليلة ونرحل عنكم» قالوا «إذا أنتم قوم قلّة فما

---

[٦٠٣] في الاصل "الى"

[٦٠٤] نفهم "ارا"

[٦٠٥] في الاصل "يعودى"

[٦٠٦] في الاصل "بدالك"

[٦٠٧] السفن Here and following

لكم والدخول علينا ؟» قالوا لهم «نريد معرفة ما أنتم عليه فأنا نحن رُسُل ذو القرنين» قالوا «من ذى القرنين ؟» قالوا «هو رجل نَبّأَهُ الله وسبب له التَمكن من كلّ شيء» قالوا لهم «وهل يمشي في البحر ؟» قالوا لهم «نعم» قالوا «في السفون وفي غيرها ؟» قال لهم افلاطُون «بل أغناه الله من السفون» قالوا لهم «نريد دخولكم على الملك»

فأدخلوهم على ملكهم فوجدوه شابّا حدث السِّنِّ [f. 248] من أجمل الناس على كرسيّ من ذهب[٦٠٨] مرَصَع بأصناف الجواهر على رأسه تاج مكلّل بالدرّ والياقوت فسلّموا عليه فردّ عليهم السلام فقالوا له أصحابه «إنّ هؤلاء يزعمون أنّهم من أصحاب ذي القرنين فسألهم عن حاله» وقال لهم «هل أنتم من أصحاب ذي القرنين ؟» قالوا «نعم» قال لهم «وما دينه ؟» قال له «دين الله أكبر بوحده ويقرّ له بالربوبيّة» قال «وكم بَلغ في الأرض ؟» قال افلاطون «بلغ مغرب الشمس ومشرقها» قال «وهل بلغ الفرس ؟» قال «نعم» قال «وهل بلغ الهند ؟» قال «نعم» قال «وما الذي أرسلكم إليه ؟» قالوا «لنعلم ما في البحر» قال «وهل رأيتم شيئا تعلموه به ؟» قال له افلاطون «ما رأينا شيئا أعجب من مدينة تمشي على الماء» قال «هذا مدينة مبنيّة من عهد أوائلنا[٦٠٩]» [f. 249] قال افلاطون «ومن يكون أوائلكم ؟» قالوا «آل علقمة ابن لوادة ابن سام ابن نوح عليه السلام» قَال لهم «فكيف ذالك ؟» قال «كان علقمة ملكا من ملوك زمانه وتار[٦١٠] في الدنيا حتّى طاعت له رقاب آل عاد وبه سُمِيَتْ العمالقة وبقا على ملكه حتّى قامت عليه آل عوص وهم من العمالقة فضرب إلى البحر فاستعمل السفون وسكنها وطال بها على [الأعداء][٦١١] في البحر و لم يأمن إلى البرّ حتّى أدعته نفسه إلى بنيان هذه المدينة فبناها وشيِّدها كما ترون وخدمتهم الآن في السفون تصلح في كلّ عام من ذالك[٦١٢] الزمان إلى زماننا هذا فاتّصل بنا خبر ذي القرنين فخفنا على أنفسنا من أمره ونحن على البحر شرقا وغربا و[سألناكم][٦١٣] بالله العظيم أن تقرءُوه منّا السلام وأن لا يقرب أثرنا [f.250] ونحن به مؤمنون وبربه

---

٦٠٨ في الاصل "دهب"

٦٠٩ في الاصل "اوايلنا" أوَلَ Root is

٦١٠ ثار

٦١١ من B. في الاصل "العداد"

٦١٢ في الاصل "دالك"

٦١٣ من B. في الاصل "سالتكم"

ولا نشرك به شيئا وأنه لا نفع له فينا ولا ملك يزيد في ملكه» فأكرمهم [الملك] وأحسن [إليـــهم][٦١٤] وعاهدوه وعاهدهم افلاطون فرجع فعلم ذو القرنين فَوَفّى لأهل تلك المدينة بما [عاهدهم][٦١٥] عليـــه افلاطون

ثمّ ارتحل إلى بحر عظيم منفجرا بالبحر المحيط مُقبلا نحو أرض تقليس[٦١٦] وهو بمشرق بـــلاد الروم على شِاطيء البحر ووصل فيها إلى مدينة عظيمة أحاطت بها جزائر كثيرة ولا ماء فيها وقد كدنا أن يهلكنا العطش فرحلنا منها إلى جزيرة أخرى كثيرة السباع والنّمور والوحوش الضّارية وفيها أســود عظام ضارية تعدوا على الخلق فنزلنا بها ووجدنا بها ماء أحلى من العسل وخرج منها من العسكر أناس يتنزّهون على شاطيء البحر [f. 251] [فإذا هم][٦١٧] بكهف عظيم في ساحل البحر وفيه عين من المـــاء فدخلوا في الكهف وَشَرَبوا من الماء فنظروا إلى الكهف فإذا فيه سارية عظيمة من الرخام الأخضر على رأسها [صنم][٦١٨] في صفة رجل أحسن ما يكون من الرجال بوجه أزهر وعين الكحل ولحية حســـنة ونقش في صدر الصنم ' هذا تمثال كوش الملك الفرس ملك الدنيا انتها ملكه وعلمه من هذا المكان إلى الشوس[٦١٩] بالمغرب وبالمشرق إلى الصّين' فنزلنا في تلك الجزيرة [ ][٦٢٠] فلمّا كان ثلث الليـــل فـــإذا بسباع قد خرجت إلينا من غيضة كانت حولها فأقبلت السباع إلينـــا فـــأرادت الهجمـــة علينـــا ثمّ [خرجت][٦٢١] عليهم حيّاتٌ وعقاريب[٦٢٢] سود وخضر وبيض [f. 252] لها قرون فجعلت لا تضـــرب أحد[ا] من الأسود إلاّ مات وهربت الأسود إلى شاطيء البحر فخرجت[٦٢٣] عليهم دوّاب كالفيلـــة لم يعرف لها صفة فتواقعت الدوّاب والسباع وهجم بعضهم على بعض ثمّ خرجت النار من شدّة نفخـــة الحيّات فأحرقت جميع تلك السباع والفيلة[٦٢٤] فأقبلت إلينا تُصْفر وتنفخ حتّى وقفت واحترق كلّ مـــن نزل بالبحيرة إلاّ كوش لم يحترق فمات من شدّة الرعب وكتب هذا ابن أخ له كان غائبا عن ذالـــك

---

[٦١٤] من B. في الاصل "اليه"

[٦١٥] في الاصل "عادهم"

[٦١٦] تغليس Alternative reading would be

[٦١٧] في الاصل "فادا هم"

[٦١٨] من B. في الاصل "اصنامُ"

[٦١٩] السوس؟

[٦٢٠] Displaced text here is cut:[فلما امسنا مرت جيوشا لى على سرير الذهب]

[٦٢١] في الاصل "حرجت"

[٦٢٢] عقارب

[٦٢٣] فخرج

[٦٢٤] مكتوب فوق "فيل" "الفيلة" . "الافيال" :B

فلمّا أتا كتب هذا الكتاب في صدر صورة وحمل السارية الفتى ابن الأخ كوش فبلّغها إلى قصر بـأرض تقليس فبنا عليها بناء في جامع الروم

فدخلنا منها إلى بحيرة مثلها شديدة الريح كثيرة الأوعار فنزلنا بجوارها فلمّـا حـسّ علينـا [f. 253] الليل وإذا بدابّة أعظم من الفيل فتبادروا إليها الناس ووقفوا بينها وبين المحلة وأمر ذو القرنـين الناس بقتالها فازندوا[٦٢٥] النار وأوقدوها من كلّ جهة حتّى أصبح فَلَمَّا انطفت النار وظهر النهار حملت على القوم فقتلت أربعين رجلا في حملتها ثمّ حمل الناس عليها بالخيل والرجال بالحديد فقتلوهـا فلمّـا قتلوها أمر ذى[٦٢٦] القرنين أن يشقّوا بطنها فشقّوا بطنها فإذا فيها حيّة طولها عشرة [أذرع بأذرعهم][٦٢٧] قد ابتلعتها والدابّة التي قتلوها هي حيّة عظيمة وأنّه لا يدخل تلك الجزيرة أحد إلاّ قتلته وهي بالنـهار لا ترا شيئا وأكثر نظرها [بالليل][٦٢٨] وإنّما منعها عن الناس في [الليل][٦٢٩] إلاّ تلك النيران التي أوقدوها

قال ثمّ ارتحلنا من تلك الجزيرة التي فيها الحيّات [f. 254] إلى غيرها فمضينا في البرّ يوما وليلـة فنزلنا في أرض عظيمة الفلوات كثيرة [الصحارى][٦٣٠] في شاطيء البحر فنزلنا فيها فإذا فيها أمّـة مـن الناس ولهم [أنيب كأنيب][٦٣١] الكلاب ووجوه كوجوه الكلاب ألوانهم سود كسواد الغُراب يـأكل القوّي منهم الضعيف ولباسهم الجلود وهم أكثر الخلق عددا لا يدينوا بدين الله ولا يعرفون حـلالا ولا حراما فلمّا نزل ذو القرين بساحتهم بادروا إليه بالحرب والقتال وليس عندهم خيـل إنّمـا أكـثرهم الرجال وبلادهم رمل وعيشتهم من نبات بلادهم ويأكل بعضُهم بعضا ويأكلون دوّاب بلادهم بغـير طبخ [فأسرعوا][٦٣٢] في الحرب معنا فحاطت عليهم جنود الخيل فدهشوا ورعبوا من الخيـل وانهزمـوا وقتل منهم مقتلة عظيمة [f. 255] وقتالهم ذكورا وإناثا كلّهم في القتال سواء وأخذ بعضهم وأتى بـه إلى ذي القرنين فسألهم عن أصْليهم فقالوا «نحن الحبشة من كوش» قال لهم ذو القرنين «وما الذي بلغكـم إلى هذه الجزيرة ؟» قالوا له «من عهد جدنا كوش أمره نوح فسكناها ونحن من تركتهم[٦٣٣] ولم نروا

---

[٦٢٥] Hans Wehr and F. Corriente under زند = kindle, *sacar chispas*

[٦٢٦] ذوَ

[٦٢٧] في الاصل "ادرع بادرعهم"

[٦٢٨] في الاصل "باليل"

[٦٢٩] في الاصل "اليل"

[٦٣٠] في الاصل "السحارى"

[٦٣١] في الاصل "انياب كانياب"

[٦٣٢] في الاصل "فاشرعوا"

[٦٣٣] نفهم "نسله"

آدميا مخالفا لِلَوْننا وصفاتنا إلاّ أنتم ومن تكون[٦٣٤] أنتم ؟» قالوا «نحن الروم وقد أمرنا ربّنا بحرب بني آدم حتّى يقرّوا له بالرّبوبيّة والواحدانيّة» فأجابوه وآمنوا به ثمّ قال لهم «هل تدفنوا أمواتكم ؟» قالوا «نأكلوها ؟» قال لهم «بئس الخلق أنتم» فأمرهم بالدِّفن وارتحل عنهم

قال ثمّ ارتحلنا عنهم فنزلنا بواد كثير الأجراف كثير البحارة[٦٣٥] كثير الشعاب لا زرع فيه ولا عمارةَ كثير الفواكه فنزلنا بساحة الوادي وأكلنا من ثماره وفواكيهه وكثر الكلام في الناس فلمّا كثر الكلام إذا نحَن بدابّة أكبر من الفيل [f. 256] لها شعر كشعر الخنزير فهجمت على الناس فأخذت إمرأة من العسكر فَقَتَلَتْهَا وأسرعت بالأكل في جوفها فأكلت منها حتّى شبعت ثمّ حمل الناس عليها فقتلوها ثمّ أمر ذى[٦٣٦] القرنين في تلك الشعاب التي فيها الدابّة فاحترقت

ثمّ ارتحلنا منها حتّى انتهينا إلى أرض كثيرة الجبال كثيرة الأودية واسعة البرارى كثيرة المنافع يوجد فيها أمّة من بني آدم لاكنهم على طول أجسامهم في الأقدام سُود الألوان لا أنوف لهم ظاهرة لا يفقهُ كلامهم وليس لهم مساكين وسكناهم في الفحوص وبقاع الأرض وكالوحوش فلمّا وصلناهم ورأونا هجموا عَلينا بالحجارة فقاتلونا وليس معهم آلات حرب فحملنا عليهم فأصبنا منهم بشرا كثيرا فانهزموا ودخلوا الكهوف والغيران فامتنعوا تحت الكهوف فنظرنا آثارهم [f. 257] في الأرض فإذا هم مختلفة أقدامهم منهم من قدمه [مثل][٦٣٧] حافر الحمار ومنهم من قدمه كحافر البغل والفرس ومنهم من قدمه كقدم بني آدم لاكنهم طوال جدّا

ثمّ ارتحلنا عنهم فنزلنا أرضا لا شجر فيها ولا حجر ولا جبل واسعة الفُحوص كثيرة الأودية فوجدنا فيها قوما رؤوسهم كرؤوس السباع ووجوههم كوجوه السباع وأجسامهم مشعرة كأجسام الخنازير ولا لهم إلاّ رجلان ويدان[٦٣٨] كبني آدم فلمّا رأونا هربوا منّا وتركناهم

ثمّ ارتحلنا إلى أرض أخرى فوجدنا فيها وادا[٦٣٩] عظيما كثير الأشجار فوجدنا في [أشجاره][٦٤٠] شجرات كلّما طلع النهار زادت طولا إلى الهوى ما دام النهار في الزيادة والأشجار في الزيادة في الهوى فإذا كان النهار في النقصان كانت الأشجار في النقصان إلى آخر النهار فإذا غبت

---

[٦٣٤] نفهم "تكونونَ"

[٦٣٥] البحار

[٦٣٦] ذو

[٦٣٧] في الاصل "متل"

[٦٣٨] رجلين و يدين

[٦٣٩] واد

[٦٤٠] في الاصل "اسجاره"

الشمسْ [f. 258] غابت تلك الأشجار فلا تزال كذالك أبدا ورائحة تلك الشّجر كرائحة المسك رأوها الناس [و]تعجّبوا من ذالك وأعلموا بها ذي القرنين فقال «[اتوني][٦٤١] بثمرة من ثمارة تلك الأشجار وورقة من أوراقها» فأراد الناس أن يأتوه بما ذكرهم , فإذا يضربون بالحجارة وهي تقع عليهم من غير أن لا يروا من يضربهم وسمعوا صوتا يقول:«لا تقطع شيئا من تلك الأشجار إيّاكم إنّ قطعتم منها شيئا هلكتم ثمّ رأينا على تلك الأشجار طيورا ليس لها مثال في الطيور لها حسن وجمال وإذا في ذالك الوادي حجارة سود في الماء فإذا خرجت من الماء أبيّضت فتعجّبنا من ذالك

ثمّ ارتحلنا منها فنزلنا بأرض فيها قوم شبه بني آدم في الصفة إلاّ إنّهم ليس لهم لحاَ[٦٤٢] ولا شعور وحمر [f. 259] الألوان وهم بشاطيء بحر المحيط بالعالمين فنزلنا بازايهم فخرجت علينا منهم طائفة فهجمت على الناس وأخذوا منّا ناسا فغاصوا بهم في البحر فلم نرا لهم أثرا بعد ذالك إلاّ عجاجة و[رجّة][٦٤٣] ولا نعلم ما هي

ثمّ ارتحلنا منها حتّى أتينا إلى أرض متّسعة جدّا فإذا فيها أناس قِصَارٌ صلع لهم أُذَانٌ مثل الأتراس إذا أراد أحدهم النوم يفترش إحدى [أذينه][٦٤٤] والأخرى أمامه يستتر بها وهم لا عُقول لهم وظننا أنّهم ليسوا بآدميّين

ثمّ ارتحلنا عن بلادهم نحو المغرب إلى أرض بابل فسرنا في جبال متّسعة كثيرة الأوْدية لا عمارة فيها فلم نزالوا فيها حتّى انتهينا إلى جبل عظيم عالي على رأسه هيكل عظيم فيه من كلّ لون طوله مائة [ذراع][٦٤٥] وعرضه خمسون [ذراعا][٦٤٦] وعلى بابه سلاسل من ذهب وفي الكرسي مائة كوّة وفي كلّ كوّة صنم من ذهب والبيت مملوءَ بصَحَائف الذهب والفضّة [f. 260] وفيه أكداس من الدرّ والياقوت والجواهر وفي وسط البيت سرير مكلّل بالدرّ والياقوت ومثل على ذالك البيت كرم من الذهب والهيكل [يَتَلالا][٦٤٧] شعاعا من كلّ جيهة فلمّا رأينا ذالك تعجّبنا منه ثمّ ذهبنا لأنظر[٦٤٨] ما في ذالك

---

٦٤١ في الاصل "اتونى"

٦٤٢ نفهم "لِحىً"

٦٤٣ من B . في الاصل "رجفة"

٦٤٤ في الاصل "ادينه"

٦٤٥ في الاصل "دراع"

٦٤٦ في الاصل "دراعا"

٦٤٧ في الاصل " يَتلآلآ "

٦٤٨ نفهم "لننظر"

شيئا ملقيا مستتيرا[٦٤٩] بثوب منسوج بخيوط الذهب وخيوط الفضّة فذهب ذو القرنين ليكشف عن وجهه فسمع مناديا يقول «يا ذا القرنين ألم ينهك ربّك عن كشف السرّ وأعلمك أنّك لن تعط الملك كلّه وأن صاحب السرير المزخرف هو مالك[٦٥٠] الجنّ فارجع بسلام»

قال أبو عبد الملك وكان مقاتلا يقول لمّا انتهى ذو القرنين إلى ذالك السرير نظر إليه فإذا فيه كدس من كبريت أحمر فيتوقد نارا فلمّا أراد الخروج أخذ منه شيئا فخرج به إلى أصحابه فتعجّبوا منه فلمّا رجع إلى بيت [المقدّس][٦٥١] [f. 261] وَضَعَهُ في فيه فكان دواء [الجذام][٦٥٢] والبرص وكان للناس فيه منافع كثيرة حتّى أخذت الروم بيت المقدّس فأخذت كلّ ما فيه من المنافع فحملوه إلى رومة فودعوه في كناسهم[٦٥٣]

قال أبو عبد الملك سمعت مقاتلا يقول قال كعب الاحبار حدّثني غير واحد من علماء الروم حديث ذي القرنين وإنّه لمّا وصل إلى هيكل ملك الجنّ ونظر إلى ما فيه من التماثيل والتصاوير المتصوّرة من الذهب والفضّة وأصناف الجواهر واليواقيت في تصاوير الأصنام [أ]لحّ في المسئلة إلى الله أنّ يخبره بذالك فنزل عليه الملك زياقيل فقال له «يا ذا القرنين هذا كلّه من عمل الجنّ العاصيّ لله وهذا الهيكل لملك الجنّ المؤمن أمره الله جلّ ذكره بمحاربة الجنّ العاصيّ فكلّما حاربهم ونصر عليهم غنم ما وجد عندهم فيأتي به إلى [f. 262] هذا الهيكل الذي ترا وإن الذي رأيت ملقا في منسوج الذهب والفضّة هو ابن الجنّ المؤمن أصابه ضرر فألقاه والده في مكانه فقال له والده «إنّ بريت وعشت رددت إلى مكاني وإن أنت مُتَّ فذالك مقامك» ومات وبقا في ذالك المكان ولاكنك يا ذا القرنين سر على البحر مغربا فإنّك ترا عجبا من عجائب الدنيا

قال فركب البحر وسار في البحر يومين وليلتان[٦٥٤] قطع فيها مسيرة شهرين كاملين فانتهى إلى جزيرة طويلة في مثل ما بين البحرين فإذا أمواج البحرين تلتطم فإذا التطمت الموجتان خلقت بينهما جوزة في صفّة الجوز لاكنها كبيضة الوز في الكبر فإذا انفقصت[٦٥٥] الجوزة ووقعت في الرمل ولا ترجع الأمواج في ذالك الموضع إلاّ مدّة في أوّل النهار ومدّة في آخره فإذا انفقصت الجوزة خرجت منها

---

٦٤٩ مستتراً

٦٥٠ نفهم "ملك"

٦٥١ من B

٦٥٢ في الاصل "الجدام"

٦٥٣ كنائسهم

٦٥٤ ليلتين

٦٥٥ انفقست Here and following

جارية من أحسن ما يكون من الجواري [f. 263] فإذا رجعت المواجتان إلى موضعها في آخر النهار [خرجت أيضا][٦٥٦] جوزة مثلها فخرج منها طير مثل النسر فيأتي لتلك الجارية فيحملها ويطير بها مقابلة البحر فلا يعرف أحدا[٦٥٧] ما يكون من أمرهما بعد ذالك فلمّا رآ ذو القرنين ذالك لحّ إلى الله في المسئلة أن يخبره بما يصنع الطير بتلك الجارية فنزل عليه الملك زِياقيل فقال له «سر على البحر ترا عجبا»

فركب البحر حتّى انتها إلى طرف البحر من خلف جبل عاليّ في الهوى فإذا هو بملك جالس على كرسي وفي اركان الكرسيّ الأربعة أربعة من الحيّات في كلّ ركن حيّة مشدودة إلى أربعة أوتاد والملك يطيل النظر إلى تلك الأوتاد يشدّ بعضا ويرخى بعضا وهذا على رأس جبل عاليّ مشرف على الدنيا ومثّل ذو القرنين نفسه حين واصل إلى الملك كأنّه في السماء العُلُوِّ الجبل فسلم عليه ذو القرنين فردّ عليه السلام فقال له الملك [f. 264] «يا ذا القرنين عجبتُ منك تريد ملك بلاد الملائكة وتشارك الله في ملكه» فقال له ذو القرنين «معاد[٦٥٨] الله أيّها الملك إنّما أنا عبد مأمور طائع لأمر ربّي ومرادي في البلوغ إليك لأسئلك عَنْ أمور أعجبتني ما هي» قال له الملك «وما هي ؟» قال له «هذه [الحيّات][٦٥٩] التي في يديك المشدودات إلى هذه الأوتاد» قال «يا ذا القرنين لولا أن الله عزّ وجلّ أمرني ما أخبرتك أعلم أن هذه الأوتاد مربوطة إليها عروق الأرض كلّها ويلقى الله الرعب في قلوب أهلها وإذا أراد الله ببلاد رخاء أو لِينةً أمرني بأرخى[٦٦٠] [الحيّات][٦٦١] فتلين عروق الأرض كلّها وذلك بقدرة الله تعالى وقضائه» قال له ذو القرنين «ما هذا الجبل العالي ؟» قال له الملك «وهل عرفت صفاهم ؟» قال «نعم» قال «وكيف صفاهم ؟ وكيف مُثِّلَ إليك ؟» قال له «أراه عالى الأطراف واسع الاركان كأنّي أرا حافته محيطة [f. 265] ولا أقدر أن نرا [٦٦٢] أركانه» قال الملك «نعم يا ذا القرنين كذالك هو وهو جبل قاف المحيط بالدنيا وكان رؤوسهما متقاربة في الرأي العيان وأركالهما لا تدرك صفاهم وصفتهم يا ذا القرنين [كصفة][٦٦٣] جفنة مرسية على الماء وكذالك الدنيا كلّها يا ذا القرنين جزيرة في البحر وهذا الجبل محيط بتلك الجزيرة فاسئل عن غير هذا يا ذا القرنين» قال له ذو القرنين «أيّها الملك ما قصّة الجارية المنفقصة من الجوزة والطير الذي يحملها ؟» قال له «يا ذا القرنين الجارية والطير لا يعلم

---

[٦٥٦] في الاصل "ايضا خرجت ايضا"

[٦٥٧] احدّ

[٦٥٨] معاذ

[٦٥٩] من B. في الاصل "حبال"

[٦٦٠] بأرخاء

[٦٦١] من B. في الاصل "حبال"

[٦٦٢] نفهم "ارا"

[٦٦٣] في الاصل "كصيفة"

الجارية المنفقصة من الجوزة والطير الذي يحملها ؟» قال له «يا ذا القرنين الجارية والطير لا يعلم منتهاها إلا الله عزّ وجلّ غير أن الملائكة يتحدثون ويقولون أن الطير طيرا[٦٦٤] يأتي إلى الجنة ويكون فيها بأمر [الله تعالى] وهو الذي يأكله أهل الجنّة ويحيا لهم وكذالك الجارية من جواري الجنّة والله أعلم لا نعلم لهم خبرا غير هذا»

قالِ ذو [٦٦٥] القرنين ثمّ ارتحلنا [f. 266] منها حتّى انتهينا إلى أرض كثيرة الخير واسعة خصيبة الفواكه والنبات مقفرة لا عمارة فيها فرآ ذو القرنين حسنها فأعجبه ما رآ منها فأمر بقوم من الفرس وقوم من الروم وقوم من الترك فأمرهم أن يسكنُ فيها إلى يوم القيامة

ثمّ ارتحل عنهم إلى بلاد كثيرة الفواكه والكهوف والغيران وثمار كثيرة فتعجّب منها ذو القرنين لّما رآ من حُسنها وجمالها وجودها ووسعها وكثرة ثمارها ليس فيها عمارة فسئل الله تعالى أن يعلمه خبر الأرض وإن يأمره بما يفعله فيها فأرسل الله له الملك زياقيل الذي كان ينزل عليه فأعلمه أن الأرض قد خلت[٦٦٦] من كثرة الظلم وإن أهلها كان سكناهم في الكهوف حتّى [سلط الله][٦٦٧] العذاب فذهبوا عن آخرهم وبقيت آثارهم فأقام فيها ذو القرنين من أوّل الصيف [f. 267] إلى آخره وهم يأكلون من ثمارها و[فواكهها][٦٦٨] فلمّا أكلوا ثمارها وفواكهها انتقلوا إلى مثلها من ثمار [الجنّة][٦٦٩] و[التلجُ][٦٧٠] فيها دائم وبردها شديد وأراد ذو القرنين أن يبقى فيها بحرية لحالها ليسكن فيها بعض من جيوشه فلمّا رآ شدّة بردها مع كثرة فواكهها[٦٧١] قال «لا يصبر على هذا إلاّ الروم» فأمر [جزاء][٦٧٢] من الروم فسكنوا فيها وهم فيها إلى يوم القيامة

قال ذو القرنين ثمّ ارتحلنا منها إلى أرض مثلها لا عمارة فيها و لم يسكنها أحد من الخلق إلاّ الجنّ ثمّ أن ذا القرنين مشى فيها بنفسه فرآ فيها أثرا ومساليك[٦٧٣] لم تشبه أثر بني آدم ولا مسالكها ولهم أسواق ومدائن وكرم غير أنّهم ليسوا بظاهرين فسئل الله تعالى أن يعلمه بذالك فنزل عليه الملك

---

[٦٦٤] طيرَ طيرٌ

[٦٦٥] في الاصل "ذو"

[٦٦٦] مَن B . في الاصل "خلقت"

[٦٦٧] من B

[٦٦٨] في الاصل "الفواكيهها" Here and following

[٦٦٩] في الاصل "الاجنة"

[٦٧٠] الثلجُ

[٦٧١] في الاصل "الفواكيهها"

[٦٧٢] في الاصل "جزءا"

[٦٧٣] مسالك

زياقيل فقال له «يا ذا القرنين هذه بلاد الجنّ لم يسلكها [f. 268] احدا[٦٧٤] من بني آدم وخلفها إلاّ البحار ولا خلف البحار إلاّ الظلمة وقد سهل الله عليك السُّلوك في المشرق والمغرب والجوف والقبلة وهذا أرض لم سلكها[٦٧٥] أحد من بني آدم قطّ إلاّ أنت وجنودك فمنّ الله عليك وفضلك على كثير ممّن خلق تفضيلا فيجب عليك أن تشكره وتحمده الذي بلّغك مَرْغُوبَك في الدنيا فسئله أن يبلّغك مقصودك في الآخرة»

ثمّ أَمر ذو القرنين بجمع الكنوز وكتب على كلّ كنوز[٦٧٦] باسمه وعدد ما فيه ومكانه وختم عليه باسمه ثمّ كتب بجميع الكنوز في كتاب وصار بالكتاب منصرفا إلى بلاده فحدّثنا وثيمةُ ابن موسا قال كتب ذو القرنين بجميع الكنوز ثمّ بعثه إلى أمّه بالإسكندريّة وكتب

بسم الله الرحمان الرحيم من ابنك [f. 269] عبد الله نصره الله على [أ]عدائه ووفقه لطاعته أمّا بعد فقد أحصيت جميع الكنوز وكتبت على كلّ كنز بعدّته ثمّ ختمت على كلّ كنز من هذه الكنوز باسمي وكتبت عدّها وعدّة ما فيها في كتاب ثمّ كتبت إليكِ بكتابي هذا بجميع ما تحصّل فيه من العدد و[سيّرتُ][٦٧٧] إليكِ به رجلا منفردا على فرس مجرّد والسّلام عليكِ ورحمة الله وبركاته

ثمّ [سارَ][٦٧٨] جنوده حتّى توسّط أرض الصّين فجاءه كتاب أمّه تُرْشِدُه وتعضده وتهديه وترضى عنه فكتبت إليه في كتابها:

بسم الله الرحمان الرحيم من أمّ عبد الله الإسكندريّ العبد الضعيف الذي لا يقوا إلاّ بقوّة الله قدر وبأمر الله صدَع وبقوّة الله منع وبغناء الله استغني وبهُدَي الله اهتدي يا بُنيّ [f. 270] لا تعجّب فإنّ العُجْبَ في خلفتك والعُجْبَ يوذيك ولا تعجل فإنّ العَجْلَة تبليك فلا تَدَعْ الغِبْطَة فيك مطمعا ولا [هرس][٦٧٩] فيك وأعلم أنّك عن قليل تحول عمّا أنت عليه يا بُنَيّ إيَّاك والشُّحَّ فإنّ الشُّحَّ يوذيك وإيَّاك والطَمعُ فإنّ الطَمعُ يوذيك وقد وصلني كتابك بجميع ما كتبتَ فيه بعدَّة كنوزك بيد رجل منفرد على فُرسٍ مجرّدٍ فالله يهديك ويُرشدك ويوفّقك والسّلام

---

[٦٧٤] احدٌ

[٦٧٥] يسلكها

[٦٧٦] كنز

[٦٧٧] في الاصل "صيّرتُ"

[٦٧٨] في الاصل "صارَ "

[٦٧٩] في الاصل "هرص". Corriente: *ser voraz o glotón.* أو يمكن نفهم "هوس"؟

وكان من سيرته يسير في البلاد ويدخل متنكرًا لا يعرفه أحدا[٦٨٠] ويَجْلس عند حُكَمائها وقضاتها فإذا رآ اشيئا[٦٨١] أنكره [و]قضى فيه بحكمه فكان كذالك في كلّ مدينة يدخلها فجلس إلى رجل من حُكّام إحدى المدائن متنكرا لا يعرفه أحد فدخل عليه رجلان يختصمان فقال [f. 271] [أحدهم][٦٨٢] للحاكم «اسمع مقالِتي وفّقك الله» فقال الحاكم «تكلّم» فقال له «إنّي اشتَرَيْتُ من هذا داراً من دياره فلمّا سَكَنْتُهَا وجدتُ فيها مالاً كثيرا فدعوته أن يأخذه منّي وأبي أن يأخذه وامتنع وقال ' والله ما لي فيه شيْءٌ'» فقال له «ما تقول أنت ؟» فقال له خصيمه «نعم كانت لي داراً فابتعتها له فوالله ما كنزته وما لي فيه شيْءٌ» فقال لهما القاضي «أ لكما أولاد ؟» فقال أحدهما «لي ولد» وقال الأخر «لي ابنة» فقال لهم «زوج أنت ابنك من ابنت خصيمك هذا ويكون ذلك المال لهما» فلمّا سمع ذو القرنين ذلك تعجّب منهما ومن الحكام وقال «ما ظننت أن أحدا في الأرض يحكم بمثل هذا ولا مثل هؤلاَء الرجلين» فقال القاضي «وهل في الأرض من يحكم بغير هذا ؟» قال [f. 272] ذو القرنين «نعم» ثمّ انصرف ذو القرنين

حدّثنا عبد الله ابن ابى بكر عن عبد الله ابن زياد عن ابى صالح عن قتادة أنّه قال لمّا توجّه ذو القرنين منصرفا من أرض الصِّين نُعِيَت إليه نفسُه واشتكا من مرض أصابه فأتاه آت في منامه فقال له «يرحمك الله إنّك تموت على أرض جديد[ة] فوقها كلّ أخضر» فلمّا أصبح قال لكاتبه «اكتب لي كتابا إلى أمّي و[اعرضهُ][٦٨٣] عليّ وعزيها فيّ ثمّ اقرأه عَلَيَّ» قال فكتب كتابا يقُول فيه:

> بسم الله الرحمان الرحيم من عبد الله ذي القرنين ابن نّباش ابن الضّحاك ابن عويلم ابن سام ابن نوح عليه السّلام إلى أمّي أعزّها الله أمّا بعد فإن هذا [الكتاب][٦٨٤] إليكِ رفيق أهل الأرض ببدَنِهِ قليلا ورفيق الملائكة بروحه كثيرا إلى الأمّ ذاتِ الصّفا[ء] [f.273] التي لم تُمتَّع ثمرتها في دار الخراب وهي بمجاورة عَمّا قليل في دار البُعْد يا أماه هل رأيتِ معطيا لم يأخذ ومهدي لا يعاطا ؟ يا أمّاه اسئلكِ برحمتك لي وبوُدّ ولادتكِ إيّاي هل وجدتِ شيء من الخلق قراراً ثابتا ؟ يا أمّاه ألم تنظري إلى الشجرة كيف يخضر وَرَقُهَا ويخرج ثمرها وتلتف أغصانُها ثمّ لا يلبث الغصن أن يتهشّمْ

---

[٦٨٠] أحدٌ

[٦٨١] شيئاً

[٦٨٢] في الاصل "اخدهم"

[٦٨٣] من B. في الاصل "ارضهُ"

[٦٨٤] في الاصل "الكتابي"

والورق أن يتحطّمْ والثَمْرُ أن يُتَمْ ؟ يا أمّاه ألم تنظري إلى النبات الأخضر كيف يَبتهِج النّظر ساعة ثمّ يَمْسَا هشيما ؟ يا أمّاه [أ] لا تنظرْ إلى النّهار كيف يضيء فإذا أمْسَا جاء من بعده ليلٌ مُظَلمٌ ؟ يا أمّاه ما رأيتِ من الماء العَذْبَ كيف يخالطه الماء المالح المتغيّر ؟ يا أمّاه ما رأيتِ إلى الخلق كيف يغترُّوا بالدنيا فأمّا مولود يموت [f. 274] وأمّا شيخٌ مسرف في [الذنوب][٦٨٥] وكلّ من خلق الله تعالى لا بُدَّ له من الفناء ؟ يَا امّاه ما تنظري إلى هذه الدار كيف قبالها روحي بأهلكِ لسْتِ لهم بدارٍ ؟ يا أمّاه هل رأيتِ مستودعا لا يرُدُّ وَديعتَهُ ؟ يا أمّاه إن كان [لأحَدٍ][٦٨٦] حقّ بالبكاء فلتَبْكِ السماء على نجومها والهوى على ظُهُوره والأرض على أوليائها وليبك الإنسان على نفسه يا أمّاه قد علمتِ وتيقنتِ أن الذي تسيير[٦٨٧] إليْه خير من الذي خرجت عنه أَخْرُجُ من دار الغروب والهمومُ والحزن والتعب والأعراض والأمراض والفناء إلى دار البقاء والجزاء والسّلام عليك ورحمة الله وبركاته من دار دليلة[٦٨٨] زائلة إلى دار طويلة باقية

ثمّ طوي الكتاب كاتبه بعد ما قرأه عليه وعزّاها في نفسه وبعث الكتاب [f. 275] إلى أمّه فلمّا وصلها قرأته وجعلت تبكى ثمّ ضمّخت الكتاب بالْعَنْبَرْ وحَبَسَتْهُ عندها

حدّثنا وثيمة ابن موسى عن سفيان ابن عيينة أنّه قال حجّ إبراهيم وإسماعيل البيت الحرام ماشِيَيْنَ فطمع ذو القرنين أن يدعوا الله تعالى له إبراهيم فسأله ذالك فقال له إبراهيم «يا ذا القرنين افسدْ بئرِ الكعبة» فقال له «يا خليل الله لم يكن فساده عن أمري و لم يخبرني أحد بفساده» ثمّ أخذ ذو القرنين فوضع السِّلاح وطاف بالبيت فأهدا له إبراهيم بَقَراً وغَنَماً

فلمّا نعيت إليه نفسه بالموت جمع علمائَه ووزرائَه ودور مملكته ثمّ أمر لهم بالذهب والفضّة والثياب الحسنة وأعطا لجميع جنوده عطاءً حسناً جزيلاً وفرّق عليهم [f. 276] [الأموال][٦٨٩] وأعطاهم

---

[٦٨٥] في الاصل "الدنوب"

[٦٨٦] في الاصل "أحدا"

[٦٨٧] اسير

[٦٨٨] ذليلة

[٦٨٩] في الاصل "الاموال"

الخيل ثمّ أمر عليهم [رجلاً صالحاً][٦٩٠] وأمرهم أن يرجعوا إلى بلادهم ثمّ توفّى وجُعِلَ على ترس من حديد وجُعِل على الترس ثوبا أخضراً[٦٩١] من تحته أغصان الرّيحان ثم جُعِلَ ودُفِنَ رحمه الله

وفي رواية أخرى قال أبو عبد الملك حدّثنا ابن [المسيّب][٦٩٢] و[الكَلْبيّ][٦٩٣] قال وصل ذو القرنين إلى بيت المقدّس ونزل بموضع يقال له دَرْمَةُ[٦٩٤] الْجَنْدَلْ فأدركه فيه أَجلُهُ فمات رحمه الله

قال أبو إسحاق وحدّثنا أبو عبد الملك عن أبي رَزْقُ الهمدانيّ عن مجاهد قال ما مات ذو القرنين حتّىَ وصل بيت المقدّس قال وسمعتُ أبا عبد الله يقول حدّثنا مقاتل عن وهب ابن مُنَبِّه أنّه قال ما مات ذو القرنين حتّى وصل بيت [f. 277] المقدّس قال وحدّثنا [ابو] إسحاق عن أبي عبد الملك عن عبد الله ابن المبارك ابن فضّالة أن الحسن حدّثهم أنّه قال ما مات ذو القرنين حتّى وصل بيت المقدّس وكان بعض الرُّوات يقولون أعطاه الله تبارك وتعالى هذه القوّةَ كلّها وهو ابن اثنين وثلاثين سنة قال أبو عبد الملك حدّثني من أدركته أنّه قال حين نزل [بذي][٦٩٥] القرنين الموت كتب إلى أمّه كتابا يذكر فيه:

هذا كتاب ذي القرنين إلى والدته أمّا بعد يا والدتي فقد أردتُ أن تصنع صنيعا
وتُكثر فيه من الطّعام وتنادي عليه جمع النّساءِ ولا يأكل طعامكِ ولا يَبْصِرُ عندكِ إلاّ
إمرأة لم يصبها ثِكْلٌ

[f. 278] قال فوصل الكتاب إلى أمّه فصنعت صنيعا لم تصنع مثله قطّ ثمّ أرسلت إلى جميع النساء وجلست على سرير ملكها فاجتمعنّ[٦٩٦] إليها النساء من كلّ ناحية فقالت لهنَّ «لا يدخل أحد منكنّ داري ولا يأكل طعامي إلاّ إمرأة ليس بها ثِكْلٌ» قال فكلٌّ من أتاها من النّساء تسئلها فتقول لها «هل أصابكِ ثِكْلٌ ؟» فتقول لها «نعم قد ثكِلْتُ بابني» قال ثمّ تدعوا بأخرى تسئلها فتقول لها «هل أصابك ثِكْلٌ ؟» فتقول لها «نعم» ثمّ تدعوا بأخرى فتقول لها «هل أصابكِ ثِكْلٌ ؟» فتقول لها «ثكِلْتُ بوالدي» قال فطلبت جميع النساء من لم يصبها ثِكْلٌ فلم تجدها إلاّ كلّ من سألتها أجابتها بابيها أو بزوجها أو بابنها أو بأخيها فلمّا رأَتْ [f. 279] ذالك وصحّ عندها استوجعتَ واحتسبته عند الله تبارك وتعالى فمات بعد ذالك رحمة الله عليه وهذا ما بلغنا من خبر ذي القرنين قال مقاتل حدّثني بعض من أدركته

---

[٦٩٠] في الاصل "رجل صالح"

[٦٩١] اخضرَ

[٦٩٢] في الاصل "السّايب"

[٦٩٣] في الاصل "الكَلْبيُّ"

[٦٩٤] دومة

[٦٩٥] في الاصل "بدي"

[٦٩٦] فاجتمعت

أنّه قال سقطت عنه النُّبُوَّةَ لأنّه لم يُرْسَلْ من دار النُّبُوَّة وإنّما أرسل في مشارق الأرض ومغاربها قال فقالوا له يا أبا الحسن يعني مقاتلا وأين هي دار النُّبُوَّة والرِّسَالَةِ ؟ قال ما بعث الله نبيّاً قطُّ إلاّ من بيت مكّة اعزّها الله أو بيت المقدّس فمنها أصُولَهُمْ وكان دار النُّبوّة ما بين هاتين البقعتين وبين العلماء في ذالك كلاما كثيراً[٦٩٧] هل هو نبيٌّ أو وليٌّ وصلّى الله على سيّدنا محمّد وعلى آله وصحبه وسلّم تسليما أمين ياَ ربّ العلمين[٦٩٨] ...

[٦٩٧] كلام كثير

[٦٩٨] العالمين

فهرس الاسماء

Please note that the references given below are to folio numbers of Ms. A indicated in brackets throughout the text.

فهرس المواضع

Please note that the references given below are to folio numbers of Ms. A indicated in brackets throughout the text.

Sample of the Variants

٣:٥ [رواية]٢ رواها ; [زياد] زيد

٣:٧ [اجرى] اسمع ; [علينا ... جزيل] علينا فضله جزيل

٣:٩ [علينا ... وفضلنا] علينا سبحانه بالنبى الاكرم مُحمّد سَيد العَرب وَالعجم صلى الله عليه وَ سَلّمُ و فضلنا

٣:١٠ [ظلام] سوَادُ

٣:١٢ [ما يكون] ما لم يكون

٣:١٣ [وهو يميتَ الأحياء] وامات الاحياء ; [فمهّدها] فمدها

٣:١٤ [فسكن كلّ ذالك] فسكن ذالك

٣:١٤ [كان...ولا حين] كان وهو الباقى بعد كل شىء مكان ولا مكان ولا حين

٣:١٦ [واحد واحْداني]

٣:١٧ [حدود] حروث

٣:١٨ [بهرت] برْهنت ; [علامته...غيره] علامته وظهرت عَلى كل شىء دلالته غيره

٤:١ [علم...الصغير] علمه محيط بكُل شىء (اذلا وابدا ؟) من الصغير

٤:٣ [لله فهو] لله تعلى فهو

٤:٤ [نبيّ] رسول الله

٤:٤ [صلعم...يظفر] صلعم فلا يبلغ داعيه ما مُوله ولا يظفر

٤:٥ [بشكره وحمده] بشكر الله وحمده

٤:٦ [محمد] سييدنا محمد

٤:٦ [عبده...أرسل] عبده نبى الله المصطفى وحبيبه المرتضى ارسله

٤:٧ [الضلالة...قال] الضلالة والردا خاتم الانبياء وامام الاصفياء زاده الله تشريفا و تكريما وصلى الله عليه وعَلى وسلم تسليما قَال

٤:٩ [قال...حدّثنا] قال عبْد الرحمن بن زند حدثنا

٤:١٠ [نعم] ; [أبي]

٤:١٤ [بالكلام] بالطعام ; [أبي]

٤:١٤ [لعلك] انك ; [على نبيّكم] عليه

٤:١٨ [جوابه] كلامه ; [وكتب]

٤:١٩ [عليه السلام] صلعم

٥:٣ [قدراً] ذكراً

٥:٥ [وبيّنتَ] وفصلت

The variants are noted by page and line number.

The bracketed text refers to manuscript A. Beside the bracketed text is the corresponding passage in B. If there is nothing beside the bracketed text, one understands that the word or phrase is not found in B.

٥:٩ [نسبه] نسبه ومَاسببه

٥:١١ [الله] الله تعلى ; [معانيها] جوابها و معانيها

٥:١٥ [ثمّ إلى الصبح]

٥:١٨ [فاغتمّوا أصحاب رسول] فاغتمّ رسول

٥:٢٠ [في غمٍّ شديد]

٦:٣ [ماَ رآ ربّي وما أمرني] ما امرني

٦:٤ [فقال له جبريلِ عليه السّلام: «يا محمّد ، عاتبك ربُّك بقولك الذي رتّبته لنفسك دون أرادت ربّك . يا محمّد ، لم قلت للنصارى]

٦:٧ [عزّ وجلّ] ; [لمّا حقق على نفسه العتاب لنسيانه لمشيئة الله . قال قتادة: عاتب الله نبيّه صلعم بأيتين في كتاب الله قوله]

٦:١١ [عزّ وجلّ] تعلى

٦:١٢ [قوله]

٦:١٣ [أبي]

٦:١٤ [قيماً] فيما

٦:١٥ [أعلمه] اعلم جبريل عليه السلام النبى ; [صلعم...وجهه] صلعم بنزول الوحى نار وجهه

٦:١٨ [سعد]

٧:١ [كان] رايت

٧:٢ [حقّا]

٧:٣ [أعلمني] بشرنى واعلمنى ; [ربّي]

٧:٤ [عزّ وجلّ] جلّ ذكره

٧:٧ [طبع على قلوبهم]

٧:٨ [جملة]

٧:١٢ [آية] آيات

٧:١٦ [الله] الله تعلى

٧:١٧ [جابرقا] جابلقا ; [الظلمة] بحر الظلمات

٧:١٨ [انتها] بلغ

٧:١٩ [إِنَّا مَكَّنَّا لَهُ فِي الأَرْضِ وَءَاتَيْنَاهُ مِن كُلِّ شَيْءٍ سَبَباً فَأَتْبَعَ سَبَباً]

٨:٢ [ربّي] الله

٨:٢ [الخمسة]

٨:٣ [علم...الله] علم الله تعلى في قوله عز وجل ان الله

٨:٥ [أن الله عليم خبيرٌ]

٨:٥ [عزّ وجلّ] جل ذكره

٨:٦ [إِنَّمآ أَنتَ مُنذرو مَن يَخْشَاها كَأَنَّهُمْ يَوْمَ يَرَوْنَهَا لَمْ يَلْبَثُوا إِلاَّ عَشِيَّةً أَوْ ضُحاهَا]

٨:٨ [ذكر]

٨:١٠ [قالوش...عبد] قالوش بن اسحاق قال عبد

٨:١٢ [سئل] سالنا

٨:١٢ [من شأنه وقصّته وما جرا له]

٨:١٦ [ذو القرنين]

٨:١٨ [بالحكمة...وكانت] بالحكمة وهو صغيرا وقد بلغ في الحكمة مبلغا عظيما

٨:١٩ [بذالك] في ذلك

٨:٢١ [يتخلّق] يتعلق

٩:١ [قال]

٩:٢ [أرسطاطاليس] ; [يفتّش] يفتش ويبحث ; [أخباره ويختبره لمّا يرا ويسمع من كلامه . فما زال أرسطاطاليس يَفتّش عليه وعلى]

٩:٤ [ما] مما

٩:٦ [نفسه...وقال] نفسه وولاه وقلده أمر الملك وتخلى له عنه وقال ; [أوّل] اولى واحد

٩:٧ [وأحقّ فيه] ; [يطيعوا...نزع] يُطيعوا امره ونزع

٩:١٢ [تبارك]

٩:١٣ [موضع] ; [بناها وفي] بناها وقيل في

٩:١٤ [سعد بن]

٩:١٥ [اسمه] يسمّى ب ; [بسياطين] بسطياطين

٩:١٦ [وقيل كان ابن عجوز و لم يكن لها ولد غيره]

٩:١٧ [الله]

٩:١٨ [يُهنّونه] يهابونه

١٠:١ [علم] ; [الروميّة] الروم ; [في ذالك الزمان]

١٠:٢ [يجيبه] ; [ما] مَن

١٠:٣ [أجابه] يجيبه

١٠:٧ [امر] انس

١٠:٧ [تهدم] تنهدمُ

١٠:٨ [لأنّه متى حاول أمر المعصيّة] ; [بفوات] بالوفاة

١٠:٩ [من نفسه] لنفسه

١٠:١١ [طلبهم] طلبه

١٠:١٣ [مضرب] من طرف

١٠:١٤ [بالرّوميّة] ; [اسكندر] اسكندرى ; [وهو احمد] ; [ومعنا اسّاس عبّاس]

١٠:١٥ ; [كلّ] جميع

١٠:١٦ [من النّاس]

١٠:١٩ [ما...أسكنها] مَا ذكر أسكنها

١٠:٢١ [طلبه] يطلبهُ

١٠:٢٢ [روميّة] روم

١١:٣ [مراسلة...على] مراسلة وحصنا افضل ما يبتغى عَلى

١١:٥ [لَوْلب] لوّب

١١:٧ [بالقدوم عليها] بالغد و

١١:٩ [انصرف] سار ; [به]

١١:١١ [العظيم...الى] العظيم الاعظم الاجل الى

١١:١٣ [الذي] ما

١١:١٦ [مسئلة] السؤال

١١:١٧ [فأتاه] فأتى به ; [بالخير] الخير

١١:١٨ [صام] قام ; [يُجنبه] يجزره ؟

١١:١٩ [مُصلّاه...ابن] مصلاه ساجدا ومتضرعا وراغبا الى الله تعلى وكان ابن ; [ساجدا وراكعا ومتضرّعا الله تعالى] ; [ثمّ] اذ

١١:٢٠ [مطيعا] مطاعا ; [وكان]

١٢:١ [ثمّ طار به في الهوا ساعة زمانيّة فأخرج رأسه من تحت جناحه]

١٢:٧ [ذلك] تلك

١٢:٧ [وقد احاط بها البحر والدّنيا ياذا القرنين كلّها]

١٢:٨ [في وسط البحر والبحر حمل الجزيرة والتحر حملته القُدْرَة يا ذا القرنين أبلا تتعجّب] ; [ربّك]

١٢:١١ [الملك] زياقيل ; [البحر اوسع من الجزيرة والجزيرة في وسط البحر]

١٢:١٣ [وأقوى خيلك] ; [عليه] عنه

١٢:١٣ [يُعلّمُكَ...فلا]يعلمك ومَن كان الله دليله ونصاره فلا

١٢:١٦ [فكيف الإهي تكلّفني ما لا أطيق]

١٢:١٨ [بحار] بحر

١٢:١٩ [فقال له الملك زياقيل] فقال له

١٢:٢٠ [أكلّفُ] يكلف

١٢:٢١ [معاني] ; [تعقل] تفهم

١٢:٢٢ [البلاد] الارْض

١٢:٢٣ [على] الا على

١٣:١ [ألقى...ذِكْرِكَ] القى في قلُوب أصْحابك الصَبر حيث ما سلكوا وفي قلوب ذكرك

١٣:٢ [ومن] وكذلك

١٣:٣ [هيبة] سبب

١٣:١٢ [مع ذي القرنين] معه

١٣:١٤ [أمر] امرهمْ

١٣:١٥ [تعالى] تبارك وتعالى

١٣:١٥ [سفر فلمّا أصبح] سفر فعولوا [و]قالوا لهُ «الى اين تريد ؟» فقال لهمْ اللهى يسبب لي سَبَباً يدلني عَلى مُراد فَلما اصبَحَ

١٣:١٨ [الله] الله تعالى

١٣:١٩ [العاسكير] جَميع العاسَكير ; [تناهز] تنهم ؟

١٣:٢٠ [وتنحنحها]

١٣:٢١ [الماء] وجه الماء

١٣:٢٣ [ان]

١٣:٢٣ [أبو]

١٣:٢٤ [بالحق ما] بالحق بشيرا ونذيرا ما ; [كما ...بقدرة] كما تضرب عَلى وجه الارض بقدرة

١٤:٢ [وكانت] و هَيَ كانت

١٤:٣ [في حينه]

١٤:٥ [كما] كَيف ; [ربي ... هو] ربّي عَنُ جبريل هو

١٤:٦ [يادون] بادون ; [حيران ... هو] حيران بن اروم ابن فاروم وهو

١٤:٨ [فكانوا] فكان

١٤:٩ [وهو ابن فروم] وهو روم بن روم بن فروم

١٤:١١ ابن [ابو]

١٤:١٤ [صلوات الله عليه وسلامه] عليه السلام

١٤:١٦ [احب الله] احب الله تعلى

١٤:٢٠ [مقفرة] قفرة

١٤:٢١ [وكهوفها]

١٥:١ [مصعدا من] مصعدا في الهوى من ; [أحد] احد من الخلق

١٥:٦ [قال فأتاه] فاتاه ; [عزّ وجلّ]

١٥:٩ [الممدودة] المعَدة

١٥:١٠ [شهادة أن] ; [أسرع مما] لانه

١٥:١٠ [كان ... صناعة] كان حين نهض للسّفر امر كل اهل صناعة

١٥:١١ [باثني عشر ألف]

١٥:١٢ [منها في صنعة العود ... والعود]

١٥:١٥ [والعبيد ... فانفتح] وَالعبيد ولهُ حركات في لوَالب كثيرة دارت بهم وَ القصر مبنى على سرير مستعمل من اصناف الرخام دَارت اللوالب بِالسرير والقصر مبنى عَلَى لواليب عَاليَة مستعملة عَلى وَسط السرير فلمّا يقرب من السرير لوح ولا نفس الا تحركت تلك اللوَاليب فَتحرك اللوْلب وتحرك القصر لتحريكهم فَدار القصر (فمسَكته ؟) الالوَاح التي في مدينة قصر ذي القرنين فوقف القَصر فدنا منهُ ذو القرنين فنظرَ الى بابه فاذا عليُه مَكتوب اشهد ان لا اله الا الله واشهد ان محمدا عبده ورسوله صلا الله عليه وَسلم فَقالها ذو القرنين فانفتح

١٦:١٦ [آدم] آدم عليه السلام ; [وتنسلوا]

١٦:١٧ [حتّى] ثم

١٦:٢٠ [الله] الله تعلى

١٧:١ [تعالى]

١٧:٢ [على] عن ; [لا يحرقهم] لا يهلكون ; [هلكت ... فأغرقهم] هلكت الامم تلك الامم الماضية خلق آدم وَ كثر نسله فَكانت القرون الذين بعده منهم مومنون وَاكثرهم (كما ؟) فرُون فبعث الله فيه نُوحا عليه السلام فدعا قومه لدين الله القويم فطغوا فَدَعا عليهم نوح فاغرقهم

١٧:٥ [الانبياء] الدنيا

١٧:٧ [يكرمه] يكرمك

١٧:٩ [ربّ العالمين] ; [بعون الله]

١٧:١٣ [أبو]

١٧:١٤ [نحو] مثل

١٧:١٦ [مسيرة]

١٧:١٧ [تَل] شيء

١٧:١٨ [الغرب] الشرق

١٧:٢٠ [حوائفهم] جوائب ؟

١٧:٢١ [تجارتهم ... فلمّا] تجارتهم وكانت جنود ذي القرنين ثلاثون مابة الف دون ارباب الصنائع فلمّا

١٨:٢ [يعلمونها] يعرفونها

١٨:٣ [الله] الله عزّ وجلّ

١٨:٤ [كلّ ... فلمّا] كلّ جهة وقال في بعض الروَايات يخرج من كلّ باب مابة الف فلما

١٨:٧ [ثالثا] اخر ; [يقال له ... يسار المدينة] يقال له شماميش بماية الف عَلى يسار المدينة

١٨:٩ [يمرّ] يخرج

١٨:١٣ [الريح] الريح من كل جهة

١٨:١٤ [تَفرْقَعَتْ] خفقان

١٨:١٥ [جنود] جيُوش ; [لمّا] ممّا ; [ضرب] صوت

١٨:١٦ [أنهم الى] أنهم اجابوه ب

١٨:١٧ [أبو عبد الملك] عبد الملك الملشوني ; [أجابتهم] اجابتهم اربعين يوماً

١٨:١٨ [فانا ... وما كان] فانا متبعون لك وطائعون لامرك وعاملون بدينك وما كان

١٩:١ [جنودنا] جنوحك ; [ثم] و

١٩:٢ [تعلمنا] نريد ان تعلمنا ; [تسوء إليه] تسوء معه

١٩:٣ [أبو عبد الملك الملشوني] الراوى

١٩:٤ [والضرب ... فرجعوا] ومن تعبد ومن تعاقب و من تجازيه فقال لهم اعبد الله ولا شرك به شيئا واعاقب من كفَر بالله تعلى واما من آمن بالله فلا سبيل لي اليه الا بالخير والامان مني ومن مني فرجعوا

١٩:٨ [وشهدوا] وذالك بعد ما شهدوا ; [أبو عبد الملك الملشوني] عبد الملك

١٩:١١ [ثمّ أتبع سبباً]

١٩:١٢ [أبو عبد الملك الملشوني] عبد الملك

١٩:١٣ [عذاب الجنود] الجنود

١٩:١٣ [وهو ... ثم يُردُّ] وهو لها والرعب منها ثم يرد

١٩:١٦ [أبو عبد الملك الملشوني] عبد الملك ; [يريد] سعيد

١٩:١٨ [امه] عمه ; [بالليل وحده وخلف عسكره]

٢٠:١ [جلّ ذكره] تعلى

٢٠:٣ [مثلها] احسا منها ولا مثلها

٢٠:٥ [والهيبة]

٢٠:٦ [في عين ... فأذا] في عين الذي تغرب فيها وجدها وجدها [sic] تغرب في عيْن حَمِية وهي عين طينها اسود يفور
ماوهاَ ويغلى كغليان القدور عَلى النار فاذا

٢٠:٨ [تكون] يكون ; [الدنيا قد ماتوا] مدينة كلها ماتوا

٢٠:٩ [لهم وقت أبدا]

٢٠:١١ [ذي القرنين ... وقال] ذي القرنين من ذلك وقال

٢٠:١١ [صوت ... تهليلهم] صوْت اهل المدينة بالتضرع والتهليل

٢٠:١٢ [المغرب ... الشمس] المغرب من شدة وقوع الشمس

٢٠:١٤ [جابرصا] جابلقا ; [جابلقا] جابرصا

٢٠:٢٠ [أقامته ... بلدنا] اقامته فان ارتحل عن بلدنا

٢٠:٢١ [نعم]

٢١:١ [يا رسول ذي القرنين]

٢١:٢ [مختلف عن] مختلف الان عن

٢١:٤ [لو رأيته ... فقال] لو رايته رأَيت علمً كثيرا وادبا وحلماً وشرفا وكرما ووقارا فَقال

٢١:٧ [لرأيت عظيما] لرأيت شيئا عظيما

٢١:١٤ [فيمن] لمن

٢١:١٦ [ملكه ؟«قال له ... باتباع] ملكه ؟ «قال له العدل في الاحكام والصدق في الاقوال والوفَاء بالعهد قال فيمَ يهدم الملك
قال باتباع

٢١:١٧ [الحكم] الاتباع

٢١:٢٠ [ويصبر] ويرضى ويصبر

٢١:٢١ [«فمن أنت منه وما هو منك ؟» قال «أنا منه و هو منّي ؟»

٢٢:٣ [كيف يميل] وما تقول في ذي القرنين كيف يميل

٢٢:٥ [صانع] صانع به

٢٢:١٠ [عضدا] عقدا

٢٢:١١ [عقدهم]

٢٢:١٢ [واصفح قال له الله عليك قال نعم]

٢٢:١٧ [المدينة] القريه

٢٢:١٨ [أمري] عمري

٢٢:١٩ [جودب] جندب

٢٢:٢٠ [ألف ... عامًا]

٢٣:١ [رويش] زوبش

٢٣:٣ [الكرذ] الكرخ

٢٣:٤ [داروم] دروم

٢٣:٩ [في الحجاب]

٢٣:١٤ [بذالك ... مكانها] بذلك فلَما وَصلت الثريا الى موضعها ومكانها

٢٣:١٦ [من] ام

٢٣:١٧ [لا] لو

٢٣:٢٠ [أن] عن

٢٣:٢١ [يجابه] يشبه

٢٤:١ [عليهما ... مبلغ تلك الدوابتان]

٢٤:٨ [يلاقي] يباشر

٢٤:١١ [احبار ... دخل] احبار رضى الله تعلى عنه دخل ; [أمر ... ابواقهم] أمر اصحابه ان يضربوا ابواقهم

٢٤:١٢ [ولا مخدرة]

٢٤:١٣ [يرفع] يصرف

٢٤:١٤ [وهو قاعد على شغله]

٢٤:١٦ [وحيله وأولياؤه]

٢٤:١٧ [كثيرة] عظاما

٢٤:١٨ [قطعت] انرثوت؟

٢٤:١٩ [أعدلهم]

٢٥:١ [عليّ من ... أنا وعيالي»] عليّ في صغري من مالهم وثلث انفقه على عيالى وهوَ الذى اسلفه فان طال عمرى معهم واحتجت اليهم رَدوا عليّ سلفى والثلث الاخر اعيش به انا وعيالى

٢٥:٣ [القرنين ... الملك] القرنين أيها الشيخ انك لحليمُ واحب ؟ ان اوليك عَلى هذه القرية وَانى لاظنك ان تقيم بها حدود الله تعلى فولاه هوَ والشيخ وَامر اهل المدينة بالسمع والطاعة لهما فسمعوا قولهما واطاعوا امرهما قال عبد الملك

٢٥:٧ [روق] زرق

٢٥:٨ [فهم ... من هَلَك] ; [من قوم ... الناجين] ; [هود] هود عليه السلام

٢٥:٩ [البحار...حتى] البحار فاقاموا بيه زمان حياته؟ عليه السلام حتى ; [الله الكفار ونجا] الله من كَفر من قومه ونجا ; [لم] ما

٢٥:١٠ [فهم في ذلك] فيبقوا هنالك

٢٥:١٢ [صحة] صحبة

٢٥:١٥ [بسراب] بضرب ; [او؟ يريهم] ان يليهم

٢٥:١٦ [فمشت] فمرّت

٢٥:١٧ [شعاري] شفارى ; [قبلهم]

٢٥:١٩ [لا بقاء لنا فيها]

٢٥:٢١ [فعسى] فعسى ان ; [فألقا ... السفن]

٢٦:٢ [الريح]

٢٦:٣ [البحر] السّفن

٢٦:٥ [الله] الله تعلى

٢٦:٦ [وَسْعِهَا] واتساعها ; [ومثلها]

٢٦:٧ [زمان] وقت ; [نبت على أحسن نبات] نبت نبات حسنا

٢٦:٩ [غرسوا ... اقاموا] غرسوا الاشجار فنبتوا على احسن نبات واقاموا

٢٦:٩ [بالاحتماع ... وطال] بالاحتماع مع بعضهم وطال

٢٦:١٠ [بينهم] مع بعضهم

٢٦:١٢ [أي] على ; [أنا] نحن

٢٦:١٥ [من]

٢٦:١٦ [ممن] عن ; [من أيّ الامم هم] من هم من الامم

٢٦:١٧ [أهلهما] هم

٢٧:٢ [أبو]

٢٧:٤ [الله] الله تعلى

٢٧:٥ [وعلّمه] معلمه

٢٧:٦ [على طهر] ; [ويقص] وهو يقص ; [أي يتبعه]

٢٧:٧ [ذكر] ذكره

٢٧:٨ [آدمي] أحد ; [وصهول]

٢٧:٩ [الورس] الورد ; [نهر] واد

٢٧:١٢ [بمن هناك]

٢٧:١٢ [بعضهم] بعض اصحابه

٢٧:١٣ [وما] ومن

٢٧:١٥ [حافاتها] صفتها

٢٧:١٦ [أعلموه ... عامرة]

٢٧:١٧ [فكتب اليهم] فيه

٢٧:١٨ [الله] الله تعلى

٢٨:١ [الطغيان] الضلالة والطغيان ; [الله] الله تعلى

٢٨:٣ [الى] بيد ; [اتاهم] انتهى اليهم

٢٨:٤ [مجيبا لدعوته] جوَاباً يقولون فيه

٢٨:٩ [اولياء] لاولياء

٢٨:١١ [باريش] اهل باريش ; [ثم]

٢٨:١٣ [ومن] ومن كان

٢٨:١٤ [حتى] وصار حتى

٢٨:١٥ [اعيالهم] برحالهم

٢٨:١٧ [من الانبياء الذين كانوا بعثوا] بعث الله

٢٨:٢١ [امرهم]

٢٨:٢٣ [منها] عنها

٢٨:٢٤ [وهي] وكانت ; [ولا تعد ولا يعلم] ; [عدّتهم] عددهم

٢٩:١ [ليس منهم] لم يكن ; [لربّه] لله تعلى

٢٩:٤ [في أثر] ; [الله] الملك

٢٩:٥ [اليها] اليهم ; [فخرج بنا الى قتال القوم]

٢٩:٦ [تفانت] التقت

٢٩:٧ [هذه]

٢٩:٨ [من بعضنا]

٢٩:٩ [بلدنا] بلادنا ; [منّا] عندنا

٢٩:١٥ [فيهم] منهم

٢٩:١٧ [بالله] مع الله

٢٩:١٨ [مخاين] خاين

٢٩:١٩ [ليس] لا ; [تغلق بها] ; [واحرص]

٢٩:٢٠ [الحكام] القضاة

٢٩:٢١ [الحكام] القضاة

٢٩:٢٢ [فكانت] فكان

٣٠:١ [قال ... القديم]

٣٠:٥ [لأن ... المال] ; [بين] من

٣٠:٦ [بنا المعاش] ; [فينا] لنا

٣٠:٨ [من قلوبنا]

٣٠:٩ [تحتاجون] تختلفون

٣٠:١٢ [السدّى] النبى صلعم ; [فتلك] فهذا

٣٠:١٣ [وارتحل] وبه ارتحل ; [يقوم] يصعد ; [فصاروا يوما وليلة]

٣٠:١٦ [ذهبا] ارتفعا ; [بطول ارتفاعهما]

٣٠:١٧ [مستوية] وهو مستوية

٣٠:١٨ [انتها ذو القرنين و] ; [منهما] بينهما

٣٠:٢٢ [ومائتان] ومابة ; [الله] الله تعلى

٣١:١ [الارتضى] الحق

٣١:٢ [ونحن طائعون]

٣١:٣ [فيعتون] فيعبون ; [فكانوا علينا] الينا ; [يسبّونا] يسلبون اموالنا

٣١:٥ [الله] ; [شود] ثمود

٣١:٨ [بارش] تاريش

٣١:١١ [وقد]

٣١:١٢ [مكوّرة] كورة ; [لمعودها] ; [عليه القدم] عليها للصعود قدم

٣١:١٤ [بين] الا من بين

٣١:١٥ [مجرا] مجريها هذه الأمور ; [غيره]

٣١:١٦ [الله] الله تعلى

٣١:٢٠ [الضلالة و]

٣١:٢١ [يقوم] يطاق

٣٢:٤ [بالله] بالخالق ; [السّموات]

٣٢:٥ [شديد ولاكنكم] شديد والشاب المرسول اليْكم والى (خيركم؟) من ذالكم ولاكنكم

٣٢:٦ [على] فكونوا على

٣٢:٨ [فيه] يذكرون فيه

٣٢:٩ [وبامر الله]

٣٢:١٠ [نباش] بن نباش ; [سلام على] سلام عليك وعلى

٣٢:١١ [بالطاعة] الله له بالطاعة

٣٢:١٩ [حتى] فدخل حتى

٣٢:٢١ [العظام وجوههم] العظيم ووجوههم

٣٢:٢٢ [كلّموه] كلهم وتكلموا

٣٢:٢٢ [فآمنوا ... قلوبهم]

٣٣:١ [وفي رواية ... قال عبد الملك] قال عبد الملك

٣٣:٦ [اصابهم] وجدهم

٣٣:١٠ [الله] الله تعلى

٣٣:١١ [يقرب] يتيقن

٣٣:١٢ [ابو]

٣٣:١٣ [باريش] تاريش ; [فلما] قال فلما

٣٣:١٥ [عالج] ابن عالج

٣٣:١٥ [قبل] من قبل

٣٣:١٧ [نوح] نوح عليه السلام

٣٤:١ [علينا] الينا

٣٤:٢ [لهم لما] لهم وما قالوا لهم لما ; [عالج] صالح ; [بيده] الميثاق بيده

٣٤:٤ [صنعه] اصنعه ; [قد]

٣٤:٨ [حضرته] اليه

٣٤:١٠ [أثنا عشر ألف] كذلك

٣٤:١١ [الأحور] اللجوج

٣٤:١٢ [الرجال ألف] الرجال والف

٣٤:١٣ [أهل] ; [فأجّل] وجعل

٣٤:١٤ [أن يثقبوها ثقبا] فيها ثقب ; [فطبعوا] فصنعوا ذلك

٣٤:١٥ [كان] كانت

٣٤:١٦ [وارتفاعه من أسفله الى اعلاه ستمائة وخمسون ذراعا]

٣٤:١٧ [خمس] خمسماية

٣٤:١٨-[ألف]

٣٤:١٩ [الله] الله تعلى

٣٤:٢١ [يخلف ألف ولد] يولف ; [ولد] ولف ; [الف ولد حينئذ] ; [أن أحله قد قرب فيستعد له] انه يموت

٣٥:٢ [عليه] ; [أي] عليه أى

٣٥:٣ [ما] مما

٣٥:٤ [طوله ولا عرضه] ; [ثقبه] ثقبه ولا الصعود عليه

٣٥:٦ [والذين] وهم الذين

٣٥:٨ [النحاس] النحاس الاحمر

٣٥:١٠ [الاحبار] الحبار رضى الله تعلى عنه

٣٥:١١ [منتهاهم ولا منتهى] ; [الواحد القهار]

٣٥:١٢ [العهود] العهد الذى عاهدهم عليه

٣٥:١٣ [الصعود] الصعود الى بنيان

٣٥:١٤ [كذالك الى يوم القيامة] وتلك حالتهم ابدا

٣٥:١٧ [أبو]

٣٥:١٩ [الى] فوصل الى

٣٥:٢٣ [بل السير اليهم بنفسي]

٣٦:١ [ولرأيك] الا رايك

٣٦:٢ [قال انا] قال لهم انا

٣٦:٤ [رسول] رسولا ; [الله] الله تعلى

٣٦:٥ [يذكر] يقول

٣٦:٦ [تاويل] ياويل

٣٦:٩ [وللالاه] ولاحسانه

٣٦:١١ [من فعلنا]

٣٦:١٢ [أطاع الله] أطاع الله ورسوله ; [الله]

٣٦:١٤ [غرفاتها ... البوّاب] غرفاتها وقيل انه ظهر منارها لجند ذي القرنين عَلى الباب قال لهُ البوّاب

٣٦:١٦ [هذا] هذا الوقت

٣٦:١٧ [لها] هنا ; [فيها اربع] هنا ; [مدائن] مدائن ثلاث اخر ; [وهذه] وهذه هى

٣٦:١٨ [العاتق] العتيق

٣٦:١٩ [رامي] ; [ألف]

٣٦:٢١ [ملوكهم] ملوككم